T0392898

THE ROUTLEDGE COMPANION
TO ASIAN CINEMAS

Balancing leading scholars with emerging trendsetters, this *Companion* offers fresh perspectives on Asian cinemas and charts new constellations in the field with significance far beyond Asian cinema studies.

Asian cinema studies – at the intersection of film/media studies and area studies – has rapidly transformed under the impact of globalization, compounded by the resurgence of a variety of nationalist discourses as well as counter-discourses, new socio-political movements, and the possibilities afforded by digital media. Differentiated experiences of climate change and the COVID-19 pandemic have further heightened interest in the digital everyday and the renewed geopolitical divide between East and West and between North and South. Thematized into six sections, the 46 chapters in this anthology address established paradigms of scholarship and viewership in Asian cinemas like extreme genres, cinephilia, festivals, and national cinema, while also highlighting political and archival concerns that firmly situate Asian cinemas within local and translocal milieus. Underrepresented cinemas of North Korea, Bangladesh, Laos, Indonesia, Malaysia, Taiwan, Thailand, and Cambodia appear here amid a broader cross-regional, comparative approach.

An ideal resource for film, media, cultural, and Asian studies researchers, students, and scholars, as well as informed readers with an interest in Asian cinemas.

Zhen Zhang is a Professor and directs the Asian Film and Media Initiative in the Martin Scorsese Department of Cinema Studies at New York University, USA. Her publications include *An Amorous History of the Silver Screen: Shanghai Cinema 1896–1937*; *The Urban Generation: Chinese Cinema and Society at the Turn of the Twenty-first Century*; *DV-Made China: Digital Subjects and Social Transformations after Independent Film*; and *Women Filmmakers in Sinophone World Cinema*. She also curates film programs and serves as a jury member for various platforms.

Sangjoon Lee is an Associate Professor of Film Studies at the School of Creative Media, City University of Hong Kong. Lee is the author of *Cinema and the Cultural Cold War: US Diplomacy and the Origins of the Asian Cinema Network* (2020) and the editor/co-editor of *Hallyu 2.0: The Korean Wave in the Age of Social Media* (2015), *Rediscovering Korean Cinema* (2019), *The South Korean Film Industry* (2024), and *Remapping the Cold War in Asian Cinemas* (2024). Lee is also a director of the Asian Cinema Research Lab (ACR Lab). His works have been translated into Korean, Japanese, Chinese, and Italian.

Debashree Mukherjee is an Associate Professor of Film and Media in the Department of Middle Eastern, South Asian, and African Studies (MESAAS) at Columbia University, USA. She is author of *Bombay Hustle: Making Movies in a Colonial City* (2020) and editor of *Bombay Talkies: An Unseen History of Indian Cinema* (2023). Her current book project, *Tropical Machines: Extractive Media and Plantation Modernity*, develops a media history of South Asian indentured migration and plantation capitalism. Debashree edits the peer-reviewed journal *BioScope: South Asian Screen Studies* and has published in journals such as *Film History*, *Feminist Media Histories*, and *Representations*.

Intan Paramaditha is a Senior Lecturer in Media and Film Studies at Macquarie University, Australia. She is the author of the novel *The Wandering* and short story collection *Apple and Knife*, and her articles have appeared in, among others, *Feminist Review*, *Visual Anthropology*, *Inter-Asia Cultural Studies*, and *Film Quarterly*. Her research and creative interests include travel, transnationalism, and decolonial feminism.

THE ROUTLEDGE COMPANION TO ASIAN CINEMAS

Edited by Zhen Zhang, Sangjoon Lee,
Debashree Mukherjee, and Intan Paramaditha

Routledge
Taylor & Francis Group

NEW YORK AND LONDON

Designed cover image: Everett Collection Inc / Alamy Stock Photo

First published 2024
by Routledge
605 Third Avenue, New York, NY 10158

and by Routledge
4 Park Square, Milton Park, Abingdon, Oxon, OX14 4RN

Routledge is an imprint of the Taylor & Francis Group, an informa business

ISBN: 978-1-032-19940-5 (hbk)
ISBN: 978-1-032-21144-2 (pbk)
ISBN: 978-1-003-26695-2 (ebk)

DOI: 10.4324/9781003266952

Typeset in Sabon
by Apex CoVantage, LLC

CONTENTS

Contents

Contents

Contents

FIGURES

TABLES

ACKNOWLEDGMENTS

First of all, this expansive, collaborative project would not have been possible without all the contributors' inspiring work, solidarity, and patience. We would like to express our deepest gratitude to each of them, as well as to several filmmakers and curators who graciously agreed to be interviewed for several chapters.

While the project was commissioned and realized over the last few years spanning the Covid-19 pandemic and beyond, its seeds were sown long ago in several seminars and lecture classes at New York University which several editors and contributors took part as doctoral students before they became leading scholars and educators in the field. Zhen is grateful to have had the opportunity to develop the courses with and learn from Sangjoon, Intan, and Debashree, along with many others over the last two decades. She is also indebted to colleagues, staff members, and students who have supported the Asian Film and Media Initiative (AFMI) at Tisch School of the Arts, NYU since its founding in 2012. Jeff Richardson and Cristina Cajulis, former and current events coordinator in the department, and Feng-mei Heberer (interim director when Zhen is on leave), in particular, have played critical roles in carrying out and expanding AFMI events and programs that have directly or indirectly contributed to the volume's conception and development.

We would also like to thank our colleagues for their support at the Martin Scorsese Department of Cinema Studies at New York University, the Department of Middle Eastern, South Asian, and African Studies at Columbia University, the Department of Media, Creative Arts, Communications, Languages and Literature at Macquarie University, and the School of Creative Media at City University of Hong Kong. Research for Sangjoon Lee's chapter was funded by the Research Grant Council (RGC) of Hong Kong, via the General Research Fund [CityU 13607323].

We are grateful for the book publication grants from Center for Research & Study, Tisch School of the Arts, NYU and NYU Center for the Humanities.

It has been a pleasure working with Routledge commissioning editor Sheni Kruger, editorial assistant Grace Kennedy, and project manager Aruna Rajendran. Thanks also go to

Acknowledgments

Hazem Fahmy and Mahima Patel for assisting with the preparation of the manuscript and Kelly Falconer (Asia Literary Agency) for reading the manuscript contract in its early stages.

Last but not least, we are thankful to our families in Asia and elsewhere for their love and support. They are very much part of who we are and inspire what we do. We dedicate this volume to them, including the spirits of those recently departed.

CONTRIBUTORS

Shi-Yan Chao is a postdoctoral research fellow at Chulalongkorn University (Bangkok). He holds a PhD in cinema studies from New York University and has taught at NYU, Columbia University, Hong Kong Baptist University, and Lingnan University. He is the author of *Queer Representations in Chinese-language Film and the Cultural Landscape* (Amsterdam University Press, 2020), along with various articles in academic journals and anthologies.

Gaik Cheng Khoo is Associate Professor at the University of Nottingham Malaysia where she teaches Southeast Asian cinema, postcolonial theory, and posthumanism. She is also the founder of the Association of Southeast Asian Cinemas Conference (ASEACC), a biannual conference that rotates throughout the region since 2004 (https://aseaccofficial.wordpress.com/). Gaik has published extensively on Malaysian independent films but also writes about food and, more recently, on Korean migrants in Malaysia and the political economy of the Malaysian durian.

Ting-Wu Cho is an independent scholar, and the programmer and board member of Women Make Waves International Film Festival. She holds a Ph.D. in Cinema Studies from New York University. Her dissertation explores Taiwan Pulp, a group of understudied exploitation films in Taiwan in the late Cold War period. Her research interests include genre studies, media industry studies, media ethnography, and Trans-Asian cinemas, with a focus on Taiwan film history.

Sanchai Chotirosseranee serves as Deputy Director of the Thai Film Archive (Public Organization). He is a programmer for the Thai Short Film and Video Festival as well as the Silent Film Festival in Thailand.

Graiwoot Chulphongsathorn is Lecturer at the Faculty of Communication Arts, Chulalongkorn University, Thailand. He published widely in the area of Thai independent films and eco-cinema studies. His work has appeared in journals including *Screen*, *JCMS: Journal of Cinema and Media Studies*, and *Antennae: The Journal of Nature in Visual Culture*. In 2018 he was awarded the British Academy's Visiting Fellowship for his project Southeast Asian Cinema and the Anthropocene. Beyond theoretical undertaking, Chulphongsathorn is a film producer and a film curator. Three of his films were selected for the Berlinale Forum Expanded.

Anne Ciecko is Associate Professor of international cinema in the Department of Communication, a core faculty member in the Interdepartmental Film Studies Program, and director of the interdisciplinary graduate certificate in film studies at the University of Massachusetts-Amherst. She is also an editor of the book, *Contemporary Asian Cinema: Popular Culture in a Global Frame* (Berg/Bloomsbury, 2006), her research articles and film culture reports have appeared in numerous journals and collections. Her DIY short experimental films and video-poems have been official selections at festivals in over a dozen countries.

Daisy Yan Du is Associate Professor in the Division of Humanities at the Hong Kong University of Science and Technology. Her first monograph is titled *Animated Encounters: Transnational Movements of Chinese Animation, 1940s–1970s* (University of Hawaii Press, 2019). She is the editor of *Chinese Animation and Socialism: From Animators' Perspectives* (Brill, 2021) and also the lead editor of *Chinese Animation: Multiplicities in Motion* (Harvard, forthcoming in 2024). In addition to being the editor overseeing Asian animation for *The Encyclopedia of Animation Studies* (Bloomsbury reference, forthcoming in 2025), she is the founder of the Association for Chinese Animation Studies (https://acas.world/), which is dedicated to introducing and promoting Chinese animation to the English-speaking world.

Victor Fan is Reader in Film and Media Philosophy, King's College London and a film festival consultant. He is the author of *Cinema Approaching Reality: Locating Chinese Film Theory* (University of Minnesota Press, 2015), *Extraterritoriality: Locating Hong Kong Cinema and Media* (Edinburg University Press, 2019), and *Cinema Illuminating Reality: Media Philosophy through Buddhism* (University of Minnesota Press, 2022). His articles appeared in journals including *Camera Obscura, Journal of Chinese Cinemas, Screen, and Film History*.

Arnika Fuhrmann is an interdisciplinary scholar of Southeast Asia, working at the intersections of the region's aesthetic, religious, and political modernities. She is the author of *Ghostly Desires: Queer Sexuality and Vernacular Buddhism in Contemporary Thai Cinema* (Duke University Press, 2016) and *Teardrops of Time: Buddhist Aesthetics in the Poetry of Angkhan Kalayanaphong* (SUNY Press, 2020). She is working on a manuscript titled "In the Mood for Texture: The Revival of Bangkok as a Chinese City" for Duke University Press. Fuhrmann teaches in the Departments of Asian Studies and of Comparative Literature at Cornell University.

Tejaswini Ganti is Associate Professor of Anthropology and core faculty in the Program in Culture and Media at New York University. She has been conducting research about the social world and filmmaking practices of the Hindi film industry since 1996 and is the author of *Producing Bollywood: Inside the Contemporary Hindi Film Industry* (Duke U.P. 2012) and *Bollywood: A Guidebook to Popular Hindi Cinema* (Routledge 2004; 2nd edition 2013). Her current research examines the politics of language and translation within the Bombay film world, the dubbing of Hollywood content into Hindi, and a social history of Indian cinema in the US.

Sangita Gopal is Associate Professor of Cinema Studies at University of Oregon and Director of the Center for the Study of Women and Society. She is the author of *Conjugations: Marriage and Form in New Bollywood Cinema* (University of Chicago Press, 2011) and co-editor of *Intermedia in South Asia: The Fourth Screen* (Routledge, 2012) and *Global Bollywood: Travels of Hindi Film Music* (Minneapolis: University of Minnesota Press, 2008). She is completing a book entitled *Mixed Media: Feminist Mediawork in India* and working on a monograph on the careers of Ivory, Merchant, and Jhabvala titled *Transnational Film Production and the Social Network*. Her recent essays have appeared in *Cultural Critique, Feminist Media Histories*, and *Journal of Cinema and Media Studies*, as well as in several essay collections.

Rachel Harrison is Professor of Thai Cultural Studies at SOAS University of London. She has published widely on modern literature and cinema, gender, sexuality, and popular culture in Thailand, in addition to a focus on the cultural effects of Siam/Thailand post-coloniality in relation to the West. She is currently working on an edited collection on culture, well-being, and public health in connection with diet and disease in Northeast Thailand. Her teaching focuses on the generation of cultural studies theory from the perspective of Asia, Africa, and the Middle East. She is also the editor of the quarterly journal *South East Asia Research*.

Lotte Hoek is a media anthropologist whose research is situated at the intersection of anthropology and film studies. She is the author of *Cut-Pieces: Celluloid Obscenity and Popular Cinema in Bangladesh* (Columbia University Press, 2014) and co-editor of *Forms of the Left in Postcolonial South Asia: Aesthetics, Networks and Connected Histories* (Bloomsbury, 2021). She is one of the editors of the journal *BioScope: South Asian Screen Studies*. She is Senior Lecturer in Social Anthropology at the University of Edinburgh.

Alicia Izharuddin teaches Southeast Asian film and gender in the Malay Studies Department at the National University of Singapore. She has published extensively on genre filmmaking, veiling practices and romance in leading journals and other publications. Her first book is *Gender and Islam in Indonesian Cinema*, published by Palgrave Macmillan in 2017.

Dal Yong Jin is a Distinguished Simon Fraser University Professor, and his major research and teaching interests are on transnational cultural studies (Korean Wave), digital platforms and digital games, globalization and media, and the political economy of media and culture. Jin has published numerous books, journal articles, and book chapters, including *Korea's Online Gaming Empire* (2010), *New Korean Wave: transnational cultural power in the age of social media* (2016), and *Smartland Korea: mobile communication, culture and society* (2017). He is the founding book series editor of Routledge Research in Digital Media and Culture in Asia, and he has been directing the Transnational Culture and Digital Technology Lab since summer 2021.

Dikshya Karki is Assistant Professor at the Department of Mass Communication, Xi'an Jiaotong-Liverpool University. She teaches, conducts research, and writes in areas of film and media.

Olivia Khoo is Associate Professor and Head of Film and Screen Studies at Monash University, Australia. She is the author of *Asian Cinema: A Regional View* (Edinburgh University Press, 2021) and co-author (with Audrey Yue and Belinda Smaill) of *Transnational Australian Cinema: Ethics in the Asian Diasporas* (Lexington, 2013). Olivia has co-edited four volumes, including *The Routledge Handbook of New Media in Asia* (with Larissa Hjorth, 2016), *Contemporary Culture and Media in Asia* (with Koichi Iwabuchi and Daniel Black, 2016), *Sinophone Cinemas* (with Audrey Yue, 2014), and *Futures of Chinese Cinema: Technologies and Temporalities in Chinese Screen Cultures* (with Sean Metzger, 2009).

Christina Klein is a film scholar and cultural historian whose work focuses on US-Asian cultural encounters during the Cold War and beyond. She is the author of two books: *Cold War Cosmopolitanism: Period Style in 1950s Korean Cinema* (2020) and *Cold War Orientalism: Asia in the Middlebrow Imagination, 1945–1961* (2003). Her articles on Korean and other Asian cinemas have been published in *The Journal of Korean Studies*, *Transnational Cinemas*, *American Quarterly*, *Journal of Chinese Cinemas*, *Comparative American Studies*, and *Cinema Journal*. She is a professor in the English department and directs the American Studies Program at Boston College.

C. Yamini Krishna has a PhD in film studies from the English and Foreign Languages University, Hyderabad. She has been the recipient of Phillip M. Taylor IAMHIST-Routledge Prize for the Best Article by a New Scholar (2021), Satyajit Ray Film and Television Institute Research Fellowship (2022), and Asian Art Archive – Shergil Sundaram Foundation Archival Grant (2022). Her work has been published in *Urban History*, *South Asian Popular Culture*, *Widescreen*, *Historical Journal of Film Radio*, and *Television and South Asia*. She has also written for the digital publications *The Wire*, *The News Minute*, *Caravan*, *Scroll*, and *Café Dissensus*. She is working on her first book, which examines the historical geography of Hyderabad through film networks. She currently teaches at the FLAME University.

Subasri Krishnan is a documentary filmmaker whose works deal with questions of citizenship through the lens of memory, migration, and interrogation of official identity documents. She led the Media Lab at the Indian Institute for Human Settlements (IIHS) from 2009 to 2024, and has curated 10 editions of the Urban Lens Film Festival. She is currently a PhD scholar and her research focuses on the citizenship crisis in Assam, a state in North-East India.

Hyangjin Lee is Professor at the College of Intercultural Communication at Rikkyo University in Tokyo. Previously, she taught in the School of East Asian Studies at the University of Sheffield and was the 2014 Kim Koo Visiting Professor of Korean Studies at Harvard University. Professor Lee is a global faculty member at Free University Berlin. She serves on the advisory board of the Pyongchang International Peace Film Festival and as a program adviser of the Showroom Cinema in the UK. She previously served as the executive director of the UK Korean Film Festival. She is the author of *Korean Cinema: North Korea South Korea Transnational* (2018), *The Sociology of the Korean Wave: Fandom, Family and Multiculturalism* (2008), and *Contemporary Korean Cinema: Identity, Culture and Politics* (2001), and has published journal articles and book chapters on the cinematic representation of war memories, gender, sexuality and transnationalism in East Asia, and the Korean Wave.

Helen Hok-Sze Leung is Professor and Chair of the Department of Gender, Sexuality, and Women's Studies at Simon Fraser University. She has published widely on Asian cinema and queer culture and is the author of *Undercurrents: Queer Culture and Postcolonial Hong Kong* and *Farewell My Concubine: A Queer Film Classic*. Her articles have appeared in journals including *positions*, *Journal of Lesbian Studies*, *TSQ*, *Journal of Chinese Cinemas*, *Urban Studies*, and *Inter-Asia Cultural Studies*. Her current research includes a SSHRC-funded project on *Transpacific Film Cities* and an audio project on queer Asian cultural activism in Vancouver during the 2000s.

Jinying Li is Assistant Professor of Modern Culture and Media at Brown University, where she teaches media theory, animation, and digital cultures in East Asia. She co-edited two special issues on Chinese animations for *The Journal of Chinese Cinemas*, and a special issue on regional platforms for *Asiascape: Digital Asia*. Her first book, *Anime's Knowledge Cultures: Geek, Otaku, Zhai* (University of Minnesota Press, 2024), explores the connection between anime culture and global geekdom. She is currently writing her second book, *Walled Media and Mediating Walls*. She is also co-editing a forthcoming collection, *The Oxford Handbook of Chinese Digital Media*.

Shuting Li is a PhD candidate in Anthropology who is also pursuing a certificate in Culture and Media at New York University. Her doctoral research project explores the ways that different generations of people in post-reform China imagine what robots or robotic technology can do for elder care. Her research interests bring together Science and Technology Studies (STS), the study of aging and care, and the family. She also directed a short ethnographic film *Chang Jiu Yuan (Year After Year*, 2021), which chronicles the everyday lives of elderly Chinese immigrants at the senior center in Chinatown, New York City, during the pandemic.

Philippa Lovatt is Lecturer in Film Studies at University of St Andrews. She is currently working on two book projects: *Reverberant Histories: Expanded Listening and Artists' Film in Southeast Asia* (under contract with Edinburgh University Press) and *Parallel Practices: Spatial Transformation and Southeast Asian Film Cultures*, which is co-authored with Jasmine Nadua Trice. She has previously published in *Journal of Cinema and Media Studies*; *Screen*; *Music, Sound and the Moving Image*; *The New Soundtrack*; *Southeast of Now: Directions in Contemporary and Modern Art in Asia*; and *Antennae: The Journal of Nature in Visual Culture*.

Ran Ma is Associate Professor in "Japan-in-Asia" Cultural Studies and Screen Studies at Nagoya University, Japan. Her research interests revolve around the intersection of Inter-Asia studies, transnational film and screen cultures, and film festival studies, for which she has published book chapters and journal articles. Currently, her focus is on exploring the dynamics of translocality, infrastructure, and affect within the context of transnational media across East Asian locales. Ma is also the author of *Independent Filmmaking across Borders in Contemporary Asia* (Amsterdam University Press, 2019). Ma has also curated screening events for Asian independent films in Osaka, Beijing, Nagoya, and Tokyo.

Daisuke Miyao is Professor and Hajime Mori Chair in Japanese Language and Literature at the University of California, San Diego. Miyao is the author of *Japonisme and the Birth of Cinema* (Duke University Press, 2020), *Cinema Is a Cat: A Cat Lover's Introduction to Film Studies* (University of Hawai'i Press, 2019), *The Aesthetics of Shadow: Lighting and Japanese Cinema* (Duke University Press, 2013), and *Sessue Hayakawa: Silent Cinema and Transnational Stardom* (Duke University Press, 2007). He is also the editor of *The Oxford Handbook of Japanese Cinema* (2014) and the co-editor of *Transnational Cinematography Studies* (2017) with Lindsay Coleman and Roberto Schaefer.

Jimena Mora holds a MA from Kyoto University of Arts and Design, Japan. Currently she teaches at the Oriental Studies Center at the Pontificia Universidad Católica del Perú. She is a member of the association DOCUPERUand ALADAA (Latin American Association of Asian and African Studies). In 2023 she was awarded an Artistic Residency at the Fukuoka

Asian Art Museum in Japan. She is co-director of Futari Proyectos dedicated to the promotion and research of Asian cinema, female Asian directors and Peruvian Nikkei cinema.

Jasmine Nadua Trice is Associate Professor of Cinema and Media Studies in the Department of Film, Digital Media at the University of California, Los Angeles. Her book, *City of Screens: Imagining Audiences in Manila Film Culture*, was published by Duke University Press in 2021.

Fathima Nizaruddin is an academic and documentary filmmaker from India. She is currently a post-doctoral researcher at University of Passau, Germany. Her articles have appeared in journals such as *HAU: Journal of Ethnographic Theory*, *International Journal of Communication (IJoC)*, *Asiascape: Digital Asia*, and *BioScope: South Asian Screen Studies*. She was Assistant Professor at Jamia Millia Islamia, New Delhi, from 2007 till 2020. She finished her PhD in 2017 from the Centre for Research and Education in Art and Media (CREAM), University of Westminster, London. Her documentary films have been screened at various international film festivals and academic spaces.

Markus Nornes is Professor of Asian Cinema at the University of Michigan, where he specializes in Japanese film, documentary, and translation theory. He has done extensive programming, especially at the Yamagata International Documentary Film Festival. He has written books on Japanese documentary, film translation, pink film, and a critical biography of director Ogawa Shinsuke. His latest book, *Brushed in Light*, is on the intimate relationship of calligraphy and East Asian cinema. Nornes has also directed several documentaries, including *When We're Together* (2020), *The Big House* (2018, co-directed with Soda Kazuhiro et al), *911* (2001), and a five-screen video installation titled *Player Played* (2019).

Hyun Seon Park is Assistant Professor in the Department of Modern and Classical Languages at George Mason University. Park's publication includes "Noir Spatiality in the Time of Violence: Allegorizing the 1960s Korean Film Noir," "Volatile Biopolitics," "The Cold War Mnemonics," and "The Sublime Objects of Affectivity." She co-edited the special issue "Cold War in Korean Cinemas" in the *Journal of Korean Studies* and recently guest-edited two special sections for the *Journal of Japanese and Korean Cinema*: "South Korean Cine-feminism on the Move" and "Cine-Gwangju: Envisioning the Gwangju Uprising in South Korean Film and Culture."

Atit Pongpanit is a lecturer at the Centre of ASEAN Community Studies, Faculty of Social Sciences, Naresuan University, Thailand. Their areas of focus include cultural studies, cinema, literature, and gender studies with reference to Thailand; literary criticism and Southeast Asian literatures in a comparative context; and cinema in Southeast Asia, with a focus on genders and sexualities.

Lisabona Rahman studied moving image preservation and presentation in Amsterdam. Her approach comes from the intersecting interests on cinema practice and history in postcolonial societies, transnational network, and women's work. She restores films, conducts performative lectures, and creates screening programs for festivals, archives, and galleries. Her works were created and shown with the support of different institutions, such as the Arsenal Institut in Berlin, Eye Filmmuseum in Amsterdam, the Film Archive (Public Organization) in Thailand, and Rubanah Underground Hub in Jakarta. Since 2018 she also conducts knowledge sharing activities related to the life history of celluloid films, which have taken place in different cities such as Berlin, Cairo, and Jakarta. Lisabona Rahman is also a founder of Sekolah Pemikiran Perempuan (School of Women's Thoughts) – a collective of artists, writers, and cultural workers that creates broadcasted programs for the circulation of feminist knowledge practices coming from the Nusantara archipelago.

Eric Sasono is an Indonesian film critic who obtained his doctoral degree in film studies from King's College London. He co-founded the Indonesian Film Society, a London-based community group to screen films regularly in London and to promote Indonesian culture to the UK public and beyond. For ten years (2009–2019), Eric was the executive board's secretary of YMMFI, the Indonesian Independent Film Society Foundation, which established the Indonesian Documentary Center (In-Docs) and organized the now-defunct Jakarta International Film Festival (JIFFest). Eric has co-written a book about the Indonesian film industry and edited a volume about Southeast Asian cinema. He is now working in a Jakarta-based civil society organization in the media sector.

Chi-Yun Shin is a Principal Lecturer in Film Studies at Sheffield Hallam University in the UK. She has co-edited *New Korean Cinema* (Edinburgh UP, 2005), which is one of the first English-language scholarly publications on Korean cinema. Her interests also expand more widely across Asian Cinema, as is evidenced by works such as the collection *East Asian Film Noir* (Bloomsbury, 2015). She has recently turned her attention to the study of South Korean women directors and organized the South Korean Women's Cinema conference in 2021, funded by the Academy of Korean Studies. She is a recipient of fellowships from Korea Foundation as well as from the Academy of Korean Studies.

Sophia Siddique holds a PhD from the University of Southern California School of Cinematic Arts. Her research interests include Singapore film, Southeast Asian cinemas, and genres like science fiction and horror. Her forthcoming publications include an essay about her participation in the making of *Shirkers 1.0* in *Incomplete: The Feminist Possibilities of the Unfinished Film*, University of California Press, co-edited by Alix Beeston and Stefan Solomon. Siddique is an associate professor in the Department of Film, Vassar College.

Gerald Sim is Professor of Film and Media Studies at Florida Atlantic University and the author of *The Subject of Film and Race: Retheorizing Politics, Ideology, and Cinema* (2014) and *Postcolonial Hangups in Southeast Asian Cinema: Poetics of Space, Sound, and Stability* (2020). His current monograph is a technopolitical study of films that shape our algorithmic imaginaries.

Enoch Yee-lok Tam is Research Assistant Professor in the Department of Digital Arts and Creative Industries at Lingnan University. His research engages with film historiography in Chinese-language film, Hong Kong film history and film policy, and East Asia's creative and media industries. Currently, he is working on a book project examining the development of Hong Kong's independent film in the post-handover period. He co-authored *Indiescape Hong Kong: Critical Essays and Interviews* in 2018, a collection of critical essays about local independent films and interviews of independent filmmakers.

Stephen Teo was formerly associate professor in the Wee Kim Wee School of Communication and Information, Nanyang Technological University, Singapore. Now an independent scholar, he is the author of several books on Asian cinema, principally *Hong Kong Cinema:*

The Extra Dimensions (British Film Institute, 1997), *Wong Kar-wai* (BFI, 2005), *Chinese Martial Arts Cinema: The Wuxia Tradition* (Edinburgh University Press, 2009), and his latest, *Chinese Martial Arts Film and the Philosophy of Action* (Routledge, 2021).

Beth Tsai is the author of *Taiwan New Cinema at Film Festivals* (Edinburgh University Press, 2023), and Visiting Assistant Professor of Film Studies at the State University of New York at Albany. Her research focuses primarily on the cinema of Taiwan, film festivals, and transnational film theory. She has published in the *International Journal of Asia Pacific Studies*, *Quarterly Review of Film and Video*, *Journal of Asian Cinema*, and *Oxford Bibliographies*.

Raymond Tsang is a lecturer in the Department of East Asian Languages and Cultures at the University of Southern California. He earned his PhD in Cinema Studies from New York University. His research interests include the geopolitical history of Hong Kong wuxia films, as well as leftist films and media. Dr. Tsang recently edited a special issue for the *Journal of Chinese Cinemas*, focusing on Hong Kong left-wing cinema and media. His broader academic pursuits encompass various topics such as cinema and revolution, genre films like sci-fi and horror, and global South films and documentaries.

Talia Vidal is an art historian trained at the Universidad Nacional Mayor de San Marcos and co-director of Futari Proyectos, a platform dedicated to the promotion and research of Asian cinema, cinema made by Asian women directors and Nikkei cinema in Peru. She is currently pursuing a Master's Degree in Asian and African Studies at the Center for Asian and African Studies of El Colegio de México. She is a member of ALADAA (Latin American Association of Asian and African Studies).

Zhuoyi Wang is Professor of East Asian Languages and Literatures at Hamilton College, the author of *Revolutionary Cycles in Chinese Cinema, 1951–1979* (Palgrave Macmillan, 2014), a co-editor of *Maoist Laughter* (Hong Kong University Press, 2019), and co-editor of *Teaching Film from the People's Republic of China* (MLA Options for Teaching, 2024).

Thong Kay Wee is a cultural worker and moving image curator based in Singapore. He is currently Program Director at the Singapore International Film Festival (SGIFF), where he is responsible for the festival's overall programming strategy. He was previously the programs and outreach officer at the Asian Film Archive (AFA) from 2014 to 2021.

Elizabeth Wijaya is Assistant Professor in the Department of Visual Studies at the University of Toronto (Mississauga) and Graduate Faculty in the Cinema Studies Institute at the University of Toronto (St. George). She is a co-founder of E&W Films and co-editor of *World Picture Journal*.

Alexander Zahlten is Professor of East Asian Languages and Civilizations at Harvard University. His recent work touches on topics such as the experience of complex media ecologies, "amateur" film/media production, and the history of the connection of electricity and the film industry in Japan. Publications include his co-edited volume *Media Theory in Japan* (Duke University Press, 2017, with Marc Steinberg) and his book *The End of Japanese Cinema* (Duke University Press, 2017) and the article "Between Two Funerals: Zombie Temporality and Media Ecology in Japan" (*positions: East Asia Critique*, 2021).

INTRODUCTION
Trans-Asian Cinemas at Home in the World

*Zhen Zhang, Sangjoon Lee, Debashree Mukherjee,
and Intan Paramaditha*

This large collaborative project was first conceived around the turn of 2019–2020 right before the COVID-19 pandemic brought shock waves and tragic loss. The pandemic has ushered tremendous changes in public health, the environment, economy, politics, and culture on varying local, national, regional, and global scales, as well as everyday life, including shopping and movie-going. The first outbreak in Wuhan, China, which had been thriving on a booming export-led, real estate bubble- and infrastructure-undergirded economy and an expanding domestic film market, suddenly put everything on brakes and in lockdown mode one city after another. And it swiftly spread across the world. The "transnational flow" of people and goods, including popular culture and movies, facilitated by trans-regional and trans-continental airlines and cargo ships, suddenly "froze" in time and space. In its wake, Zoom and other online platforms replaced myriad forms of in-person inter-personal exchanges, especially in education, socialization, and cultural and artistic production and consumption. Film festivals around the globe, which embody the global flow of movies, film personnel, and audience par excellence, with some initial hesitation, took on a phantom, virtual existence by going online. Booming film industries in countries like China and South Korea, as in Hollywood and Bollywood, took a nosedive to reach near collapse, as the relation of commercial films with theatrical "box office" revenues was transformed drastically (Fortmueller 2021; Li, Wilson, and Guan 2023). It is not until the spring of 2023, when the WHO officially declared the end of the pandemic and the world has learned to live with the virus, that things began to approach a semblance of normalcy.

Views from Two Film Festivals Across the Asia-Pacific

By fits and starts, having coursed on the Internet over more than three pandemic years, including a workshop and several editorial meetings on zoom, this anthology project also arrived at its conclusion. Personally, some of us editors were able to enjoy movie-going as before (save for a few voluntary masks) in two global cities on two sides of the Pacific in the summer of 2023: the Shanghai International Film Festival in June and the New York Asian Film Festival in July. The many riveting Asian films across fictional and non-fictional modes we watched at these two festivals have also provided inspiration for introducing this

DOI: 10.4324/9781003266952-1

Companion by anchoring it in the present. Exhibition, spectatorship, and film festivals are among the important sites of fieldwork and frameworks of the volume; where and how films are shown and received can reveal a great deal about the shifting conditions of production and trajectories of circulation. The two festivals were very different in nature and spectatorial address. Founded in 1993 and the largest in China, the Shanghai International Film Festival (SIFF), the only International Federation of Film Producers' Associations (FIAPF) accredited A-list festival in the country, is a government-sponsored humongous operation screening hundreds of films at its flagship Shanghai Cinema Center and across the city. It encompasses several categories of competition, a film market, a pitch program, a restoration program, a festival forum, and other ancillary events.[1] The festival was suspended in 2022 due to a protracted city-wide lockdown in Shanghai, which exacerbated the sadness of residents and pessimism about the health and prospects of the country's film industry, arts, and culture more generally.

SIFF's resumption in 2023 was certainly meant to be a booster against despair and a major public relations campaign to resuscitate the city and Chinese film industry on a global stage. "International" guests, especially those from North America, Australia, Europe, and even South Korea,[2] were far fewer than pre-pandemic times, but many young people traveled to the festival from other parts of China. Though domestic independent films (without the "dragon seal" approval for theatrical release) and Taiwan films were virtually absent, Shanghai audiences still enthusiastically welcomed an enormous program of diverse offerings after the previous year's hiatus and trauma. These included a large body of films by veterans and emerging filmmakers from Japan (e.g., the 91-year Yamada Yoji and Kumakiri Kazuyoshi), a number of small-to-medium-budget films from young filmmakers in mainland China and Hong Kong, and a sizable selection from other more or less "friendly" Asian countries or regions (India, Laos, Indonesia, Sri Lanka, Iran, Kazakhstan, Uzbekistan). These were presented in different slates – from the competition section to the Belt and Road Film Week, a pre-festival sidebar program. Women filmmakers were notably well-presented. Liu Jiayin's (China) new film *All Ears* won Best Director, and Spanish (Catalan) newcomer Marta Lallana received the Grand Jury Prize for *Muyeres*, an evocative meditation on cultural heritage and women's voices. Japan's Kaneko Yurina (*People Who Talk to Plushies Are Kind*) and China's Chen Xiaoyu (*Gone with the Boat*) were in the Asian New Talent competition. Yang Lina was the sole woman filmmaker with the only Asian and Chinese-language film (*Leap of Faith*) featured in the Documentary Competition (a small selection of five films), which says something about the stricter censorship on this truth-seeking form of filmmaking. Nonetheless, SIFF presented a one-of-a-kind opportunity for Shanghai and Chinese audiences to see the outside world, appreciate kaleidoscopic cinematic visions and touching stories, which also helped channel pent-up emotions. Films about the elderly in isolation (during the pandemic or otherwise), intergenerational bonds, mutual aid among the marginalized, and protests against injustice and state violence, such as *Anxious in Beirut* (2023; Golden Goblet Best Documentary, Lebanon), *The Newspaper* (Sarath Kothalawala and Kumara Thirimadura 2020, Sri Lanka), and *The Village* (Fujii Michihito 2023, Japan), resonated strongly. It is as though subjects that would be hard to get past Chinese censors locally, found their way to the Chinese audience via these "foreign" films that tell familiar stories about human rights, civic disobedience, press (un) freedoms, poverty, environmental disaster, and abuse of power.

Back in New York, summer 2023 in Gotham was fully abuzz with culture and arts activities as in pre-pandemic times. The Lincoln Center, where the New York Asian Film Festival

(NYAFF) has been held for the last decade, at the Walter Reade Theater, is a vibrant hub of music, dance, and movies, both indoor and outdoor. Founded by a few North American male fans of popular Asian genre cinema in 2002, the non-profit organization has grown into a substantive institution with a large multicultural audience base, offering a high-caliber annual event of blockbusters and art house gems from a wide spectrum of Asian countries every July.³ The 2023 edition again boasted solid representation from South Korea, Hong Kong, and Taiwan, co-sponsored by their respective government agencies in the city as a means of nation branding. Bold and innovative works by emerging filmmakers included the exquisitely photographed *Glorious Ashes* (2022), by the Vietnamese director Tro Tàn Rực Rỡ, based on short stories by renowned female author Nguyen Ngoc Tu; *Gaga* (2022), a masterfully directed fiction and non-fiction blend on intergenerational love and tribal conflict by Taiwan's Atayal woman filmmaker Laha Mebow; *The Cord of Life* (2022), an impressive feature debut by Chinese-Mongolian woman director Qiao Sixue; Anastasia Tsang's *A Light Never Goes Out* (2022, starring Sylvia Chang), a love poem to a vanishing Hong Kong; and Zhang Wei's (director in focus) *The Rib* (2018), an independent film about the ambivalent relationship between the transgender and Christian communities in China.⁴ Malaysian film *Abang Adik* (2023, feature debut directed by Jin Ong), about two undocumented orphans who adopted each other as brothers and get fatefully implicated in immigrant smuggling, received the Uncaged Award for Best Feature Film Competition.

Visiting these two festivals in the East and West, divergent in nature and scale, helped refresh the ideas and perspectives behind the work that we as a collective have been engaged in over the pandemic years. What the two festivals share most visibly is the audience's joy in resuming movie-going in person as a social and public activity (screenings with Q&A sessions are the most popular), and their thirst for new films and visions that are compassionate, innovative, and provocative. While certain films shown at NYAFF would not be accepted by SIFF, the latter's programmers seemed to have tried their best to balance popular crowd-pleasers and bold alternative cinema, along with shorts and animations. SIFF's top-down official façade is softened by the horizontal spread of its exhibition venues all over the city – from high-end luxury theaters downtown to old theaters in working class neighborhoods and multiplexes in suburban shopping malls. NYAFF also has a secondary site in New Jersey catering to a large Asian population and other cinephiles in the Garden State, beyond the rarefied Lincoln Center location. The institutional and aesthetic tendencies of SIFF and NYAFF, and their varying cultural and socio-political ramifications locally and globally, resonate with many of the issues in this volume: women's filmmaking and queer film practices, trans-Asian circulation of images and imaginaries, national cinema redefined, mixed genres and modes, blurring boundaries between commercial and independent films, and the politics of festivals and archives.

Once More, "Asian Cinema" or "Asian Cinemas"?

This *Companion* endeavors to offer fresh perspectives on Asian cinemas and charts emergent constellations of the field. Asian cinema studies, at the intersection of film/media and area studies, has rapidly expanded and transformed under the impact of globalization, compounded by the resurgence of a variety of nationalist discourses, sentiments, and institutions, as well as counter-discourses, new socio-political movements, and the possibilities afforded by digital media. Differentiated experiences of climate change and the COVID-19 pandemic have further heightened interest in local politics and cultural activism, newer media and the digital everyday, and a renewed geopolitical divide between East and West and between North and South. A new "companion" to Asian cinemas therefore feels necessary and urgent in these times.

In 1993, evoking the 1985 Asian Cinema symposium, which Wimal Dissanayake organized in conjunction with the Hawaii International Film Festival, William Rothman (1993) wrote: "other than martial arts films, few of us had seen a single film from Hong Kong, Taiwan, or mainland China. And it goes without saying that the cinema of Korea, the Philippines, Indonesia, and Southeast Asia was completely unknown to us" (255). The SIFF and Taiwan's Women Make Waves International Film Festival (WMFIFF, the first in Asia; see Chapter 43, by Beth Tsai) were founded that same year. Even older film festivals like the Tashkent Film Festival of African and Asian Cinema (since 1968, see Chapter 15 by C. Yamini Krishna), or those in the diaspora, such as the Asian American International Film Festival in New York (AAIFF, founded by Asian CineVision in 1978), seemed to have not yet entered these scholars' viewfinder. Asian cinema was largely perceived to be a territorially bound phenomenon in terms of national origins, "representative" masters and genres. Two years later, in a special "Asian cinema" issue of *Film History*, Kristin Thompson (1995) began her editorial with this confession:

In the early 1970s, when I began graduate school, Asia occupied a relatively small place in the film studies curriculum. For most students, a few classics of Kurosawa, Mizoguchi and Ozu – all of them from the postwar period – and the work of Satyajit Ray seemed to be the sum of what one needed to see from the Asian cinema." (3)

Thompson problematized the fact that American film studies had traditionally given diminutive critical consideration to Asian cinemas, paying lip service to the question of "world cinema" representation by drawing on a handful of auteurs feted in the West. For many decades before the 1990s, India and Japan had been the only film-producing countries that secured their places in the official narrative of world cinema. Joseph Anderson and Donald Richie's *The Japanese Film: Art and Industry* (1959) was the first English-language academic book on Asian cinema, followed by Erik Barnouw and S. Krishnaswamy's *Indian Film* (1963). The early successes of Kurosawa Akira, Mizoguchi Kenji, and Satyajit Ray at various film festivals in Europe helped ignite enthusiastic responses in Western film studies during the period and remained for several decades as "the sum of what one needed to see from the Asian cinema." Much of the interest in these Eastern masters was also a manifestation of Cold War politics combined with a new brand of postcolonial exoticism enabled in part by the three major festivals in Europe (see Chapter 41, by Anne Cieko).

At the time of their writings, Rothman, Thompson, and Dissanayake could never have imagined that, in two decades, one whole floor of their library bookshelves would be filled with books on Chinese-language cinemas alone, and Asian cinema studies would fully blossom in the new millennium. Three important volumes dedicated to "Asian cinema" as a regional category appeared in the early 1990s: John Lent's *The Asian Film Industry* (1990), offering a preliminary inventory of national cinema industries, and *Melodrama and Asian Cinema* (1993) and *Colonialism and Nationalism in Asian Cinema* (1994), both edited by Wimal Dissanayake. Despite their "national cinema" divisions and overreliance on ideology critique, several contributions in the Dissanayake volumes demonstrated conscious critical engagement with theoretical paradigms widely debated at the time. Meanwhile, scholarly articles and criticism on Asian films were mostly published in *Cinemaya* (1988,

India), *East-West Film Journal* (1986–94, East-West Center at University of Hawaii, Honolulu), and *Asian Cinema* (1995–), a modest publication of the Asian Cinema Studies Society, all largely outside the purview of the Anglophone mainstream academia.

Today, the field boasts not only a large corpus of scholarly works (monographs, anthologies, specialized journals and special issues, and countless articles) on well-known old and new cinema traditions or new waves from Japan, India, Thailand, Hong Kong, Taiwan, South Korea, and the People's Republic of China, but also on large and small countries in Southeast and South Asia that had been largely excluded from cinema studies curricula in the past. There are several anthologies focusing on Southeast Asia, including *Glimpses of Freedom: Independent Cinema in Southeast Asia* (Ingawanij and McKay 2012), *Southeast Asian Independent Cinema* (Baumgärtel 2012), *Film in Contemporary Southeast Asia* (Lim and Yamamoto 2012), *Southeast Asia on Screen: From Independence to Financial Crisis* (Khoo, Barker, and Ainslie 2020), and *Independent Filmmaking in Southeast Asia* (Meissner 2021). More importantly, this effervescence of Asian cinema studies scholarship in the last three decades emanates from a very diverse, multicultural, and cosmopolitan scholarly community composed of many people of Asian descent who are based in Asia, the Asian diaspora, or have recently immigrated to the West or migrated within Asia. Their presence and influence are also visible in new, more specialized journals, such as *Journal of Chinese Cinemas* (2007–), *Journal of Chinese Film Studies* (2021–), *South Asian Film and Media* (2009–), *Journal of Japanese and Korean Cinema* (2009–), *Bioscope: South Asian Screen Studies* (2010–), *Pelikula: A Journal of Philippine Cinema* (1999–), and so on. Trans-regional affiliations have grown and pushed for conversations and collaborations across the Asian regions (Lovatt and Trice 2021). Some of the initiatives are ASEAC (Association of Southeast Asian Cinemas), a regional collective in SEA involving academics, filmmakers, critics, archivists, and art activists based in the region and beyond. ASEAC and the Southeast Asia-Pacific Audiovisual Archive Association (SEAPAVAA) organize conferences regularly in different cities in Asia to foster regional knowledge production and circulation.

A reference bibliography for an introductory course on Asian cinema today would easily span several pages. Some syllabi cover "Asia" as a whole; others restrict themselves to regional markers inherited from the Cold War discourse, typically "East Asia" and "Southeast Asia." In terms of their comprehensiveness and depth, we are in most direct conversation with three anthologies and we have tried to extend their contribution to the field. These volumes are *Contemporary Asian Cinema: Popular Culture in a Global Frame* (2006), edited by Anne Ciecko; *Asian Cinemas: A Reader and Guide* (2006), edited by Dimitris Eleftheriotis and Gary Needham; and *The Palgrave Handbook of Asian Cinema* (2018) edited by Aaron Han Joon Magnan-Park, Gina Marchetti, and See Kam Tan. The first two offered a perfect combination of introductory surveys and theoretically probing at a time when many of us first started creating specialized courses on Asian film history and historiography. *Contemporary Asian Cinema*, designed for a semester-long course with a focus on popular cinema within historical and global contexts, covers fourteen national cinemas in a sequence that provocatively reverses the reception of Asian cinema traditions in Western festivals and academia, from Southeast Asia (starting with the Philippines), to South Asian (with Sri Lanka and Bangladesh preceding India), and then East Asia (ending in Japan). Leading and emerging scholars in respective national cinemas composed concise historical overviews informed by conceptual and thematic interests. Placing the book in dialogue with postcolonial critiques of Orientalism and emphasizing the diversity and complexity of Asia, especially considering intensified transnational movements around the turn of the new century, Ciecko asserts in her introduction, "[t]here is no one Asian cinema" (5), "[t] here is no homogenous Asian monoculture" (7), and, heeding the immensely rich array of languages, dialects, topolects, and accents, "Asian cinema is polyglot" (14). The volume's two key interventions are the ground-up Asian perspectives in which the subjectivities of local film culture producers, critics, and audiences are taken seriously, and a departure from the existing "fetishism" of art cinema by a few national masters. The book remains a useful introductory text, though it sorely needs to be updated. Its brevity, however, and its focus on "contemporary cinemas," predominantly live action narrative features, leave many gaps in other important periods and areas of inquiry.

Instead of an introductory textbook, *Asian Cinemas: A Reader and Guide*, also published in 2006, is quite unique in its theoretical ambition and geographical selectiveness. This pioneering collection of twenty-three essays by a wide range of academic specialists situates Asian cinema scholarship within the ongoing theoretical debates in film and cultural studies. As the editors wrote in their introduction, *Asian Cinemas* is "a collection of important (but limited) readings and a guide to an initial exploration of key aspects of Asian cinema" (4). And they hoped that it would "stimulate the appetite of students of Asian cinemas for further reading and more thorough explorations" (4). Notably, it explicitly departs from "Asian cinema" as a singular entity. Instead of a long list of countries (which is impossible to exhaust for any volume), it focuses, thematically, on several larger or significant "national cinema" phenomena variously defined, including Japan, China, Taiwan, India, and Turkish cinema. The volume sources the bulk of its content from articles previously published in the 1970s and 1980s that were considered seminal and provocative and adds six newly commissioned chapters. More suitable as supplementary reference for an advanced seminar today, the volume highlights important trends in Asian film studies and critical theory that had acquired a canonical or cult status by the 1990s (especially Ozu Yasujiro, Bruce Lee, the *Godzilla* movies, Hindi "social film" or melodrama, China's "fifth generation," and Taiwan New Cinema's auteurs), whereas all the "rest" of Asia's cinemas are eclipsed. The concentrated case studies provide fodder for thought on specific figures and problematics, both familiar and less attended to (e.g., the section on Turkey). The cases serve to interrogate the validity and limits of Euro-American perspectives by engaging theories on Orientalism, postcoloniality, national cinema, genre, authorship, and stardom with commentaries by established senior scholars, including Rey Chow, E. Ann Kaplan, Ackbar Abbas, David Desser, and Ravi Vasudevan. Their textual reading and ideological/ cultural critique are often illuminating and polemical. At nearly 500 pages, this "Reader and Guide" unfortunately has very little to teach students about other critical aspects of film history and culture, such as technology, infrastructure, early cinema, queer cinema, intermediality, distribution, archiving, preservation, migration, film festivals, activism, and non-fiction and animation.

The most expansive anthology to date is the 700-plus-page tome, *The Palgrave Handbook of Asian Cinema*, which advocates the continued need for "Asian cinema" as an integrated, forward-looking conceptual framework. The volume is largely based on the papers presented at the Asian Cinema Studies Society conference held at the University of Hong Kong in March 2012. Thirty-three chapters grouped into six sections covering theory, history, cultural identity, and geopolitics address an impressive range of topics. The volume covers regions from "Turkey to the edges of the Pacific," comments on new phenomena "[f]rom the revival of the Silk Road as the 'belt and road' of a rising China" and offers "historical ruminations on the legacy of colonialism across the continent" (back cover).

The impressive geographic range forms the basis for co-editor Magnan-Park's passionate call for a "Poly-Asia continental film movement" comprising "East Asia, Inner Asia, Southeast Asia, South Asia, and Central Asia as well as the Middle East and Oceania" (18). The chapters concerning Armenia, Iran, Iraq, and Turkey indeed serve to illustrate such a "continental" reach. Acknowledging the historical, cultural, linguistic, philosophical, religious, and other differences among Asian countries and sub-regions, the *Handbook* endeavors to undo Orientalist and Cold War legacies – " 'Asia' as a figment of the Western imagination" (2). The editors argue that a more unified community of Asians in their homeland or in the diaspora could more effectively combat Western powers and Hollywood dominance in the new "Asian century." The *Handbook* aspires to transcend "the limitations of national borders to do justice to the diverse ways in which cinema shapes Asia geographically and imaginatively in the world today" (back cover).

Despite the sweeping "continental" scope and a few case studies on West Asia, subjects centered in or around East Asia take up most of the space and remain a normative, if not hegemonic, analytic lens. Southeast and South Asian regions beyond India, as well as women filmmakers, are regrettably under-represented.[5] These are the areas our *Companion* extends and explores further, both in thematic range and critical investment. The optimistic post–Beijing Olympics and pre-pandemic trends toward expanded film markets in the region, Pan-Asian co-production and circulation, an elongated list of Asian film festivals or programs inside and outside Asia (Hong Kong, Busan, Shanghai, Singapore, Udine, Los Angeles, New York, Toronto, and so on), media synergy, digital platforms, and other developments seem to have spurred passionate research on past and present manifestations and trends that anticipate a more inclusive, yet ultimately utopian "poly-Asian continental film movement."

The ascendance of neo-autocratic regimes across Asia and the world, the conservative backlash and the global impact of the Trump era, the COVID-19 pandemic and the ensuing escalated neo–Cold War tension across the Taiwan Strait and the Pacific, intensified climate change, war in Ukraine and elsewhere, and crumbing IT giants (from Silicon Valley to Alibaba) have not just caused slowdown in the global economy and reduced transnational travels and transactions but also brought depression, pessimism, and renewed critique of neoliberal capitalism, racism, ethno-nationalism, and authoritarianism in various forms. This *Companion* is conceived in this turbulent era that affords retrospections and introspections on Asian cinemas in decidedly plural terms, and their historically differential temporalities and new formations. Conditioned by the recent past and by the current climate, we excavate stories of suspicion as well as solidarity, record ongoing experiments, and envision possibilities for hopeful futures.

Trans-Asian Practices and Networks

In the footsteps of the aforementioned key anthologies on Asian cinema(s), we are also marking a departure from narrowly defined "national cinema" or superficially signaled "transnational cinema" models, while not entirely giving up on their historical valence and conceptual purchase within concrete contexts. Instead of an overarching "Asian cinema" as an abstract concept (Teo 2012) or an aspirational "movement" vis-a-vis Hollywood on a grand scale, our overall guiding principles are historically minded, trans-Asian, critical, and decolonial Asian studies, alongside interdisciplinary, comparative approaches. Ciecko, Miyao, Ma, and Teo, whose work appeared in *The Palgrave Handbook*, join forces with us by sharing their new research and thinking on the concepts, practices, and institutions of "Asian cinemas" and what we prefer to call "trans-Asian cinemas." Yet we are cognizant of regional, national, and sub-national specificities in a world that still operates in the framework of the nation state and the UN grid that excludes or mis-recognizes many peoples and cultures. Our geographic coverage is not motivated by the purported "Asian century" and "rise of China" (and its ambitious "continental" reach via its "Belt and Road"),[6] but more inspired by varying kinds of exchange and circulation in practice and ideas beyond government agendas and large-scale industrial relations, be it across oceans, borders, archipelagoes, or mountain ranges. We have consciously allocated more space to Southeast Asian archipelagic nations, to South Asia beyond Bollywood, and trans-hemispheric linkages across the Pacific, including South America.

Dissatisfied with an academic publishing convention that "theory" must always preside over "practice," we have adopted instead a non-hierarchical approach firmly grounded in urgent concerns of the present that allow new assessments of film and media studies paradigms. Thus, we begin with a section on radical screen practices and feminist and queer film aesthetics. While gender and activism-themed essays are often tucked into unassuming sections of an anthology, our editorial choice is meant to foreground the critical importance of these perspectives in rethinking cinematic history, screen culture, and theorization. To accentuate our commitment to practice *as* theory, and inspired by the model of *Southeast Asian Independent Cinema: Essays, Documents and Interviews* (Baumgärtel 2012), we also invited several filmmakers and festival curators, including Deepa Dhanraj (India), Anocha Suwichakornpong (Thailand), Yim Soon-Rye (South Korea), Tan Pin Pin (Singapore), Roger Garcia (Hong Kong), and Futari Proyectos (Peru), to take part in conversations about their work and views on the current state of Asian cinemas at home and in the world. These components will hopefully provide readers with a heightened awareness of the relationship between cinema and social change both on and off screen, throwing new light on and adding new twists to existing analytic frames.

Our overall trans-Asian framework is informed by the "trans-Asia" methodology that has been developing within the community of critical Asian studies scholars in film, media, and cultural studies in the new century. In 2004, Australia-based cultural and media studies scholar Iwabuchi Koichi presented the term in Japanese (Iwabuchi 2004). Film scholar Yoshimoto Mitsuhiro took it up in his article "National/International/Transnational: The Concept of Trans-Asian Cinema and the Cultural Politics of Film Criticism," in *Theorising National Cinema*, edited by Valentina Vitali and Paul Willemen (2006).[7] Deconstructing the Euro-American-centric kernel in the East-West dichotomy inherent in the term "national cinema" and "Asian cinema," as well as the specter of the Cold War and the logic of capital inherent in the "international" and "transnational," Yoshimoto declares, "[a]s a critical category, trans-Asian cinema refuses any unproblematic assertion of the uniqueness of Asian cinema as such, and of the various national cinemas in Asia." Therefore, the trans-Asian approach must always have a "genuine comparative perspective" sensitive to historicity and power dynamic (260). More as a proposal at the end of his polemical article, Yoshimoto stops short of elaborating or demonstrating how one might go about doing "trans-Asian cinema" studies. *Trans-Asia as Method: Theory and Practice*, edited by Jerome de Kloet, Yiu Fai Chow, and Gladys Pak Lei Chong, presents a constellation of interdisciplinary efforts in further developing the method with applications in critical theory, historical studies, cultural studies, and film studies, while alerting to the reductive dichotomization of the West and Western theory vis-a-vis "Asians (and the rest)" (de

Kloet, Chow, and Chong 2019, 6). In his chapter in the volume, Iwabuchi rearticulated his proposal for "trans-Asian" method as a means to "envision and actualize Asia as a dialogic communicative space in which people across borders collaborate to connect diverse voices, concerns, and problems in various, unevenly intersecting public sites in which the national is still a major site but does not exclusively take over public interests" (2–3). With other empirical cases that illustrate the numerous forms of border-crossing of peoples and cultural products, what we found most constructive in that anthology were the trans-Asia comparisons, referencing and collaboration, as well as a politics of transformation (instead or on top of deconstruction) inspired by intersectional feminism.

Beyond mostly cultural studies cases studies related to East Asia in *Trans-Asian as Method*, several recent significant monographs (Hee 2019; Lee 2020; Ma 2020; Mukherjee 2020; Sim 2020; Siddique 2022; Khoo 2021) and anthologies (especially *Early Cinema in Asia* [Deocampo 2017] and *Theorizing Colonial Cinema: Reframing Production, Circulation, and Consumption of Film in Asia* [Kwon, Odagiri, and Baek 2022]) have productively engaged in trans-Asian cinema studies aided by discoveries of "new" archives and rigorous, imaginative historiographical methodologies. We join their effort in implementing and complicating the trans-Asian method with a concentrated focus on cinema practices (defined in widest sense), in conversation with critical theory and decolonial and feminist historiography. We chose to keep the hyphen between "trans" and "Asia" for its emphasis on process, change, and unevenness, but adopt the lowercase for "trans-" and more fluid adjective form of "Asian" for articulating a critical distance to neoliberal or ethno-national grand narratives (such as the "Asia-Pacific century" or the "rise" of China and India) and a commitment to heterotopic, alter-geographic, anti-imperial, indigenous, vernacular, trans-regional, and transhemispheric experiences and practices spanning over a century of Asian and world film history.

We use the term "trans-Asian" to describe crossovers, exchanges, and migrations that take place across and beyond the territorial and imagined limits of "Asia." As the term "transnational" does for the category "nation," the term "trans-Asian" brings into question the stability or givenness of the category Asia. A sense of movement is implied by the prefix "trans-" and indicates not a static or ontological given but a processual and fluid state of becoming. By linking "trans" with the many multifaceted "Asias," we question received assumptions about what Asia *is* as a continent, what Asia *represents* as a distinct civilizational Other, or whether a stable corpus of Asian cinema informed by an Asian consciousness is either possible or desirable. Thus, we approach Asia as contingent and historical, made up of transnational trajectories and transmigrations, engendered through translations and transmissions. The local and the global are kept in tense relation through the prefix "trans-" and the hyphen underlines the unresolved and ongoing negotiations between identity and its breakdown. The gendered meaning of trans is implicit here, and as Mel Y. Chen has noted, "*trans-* is not a linear space of mediation between two monolithic, autonomous poles, as, for example, 'female' and 'male'. . . Rather, it is conceived of as more emergent than determinate, intervening with other categories in a richly elaborated space" (M. Chen 2012, 136). It is also in affinity with the idea of "transtopia" (borrowed from Hong Kong author Dung Kai-cheung) as conceptualized by queer theorist and historian Howard Chiang, in its two-pronged intervention to minoritarian identity politics; first, in its reference to "different scales of gender transgression that are not always recognizable through the Western notion of transgender," and second, because "transness appears less as a fixed entity than as individual and structural gradations that fundamentally ground most, if not all, facets of human life" (Chiang 2021, 4). In this spirit, our hope is that this volume foregrounds process and practice, movement and meaning, in an undulating continuum of combinations and contradictions. A trans-Asian method, as many of the chapters demonstrate, can signal misalignments between nations and languages, even as it can affirm attempts to understand and converse across difference.

The *Companion* is strung together by six sections, with each containing approximate equal weight. While the themes and rubric of each section organize the relevant chapters under one umbrella term, such as "Cine-activism," "Beyond Genre," "Independent Practice," and "Archives, Festivals, and Film Pedagogy," the sections are hardly mutually exclusive. Instead, they interconnect and supplement each other, presenting multifaceted views on clusters of film cultures, phenomena, practices, and institutions in varying scales, manifestations, and relations. The short introductions of each section highlight the key issues, approaches, and crisscrossing lines of thought and action that connect the chapters; they serve as anchors for each section and as relay junctions across sections. While most survey-style anthologies begin with a section featuring reprints of canonical essays or articles that provide grand theoretical frames of analysis, we seek to make a small departure from this conventional structure. Section I, on feminist, queer, anti-caste, and other activist practices, marks a critical area of Asian cinematic churning that has long sustained cross-regional solidarities of imagination and politics across linguistic, regional, religious, and national boundaries. Section II brings together different iterations of how cinema mediates imaginations of place and affective affiliations between places. What role has cinema played in both fortifying and contesting the modern nation-states of Asia? Essays in this section offer rigorous critiques of nationalist academic methodologies, filmic ideologies, and state policies by engaging with political films, the vexing question of a national language, and media industrial maneuvers.

We are equally mindful of cinema as industry and culture, apart from aesthetic form and social text. Section III takes up this concern directly as we explore a long arc of film cultures and industrial practices across Asian cinema centers. If on one hand, material media infrastructures like cables can mark out alternate imaginations of place and territory, we also see the ways in which streaming platforms like Netflix have both complicated and sharpened ideas of cinematic time and place, as well as hybrid content on the Internet and social media. In Section IV we complicate the fetishistic conflation of contemporary Asian cinemas with so-called extreme genres. The hugely popular branding of Asian horror genres as "Asia Extreme" was tied to the DVD rental boom in the early 2000s and helped bridge the gap between art cinema and popular culture. Here we discuss genre beyond the rubrics of art or extreme and excavate histories and futures of tropes, themes, and modes that have been important to Asian cinema and its viewers. Filmmakers disrupt and rework genres by activating imagination across national and cultural borders and reconnecting their works and those of their predecessors in film history. Section V is devoted to the vibrant independent film practices of various kinds, from Malaysia, the Philippines, and feminist documentary making and animation experiments across the Taiwan Strait, to resistance against censorship in Singapore and India, echoing several cases in Section I. Contributors discuss challenges of production and sustainability, marginal and subversive voices, and issues of care and labor in creative practice and community making. Finally, Section VI highlights our commitment to foregrounding extra-textual and non-representational sites and practices that have been critical to the discourse on and reception of Asian cinemas. Film pedagogy, festivals, retrospectives, and archival efforts come together here as we examine the role of cultural commentary in the material lives of film and its preservation, as well as the affective work done by curators and cinephiles in keeping certain memories of cinema afloat.

The ramifications of climate change and COVID-19 have highlighted and reframed some salient keywords such as care, collectivity, and solidarity in this volume. These keywords continue to push the ways of thinking about trans-Asian frameworks in collaborative practice: what does it mean to make and talk about connection and exchange beyond the transactional, imperial, patriarchal logic? This volume is a way for us, scholars operating between cultures, borders, and languages, to nurture our academic, artistic, and cultural activist networks across continents and oceans, and amplify issues that may not fit the imagination of neoliberal creativity or film/academic market visibility. At the same time, as we have dealt with our own challenges and losses in the span of four years, which affected the speed of preparing for the publication of this book, we cannot further emphasize the feminist perspective of care work as an inseparable factor involved in the labor of producing academic work. A trans-Asian collaborative practice is an ongoing endeavor to critically assess not only histories and structures that enable the mobility (and immobility) of cinemas but also notions of production, creativity, and legibility, as well as the kind of knowledge that we produce and share with our students and the public at large.

Notes

1 For more about the history of SIFF, see Berry (2017) and Ma (2012, 2017).
2 This is in part due to both a strained bilateral relationship between the PRC and some of these countries that have been critical of China's human rights problems, COVID-19 cover-up and excessive restrictions, and tensions in trade and copy rights, etc. "Taiwan's Golden Horse Awards" and "COVID-19" were among the sensitive words during the festival.
3 NYAFF was founded by the New York–based Subway Cinema. Grady Hendrix, one of the founders of Subway Cinema, explains the reasoning: "It seems there's only room for two things in releasing foreign films: one is 'world cinema masterpieces' and the other is 'trash' or what gets lumped under that label. There's not a lot of room left for plain old good movies . . . One of the reasons we've been able to do well is that there's a gap. These movies are being made, and they're not being picked up, but there's clearly an audience who wants to see them" (Palmer, August 14, 2001). Throughout its early years, NYAFF brought Johnnie To, Tsui Hark, Park Chan-wook, Bong Joon-ho, Takashi Miike, Kim Jee-woon, Ryoo Seung-wan, and Sion Sono to New York's discerning cinephiles and genre cinema enthusiasts.
4 Largely due to the "sensitive" subject matter, this is the only film without the "dragon seal," hence not released publicly in China. His earlier and most recent films all passed censorship and the so-called "technical standards" assessment for theatrical and/or online exhibition.
5 The last chapter by Gina Marchetti is about the Hong Kong–Australian director Clara Law's 2004 documentary, *Letters to Ali*, with an activist orientation.
6 The absence of central and west Asia in this *Companion* is also admittedly due to our lack of expertise on these areas. Instead of soliciting token contributions, we decided to concentrate on the areas our research and resources can address adequately.
7 Zhen Zhang and Yoshimoto co-taught a graduate seminar on topics in Asian film studies at New York University in the early 2000s where the group probed these terms including "trans-Asian cinema." Sangjong Lee, co-editor of this *Companion*, was one of the seminar participants who developed an original dissertation project on East Asian co-production during the Cold War, putting transnational film history and "trans-Asian cinema" studies into practice. Lee's recent book, *Cinema and the Cultural Cold War: US Diplomacy and the Origins of Asian Cinema Network* (2020), is an exemplary work of trans-Asian film historiography.

Bibliography

Anderson, Joseph, and Donald Richie. 1959. *The Japanese Film: Art and Industry*. New York: Grove Press.

Barnouw, Erik, and S. Krishnaswamy. 1963. *Indian Film*. New York: Columbia University Press.

Baumgärtel, Tilman, ed. 2012. *Southeast Asian Independent Cinema: Essays, Documents and Interviews*. Hong Kong: Hong University Press.

Berry, Chris. 2017. "Shanghai and Hong Kong: A Tale of Two Festivals." In *Chinese Film Festivals: Sites of Translation*, edited by Chris Berry and Luke Robinson, 15–33. London: Palgrave Macmillan.

Chen, Mel Y. 2012. *Animacies: Biopolitics, Racial Mattering, and Queer Affect*. Durham, NC: Duke University Press.

Chiang, Howard. 2021. *Transtopia in the Sinophone Pacific*. New York: Columbia University Press.

Ciecko, Anne T., ed. 2006. *Contemporary Asian Cinema: Popular Culture in a Global Frame*. London: Bloomsbury Academic.

de Kloet, Jerome, Yiu Fai Chow, and Gladys Pak Lei Chong, eds. 2019. *Trans-Asia as Method: Theory and Practice*. London; New York: Rowman & Littlefield.

Deocampo, Nick, ed. 2017. *Early Cinema in Asia*. Indiana University Press. Bloomington, IN: Indiana University Press.

Dissanayake, Wimal, ed. 1993. *Melodrama and Asian Cinema*. Cambridge/New York: Cambridge University Press.

———. 1994. *Colonialism and Nationalism in Asian Cinema*. Bloomington: Indiana University Press.

Eleftheriotis, Dimitris, and Gary Needham, eds. 2006. *Asian Cinemas: A Reader & Guide*. Honolulu: University of Hawaii Press.

Fortmueller, Kate. 2021. *Hollywood Shutdown: Production, Distribution, and Exhibition in the Time of COVID*. New York: University of Texas Press.

Hee, Wai-Siam. 2019. *Remapping the Sinophone: The Cultural Production of Chinese-Language Cinema in Singapore and Malaya before and during the Cold War*. Hong Kong: Hong Kong University Press.

Ingawanij, May Adadol, and Benjamin McKay, eds. 2012. *Glimpses of Freedom: Independent Cinema in Southeast Asia*. Ithaca: Cornell Southeast Asia Program Publications.

Iwabuchi, Koichi, ed. 2004. "Houhou to shite no toransu ajia [Trans-Asia as a Method] (in Japanese)." In *Koeru bunka kousaku suru kyoukai* [Transgressing Cultures and Intersecting Boundaries], 3–24. Tokyo: Yamakawa Shuppan.

Khoo, Gaik Cheng, Thomas Barker, and Mary J. Ainslie, eds. 2020. *Southeast Asia on Screen: From Independence to Financial Crisis (1945–1998)*. Amsterdam: Amsterdam University Press.

Khoo, Olivia. 2021. *Asian Cinema: A Regional View*. Edinburgh: Edinburgh University Press.

Kwon, Nayoung Aimee, Takushi Odagiri, and Moonim Baek, eds. 2022 *Theorizing Colonial Cinema: Reframing Production, Circulation, and Consumption of Film in Asia*. Bloomington, IN: Indiana University Press.

Lee, Sangjoon. 2020. *Cinema and the Cultural Cold War: US Diplomacy and the Origins of Asian Cinema Network*. Ithaca, NY: Cornell University Press.

Lent, John. 1990. *The Asian Film Industry*. Austin: University of Texas Press.

Li, Qiao, David Wilson, and Yanqiu Guan, eds. 2023. *The Global Film Market Transformation in the Post-Pandemic Era: Production, Distribution and Consumption*. Abingdon, Oxon; New York, NY: Routledge.

Lim, David C. L., and Hiroyuki Yamamoto, eds. 2012. *Film in Contemporary Southeast Asia: Cultural Interpretation and Social Intervention*. London/New York: Routledge.

Lovatt, Philippa, and Jasmine Nadua Trice. 2021. "Theorizing Region: Film and Video Cultures in Southeast Asia." *JCMS: Journal of Cinema and Media Studies* 60, no. 3 (Spring): 158–62.

Ma, Ran. 2012. "Celebrating the International, Disremembering Shanghai: The Curious Case of the Shanghai International Film Festival." *Culture Unbound: Journal of Current Cultural Research* 4: 147–68.

———. 2017. "Programming China at the Hong Kong International Film Festival and the Shanghai International Film Festival." In *Chinese Film Festivals: Sites of Translation*, edited by Chris Berry and Luke Robinson, 237–57, London: Palgrave Macmillan.

———. 2020. *Independent Filmmaking Across Borders in Contemporary Asia*. Amsterdam: Amsterdam University Press.

Magnan-Park, Aaron Han Joon, Gina Marchetti, and See Kam Tan, eds. 2018. *The Palgrave Handbook of Asian Cinema*. London: Palgrave MacMillan.

Meissner, Nico. 2021. *Independent Filmmaking in Southeast Asia: Conversations with Filmmakers on Building and Sustaining a Creative Career*. Abingdon, Oxon; New York, NY: Routledge.

Mukherjee, Debashree. 2020. *Bombay Hustle: Making Movies in a Colonial City*. New York, NY: Columbia University Press.

Palmer, Augusta. 2001. "Nowhere to Hide: *Subway Cinema* Stages Korean Invasion." *IndieWire*, August 14. https://www.indiewire.com/2001/08/festivals-nowhere-to-hide-subway-cinema-stages-korean-invasion-80821

Rothman, William. 1993. "Overview: What is American about Film Study in America?" In *Melodrama and Asian Cinema*, edited by Wimal Dissanayake. Cambridge: Cambridge University Press.

Siddique, Salma. 2022. *Evacuee Cinema: Bombay and Lahore in Partition Transit, 1940–1960*. Cambridge: Cambridge University Press.

Sim, Gerald. 2020. *Postcolonial Hangups in Southeast Asian Cinema: Poetics of Space, Sound, and Stability*. Amsterdam: Amsterdam University Press.

Teo, Stephen. 2012. *The Asian Cinema Experience: Styles, Spaces, Theory*. New York, NY: Routledge.

Thompson, Kristin. 1995. "Asian Cinema History Today." *Film History* 7 (1): 3–4.

Yoshimoto, Mitsuhiro. 2006. "National/International/Transnational: The Concept of Trans-Asian Cinema and the Cultural Politics of Film Criticism." In *Theorising National Cinema*, edited by Valentina Vitali and Paul Willemen, 254–61. London: BFI.

SECTION I

Cine-activism and Feminist Aesthetics

INTRODUCTION

Zhen Zhang

On a warm but breezy summer night in 2023, *In Search of Bengali Harlem* (2022), a heartrending documentary about immigration, history lost and found, generation and community, was shown as part of the Rooftops Film summer program in Kensington Plaza, Brooklyn. The triangle-shaped space surrounded by South Asian grocers and restaurants had rows of folding chairs occupied by a diverse audience, but mostly South Asian people living in the area or coming from elsewhere. Co-director and main character Alaudin Ullah, district representative Shahana Hanif, and several other community leaders introduced and talked about the film before and after the screening. Their impassioned speeches and conversations with the audience about forgotten histories, ambivalent relationships between the homeland and the diaspora, and between different generations turned the outdoor screening into a platform of public education and community activism.

This scene is half a world away from the open-air cinema in the streets of Dhaka, Bangladesh, described in rich detail by Lotte Hoek in the first chapter. But the high emotions and political energies I witnessed in Kingston Plaza resonated with those galvanized by the mobile projection of films by activist filmmakers embedded in the political crowd in Bangladesh. Taking seriously the critical role of exhibition practices in broadening the public sphere, we open the volume with Hoek's insightful analysis of film societies' role in Bangladesh's radical social and political movements since around the independence from Pakistan in 1971. They have screened experimental or non-commercial films by members and others outside of theaters, often literally amid protests and rallies. In 2013, for example, several film societies, alongside other cultural organizations, held free screenings, painted, sang, and staged plays during a mass protest in reaction to the International Crimes Tribunal on 1971 war crimes perpetrators. Bangladesh Film Society's publication featured women filmmakers in action. Among them, Reshmi Ahmed (a founding member of the Bangladesh Documentary Council) made *My Protests* (2014) documenting and tracing the historical roots of the 2013 protests, including, among other things, a 2008 outdoor screening of the avant-garde documentary *Stop Genocide*, made by Zahir Raihain in 1971. Functioning as a modular political form across several Asian societies against varying socio-cultural backgrounds, the mobile projection on a large screen, Hoek contends, holds the potential to mobilize or harness the political energy of the crowd.

DOI: 10.4324/9781003266952-3

Socially engaged filmmaking and alternative spectatorship formation as part of the "wider media ecology" enmeshed in social transformation are echoed in the rest of the section and elsewhere in the volume. Sangita Gopal's chapter delves into what she calls "genres of ecofeminism" and explores the social and aesthetic ramification of Indian women filmmakers' engagement with environmental movements in 1970s–'90s. She argues that these filmmakers working across media platforms including print journalism, radio, television, and theater activate affective agency of narrative conventions (specifically, horror, romantic comedy, and the domestic melodrama), and make sense of the "raw" material of environmental disasters and struggles from the ground up. These vernacular strategies, employed reflexively, reveal deep structural inequities that distribute environmental risk differentially among the population, while educating and mobilizing a wider middle-class audience.

Women filmmakers began to emerge in East Asian New Wave cinemas as well. Tang Shu-shuen and Ann Hui spearheaded the Hong Kong New Wave with their genre-bending works. Tang's *The Arch* (1968), in evocative black and white montage, is a bold modernist costume-drama indicting the repressive Confucian moral codes (Yau 2004). Ann Hui's *Boat People* (1982) made a big splash in international film scene and has become arguably the most prolific and well known Sinophone woman filmmaker (Erens 2000). In South Korea, women filmmakers like Yim Soon-rye (the sixth woman filmmaker to complete and release a feature narrative in Korean film history) began to ride the Korean New Wave in the 1990s (Park 2020). Chi-Yun Shin's interview with Yim traces a fascinating creative career from her film education in Paris to continuity supervisor upon entering the Korean film industry, from her early independent features exploring marginalized masculinity from a woman director's perspective to both popular and critically acclaimed *Little Forest* (2018) about a young woman rediscovering her roots and selfhood in the rural hometown. Along the way, Yim became more invested in women's, human, and animal rights activities and organizations dedicated to consciousness raising and social change about equality and diversity in the film industry and in the society.

Meanwhile, a younger generation of Korean women filmmakers have made significant strides with innovative works. Hyun Seon Park identifies and conceptualizes a "renovating vision of cine-feminism" in two independent debut features, Kim Bo-ra's *House of Hummingbird* (2018) and Yoon Dan-bi's *Moving On* (2020). Their preoccupation with urban and domestic space inherits a major trope *jip* (home or house) in postwar South Korean cinema (e.g., Kim Ki-young's *The Housemaid* 1960), as a place of modernity or capitalist desire or a source of uncanny anxiety. But they depart from the cannons by inserting an agentive female adolescent gaze and a gynocentric intergenerational framework for healing, memory retrieval, and opening an affective "relational space" or a "home-world" structured around everyday temporality that deconstructs the scale, intensity, and categories of the male-centered representational system.

The following two chapters focus on women filmmakers in Southeast Asian contexts. We encounter Thai filmmaker Anocha Suwichakornpong in Graiwoot Chulphongsathorn's profile interview. Her films defy genre expectations and rewrite recent Thai socio-political history by blurring the lines between narrative, documentary, and experimental films. At once pensive and incisive, her works challenge existing historiography (or its erasure) of popular protests and gender politics. Akin to Yim in South Korea, Suwichakornpong has played a leading role in community building. She co-founded a female-led film collective *Electric Eel Films* and *Purin Pictures*, an initiative which supports Southeast Asian cinema, which also supported Indonesian filmmaker Mouly Surya's film discussed in Intan Paramaditha's chapter. Paramaditha examines the potential and limits of Euro-American transnationalism theories in a locally and regional specific context. Using Surya's *Marlina Si Pembunuh dalam Empat Babak* (Marlina the Murderer in Four Acts, 2017), a feminist intervention in the Western genre, Paramaditha's nuanced analysis of this "Western" is situated within the evolving landscape of women's cinema in Southeast Asia as a whole. The independent movements and digital technology have enabled many women to enter the film industry and an expanded space for alternative perspectives and storytelling. Entangled in local networks, cultural activism, and transnational arts and festival circuits, the film-makers explore ways of connecting grassroots experiences and cosmopolitan aspirations. Educated abroad as Tang and Yim mentioned above, as well as her fellow Indonesian women directors, such as Nia Dinata, Nan Achnas, and Mira Lesmana, Surya's privileged class and educational background place her work in a complex web of symbolic capital and local, political commitment. Labeled as "Satay Western" and "Feminist Western," *Marlina*'s appropriation of the Western demonstrates its affinity with the new "Asian west-erns," transnational feminist cinema and the recent #MeToo movement, through a gender reversal of the hero(ine), female revenge, and bonding, a reflexive, creative use of the land-scape, among other strategies. "Yet what does *Marlina* mean to Indonesian women?" Para-maditha turns to the Eastern Indonesian writers and activists for understanding the film's ambivalent reception in a regionally concrete context, as well as her personal involvement in a trans-archipelagic feminist collective beyond the urban-center middle-class perspective. The lack of ethnographic sensitivity and accuracy in representing the Sumbanese culture and women, and the fact the film was not shown in the region while it garnered attention in the capital and international festivals, raise questions about the power imbalance and geo-cultural complexity in transnational cinema and feminist practices. The trans-Asian method pertains not simply to exchanges between Asian nations in Asia and across the continents and oceans but, more crucially, to urban-rural, inter-regional, and trans-archi-pelagic dynamics shaped by colonial and post-colonial experiences and discourses.

Shi-Yan Chao takes us further into the dynamic relationship between the national and the transnational in his chapter on Taiwan queer cinema's engagement with the marriage equal-ity campaign in the island nation. The recent synergy of the *tongzhi*/queer movement and the strengthening Taiwanese consciousness has contributed to an emerging "homo(trans) nationalism" that recast Chao's previous conceptualization of the "Chinese queer diasporic imaginary" undergirding an entrenched symbiotic Chinese patriarchy and state relationship in a changing local and cross-Strait context. The democratization process and the *tong-zhi*/queer movement, entwined with the rising "Taiwanese consciousness" (as a defensive identity formation vis-a-vis the PRC), has destabilized the traditional Chinese "family" and "state" strongholds and *transformed* the domestic and national space to accommo-date queer kinship. *Dear Tenant* (2020) and *Your Name Engraved Herein* (2020) from the immediate post-gay-marriage era,[1] however, do not visibly celebrate the gay marriage as a transnational liberal value, but instead reflect on the lived experiences of being *tongzhi* in earlier time periods. They achieve their compelling emotional appeal through innovative revision of TV family drama tropes (*Dear Tenant*) and a reflexive historiographic approach to the *tongzhi*/queer movement in the post–martial law era (*Your Name*). The dual tempo-ral structure in the latter coincides with a reshaping of queer temporality and affect in many *tongzhi* lives in Taiwan and the hopeful ending departs from earlier melancholic *tongzhi*/queer narratives.

Helen Hok-Sze Leung's chapter concludes the section by taking us across the Pacific, to Vancouver, Canada's vibrant diasporic Asian screen culture scene, an integral part of what critics have called the "Pacific New Wave." In a city whose film (location) industry and tourism depend a great deal on Hollywood productions and rising East Asian cinemas, the local Asian independent filmmakers have persevered and thrived through their commitment to place-specific aesthetics, experimentation with hybrid styles, and a multimedia and collaborative approach to filmmaking. Leung highlights the pioneering work of Mina Shum (her debut feature *Double Happiness* [1994] launched Sandra Oh's career) and her influence on a younger generation of Asian diasporic filmmakers. The commitment of place inspired Asian filmmakers to explore issues of land and Indigenous community. Japanese-Chilean Canadian filmmaker Alejandro Yoshizawa's *All Our Father's Relations* (2016) is one of the first films to explore Asian-Indigenous relations in the region. Echoing the film societies' political engagement in Bangladesh in the opening chapter, the "artist-run-center" counterculture movement in Vancouver's Asian film scene engages with issues of gender, sexuality, and race, along with alternative practices in production, exhibition, and distribution. More excitingly, a group of queer filmmakers have made and exhibited their film and multimedia work not only in theaters but also in outdoor places laden with historical significance for Asian immigrants.

Note

1 In May 2019, Taiwan became the first nation in Asia to legalize same-sex marriage.

References

Erens, Patricia Brett. 2000. "The Film Work of Ann Hui." In *The Cinema of Hong Kong: History, Arts, Identity*, edited by Poshek Fu and David Desser, 176–96. Cambridge: Cambridge University Press.

Park, Hyun Seon. 2020. "South Korean Cine-Feminism." *Journal of Japanese and Korean Cinema* 12 (2): 91–97.

Yau, Ching. 2004. *Filming Margins: Tang Shu Shuen, A Forgotten Hong Kong Woman Director.* Hong Kong: Hong Kong University Press.

1

A SCREEN IN THE CROWD

Film Societies and Political Protest in Bangladesh

Lotte Hoek

Screenings in the Crowd

In 2013, a huge public protest sprung up in Dhaka, the capital of Bangladesh. As protest-ers gathered in their thousands, films were screened among them. Amid the giant crowd, student activists of the Dhaka University Film Society (DUFS) hitched a cloth painted with a reflective coating to bamboo poles and erected a large improvised film screen. With a generator, a laptop and a projector set up in the street, they screened documentary and feature films late into the night. The large screen raised by the collective of film society activists addressed no particular audience but accrued spectators and passersby from within the crowd, many of whom held smaller digital screens individually. What was the place of this large screen within the digitally enabled crowd? A closer look at the large screen rigged up by film societies in the political crowd illustrates the intersections between cinema and social change, in which textual and aesthetic forms are springs to action for activities around the screen that call into being publics and modes of reception that may or may not be in sync with the aspirations of the political protests that they participate in.

Film is among a range of cultural forms that have been part of public contestations at moments of heightened political conflict in Bangladesh. Artists and cultural movements were at the heart of the political mobilizations of the 1950s and '60s that would eventu-ally become the struggle for Bangladesh's independence from Pakistan in 1971. Filmmak-ers and film texts have participated in myriad ways in social and political movements and moments of acute public dissent and protest. A key vector by which cinematic activism has taken place are film societies. Film societies are cine-clubs that screen critically acclaimed, experimental or non-commercial films outside of theaters and organize film related activi-ties for their membership. Built around a shared conviction about the social importance and political power of art cinema, the activities of film societies have been understood as a "movement." With a collective goal to improve the quality of films and spread awareness of a distinct canon of worthy films, the film society movement in South Asia originating in the 1950s and '60s, has been particularly linked to progressive and radical political orienta-tions (Majumdar 2021; Venkiteswaran 2009). Simultaneously, film societies have been in the crosshairs of global political wrangling through their reliance on international cultural

DOI: 10.4324/9781003266952-4

Figure 1.1   A film screening by Moviyana Film Society on the roads of Dhaka's busy Shahbag intersection. Credit: Belayat Hossain Mamun and Moviyana Film Society.

organizations and foreign embassies who use their supply of film reels and access to audi-
toriums as soft political power.

There are moments when the practices of the film society, normally focused on film
screening and collective viewing that are largely contained in festivals and small-scale
screenings, burst their banks to emerge in the public domain as part of larger political
mobilizations and broad coalitions. In these moments, the screen is not the object that
constitutes the crowd around itself. Rather, the screen emerges in a crowd created by a
constellation of other actors and objects. I focus on these moments in this chapter. Nusrat
S. Chowdhury identifies mass gatherings as the key form by which political participation
and contestation unfolds in Bangladesh. She writes that "in Dhaka, political groups aim
to take over historically meaningful spaces of public gathering. . . . Whichever political
side one is on, the goal is to take over the street" (2019, 9). She argues persuasively that
such occupations are "a first step in making an effective political statement. These are not
spontaneous crowds of angry citizens . . . but are more or less rehearsed *spectacles of presence*" (2019, 9–10, my emphasis). Building on her work, I show that the large open-air
film screening has been one facet of such "spectacles of presence," one that has a robust
presence in moments of popular political dissent in Bangladesh. These include during the
movement against dictatorship in the 1980s, for the recognition of war crimes in the early
1990s and again during mass protest against the International Criminal Court's rulings in
the 2010s. Inspired by discussions of the political nature of the crowd in postcolonial South

Asia, I ask what the place is of the large temporary screen within this crowd. While "we now have a platform infrastructure where online and device-led participation is increasingly transforming the collective or even displacing older phenomenologies of the crowd as a key reference for political subjectivity" (Sundaram 2022, 267), I suggest that the large, temporary film screen retains a place and political potency within this new type of digitally enabled political crowd.

Describing, first, the longstanding political nature of film society practice and, second, the form of free, open-air film screenings in political crowds, in this chapter I argue, first, that improvised film screenings within mass gatherings have a political history in the 20th century that continues to be part of the politics of the digitally enabled crowds of the 21st century, where the small screen of the mobile phone exists alongside the large screen onto which moving images are projected. Second, I argue that this screen in the crowd is a *modular* political practice, one that has stable formal characteristics, is portable and adaptable between different political contexts and moments, and is already understood to have particular types of outcomes or impacts. This political form and practice can be found during large-scale occupations of public space in major cities across the world, including in the form of Tahrir Cinema and Kazeboon screenings in Egypt (Lebow 2018; Mollerup and Gaber 2015) and film screenings within the street occupations in Hong Kong's umbrella movement (Ho 2020, 715; Veg 2015, 64). To account for the political efficacy of this modular form, I theorize the Bangladesh film society movement's outdoor screenings by engaging discussions of similar and adjacent practices of outdoor and mobile cinema elsewhere in Asia (Ingawanij 2018; Li 2020; MacDonald 2017; Zhou 2021) that have stressed the transformed nature of both spectatorship and social space in such forms of film screening. Within the crowd, film projection's transformative effects animate already existing political potentials of the crowd. Finally, I show that while film screening in and through film societies is part of the domain of the political, by its very crowd-like nature such screenings are unpredictably tethered to aspirations for social and political transformation.

Film Societies and Cinema's Political Forms

A year after the Shahbag protests had ended, I visited the offices of DUFS. The airy modernist buildings of the Teacher-Student Centre (TSC) were designed by the Greek architect Constantinos A. Doxiadis in 1962 and sit at the heart of the campus. Along its corridors are the offices of many student associations. The room occupied by DUFS was lined with glass-fronted bookshelves and the spare wall space was decorated with framed film posters and flyers from the society's past, including for an event called Assembly and Film Screening Against War from 2003. Presiding over the room was a giant portrait of a smiling Satyajit Ray, the Indian Bengali filmmaker who exerted such influence over the film society movement in India and whose films are routinely screened in Bangladeshi film societies.

A number of students leaned over the heavy wooden table that took up most of the space in the middle of the room. They turned the pages of a picture book excitedly. The book, titled *Jagoroner Kotha* (Words of Awakening, Haque 2014), contained photographs from the mass protests that had erupted in February 2013 at the Shahbag intersection, on the edge of the Dhaka University campus. Members of DUFS had been actively involved in these mass protests. When the Shahbag movement unfolded on their doorstep, the DUFS activists brought their screening practice into the street, showing films related to the Liberation War. The students exclaimed and chatted excitedly as they flipped through the book and came across portraits of friends and comrades, bringing up small anecdotes and reminiscing about those heady days of the year past.

The mass protests in 2013 had started online when Bangladeshi bloggers expressed their discontent over a verdict of the International Crimes Tribunal that had sentenced a war criminal to life imprisonment instead of sentencing him to death. The Tribunal was instated to try those who had collaborated with the Pakistan army during the Bangladesh Liberation War in 1971 and its judgments were understood to answer major questions facing the polity, such as the place of secular politics, the direction of social development, and the nature of Bengali culture within public life and the state in Bangladesh (Mohaiemen 2013; Chowdhury 2019; Roy 2019; Sabur 2013). The bloggers called for a gathering at the Shahbag intersection, where a small segment of pavement opposite the National Museum had been set aside for protest (Chowdhury 2019, 9). Within hours the numbers gathered at Shahbag had grown exponentially to a vibrant mass protest where a broad coalition of activists and sympathizers had gathered.

Among the crowd were many cultural organizations, including film societies. "We held free screenings at Shahbag," a DUFS member explained to me. They had screened classic war films that captured the fervor and despair of the 1971 Liberation War, including canonical film society films about 1971 such as *Stop Genocide* (1971) and *Muktir Gaan* (Song of Freedom, 1995). Their public screenings were their protest. The film societies were part of the wider media ecology of Shahbag that included drawing, theater, music, dance, and rhetorical performances both in the streets and online. The DUFS students came out into the street alongside those who drew and painted, sang, and staged plays. Films were only one among many styles and forms of publicity by which subjects were moved and mobilized.

"It is our responsibility," one of the students explained to me, "DUFS has always been the most activist film society in the movement." The convictions about cinema's place and efficacy in social and political mobilizations ran deep at DUFS. The Students Film Federation had been set up at Dhaka University in 1963 (Banglapedia 2014), the same year the Pakistan Film Society (later the Bangladesh Film Society) was founded (Raju 2015: 19). These film clubs, and others that were set up over the years, focused on screening and discussing films, mostly internationally renowned ones and whatever reels passed through the various diplomatic circuits into Bangladesh. The active members of these societies have come to be described as film activists. Their screening and discussion of a canon of films aimed to create access to these texts and to realize particular modes of engaging them. In this way they built a social and intellectual life around film texts and made cinema a particular social and ritual practice. Key activists moved between the societies, reviewing films for newspaper, publishing periodicals related to the societies and films. The belief in the social power and efficacy of cinema was a shared assumption across these fora. The gathering storm of popular unrest and military rule in the late 1960s, alongside the longstanding left political engagements of many of the society's key figures, pushed the conceptualization of cinema as a political tool that has since animated the film society movement in Bangladesh.

Core ideas about the forceful nature and political power of cinema are articulated explicitly in the 1980 special issue of the Bangladesh Film Society's periodical *Film Bulletin*. Titled *Camera Jokhon Rifle* (When the Camera Is a Rifle), the issue includes essays by film society activists and renowned Bangladeshi filmmakers, including Zahir Raihan, Mohammad Khusru, Alamgir Kabir, and Tanvir Mokammel, as well as an essay by feminist philosopher Hasna Begum on Humberto Solas' *Lucia* (1968). Published less than ten years after Bangladesh gained independence through a popular armed struggle, *Camera Jokhon Rifle* places the film text and director's vision at the heart of the political potential of the cinema. But the activation of this potential required the expert introduction of these films to audiences outside of the capitalist frames of film production and distribution interests. The generation of film activists writing in *Camera Jokhon Rifle*, under the guidance of Kabir and with the inspiration of the late Raihan, would reshape the film society's practices of exhibition and embrace a mobile projection format to screen films they made themselves, often on 16 mm. *Camera Jokhon Rifle* engaged the legacies of the Third Cinema and was in lockstep with developments elsewhere in South Asia, where filmmakers such as Anand Pathwardan also considered that "films are living weapons, not things to appreciate in the cinema" (in Cubitt 1986, 63). DUFS and other film societies like it in early-21st-century Bangladesh have inherited the practices and ideals of the film society movement that developed since the 1960s.

The participation of film societies in the 2013 Shahbag movement was documented in the slim *Jagoroner Kotha* volume. Cultural activists of all sorts were well represented during the protests and among the many portraits in the volume were photographs of film society activists. Published on the occasion of International Women's Day, the photographs were all of women during the protests, some of whom were named in the captions. The DUFS students leafed through the volume and exclaimed and chatted excitedly as they came across portraits of friends and comrades, reminiscing about those heady days of the year past. One of the portraits showed filmmaker and film society activist Oddri Hridesh, lifting her digital camera above her head. Her face shows great concentration as she looks at the small digital display while she documents the movement unfolding before her. In another photograph, Reshmi Ahmed, one of the founders of the Bangladesh Documentary Council, is shown with her fist raised.

A year after the protests, Reshmi Ahmed made a Bengali-language documentary film titled *Amar Protibad* (My Protest, 2014) that documents her own involvement in the political movement. This film illustrates effectively how political protest has incorporated film-based activism, whether through documentation or as free outdoor film projections. The voiceover in the film is by Shameem Akhtar, one of the most significant female independent filmmakers in Bangladesh, who is also interviewed in the film. Akhtar's voice narrates Ahmed's life story over new and archival images documenting major political transitions in East Pakistan/Bangladesh by which the ideals of the Liberation War (democracy, socialism, nationalism, secularism) are pushed aside and collaborators and war criminals return to public life and political power. The film is punctuated by the statement "I was unable to protest" (আমি প্রতিবাদ করতে পারি নেই), that closes out each sequence of the film.

The film's refrain changes in the sequence that tracks the 2008 Movement for Bengali Culture, which gathered young people in the capital associated with left and progressive political positions to protest the perceived Islamization of the public domain in Bangladesh. One still image in the sequence shows Reshmi Ahmed during these protests with a small video camera in hand, on an open-backed lorry, alongside other filmmakers and photographers, including renowned photojournalist Abir Abdullah. The voiceover says: "The young people could no longer sit idly. I went and saw my friends protesting. . . . I joined in with my camera. Let's see if something can be done." Ahmed singles out the camera as her political tool of choice. As this statement is made, a still photograph shows young people holding a banner of the Conscious Artists' Society. The montage that follows shows large protests at Dhaka University and the Institute of Fine Arts. Footage from several outdoor cultural events is cut together. Filmmakers and activists present at these protests, such as Naeem

Mohaiemen, Nasrin Siraj Annie, and Molla Sagar, make fleeting appearances, and footage shot by them is also incorporated into the film.

One of the events Ahmed shows as part of the 2008 sequence is an outdoor screening of the avant-garde documentary *Stop Genocide*, made by Zahir Raihain in 1971 as an awareness raising film (Akhter 2020). This outdoor screening at Dhaka University was part of the protests. As Mohaiemen reflected at the time: "We write and film and photograph and protest, not to stop an 'Islamist threat' but to take control of the terms of the debate" (2008: online). It is not for nothing that when Ahmed decides the time had come for her protest, she picks up her camera. The final scene of the film shows the 2013 Shahbag protests. The voiceover concludes that "I took to the streets with my camera. At last I protested" (আমি আমার ক্যামেরা নিয়ে বেরিয়ে পড়লাম। অবশেষে আমি প্রতিবাদ করলাম).

Reshmi Ahmed's film and the events it documents illustrate how film and film societies have been active participants in the "spectacles of presence" that are central to mass politics in Bangladesh. Filmmakers and film screenings have a well-established and oft-reprised part in political mobilization. Film society activists, for their part, are clear about the urgency of their free outdoor screenings as part of the political crowd. But how might we understand more precisely in what ways the large temporary film screen forms part of mass protest? And what sort of political action it precipitates within the crowd?

Mobile Projection in the Crowd

Open-air and itinerant film screenings have been used for explicitly political projects of the colonial, postcolonial, or socialist state and have been studied as such (Larkin 2008; Ingawanij 2018; Cooper 2020; Zhou 2021). Early film projection in South Asia often took place in tents that were erected temporarily as part of itinerant shows and plein air entertainments (Chatterjee 2011; Mahadevan 2015), but the advent and ubiquity of built theaters largely brough commercial screening of cinema indoors. While outdoor entertainment cinema has persisted across Asia (Imanjaya 2016; Mahadevan 2015, 4), outdoor film screenings largely became the domain of political consciousness raising and publicity efforts on the part of the state, political groups and social movements over the course of the 20th century. Linked to associations of education with the outdoors in South Asia, where "true Enlightenment cannot be achieved within the closed box of a room – one needs to be outdoors, under the open sky" (Charles Correa in Brown 2009, 24), outdoor and mobile film projection in East Pakistan/Bangladesh has taken the shape of government publicity vans, carts, and boats bringing government films of instruction and persuasion into rural areas, 16 mm NGO projectors displaying awareness raising shorts, and films made by activist filmmakers taken on the road to screen in village fields from the 1980s onward. These types of screenings were open to the air, itinerant or mobile in their set up and screening schedules, as well as frequently improvised in the sense of making do with the limits and affordances of the particular spaces and social settings in which the screenings were held.

A film screening in the open-air in the midst of a crowd, and outside the disciplining structures of commercial exhibition in purpose-built spaces, requires a rethinking of the nature of film exhibition and spectatorship. In their respective discussions of open-air film screenings in 20th-century China, Li (2020) and Zhou (2021) both emphasize that what is on the screen is only one aspect of the wider social and material environment around the open-air screen. "One dimension of cinematic experience, which open-air cinema particularly foregrounds, is the 'air,' or the overall atmosphere of an exhibition space that engages viewers through multiple senses" (Zhou 2021, 105). Li calls this "hot noise," "a broader sensory environment, ambience, and vibe" (2020, 11). Working with memories of mobile cinema in mid-20th-century China, both Zhou and Li ask how this immersive and extended experience might recalibrate what we understand as cinema and the forms of spectatorship this makes possible. "Instead of drawing audiences into the film . . . , Chinese mobile cinema created an electrifying environment that radiated outward, entangling viewers" (Li 2020, 11). Zhou calls this " 'atmospheric spectatorship,' a mode of cinematic experience that does not necessarily privilege the film as an object of attention but is characterized by presence in an experiential milieu that surrounds the viewer" (2021, 105). In relation to Thailand's "itinerant makeshift cinema," May Adadol Ingawanij emphasizes how peripatetic modes of display are embedded within existing ritual and artistic practices, where the human sensorium is animated by non-human entities and artifacts, including spectral agents (2017). Complementing these foci on expanded and entangled modes of spectatorship, MacDonald notes that film screenings in outdoor spaces as part of Daoist ritual practice in contemporary Thailand transform those spaces. He argues that "projection technology measures out a space for the viewer and has a social implication" so that when the projector is placed in an open urban space, we can "see street cinema as a space momentarily changed by the projection of light and by the uninvited presence of viewers, their bodies attracted and oriented to the screen" (2017, 159). The analyses of mobile cinema by Li, Zhou, Ingawanij, and MacDonald help imagine the changed natures of both spectatorship and public space that occurs when film projection happens outdoors, non-theatrically, and sometimes unannounced. In such cases, spectatorship is "atmospheric," the public space transformed by the arrival of the cinematic apparatus, while the film text takes its place among the many other types of practices, durations, and entities that inhabit the surroundings of the screen that interpellate and entangle passing spectators.

The emphasis in much of the literature on mobile cinema is on historical case studies and building analyses from recollections by the elderly and encounters in the archive. But "thriving vestigial media" (Mahadevan 2021, 136), such as film projection onto temporary screens in the field or street, unsettle the technological episteme that posits the erasure of such forms of projection as either withered away by the consolidation of film form within the theater or as an Asian "survival" that speaks to cinema's improper or belated transition. The large, temporary, open-air screen in the public domain, with un-ticketed access, generating "atmospheric" forms of spectatorship and transforming public space is not a vanished scene however. In Dhaka, film societies such as Moviyana and DUFS continue to project films on large screens in the roads for non-paying spectators who wander in and out, not unlike MacDonald's Thai laborers who find repose in the car park turned projection space (2017, 160). It illustrates that "the cinema's manifestations, what it means, and how it becomes viable remain unpredictable and open to a process of reinvention and improvisation" (Mahadevan 2015, 9).

The legacy of the cinema as "rifle" and state publicity, alongside the proximity of cultural movements to social and political activism in Bangladesh, means that when the activists of DUFS rig up their screen, setting up laptop and projector in the street, it is not merely one manifestation of cinematic experience but also a screen practice that is a modular political form. It is modular as the format of the open-air, non-ticketed screening of relevant films on a big screen set in the public path is portable between different contexts, from the documentary screenings during labor union actions to popular protests against environmental destruction to being part of annual commemorative events. It is also modular because its form is emulated across these spaces and is immediately recognizable as a particular sort of cultural politics. It is political in that this screen practice is one way of participating in and contributing to Chowdhury's "spectacles of presence" that are central to making political statements and forcing action in Bangladesh. The particular political nature of this screening practice lies in its capacity to generate an "atmospheric spectatorship" that connects particular film texts to its environment of protest and gathering by transforming the social space around it, thus connecting the temporalities, aesthetics, and sentiments of the screen and the street. The crowd is the medium of mass politics in Bangladesh, "a repository of the nuances of postcolonial sovereignty, where the popular and uncivil come together" (Chowdhury 2019, 6). In the crowd "imperceptible potentials" emerge in a "tangle of representations and practices" (Chowdhury 2019, 20), generating "political affect," constituted by "a mix of corporeality and public feelings" (Chowdhury 2020a, 265). The large screen becomes part of this crowd formation and contributes to its "tangle of representations and practices" that generate public feelings.

The moving image screened on a large temporary screen within the political crowd is not about immersive spectatorship and transparent representation. This is what the historical accounts of the mobile cinema underscore: the force of the moving image by which the film text is refracted through an atmosphere thick with bodies, sounds, images, and objects surrounding the screen. In their discussion of film screenings in Tahrir Square during Egypt's revolutionary movement, Mollerup and Gaber suggest that "revolutionary street screenings enable particular paths to knowledge because they make media engage with and take place within quotidian spaces that the revolution aims to liberate and transform" (2015, 2906). It is in the concatenation of objects, bodies, images, and sensations that political knowledge and affect is realized that is not the effect of immersive spectatorship. More-than-clear articulations by recognizable actors whose claims emerge apparently unmediated and transparently from its grounds, and unlike the plentiful giant digital screens that beam advertisement films and government messages at commuters as they idle in Dhaka's traffic jams, the moving image projected by protesters in the crowd are received in a manner that entangles them rather than communicating directly to them.

While in Tahrir Square and neighborhoods across Egypt images from the Internet and social media that documented the revolution were remediated by projection onto large screens in the street (Alexander and Aouragh 2014; Mollerup and Gaber 2015), at Shahbag the crowds were offered screenings of feature films and documentaries related to the 1971 Liberation War. These were not images *of* the protests but images that were already part of the mobilizing discourse that animated these protests, the so-called "spirit of the liberation war." The "*muktijuddher chetona* or spirit of the liberation war is now as much a powerful commodity as a political tagline" (Chowdhury 2019, 182), and most images related to the 1971 war have been reduced to this shorthand. It made such films the obvious choice for screening at Shahbag.

One of the films screened at Shahbag was *Muktir Gaan* (Song of Freedom, 1995), the partly dramatized documentary film about a Bengali musical troupe that traveled to the front during the 1971 Liberation War by Tareque Masud and Catherine Masud. *Muktir Gaan* is a staple of the 1971 war cinema genre and is frequently screened on national holidays. As such, it participates in the wider "political iconographic culture" (Chowdhury 2020b, 29) in which particular images have been invested with a direct link to the "spirit of the liberation war," while divesting them of other associations, undoing their polysemy through repetition and censorship. A glimpse of the eye is sufficient to establish the nature of such images even in crowded open-air conditions that may dissuade more attentive modes of reading. Iconic films are well suited to an atmospheric spectatorship.

At Shahbag, *Muktir Gaain* was braided with other iconic forms in the wider media ecology of the protest, where different forms and temporalities are folded together (Cody 2020). These prominently included digital media environments. In a blog post during this time, dancer and cultural activist Lubna Marium (2013), who had actively participated in the war herself, warned against the dehumanizing effects of the call for more death that animated the crowds at Shahbag. In her powerful post, she recalled her younger brother, who was a liberation fighter and witness to the war's atrocities. He "took his own life six years after Bangladesh's Independence" (Rahman 2018). Marium's refusal to join the calls for more violence and death in Shahbag's central demand for the death penalty made her the target of virulent criticism and abuse online. In a short reflection on the same blog, Naeem Mohaiemen wrote: "As I read harsh comments directed against [Lubna Marium] online . . . I wondered if anyone remembered that the film playing in the background of Shahbagh's giant screen was *Muktir Gaan*. . . and the two women in the singing troupe were Lubna Marium and her sister Naila Sattar?" (Mohaiemen 2013). It seemed no one remembered. While the film societies screened documentary footage of Lubna Marium on the front lines with her cultural troupe on a large screen at Shahbag, activists in the crowd hurled abuse at her on smaller digital screens. The details of the film dispersed and evaporated as the film's mode of address was transformed through its screening in the crowd.

The screening of *Muktir Gaan* at Shahbag illustrates how the large screen in the crowd generates a particular type of spectatorship that activates political potentials imminent in the crowd in excessive and unpredictable ways. The activities of film societies within political crowds should be understood as part of Chowdhury's "imperceptible politics." Chowdhury highlights hearsay, accident, and excess as the form potentials that lead to political action take in the crowd (2019, 21). Within the "hot noise" of the crowd, excess and misrecognition emerge as forms of interpellation by the large screen. This is what the moving image on the mobile screen in the crowd provides: immanent potentials animated by the moving image that channels forces between the human, the material and the spectral. A dispositive emerges of which the screen and the moving image, the film activists and their curations, form only one part. The point is not that spectators were paying unjustifiably little attention to *Muktir Gaan* or any of the other films screened but rather that the screen in the crowd encourages an "atmospheric spectatorship" that has a role to play in fanning the possibilities of an imperceptible politics immanent in the crowd. Asking whether the crowd knows who the figure on screen is remains important but is futile. This is not because social media users or political crowds are somehow worse readers of film but because of the ways in which the big screen comes to be braided within the media logics of the 21st century. Impromptu film projection onto a large temporary screen in the crowd is part of the "deep mediatization" (Hepp 2020) of contemporary life. Between mediatized bodies and the large screen onto which are projected films that are already short-hand for particular political messages within a wider political economy of slogans and visuals, a visceral and enervated co-presence in the crowd in which "imperceptible potentials" are activated by those screenings are more significant than the information loss that occurs in the process.

The Cinema of the Movement, the Movement in the Cinema

A year after the spectacular political crowds had gathered at the Shahbag intersection, Moviyana Film Society organized a series of film screenings on the street outside the National Museum to commemorate the events of February 2013. Titled "Cinema of the Shahbag Movement, the Shahbag Movement in Cinema" (শাহবাগ আন্দোলনের চলচ্চিত্র, চলচ্চিত্রে শাহবাগ আন্দোলন), Reshmi Ahmed's *Amar Protibad* was screened. The crowds of last year had splintered and then melted away but smaller groups of spectators gathered, sharing in that film society conviviality of dedicated cinephiles, film activists, friends of friends, accidental passersby, and hot sweet tea. Despite the dissipated effervescence, film society activists returned. They would continue their movement, sharing and spreading modes of gathering around the screen that erupt into public spaces among small and large crowds.

The large temporary screen within the political crowd indicates a new conjugation of media regimes. Francis Cody argues that while publicity has changed in the era of social media, earlier media formations are recast rather than replaced in the present (2020). The appearance of a large screen in a crowd of people each holding their own mobile phones should be understood in this light. Rather than a throwback to an earlier era of cinema as a mobilizing and political form, the large film screen is a modular political form in the digitally enabled crowd of the 21st century. Here the relaying of the message, requiring a particular type of attention and spectatorial position, is not the central task of the large screen. Instead, within the visually oriented political cultures of contemporary protest, moving images function as shorthand and are refracted through the atmosphere thick with bodies, objects, technologies, sounds, and images. Actualizing potentials immanent in the crowd, these moving images and large screens are live wires that are unpredictably tethered to the social and political movements of which they are a part.

Acknowledgments

I'm deeply grateful to Debashree Mukherjee, Oddri Hridesh, Belayat Hossain Mamun, Dhrubo Das, Saydia Gulrukh, and Magnus Course for their comments and support in developing this chapter.

References

Akhter, Fahmida. (1971) 2020. "Zahir Raihan's Stop Genocide: A Dialectical Cinematic Message to the World." In *South Asian Filmscapes: Transregional Encounters*, edited by Elora Halim Chowdhury and Esha Niyogi De, 233–49. Seattle: University of Washington Press.

Alexander, Anne, and Miriyam Aouragh. 2014. "Egypt's Unfinished Revolution: The Role of the Media Revisited." *International Journal of Communication* 8 (1): 890–915.

Brown, Rebecca M. 2009. *Art for a Modern India, 1947–1980*. Durham: Duke University Press.

Chatterjee, Ranita. 2011. "Journeys in and Beyond the City: Cinema in Calcutta 1897–1939." PhD diss., University of Westminster.

Chowdhury, Nusrat Sabina. 2019. *Paradoxes of the Popular: Crowd Politics in Bangladesh*. Stanford: Stanford University Press.

———. 2020a. "Death, Despair and Democracy in Bangladesh." In *Emotions, Mobilisations, and South Asian Politics*, edited by Amélie Blom and Stéphanie Tawa Lama-Rewal, 264–80. Delhi: Routledge.

———. 2020b. "A Second Coming: The Specular and Spectacular 50 Years On." *Sudasien Chronik – South Asia Chronicle* 10: 31–58.

"Cine Club." 2014. *Banglapedia*. Accessed July 1, 2022, https://en.banglapedia.org/index.php?title=Cine_Club.

Cody, Francis. 2020. "Metamorphoses of Popular Sovereignty: Cinema, Short Circuits, and Digitalization in Tamil India." *Anthropological Quarterly* 93 (2): 57–88.

Cooper, Timothy. 2020. "The Kaččā and the Pakkā: Disenchanting the Film Event in Pakistan." *Comparative Studies in Society and History* 62 (2): 262–95.

Cubitt, Sean. 1986. "'Bombay our City': Interview with Anand Patwardhan." *Framework* 0 (30): 60–66.

Haque, Shammi, ed. 2014. *Jagoroner Kotha* [Words of Awakening]. Dhaka: Lucky Akhtar.

Hepp, Andreas. 2020. *Deep Mediatization*. New York: Routledge.

Ho, Ming-sho. 2020. "How Protests Evolve: Hong Kong's Anti-Extradition Movement and Lessons Learned from the Umbrella Movement." *Mobilization: An International Quarterly* 1, no. 25 (SI): 711–28.

Imanjaya, Ekky. 2016. "The Cultural Traffic of Classic Indonesian Exploitation Cinema." PhD diss., University of East Anglia.

Ingawanij, May Adadol. 2018. "Itinerant Cinematic Practices In and Around Thailand during the Cold War." *Southeast of Now: Directions in Contemporary and Modern Art in Asia* 2 (2): 9–41.

Larkin, Brian. 2008. *Signal and Noise: Media, Infrastructure, and Urban Culture in Nigeria*. Durham: Duke University Press.

Lebow, Alisa. 2018. *Filming Revolution*. Stanford: Stanford University Press.

Li, Jie. 2020. "The Hot Noise of Open-Air Cinema." *Grey Room* 81: 6–35.

MacDonald, Richard L. 2017. "Projecting Films to Spirits: On Shrines as Conjunctural Space and the Ritual Economy of Outdoor Cinema in Bangkok." *Visual Anthropology Review* 33 (2): 152–63.

Mahadevan, Sudhir. 2015. *A Very Old Machine: The Many Origins of the Cinema in India*. Albany: SUNY Press.

———. 2021. "Obsolescence." *BioScope: South Asian Screen Studies* 12 (1–2): 134–36.

Majumdar, Rochona. 2021. *Art Cinema and India's Forgotten Futures*. New York: Columbia University Press.

Marium, Lubna. 2013. "Lubna Marium on Shahbag." *Alal o Dulal*. Accessed June 30, 2022. https://alalodulal.org/2013/02/12/marium/.

Mohaiemen, Naeem. 2008. "Smash Palace." *The Daily Star*, November 3. https://www.thedailystar.net/news-detail-61520.

———. 2013. "Shahbagh: The Forest of Symbols." *Kafila*. Accessed April 30, 2022. https://kafila.online/2013/02/22/shahbagh-the-forest-of-symbols-naeem.

Mollerup, Nina Grønlykke, and Sherief Gaber. 2015. "Making Media Public: On Revolutionary Street Screenings in Egypt." *International Journal of Communication* 9 (19). https://ijoc.org/index.php/ijoc/article/view/3655.

Rahman, Sadiqur. 2018. "Lubna Marium: An Artiste-Activist on the Move." *New Age*, November 23. Accessed March 31, 2023. https://www.newagebd.net/article/56787/an-artiste-activist-on-the-move.

Raju, Zakir Hossain. 2015. *Bangladesh Cinema and National Identity: In Search of the Modern?* London: Routledge.

Roy, Ratan Kumar. 2019. "Online Activism, Social Movements and Mediated Politics in Contemporary Bangladesh." *Society and Culture in South Asia* 5 (2): 193–215.

Sabur, Seuty. 2013. "Post Card from Shahabag." *ISA e-Symposium for Sociology* 3 (1): online.

Sundaram, Ravi. 2022. "The Fringe as Media Infrastructure." In *Media and the Constitution of the Political: South Asia and Beyond*, edited by Ravi Vasudevan, 261–84. Delhi: Sage Spectrum.

Veg, Sebastian. 2015. "Legalistic and Utopian: Hong Kong's Umbrella Movement." *New Left Review* 92 (March): 55–73.

Venkiteswaran, C. S. 2009. "Reflections on Film Society Movement in Keralam." *South Asian Popular Culture* 7 (1): 65–71.

Zhou, Chenshu. 2021. *Cinema Off Screen: Moviegoing in Socialist China*. Oakland: University of California Press.

2

GENRES OF ECOFEMINISM

Women Filmmakers in India and the Environment

Sangita Gopal

In an essay titled "Do I know the Anthropocene when I see it?" Jennifer Fay examines eco-centered documentary films to suggest that as spectators it is difficult to see the Anthropocene and perplexing to be "responsible for environmental evil at imponderable scales that may elude both perception and intention" (Fay 2022, 44). I take up this provocation to explore three narrative features – made by the Indian women directors Aruna Raje, Sai Paranjpye, and Aparna Sen – that use genre conventions to draw the connection between environmental crisis and human complicity that lies at the basis of concepts such as the Anthropocene, the Capitalocene, and the Great Acceleration. As a phenomenon, the Anthropocene, Jennifer Petersen suggests, has structural and affective affinities with "horror and melodrama" (Peterson 2019, 162). In what follows I will add to this list another genre – the romantic comedy – to argue that the narrative conventions codified by certain genres do successfully bridge the scalar problems identified by Fay more effectively than indexical formats such as the documentary. Genre films – the meeting ground of industrial logics and audience desires – are not obliged to reflect reality but rather use conventions to lend narrative and cognitive shape to messy events and emerging phenomena. Different generic takes on environmental crises, as I shall show here, help viewers apprehend the responsibilities that different actors bear for large-scale planetary disasters and perhaps even discern how things might be different.

Though the affordances of the documentary are not particularly attuned to represent such crises, paradoxically, it is to this form that one invariably turns to gather evidence of the Anthropocene and this is also true in the Indian context. Starting in the late 1970s, we witnessed in India the rise of broad-based environmental movements – particularly ecofeminism and deep ecology – that responded to the destruction inflicted by large-scale development projects to forest ecologies and traditional lifeways (Sinha, Gururani, and Greenberg 1997). The best known of these – Chipko and the Narmada Bachao Andolan – are mostly remembered today through several landmark documentaries while the genre films that engaged these same events – Aruna Vikas's *Geherayee* (Depth, 1980), Paranjpye's *Papeeha* (The Song Bird, 1994), and Sen's *Yugant* (What the Sea Said, 1995) – are almost completely forgotten and can only be viewed as utterly degraded copies on YouTube or in scattered private collections. The features I examine here bookend a decade or so of intense

DOI: 10.4324/9781003266952-5

Figure 2.1   Seeing the Anthropocene: A troubled marriage is engulfed by an ocean set aflame by an oil spill thousands of miles away (*Yugant*, What the Sea Said, 1995).

protests between environmental activists – peasants, indigenous peoples or adivasis, and their allies – and the state. These movements were extensively reported on and debated by local, national, and international print and broadcast media, expressed through artworks, street theater, and popular music, as well as the subject of several independent documentaries – K.P. Sashi and Ratha Mathur's *A Valley Refuses to Die* (1988), Simantini Dhuru and Anand Patwardhan's *A Narmada Diary* (1995), Ali Kazimi's *Narmada: A Valley Rises* (1992), and state-sponsored educational films. While these non-fiction works have benefitted from scholarly attention as paradigmatic examples of the "eco-doc" and "activist media" (Demos 2013), the feature films have received little critical consideration in discussions of the oeuvres of these fairly prominent women auteurs. This might owe partly to the overt "topicality" of these films – they are tethered to a time and wax and wane with it – but their obsolescence may also be ascribed to their status as "genre films" – *Geherayee* is a horror film, *Papeeha* is a rom-com, and *Yugant* is a domestic melodrama. Neither possessing the indexical value of a documentary nor the gritty realism of alternative cinema, these films were hard to classify except through the framework of gendered authorship and even here, as genre films they are considered anomalies in the "feminist" oeuvres of Raje, Sen, and Paranjpye. I return to them here as works of eco-cinema that share some aesthetic and political inclinations: First, they mine the affective agency of genre conventions to make the environment a matter of concern to the urban, middle-class audiences far removed from the scenes of tribal dispossession typically received as news. Second, they use narrative to "process" this news and make sense of raw data, since environmental degradation is so hard to "see" and must therefore be apprehended. And third, the films are motivated by an aesthetic of allyship that tries to mitigate the ethnographic impulse in upper-class, upper-caste explorations of what Ramachandra Guha and Martinez-Alier have called the "environmentalism of the poor" (Martinez-Alier 2012).

Let me begin by briefly locating this eco-cinema within broader tendencies found in women's mediawork at this time. Making films on issues of public interest – what was in the news – as well as drawing the public's attention to what ought to be in the news – is a feature of women's media work at this time. As I have argued elsewhere, we might attribute these tendencies to the intermedial nature of women's careers – the directors I research worked in print journalism, radio, television, and theater – all environments much closer to the "here and now" and they carried this disposition over to their narrative features as well. Environmental activism was a particularly attractive subject for women mediamakers for not only was it in the news, but peasant and indigenous women were at the forefront of these movements for they had the greatest stakes in protecting the ecologies on which their subsistence depended. Upper-caste, upper-class, urban women were seeking common cause with their social and spatial others, and women-led environmental activism offered rich grounds for intersectional politics – an opportunity for elite feminists to "learn from below." But how should these encounters be represented? One mode as Bishnupriya Ghosh (2011) has noted was the eco-doc featuring testimonies from indigenous communities displaced by development projects. The objective was to activate audiences into solidarity not only through a direct encounter with victims but also through a poetic realism that evoked the land and peoples that development would devastate.

Women filmmakers, however, made a different aesthetic choice – away from ethnography and toward genre, motivated perhaps by the insights of feminism. As scholars have noted, the expansion of media platforms in India through the 1980s led to greater representation of social and cultural difference. But upper-class, upper-caste feminists – themselves the beneficiaries of such visibility – were keenly aware of how the divisive logic of representational politics hampered the building of solidarity with their social "others." Rather than conferring visibility on the dispossessed, these filmmakers sought an aesthetic practice that could reflect on the political limits of visibility politics and signal their own privileged access to the means of production. In what has been called the Indian New Wave, various aesthetic strategies associated with Third Cinema such as the commingling of fictional and non-fictional modes and the uses of agit-prop art, posters, animation, and direct address were employed to disturb realistic absorption (Majumdar 2021), but Aruna Raje, Sai Paranjpye, and Aparna Sen interestingly pick genre as a heuristic that selects, processes, and gives significance to data and as such has reflective and affective agency.

In what follows, I will briefly explore how *Geherayee* and *Yugant* use generic conventions to effect scalar connections between our everyday actions and environmental disaster to underline how "ordinary complicity underlies modern catastrophe" (Fay 2022, 47). I will then conclude with a slightly more expansive case study of Paranjpye's *Papeeha* – perhaps the least remembered of the three to explore how Paranjpye uses the conventions of rom-com to craft an ethics of intersubjectivity.

Aruna Raje's *Geherayee* (1980) is a horror film that draws on anthropological and historical research into spirit possession, indigenous epistemologies about the relation between human and non-human agents, and strategies marginalized communities have used to designate certain lands as protected. The film opens in the country estate of Chennabasappa who has come from the city and is being shown around by his steward Baswa who says that by the grace of the resident deity of the forest – Yellama[1] – the estate is thriving. Chennabasappa brusquely informs Baswa that the health of the estate is no longer relevant since the land has been sold to build a factory where all the peasants will find higher-paying jobs. In response, Baswa asks, "What about these trees – will they be uprooted? If these trees are buried under bricks and concrete – it is 'balatkar' – rape. The land is not mine, but I have tended it like my mother. It gives me sustenance." But his concerns are unheeded. Back in the city,

Chennabasappa's daughter, Uma, and wife, Saroja, are both distressed by this redevelopment project and their attunements to the land and its people are contrasted with Chennabasappa's irrational attachment to development. That same night, the first signs of possession manifest as Uma wakes up clutching her neck as though she is being strangled and the camera cuts to a tree outside her bedroom. Later Uma begins to speak in Baswa's voice and accuses her father of raping Baswa's wife and causing her death by suicide. Neither doctors nor exorcists are able to "cure" Uma and the film ends as the spirits – human and arboreal – leave Uma's body and take up residence in her brother's, thus commencing another cycle of possession.

The film upon its release was credited with "planting a bhoot or supernatural creature in your living room" – and this relocation of the supernatural from decaying country estates and forests predominant in the Indian horror genre's revival in the late 1970s and '80s to a bourgeois home in the southern Indian city of Bangalore, I suggest, is an Anthroposcenic gesture, as spirits robbed of their habitats take possession of ours. The film also triangulates this face-off between man and nature by connecting the capitalist and patriarchal exploitation of women, dalit, and indigenous peoples to environmental degradation. For Chennabasappa not only cuts down forests to build factories but also displaces indigenous peoples and eradicates their lifeways and kinship conceptions. As Kali Simmons (2019) suggests, ecological thinking must "remember what kind of life was possible to begin with" and thus engage indigenous epistemologies and ontologies. *Geherayee* uses the horror genre and its trope of possession to precisely imagine these other ways of being in the world.

Let us turn briefly now to look at the production history as well narrative features of *Geherayee* to suggest how a generic feature – the ghost – becomes a thinking tool to conjure a more complex ethico-political relationship between humans and non-humans and attend to the multiple and incommensurable scales along which the human must be imagined (Chakrabarty 2009). In the Hindu context, the ghost's significance does not lie in repudiating the boundary between the living and the dead but rather ghosts (bhoots) and spirits (prets) were figures of justice, territoriality, and community who occupied the same ecosystem as humans – if in spirit form (Seale-Feldman 2019). Anthropologists and historians working in diverse historical and regional contexts have noted that ghosts and spirits served as figures who secured some minimal power for the dispossessed (lower caste/dalits) especially with regard to land and property (Prakash 1986). Spirits prevented further exploitation and denudation by taking up residence in marginal lands, water bodies and trees. If these boundaries guarded by the spirit were violated or if indeed the spirit lost its habitat owing to the capture of land or the felling of trees, it might take up residence in human dwellings and human bodies. Further, such afflictive spirits were much more likely to haunt women and girls, whose comportment and bodily dispositions were more bounded and regulated to begin with. Possessing these bodies thus offered the greatest opportunities for performing insurgency and transgression (Ram 2012; Moore 1993).

Writing about animism as an ecological idea, May Ingawanij (2021) has noted,

Humans' maintenance of the capacity of ritual to address spirits, and to sensorially perceive communicative exchange with them, constitutes . . . a way of harnessing the prospect and hope of the continuing liveability of one's life and one's habitat as well as an orientation towards possible futures (551).

Aruna Raje (2017) recalls her childhood fascination with such communicative practices that she witnessed all around her. Her family would often find lemons marked with red powder (kumkum) or weird straw dolls with pins strewn in their garden. Her mother tossed these objects out without a thought, but for Raje, they were the material traces to another way of thinking, other beliefs that are, a part of real life – a world of mantriks, tantriks, spells and curses, wandering souls, and vengeful sprites. For the adult Raje, these other epistemologies were a matter of neither belief nor fascination but rather an anthropological fact – a part of the ecology in which she grew up (92). Thus, when Raje in the wake of the horror boom in India, and the success of *The Exorcist*, was offered a horror film she knew right away that that she would make a "real" horror film – grounded in reality. And this decision was not an aesthetic matter but rather inhered in Raje's belief in multiple epistemologies, theologies, and lifeworlds. The script for *Geherayee* was a kind of composite then, ecumenically drawing on these ethnographies of the supernatural that Raje had gathered over the years. The film is anthropological in assembling traditional beliefs about possession and exorcism, curses, and talismans that inhabit the everyday. For Raje these are "transmitted wisdoms – not reducible to knowledge, beyond validation or invalidation – can be captured in stories but cannot be told as a story" (Mubarki 2016). They might have roots in religion but, through ritual praxis and social engagement, touches both secular and ritual spheres that may repress or amplify them. As Gyan Prakash has shown, upper-caste Hindus repressed the spirit world of the lower castes to maintain caste hierarchies by subordinating them to Hindu ritual practices, such as offering "pinda" to propitiate ancestors, assuring that ancestral spirits could not be possessed by "lower-caste" bhoots (Prakash 1986, 215). As such, this link between ghosts and caste hierarchies suggest once again the intimacy between savarna Hinduism and the so-called "rational" mindset that does not believe in the spirit world. Upper-caste Hindu practice was sequestered from the ghost world. This world of spirits was against the taxonomies of modernity – it offered rather perpetual transmutation, "no realm of being, visible or invisible, past or present, is absolutely discontinuous but all are equally accessible and mutually dependent" (Mubarki 2016, 216). As Raje recalls, "after release of film many people asked us about our beliefs and we do not believe but nor can we deny that such phenomena existed and affected people. I guess during the making of the film, we became temporary believers" (202). These ethnographies present then a formal problem – they cannot be told as a story – thus, horror as a "genre," with reliable conventions that bring diverse orders and epistemologies into confrontation, might be used to solve this narrative problem.

A similar problem of incommensurability structures Aparna Sen's *Yugant* (The End of Times, 1995). How to articulate the miscommunications and divergent desires that lead to a failed marriage with how modernity and its economic systems have failed the world and its indigenous peoples? The film draws on the conventions of melodrama – improbable coincidences, forced causalities, moral polarities – to make this audacious connection between the scenes from a marriage and the environmental catastrophe unfolding in India at the time. The film's opening voiceover links the exhaustion of a marriage to the earth's depletion as Anusuya and Deepak return after 17 years to the site of their honeymoon – a seaside village in the eastern Indian state of Orissa – to give this moribund relationship another chance. The film unfolds through a series of flashbacks that demonstrate how far apart this once-loving couple has grown, even as the ocean ecology and the fisherfolk who lived in consonance with it have been subject to the Great Acceleration (Steffen et al. 2015). Though Anu and Deepak both critique deforestation and big dam projects that have displaced indigenous communities, we learn that Deepak has bought a gas-guzzling vehicle, while Anu makes aesthetic capital out of media images of petro-disasters. If melodrama was described by Peter Brooks (1976) as a "clarification of the cosmic moral sense of eve-ryday gestures" (7) – an essentially anaphoric form – then indeed it is a genre capable of connecting across time scales – the 17 years in the couple's life and the temporality of the Anthropocene. At the beginning of their marriage, we learn, Anu could make kin with the ocean and its creatures, but in 17 years, that bond has severed. Deepak, on the other hand, has always conceived of nature as the indifferent spectator to human frailty rather than as something human actions continuously degrade. Though alienated from his capitalist exist-ence, his critique is always directed outward – mostly toward Anu. Wrapped up in a haze of malaise and recrimination, this couple fails to see that the real victims of their narcissis-tic, consumerist lifestyles are the environment and the indigenous peoples. While the film's treatment of the marriage plot is realistic, its staging of the Anthropocene makes full use of the expressive potential of melodrama. In the film's improbable denouement – in strict consonance with the moral polarities that govern melodrama – only the villains – Anu and Deepak – are punished by the burning seas for their failures at worlding but the indigenous fishing community is spared. Both films explore the links between patriarchy, settler colo-nialism, extractivism, and environmental devastation, but, as I have shown, they use genre conventions of horror and melodrama to keep the moral framework of the Anthropocene firmly in view.

While Raje and Sen use genre to reconcile the scales that often overwhelm the representa-tions of the Anthropocene and clarify human complicity in ecological degradation, I would like to conclude with Sai Paranjpye's romantic comedy *Papeeha*. As mentioned, during the 1980s and into the next decade, forests were the subject of vigorous debates as the state's control over forests under the sign of preservationism accelerated and the state began to designate even smaller areas with higher human densities as protected. There is much excel-lent research that shows that this rush to notify, though putatively conservationist, actually sought control over these forests for development projects, including agrobusiness and big dams.[2] There was pushback by the deep ecology movement that urged that authority over landscape should devolve to local communities for they are the most skilled and motivated to use it in a sustainable fashion, and as Guha notes, India needed to move away from the false binary of "impoverishment of resources versus impoverishment of the population" by imagining new models of development that took into account deep ecological insights.

It is precisely this false binary that Paranjpye wanted to translate into film so that the "public" could affectively engage with and emotionally invest in these issues beyond the modes of news and documentary. With this goal, Paranjpye and her team researched this film for two years. First, they consulted books such as Jagdish Godbole's *Paradh* (The Prey), Verrier Elwin's *The Aboriginals*, and S.D. Kulkarni's *Class and Caste in a Tribal Movement*. Then they visited the Tribal Museum in Bhopal and traveled through many forests and met with communities. And yet when it came to deciding where to set her film, Paranjpye (2020) realized that each forest and its ecosystem was so distinct that the process of selec-tion would be arbitrary at best and expedient at worst. Unable to find a rationale for pick-ing a particular forest – Sanjay Gandhi Udyan, Vikram Garh, Dahanu, Palghar, Hemalkasa, Navegaon, and its people – Warli, Madia, Bhil, Gond, Koli – over another, she decided to "forget realism and embrace fantasy" (369).

So like Raje, she created a composite. She made up a tribe, a forest – Mantarban, and an adivasi language. She realized early on that the budget for the film would not allow for the kind of infrastructural investment required to shoot in one location – a specific forest inhabited by a particular indigenous community, nor did she know how to involve the inhabitants of the forest in the film, so she decided that her imaginary forest would be a placeholder for any/all of the forests of Maharashtra, wherever the crew could receive permission to film and on whatever schedule the weather allowed. Indeed, while the film is shot "on location" or rather on any number of locations whatsoever, these "real" forests stand in for a fantastical one. She observes how a shot might begin with a character climbing up one tree, but in the reverse shot the camera might be looking up at an entirely different tree. Film space is created through purely cinematic means and, rather than immersing the audience in a "world," she wanted them to encounter and cognitively process other worldviews. Thus, the film has two narrators – a voiceover that represents statist ideologies of conservation and a diegetic narrator – Baba Gurung and his gang of rascals – who express the adivasi worldview and offer deep ecological critiques of these positions. Paranjpye states that she gleaned these critiques from her many conversations with adivasis (350–368).

Given the film's interest in adivasi worlding, rather than world-building, Paranjpye decided that the genre of the romantic comedy was best suited to expressing the clash between worldviews and their resolution. As Stanley Cavell (1984) has told us, it is through the erotically charged, witty banter of the romcom that we learn to "speak the same language" (87–88). The rom-com teaches us how to cherish sovereignty – of oneself and others – in order to gain the equality of a union. That is why the couple must meet and then part to retain their own sovereignty and then commence on a course of self-education where they learn to value the sovereignty of the other. It is only after this process that they are ready for a final union. But *Papeeha* triangulates this schema by inserting the forest between girl and boy. So here not only must girl and boy learn to speak the same language, they must also unlearn the language of worlds and embrace the process of worlding. Thus, Paranjpye's couple – Kabir the forest officer and Jiya the anthropologist – are initially aligned with different factions of the forest ecology. While Kabir cares only for the non-human elements of the forest, especially the trees, and is blind to the tribals who work for him including his man Friday Bicchua – Jiya is wholly on the side of the tribals. But her view of them is Rousseauist, and so she is disenchanted when the adivasis sport Nylon shirts over their "langotis" – loincloths, crave toothpaste and baubles and trinkets from the city. As is conventional in the genre they spar continuously – they are attracted to each other but unwilling to let go of their ideological orientations vis-à-vis the forest. And so their union is threatened but then each undergoes a reorientation that forces them to recognize the sovereign claims of this third party – the forest. Their final reunion is only possible when each comes to see that the forest is an ecosystem comprising the human and the non-human and most efficiently managed by its stakeholders. They imagined themselves as saviors of trees and tribals but must now try to be an ally. Both Kabir and Jiya must learn with and from the adivasis and enter into a collaborative relationship with them in order to fend off the true antagonists – predatory capital (a multinational rayon company) and an extractivist state. Kabir and Jiya's re-education – a precondition to their union as dictated by the structure of romantic comedies – involves that each reassess their relationship to this ecology by learning to learn. Kabir, who has always viewed himself as the protector of the trees and never trusted the adivasis with managing their own resources, must acknowledge that by taking away their means of subsistence, no matter how pure his intentions, he does the bidding of a settler-colonialist state. When the big developers move in, all his corrupt boss has to do is transfer him for a few months, and it is the adivasis – primarily the women and children – who most rely on and therefore defend most rigorously their habitats and push back the developers, and Kabir has to take his lead from them. Kabir has to rethink his relation to space as possession. Jiya, in turn, has to learn that though she is a camera-wielding researcher who has come to gather field notes, she, too, is being studied by her "tribe." She has no epistemic vantage. Her inappropriate clothes and footwear are liabilities in the forest and slow her down, her desire for privacy in a household, where cattle and humans dwell together, is met with bemusement and the women find her coyness in matters of sex and desire quaint. Most significantly, Jiya has to relearn her temporal orientation vis-à-vis the adivasis and recognize that they are her contemporaries and their onto-epistemologies have co-evolved with their habitats and perfectly adequate to it. She has to learn to neither fetishize nor chastise their ways but just stay by their side in their quest for sustainability. The adivasis occupy a diversity of gendered positions regarding what the future should look like – while some men embrace development with its promise of telephones, televisions, videos, and even computers, others reject it as culturally other to the mores of the forest. The women, in contrast, value the tree as their ancestral mother for it provides resources that they have learnt to use prudently. They use dead branches and twigs for fuel and warmth, prune new growth, and sell it in the market for commodities, and so they defend the trees with their bodies – Chipko style – not as Kabir might have for the "thing" itself but for its use and exchange values and its role in maintaining ecological processes and services. I make this sound dry but really it is sparkling romantic comedy – witty, humorous, and self-reflexive – that uses genre conventions to thoroughly eschew the modes of ethnographic capture through which one's social others become a locus for knowledge production. The details of tribal life that the film incorporates – though based on fieldwork – serve purposes entirely other than verisimilitude – they have affective, conceptual, and pedagogic functions. Let me give a couple of examples. Jiya knows that adivasis hunt for and eat rats, but what she doesn't know is that adivasis know how to recover rice stolen by rats from their homes and hidden in the burrows. This brings home to her what a subsistence lifestyle really means. In another instance, Paranjpye had heard that in a certain tribe, if a woman finds lice in her comb, it is a sign that her desire is returned and she has made her beloved her own. Jiya's delight at finding a louse in her comb and the joyful song and dance sequence that follows is the first time she admits her attraction to Kabir. Details – and there are numerous others – function here not to build a world but express a worldview, a way of being in the world that provides an alternative to the Anthropocene. Perhaps such processes of worlding can only be apprehended by forgetting realism/embracing fantasy.

The embrace of familiar industrial genres such as horror, domestic melodrama, and romantic comedy by women filmmakers from India to tackle the problem of representing environmental crises as well as address questions of environmental justice is indeed a remarkable and under-investigated aspect of Indian film history in the 1980s, when women's contributions have mostly been viewed through the lenses of feminism and auteurship. The corpus of films I have described here use genre conventions astutely to figure environmental crisis whose planetary scope and temporal scale do not easily lend themselves to the realist modes that were embraced by the new cinema of the time. Even more significantly, genre allows these films to elaborate on how humans are implicated in this crisis as agents who must at once take responsibility for environmental degradation and work together to imagine other futures. At the same time, these are also feminist films that show how patriarchy is secured by exploiting both human and non-human actors and how these extractive processes can be critiqued by learning to look from the vantage of our human and ecological others – ghosts, spirits, fisherfolk, sea creatures, the forest and its dwellers. Genre codes play a crucial role in expressing these diverse forms of worlding.

Notes

1 Yellama is a deity worshiped by Dalit castes.
2 See Sivaramakrishnan (2011), Agarwal (1998), and Jewitt (1995).

References

Agarwal, Bina. 1998. "Environmental Management, Equity and Ecofeminism: Debating India's Experience." *The Journal of Peasant Studies* 25 (4): 55–95.
Brooks, Peter. 1976. *The Melodramatic Imagination*. New Haven, CT: Yale University Press.
Cavell, Stanley. 1984. *Pursuit of Happiness: The Hollywood Comedy of Remarriage*. Cambridge: Harvard University Press.
Chakrabarty, Dipesh. 2009. "The Climate of History: Four Theses." *Critical Inquiry* 35 (2): 197–222.
Demos, T. J. 2013. "The Art and Politics of Ecology in India: A Roundtable with Ravi Agarwal and Sanjay Kak." *Third Text* 27 (1): 151–61.
Fay, Jennifer. 2022. "Do I Know the Anthropocene When I See it?" *Representations* 157 (2): 41–57.
Ghosh, Bishnupriya. 2011. *Global Icons: Apertures of the Popular*. Durham: Duke University Press.
Ingawanij, May Adadol. 2021. "Cinematic Animism and Contemporary Southeast Asian Artists' Moving-Image Practices." *Screen* 62 (4): 549–58, 551.
Jewitt, Sarah. 1995. "Europe's 'Others'? Forestry Policy and Practices in Colonial and Postcolonial India." *Environment and Planning: Society and Space* 13 (1): 67–90.
Majumdar, Rochona. 2021. *Art Cinema and India's Forgotten Futures: Film and History in the Postcolony*. New York: Columbia University Press.
Martinez-Alier, Joan. 2012. "The Environmentalism of the Poor: Its Origins and Spread." In *A Companion to Global Environmental History*, edited by Erin Stewart Maudlin and J. R. McNeill, 513–29. Hoboken, NJ: Wiley Blackwell.
Moore, Erin P. 1993. "Gender, Power, and Legal Pluralism: Rajasthan, India." *American Ethnologist* 20 (3): 522–42.
Mubarki, Meraj Ahmed. 2016. *Filming Horror: Hindi Cinema, Ghosts and Ideologies*. New Delhi: SAGE Publications India.
Paranjpye, Sai. 2020. *Patchwork Quilt: A Collage of My Creative Life*. New Delhi: Harper Collins.
Peterson, Jennifer. 2019. "Ecodiegesis: The Scenography of Nature Onscreen." *Journal of Cinema and Media Studies* 58 (2): 162–68.
Prakash, Gyan. 1986. "Reproducing Inequality: Spirit Cults and Labor Relations in Colonial Eastern India." *Modern Asian Studies* 20 (2): 209–30.
Raje, Aruna. 2017. *Freedom: My Story*. New Delhi: Harper Collins India.
Ram, Kalpana. 2012. "How is Afflictive Possession 'Learned'? Gender and Motility in South India." *Ethnos* 77 (2): 203–26.
Seale-Feldman, Aidan. 2019. "Relational Affliction: Reconceptualizing 'Mass Hysteria'." *Ethos* 47 (3): 307–25.
Simmons, Kali. 2019. "Reorientations; or, an Indigenous Feminist Reflection on the Anthropocene." *Journal of Cinema and Media Studies* 58 (2): 174–79.
Sinha, Subir, Shubhra Gururani, and Brian Greenberg. 1997. "The 'New Traditionalist' Discourse of Indian Environmentalism." *The Journal of Peasant Studies* 24 (3): 65–99.
Sivaramakrishnan, Kalyanakirsha. 2011. "Thin Nationalism: Nature and Public Intellectualism in India." *Contributions to Indian Sociology* 45 (1): 85–111.
Steffen, Will, Wendy Broadgate, Lisa Deutsch, Owen Gaffney, and Cornelia Ludwig. 2015. "The Trajectory of the Anthropocene: The Great Acceleration." *The Anthropocene Review* 2 (1): 81–98.

3

RIDING THE WAVES

An Interview with Yim Soon-rye

Chi-Yun Shin

South Korean (hereafter Korean) director Yim Soon-rye made her feature debut in 1996 with *Three Friends*, which made her the sixth female director in the history of Korean cinema. With only five women directors who managed to complete feature length fictional films that received theatrical releases before her, Yim has been the leading woman filmmaker in Korea, directing a number of films ranging from critically acclaimed independent films, such as *Three Friends* and *Waikiki Brothers* (2001), to crowd-pleasing dramas, such as *Forever the Moment* (2008) and *Little Forest* (2018), as well as her salient collaborations with the National Human Rights Commission of Korea, as in *The Weight of Her* (2003) and *Fly Penguin* (2009). As a bona fide pioneer in a highly male-dominated field, Yim has negotiated and adapted to the shifting dynamics of the Korean film industry, which may explain the diverse styles and topics of her oeuvre. In August 2023, we met online via Zoom, and had email correspondences to talk about her career, starting from what attracted her to filmmaking, and how she got to make her much lauded first short film *Promenade in the Rain* (1994), to her latest foray into big-budget action filmmaking with *The Point Men* (2023).

Chi-Yun SHIN (hereafter CYS): **I'd like to take you to the beginning. When and how did you get attracted to the medium of cinema? Was there any film or filmmaker that made you interested in cinema?**
YIM Soon-rye (hereafter YSR): There wasn't anyone or anything special initially, but I did like going to the movies during my middle and high school days. I've seen a lot of, mostly commercial, movies from Hong Kong and Hollywood, as well as Korean movies. I'm speaking of the mid to late 1970s, when teachers would go around and check movie theaters, and I got caught several times watching movies we were not supposed to and got reprimanded the next day. Although briefly, I even considered majoring in theater and film when I applied for a university place. But at that time, the department of theater and film was the destination for the good-looking kids who wanted to become

DOI: 10.4324/9781003266952-6

actors. So, I couldn't tell anyone – including my parents, who would have been totally puzzled as to why I would want to be an actor – even though it was directing that I was interested in. As I've said in other interviews before, I had dropped out of school when I was in my third year of high school and hadn't done much for two years. So, in the end, I went for a more "serious" subject and did an English degree at Hanyang University.

Then, one day, a classmate in the English department spoke of a certain French film she watched at the French Cultural Center, which immediately piqued my interest. So, I decided to check it out myself and went there, and the first film I saw was *Pastoral Symphony* (1946), featuring Michèle Morgan, with English subtitles, which was nothing like the Hong Kong or Hollywood or Korean commercial films I had seen so far. That's when I got properly drawn to film. For well over a year, I went to the French Cultural Center every weekend and watched all the movies that were shown on Saturdays and Sundays, usually eight films a weekend, until I'd seen most of the films they had had there. From watching French films, particularly the French *nouvelle vague* films, I began to think about the possibility of making films myself rather than watching and just consuming films.
CYS: That explains why you're considered to be part of the famous Cultural Center generation![1]
YSR: That's right. I lived in Incheon then, and the French Cultural Center was located near Gyeongbokgung Palace. So, it took me about an hour and half to get home, and I used to savor the lingering feelings from watching the films all the way home. This experience made me realize how films can communicate deep thoughts about life that I thought only possible through serious literature in the past.

So, when the time came to decide what to do after graduation, I decided to become a filmmaker, even though it offered the riskiest and most uncertain future. Because I was a good student with great grades, I could have easily worked for a big company, or joined the graduate program at the English department. In fact, a few of my professors in the English department encouraged me to carry on studying. But life as an academic or an office worker seemed rather boring. The Korean film industry, however, was not systematic back then in 1984. A typical route to become a film director was to "go under" one of the well-known directors – the three big names at the time were Im Kwon-taek, Bae Chang-ho, and Lee Jang-ho – and follow one of them around for about ten years, learning everything from the director. I mean, ten years is a long time to invest, and I also realized that I hadn't studied film broadly or systematically. So, I decided to do a master's degree in theater and film at Hanyang University in 1985. But the postgraduate program at the time was not fully established, and the biggest issue was that there weren't many opportunities to watch all those films mentioned in the textbooks we studied, let alone in good condition. There was no Internet back then. On top of that, though it is a kind of excuse, my thesis adviser kept rejecting passing my thesis, which added frustration. So, instead of completing the master's degree, I set out to watch films in France. My goal was becoming a film director, so I thought I didn't need this degree. Someone had told me about the Cinematheque in Paris and how almost all movies from around the world were released in Paris. Initially, I went to France with the sole purpose of watching movies, but because of my visa status . . . I had to go to school. So, I went to Paris 8 University, where I took 12 modules plus 5 more to get a bachelor's degree. After that, since I felt I needed to watch more movies, I continued on and did a master's degree there. Even before I started, I had a thesis plan to work on the films of Mizoguchi Kenji. I noticed that his films were relatively lesser known compared to Ozu Yasujiro and Kurosawa Akira, or any other famous Western directors I liked. I actually spent three months in Japan watching Mizoguchi films as there happened to be a Mizoguchi retrospective in Japan before I wrote my master's thesis. So, I went to France in 1988, and returned to Korea in 1992, so I spent about four years abroad.

CYS: **How did you get into the film industry when you returned to Korea?**

YSR: In Paris, I had met and become friends with someone who used to work in Chungmuro,[2] so I built a network through him. He actually worked on the movie *Chilsu and Mansu* (1988), and when its director, Park Kwang-soo, came to Paris when he was making *The Berlin Report* (1991), we met with him and his team that included director Yeo Gyundong. When I returned to Korea, again through that friend, I managed to meet up with the famous director Im Kwon-taek, but several opportunities to get into the industry, including working for Im's *Taeback Mountains*, fell through for various reasons. Thinking maybe Chungmuro wasn't for me, I was getting ready to make a documentary about the last circus troupe, the Dongchun Circus. But then, director Yeo got in touch with me – he was starting his debut feature *Out to the World* (1994) and suggested that I join his team as a script supervisor. So, that became my first proper Chungmuro gig.

CYS: **Was that experience helpful when you started your own film project?**

YSR: Very much so. I got to know how the Chungmuro system works, and the crew members I worked with including the cinematographer, lighting director, recording engineers, etc. were all top-class. They were very experienced, super competent and nice, and they helped me a lot when I directed my first short film, *Promenade in the Rain* (1994). What was lucky was that as soon as I finished the film, the Seoul International Short Film Festival was launched, and I won the Grand Prize and the Press Award there.

CYS: **Ah, yes, your legendary first film, *Promenade in the Rain*, was showcased there! Didn't Samsung set up the Seoul International Short Film Festival?**

YSR: That's right, the Samsung Entertainment Group. The mid-1990s were when large corporations began investing in the movie industry and also founded and funded such events.

CYS: **In addition to winning big prizes, *Promenade in the Rain* received rave reviews. The prominent film critic Jung Sung-il, in particular, enthusiastically praised the film. Do you remember the excitement?**

YSR: I do remember. I set out to make a short film mainly to test my ability, so I was a little surprised to get such responses. I mean nowadays anyone can easily make short films, but back then in the mid-'90s, it was hard to get access to the equipment and other resources, unless you did a film production degree at a university. Possibly because of the education system, the short films produced then tended to have certain mannerisms, while my film didn't follow a sort of short film grammar that existed in Korea. So, it stood out as fresh and different. I heard that some critics were puzzled that the film didn't really show any French style either. Anyways, I didn't make it with a film festival in mind, but the Seoul Short Film Festival was created right after I made it, and since I won awards there, I got a lot of attention from the media and producers.

CYS: You made it with all amateur actors, except the actor Myung Gye-nam, right? And how did you come up with the title? It's such a cool title.

YSR: I had known the actor Myung from working on *Out to the World,* and the rest of the cast were amateurs, although the lead actress had a little bit of experience in stage acting. I like the title too, though it sounds a bit like a Hong Kong movie title. I called it *Promenade in the Rain* as the protagonist walks in the rain and realizes the gap between reality and ideals.

CYS: Ah yes, at the end of the film, the heroine realizes that the guy she's been waiting for all day is bald with a wet wig, and he seems rather disappointed at her, who's all soaked from her walk in the rain. That was an emotionally quite complex ending.

YSR: I guess that's the sentiment I was going for, looking at the sad or pitiful reality of the people who are ordinary, or a little worse than average by society's standards. They have no choice but to accept the reality, and life continues, and so on.

CYS: You finally made your feature debut in 1996 with *Three Friends*, and that film also got a lot of attention.

YSR: It was also fortunate that the Busan International Film Festival was just launched as soon as I finished the film, and it won the NETPAC (Network for the Promotion of Asian Cinema) Award there. So, while both *Promenade in the Rain* and *Three Friends* may have their own strengths, they got a lot of help from the newly established film festivals. Because of these festivals, I was able to attract attention from other festivals such as Berlin or Vancouver.

CYS: In many ways, the year 1996 was quite special to the history of Korean cinema – it was the birth year of the first international Film Festival in Korea, and it's also when you debuted, and directors Hong Sang-soo and Kim Ki-duk debuted with *The Day a Pig Fell into the Well* and *Crocodile*, respectively. Three of you are the same age and debuted in the same year.

YSR: It's also the year when the film magazine *Cine 21* was first published. I think they were looking for worthwhile films to discuss in their magazine. My works and the works by Hong and Kim caught their attention because we all came back from abroad, and our films displayed something different from Korean cinema.

CYS: You then directed your second feature *Waikiki Brothers* (2001). From the outset, I'd like to say that I love this film. I think it's a masterpiece. It captures so many complex emotions – there are moments of desperation, elation, and sadness, and it's also very funny. I hope you realize you have talents for comedy too.

YSR: [*Laughs*] Well, I don't tend to do laugh-out-loud comedies, but I like making people laugh with subtle comedies.

CYS: Yes, humor comes from little things like expressions or the timing! I actually watched the film again recently, and really appreciated its editing this time. You cut back and forth between the past and present of the protagonist Sung-woo. He was a lead guitarist and vocalist in a high school band, but grown-up Sung-woo is in a third-rate band and works in seedy nightclubs or karaoke bars. The stand-out scene is where he is forced to perform naked in a private party, among drunk and naked people. He is only "wearing" his guitar and sings the same song he performed in his high school days. The camera then closes onto a TV monitor in the room, which shows a nice beach. It then cuts to the beach where high schooler Sung-woo runs around naked with his friends. His nakedness here, of course, expresses his carefree and uninhibited status, while naked Sung-woo in the present is desperate and humiliated. It wonderfully contrasts ideals vs. reality.

YSR: Well, in that sense, *Promenade in the Rain*, *Three Friends*, and *Waikiki Brothers* have similar sentiments.

CYS: It has been over 20 years since *Waikiki Brothers* was released.

YSR: That's right. In 2021, we had the 20th anniversary screening at the Jeonju International Film Festival. *Waikiki Brothers* was the opening film there in 2001, in their second year. It was during the COVID-19 pandemic then, so the audiences were in the theater, and some of us – me and actors Park Won-sang and Park Hae-il – were in the theater office and had a Zoom conversation with them. Since it's an old movie, I thought that it'd be older people who had enjoyed it in the past who came to see it again, but surprisingly, there were lots of young people in their 20s and 30s. There was a young woman who came with her mother. I was also curious how these younger audiences would think of the movie, and many found it very interesting.

CYS: That is great to hear! Jeonju has very discernible audiences! Another film I watched again recently is director Kwak Kyung-taek's *Friend* (2001), and I found there are a lot of similarities between the two films. Both films came out in 2001, the story goes back to school days in the '70s when the main characters fall in love with a charismatic female lead vocalist in a girl's school band. Both feature seaside hometowns and were rated Adults Only.

YSR: [*Laughs*] Because of the nude scene. Well, *Friend* is a very famous work, and there are lots of lines that have been quoted and talked about.

CYS: Despite the similarities, responses from the audiences were very different.

YSR: That's right. *Friend* was a huge hit (eight million viewers), and Waikiki Brothers was pulled out of the movie theaters early, but the audiences rented a theater to screen it, and in the end, it drew about 100,000 viewers altogether. Still, there was a demand for diversity in cinema. In 2001, low-budget commercial films like *Failan* and *Oasis* also came out, and I think it was the last period when people wanted and supported a variety of movies, not just mainstream stuff.

CYS: That's right. Not just Korean films, but all sorts of foreign movies were released then – a multiplex had a true sense of multiplex.

YSR: Yes, I remember Tarkovsky movies attracting 150,000, even 300,000 audiences at the end of the 1990s [*laughs*].

CYS: **Among the films you've directed, is there any one in particular you're most satisfied with?**

YSR: Well, like most creators, I have various regrets for all of them, but *Waikiki Brothers* seems to be the one that has my style and sentiment the most.

CYS: **How would you describe your style and sentiment?**

YSR: Emotionally, it's a bit gloomy, and thematically, I tend to deal with outsiders. There's not a lot of camera movement or close-ups, and I use a lot of long takes. The film has about half the average number of cuts of other movies at the time. I resisted using lots of music or close-ups and fast cutting, because it seemed too direct to say what's intended by using them. I wanted the audiences to find their own rhythm or deepen their thoughts through having a sense of distance. I thought I was providing scope for them, but it is very unpopular and not commercial, ultimately boring for the audiences who want fantasy or beauty. My films keep bringing out the ugly or pathetic aspects that they do not want to see.

CYS: Perhaps because you studied in France, you seem to have been influenced a lot by European art film traditions. Giving the audience a choice through long takes is the principle of the kind of films that André Bazin championed, and being gloomy reminds me of Italian neorealism.

YSR: I'm not sure. I think being gloomy comes from my perspective on Korean society. It did get brighter, say, in *Little Forest* (2018), but as you probably have experienced yourself, when you come back to Korea after living abroad for a while, you come to look at Korean society objectively with sharper eyes. So, when I came back from France, I can see that Korean society lacks diversity and is quite violent, and how I saw Korean society then is reflected in *Three Friends*. In the case of *Waikiki Brothers,* I wanted to show how dreams wear out as time goes by, faced by reality. Though it's set in regional towns in Korea, that can happen anywhere in the world. In terms of visual styles, there may be influences from European films, but I think my long takes or full shots are similar to those of Asian filmmakers such as Hou Hsiao-hsien or Kenji Mizoguchi. I found theirs more impressive.

CYS: Of course, you wrote your MA dissertation on the films of Mizoguchi!

YSR: It's also not my style to say directly how things are. Similarly, I want the audiences to actively find meanings in the movies, rather than me telling them how to think – and I thought the movies that allow a room for the audience are good movies.

CYS: It makes sense that you described your next film, *Forever the Moment* (2008), as a popular success obtained by conceding some of your colors.

YSR: I mean, *Three Friends* was praised at the Busan Film Festival, and *Waikiki Brothers* was in the limelight at the Jeonju Film Festival, but when they were released, *Three Friends* drew about 30,000 viewers, while *Waikiki Brothers* managed to attract 100,000. Then, as a filmmaker, I had to accept that some people like the type of films I make, but the majority don't. I also had to ask myself if I should continue making movies for a small number of viewers, hence ignoring the majority.

CYS: *Forever the Moment* was certainly a turning point in your career in many ways, including the fact that female characters are fully highlighted. But you didn't completely turn to commercial filmmaking with the film.

YSR: That's right. The film did have a lot more close-ups, music, and camera movements than my previous films. Nevertheless, it is not a typical sports film and doesn't follow the mold of a typical commercial film. I did go a little closer to what the audience wanted, though. In terms of casting, for instance, all but two people in *Promenade in the Rain* have ever acted before, all of *Three Friends*' actors are amateurs, and in *Waikiki Brothers*, most of the cast were then unknown actors from theater. But I cast well-known actors in *Forever the Moment*. The story itself had a popular appeal too. So, I was a little more flexible and compromised, if you like, and in the end, it was well received by the public. Still, I didn't give up the principles that mattered to me, such as my interest in outsiders and people who are not noticed in society.

CYS: I think you certainly have affection for the underdogs. *Forever the Moment* is about a women's handball team, not a popular or mainstream sport in Korea, and you also focus on the "older" members of the national team and their various trials and tribulations.

YSR: I do. I'd like to protect certain aspects that I regard to be fundamental, while being more flexible on other factors such as casting or filming methods if these let the audiences find my films to be more accessible.

CYS: In 2009, you directed *Fly Penguin*, which was produced by the NHRCK (National Human Rights Commission of Korea). It's an omnibus film, and I really like the way the four different stories are told, and how the characters of each episode are all connected. The film portrays a cross section of middle-class lives in Korea so well that I wondered how you know it in such detail.

YSR: *[Laughs] As you said, it's a work commissioned by the NHRCK. Human rights can be big subjects such as the rights of migrant workers, but I wanted to find human rights issues in our daily lives, in the family and workplace relations. So, excessive interference of parents can be a violation of children's rights, even though they may think of it as a way of loving their children, and I look at the controlling behavior of a spouse, or discrimination people unconsciously commit toward vegetarians or non-drinkers as human rights issues. Being a NHRCK project, the budget was very small, but the money was there, so I was able to say what I wanted to say about Korean society. I like that.*

CYS: After that, you directed *Rolling Home with a Bull* (2010).

YSR: *It's based on a novel, and I really liked the original novel. I'm also very interested in Buddhism, so I decided to take on the project, even though this was, again, a small-budget film.*

CYS: *Rolling Home with a Bull* reminded me of *Waikiki Brothers* a lot, probably because of its road movie aspect and its focus on a rather tangled past relationship. I also find the male protagonists of both films frustrating and somewhat irritating.

YSR: *[Laughs]* It's not like I like frustrating people in real life, but my male characters tend to be slightly gloomy in temperament, lacking machismo, and not good at decision-making. I think I have compassion for such men as they aren't validated in Korean society. British critic Tony Raynes once commented that the men portrayed in *Waikiki Brothers* are so different from the men in other Korean films, deviating from the typical Korean masculinities, possibly because I'm a female director.

CYS: **That's an insightful comment. I agree that your films offer a unique perspective on men. Come to think of it, director Hong Sang-soo's protagonists are often unmanly guys. How would you compare your male characters to those in director Hong's films?**

YSR: You're right, but director Hong's characters are mostly intellectuals – university professors, writers, or artists, while my characters are outsiders in terms of social status or class. The male protagonist in *Rolling Home with a Bull* is a poet, but he's more a small-scale farmer's son than an artist. I have interest, affection, and compassion for those atypical male outsiders.

CYS: **In both *Waikiki Brothers* and *Rolling Home with a Bull*, the characters travel around a lot, and it seems to me that you've traveled around Korea a lot and know the countryside really well – not tourist spots, but small and ordinary places, and your affection for such places is reflected well on the screen. Am I right in thinking that you like to travel around Korea?**

YSR: Yes, I do like traveling. As you pointed out, I don't do tourist destinations, but I like the Korean countryside a lot and its beautiful nature. I remember getting a phone call from director Bong Joon-ho, who wanted to know the location of the scene where the bull is sitting on the sandy beach in *Rolling Home with a Bull*.

CYS: Ah, I remember the scene, too. The color of the sea is almost unrealistically clear blue. That was where a kind of reconciliation takes place, too. Very peaceful. Still, after *Forever the Moment*, your films continued to be sluggish in terms of box-office performance, that is, until *Little Forest* (2018).

YSR: Yes, *Little Forest* did pretty well – its break-even point was 500,000 admissions, but it drew 1.5 million viewers. I was glad to see that young people, particularly female audiences in their 20s and 30s, responded to the film. Many of them told me that they watched it several times.

CYS: **The film is about a young woman who's trying to figure out what she wants to do with her life, so I can see why it resonated with so many young women in Korea. I think a huge factor behind its success is the actress Kim Tae-ri who did an amazing job at portraying the main protagonist. How did you get to cast her?**

YSR: You're right that the leading actress is so important to this film. First and foremost, I was looking for an actress who has a natural look, then I saw *The Handmaiden* (2016), the film that introduced us to the actress Kim Tae-ri. I thought she had such a natural charm, and when I met her in person, she really didn't disappoint. She was smart and thoughtful, and she even ate with great appetite, which was important for the role! It worked out well for her too, as her agency was keen for her to take on a more "ordinary" role, so to speak, after playing a strong character with lots of nudity in *The Handmaiden*. If it had not been for the actress Kim Tae-ri, the film wouldn't have been that successful.

CYS: She's been in lots of other high-profile films and drama series since then such as *1987: When the Day Comes* (2017), *Mr. Sunshine* (2018), and *Twenty-Five Twenty-One* (2022), and she's a bona fide leading actress now! Other cast members were great, too, but in particular, I really like the role of the mother, played by the great actress Moon So-ri. She's wise and also mysterious. I wish there was a sequel centered around the mother character.

YSR: [*Laughs*] Yes, if Moon hadn't played the role, it wouldn't have worked so well. She plays a mother who leaves her child behind, and that normally doesn't sit well with Korean audiences' sentiments, but Moon made them understand. Although it wasn't a big role, Moon captured the depth of the character and the film just right.

CYS: She also directed and starred in *The Running Actress* (2017), which is one of the string of women-directed exciting films that have come out in the past few years. Examples include *Microhabitat* (2017), *Maggie* (2018), *House of Hummingbird* (2018), *Moving On* (2019), *Lucky Chan-sil* (2019), *Voice of Silence* (2020), and they're all so fresh and interesting.

YSR: You're right. They're all very good films. In fact, I'd say that 70–80% of talented film directors in Korea are women. The problem is that these directors have now shown their colors and talents through independent feature films, but they're not absorbed into the mainstream system. The current system favors directors who are already in the system rather than new directors. The industry hasn't yet recovered since the COVID pandemic, and new directors are given much fewer opportunities.

CYS: **My understanding is that because big films were not released during the COVID pandemic, smaller films were able to fill in the gap. Is that right?**

YSR: That may be so, but the current audience pool for independent or art films in Korea is quite small, and Korean audiences tend to flock to the already popular ones.

CYS: From outside, looking at such talented women directors, I'm thinking that the future of women's cinema in Korea is really bright, but your view seems more pessimistic, probably because you know the system and its mode so well.

YSR: Well, women directors' works tend to be a lot less typical in terms of genre expectations, and less sensational, so not many commercial projects go to women directors. Actually, I think we're going through a transitional period now. So, we'll have to wait and see, but so far, I'm a little bit skeptical.

CYS: **You also acted as a co-chairperson for the Korean Center for Gender Equality in Film (Deun-deun), which was established in 2018. I understand that the aims of the center are to prevent sexual abuse and discrimination, as well as to promote film policies that attempt to improve gender inequalities in the film industry. What practical things does the center do to achieve its aims?**

YSR: In 2021, I actually stepped down from all the representational positions in organizations, including the Gender Equality Center, but Shim Jae-Myung of Myung Films is still keeping the chairperson position, partly because it's hard to find a successor. As I said before, most of the talented and good filmmakers in film schools or independent film circuits are women, but they are not picked for commercial films, while it's relatively easier for men to enter. So, in the end, we're trying to reduce that barrier, but, since movies are made with private capital, you can't tell a film company to use a woman, so we lobbied public institutes, such as the Korean Film Council to give extra points to women when assessing projects. In this way, we want to create an environment where it is a little easier for women filmmakers to enter the film industry. The center also offers sexual violence prevention education, supports victims of sexual violence legally and medically, and has signed an MOU (memorandum of understanding) with unions, such as the Director's Guild or Cinematographer's Guild, to terminate contracts with people who commit sexual violence. We have seen a cultural change in the industry, and the center led it.

CYS: **That is great to hear. Hope the center is able to continue the good work. Now, your latest film *The Point Men* was released in Korea early this year [2023]. The film is based on a strange case that happened in 2007 when Korean Christian missionaries went to Afghanistan despite the warnings from the government and were kidnapped by the Taliban. Can I ask what motivated you to take this project on?**

YSR: I accepted it because I thought I could explore how religion is used as an excuse for nonsensical acts, whether it's Christianity or Islam, rather than guiding people to lead their lives more wisely and peacefully. The main character here is a Korean diplomat who tries to save the hostages, and the central story is his dilemma of having to save the hostages who voluntarily went to a destination they were told not to go.

CYS: I heard that the budget is over 15 billion won ($13 million), which is the highest amount "entrusted" to a woman director in Korean film history.

YSR: Yes, I heard that, too. The cost went up mainly because a lot of production took place overseas in Jordan. The budget was set at about 15 billion, but there was an extra increase due to the COVID-19 pandemic, so it went up to about 17 billion won in the end. The most amount I had spent on a movie was 4 or 5 billion before this, so it was a weighty responsibility.

CYS: **I understand that filming finished in 2020. I presume the release has been delayed because of the pandemic?**

Figure 3.1   Director Yim Soon-rye on the set of *The Point Men* in Wadi Rum desert in southern Jordan during filming in late August 2020.

YSR: Yes, we finished filming in September 2020, and post-production in 2021. But it cost so much money, it couldn't be released when film theaters were not quite reopened. There were also a few other big films looking for the right timing, so we needed to avoid each other as well.

CYS: **Despite careful considerations, maybe because it has such a high break-even point, the film was a box-office failure (just over 1.7 million admissions against the BEP point of 3.5 million). How do you assess it? Do you have any complaints about marketing or publicity?**

YSR: I have no complaints about distribution, but if I were to analyze the cause of its failure, firstly the Korean film market is not buoyant at all. Simply, audiences do not come to the theaters. Second, as I implied earlier, Korean audiences tend to be easily swayed by quick judgments or rumors on content. Public opinion on the whole kidnapping incident has never been great, and I think we failed to persuade the audiences why the hostages needed to be rescued even though they went to a dangerous place of their own accord.

CYS: I wonder if the Korean audience misunderstood the core ideas that the film was trying to convey.

YSR: I feel that it was not so much how they misunderstood what the film was trying to say as lacking in their efforts to understand it. I was also lacking in my skills to bring in efficient cinematic logic, style, and organization to reverse the hostile public opinion. In April this year, the film was screened at the Korean Film Festival in Florence, Italy, and the audience response there was a lot better than in Korea, probably because the Italian audiences don't have negative emotions associated with the actual incident.

CYS: **It is a shame as I think the film certainly offers lots of cinematic pleasures as well as humanist ideas. Lastly, are you preparing your next project? I wonder if you've got any offers to direct a TV series?**

YSR: Actually, I have jumped on the bandwagon and am preparing to do a series. Simply, money has dried up in the Korean film industry. Because of the pandemic, films hadn't been properly released for almost three years – basically, they needed to make money first to invest in the next one. There's still a lot of money going around in streaming platforms though, and I received an offer that's interesting to me. There's nothing I can say in detail yet.

CYS: I understand. I'll look forward to seeing your next work soon then. Thank you so much for your time and sharing your stories.

Notes

1 The Cultural Center generation refers to a group of Korean filmmakers (such as Chung Ji-young, Park Kwang-su, Kim Hong-Joon, Yim Soon-rye, and Kim Ji-woon) and critics (notably Jung Sung-il and Yang Yun-mo) who encountered European art films through attending regular film screenings at French and German Cultural Centers in Seoul in the 1970s and '80s, when types of films from abroad were very limited and regulated by the authoritarian governments.
2 Chungmuro is a street and area nearby in Seoul where many film companies were based, hence a byword for the Korean film industry.

4

THROUGH THE LENS OF SOUTH KOREAN CINE-FEMINISM

House of Hummingbird (2018) and *Moving On* (2020)

Hyun Seon Park

South Korean Feminist Revival[1]

In recent years, feminism in South Korea has gained unprecedented visibility, fueling the rise of South Korean cine-feminism. This feminist resurgence can be attributed to various factors, including the emergence of young feminists on online platforms and social networks, as well as collective demands for justice sparked by the Gangnam Station murder case in 2016. Additionally, the alarming rise of overt misogyny and what can be described as a "backlash" against feminism has contributed to the urgency and intensity of the movement. The viral movements of #IAmAFeminist, #MeToo, and #WithYou have shed light on the violence and abuse that permeate all sectors of strongly patriarchal societies. The film industry was one of the first spheres where the #MeToo movement gained traction, with accusations of rape and sexual misconduct being made against filmmaker Kim Ki-duk, a Golden Lion award winner, and his "alter ego" (*pereusona*) actor Jo Jae-hyun. To prevent sexual abuse and discrimination, Women in Film Korea (Yeosungyounghwainmoim) and the Korean Film Council (KOFIC) founded the Korean Film Gender Equity Center (*Deun Deun* in Korean) in 2018. However, anti-feminism was also rapidly spreading among young men who expressed hostility against feminism and it continued to accelerate in the "gender war." A notable case that exemplifies this is the controversial reaction to the theatrical release of Kim Do-young's *82-nyeonsaeng gimjiyeong* (Kim Ji-young, Born 1982, 2019). The film, based on a feminist novel of the same title, triggered a fierce and deeply sexist battle within South Korean society, and leading actress Jung Yu-mi received a barrage of hateful comments on social media (Kim 2019). This incident poignantly demonstrates the current landscape of cine-feminism in South Korea, which is marked by the intricate interplay between deeply ingrained sexism and gender discrimination. Additionally, the industrial demography of South Korean film faces significant challenges in addressing gender inequality. For instance, despite comprising 60% of theater and film school students, only 11.5% of debut films, 8.5% of commercial films, and 4.1% of high-budget films are directed by women. The underrepresentation highlights the persistent struggle for gender parity and underscores the obstacles faced by women directors in South Korea's film industry (Park and Sim 2020, 236).

DOI: 10.4324/9781003266952-7

Nonetheless, South Korean women directors continue to create compelling works that center around female narratives and explore the complexities of female experience.[2] Even within the realm of low-budget and independent filmmaking, these filmmakers have emerged as a catalyst for a new wave of women's independent cinema. Including Jeong Ga-young with *Bamchigi* (Hit the Night, 2017), Kim Bo-ra with *Beolsae* (House of Hummingbird, 2018), Yoon Ga-eun with *Urideul* (The World of Us, 2016) and *Urijib* (The House of Us, 2019), and Lee Ok-seop with *Megi* (*Maggie,* 2018), women filmmakers have been recently signaling a new wave of women's cinema, "leading South Korean cinema to the next century" (Chau and Ng 2020). Their works reflect a growing emphasis on female-centric perspectives and address how the potential of the private intimacy transforms into the universal and public sphere.

This chapter highlights two feature debuts by young female directors: *House of Hummingbird* by Kim Bo-ra and *Nammaeui yeoreumbam* (Moving On, 2020) by Yoon Dan-bi. Their subsequent appearances indisputably breathed fresh vitality into South Korean cine-feminism. *House of Hummingbird*, written, produced, and edited by director Kim, was first introduced at the Busan International Film Festival in 2018 and achieved unprecedented box office and critical success at home and abroad. Director Yoon was also acclaimed for her remarkable debut film, *Moving On*, which she made as a graduation project from Dankook University's Graduate School of Cinematic Content. Many critics find it reminiscent of Asian filmmakers, such as Oz Yasujiro, Hou Hsiao-hsien, and Kore-eda Hirokazu. Around the same time, the Korean film industry showed the potential of the so-called K-culture by receiving global recognition in Europe and the United States with films like Bong Joon-ho's *Gisaengchung* (Parasite, 2019) and Lee Isaac Chung's *Minari* (2020). However, the recent emergence of young female directors has a peculiar significance to contemporary Korean cinema as they show the relationship between cinema and the world in a renovating vision of cine-feminism. What I refer to as cine-feminism is a new method for critically reshaping Korean film historiography and media ecosystems from a feminist perspective. These female directors often write screenplays themselves, bringing their childhood memories and women's experiences into the cinematic world, thereby showing the world of young women filled with vulnerability and affectivity. Renewing the relationship between film and the world, they spawn plural "worlds" since their films deconstruct the scale, intensity, and categories of the male-centered representation system and *dominant fiction* as a way of reserving social hegemony (Silverman 1992), which tend to take place in the "large world" of the grand narrative.

House of Hummingbird and *Moving On* are two cinematic works that skillfully navigate plural strata of the world through the trope of *jip* (집), which conveys the concepts of both "home" and "house." This chapter endeavors to elucidate the intricate significance of the dwelling on the screen and discuss how *jip* signifies multifaceted things, ranging from the catalyst of developmental urbanity to the juncture of the personal and the socio-political. Subsequently, a meticulous analysis of these films will unveil alternative ways of understanding and envisioning this intrinsic world of *jip* as perceived through the vantage point of adolescent girls.

The Trope of the House in Korean Films

Korean cinema has explored various representations of home/house, including its roles as a physical space, an urban cornerstone, and a symbolic construct. The trope of *jip*, deeply ingrained in the cultural context, has fostered an intimate connection with a diverse array of Korean films spanning various genres and historical epochs. The uniquely conspicuous, visual presence of the house prominently comes to the forefront, particularly in horror films. In "The Uncanny" (1919), Sigmund Freud demonstrates how the German adjective *heimlich* and its antonym *unheimlich* are tied to the double meaning of *heimlich* that signifies not only "belonging to the house, not strange, familiar, tame, intimate, comfortable, homely, etc." but also "concealed, kept from sight, so that others do not get to know about it, withheld from others" (Freud 2003, 222; 223). Such a familiar and comfortable place as the home comes to generate one of the most unfamiliar and unhomely feelings. This ambivalent duality is why many horror/mystery/thriller film genres center on the house. For instance, these horror films – Yoon Jong-chan's *So-reum* (Sorum, 2001) and *Sainyong sigtak* (The Uninvited, Lee Soo-Yeon 2003) – conjure up, respectively, the grotesqueness of an apartment just before demolition and the deep-seated trauma in the house interior. Also, the recent thriller films – Heo Jung's *Sumbakkoggil* (Hide and Seek, 2013) and Lee Kwon's *Do-eolak* (Door Lock, Lee Kwon 2018) – deal with intruders in the house. They address the urban anxiety that the safe boundary of the house could easily be trespassed on by others.

Besides the generic formulation, *jip* has become intertextual on the road to global modernity. From a two-story western house with a piano and stairs in Kim Ki-young's *Hanyeo* (The Housemaid, 1960) to the semi-basement and the upper-class house in *Parasite*, the house is at the core of developmental mentality and class discourse in South Korea. Bong Joon-ho, who pays homage to Kim Ki-young's films, expands a vertical rhythm of rise and fall to the entire city in *Parasite*. In a scene where the stream of heavy rain flows unstoppably downward, director Bong contrasts the hillside residency of the upper class, who enjoys camping in an outdoor garden, with an emergent situation of proletariats at a disaster shelter in a low and flooded area. Borders in the polarized map of the class become visible while their dissolution occurs through the secret room and hidden niches inside the house.

The visual economy of the house has an intriguing portrayal in Jeon Go-woon's *Sogongnyeo* (Microhabitat, 2018). This whimsical film embraces the bittersweet existence of a young housekeeper in the era of neoliberalism. To secure a bit of freedom and joy, which means a pack of cigarettes and one glass of single malt whiskey daily, the protagonist gives up her house as the rent increases. In a scene where the protagonist wanders off in search of an affordable home, the film satirizes how a new millennial precariat survives in such an environment as what can be called a four-walled box rather than a home. Nobody seems to care for the livability of these environments, including semi-basements, rooftop rooms, dens of cockroaches, or studios without kitchens or toilet facilities; Money is the operative "moral law" of the rental market.

However, *House of Hummingbird* and *Moving On* suggest alternative approaches to the meaning of the home/house through the lens of cine-feminism. *House of Hummingbird* shows the catastrophe of a middle-class family and urbanized Seoul in the mid-1990s, while *Moving On* shows an affective image of a place where traces of life are imprinted across generations and addresses the non-singular flow of time in *jip*. Notably, the utilization of *jip* as a suffix introduces the notion of "the place where something formed" or "the trace of something." The former is turning the familial space into a social and political sphere, while the latter is returning its significance to the affective environment. In the different modes of the two films, at stake is the question of "What political, aesthetic, and ethical questions can be raised in the trope of *jip*?" Posing the house as the affective and relational world, both contribute to expanding the potential of the *home-world* by meticulously weaving a small space (house) and a small time (everyday life). Furthermore, through their cine-feminist approaches to the urban and familial topology of a house, the two films foreground the physical mobility and affective transition and reconstruct the aesthetics of gaze, memory, and writing from a female adolescent's perspective.

The Affective and Relational Entanglement of Home-World

Cine-feminism's practices have deconstructed the house's ideology that has bound women and re-established the relationship between women and the domestic space through critical intervention and alternative representation. An excellent instance is *Jeanne Dielman* (1975); for 3 hours and 21 minutes of screening time, Chantal Ackermann depicts three days of a widowed single mother staying in her apartment while cooking, cleaning, bathing, and having dinner with her son, except the time she goes shopping for groceries. The film ultimately reveals that her labor for a living is prostitution at home. Overturning the conventional image of home and controlling the male gaze, *Jeanne Dielman* demonstrates that the house is no different from a space of sexual oppression and economic exploitation. Likewise, the patriarchal *oikos* discourse has reproduced female oppression and gendered division. *Oikos*, an ancient Greek term, refers to family, household, and the house. As a private sphere, *oikos* is divided from the public sphere, called *polis*. Ancient Greek society designated women, children, and enslaved people to the realm of *oikos*, which consisted of the domestic and interior places such as the bedroom, kitchen, bathroom, and closet (Hannah 1958). The role of women has limited interior spaces such as the bedroom, kitchen, or closet. Likewise, a prominent feminist thinker Luce Irigaray criticizes the house's long history as a mechanism for locking women into an "internal exile" (Irigaray 1993, 144).

Then, what can be an alternative approach to the house? It would set a theoretical limit on this peculiar space to cancel it merely as a place of violence to be disclosed or a patriarchal *oikos*. How can we develop the concept of the house into a more inclusive and empowering space? This chapter explores a new aspect of "home-world" as a sense of being connected and of multi-strata, reconfiguring the home/house in two modes: the affective and the relational. As discussed in affect studies, emotion is not simply an individual and psychological status of the subject but a socially and culturally constituted mode of feeling in the surrounding environment (Ahmed 2014). This reinterpretation offers the feminist recalibration of house and home, where emotion extends beyond personal experience to encompass transpersonal experience and shared understanding. Emotion becomes an affective force that interconnects individuals with their surroundings, fostering a deeper and more meaningful relationship with the space they inhabit. The second mode of home/house as relational space poses a pluralistic space that goes against the idea of absolute and measurable Euclidean space (Thrift 2006). In this mode, home becomes the entangled world as a network of power, labor, sexuality, unconsciousness, and the capabilities of the agency. In a significant way, affective space and relational space are connected because the critical shift from absolute to relational space is abandoning "representation" as an image that replaces and duplicates something. Likewise, if we look at the house again as a relational space; we can see the "past, present, and future space-time created by exchanging influence with power, labor, sexuality, unconsciousness, and the capabilities of actors" (Thrift 2003, 99–100).

Instead of drawing boundaries around the home/house, these films engage in questions such as "What if we regarded the world as made up of flows and tried to change our style of thought to accommodate that depiction?" (Urry 2000, 23). Feminist theorist Elizabeth Grosz searches for spatial figures that can convey the ambition to build different, more fluid kinds of space (Grosz 1994). In that sense, the house must also be free "from the straitjacket of container thinking" (Thrift 2003, 100). In both *House of Hummingbird* and *Moving On*, the notion of home and the domestic space transcends its conventional role as a mere container mediating family relationship. Instead, it emerges as a dynamic framework characterized by a series of affective and relational metamorphoses. At the same time, in these films, the home-world becomes deeply interwoven with the domain of social practice. The spatial construct of home is far from a passive medium; rather, it assumes the mantle of a strategic representation that actively participates in all practices and discourses of relational dynamics.

Ruptured Home and Emerging Gaze in *House of Hummingbird*

House of Hummingbird is set in 1994, a time when Seoul underwent an economic upturn. This era witnessed an accelerated and forceful pace of urban development and expansion, leading to a series of rapid and often disruptive interactions within South Korean society. The film observes the world through the perspective of Eun-hee, a 14-year-old girl living in the Gangnam district, known for upscale modernity and prosperity during the time. Eun-hee's narrative of self-discovery during her coming-of-age journey stands in stark juxtaposition to the society's ambivalent transformation, which is expressed in two distinct yet interconnected manifestations: the familial struggle and the urban upheaval that verges on disastrous collapse.

The opening sequence of *House of Hummingbird* takes place in front of a closed apartment door where the main character Eun-hee finds the wrong house and persistently rings the bell which is unanswered. It reminds us of Korean writer Pak Wan-suh's short story *Dalmeun bang* (Identical Apartment, 1974), which was written amid the 1970s construction boom of the apartment complex in Gangnam and showed the uncanny uniformity of apartment space and the hypocrisy of the emerging middle class. Similar to Pak's description of apartments in the story, the beginning of *House of Hummingbird* depicts the long line of apartment corridors and floors in a symmetrical pattern. Then, the temporal and spatial indicator of "1994, Eunma Apartment" appears over the geometric image of apartment corridors to give a glimpse of the socio-cultural status of the urban space.

Eun-hee's family runs a rice cake business in the Gangnam district and tries hard to catch up with the mythology of the middle-class. The film frequently depicts the family gathered around the dinner table, showcasing the patriarchal structure of a Korean family in the 1990s. Then, as the narrative unfolds, Eun-hee's family story intertwines with the tale of a societal disaster. The house that does not welcome its habitats parallels with other spaces that Eun-hee explores in the film, creating a somewhat unstable and cracked topology of home and the city. More specifically, Eun-hee's daily rhythm – going back and forth between home, school, and *hak-won* (private academy institutions) – is punctuated by instances of isolation, dissonance, and even physical maltreatment. Her journey later encompasses a hospital where she undergoes surgery for an unusual lump beneath her ear; a redevelopment site cloaked in protest banners and slogans; and ultimately, the catastrophic event of the severed Seongsu Bridge over the Han River, an actual occurrence in Seoul in October 21, 1994.

The feminist approach of *Hummingbird* prominently highlights the power of the female gaze, shedding light on emotions and intimate moments as opposed to the male gaze, which often depicts and objectifies women and the female sphere through the camera lens of appearance and visual pleasure. The gendered economy of visuality is dismantled by two distinct female gazes that emerge in the film: one emanates from Eun-hee, an adolescent girl, while the other emanates from Young-ji, a college student who takes a leave of absence ostensibly for political reasons, and who works as a temporary instructor at a private academy. Most of the time, Young-ji appears as a perceptive observer and empathetic listener. Yet she taught Eun-hee how to see the world with a keen eye as well as how to react in an unjust situation. This intricate dynamic converges Eun-hee's gaze, marked by its inherent instability and peripheral nature, with Young-ji's socially conscious perspective. Eun-hee's unstable and peripheral gaze and Young-ji's socially critical gaze meet and create an intimate space, where both perspectives merge to create a unique and meaningful symbiosis.

Beyond the convergence of two women's perspectives, the film connects the significance of the gaze – as a way of seeing – to the fluidity and dynamism of a moving body. The female gaze, often perceived as a confined term, evolves into an integral facet of an engaged and immersive bodily experience. Notably, Eun-hee broadens her horizons through her physical crossings. As mentioned, the film shows an array of various places, from her home to her educational institution, and even popular locations such as a karaoke room and a non-alcoholic dance club for youngsters in the mid-1990s. Each of these locales serves as a tableau, emblematic of the mid-1990s Korean societal mosaic. This intricate canvas encapsulates the comprehensive spectrum of Korean societal structures: the delineations between public and private domains, the interplay between endurance and pleasure, and the layered complexities of hierarchical boundaries.

The film, at its core, unveils an alternative perspective, one that extends beyond the mere act of visual observation. Eun-hee's bodily sojourns through these multifaceted spaces become a motif for her personal metamorphosis and an avenue for exploring the connections between visual narratives and corporeal experiences. The unfolding narrative implicitly urges the audience to recalibrate their understanding of the young female subjectivity, transcending the conventional boundaries of the gaze and embracing a more immersive and dynamic embodiment of lived experiences. One remarkable aspect of this film lies in the expansive nature of Eun-hee's gaze, stretching its horizons through spatial intersections. For instance, a particularly poignant scene portrays Eun-hee's solitary return to her home from the hospital. Adorned with white bandages encircling her ear, Eun-hee occupies a seat on the bus, her gaze fixated beyond the windowpane. In this moment, she appears not lonely but independent as a young woman traversing the world unaccompanied. Within the realm of spatial dynamics shaped by her gaze and movement, a paradoxical fusion of vulnerability and strength emanates from her visage.

Toward its culmination, *House of Hummingbird* unfurls a profoundly evocative landscape. At the heart of this scene stands a trio of teenage souls – Eun-hee, her sister, and her boyfriend – gathered along the banks of the Han River. Here, under the blue ambience of the breaking dawn, they bear solemn witness to the wreckage of a bridge, which looks surreal because of its severance. This crystalline moment poses a reflective question about the violence of relentless urban development and the distorted facets of familial relations. Eun-hee, embodying a poignant determination, directs her gaze unwaveringly toward the scene of tragic desolation. It is a gaze that transcends the mere act of looking; it's an act of bearing witness, a communion with the weight of remembrance and the pain of loss. Her solemn vigil bespeaks a resolute yearning to honor the memory of Young-ji, whose existence was tragically snuffed out on the day the Seungsu bridge collapsed. Through Eun-hee's eyes, the film unveils a multidimensional narrative tapestry, one that juxtaposes together

Figure 4.1 House of Hummingbird – Eun-hee's bus journey and seeing the world through her eyes.

the intimate threads of her own family's problem, the echoes of the lyrics that Young-ji once sang of severed factory workers' fingers, and the fractured remains of the bridge itself in the very heart of Seoul's urban landscape. The bridge, once a connector of worlds, now stands as an emblem of division, a striking embodiment of the perils entailed in the relentless pursuit of progress. In short, *House of Hummingbird* ingeniously dissolves the barriers between the personal and the societal, the microcosmic and the macrocosmic. It is a young female subject's witnessing body that encapsulates a myriad of interconnected narratives and distills them into an emotionally charged landscape.

The Ethics of Memory and Time in *Moving On*

While *House of Hummingbird* explores the uncanny rupture in urban history through the crossing gaze of a teenage girl who tries to reach her world, *Moving On* addresses the ethical aesthetics of remembering traces and imprints in a family across generations. The opening sequence of *Moving On* introduces Ok-ju, a teenage girl with her divorced father and her younger brother. She stands in a vacant living room just before moving out of the house, looking over the kitchen and the walls. Ok-ju looks at a framed picture still hanging on the empty wall when she goes out, which must be her family picture but is not shown to us. The camera movements create a unique atmosphere in the following scene as Ok-ju's family leaves home. The camera tracks backward while showing the front of the van in a long take; as the camera moves back, the space expands, and the empty townhouses and demolition signs come into the screen. The next scene shows Ok-ju's family moving into Grandpa's house without further explanation.

Implicit within the Korean title *Summer Night of Brothers and Sisters*, the film depicts the dual narrative of two siblings in the film: the one for Ok-ju and her younger brother, the other one for Ok-ju's father and aunt. Amid the backdrop of the elder generation's deteriorating health, particularly Grandfather's dementia, the exploration of familial dynamics takes center stage. When adults bring their father to the hospital, a teenage girl and a young boy inquisitively venture through the house. Grandpa's home becomes more than an old two-story house as if it is breathing with memory and traces. The house pulsates with an embodiment of object-life ontology, a fusion of inanimate objects and the essence of life. Among these relics, aged vinyl records and vintage speakers coexist alongside an ancient wall clock and a manual sewing machine perched upon the second floor. Even the gateway garden, adorned with cherry tomatoes, peppers, and grapes, bears testament to the continuity of life amid the passage of time. Walter Benjamin illustrates the relationship between the traces left in the interior and residence:

> The interior is not just the universe but also the étui of the private individual. To dwell means to leave traces. In the interior, these are accentuated. Coverlets and antimacassars, cases and containers are devised in abundance; in these, the traces of the most ordinary objects of use are imprinted. In just the same way, the traces of the inhabitant are imprinted in the interior.
>
> *(Benjamin 2008, 104)*

A house is a space where the most intimate traces of life remain, our world, and an ontological archive. This shows how the various items and elements within the house carry a deeper significance, embodying the lives, stories, and memories of the characters and their shared history.

Moving On captures the world of the house as a constant process in which family intimacy gets emptied and filled while also capturing the elongated temporality of midsummer. Here, the house itself emerges as an image of affect, reflecting Baruch Spinoza and Gilles Deleuze's concept of affect as a temporal cascade of fluctuations and metamorphosis (Deleuze 1988). Time passes differently in the house as an affective space. This is particularly exemplified in a scene that stands out prominently. Here, a father is reading a book on the sofa and Dong-ju sleeping on the living room floor. The wall clock reads 7:50. The sound of the second-hand flowing is loud. Suddenly, his father shakes Dong-ju to wakes up. Fearing that he's running late for school, Dong-ju hastens to prepare, only to realize that the season is that of summer vacation, alleviating his initial apprehension. This episode carries echoes from the past, a delightful connection to Dong-ju's grandfather, who employed a similar trick on his own father. In his father's childhood, his grandfather just woke up the father for school, but when he went out with his bag, it was 8:30 in the evening, not 8:30 in the morning. Although the clock on the wall indicates a time of the day with spatialized temporality moving from one point to another, the film transforms the movement of time into poetic events. The clock's hands whimsically increase and decrease, just like in *Alice in Wonderland*, and undulate in a manner that seemingly elongates and compresses time. As if imbued with a narrative agency of its own, the clock evolves into an affective object, each moment it points to carrying a distinct temporal significance – a poignant reminder that time's essence is more intricate and layered than its mere measurement.

By capturing the affectivity and temporality within the household, *Moving On* suggests an alternative contemplation of interior space and the home. From a feminist point of view, it builds the image of the house as an affective realm, an evocative repository of temporal traces, diverging from a house connected to the *oikos* discourse of patriarchal order and household management. In this cinematic world, Grandpa's house permeates boundaries and gives rise to a porous expanse of memory. Everyday objects like doors that swing open and shut, stairs connecting the first and second floors, and mosquito nets that are built and torn down connect each person, create a bond of longing, and mix different memories, dreams, and the present. In this way, *Moving On* reframes our conception of the domestic realm. It subtly subverts the confines of patriarchal constructs, inviting us to perceive the house as a living entity pulsating with emotions and echoes of time, a sanctuary that nurtures a multiplicity of experiences beyond the conventional notions of order and management.

In a feminist lens, the film nurtures a very vibrant connection between the home-world and the teenage girl. In a sequence, Ok-ju sits on a staircase and unnoticeably looks at her grandfather as he indulges in his music. Regarding the relationship between Ok-ju and her grandfather, the two do not share many conversations or direct interaction. Still, an unspoken understanding binds them, revealing an intricate form of empathy that transcends words.

This profound connection deepens as the story draws to a close. After her grandfather's funeral, Ok-ju finds solace and grows from within. Upon returning grandpa's home, shared moments around a meal stir tears, and her overwhelming emotions guide her toward a moment of solitude. She retreats to a room, surrendering herself to sleep. The film concludes on a poignant note, offering a retrospective glimpse into the past through her grandparents' wedding photographs, swaying laundry, and a coiled hose nestled amid the lush greenery of the garden. Through Ok-ju's perspective, the film underscores a crucial insight: the house is not a static container for relationships but a living tapestry onto which the ever-changing interplay of the world is woven.

From an ecofeminist perspective, Verena Conley emphasizes that feminine writing can embody ecological and environmental consciousness rather than being solely self-centered. She posits that in ecofeminist politics, writing should engage in an ongoing dialogue with issues that extend beyond the human realm, emphasizing interconnected elements within specific environments (Conley 2006, 119). This concept aligns harmoniously with the image of a relational and ecological home-world depicted in *Moving On*. To take an instance of a striking visual moment, within the living room on the first floor, three generations of the family come together to share a meal and celebrate a birthday. From outside the house, this scene is visible through the expansive window. The family and the indoor space are surrounded by the frame of the window, the exterior wall of the house, and the lush grass and trailing vine leaves in the front yard. Home/house is presented not as a building or an indoor space but as an environment that surrounds the lives of various objects. The film refrains from orchestrating grand compositions that counterpoint one another. Instead, it deftly interweaves the imprints of the house's inhabitants and the memories carried by various small objects. When many memories coexist and interact, the affective images emerge. These images, in turn, unfurl layers of themes encompassing life and death, the symbiotic relationship between objects and existence, and the coalescence of presence and absence. In this vein, *Moving On* resonates with the ethos of ecofeminist politics by forging a cinematic space that not only contemplates the intricacies of life within the home-world but also extends into the broader web of time and memory.

In conclusion, both *House of Hummingbird* and *Moving On* ingeniously shape the cinematic portrayal of home and house through the unique lens of young women. Concurrently, these films carve out a fresh panorama of diverse and pluralistic worlds. Teenage girls in the films not merely belong to the family but dynamically participate as agents of creation and transformation in reforming, negotiating, and rupturing the given world of home/house. In parallel, the cine-feminist filmmakers adeptly demonstrate the exploration of spatial and affective dimensions. This involves a dynamic interplay of the gaze, punctuated by its corporeal traversal and poetic reconstruction. The cinematic canvas becomes a medium through which to experiment with the interplay of affective images, inviting viewers to engage with the ever-evolving landscapes of emotions and connections. Moreover, the filmmakers venture into the realm of ecological potential, weaving together the subjective existence with the objects and the environment. Through their cine-feminist lens, these South Korean women filmmakers illuminate paths toward reimagining the notion of home, fostering dialogues between the personal, the social, and the ecological realms.

Notes

1 This part draws on the introductory essay for the special section titled "South Korean Cine-Feminism," which I had the privilege of guest-editing in *Journal of Japanese and Korean Cinema*.
2 For instance, at the New York Asian Film Festival in 2020, among the ten female directors represented in the lineup, five hailed from South Korea. They include *Kim Ji-Young: Born 1982*, *Lucky Chan-sil*, *Moving On*, and two episodes from the television series *SF8* (Chu 2020). Likewise, at the Korean Film Festival in Australia in 2020, 8 of its 18 invited films were made by women.

References

Ahmed, Sara. 2014. *The Cultural Politics of Emotion*. Edinburgh: Edinburgh University Press.
Benjamin, Walter. (1935) 2008. "Paris, the Capital of the Nineteenth Century." In *The Work of Art in the Age of its Technological Reproducibility and Other Writings on Media*, edited by Michael W. Jennings et al. Cambridge/Massachusetts/ London: The Belknap Press of Harvard University Press.
Chau, Hie, and Natalie Ng. 2020. "The Women Directors Leading South Koren Cinema Its Next Century." *Filmedinether*, October 26. Accessed December 22, 2022. https://www.filmedinether.com/video-essays/the-women-directors-leading-south-korean-cinema-into-its-next-century/.
Chu, Beatrix. 2020. "A Long Road for Women Directors in South Korea: NYAFF's Female-led Korean Films and the Ongoing Struggle for Gender Equality." *Filmmaker Magazine*, October 21. https://filmmakermagazine.com/110485-a-long-road-for-women-directors-in-south-korea-nyaffs-female-led-korean-films-and-the-ongoing-struggle-for-gender-equality/#.Y7JyvnZByUk
Conley, Verena Andermatt. 2006. *Ecopolitics: The Environment in Poststructuralist Thought*. London/New York: Routledge.
Deleuze, Gilles. 1988. *Spinoza, Practical Philosophy*. Translated by Robert Hurley, San Francisco: City Lights Books.
Freud, Sigmund. (1919) 2003. "The Uncanny." In *The Uncanny*, translated by David McLintock and Hugh Haughton. New York: Penguin Books.
Grosz, Elizabeth A. 1994. *Volatile Bodies: Toward a Corporeal Feminism*. Bloomington: Indiana University.
Hannah, Arendt. 1958. *The Human Condition*. Chicago: University of Chicago Press.
Irigaray, Luce. 1993. *An Ethics of Sexual Difference*. Translated by Carolyn Burke and Gillian C. Gill. London: Continuum.
Kim, Hyung Eun. 2019. "Kim Ji-young, Born 1982: Feminist Film Reignites Tensions in South Korea." *BBC News*, October 23, 2019. https://www.bbc.com/news/world-asia-50135152.
Park, Hyun Seon. 2020. "South Korean Cine-Feminism." *Journal of Japanese and Korean Cinema* 12 (2): 91–97.
———, and Hyekyong Sim. 2020. "Sinepeminijeum 30nyeon, yeoseongui nuneuro bon hangukyeonghwa [The 30 years of Cin-Feminism: Korean Cinema through Women's Eye]." *Munhwa/gwahak* [*Culture/Science*] 101: 224–40.
Silverman, Kaja. 1992. *Male Subjectivity at the Margins*. New York: Routledge.
Thrift, Nigel. 2003. "Space: The Fundamental Stuff of Human Geography." In *Key Concepts in Geography*, edited by Nicholas Clifford, Sarah Holloway, Stephen Rice, and Gill Valentine. London: Sage Publications.
———. 2006. "Space." *Theory, Culture & Society* 23 (2–3): 139–46.
Urry, John. 2000. *Sociology beyond Societies: Mobilities for the Twenty-First Century*. London: Routledge.

5

REWRITING HISTORY, CHANGING THE STORY

An Interview with Anocha Suwichakornpong

Graiwoot Chulphongsathorn

Graiwoot Chulphongsathorn (GC): **When did you realize the idea of being a filmmaker could be your life choice?**

Anocha Suwichakornpong (AS): I can't really give a straightforward answer to what is seemingly a very straightforward question. I can say that when I was younger, not being from Bangkok – I grew up in Pattaya, a seaside city, two-hour drive from Bangkok – my sisters and I used to rent VHS tapes from our local store, so I did like watching movies as a kid. But I was not really thinking about it deeply or in a serious way. When I was younger, I was more interested in literature. But when I went to study in the UK, there was maybe a little bit of a shift. At one point, it became more obvious that I was more interested in movies than literature. And this had to do with the fact that I discovered world cinema. Somehow, world cinema opened up to me when I was living in London, and I watched movies from Europe, like Italian films, French films.

The more I watched, the more I became interested in reading about films, as well. This was when I was doing my bachelor's degree, which incidentally had nothing to do with film. But since I took an interest in it, I wanted to do my dissertation on something that had to do with cinema. And so I asked my thesis adviser, if I could write about Chinese cinema. At the time, the fifth-generation filmmakers were really hugely popular in the UK and in many parts of the world. Like Chen Kaige and Zhang Yimou, they were the stars of international cinema with films such as *Da hong deng long gao gao gua* (Raise the Red Lantern, 1991) or, those like –

GC: ***Ba wang bie ji*** (Farewell My Concubine, 1993).

AS: Yes. So those were the movies that really captured the public imagination, talking about Asian cinema, but not just Asian, in the world cinema stage. I wanted to know more about these filmmakers. So I . . . made a self-study research and wrote about the fifth-generation filmmakers as my dissertation when I was doing a degree in jewelry design. It was fine that my supervisor was cool with it. I was doing research at the British Film Institute library. I was just reading about [the] Beijing Film Academy and the fifth-generation filmmakers, and reading the news and micro films. After that, I did a master's degree at Warwick University in arts education and cultural studies. Incidentally, Warwick has a very

DOI: 10.4324/9781003266952-8

strong film studies program. I was not a film student, but being from the education department, I was able to take a class in the film department as an optional course. I enrolled in Intro to Film Studies, and it was really an eye-opening experience for me because the other students, they were all film majors, and I was the only one who came from another department. In that one semester, I really learned a lot about cinema . . . to be engaged with it in a more critical approach. I could say, that was also a turning point, but still I wasn't thinking of it as a career choice. I was just really interested in it. And it was like for the first time, I felt that I could understand the thinking behind the construction of a scene and things like that. It planted the seed for what I'm doing now.

GC: Asian cinema is famous for genre films, such as ghost cinema, action cinema or local comedy. But it seems to me that these genres did not influence you much, which in a way is a good thing because it makes your films unique. Can I say that you are a part of current Asian filmmakers who want to make a new kind of Asian films, which have their aesthetic and are influenced by global culture?
AS: I think that's a fair assessment of what I do, because as I was just saying, and you rightly put it, I was not really influenced by genre films. I took an interest in cinema when I discovered world cinema, particularly European cinema, and then with the Chinese films of the '90s. I was influenced by those films more. And it's true that I'm still trying to come up with – I don't know if "language" is the right word – but something that for me is very important. But I don't even think of it in terms of something that is specific to Asian or not Asian. I want to make a film that I myself want to see, but also [with] every film I try to not repeat myself. I try to experiment with every film that I make because there's still a lot to discover, I feel. It's still very much alive, I think, what cinemas can be.

GC: In terms of the language or the aesthetic, in the past decade, there is a term in art-house cinema called slow cinema. But your film is not a part of that group. In contrast, it seems to me that your films are a part of the other groups, which explore the idea of in-betweenness, such as the space between reality and fiction; professional actors and non-professional actors; the mix of narrative, documentary, and experimental films; or even the idea of the mix between cinema and performance art. Do you see yourself as a part of this tradition or this wave of filmmakers who explore this in-betweenness?
AS: I'm glad to hear that. I don't really consciously think about it, but now that you put this question to me, I'm thinking about it. Yes, I do see myself like that. The term "slow cinema" is a bit of a blanket term. Sometimes it's used . . . in a very liberal way. In fact, when I was making *Jao Nok Krajok* (Mundane History, 2009), I thought I was not going to make a slow [film]. Even back then, this was . . . 2008 when I was shooting *Jao Nok Krajok.* I was conscious of this term, slow cinema, as being used to describe a lot of Asian films and I didn't want to fall into that category.

Maybe the term's used differently now, but in 2008, I had this feeling that the connotation was a little bit . . . like a stereotype. And I wasn't really keen on it, so I wanted to design the look of the film, the aesthetics, the cinematography, to actually go against what I thought would be classified as slow cinema. The character in *Jao Nok Krajok*, he's paraplegic and he has to stay in bed the whole time, so I deliberately did not want to use too much static camera, so it was handheld. That was a decision that was related to this whole idea of slow cinema, actually. Yet, when the film came out, some people still said that it was really slow, which was surprising to me. Having said that, nowadays I don't think about it as much. If people call my films slow cinema, I'm fine with that . . . to each their own and everyone has their own way of approaching themselves.

GC: **You have already mentioned** *Jao Nok Krajok*. **I think the film defies any expectation of Asian cinema. Could you talk a little bit about the first idea behind it?**

AS: I had made a few shorts and was getting a little bit more into the politics in Thailand at the time. This was the time just after Thaksin Shinawatra was ousted in 2006.[1] That was a turning point for me as well, to witness the kind of mentality of people in Bangkok . . . who went out . . . giving . . . flowers to [support] the army riding the tanks. Yeah, it did something to me. And then I became more aware of what was going on in Thailand . . . historically as well, because then I started to read more about . . . politics in the '70s . . . and it has to do with *Jao Nok Krajok* because I felt there was [a] parallel between what was happening politically in the '70s and around this time, 2006–2008, with the red shirt protestors that were in full force then. And then how the king was seen as this father figure of Thailand and was supposed to solve all kinds of crises just by the virtue of his divine being. It was [a] very strange time. Well, I actually wrote a short story, first. It was basically the basis of the script for *Jao Nok Krajok*. But this short story only had two characters and it was written in a kind of first-person narrative. It was just one page, almost like a diary entry, where the son talks about the relationship with his father. After that, I decided to write a screenplay based on the same idea, but . . . a script form. You would need a lot more elements to fill in . . . more characters. It also became more plotty. The script of *Jao Nok Krajok* was written in a chronological order, and we shot the film thinking it was going to be in a chronological order.

GC: **But the outcome is a very non-linear film. I am curious about the ways in which you work with your editor, Lee Chatametikool.**

AS: Lee also edited *Graceland* (2006). That was the first time I worked with him. *Graceland* turned out to be quite successful, in terms of festivals. It gave us the confidence to work together again. In the beginning, he was still editing according to the script. The first few drafts were linear, and I remember him commenting on that, because the main character's just in bed, and then you would have scenes where someone walks into the room, and leaves the room, like the father or the housekeeper. It's a little bit monotonous, this day-to-day existence. Lee commented, "It's funny watching this, you could almost loop the scene." At some point when we reached [the] fourth or fifth draft of the edit, we both felt that it could still be better. And what he said came back to me. Then I had this idea . . . what if we tell the story not in the chronological order [but] start in the middle of the story, let's see if that would work.

There is that famous quote from Godard, that the story has [a] beginning, middle and end, but not necessarily in that order. I was also thinking about . . . telling a story somewhere in the middle and then the audience has to be really [be] active and try to follow the story. In terms of practice, what we had was the index cards with each scene written on them. We already had this in practice, even before we constructed the film. So all these index cards were just on the floor. Lee said, "Why don't [you] play around with these cards and I'll come back in 30 minutes." So I rearranged basically the first 15 minutes of the films. Then Lee came back in and he edited this first 15 minutes. And he said, "Okay, let's watch it to see if it's watchable at all. If it actually makes sense." And then we sat down to watch it. And after 15 minutes he said, "I think it could work."

Interestingly enough, the 15-minute structure stayed throughout the film. If you watch closely, every 15 minutes something shifts, but it's not like once you have the first 15 minutes, and then you have the second 15 minutes. Each one has to make sense in its own terms, but also in relation to the other blocks. That's how we did it. And it took a long time because it was the first time for me to try to do that. I really learned a lot in this process and I think I got to understand a little bit more about non-linearity just by doing it. Also, I felt that the final film ended up being closer to the short story rather than the script because it was more internal. The problem with the linear drafts, the edits that we had . . . was that it was lacking in this kind of emotional journey for the character. It became just . . . you just follow plots. One thing happens, another thing happens, but you are not enough with a character. With this kind of [non-linear] structure . . . you are more invested [in] the character, at least that's what I try to do. Because you are not following the incidents, you are more with the character internally, emotionally.

GC: **For *Jao Nok Krajok* you did not only make your first feature film, but you also founded your first company Electric Eel Films. What separates Electric Eel Films from other film collectives in Thailand is that it is a female-led. Electric Eel Films is a very rare company that has an in-house woman cinematographer, a woman producer, a woman editor, a woman director. There are male filmmakers blended beautifully into the collective too. Are you conscious that you support other young female filmmakers?**
AS: I think half-conscious, and also half-organic. In the beginning, maybe it happened quite organically that . . . young female filmmakers, like Ohm [editor Aacharee Ungsriwong] or Nan [cinematographer and producer Parinee Buthrasri], enjoyed hanging out with me because it is kind of like a sisterly feeling. And we work well together. I have to say that I have three older sisters, no boys in my family, I'm very used to being surrounded by women. My mom is also an important, strong character in our family. And I went to convent school when I was young. So I'm very used to hanging out with a lot of women. It just happened naturally that I surrounded myself with more women, and they probably felt more comfortable in the same environment. But after a while, it became apparent to me that it can be difficult for some of them to be noticed or to be given an opportunity. So I try to encourage this to happen. If there's a way for me to form a connection between one filmmaker and another, I try to link them in some way to create work, then I try to do it.

GC: **Let's shift to *Dao Khanong* (By the Time It Gets Dark, 2016). Both you and I are in the same generation that doesn't have a direct experience with the 6 October massacre, but do you believe that it is our duty to acknowledge its existence, or find ways to remember it?[2] As I see it, *Dao Khanong* is not directly about the massacre, but it is about the ways in which people try to remember it.**
AS: I think it is a responsibility for sure. I don't think we can deny that, even though we don't have, as you said, direct experience with the massacre, that doesn't mean that we cannot think about it. It's all the more that we should think about it because we, the generation just right after . . . if we don't think about it . . . then the next generation will not think about it. I think it would be a great mistake, if such brutality is forgotten. Because it has not been solved, it hasn't been brought to justice and the people who were of that generation, the people who were directly involved, they have it with them, they carry it with them. Someone like Thongchai Winichakul, he's been spending every day thinking about it.[3]

And if our generation . . . ignores it, or doesn't keep this memory . . . it shouldn't just be a memory, too. It's not our memory, but it's a real incident. If we don't try to create the space for it, not only to remember, but try to keep it alive and push it forward, then nothing will happen. I still think that something could happen in the future, that maybe the families of the victims or the people who have disappeared will receive justice. I'm not saying that my film can do that, I don't think it can, but [if] it can still engage in this discourse, then I'm happy. I'm happy enough that it has . . . a small part for the people to keep on thinking and doing something about it.

GC: After a big project like *Dao Khanong*, it seems like you choose to enter into smaller double features, *Krabi 2562 (2019)* and *Jai Jumlong* (Come Here, 2021). I find both films are linked together as they are films about a particular province known for tourism in Thailand, but the way that you show the city in both films is quite different. Can you explain a little bit about the idea of going to these particular provinces and making a film about them?

AS: *Jai Jumlong* was supposed to come out first. Actually, I did shoot it before *Krabi 2562*. As you said, *Dao Khanong*, which for me was a big project, took a lot of me, but also the process of getting it made really took a long time. So I was looking for another way of making a film, to explore other possibilities, to see if I could make a film that would be a bit more spontaneous . . . with very few characters, and would not have to rely on huge funding from so many places. And without a script.

Figure 5.1   The re-enactment of the 6 October 1976 massacre. *Dao Khanong* (By the Time It Gets Dark, 2016). Courtesy of Electric Eel Films.

That was the basis of *Jai Jumlong*. I handpicked a group of actors, and some of them, as you know, are not really professional actors. And one in particular, had never acted before. I wanted to work with these five young actors who are very different in terms of their backgrounds and acting experience, and to work together, to come up with a story. I had a basic idea for the story, but I had no script. I had a rough treatment based on a group of people going to Kanchanaburi. I went to Kanchanaburi with Electric Eel friends, and that was some years before *Jai Jumlong* was shot.

Kanchanaburi has many different facets. On the one hand, it's . . . a very touristy town, both for Thais and non-Thais, but very different for different purposes. When you ask Thai people what Kanchanaburi is for, rafts and waterfalls are what they think of. For a lot of non-Thais, they go [for] the Bridge of River Kwai, the death railway, and the cemetery. For Thai people too, but I think to a lesser degree.

I'm quite interested in these different ways of looking at Kanchanaburi from the touristic perspective, but also on the other hand, there is this idea of Kanchanaburi being a movie town and connected to Prince Chatrichalerm Yukol's films . . . all the war, epic propaganda films, which I was really intrigued by.[4] So I thought Kanchanaburi would be a good setting for a very different kind of film. This is in retrospect. At the time I was not thinking, "I'm going to make a film one day." And so a few years later when I wanted to make this small film with a group of young actors, I immediately thought of Kanchanaburi and to set it there. We spent the pre-production period mostly on workshopping with the actors, because they really were from such diverse backgrounds that it took time to make it gel. Like Saipan (Apinya Sakuljaroensuk) is a movie star, but Sorn (Sornrapat Patharakorn) never acted before, ever.

GC: I think he's great in the film.

AS: I'm glad to really hear that because he was very nervous in the beginning. Because he knew that he would have to play alongside Saiparn. But actually, during the workshopping period, I hadn't dedicated specific roles to the three male actors yet. So they were rehearsing with the ideas that they might be playing any of these characters. We would alternate . . . having them play different characters every day to see who would be the best fit forward.

GC: Can I shift the conversation to another part of your work, Purin Pictures – an organization which gives production grants to Southeast Asian filmmakers and film workers? Could you talk about the idea behind the organization?

AS: I was in a conversation with Visra Vichit-Vadakan, who, as you know, is a filmmaker herself, and we became good friends because she was a leading actor in my film. We had known each other even years before that. But the process of making *Dao Khanong* made us more attuned to each other's ideas and ways of thinking about cinema. So we were talking about Thai cinema and art-house cinema, and then Visra said, "Well, if there's a way for us to support independent films in this region, then that would be very good." Visra was already doing Purin Foundation . . . another organization. They do other work as well, like education work and other projects. Purin Pictures being a part of Purin Foundation, which focuses only on film work. In the beginning, we didn't really have . . . a clear idea. I was more connected to the scene here because she lives in the US. In the beginning – before we had a structure in place [like we do] now, with the open call, with submissions – it was more [about] identifying which projects might have potential. I knew about Mouly Surya's film, *Marlina the Murderer in Four Acts*, that was the very first film we supported.

In the beginning, it was just about scouting films and identifying them and discussing with the producers of those projects to see if there was a way for us to support them. But this didn't go on for a long time [because] we realized that it would be much better if we had a real structure. And with Aditya Assarat, we modeled the fund after the already well-known existing funds, like the Hubert Bals Fund or Asian Cinema Funds and some other European funds. We opened up to any filmmakers who might be interested to apply. And right from the beginning, both Visra and I, being female filmmakers, we also wanted to give a little bit further support . . . to give more opportunity to women filmmakers. So we made it a rule to earmark at least one award for each round, that would go toward first and second time female filmmakers.

We don't only give grants to the productions, as you know, we give it to cinema related activities, as well. That is an important part of what we do. It's not just producing films and supporting producers [and] filmmakers, but the people who are film workers in the areas of films, like archivists, educators, festival programmers, and people who are engaged in Southeast Asian cinema, we also support them. And it's an area that, for us, is as equally important as producing.

GC: **Talking about supporting women filmmakers, what do you think of the gender issue in the Thai film industry? For me, I find it frustrating because it is treated as a nonissue. This is in contrast to Hollywood where gender issues have been at the forefront of the industry in the past few years. Yet, in Thailand, we talk about something else because the film industry has so many problems.**

AS: I'm glad you brought this up. I also don't think that it's being talked about enough, but . . . if I say this, I'm such a target. I'm a woman, I'm a practicing filmmaker. But if you hear it from non-filmmakers such as yourself . . . I know you are filmmakers, but you are academics as well. Why is it a nonissue? I don't know. I think in Korea, #MeToo was really strong a couple of years ago, to the point that there was a backlash against it. And in the US as well, to some degree, because it kind of went so far one way and it kind of bounced back. I would like to say that in Thailand, I don't think we've gone far enough, but even though we haven't gone far enough, there's already backlash. It's weird.

GC: **Because even for me, when I see a curation of short films in Thailand, I am often curious about the lack of female filmmakers in the program. In the past few years I made a decision that whenever I curated a film program, I needed to think about the percentage of genders in the choice of those that I choose.**

AS: I appreciate that. I think about it and I do that too, and it's good to hear that because it's encouraging. Did you remember the director roundtable with the Hollywood Reporter Thailand, when they only invited male directors? There were six of them. And I questioned [in public] that not all of those six men were even active that year, in terms of having a film out. Then, when they did the second roundtable, this time they included me and Tanwarin Sukkhapisit, who is a transgender director. I also thought that was very strange. But still, at least they took note of it. That was many years ago, and even now it hasn't really taken off. Now it is my turn to ask you, what can we do to bring this issue to light?

GC: **As a film lecturer, I show many works by female filmmakers per academic semester. I believe that if the students, both male and female, see that films are made by all types of** genders, they can imagine the landscape of the film industry in a different way than what we have today.

AS: Because really, there have been more female film students than male for a long time now, but that doesn't translate into working professions. When female film students graduate, they go do something else.

One of the things that maybe sometimes people forget when we talk about it, is why is there a need to do it? This is a part that we also have to keep talking about, that sometimes you get different perspectives from the films made by women, like the way of looking at the world. Sometimes – not all the time, but sometimes – I really see that there is a difference between a film made by men and a film made by women. Like I said, I'm not going to say all the time, but it happens. I don't know if it's even true, but a film like *Petite Maman* (Little Mother, 2021), if I didn't know that Celine Sciamma made the film, I probably could guess that it was made by a female director. Is that fair?

GC: I think it's fair. It is not just about the tenderness in the film, but I think there is a chemistry that is very different from other wavelengths that are in the world. It is a very different voice and we need to cherish it.

AS: Yeah. So to have more diversity in perspectives. I think it's important for the landscape of cinema.

Notes

1 In 2006, Thai prime minister Thaksin Shinawatra was ousted by a military coup.
2 The 6 October 1976 massacre is the assault and massacre of students at Thammasat University. The incident was one of the bloodiest events in Thai history.
3 Thongchai Winichakul is the emeritus professor of history at the Department of History, University of Wisconsin-Madison. He is one of the survivors of the 6 October 1976 massacre.
4 Prince Chatrichalerm Yukol is a Thai director who is famous for nationalist epic films, including *Suriyothai* (The Legend of Suriyothai, 2001).

6

TRANSNATIONAL WOMEN'S CINEMA IN SOUTHEAST ASIA

Mouly Surya's *Marlina the Murderer in Four Acts*

Intan Paramaditha

The increasing transnational mobility of cinemas and filmmakers through various venues, from small independent film festivals to global streaming platforms, has challenged approaches in film studies not only regarding debates around national cinema, but also the study of women's cinema and feminism. In Southeast Asia, the discussion of transnational women filmmaking practice as well as its connection to feminist film studies is still limited despite several articles about Southeast Asian women filmmakers (Chaiworaporn 2014; Trice 2019). In this essay, I situate films by and about women in Southeast Asia as transnational women's cinema to highlight how women filmmakers in the region challenge dominant discourses, reclaim cosmopolitan film aesthetics, navigate local and transnational structures of production, distribution, and exhibition, and forge trans-Asian connections. I will focus on Mouly Surya's *Marlina Si Pembunuh dalam Empat Babak* (Marlina the Murderer in Four Acts, 2017) as a case of transnational women's cinema in its feminist intervention of the Western genre, mobility in film festivals and networks, and embeddedness in the sphere of global feminism, particularly the #MeToo discourse. The film contributes to the national and transnational discourses around feminism and sexual violence, yet it also raises questions around whose feminism is visible and recognized in the transnational sphere. This chapter argues that transnational feminism as a framework is essential to the analysis of transnational cinema. It also argues that adopting the transnational feminist approach means delving into not only what is enabled by transnational trajectories, that is, what new productive spaces beyond national boundaries women filmmakers can access and create, but also what is excluded from or disabled by the transnational imagination.

Transnationalizing Feminist Film Studies

The transnational frame in film studies has been seen as a productive tool that acknowledges the complexity of cultural and economic factors that support and shape cinemas beyond national borders as well as the filmmakers' experience of migration and border crossing that affects themes and contexts of filmmaking. Higbee and Lim (2010) map out three approaches in theorizing the question of the transnational in film studies. The first

DOI: 10.4324/9781003266952-9

one views the limitation of the national cinema model and focuses on the questions of production, distribution, and exhibition transcending national borders, as shown in publications such as Ezra and Rowden's *Transnational Cinema: The Film Reader* (2006). The second approach analyzes film cultures as a regional phenomenon that challenges geopolitical boundaries, as exemplified in Sheldon Lu's analysis of transnational Chinese cinemas (1997). The third direction of transnational cinema framework focuses on cinemas of diasporic, exilic, and postcolonial filmmakers that destabilize ideas of cultural identity, nation, and national cinema, which can be seen in Hamid Naficy's work, *An Accented Cinema: Exilic and Diasporic Filmmaking* (2001). Critiques of transnational cinema have been posed, including some tendencies to celebrate the transnational over the national without acknowledging global inequalities that make transnational encounters and circulations possible. However, film studies' debates around transnational cinema as a framework have been quite slow in engaging with the discourse of postcolonial and feminist studies. For instance, in proposing the framework of critical transnationalism, Higbee and Lim call to pay attention to "postcoloniality, politics, and power" and how they reveal "new forms of neocolonialist practices" (2010, 18) without acknowledging that these questions have also informed theories of transnational feminism in feminist studies.

In feminist film studies, feminist film theory grounded in the universalizing ideas of "woman" through psychoanalytic and structuralist approaches has been contested since the early 1990s. The concept of women's cinema, first introduced in Claire Johnston's canonical essay, "Women's Cinema as Counter-Cinema" (1973), has led to productive conversations in the 1970s and 1980s on women's agency behind the camera, whether or not women filmmakers should adopt the dominant film aesthetics to reclaim pleasure (Johnston 1973) or to destroy pleasure through avant-garde cinema (Mulvey 1975), as well as the notion of female spectator (Doane 1982) and the public sphere of women's cinema (De Lauretis 1987). Yet, as bell hooks (1992) suggests in her essay that critiques Mulvey's "Visual Pleasure and Narrative Cinema," an analysis of race is significantly missing from universalizing feminist film theory. Informed by black feminist theories and postcolonial theory, feminist film scholarship in the 1990s started to adopt a more intersectional and transnational perspective. Ella Shohat has consistently proposed a more transnational view of film studies through her work, *Unthinking Eurocentrism* (Shohat and Stam 1994) and *Talking Vision: Multicultural Feminism in a Transnational Age* (Shohat 1998).

In feminist studies, transnational feminism emerged as a response to transnational flows of capital, migration, new forms of colonialism, and the universalizing rhetoric of global feminism, themes that are prominent in the works of Inderpal Grewal, Caren Kaplan, Chandra Mohanty, and Jacqui Alexander. Grewal and Kaplan's conceptualization of the "transnational" in transnational feminism is crucial; it "signals attention to uneven and dissimilar circuits of culture and capital. Through such critical recognition, the links between patriarchies, colonialism, racism, and other forms of domination become more apparent and available for critique or appropriation" (2000). The influence of transnational feminist scholarship was not apparent in the early discourse of transnational cinema in film studies. It was only in the past decade that feminist film studies started forging a link between transnationalism in film studies and transnational feminism, as shown in a few works by feminist film scholars (Wang 2011; Marciniak, Imre, and O'Healy 2012; McHugh 2009; White 2015). Linzhen Wang writes that because the concept of transnational cinema emerged as a response to economic and media globalization and the development of technology, some applications of it "have projected an apolitical and utopian vision of transnationalism . . .

in which people will gain greater access to the means of global representation" (2011, 18). Transnational feminism is important to provide a political perspective by exposing "dispro-portioned movements across borders" (18).

This essay responds to two conditions in the field of film studies. First, despite the emerging works in feminist film studies that underline the importance of the transnational, an analysis of transnational cinema has not fully engaged with transnational feminism and its critique of global economic structures, colonial power, and universalizing ideas of feminism. Second, even in works that focus on transnational women's cinema that are critical of Hollywood, global funding, and Eurocentrism, a discussion of women filmmaking practice in Southeast Asia is still largely limited.

Women Filmmakers in Southeast Asia

In her 2014 article, Anchalee Chaiworaporn provides a useful introduction to women film directing in eight out of ten ASEAN countries: Cambodia, Indonesia, Laos, Malaysia, the Philippines, Singapore, Thailand, and Vietnam. Chaiworaporn demonstrates that women film directors have played an important part in Southeast Asian film cultures and that the development of independent cinema and digital technology since the 1990s was influential in nurturing the growth of women filmmaking. Prior to the independent film movements in Southeast Asia, only a few women could become directors due to their connection to the industry; in the Philippines, for instance, women made their own films after working as actresses or scriptwriters. Independent film culture and digital filmmaking opened up more spaces for storytelling and a wider possibility for women to enter the film scene. In post-authoritarian Indonesia, the early 2000s were marked by the entrance of more women filmmakers into the film scene and the interrogation of norms, including gender and sexuality. Whereas from 1926 to 1998, only four women filmmakers were recorded in official books on Indonesian film history, in 2015 there are 85 women filmmakers actively making films in Indonesia, with some internationally renowned names, including Nia Dinata, Nan Achnas, Kamila Andini, and Mouly Surya.

Problems of opportunities still persist, Chaiworaporn notes, even in the more democratic era of filmmaking. Since Thai cinema entered the era called New Thai Cinema in 1997, there have been 26 women directors with 32 features and documentaries made commercially or independently. Yet, as Chaiworaporn also observes, "Most Thai women directors only began making films after 2003, and sadly, their directorial debuts, no matter if they were commercial or art-house in nature, often became the first and the last film they were to make" (2014, 167). Fewer Thai filmmakers, such as Pimpaka Towira, and the younger generation, such as Anocha Suwichakornpong and Visra Vichit-Vadakan, consistently make films. The link between how gender ideology and funding infrastructure contribute to career sustainability opens up spaces for further research. Yet overall, independent filmmaking – the ability to create without depending on state funding and institutions – allows women filmmakers to challenge dominant discourses. For instance, Malaysian filmmaker Tan Chui Mui uses independent filmmaking as a site of creativity to question national identity through the use of Chinese language. For decades, Malay language cinema was normalized as Malaysian national cinema even though, as writer and film journalist Hamzah Hussin puts it, the "Malaysian film industry was founded on Chinese money, Indian imagination, and Malay [labor]" (Van der Heide 2002, 105). With the rise of Malaysian independent filmmaking in the early 2000s, there have been more films portraying Chinese Malaysian characters using Chinese languages (Mandarin, Cantonese, or Hokkien) and English.

Women filmmakers in Southeast Asia navigate between local networks, often related to cultural activism, and transnational arts and festival circuits. In her study of three women filmmakers in Southeast Asia, Jasmine Nadua Trice highlights that all three filmmakers participate in "running arts organizations that cultivate local, grassroots networks" while actively aligning themselves with "cosmopolitan channels that work outside of global mass culture" (2019, 11). Anocha Suwichakornpong (Thailand) is involved in the production companies Electric Eels Films and Purin Pictures, which have supported projects from Southeast Asia, including Mouly Surya's *Marlina the Murderer in Four* Acts; Shireen Seno (the Philippines) cofounded the film and video studio Los Otros to produce films and facilitate cultural exchange; and Nguyễn Trinh Thi (Vietnam) runs a center for documentary, experimental films, and video art called Hanoi Doclab. Women filmmakers in Southeast Asia are often makers and organizers who take part in "an ongoing process of negotiating scale, working across local, national, and transnational spheres" (Trice 2019, 17).

Further, the category of "women" often mobilizes trans-regional affiliation and connection. In addition to categorization by the media in articles such as "Southeast Asian Women Filmmakers to Watch," festivals and art forums tend to locate women filmmakers based on regional and gender categories. Film funding and sites of circulation help create connections, "uniting them within various scalar rubrics, where authors are seen as 'Asian,' 'Southeast Asian,' or 'women,' and films become regional or national" (Trice 2019, 14). Patricia White uses the term "network narratives" (2015, 133) to describe "regional, gendered dynamics in world film culture," networks that connect women with political and aesthetic agendas, exemplified by programming such as the competition of films by Asian women directors at the International Women's Film Festival in Seoul. "Women" as a category enables encounters, collaboration, and, as we later learn in the case of Mouly Surya's *Marlina,* a discursive space where conversations take place.

It is notable that transnational trajectories and cosmopolitan middle-class backgrounds are important to the making and positioning of women filmmakers in Southeast Asia. As Chaiworaporn writes, "The progress of women film directors is largely due to the development of education, the arrival of digital filmmaking, the mushrooming of film festivals, and the fact that many South-east Asian women directors come from [a] privileged background" (177). Many women filmmakers were educated abroad, and this reminds us that an analysis of class is indispensable in researching transnational cinema. Recent research on African filmmakers shows that being members of a transnational middle class, with transnational experiences and tastes, influences how the filmmakers think about the production and circulation of their film (Steedman 2019; Haynes 2016). I propose that when we deploy a transnational feminist approach to transnational cinema, we consider not only what women filmmakers accumulate due to the privilege of class and cosmopolitanism, but also what may have been sidelined. In the following section I will locate a film by feminist film director Mouly Surya as an example of transnational women's cinema; cinema made by a woman director about women's resistance using the framework of transnational feminism to complicate universal ideas of women and feminism.

Mouly Surya's Transnational Feminist Cinema

Mouly Surya, born in Jakarta in 1980 and educated in Australia, has made three feature films of critical acclaim, including a directorial debut, *Fiksi* (Fiction, 2008), which won the Citra Award for Best Film at the prestigious Indonesian Film Festival. Yet it was *Marlina the Murderer in Four Acts* (2017) that established her as a rising star from Southeast Asia and contributed to her reputation as a young feminist film director. The film was written by Mouly Surya and Rama Adi based on a story conceived by filmmaker Garin Nugroho. A revenge tale set in Sumba, an island in Eastern Indonesia, part of the Nusa Tenggara province, the film focuses on a young widow, Marlina, in four acts ("The Robbery," "The Journey," "The Confession," and "The Birth"), following her journey after decapitating her rapist, Markus, and poisoning his followers/robbers to death. Marlina travels to seek refuge from a justice system that fails to offer protection to women, and along the way she meets and bonds with other women. The poster of the film projects a provocative tone with a striking image of Marlina carrying the head of her perpetrator while riding a horse. The film was screened at the Director's Fortnight at the Cannes Film Festival as well as other international festivals, and received positive reviews from film critics worldwide.

Mouly Surya shares a similar background with other Indonesian filmmakers who emerged after the end of authoritarian regime in 1998. Recently stepping into a more democratic period, coupled with the mushrooming of independent cinema and digital technology in Southeast Asia, members of this generation actively interrogate national constructions of identities, gender, and sexuality in the post-authoritarian period. Like other renowned Indonesian women filmmakers, such as Nia Dinata, Nan Achnas, Mira Lesmana, and Kamila Andini, Mouly Surya was privileged with Western education, mobility, and taste that came with her urban middle-class background. The allusion to the cinematic style of the Western film genre in *Marlina* is part of Mouly Surya's cosmopolitan sensibility, although traces of global influences have been seen quite early in her films. The title of her second feature film, *Yang Tidak Dibicarakan Ketika Membicarakan Cinta* (What They Don't Talk About When They Talk About Love, 2013), is an homage to Raymond Carver's book, *What We Talk About When We Talk About Love* (1981). It was screened at more than 50 film festivals, including the Sundance Film Festival and International Film Festival Rotterdam.

The post-1998 generation of Indonesian filmmakers imagines networks beyond national boundaries, resulting in various efforts to locate their work in the transnational film circuit through global funding and film festivals. In the case of Mouly Surya, this can be seen from her career at various festivals that lead to funding opportunities. *Marlina the Murderer in Four Acts* was co-produced by Indonesia's Cinesurya and Kaninga Pictures, Malaysia's Astro-Shaw, the Singapore-based streaming service HOOQ, Thailand's Purin Pictures, and France's Shasha & Co-production, and its international rights were picked up by the Hong Kong–based company Asian Shadows (Shackleton 2017). After receiving much recognition through *Marlina,* Mouly Surya was invited to direct a Netflix film, *Trigger Warning,* an action thriller starring Jessica Alba (Couch 2020).

The transnational itinerary of *Marlina the Murderer in Four Acts* is captured in the labels that international media have attached to the film: "Satay Western" and "Feminist Western." These labels encapsulate Mouly Surya's transnational women's cinema practice in which her feminist politics and aesthetics create a greater connection through the film's appropriation of the Western genre and its embeddedness in global feminist discourse. The Western itself has evolved from a genre interwoven with American culture to a transnational one that has gone through multiple global iterations (Paryz and Leo 2015). Throughout 2000s, auteur films like *Django Unchained* (2012), by Quentin Tarantino; *No Country for Old Men* (2017), by the Coen Brothers; and *There Will Be Blood* (2007), by Paul Thomas Anderson, have expanded the Western's themes, narrative, and symbolism, and rejuvenated interest in the genre among the international art-house film audience. Revisionist Western films also include films that subvert constructions of gender, including films like Ang Lee's *Brokeback Mountain* (2006) and Jane Campion's *Power of the Dog* (2021), which disrupt the myths of masculinity attached to the genre. Scholars have discussed the reappropriation and revival of the Western in the transnational mediascape, particularly in Asian contexts. Focusing on Japan, South Korea, and China, Vivian P.Y. Lee argues that the Asian Western "should not be seen as a derivative or imitation" of the American Western; rather, it is "a site of 'ongoing intergeneric dialogues' between the Western genre and Asian cinema" (Lee 2015, 163). In this context, *Marlina*'s "Satay Western" could be placed alongside other Asian Westerns – with food names, suggesting diversity in global consumption – including Takashi Miike's *Sukiyaki Western Django* (2007) or Kim Ji-woon's Kimchi Western *Jo-eun nom nappeun nom isanghan nom* (The Good the Bad and the Weird, 2008), which was inspired by Sergio Leone's Spaghetti Western *Il buono, il brutto, il cattivo* (The Good the Bad and the Ugly, 1966).

With a few exceptions, most of the Western adaptations are directed by men and are still centered around male protagonists. Marlina contributes to the large discourse of global film history through its revision of the Western by offering a non-Western feminist viewpoint. As such, the film demonstrates several aesthetic strategies that respond to the genre's iconography as well as narrative. One of the strategies deployed by Mouly Surya is to explore the relationship between characters and the landscape. Thomas Schatz describes the American Western genre as a "formalized vision of the nation's infinite possibilities and limitless vistas, thus serving to 'naturalize' the policies of west-ward expansion and Manifest Destiny" (1981, 47). A mythic landscape of the American frontier with plains, deserts, and mountains is part of Western iconography. The Western trope of a lone cowboy in the wilderness, entering and transforming the wide-open space, is evoked and twisted in *Marlina*.

In the opening sequence, we see a wide shot of savanna, and a man appears from a distance. He is Markus, who seems to be a Sumba-style male hero, riding a motorcycle instead of a horse. The camera follows Markus, as he journeys through the arid Sumba landscape under a cloudy sky. The reference to the Western is made even clearer through the soundtrack, which according to composer Yudhi Arfani, was influenced by Western scores composed by Ennio Morricone. The opening sequence sets up and betrays the expectations of the audience. We assume that Markus is a hero with a goal, a reminder of the masculine discourse of the frontier myth in the Western genre. Indeed, Markus has an aim; he entered the house of the recently widowed Marlina, telling her that seven men, including himself, will rape her and take all of her cattle as payment for a debt. However, the house immediately becomes a battlefield for Marlina. She kills Markus' friends by poisoning their chicken soup, and when Markus rapes her, she mounts on him and decapitates his head with a machete. This ends the first act of the film and establishes the second in which Marlina travels to town to report the crime to the police.

In disrupting the traditional relationship between character and landscape, Mouly Surya interrogates the private-public divide. Strategies of resistance are not made outside but within the domestic space. Marlina is not engaged in a duel in the sun; rather, she navigates between Marcus sleeping in her bedroom, his friends invading her living room, and the kitchen. Marlina pretends to brush her hair, silently grabs poisonous herbs from her dressing table, and returns to her kitchen to blend the herbs in the chicken soup. In these feminine spaces, she chooses her weapons. The open road, on the other hand, is not a site for colonial conquest. If there is such thing as the frontier for Marlina, it is redefined as a space in which she finds connections and solidarity with other women. It is on the road that

Marlina meets an older woman and her friend, Novi, who is nearly ten months pregnant and is anxious about giving birth. Marlina, who has lost her baby and husband, is forced to listen to these women talking openly about motherhood and sex. The bonding between Novi and Marlina is solidified when, in the end, Novi assists Marlina in killing the rest of Markus' followers.

The feminist politics of the gaze in the film can be seen from two strategies. First, the film portrays Marlina as someone who observes and makes decisions. All events in the film unfold and progress from the perspective of Marlina, and the audience is positioned as an observer through Marlina's eyes. Second, the camera prevents objectification of the female characters, and this includes not seeing Marlina as a victim. When Marlina finally arrives at the police station, they tell her that she needs to prove that she has been raped, although ironically the test will only be available in a month. Marlina walks out of the station, sits at a satay stall, and weeps. The child of the satay seller holds her, giving a glimpse of mother-daughter bonding that Marlina never had. The audience, however, does not see her crying. She turns her back on the audience, as if refusing to be framed by the camera's gaze as an object of pity.

Both the Western style and feminist themes are recognizable features in the film that immediately attract international media attention and connect Mouly Surya to a wider audience. The *Toronto Star* describes *Marlina* as a film that "recalls the oaters of Sergio Leone and his brethren . . . but it upends the usual male concerns for some serious and satisfying payback" (Howell 2018). *Variety* even explicitly suggests that the mix of Western genre and art-house serves as a measurement for potential success in distribution: "this savvy blend of genre and art-house sensibilities will kill it at festivals, but needs adventurous distributors to put it into theatres where it can be viewed in its widescreen beauty" (Lee 2017). The website rogerebert.com recognizes that the film fits the style of global art-house

Figure 6.1   In Mouly Surya's feminist Western *Marlina the Murderer in Four Acts*, strategies of resistance are made within the domestic space.

cinema and underlines the feminist theme as an element that connects *Surya* with new audiences: "It's one of those features from a distant part of the globe that seems like it may have been created primarily for Western art houses and festivals, where its exemplary direction and feminist theme are indeed likely to win *Surya* new fans" (Cheshire 2018).

The alignment between *Marlina* and feminist discourse is heightened by the globalized Women's March and #MeToo. Marlina premiered at the Cannes Film Festival in May 2017 and circulated just when the #MeToo movement took off. The connection of keywords attached to *Marlina* – Western, Asian, woman who fights – is summed up by producer Isabelle Glachant: "an incredible film that mixes a powerful universal story of a woman fighting for justice with elements of a Western in a surprising Asian setting" (Shackleton 2017). Similarly, while suggesting victimization of women in the Global South as something that happens remotely, *Slant* magazine uses gender and feminism as a way of connecting the film and its potential audience: "The film is enlivened by an acute grasp of the impossibilities that abused Indonesian women face in a society predicated on their continued physical and emotional subjugation to men" (Dillard 2018).

The #MeToo discourse strengthens the link between *Marlina* and what Patricia White calls "network narratives" that connect feminist texts, feminist politics, and feminist networks (2015, 133). Yet what does *Marlina* mean to Indonesian women? In the context of massive public support for the Anti-Sexual Violence Bill and the higher visibility of feminist language, mainly in urban areas, *Marlina* was seen as urgent and timely, yet critique from Eastern Indonesian writers and activists reveals concerns around locations and asymmetrical situations. What Isabelle Glachant describes as a "surprising Asian setting" becomes a site of contestation that disrupts singular notions of women or feminism.

Anti-Sexual-Violence Discourse and Critique of the Center

My reception of *Marlina* was influenced by my position as a feminist who has done research on Indonesian cinema and struggled with its lack of visibility in film studies. Watching the film in 2017 was an emotional moment; I found myself admiring the film style and its bold feminist statement as, after many years, it was the first time that I had seen an Indonesian film with a strong feminist aesthetic since Nan Achnas' *Pasir Berbisik* (Whispering Sand 2001). I was proud of the international attention that *Marlina* deserved, and I kept promoting it by incorporating it in my syllabus and introducing it at various events, including in a 2019 program to celebrate women filmmakers at the Art Gallery of New South Wales. I was disturbed by male critics who problematized the film by asking whether or not the beheading was necessary or why feminism had to be visualized through violence. Similar to cases of patronizing male attitudes toward *Whispering Sand*, some male critics undermined the cinematic experimentation in *Marlina* to foreground their own concerns regarding the proper ways of expressing feminism. It took some time for me, through my process of being involved in a trans-archipelagic feminist collective, to view that my admiration for *Marlina*'s feminist aesthetics can coexist with valid critique around cultural representation.

Reception of *Marlina* in Indonesia is informed by three discourses: first, conversations around why feminism promotes violence, mostly driven by male viewers and critics; second, *Marlina* as part of the feminist discourse of sexual violence in Indonesia; and third, the discourse of cultural appropriation of Sumba. The second discourse, embraced by women viewers, feminist critics, and feminist publications, was prominent in the media due to heated debates on sexual violence, heightened by both global and national movements. In

2017, the campaigns of feminist groups to push the government to ratify the Anti-Sexual Violence Bill, a struggle that had already started in 2014, coincided with the globalized #MeToo movement, and Indonesia's Women's March. *Marlina* contributed to national discourses of sexual violence and feminism in the year when feminist articulations in Indonesia became more visible than ever, with anti-sexual-violence rhetoric served as a common language. Yet it is notable that these discourses were mobilized and dominated by the metropolitan centers – in other words, feminists and organizations based in Jakarta and Java. The Women's March, for instance, was initiated by the Jakarta Feminist Group, a collective of urban, transnational middle-class women in Jakarta.

Looking at *Marlina*'s impact from the center, i.e., my privileged location as a feminist raised in Jakarta and benefitting from the hegemony of Java and uneven development in Indonesia during the authoritarian regime, I had to de-center my feminism to truly listen to perspectives from Eastern Indonesia. A critique of *Marlina* came from feminists and activists from Eastern Nusa Tenggara (NTT), where the film is set. Dicky Senda, community activist from Mollo, NTT, states in a Facebook page that after waiting for the film with much enthusiasm, he was disappointed because the depiction of Sumbanese culture felt "enforced." (2017) Maria Pankratia, writer and cultural activist from Ruteng, NTT, elaborated on her critique in a longer article. She was in Waingapu, the shooting location, when she and her two friends "saw people walking around with sophisticated equipment" (2017). Being drawn to the potential of watching a Sumbanese woman as a protagonist, Pankratia decided to gather all reviews and articles about *Marlina*. Like Dicky Senda, she found problems in how Sumbanese culture was represented, including details such as clothing, dialect, and food. She had many questions about *Marlina* after watching the film and tried to answer them by watching the behind-the-scenes videos: "I can't be angry just because I am a woman from Eastern Nusa Tenggara who feels that there is something wrong. I do not want to return to the same complaint: 'Jakarta people will only make films according to their wish'" (2017).

Some of Pankratia's criticism can be categorized as minor details, such as the fact that the Sumbanese do not recognize "chicken soup" (*sup ayam*), which Marlina uses to kill her abusers, or how it is almost impossible to find a satay stall in Sumba. Yet some other comments lead to a larger question of whether the film has been framed through the lens of the dominant Muslim Jakarta/Java framework. Commenting on the scene in which Novi kisses her husband's hand, a sign of wife's obedience to the husband in conservative Muslim families, Pankratia argues that such behavior may be found in other parts of Eastern Nusa Tenggara that have been influenced by Islam, but it is not a common practice among Sumba women. She then asked why there are no local Sumbanese actors other than the child actor playing Topan: "This film is about Sumbanese women. The crime, the society, and the police office are all in Sumba. It takes place in Sumba but no Sumbanese actors are involved." She concludes, "It seems that Sumba is borrowed; the spaces and daily lives of its society are temporarily exploited for this film" (2017). Questions from local activists echo the critique of film scholar Umi Lestari, who calls *Marlina* "a cinema of integration" in its ability to "comfort the spectator with *mooi* (beautiful) Sumba image" and yet fails to "cultivate the communal side and the collective struggle" of the Sumba ethnic group (2019). A similar critique has also been posed by Sharon Y.X.R. Ndoen, a film scholar of NTT heritage, who reminds us that the idea for the story itself, which came from prominent Javanese film director Garin Nugroho, reflects an observation filtered through the Javanese colonial fantasy of Eastern Indonesia (2023).

Finally, Maria Pankratia's question in her article requires us to critically view transnationalism from the margins. She asks, "Why was *Marlina* not screened for the first time in Sumba?" Pankratia underlines the travels that *Marlina* have made and, implicitly, the cultural capital that has been accumulated in each transnational encounter:

> The film was shot in Sumba, using the cultural background, tradition, and daily lives of the Sumbanese. Yet, even though the film has traveled to Cannes, Toronto, Melbourne, Poland, the Philippines, Busan, and Tokyo, it has never been shown to the Sumbanese community. Did the filmmakers think about how indigenous Sumbanese people would watch their own lives recreated on screen, played by well-known Indonesian actors and actresses?
>
> *(2017)*

The question about audience and the sphere of circulation reminds us to adopt a transnational approach to Teresa De Lauretis's essay "Rethinking Women's Cinema: Aesthetics and Feminist Theory," in which she asks, "Who is making films for whom, who is looking and speaking, how, where and to whom?" (De Lauretis 1987, 135).

While it is important to amplify the works of women who make films about women especially in the contexts of non-Western and Global South productions, we also need to keep exploring how women's cinema imagines the public in a feminist way. Who counts as a transnational public? Which women, and which feminists? Pankratia's essay triggers further thoughts about transnational women's cinema not only as counter-cinema that challenges mainstream/Hollywood cinema, but also as a category that invites an analysis of power asymmetry within feminist filmmaking. As Grewal and Kaplan remind us, "There IS NO SUCH THING as a feminism free of asymmetrical relations"; transnational feminist practices "involve forms of alliance, subversion, and complicity within which asymmetries and inequalities can be critiqued" (2000). In the time when #MeToo seems to function as a global feminist language, transnational feminist analysis of women's cinema must continue questioning universalizing views of women, feminism, and the notion of resistance.

Conclusion

In this chapter I have outlined the importance of looking at films made by women in Asia through a transnational lens and adopting transnational feminism as a framework. I have provided a general view of women's film practice in Southeast Asian cinema and focused on Mouly Surya as an example of transnational women's cinema. The film intervenes in aesthetic forms that have been associated with male directors and male experience, and its politics aligns with contemporary transnational feminist discourse. Through its connection to the #MeToo movement, *Marlina* opens up the potentials for feminist connection and exchange at both national and transnational levels. My discussion of critical voices here aims not to diminish the important contributions of Mouly Surya and *Marlina* to the transnational women's cinema discourse but to invite a reflection: How does transnational women's cinema resist universalizing tendencies in global feminism and engage with issues of power relations, friction, borders, and difference?

Transnational women's cinema needs to focus not only on what has been enabled by transnational production and circulation; transnational feminism at work must consider what has been disabled or excluded through an analysis of inequality based on class, location, and structures of coloniality. By complicating issues of power, knowledge, and borders in transnational women's cinema, we allow ourselves to discuss the productive spaces (encounters, collaboration, co-production) but also reflect on spaces of tension and discomfort. Transnational feminism also requires us to keep interrogating our positions as researchers who are privileged due to our locations (whether urban or Western), transnational connection, and mobility, and how such privilege affects the way we view cinema.

References

Chaiworaporn, Anchalee. 2014. "Moving Up: Women Directors and South-East Asian Cinema." In *Celluloid Ceiling: Women Film Directors Breaking Through*, 160–78. London: Aurora Metro Books.

Cheshire, Godfrey. 2018. "Marlina the Murderer in Four Acts." rogerebert.com. June 22. Accessed January 24, 2024. www.rogerebert.com/reviews/marlina-the-murderer-in-four-acts-2018

Couch, Aaron. 2020. "Jessica Alba to Star in Netflix Thriller 'Trigger Warning'." *Hollywood Reporter*. May 14. Accessed January 24, 2024. www.hollywoodreporter.com/movies/movie-news/jessica-alba-star-netflix-thriller-trigger-warning-1294873/

De Lauretis, Teresa. 1987. "Rethinking Women's Cinema: Aesthetics and Feminist Theory." In *Technologies of Gender: Essays on Theory, Film, and Fiction*, 127–48. Bloomington, IN: Indiana University Press.

Dillard, Clayton. 2018. "Review: Marlina the Murderer in Four Acts." *Slant Magazine*. June 18. Accessed January 24, 2024. www.slantmagazine.com/film/marlina-the-murderer-in-four-acts/

Doane, Mary Ann. 1982. "Film and the Masquerade: Theorising the Female Spectator." *Screen* 23 (3–4): 74–88.

Ezra, Elizabeth, and Terry Rowden. 2006. *Transnational Cinema: The Film Reader*. London: Routledge.

Grewal, Inderpal, and Caren Kaplan. 2000. "Postcolonial Studies and Transnational Feminist Practices." *Jouvert: A Journal of Postcolonial Studies* 5 (1). Accessed May 8, 2022. https://legacy.chass.ncsu.edu/jouvert/v5i1/grewal.htm

Haynes, Jonathan. 2016. "Neoliberalism, Nollywood and Lagos." In *Global Cinematic Cities, New Landscape of Film and Media*, edited by Johan Andersson and Lawrence Webbs, 59–75. New York: Columbia University Press.

Higbee, Will, and Song Hwee Lim. 2010. "Concepts of Transnational Cinema: Towards a Critical Transnationalism in Film Studies." *Transnational Cinemas* 1 (1): 7–21.

hooks, bell. 1992. "The Oppositional Gaze: Black Female Spectators." In *Black Looks, Race and Representation*, 115–31. Boston: South End Press.

Howell, Peter. 2018. "Marlina the Murderer in Four Acts: Feminist western speaks softly but carries a big blade." *Toronto Star*. June 28. Accessed January 24, 2024. www.thestar.com/entertainment/movies/marlina-the-murderer-in-four-acts-feminist-western-speaks-softly-but-carries-a-big-blade/article_3c314c57-ab8f-5301-b666-f20d42b351a0.html

Johnston, Claire. 2014. "Women's Cinema as Countercinema 'UK, 1973." In *Film Manifestos and Global Cinema Cultures*, 347–56. Oakland: University of California Press.

Lee, Maggie. 2017. "Film Review: 'Marlina the Murderer in Four Acts." *Variety*, May 26. Accessed May 8, 2022. https://variety.com/2017/film/reviews/marlina-the-murder-in-four-acts-review-1202446324/.

Lee, Vivian P. Y. 2015. "Staging the "Wild Wild East": Decoding the Western in East Asian Films." In *The Post-2000 Film Western: Contexts, Transnationality, Hybridity*, edited by Marek Paryz and John Leo, 147–64. London: Palgrave Macmillan UK.

Lestari, Umi. 2019. "Sumba From Jaa: Notes on Garin Nugroho, Ifa Isfansyah, and Mouly Surya Films." *Inter-Asia Cultural Studies Conference*. Unpublished Paper. Accessed May 7, 2022. https://umilestari.com/wp-content/uploads/2019/01/UmiLestari-SumbafromJava2019.pdf.

Lu, Sheldon Hsiao-peng. 1997. *Transnational Chinese Cinema: Identity, Nationhood, Gender*. Honolulu: University of Hawaii Press.

Marciniak, Katarzyna, Anikó Imre, and Áine O'Healy. 2012. *Transnational Feminism in Film and Media*. Basingstoke: Palgrave Macmillan.

McHugh, Kathleen. 2009. "The World and the Soup: Historicizing Media Feminisms in Transnational Contexts." *Camera Obscura: Feminism, Culture, and Media Studies* 24 (3): 111–51.

Mulvey, Laura. 1975. "Visual Pleasure and Narrative Cinema." *Screen* 16, no. 3 (Autumn): 6–18.

Naficy, Hamid. 2001. *An Accented Cinema: Exilic and Diaspora Filmmaking*. Princeton, NJ: Princeton University Press.

Ndoen, Sharon Y. X. R. 2023. "Voices from the Undercurrent: Decolonising *Marlina The Murderer in Four Acts*." *Cine Excess*, Issue 5, April. Accessed August 9, 2023. https://www.cine-excess.co.uk/issue-5-bodies-as-battlefields.html.

Pankratia, Maria. 2017. "22 Pertanyaan tentang Marlina, Si Pembunuh dalam Empat Babak." Accessed May 7, 2022. https://balebengong.id/22-pertanyaan-tentang-marlina-si-pembunuh-dalam-empat-babak/.

Paryz, Marek, and John Leo, eds. 2015. *The Post-2000 Film Western: Contexts, Transnationality, Hybridity*. New York: Springer.

Schatz, Thomas. 1981. *Hollywood Genres: Formulas, Filmmaking, and the Studio System*. New York: McGraw-Hill.

Senda, Dicky. 2017. "Facebook Post." November 27. Accessed May 8, 2022. https://www.facebook.com/1348706932/posts/10215465686579181/?d=n.

Shackleton, Liz. 2017. "Astro, HOOQ, Purin Board 'Marlina the Murderer in Four Acts.'" *Screen Daily*, April 12. Accessed May 8, 2022. https://www.screendaily.com/news/astro-hooq-purin-board-marlina-the-murderer-in-four-acts/5116766.article.

Shohat, Ella. 1998. *Talking Visions: Multicultural Feminism in a Transnational Age*. Cambridge: MIT Press.

Shohat, Ella and Robert Stam. 1994. *Unthinking Eurocentrism: Multiculturalism and the Media*. London: Routledge.

Steedman, Robin. 2019. "Nairobi-Based Middle-Class Filmmakers and the Production and Circulation of Transnational Cinema." *Poetics* 75: 1–10.

Trice, Jasmine Nadua. 2019. "Gendering National Histories and Regional Imaginaries: Three Southeast Asian Women Filmmakers." *Feminist Media Histories* 5 (1): 11–38.

Van der Heide, William. 2002. *Malaysian Cinema: Asian Film: Border Crossings and National Culture*. Amsterdam: Amsterdam University Press.

Wang, Lingzhen. 2011. *Chinese Women's Cinema: Transnational Contexts*. New York: Columbia University Press.

White, Patricia. 2015. *Women's Cinema, World Cinema: Projecting Contemporary Feminisms*. Durham: Duke University Press.

7

TAIWAN QUEER CINEMA, MARRIAGE EQUALITY, AND HOMO(TRANS)NATIONALISM

Shi-Yan Chao

Introduction

In my previous research on Chinese-language film, I proposed the idea of the "Chinese queer diasporic imaginary" as the foundation of Taiwan queer cinema (Chao 2020, 39–98). This imaginary appeals both to the *theory* of "diasporizing the queer" (Puar 1998) exist-ence in general (Watney 1995; Sinfield 1998) and the *experience* of being queer in a Chinese cultural setting. It is mediated by several tropes, including *niezi* (literally "unfilial son"), the folkloric figure of Nezha, AIDS, apparition, and Chinese/Taiwanese operas. While these tropes reflect on the seemingly insoluble tension between Chinese *tongzhi*/queer subjects and their family-based social settings, the meaning of the diasporic is rendered through an emphasis on its metaphoric use, namely, internal exile (*neizai liufang*), or exile domestically and psychologically.

Crucially, the Chinese queer diasporic imaginary also enlists a strong *historical* dimen-sion. With its strengthened nexus between family (*jia*) and state (*guo*) through a selec-tively appropriated Confucian tenets of filiality (*xiao*) and loyalty (*zhong*), this imaginary was maneuvered to great political effect by the authoritarian Nationalist regime (Chinese Nationalist Party, KMT) in Taiwan under martial law (1949–87). Constitutive of the social institution was heteropatriarchal familialism, wherein homosexuality was rendered a trait of non-subjectivity for its failure to fulfill the primary mandate of filiality, namely, to pro-duce (male) offspring to continue the family line (Brainer 2019, 42–47). Meanwhile, the state projected by the Nationalist regime was admittedly filtered through China-centrism, that is to say, the homeland for the Nationalist followers was not Taiwan itself but an expanded version that further included the territory of mainland China (Chang 2015, 24–66).

Taiwan's nativist literary movement (*xiangtu wenxue yundong*) in the 1970s began to challenge this hegemonic view about the state with its famous agenda of "back to the soil" (*huigui xiangtu*). It opened the possibility to reorient nationalist sentiment away from mainland China to Taiwan *per se*. Taiwan New Cinema from the early 1980s also mani-fested a deep concern for local experience and Taiwanese history (Yip 2004). The most crucial factor that afforded a rethinking of the family-state discourse came with the process

DOI: 10.4324/9781003266952-10

of democratization (Jacobs 2012) following the lifting of martial law in 1987. Democratization in Taiwan has led to a "changing political environment" (Makeham 2005, 3) on the one hand, and the rise of a "vibrant civil society" (Huang, Davies, and Fell 2021, 13) on the other. Taiwanese citizens elected the first president born in Taiwan in 1996, and in the year 2000, Taiwan ended the five-decade reign of the Chinese Nationalist Party by electing the first president from the oppositional Democratic Progressive Party (DPP) into office. This notably reverberated through a growing impulse of "Taiwanese consciousness" (Jacobs 2005, 38), among Taiwan's residents, who increasingly embraced different views on the nation's status.[1] An emerging vibrant civil society has been animated, and further empowered, by various social groups and individuals with wide-ranging agendas (Fan 2019). Taiwan's *tongzhi*/queer movement was set in motion in the 1990s, accelerated in the 2000s, and saw its momentum with the passage of the marriage equality bill in May 2019.

This rising Taiwanese consciousness has afforded a crucial intervention into the discursive construct of the state. At the same time, the *tongzhi*/queer movement, concomitant with the consolidating civil society, has gradually contributed to a rethinking of the discursive formation of the family. The two appear to pose challenges to two sides of the KMT-sanctioned family-state ideology separately. Have these two forces joined hands somewhere in practice? If so, on what ground and to what political effect? As I will show, the two merged in a form of "homonationalism" during Taiwan's marriage equality campaign amid the intensified political situation across Sinophone societies in the mid 2010s. In what ways, then, might have the process of Taiwan's marriage equality campaign, along with its eventual legalization, impacted queer Taiwanese cinema? This chapter's third and fourth sections offer close readings of two highly popular *tongzhi*/queer films from the immediate post-gay-marriage era: *Qin'ai de fangke* (*Dear Tenant*, Cheng Yu-chieh 2020) and *Ke zai ni xindi de mingzi* (*Your Name Engraved Herein*, Liu Guang-hui 2020), respectively. With their differed recourses to localist melodrama, Taiwanese history, and queer temporality, these two films, I contend, respond to *tongzhi*/queer politics by negotiating the Chinese queer diasporic paradigm through the more recent homonationalist sentiment.

Marriage Equality, State Identity, and Homo(trans)nationalism

In May 2019, Taiwan's *tongzhi* movement attained a historic momentum, making Taiwan the first nation in Asia to legalize same-sex marriage (Chiang 2019). In three years, about 8,000 same-sex couples have registered their marriages across Taiwan (Teng 2022). While celebrating the advancement of same-sex marriage rights, we should, however, remain aware that marriage equality is not the only goal for the *tongzhi*/queer movement (as marriage equality does not automatically nullify forms of discrimination against LGBTQ+ people). There are still unsettled grounds surrounding Taiwan's same-sex marriage itself, such as marriage rights for same-sex unions involving one party from countries that disallow same-sex marriage (Teng 2022). Also, because Taiwan's marriage equality took the form of special law, instead of an amendment of the Civil Code (Tseng 2022, 235), lesbian/gay couples do not automatically enjoy the same rights as their straight counterparts but are faced with legal obstacles regarding co-parenting, childbearing, and child adoption (Chiang 2022). Friedman and Chen (2021) have underlined the discrepancy between marriage rights and family equality, which is a continuing battle, surrounding Taiwan's same-sex marriage campaign.

On the other hand, an examination of the *process* of Taiwan's marriage equality campaign shall further reveal that this movement is not just about marriage rights for lesbian and gay individuals but is also imbricated in a form of "homonationalism," wherein homosexual subjects and their cultural/legal rights are simultaneously negotiated through nationalist concerns (Puar 2017). In her elucidation of the idea in the US context, Jasbir Puar notes that homonationalism highlights a critique of "how lesbian and gay liberal rights discourses produce narratives of progress and modernity that continue to accord some populations access to cultural and legal forms of citizenship at the expense of the partial or full expulsion from those rights of other populations" (Puar 2017, 228), along such axes as race, class, and sex. While Puar's critique has its footing in the US and its top-down nationalist agenda, recent scholarship on Taiwan's same-sex marriage has directed attention to the process of the movement, highlighting the activists' everyday struggles and their bottom-up strategies informed by the nationalist concerns figuring through the "transnational" politics across Sinophone societies in Taiwan, China and Hong Kong (Ho 2019b; Chen-Dedman 2022; Liu and Zhang 2022; Kao 2021). With Liu and Zhang's (2022, 42) rearticulation of "homotransnationalism" in place of homonationalism to better capture the regional Sinophone circuits, Chen-Dedman (2022) unpacks the nationalist element through the lens of decoloniality in respect to the China factor in play. This lens articulates a pluralistic vision of Taiwanese subjectivity, privileging "an ethic of self-determination and pluralistic self-identification against Sinocentric claims to the contrary" (Chen-Dedman 2022, 4). In his explication, many in Taiwan also take decoloniality as "fundamentally connected to the assertion of a Taiwanese identity that prioritizes the defense of their country's liberal democratic system and sovereign self-determination free from PRC interference" (Chen-Dedman 2022, 8). Under the renewed tension across the strait, Taiwan's "defensive identity formation – including its *tongzhi* rights movement – mirrors [a deep] concern of being existentially erased" (Chen-Dedman 2022, 8). For many in Taiwan, the support for *tongzhi* rights thus also represents their belief in what have been called "Taiwanese values" (*Taiwan jiazhi*) such as inclusivity and expansive human rights protections; the progress on *tongzhi* rights thus simultaneously represents "a selective way for the Taiwanese state to liberally distance itself from China" (Chen-Dedman 2022, 12).

Many in present-day Taiwan, especially those of the younger generations (Lin 2020, 22), support building an inclusive society where every resident, despite their differences, can enjoy equal rights and comfortably call it *home*. This inclusive, democratic civil society, however, also resonates *against* both our past dominated by the authoritarian KMT and our present threatened by the increasingly authoritarian CCP (Chinese Communist Party). A defensive mechanism thus figures an identity formation defined by what Taiwan is perceived to represent. This identity formation not only involves a decolonizing process against any Sinocentric claims, but more importantly, it involves a strengthening of the autonomous self-determination for Taiwan to become a more inclusive, democratic civil society that has de facto enjoyed *state* sovereignty. This processing behind the Taiwanese marriage campaign and the rewriting of the traditional family-state discourse is inseparable from the Taiwanese public's shifting ideas about their national identity, which is moving toward supporting an autonomous statehood firmly based in Taiwan's inclusive, democratic civil society.

Symptomatically, the two most popular *tongzhi* films from the immediate post-gay-marriage era, *Dear Tenant* and *Your Name Engraved Herein*, do not jump to celebrate gay marriage. They instead highlight the lived experiences of being *tongzhi* in earlier time periods: the early 2010s and the late 1980s, respectively. While *Dear Tenant* focuses on the socio-familial issues pertinent to the contemporary *tongzhi* rights movement, *Your Name* gravitates toward an unrequited gay love drained by the socio-political environment of the time. The latter notably ends in the present-year of 2020, which – with marriage equality in mind – does imply a fresh gleam of hope and redemption. I will discuss the varying ways in which each film redefines the family and reflects upon the Taiwanese identity/experience question. The new Taiwanese consciousness underpins the changing public understanding of the state and, more recently, merges with homo(trans)nationalism to challenge the Chinese queer diasporic imaginary.

Dear Tenant: Negotiating Homo(trans)nationalism with Taiwanese Melodrama and Tongzhi Politics

Dear Tenant unfolds around Chien-yi, who, for the past five years, has been looking after his deceased boyfriend's nine-year-old son, Yo-yu, and the boy's elderly grandmother, Mrs. Chou. They live together like a family, and it is Chien-yi's particular way of mourning over his late boyfriend, Li-wei, by remaining in the life Li-wei once had and loving the people Li-wei loved. But when Chou passes away, her other son Li-gang returns from mainland China and discovers that Chou's property has been passed down to Yo-yu, whom Chien-yi has legally adopted. Li-gang contacts the police, suspecting Chien-yi of killing his mother for attempting to own the property. With evidence mounting, Chien-yi is charged with attempted murder and illegal drug possession. What lies behind all this, as the film gradually reveals, actually involves Chou's willed plan (to let Chien-yi continue looking after her grandson in her house after she passes), an accident involving Yo-yu (who innocently overdoses Grandma with Fentanyl, a sort of painkiller Chien-yi has illegally purchased at Chou's insistence that, unknown to him, would serve Chou's plan to free herself from her deteriorating health). Chien-yi is determined to protect Yo-yu from bearing the sense of guilt, particularly because he himself feels guilt over Li-wei's death in a mountain-climbing accident.

    Dear Tenant negotiates with the Chinese queer diasporic imaginary on two levels. On one level, the film manifests a clear sense of Taiwaneseness. On the other, it illustrates a reconciliation between a *tongzhi* subject and his family. Regarding the former, Mrs. Chou's characterization, for instance, echoes the veteran actor's (Chen Shu-fang) public persona, "national grandma" (Chen 2020), through Taiwanese-language media, showcasing a highly recognizable embodiment of local Taiwaneseness that extends from her way of speaking and acting, to her delicate interaction with the other characters. The sense of Taiwaneseness also finds expression in the film's generic affinity and affective expression. The tension between Mrs. Chou and Chien-yi, in large part, incarnates a common subject of Taiwanese primetime TV serials and other media that routinely melodramatizes the conflict between mothers-in-law and daughters-in-law (*poxi wenti*). While switching the gender of the daughter-in-law to male, the film's narrative is fleshed out through a format and affect or sensibility quite familiar with local audiences. Meanwhile, mainland China here comes into frame only through the (unflattering) character of Li-gang, who is merely marked as a Taiwanese businessman (*taishang*) working in Shanghai.

    Tongzhi/queer narratives normally focus on the reconciliation pertinent to nuclear families. *Dear Tenant* is the first Taiwanese film that features tension and reconciliation between a gay man and his quasi mother-in-law. The uneasy family dynamic is epitomized by an early scene concerning the family worship of the ancestors on the Lunar New Year's Eve, led by Mrs. Chou and joined by Li-gang and Yo-yu. Shortly after the worship starts, someone suddenly rushes across the foreground of the long shot appearing as a shadow. In the next medium shot, that ghostly figure is revealed to be Chien-yi, now in clear focus in the background holding a hot dish from the kitchen. While busy preparing the New Year's meal, Chien-yi is not even invited to participate in the family ritual, meaning he lacks any acknowledged status in that family. He only quietly pays respect from the sideline when his deceased partner Li-wei's name is mentioned. In that scene, though, a special bond between Chien-yi and Yo-yu is implied by their eye contact.

The reconciliation, or rather Mrs. Chou's sincere acceptance of Chien-yi into the family, is gradually played out in several scenes. Halfway through the film, when Mrs. Chou is in the hospital, she shows a softened attitude for the first time toward Chien-yi. She compliments his good looks ("You are handsome. No wonder my son fell in love with you"), before exhorting him to find out the procedures of child adoption. On the day of Chien-yi's legal adoption of Yo-yu endorsed by Chou in court, the three take a "family" picture outside afterwards. In a highly emotional scene near Chou's final moment, Chou speaks to Chien-yi: "There is something I always want to ask you. When my son was with you, was he happy?" With Chien-yi's confirmation, Chou continues, "That's good. In fact, I stopped blaming you [for my son's death] a long time ago. You need to stop blaming yourself too, okay?" This indicates the full reconciliation between the two that hinges on their mutual lost love of Li-wei and helps Chien-yi move on. The morning when Chien-yi realizes that Chou has gone, he whispers to her, "Thank you for treating me like family. I will take good care of Yo-yu." Looking after Yo-yu, it is later revealed, was also the promise Chien-yi had made to his partner at his final moment.

Extending the recent debates surrounding *tongzhi* rights, *Dear Tenant*, with its story set in the early 2010s (denoted by the new building title under Yo-yu's name dated May 2011), also reflects the politics of the *tongzhi* movement more broadly. In the film, Mrs. Chou's original plan (to have Yo-yu inherit the house and Chien-yi adopt Yo-yu) could have been the ideal arrangement. However, the rights to inheritance and adoption do not necessarily work to the benefit of those who lack legally recognized statuses vis-à-vis the deceased (thus, Chou's other son, as the child's next of kin, can pose a challenge to Chien-yi). The film ends somewhat ambiguously: it appears that Chien-yi has just finished a light sentence of several months (on the charges of illegal drug possession and Chou's death due to overdose), while he has in the meantime lost custody, and thus, the house to Yo-yu's uncle. In comparison with this ending, the scene following the legal adoption segment, with Chien-yi looking at the new family picture saying, "I wish you [Li-wei] were here," acutely resonates with the heartfelt desire for "co-parenting" alongside marriage rights for same-sex couples in the *tongzhi* movement. Co-parenting is an ongoing battle after marriage equality, as mentioned). (See Figure 7.1.) The sequence where the ninth-grader Yo-yu is bullied by a classmate over Yo-yu's relation to Chien-yi likewise hints at another fierce battle in the *tongzhi* movement: "the introduction of gender equality education which included cultivating an awareness and tolerance of the LGBT population through the curriculum" (Ho and Huang 2022, 147) in junior high and elementary schools. The expansive gender equality curriculum is also expected to foster a more open attitude among youngsters to different forms of familial relationship, alongside "recognition and respect for different genders, gender characteristics, gender temperaments, gender identities, and sexual orientations" as has now been put into law (Ho and Huang 2022, 162).

Figure 7.1   The new "family" picture and the "coparenting" wish from *Dear Tenant*.

While showcasing some liberal-minded sympathizers in society when it comes to Chien-yi's case (such as the female prosecutor and Chien-yi's female boss), the film, more importantly, points to the contagious presence of homophobia in the system, which runs from the uncle (who literally calls Chien-yi "abnormal") to the counseling agency (which helps diagnose whether or not Yo-yu has been sexually abused based on the uncle's biased presumption), to the police sergeant (who moralistically condemns Chien-yi for "hooking up with random men" while having adopted "a young boy"), and to the panicking parents (who are connected to each other via social media in their overreaction to the police sergeant's investigation at the tutorial center where Chien-yi teaches piano). Such a contagious presence of homophobia was, indeed, also highly symptomatic of the anti-gay mobilization faced by the more recent marriage equality campaign. Finally, while offering a highly sympathetic portrayal of the gay protagonist, the film does not try to "sanitize" Chien-yi's image and gay social life in general. Not only does Chien-yi use "hookup apps" to solicit sex without any intention to build a "serious" relationship, but the film also confronts the unflattering issue of drug (ab)use in gay social life. This deviates from the normalizing tendency and positivist politics expected from the ongoing mainstreaming of gay lifestyle. This *un*sanitized picture thus indexes the film's more complex positioning vis-à-vis the normalizing appeal of the *tongzhi* movement.

Your Name Engraved Herein: Approaching Homo(trans)nationalism via Taiwan History and Queer Temporality

Your Name Engraved Herein is set against the backdrop of Taiwan's immediate post-martial-law era, where two teenagers, Chia-han and Birdy, fall in love amid family pressure, homophobia, and broader social change. As students at an all-male Catholic high school in Taichung, Chia-han and Birdy befriend each other through the school band; they engage in antics while exchanging long glances. The school's priest and band leader, Father Oliver, reminds the students to "*profiter du moment*" (live in the moment), leading Chia-han to strengthen his bond with Birdy. The two, using the excuse of attending the public funeral for President Chiang Ching-Guo's death in early 1988, take a trip to Taipei and grow closer through their adventures in the capital city. Despite mutual interest, the pair remain hesitant to act on their budding attraction. The introduction of the co-educational system, then, adds a wrinkle to their relationship. Birdy catches the eye of a female junior, who offers Birdy the hope of a socially acceptable heterosexual romance, but Chia-han holds onto his affection for Birdy. Repeated conflicts and reconciliations draw the pair together and break them apart, before fate takes them in different directions, until three decades later, their paths cross again in 2020.

Picking up the "historical" approach to contextualizing *tongzhi* liberation in Taiwan's democratization as set up by Yang Ya-che's *Nüpengyou nanpengyou* (Girlfriend Boyfriend, Yang Ya-che 2012), *Your Name Engraved Herein* negotiates with the Chinese queer diasporic imaginary by offering a nuanced picture of individuals growing up in Taiwan in a particular historical period. Imbricated in the social transition in the immediate post-martial-law era and reflecting on that transition's impact on everyday life, the relevant experience portrayed is undeniably local and Taiwanese. This experience finds expression in an array of interrelated aspects: politics, school, family, urban landscape, popular culture, and interpersonal communications.

Preceded by the extra-diegetic insert of historical news footage of the Taiwanese government's official announcement to end martial law in the summer of 1987, the film's story starts shortly "after martial law [is] lifted" (as indexed by the overlay), where Chia-han, a second-year high school student of the *sciences* concentration (*lizu*), meets his newly transferred fellow student, Birdy, of the *humanities* concentration (*wenzu*) for the first time during a swimming class. In the immediate post-martial-law era, not only do we sense the lingering influence or legacy of the authoritarian institution in society, such as the penetrating existence of police in plainclothes and, as trivial as it may seem, the obsolete practice of Chinese writing from right to left (to avert the "left"-leaning association of writing in the reverse direction), as seen on the headrest covers on the train that reiterates the nationalist New Life Movement, initiated by Chiang Kai-shek decades ago to boost the quality and morality of citizens. We also witness the remaining presence of an illiberal organization through the school system, such as the presence of military officers (*jiaoguan*) and the disciplinary implementation of dormitory checks and physical punishments on campus, together with the militarizing practice of patriotic singing competition across campuses. In general, the social milieu and campus environment remained rather conservative. Not only were male and female students largely separated with all close relationships forbidden before college (age), but the educational system was hierarchical on a gendered basis. As hinted at in the film, the choice between sciences and humanities concentrations (to be made by students prior to their second year in high school and that would subsequently decide the subjects of their college entrance exams) was heavily laden with social and famil-ial expectations, wherein the sciences and humanities concentrations were largely aligned with the perceived precincts for men and women, respectively. Against such a gender-biased perception, to choose a humanities concentration, for male students, usually also implied that their academic performances might be inferior to those of their male peers in sciences – hence the tension in Chia-han's family when he has to switch or "downgrade" his concen-tration from sciences to humanities (which allows Chia-han easier access to Birdy) by the end of the second year. The father considers it embarrassing – "face-losing" (*diulian*) – to the family, while the mother is alerted to the potential temptation to be faced by Chia-han from the incoming girls predominantly with the same humanities concentration. Other instances particular to contemporary campus life include male juveniles' coping with sexual taboos, their strong desire for motorbikes (for an enhanced sense of freedom as well as to impress girls), their gross prank called *a-lu-ba* (featuring a kind of group assault, jokingly or otherwise, on targeted fellow male students' lower bodies) that connoted male juveniles' heightened awareness of their physical change during puberty.

The composition of Chia-han's family, with the father ethnically a mainlander (*waisheng-ren*) and the mother a local Taiwanese (*benshengren*), is not uncommon in contemporary Taiwan.[2] With the father's age markedly higher than the mother's (also a marker common to such cross-ethnic unions), the father only speaks accented Mandarin, while the mother switches between Mandarin and Taiwanese, with the use of Taiwanese mainly applied to her private conversations with Chia-han. Moreover, the escalated tension between Chia-han and his father is not only rendered through Chia-han's recent change of concentration but also through Chia-han's dissatisfaction with the father's heavy spending on his recon-nected "old family" (*laojia*) in China, which was indeed part of the social phenomenon facilitated by the policy change in late 1987 that started to allow Taiwanese citizens with family in China to visit them in the mainland. Such a depiction of Chia-han's family, in brief, resonates with the experience of many (or some public imaginary?) based in Taiwan at that historical juncture.

In addition to the political, educational, and family dynamics, the particular Taiwanese experience is also portrayed through urban landscape, popular culture, and interpersonal communications. Among the urban settings depicted, most remarkable is the simulated par-tial reconstruction of the historic locale of Chung-hua Commercial Complex (*Zhonghua shangchang*) in downtown Taipei, along with the hallways of the nearby Lion's Plaza Com-mercial Building in the Xi'men district, the private box of the then-popular movie-viewing venue called MTV (Movie TV), the precinct of an old-fashioned movie theater, the interior of a taxi equipped with an old-style meter, and so on. Spaces like these lay the foundation of an urban environment reminiscent of Taipei of the late 1980s, which pertains to the nation-wide landscape (stretching, for instance, from Taichung to Penghu Island, as highlighted by the protagonists' second trip together) and is further enlivened through the popular culture of the time. The latter ranges from acclaimed movies like Alan Parker's *Birdy* (1984) and Stanley Kwan's *Yanzhi kou* (*Rouge*, Stanley Kwan 1987), to beloved writings by the legend-ary female author San Mao, to (gay-identified) pop artists like Leslie Cheung and George Michael, and to immensely popular Mandarin songs at the time like "This World" (*Zhege shijie*), "The Crowded Paradise" (*Yongji de leyuan*) and "Meet by Chance" (*Pingju*). In particular, "This World" and "The Crowded Paradise," performed respectively by Tsai Lan-chin (whose posthumous debut album was released in 1987) and Chen Sheng, who, with *The Crowded Paradise* being the title of his debut album from 1988, remains widely popular and has become known for his localist Taiwanese persona (Xian 2005, 139), comprise two thematic motifs on the soundscape. Whereas the former is aligned both with the students' yearning for freedom from the institution and with Chia-han and Birdy's private world, the latter is more associated with the view on precarious modern relationships and specifically with Chia-han's take on Birdy's betrayal of their bonding. And of course, in a time before Internet and mobile phones, interpersonal relations are further mediated by the tele-communicative methods of landlines, public pay phones, and, notably, pagers, which were popular in the late 1980s and 1990s. For pager users, coding was rather common, and some local codes like "wanan," as highlighted in the film, could be deciphered either as "good night" (*wan'an*) or, more creatively, as "I love you, love you" (*wo ai ni ai ni*, with its five initials encoded into "wanan"). Just as the code of "wanan" is important to the main characters with an enduring effect even in 2020 (their repeated exchange of "good night" can virtually mean an affirmative "I love you" now), so does their use of pager and coding echo the lasting memories for many audience members about their similar experience during that time.

How, then, does the film speak about the *tongzhi* movement or its politics? Here I would like to highlight three interrelated aspects. First, the film pays homage to veteran gay activist Chi Chia-wei (a.k.a. Dayway Chief). Known as "the first openly gay Taiwanese person" and "senior AIDS assistance and prevention volunteer" (Yeh 2016), Chi had also been fighting for same-sex marriage rights through various legal and non-legal measures since 1986. This included his more recent appeal to a constitutional interpretation in 2015 that proved decisive in the passage of the same-sex marriage bill in 2019. In the film during Chia-han and Birdy's trip to Taipei, they witness a one-person protest near the Chunghua Commercial Complex. Holding a sign that reads "The right to marry is for everyone! Homosexuality is not a disease!" and wearing a self-made white costume covered with condoms, that person is identified as Chi when the police in plainclothes yell his name ("You again, Chi Chia-wei!") while dragging him away from the scene. Based on Chi's vivid persona from the time, that character is meant to pay homage to Chi for his persevering activism for gay rights, marriage equality, and AIDS prevention, which predates the perceived start of the *tongzhi* movement in the 1990s (with its broadened base and scale) and is directly connected to the current developments of *tongzhi* rights (as highlighted by the passage of the marriage equality bill). This spans the whole trajectory of Taiwan's *tongzhi* movement to the mid to late 1980s.

Second, the film proffers a nuanced depiction of the individuals growing up in Taiwan in the immediate post-martial-law era, simultaneously filtered through the gay protagonists' bodily presence and sensual perspectives. Whereas the turning points in history have been the settings for numerous film narratives which have, however, tended to be characterized by male dominance and an absence of gay agency, what *Your Name* does, accordingly, is to go against this convention and rewrite gay presence back into history. Not only is a parallel drawn between the path of national history and the trajectory of the *tongzhi* movement in the post-martial-law era, this parallel also reverberates through the more recent "homo(trans)nationalist" tendency in Taiwanese society that merges LGBT rights with some (grassroots) nationalist agenda, or, in the case of *Your Name*, addresses *tongzhi* subjects by re-incorporating their presence into the writing of the nation's history.

Third, the film is characterized by a particular temporal structure, with its main body set in the late 1980s ("after martial law [is] lifted") and the last part set in 2020 (read:

after the marriage equality bill passed). The present-day section starts with a reunion of the school band members, which in part is to commemorate their leader, Father Oliver, who has lately passed away in Montreal. During the gathering, Chia-han is shown anxious about something (the potential appearance of Birdy), while Chia-han himself is revealed to have remained withdrawn from such socializing events. Implicitly, Chia-han has just come out of a certain "internal exile," which is not uncommon for queer subjects who find themselves alienated from their straight peers' lifestyles, while Birdy, as Chia-han later finds out, has gone through a straight marriage and divorce (as Birdy's ex-wife admits: sexual orientation cannot be changed as she wished). Chia-han and Birdy finally reunite in Montreal through their respective trips to pay respect to Oliver and his survived husband. The film ends with some sweet indications of Chia-han and Birdy's relationship potentially rekindled by way of their reluctance to say goodbye, along with their repeated verbal exchanges of the coded term of "wan'an" (as both "good night" and "I love you"), after three decades of delay.

The film's dual temporal structure in effect coincides with a reshaping of queer temporality and affect in many *tongzhi* lives at this historical juncture. Instead of the sense of futureless melancholia mediating what Fran Martin (2010) has coined the "memorial mode" prevailing earlier lesbian/tomboy narratives in Sinophone cultures, now with the possibility of same-sex marriage and family for lesbians and gay men in Taiwan, the future vis-à-vis the present may start to mean something more imaginable or projectable in many *tongzhi* lives, while looking back may as well start to designate something beyond loss and melancholia. For *Your Name* in particular, its focus on the bitter memory of an unrequited gay love is indeed melancholic, but the protagonists' reunion in 2020, together with the sweet indications of their potentially rekindled relationship, represents a heartwarming redemptive intervention. With a homonationalist resonance through its socio-political context, the film's dual temporal structure also serves to remind us of how far we – as both the *tongzhi* community and our nation – have come against authoritarian puissance over the past four decades, toward a hard-earned liberal democracy.

Conclusion

This chapter examines Taiwanese queer cinema in relation to the marriage equality campaign. I first unpack the idea of the Chinese queer diasporic imaginary and its underpinning family-state discourse by identifying the dual forces of the *tongzhi*/queer movement and the Taiwanese consciousness, with the former having led to a rethinking of the discursive figuration of the family while the latter having lent a crucial intervention into the discursive construct of the state. I, then, highlight the synergy of these two forces during the more recent marriage equality campaign through what has become known as homonationalism or even homotransnationalism. Although *Dear Tenant* and *Your Name Engraved Herein*, the two best-known *tongzhi* films since marriage equality, do not jump on the bandwagon of gay marriage, they nonetheless emphasize the lived experiences of being *tongzhi* historically: the early 2010s and the late 1980s, respectively. While *Dear Tenant* focuses on the socio-familial issues pertinent to the contemporary *tongzhi* rights movement, *Your Name* gravitates to an unrequited gay love drained by the socio-political ambient of the time. The latter notably also features a dual temporal structure that reshapes queer temporality while gesturing at a belated redemption enabled only by the recent marriage equality. Aside from the *tongzhi* movement/politics that helps rewrite the family definition to include *tongzhi*, the two films also underscore varied aspects of Taiwanese identity and experience, which manifests the Taiwanese awareness at once underpinning the changing public opinions about the statehood and merging through homo(trans)nationalism to challenge the Chinese queer diasporic imaginary.

Notes

1 Among Taiwanese citizens' self-identification as Taiwanese, Chinese, or both, "Taiwanese identity began to overtake Chinese identity in 1995, and by 2014 the former had evolved into a solid majority (60.6 percent), while the latter had shrunk to a mere 3.5 percent" (Ho 2019a, 60).
2 Though relatively small in number, Indigenous peoples comprise a crucial ethnic group, along with three other major ethnic groups of the Han Chinese on the island: Hoklo, Hakka, and the mainlander. While the mainlander, consisting mainly of those who came to Taiwan from China after 1945, is also called *waishengren*, the other three ethnic groups are considered *benshengren*, generally those "who lived in Taiwan and whose ancestors migrated to the island before the [postwar] Chinese takeover" (Chang 2015, 4).

References

Brainer, Amy. 2019. *Queer Kinship and Family Change in Taiwan*. New Brunswick: Rutgers University Press.

Chang, Bi-yu. 2015. *Place, Identity and National Imagination in Postwar Taiwan*. New York: Routledge.

Chao, Shi-Yan. 2020. *Queer Representations in Chinese-Language Film and the Cultural Landscape*. Amsterdam: Amsterdam University Press.

Chen, Hsing-ying. 2020. "'National Grandma' Chen Shu-fang: Acting is My Life Career, I Must Do My Best, Whether People Can See It or Not." *The Reporter*, November 5, 2020. Accessed July 4, 2022. https://web.archive.org/web/20201122093809/https://www.twreporter.org/a/2020-taipei-golden-horse-film-festival-chen-shu-fang.

Chen-Dedman, Adam. 2022. "Seeing China Differently: National Contestation in Taiwan's LGBTQ (*Tongzhi*) Movement." *Nations and Nationalism* 1–18.

Chiang, Howard. 2019. "Gay Marriage in Taiwan and the Struggle for Recognition." *Current History: A Journal of Contemporary International Affairs* 118 (809): 241–43.

Chiang, Yi-ching. 2022. "LGBT Rights/Despite Same-Sex Marriage Law, Parental Rights Still Lacking." *Focus Taiwan*, June 4, 2022. Accessed June 5, 2022. https://focustaiwan.tw/society/202206040004.

Fan, Yun. 2019. *Social Movements in Taiwan's Democratic Transition: Linking Activists to the Changing Political Environment*. New York: Routledge.

Friedman, Sara L, and Yi-Chien Chen. 2021. "Will Marriage Rights Bring Family Equality? Law, Lesbian Co-Mothers, and Strategies of Recognition in Taiwan." *Positions* 29 (3): 551–79.

Ho, Ming-sho. 2019a. *Challenging Beijing's Mandate of Heaven: Taiwan's Sunflower Movement and Hong Kong's Umbrella Movement*. Philadelphia: Temple University Press.

———. 2019b. "Taiwan's Road to Marriage Equality: Politics of Legalizing Same-Sex Marriage." *The China Quarterly* 238: 482–503.

Ho, Ming-sho, and Chun-hao Huang. 2022. "The War of Referenda in 2018: Analyzing the Interaction between Social Movements and Political Parties." In *Taiwan During the First Administration of Tsai Ing-wen: Navigating in Stormy Waters*, edited by Gunter Schubert and Chun-yi Lee, 142–66. New York: Routledge.

Huang, Chia-yuan, Daniel Davies, and Dafydd Fell. 2021. "Taiwan's Contemporary Indigenous Peoples." In *Taiwan's Contemporary Indigenous Peoples*, edited by Chia-yuan Huang, Daniel Davies, and Dafydd Fell, 1–17. New York: Routledge.

Jacobs, J. Bruce. 2005. "Taiwanization in Taiwan's Politics." In *Cultural, Ethnic, and Political Nationalism in Contemporary Taiwan: Bentuhua*, edited by John Makeham and A-chin Hsiau, 17–54. New York: Palgrave Macmillan.

———. 2012. *Democratizing Taiwan*. Leiden: Brill.

Kao, Ying-Chao. 2021. "The Coloniality of Queer Theory: The Effects of 'Homonormativity' on Transnational Taiwan's Path to Equality." *Sexualities*: 1–18. Accessed January 30, 2022. http://doi.org/10.1177/13634607211047518

Lin, Pei-ting. 2020. "Who Supports Same-Sex Marriage? Exploring the Mass Bases of the Same-Sex Marriage Issue in Taiwan." *Journal of Social Sciences and Philosophy* 32 (2): 207–38.

Liu, Wen, and Charlie Yi Zhang. 2022. "Homonationalism as a Site Contestation and Transformation: On Queer Subjectivities and Homotransnationalism across Sinophone Societies." In *Homonationalism, Femonationalism and Ablenationalism: Critical Pedagogies Contextualized*, edited by Angeliki Sifaki, C. L. Quinan, and Katarina Loncarevic, 31–47. New York: Routledge.

Makeham, John. 2005. "Introduction." In *Cultural, Ethnic, and Political Nationalism in Contemporary Taiwan: Bentuhua*, edited by John Makeham and A-chin Hsiau, 1–14. New York: Palgrave Macmillan.

Martin, Fran. 2010. *Backward Glances: Contemporary Chinese Cultures and the Female Homoerotic Imaginary*. Durham: Duke University Press.

Puar, Jasbir K. 1998. "Transnational Sexualities: South Asian (Trans)nation(alism)s and Queer Diasporas." In *Q&A: Queer in Asian America*, edited by David L. Eng and Alice Y. Hom, 405–22. Philadelphia: Temple University Press.

———. 2017. *Terrorist Assemblages: Homonationalism in Queer Times*. 2nd ed. Durham: Duke University Press.

Sinfield, Alan. 1998. "Ethnicity, Diaspora, and Hybridity." In *Gay and After*, 18–44. London: Serpent's Tail.

Teng, Pei-ju. 2022. "LGBTQ Rights/Same-Sex Cross-National Couples Continue Fight for Marriage Equality." *Focus Taiwan*, May 28, 2022. Accessed June 5, 2022. https://focustaiwan.tw/society/202205280014

Tseng, Yu-chin. 2022. " 'It's Not Marriage!' Framing and Mobilizing in the Anti-Same-Sex Marriage Movement." In *Taiwan During the First Administration of Tsai Ing-wen: Navigating in Stormy Waters*, edited by Gunter Schubert and Chun-yi Lee, 234–53. New York: Routledge.

Watney, Simon. 1995. "AIDS and the Politics of Queer Diaspora." In *Negotiating Lesbian and Gay Subjects*, edited by Monica Dorenkemp and Richard Henke, 53–70. New York: Routledge.

Xian, Yi-ying, ed. 2005. *Call Me Tai-ke!* Taipei: Net and Books.

Yeh, Yu-juan. 2016. "From a 1 Person March to 250,000 Strong: Chi Chia-wei's LGBT-Rights Marathon." *The Reporter*, December 15, 2016. Accessed July 20, 2022. https://www.twreporter.org/a/lgbt-rights-activist-qi-jia-wei-english.

Yip, June. 2004. *Envisioning Taiwan: Fiction, Cinema, and the Nation in the Cultural Imaginary*. Durham: Duke University Press.

8

LOVE IN PACIFIC TIME

Asian Screen Culture in Vancouver

Helen Hok-Sze Leung

diaspora babies, we
are born of pregnant pauses/spilled
from unwanted wombs/squalling invisible-ink poems/written in the margins
of a map of a place
called No Homeland

– Kai Cheng Thom

Poet Kai Cheng Thom's recitation of "Diaspora Baby" accompanies a series of drone aerial shots of a lush, mountainous coastline typical of British Columbia's landscape. The camera focuses on a tiny spot of red on a rocky beach, gradually zooming in to reveal drag performer Maiden China, sumptuously dressed in flowing layers of red. Her figure embodies at once the extravagance of a drag queen's costume and the blushing bridal wear of a traditional Chinese wedding, startlingly juxtaposed against the expansive wilderness of the coastal backdrop. This sequence ends on an extreme close-up of Maiden China's face, beautifully painted with the stylized makeup reminiscent of a Chinese opera performer, her haunting gaze smoldering behind a beaded veil cascading from a colorful headwear.

This memorable series of images which opens *Yellow Peril: Queer Destiny* (2019), a short film by Love Intersections – a queer arts collective based in Vancouver, Canada – exemplifies a West Coast Asian screen culture that has survived and thrived in the complex dynamics of a filmmaking city on the Pacific Coast, north of Hollywood, east of East Asia, and intimately connected to both regions through relative geographical proximity and generations of migration history. This article tells the story of this film scene and maps its survival in the at times "unwanted" and "invisible" margins of a city's dominant film culture.

In the Shadow of Hollywood North

Whenever Vancouver is mentioned in the context of film, it is unlikely that *Yellow Peril* or the homegrown independent filmmaking scene that nurtures such works would be the focus. Whether in a glossy tourism profile in *Vanity Fair* (Destination Canada 2022) or

DOI: 10.4324/9781003266952-11

Figure 8.1   Still from *Yellow Peril: Queer Destiny*. Image used with permission.

a seasonal reportage of "what's filming" in the *Vancouver Sun* (Ruttle 2022), the city is invariably associated with its success as "Hollywood North," a moniker given to the wildly successful location industry that has continued to flourish. As one of the earliest cities to pivot its resource economy to the provision of location services for Hollywood (Gasher 2002, Ch. 4–5; Scott and Pope 2007), Vancouver has served as a pioneering model for cities all over the world to transform itself as a runaway production hub (Tinic 2012). Furthermore, there have also been many public and private initiatives to leverage its Hollywood North reputation, a large Asian immigrant population, and relative geographical proximity to East Asia to attract financing, collaborations, and access to markets in parts of Asia, especially China. These efforts include courting Asian productions to film on location in the city, organizing film festivals and screen writing contests with the aim to attract investors to fund local filmmakers, and developing joint film school programs (Leung 2015, 34–39; Leung 2016, 124–26). Even with the interruption of the pandemic, the industry has earned the province a "record-shattering" $4.8 billion spendings during 2021, according to a report by the Vancouver Economic Commission, which calls the industry one of the first sectors to "roar back" from the pandemic (2022). The website Hollywood North Buzz and the @YVRShoot twitter handle track and crowd source production sightings daily. *This Is Vancouver*, a massive oral history project commissioned by the Vancouver Public Library, devotes an entire section titled "Hollywood North" that collects stories about Vancouverites' "personal encounters with the industry." Ironically, an industry that thrives on erasing the city's history and identity on screen (Todd 2013, 8–9) has nonetheless become one of the most significant economic and cultural drivers of the city in the twenty-first century.

The impact of this thriving industry on local creative talents is double-edged. On the one hand, it has sustained growth and innovation in the sector (most notably in the areas of film and television production and more recently, video games, digital media and VFX), attracting investments and creating a vibrant job market for home-grown, especially below-the-line, talents who are established and qualified enough to fill even the biggest Hollywood productions. On the other hand, it has exponentially pushed up production costs in an already expensive city; hijacked resources, access to infrastructure, and distribution opportunities from smaller productions; and contributed to the deterioration of labor conditions even in one of the most unionized creative sectors in the world (Curtin and Sanson 2017, 449–50). Furthermore, the dynamics have intensified the irony that, while the city is ubiquitous on screen, variously disguised as different cities, small towns, or even alien planets – what Creative BC, the film commission agency for the province of British Columbia, proudly advertises as "a world of looks" – local productions that set their stories in Vancouver can barely afford to shoot in the city. Thus, while we see ample scenes of Vancouver as a nameless metropolis in *Deadpool* (2016), a generic small American town in *Juno* (2007), a recognizably fake Seattle in *Beijing aishang Xiyatu* (Finding Mr. Right, 2013), or a blatantly fake New York in *Hongfan qu* (Rumble in the Bronx 1995), we see very little of the city in productions where a sense of place matters. For example, the cult queer classic *Better Than Chocolate* (1999) sets its love story between an artist and a bookstore owner in and around Commercial Drive, a historic hub for Italian, Portuguese, and Eastern European immigrants that has also developed into a bohemian countercultural space with a vibrant lesbian community. Such a film would have been enriched by a distinctive evocation of its setting, but with a minimal budget of CAD 1.6 million, it could ill afford to shoot much on location in Vancouver. Similarly, while the city has appeared so often in US crime shows, such that one critic suggests "it is haunted by its American doppelgänger" (Steenberg 2013, 92), the Vancouver-set production *Blood and Water* (2015–21), an Asian-led, multilingual TV crime show (in which then future Marvel star Simu Liu landed his first significant role), had to shoot many of its scenes in a Toronto studio in order to lower production costs, rendering its Vancouver visually much less distinctive than what passes as a gritty, rain-soaked Seattle in *The Killing* (2011–14) or the conspiratorial, shadowy spaces FBI agents investigate in *The X-Files* (1993–2002, 2016–18). It seems that the more the city becomes a successful commercial filmmaking hub, the more challenging it is for its own sense of place to find expression on screen.

Pacific New Wave

This struggle for representation and for a sense of place and identity has, from the beginning, animated the independent filmmaking culture that has persisted in the margins of the city's location industry. A group of filmmakers that critics dub the "Pacific New Wave" (Burgess 2003, 29–33) or the "West Coast Wave" (Spaner 2004, 91–109) emerged in the 1990s. Film journalist David Spaner, who has documented the complex interactions of independent filmmaking with a dominant corporate film culture in places as diverse as Mexico, France, and Canada (Spaner 2012), characterizes this group of filmmakers as the first significant independent filmmaking scene in Canada outside of both the Hollywood-centered infrastructure, and the much-better-known film scene in Toronto where the careers of David Cronenberg, Atom Egoyan, Patricia Rozema, and John Greyson started (Spaner 2004, 92). The Vancouver group, which consists not only of directors but also producers, cinematographers, camera operators, and editors who work in various roles on each other's projects, is noted for contrasting influences inherited from film programs in the city's two universities: the theater tradition and narrative-driven filmmaking at the University of

British Columbia, where many of the group's directors were students, and the experimental and interdisciplinary ethos of Simon Fraser University where students previously trained in photography and other visual arts brought different skill sets and a countercultural mindset to filmmaking. It is notable that the most prominent women in the group, Lynn Stopkewich and Mina Shum, have maintained career longevity and versatility as directors, despite the profession's well-known male dominance. Shum was also among the first in the group to garner critical acclaim and some degree of mainstream recognition and box-office success with her debut feature *Double Happiness* (1994), the film that launched Sandra Oh's career. Set in Vancouver, the film tells the story of an aspiring actress and the complicated family dynamics of her Asian immigrant family through very distinctive spaces in the city. Critics have noted the detailed ways in which the film evokes specific neighborhoods: from the claustrophobic interiority of an immigrant enclave, to metropolitan spaces of transcultural interactions, to the wide-open green spaces that surround and permeate the city (Melnyk 2014, 229–53; Hanley 2014). Shum made two more features after *Double Happiness* but primarily worked in documentaries and television for almost two decades before returning to feature filmmaking and reuniting with Sandra Oh in *Meditation Park* (2017). Set again in Vancouver and about an Asian immigrant family, the film tells the story of a middle-aged housewife, Maria, played with emotional depth and sharp comedic timing by Cheng Pei Pei. After 30 years of marriage, she slowly discovers that her husband has been cheating on her with a younger woman. Maria's gradual journey toward gaining her independence is similarly evoked through the distinctive spaces she moves through in her daily life in Vancouver: the cloistered domestic interiors of a middle-class household which has kept her isolated and dependent; the social spaces of the residential front yards, public parks, and community centers in East Vancouver, where neighbors from different backgrounds gossip, fight, scheme with and against each other while developing unlikely friendships; the cheery haunts in Chinatown where Asian women from different immigrant generations gather; and the snowy mountains and expansive oceanscape captured in the final shot as Maria stands alone on the deck of a BC Ferry, for the first time charting a life path for herself independent from her marriage.

Asian Film Scenes

Diasporic Asian filmmakers in Vancouver who are influenced by Shum and her generation of filmmakers continue to honor this commitment to place and deftly explore the interplay among domestic, urban, suburban, and natural spaces of the city in features as well as in shorts and documentaries. Julia Kwan's debut feature, *Eve and the Firehorse* (2005), films its story about an imaginative child in interior spaces set at a deliberate distance from the hustle and bustle of Chinatown, the metropolitan downtown, or open natural spaces, to denote a close-knit, first-generation Asian immigrant suburban community where isolation and over-protectiveness fuel a child's rich fantasy life (Leung 2015, 42–44). Kwan's subsequent feature documentary, *Everything Will Be* (2014), turns its focus to Vancouver's Chinatown at a time when the neighborhood is caught in a flux of rapid urban changes, where the dynamics of gentrification intersect revitalization and preservation efforts while bypassing the most vulnerable residents in the neighborhood.

The attention to place also involves reflecting on Asian migrants' relation to the land and to Indigenous communities. Japanese-Chilean Canadian filmmaker Alejandro Yoshizawa's film, *All Our Father's Relations* (2016), is one of the first films to shine a light on the largely undocumented history of Asian-Indigenous relations in the region. The film was made in collaboration with its subjects: four elderly siblings in the Grant family who were raised Indigenous by their mother in the First Nation community of the Musquem people. Guided by fading memory of their father, a migrant worker from China who married their mother while working on leased farmlands on the Musquem Reserve during the 1920s, but who later became estranged from the family following his divorce from his wife and subsequent departure from the reserve, the siblings were determined to find out more about their Chinese heritage. The film follows the siblings as they trace their late father's migration journey which eventually took them all the way to Guangdong to meet with relatives on their father's side. As the film explores this intimate family story, it also tries to unravel the larger interconnected histories of Indigenous peoples and Asian migrants, the social as well as legal contexts of racism and exclusion, and the entangled dynamics between the exploitation of Asian migrant labor on the one hand, and Indigenous dispossession on the other. Indigenous filmmaker Kamala Todd has described Hollywood as "a powerful place maker, writing its own narratives and geographies onto the land" (Todd 2013, 9). Films like *All My Father's Relations* is important for countering such erasure while demonstrating the need for Asian filmmakers to work with Indigenous communities to reinscribe unremembered and ignored histories on screen.

Directly commenting on the city's weak sense of place, film editor Tony Zhou – whose YouTube channel Every Frame A Painting (2014–2016), where he posts thoughtful video essays on film form, is immensely popular and beloved by film buffs – made a brilliant short video, *Vancouver Never Plays Itself* (2015). Narrated by Zhou with his signature humor and made with an editor's cinematic eye, the video essay assembles clips from Hollywood's most famous productions and analyzes the technical expertise and artistry with which they disguise Vancouver's location while simultaneously lamenting the impact the location industry has on the city's own "lack of film identity." Zhou then pays homage to films from the Pacific New Wave where "Vancouver does plays itself." For Zhou, these indie films offer perspectives of the city that he, "as a child of immigrants, who mostly explored the city on foot," could relate to. Zhou's plea to filmmakers to diversify settings and to challenge the "ubiquity but invisibility" of the "third largest filmmaking city in North America" very much echoes that of filmmakers from the Pacific New Wave generation, many of whom view it as a matter of ethics. Larry Kent, who appears in Zhou's short, once said in an interview that he considers films that set Seattle in Vancouver to be a "lie" that betrays each city's "completely different emotional feeling" (Spaner 2004, 44), while Bruce Sweeney, whose film *Excited* (2009) Zhou quotes in the video, once called shooting in Vancouver while setting a film elsewhere "reprehensible behaviour" (Spaner 2004, 159).

The connection that Zhou's video essay makes between the indie ethos of the Pacific New Wave films and his Asian immigrant experience has resulted in a distinct "West Coast Asian" film culture, which Su-Anne Yeo describes as "eclectic, elusive, sometimes collaborative, and frequently contradictory" (Yeo 2007, 114). Among the many place-specific circumstances that Yeo has identified as defining factors, two strike me as most illustrative of the contradictory as well as collaborative nature of this film scene. First, Yeo suggests that while Vancouver is marginalized from the main national cultural institutions located in Toronto and Montreal, and never benefitting from the same level of funding or infrastructural development, the city's inferior cultural status affords local filmmakers the creative freedom to flout conventions favored by revered public institutions like the National Film Board (NFB) and the Canadian Broadcasting Company (CBC) (117). Yeo contrasts the hybrid works by Asian diasporic filmmakers like Anne Marie Fleming and Karen Lee, who blend fictional and documentary elements in their films, with the documentary realism favored by NFB and CBC. This realist style was especially expected from racialized film-makers making "serious" films about social justice during the 1990s and 2000s, when the earlier influence of John Grierson and the British documentary film movement was very dominant. Anne Marie Fleming's most acclaimed work, *The Magical Life of Long Tak Sam* (2003), very much goes against such expectations by deploying an atypical whimsical visual and narrative style to trace the life of Fleming's great-grandfather who left China to tour the world as an acrobat and magician. The film comprises a playful pastiche of ani-mation, comic strips, found photographs, and a highly self-reflexive personal travelogue. The fantastical style does not hinder the film's rich evocation of a turbulent global history of war, migration, and racism, but it steadfastly refuses to pin down any "truth" about its subject's relation to this history. The film's emphasis on illusion (it is about a magician after all) and the unreliability of memory has even been characterized as its own kind of magic trick (Trimboli 2015). After making the film, Fleming also published an illustrated graphic memoir (Fleming 2007), thereby giving the film an "afterlife" in a different artistic medium. This multidisciplinary approach to filmmaking is still very much embraced by independent filmmakers working in the city today. The interest in and ease with connecting filmmaking with other art practices stems, in part, from a long history of artist-run-center movement in Vancouver, which is another defining factor Yeo attributes to the distinctive style of Vancouver's Asian film scene (Yeo 2007, 121–22). Rooted in the countercultural resistance against institutionalized art that erupted during the 1960s–'70s and has since continued in response to the ongoing paucity of resources for cultural production and distribution in the region, the artist-run-center scene in Vancouver has influenced filmmakers not only to work collaboratively with artists in other disciplines but also to be actively involved in creating alternative avenues for distribution, exhibition, and curation, in addition to making and producing their own films. Moreover, the movement's politicized ethos has created a space where it is normal for artists to tackle potentially controversial issues: much of the scene's activism in the 1990s and 2000s is "preoccupied with issues of gender and sexuality as they are implicated with race" (Yeo 2007, 122), and the notion "that art and aesthetics are ideo-logically inflected . . . is presumed as a baseline for aesthetic production in the Vancouver context, where artists either play with the ideological implications/potentials or else wage open war against them" (Betts and Polyck-O'Neill 2017, 6).

Many of the Asian-led, film-focused artist-run collectives in the city today have retained this multidisciplinary focus and political orientation. Even as digital technology has expanded the capacity for online and transnational initiatives, these collectives have also demonstrated a renewed commitment to place-specific projects and local engagement. For example, the arts collective Cinevolution – co-founded in 2007 by three Asian women and currently run by a diverse team of Asian filmmakers, producers, visual artists, and curators – is based in the city of Richmond, a suburb south of Metro Vancouver where, according to a 2021 census, the current population is close to 75% Asian, with a diversity of backgrounds including early-19th-century Japanese settlement in the adjacent fishing town, influx of Hong Kong immigrants during the late 1960s and again in the 1980s–'90s, as well as more recent waves of immigrants from China and parts of South and Southeast Asia (Statistics Canada 2023). Cinevolution characterizes itself as "grassroots, women-led, migrant-driven" (Cinevolution n.d.). It organizes film festivals and digital media skills workshops, makes podcasts, and mentors young artists, in addition to making and producing films and multimedia projects. While its projects are not confined to one place, the collective devotes a lot of efforts to collaborating with Richmond's local art gallery and public library to program projects that directly engage communities in the neighborhood.

Queer/Asia Intersections

Similarly collaborative and multidisciplinary, Love Intersections is another artist-run collective that continues to animate the city's independent film scene. Based in Vancouver's Chinatown, which is located near the downtown core, Love Intersections was co-founded by Asian filmmakers David Ng and Jen Sungshine, who use screen media to tell queer migrant stories and explore the intersections of sexuality, race, and intergenerational dynamics. With the explicit aim of connecting the experiences of racialized queer communities, the collective has made short films on queer subjects' Deaf identity, Muslim faith, experience as refugees, Two-Spirit identity, and involvement in Black Lives Matter, among other themes (Love Intersections n.d.).

The collective's 2019 short film, *Yellow Peril: Queer Destiny*, consciously situates their work within the city's indie lineage by paying homage to the work of openly gay artist Paul Wong, who has been an important figure in the city's queer and arts scenes since the 1980s. Wong curated *Yellow Peril: Reconsidered*, a major exhibition that toured the country in 1990–91 with the works of 24 multidisciplinary visual artists of diverse Asian backgrounds from different parts of Canada, all of which explored the history of anti-Asian racism and exclusion through experimental perspectives. The project was groundbreaking not only for the unprecedented national spotlight it shone on Asian artists but also its frank critique of institutional racism against Asians as well as of Asian immigrant communities' own conservatism and indifference toward alternative art (Wong 1990, 8). Wong also pointedly highlighted the works of gay and lesbian artists, including Richard Fung, Helen Lee, and Chick Rice, whose film and photography works explicitly explore sexuality and gender in relation to race (Wong 1990, 12). By invoking Wong's work in the film's title, Love Intersections connects *Yellow Peril: Queer Destiny* to a long history of independent artistic practice and activism in the city and the seminal role queer Asian artists have played in this history. *Yellow Peril: Queer Destiny* follows drag artist Kendall Yan, a.k.a. Maiden China, as her colorfully clad figure lusciously inhabits spaces in the city: posing against the expansive coastal vista in the opening sequence, crouching down to burn incense in front of a make shift ancestral shrine in a leaves-strewn downtown parking lot, sauntering on the railway tracks built on the backs of migrant Chinese labor in the late 19th century, standing in full drag in the middle of a formal hall in a Ming-dynasty-style house, and riding on a cycle rickshaw on a rooftop overlooking the city's skyline. Interspersed between these visually enigmatic shots is *vérité* footage of Kendall navigating daily life: chatting about childhood stories in her father's kitchen, swapping coming out stories with her brother while playfully balancing on a mini seesaw together, and reflecting on changes in the drag scene with fellow House of Rice performer Shay Dior. The most affecting of these everyday scenes is a discussion Kendall has with lion dance performers Kimberly Wong and Dora Ng, who describe the panful experience of being told they are "disrespecting" a traditional practice that others have perfected with blood and sweat. Often, the perceived "disrespect" is felt by those offended by a traditionally male practice being taken up by women or trans people and performed in queer spaces, such as a lion dance performed during a drag show. Kendall recalls being accused of "commodifying" a cultural practice and turning something solemn into a "gimmick." This crucial conversation was shot in an observational mode and the filmmakers refrain from leading the audience to any easy answer or clear-cut judgment on the issue. Nonetheless, the painful conversation in this scene indirectly gives meaning to the more abstract sequences of Maiden China's visually flamboyant presence in the city's various spaces, always with a somber expression and embodying, or in the vicinity of, a "traditional" Asian symbol whether in the form of bridal wear, an ancestral shrine, or sticks of incense. Furthermore, the film is divided into sections titled after five elements: wood, fire, air, earth, and water. Its visual evocation of a visibly queer figure ostensibly "out of place" in both her surrounding and with traditional objects of her heritage seems to be the film's way of rebalancing the elements to acclimatize its viewers to what may initially be perceived as cultural "dissonance," but which may, in time, be experienced as a new kind of queer harmony.

Continuing the multidisciplinary approach of previous filmmakers, Love Intersections has gone on to develop *Yellow Peril: Queer Destiny* into various "afterlives," one of which was an installation in the heart of Chinatown in 2020, just before the COVID-19 lockdown. At the installation, footage from the film was projected onto two giant double screens mounted on the walls of a room where queer objects, such as a dildo or an erotic text, were displayed among traditional ceremonial objects. The installation was also accompanied by "place activation" events including a lion dance in the middle of Chinatown and an ancestral veneration ceremony at the nearby historic site of a violent anti-Asian riot that took place in 1907. Subsequently, the filmmakers added another chapter to the film, titled *Yellow Future: Queer Destiny 2.0* (2022), which follows Maiden China's reflection on her trans identification and experience during the pandemic and related incidents of anti-Asian racism. This "afterlife" of the film was similarly "activated" by place-specific events featuring intergenerational dialogues on the potential of arts practices and the future of local community-building.

For the Love of a Place

Asian diasporic filmmaking is often studied primarily through the lens of the filmmakers' identity, which sometimes runs the risk of homogenizing works that come from very distinctive filmmaking contexts while also overlooking works that are produced and disseminated outside of major filmmaking centers. I have tried in this article to offer a case study to highlight the place-specific dynamics of a diasporic independent filmmaking culture that has continued to survive despite (and at times because of) its proximity to a mammoth commercial film industry. An Asian film scene in a city that is projected to comprise 59% of "visible minorities" who are predominantly Chinese, South Asians, Filipinos, Koreans, and West Asians by 2031 (Hiebert 2012) is bound to be dynamic in its interpretation of what constitutes "Asian" and constantly evolving its ongoing creative directions. It may also seem surprising that such a film scene would produce so many significant female and openly queer filmmakers, considering the generally challenging climate of the industry toward such creators. On deeper reflection, it seems logical that a film culture eking out its existence on the margins of dominant institutions and industries would, by its very nature, value and nurture similarly marginal experiences.

The unexpected recent mainstream success of *Everything Everywhere All at Once* (2022), an Asian-led indie production that has become both a box office hit and critical sensation in Hollywood, will likely bring increased visibility to diasporic Asian filmmaking.

Under this welcomed spotlight, it is worth also making the critical efforts to highlight other distinctive contexts where lesser-known diasporic Asian filmmaking scenes have been producing daring and unconventional works for a long time and is poised to continue to do so for many generations to come.

References

Betts, Gregory, and Julia Polyck-O'Neill. 2017. "Contesting Vancouver: Case Studies in a Cultural Imaginary." *Canadian Literature* (235): 6–11.

Burgess, Diane. 2003. "Charting the Course of the Pacific New Wave." *CineAction* 61 (Spring): 29–34.

Cinevolution. n.d. "Our Organization." Accessed March 1, 2023. https://cinevolutionmedia.com.

Curtin, Michael, and Kevin Sanson. 2017. *Voices of Labor*. Oakland: University of California Press.

Destination Canada. 2022. "Welcome to Hollywood North." *Vanity Fair*. Accessed March 1, 2023. https://www.vanityfair.com/sponsored/story/welcome-to-hollywood-north.

Fleming, Ann Marie. 2007. *The Magical Life of Long Tack Sam: An Illustrated Memoir*. Toronto: Penguin Random House Canada.

Gasher, Mike. 2002. *Hollywood North: The Feature Film Industry in British Columbia*. Vancouver: University of British Columbia Press.

Hanley, David. 2014. "Contextualizing Questions of Identity and Space in Mina Shum's *Double Happiness*." *Off Screen* 18, no. 11–12 (December). https://offscreen.com/view/double-happiness.

Hiebert, Daniel J. W. 2012. "A New Residential Order: The Social Geography of Visible Minority and Religious Groups in Montreal, Toronto, and Vancouver in 2031." Accessed March 5, 2023. https://www.canada.ca/en/immigration-refugees-citizenship/corporate/reports-statistics/research/a-new-residential-order-social-geography-visible-minority-religious-groups-montreal-toronto-vancouver-2031.html.

Leung, Helen Hok-Sze. 2015. "Asia/Canada Reframed: Perspectives From a Transpacific Film Location." *Canadian Literature* (227): 114–32. https://doi.org/10.14288/cl.v0i227.187796.

———. 2016. "Hollywood North, Asiawood West." In *Contemporary Culture and Media in Asia*, edited by Daniel Black, Olivia Khoo, and Koichi Iwabuchi, 31–48. London: Rowman & Littlefield.

Love Intersections. n.d. "Film Work." Accessed March 1, 2023. https://loveintersections.com/videos/.

Melnyk, George. 2014. *Film and the City: The Urban Imaginary in Canadian Cinema*. Athabasca, Alberta: Athabasca University Press.

Ruttle, Joseph. 2022. "Hollywood North: What's Filming Around Metro Vancouver This Summer." *Vancouver Sun*, July 7.

Scott, Alan J., and Naomi E. Pope. 2007. "Hollywood, Vancouver, and the World: Employment Relocation and the Emergence of Satellite Production Centers in the Motion-Picture Industry." *Environment and Planning A* 39 (6): 1364–81. https://doi.org/10.1068/a38215.

Spaner, David. 2004. *Dreaming in the Rain: How Vancouver Became Hollywood North by Northwest*. Vancouver: Arsenal Pulp Press.

———. 2012. *Shoot It!: Hollywood Inc. and the Rising of Independent Film*. Vancouver: Arsenal Pulp Press.

Statistics Canada. 2023. *(Table). Census Profile. 2021 Census of Population. Statistics Canada Catalogue no. 98-316-X2021001*. Ottawa. Released February 8, 2023. Accessed March 21, 2023. https://www12.statcan.gc.ca/census-recensement/2021/dp-pd/prof/index.cfm?Lang=E.

Steenberg, Lindsay. 2013. "World Film Locations: Vancouver." In *World Film Locations: Vancouver*, edited by Rachel Walls, 92–93. Bristol: Intellect.

Tinic, Serra. 2012. "Hollywood Elsewhere: The Runaway Locations Industry and Transnational Production Cultures." *The International Encyclopedia of Media Studies*. https://doi.org/10.1002/9781444361506.wbiems053.

Todd, Kamala. 2013. "World Film Locations: Vancouver." In *World Film Locations: Vancouver*, edited by Rachel Walls, 8–9. Bristol: Intellect.

Trimboli, Daniella. 2015. "Memory Magic: Cosmopolitanism and the Magical Life of Long Tack Sam." *Continuum* 29 (3): 479–89.

Vancouver Economic Commission. 2022. "B.C. Film Roars Back with Record-Shattering $4.8 Billion Spend in 2021." September 12, 2022. Accessed March 1, 2023. https://vancouvereconomic.com/blog/media/bcfilm-spends-4-8-billion-in-2021/.

Wong, Paul. 1990. *Yellow Peril: Reconsidered*. Vancouver: On Edge.

Yeo, Su-Anne. 2007. "Vancouver Asian." In *Reel Asian: Asian Canada on Screen*, edited by Elaine Chang, 114–25. Toronto, ON: Coach House Books.

SECTION II

Mediating Place
Colonial, National, and Trans-Asian Imaginaries

INTRODUCTION

Debashree Mukherjee

This section demonstrates the many ways in which cinema has historically been mobilized for imperial, colonial, and nationalist purposes, and the many sites through which film scholars today can unpack, interrogate, and perhaps even undo the harms coded into the cinematic archive. Be it British newsreels about tribal peoples of "the East" or Hollywood films about mythic "Shangri-Las," an Orientalist-filmic gaze that privileges the West in a planetary hierarchy based on skin color and geography continues to feed anti-Asian sentiments even today. It is this shared racialization that prompted many scholars in the era of decolonization to propose a vision of "Asia as method." However, as we point out in our general introduction, the category of "Asia" is not only slippery but can occlude various forms of colonial violence that divide up Asia from within. This section goes beyond a discussion of European colonialism or 19th-century imperialism and applies pressure on the modern postcolonial nation-state itself. While critiques of Japan's imperial ambitions both pre– and post–Cold War are as necessary to discuss as China's continued territorial ambitions vis-à-vis Taiwan, each author applies new methods to approach these histories and open them up for more than a simply accusatory orientation to the past.

The postcolonial nation-state produces its own inequities, specifically along axes of class, gender, caste, language, and race. Ting-Wu Cho's chapter, for example, is an important reminder of the indigeneity that continues to be pushed toward the borders of national imaginations, a minoritization and exoticization that survives across different imperial regimes. C. Yamini Krishna's chapter can also be read subtextually to gesture toward the relative invisibility of Telugu-language imaginations within India's mainstream national politics that is geared toward New Delhi and Hindi. Cinema thus emerges as an important ground for examining the cultural tensions that invariably tear away at the nation-state's drive toward coherence.

Place, place-making, and cinema's particular modes of spatial production are central to many of the essays in this section. By dragging place to the center of the discussion, these authors apply new pressures to the old paradigms of national cinema. But the methods and frames of analysis here are diverse. Using innovative methods such as textual analysis of pedagogical and popular literature on cinema, the study of film subtitles and shifts in subtitling choices over decades, the use of curation and film programming as a decolonial mode

DOI: 10.4324/9781003266952-13

of return into the archive, or close film analysis, our contributors offer multiple strategies that can be used in our continued questioning of the national cinema paradigm. As we move from Japan to Taiwan to Singapore, South Korea, Nepal, and into India, our authors focus on alternate parameters of comparison and grouping such as region (Himalayan, oceanic, urban), film philosophical concepts, transnational archive production, and linguistic identity.

We begin this section with imperial desires explicitly played out on the terrain of cinema. Daisuke Miyao considers the meaning of "Asian Cinema" as a conceptual, geographic, commercial, and political category when thought from Japan, and explores its shifting valences and purview before and after World War II. Drawing on an impressive range of textual materials – from academic and popular books on cinema to film magazines and economic theory – Miyao traces changes in the use of the category "Asian cinema" from an early 20th-century Japanese Asian studies formulation where the East was pitted against the West, to a post-1941 triangulated understanding where there was Asia, there was the West, and then there was Japan. In the process we get a fascinating glimpse of the imbrications of cinema, capitalism, and colonialism in Japan's paternalist approach to the idea of Asia, one which was focused on its geopolitical interests in Southeast Asia and left Japan itself conveniently beyond the remit of a potential "trans-Asian" vision. The implications of this essay are several–from a nuanced caution to historicize claims to approach "Asia as method," to insights that the history of "area studies" is not solely a product of Cold War research needs that emanated in the United States but has longer histories in Japan (where Asian studies was instituted in 1908).

Zhuoyi Wang does a deep dive into the production history of *Taiwan Wangshi* (*My Bittersweet Taiwan,* 2004) and argues that the film represents a transitional moment in the PRC's cinematic treatment of Taiwan. In 1979 the PRC announced its new policy toward Taiwan as an "inalienable part of China since ancient times," departing from a 30-year stance as enemy territories during the Cold War. Chinese filmmakers were pressed into service in the early 1980s to make melodramas that affirmed "the Message" about deep cross-strait histories of affect and unity. Wang argues that the commercial failure of these '80s films was finally repaired by *Taiwan Wangshi* in 2004 which successfully navigates multiple ideological nuances including Chinese nationalism, lingering affections for Japan, and Taiwanese self-identity. These nuances, Wang shows, emerged through a struggle or *douzheng* between artistic principles and the political mandates of propagandistic filmmaking. "Filming Taiwan Between a Quest for Artistic Purity and Propaganda in the People's Republic of China" thus tracks the production struggles of the makers of *Wangshi* as they tried to reconcile a mandate to send a direct political message with more humanistic emotional truth. In a sense this is an excavation of film philosophy, where the filmmakers' investment in traditional Chinese aesthetic principles such as *qiyun* (lit. "flowing energy and lasting charm") and Confucian concepts such as such as *cheng* (sincerity) and *zheng* (truth) are examined through their own critical writings and interviews. For example, Huang Dan, the writer and producer of *Wansghi*, who is also a film studies professor, developed the concept of *qingzhenyiqie* (genuine feelings and sincere attitude) and has advocated it over the years as an ideal for Chinese cinema.

Early cinematic representations of indigenous peoples, be they from Hawaii, the Andaman Islands, or the South Pole, are tainted by the racial-colonial logics that undergirded their conditions of production, that is, the infrastructures and imaginations of their creation. But these are often the only extant visual traces of marginalized communities and practices, doubly erased under colonialism but also by postcolonial regimes. If return thus becomes necessary, how might a decolonial lens be applied to these overdetermined archives? Ting-Wu Cho's "In the Name of Love: Screen Representations of Taiwan Indigenous Peoples (1920s–1940s)" takes an inventive approach to recovering histories of indigenous subjectivity. Cho examines American newsreels shot in Taiwan by Fox Movietone in the first half of the 20th century, and juxtaposes these with Chinese-language feature films made in Taiwan between 1937 and 1950. This film selection, spanning three different eras of political transition for the Taiwan archipelago, offers a complex interplay of imperial visions. Cho first presented this footage in a curated program of archival film clips at the 11th Orphan Film Symposium in 2018. The author's choices of selection and juxtaposition form a central part of the argument toward a decolonial re-reading of colonial film archives.

In 2016, two lost films about "overseas Chinese" that were made in Singapore in 1946 resurfaced: *Huaqiao xuelei* (*Blood and Tears of the Overseas Chinese*, dir. Tsai Wen-chin 1946), and *Haiwai zhenghun* (*Spirit of the Overseas Chinese*, dir. Wan Hoi-ling 1946). Elizabeth Wijaya takes this moment of archival rediscovery to examine 1946 as a transitional time "between nations," when the contours of China, Singapore, Malaysia, and even Japan were still fluctuating. She examines the films at two levels simultaneously, the imaginative space of diegesis and dialogue, and the institutional space of archiving and restoration. The films center the identity of the overseas Chinese and display ambivalent yearnings for the "homeland." At the same time, a broad idea of "Nanyang" as a tropical "second home" for Chinese persons is constructed through mise-en-scene and sentimental encounters between recent migrants to Singapore and those born there. Both the films treat these questions with varying degrees of force, *Huaqiao xuelei* perhaps more ready to center Singapore itself as a multilingual, multiracial place marked by contingency. Moving beyond plots about belonging and citizenship to the circulation of the films, Wijaya examines multilingual subtitles of these films and the contexts from which these emerge. The chapter poignantly pursues how institutions such as national film archives serve to further entrench the framework of a national cinema. Even as the filmmakers once moved between Hong Kong and Singapore, between Japanese occupation and British control, between Mandarin, Malay, and Hokkien, the films today reside in the China Film Archive performing a kind of cinematic citizenship.

Dikshya Karki offers us a rare look at the relationship between cinema and Nepal, looking not at films made in Nepal but at cinematic fantasies of a place like Nepal. The dream of Shangri-La, a mythical place marked by Himalayan topography, Buddhist architecture, and a soft-focus Eastern mysticism, is one that has been forged intermedially between literature, travelogues, and movies. Karki argues that is overwhelmingly Nepal, via its capital city Kathmandu, that has served as the historical-geographical referent for these fantasies. The chapter does a close and multifaceted reading of two films, *The Night Train to Kathmandu* (1988) and *Doctor Strange* (2016), to unpack the colonial-Orientalist visions that blur the specificity of culture and region, and offers new spatial coordinates that mediate local understandings of place with a tourist economy that is buoyed by a history of exotic stereotyping.

The theme of place-making continues with the next essay by Ran Ma, where she examines four films by the Korean Chinese filmmaker Zhang Lu, made between 2014 and 2019, and situates them as "inter-Asian" texts made by a diasporic filmmaker. Mobilizing theories of affect and spatiality, Ma mounts an aesthetic-philosophical critique of methodological nationalism. However, Ma is careful not to turn the problematic of place and identity into an abstraction and grounds her study in material practices such as location shooting. The reader drifts in and out of the registers of representation and production while following the urban drifters in Lu's films. It is through these spatial itineraries of aimless roaming that Lu's border-crossing characters (North Korean defectors, returnees from Japan, migrant workers) produce what Ma terms "affective-scapes," i.e., place-person relations of embodied emotion that are wrought through cinematic techniques of movement, mise-en-scene, and subject.

In "Postcards from Russia," C. Yamini Krishna maps a fascinating and understudied network of ideas, aesthetic forms, media, and filmmakers that stretched between Soviet Russia and the Telugu-language cultural spheres of southern India. Inspired by socialist politics and a utopian faith in the transformative potential of the arts, scores of writers, lyricists, poets, actors, composers, producers, and directors in India actively crafted stage plays and films that railed against the exploitation of peasants and workers and, frequently, urged a people's revolution. Krishna not only reads leftist messaging in film plots, characters, symbolism, and song lyrics but also considers industrial exchanges across the two filmmaking regions via film festivals, diplomatic tours, and awards ceremonies through the decades of the Cold War. Thus, ideological and cultural traffic emerge as important nodes in mid-century trans-Asian cinematic imaginations, nodes that would be overlooked if we continued to restrict our scholarly gaze to national and nationalist cultural formations.

9

WHAT IS "ASIAN CINEMA" IN JAPAN?

Film and Political Economy in the 1940s

Daisuke Miyao

The category of "Asian cinema" (*Ajia eiga*) has been widely used in Japan since the 1950s. Curiously, though, the category does not usually include Japanese-made films, despite Japan's geographical location in Asia. Such a strange exclusion indicates Japan's unique geopolitical positionality within broader Asia, specifically as a colonial power with an imperial past and potentially imperial futures. The major goal of this chapter is to ask what "Asian cinema" means in Japan with its colonialist sensibility that lingers on to this day.

Amid the *Anpo* protests of 1960 (*Anpo tōsō*) – a series of massive protests that took place throughout Japan against the revision of the United States–Japan Security Treaty (1952), which allowed the US to maintain military bases on Japanese soil – a Japanese scholar of Chinese literature, Takeuchi Yoshimi, gave a pair of lectures titled "Asia as Method." What Takeuchi proposed was to develop Asia's "own cultural values," which "do not already exist, in substantive form" (Takeuchi 2005, 165). These lectures appear to have at least three goals. First, Takeuchi tried to reassess Japanese imperialism which led to an aggressive invasion of its neighboring countries. Second, he wanted to overcome Asian intellectuals' complex toward their "superior" counterparts in Europe and the United States. Third, he critiqued Western ideals of freedom and equality that had been considered to be universal values by providing a different perspective. To create its own cultural values, Takeuchi emphasized the significance of a comparative Asian viewpoint. For Takeuchi, European nations or the United States were not the appropriate "interlocutors who share the same structural anxiety" (2005, 150). Elaborating on Takeuchi's idea, a Taiwanese critical theorist, Chen Kuan-Hsing argues that "the back and forth dialogue process" between Euro-America and Asia cannot overcome the inferiority complex nor challenge the innate Eurocentric hierarchy in so-called Western universal values, but only through inter-referencing places, which are closer to each other or share similar historical experiences, can we leave the mistake of the "catch up" type of normative mode of knowledge, and to produce more grounded knowledge and understanding that come closer to historical reality (Chen 2012, 323). The basis of the formation of the Asian "cultural values" for

DOI: 10.4324/9781003266952-14

both Takeuchi and Chen is, thus, the "common destinies" of the "impact, subjugations, and resistance brought by imperialism, colonialism, and the Cold War" (Chong, Chow, and Kloet 2020, 3).

However, Gladys Pak Lei Chong, Yiu Fai Chow, and Jeroen de Kloet warn us that emphasizing commonalities could run "the risk of ignoring the power structures that render some Asian (or European, or Western) voices more vocal than others" (2020, 4). What they stress is that the power imbalance is not limited to the West and Asia but is far more complex if we look from an intra-Asia perspective. Mitsuhiro Yoshimoto raises questions about "power structures" implicit in the notion of Asian cinema:

> [L]et us first note that the notion of Asian cinema itself is not a self-evident idea. . . . Asian cinema is a construct that needs to be scrutinized from a range of critical perspectives. What has contributed to the emergence of the idea of Asian cinema? What purpose does it serve in film scholarship and criticism? What position does it occupy in the study of national cinemas?
>
> *(254)*

According to Yoshimoto, the emergence of Asian cinema is "inseparable from the globalization of the American economy and the rise of East Asia as an important region for it." Secondly, the idea of Asian cinema has partly been embraced "in search for an alternative to the form of essentialism" that interprets the cinema of a particular nation as "a reflection of national character, sensibility or spirit" and eventually enhances the dichotomy between Hollywood as the center and the cinemas of the rest of the world as periphery. Finally, the construction of Asian cinema is strongly influenced by "international film festivals and a new global-ecumenical film culture" (254–55). To accomplish this difficult job of re-conceptualizing Asian cinema outside Eurocentrism, what Yoshimoto proposes is "trans-Asian cinema":

> As a critical category, trans-Asian cinema refuses any unproblematic assertion of the uniqueness of Asian cinema as such, and of the various national cinemas in Asia. It also resists the logic of transnational capital, which de-historicizes and de-politicizes difference and very real boundaries in the name of multiculturalism.
>
> *(Yoshimoto 2006, 260)*

Yoshimoto's reaction is to the construction of "Asian cinema" by the "West." His "trans-Asian cinema" offers "a genuine comparative perspective," which would be "a historically defensible understanding of any national cinema in its unique cultural specificity, that is to say, not as the 'other' of some other national cinema, which for its commercially dominant or aesthetically influential position on a global scale, is equated to 'the cinema' as a whole" (Yoshimoto 2006, 260). Yoshimoto's proposal seems very similar to Takeuchi's emphasis on an intra-Asian comparative view because both of them presuppose the "unique cultural specificity" of each country but try to explore commonalities among them that could collectively distinguish them from non-Asian films. While their arguments maintain the dichotomy between the West and the East, they do not subscribe to the Eurocentric notion of the self/other categorization that ignores the unique cultural and historical specificity of each region and people.

In this chapter, I extend Takeuchi and Chen's idea of "Asia as method" to film studies. But my focus is not on exploring inter-Asian commonalities. Instead, I critically engage with Yoshimoto's notion of "trans-Asian cinema" in the context of Japanese film history. Reviewing the discursive construction of "Asian cinema" in Japan in the 1940s right before the notion started to be used broadly, this chapter questions if a "trans-Asian cinema" is possible.

1. The Emergence of "Asian Cinema" in Japan: Ichikawa Sai's *The Creation and Construction of Asian Cinema* (1941)

Filmmaking cooperation among Asian countries started as early as 1931. But the notion of Asian cinema did not exist in Japan until the late 1930s, especially after the 1937 China Incident and the founding of the Manchurian Motion Picture Association (Manshū Eiga Kyōkai, aka Manei) in Manchukuo. Markus Nornes claims that it was at that moment when "pan-Asian industrial film criticism" started to flourish and "writers [in Japan] increasingly evaluated films, filmmakers, and studios in their collective effort to imagine and construct 'Asian cinema'" (Nornes 2013, 176).

However, during the Second Sino-Japanese war period that followed the 1937 China Incident, the term that was given to such pan-Asian imaginations of film culture was not "Asia" but "continent" (*tairiku*) as the latter term entered daily use in Japanese media to refer to the continent of Eurasia, where Imperial Japan intended to expand its colony. The immediate focus in this Eurasian imaginary was China, including Manchuria. Accordingly, a discourse of "continent films" (*tairiku eiga*), as a loosely defined genre started to appear. Roughly speaking, "continent films" meant Japanese-made films whose stories were set in the Asian continent, mainly in China, Manchukuo, and/or Mongolia, as well as the films made by three Japanese-funded companies in China: Chūka Denei, Manei, and Kahoku Denei (An 2004, 132).

Three weeks before the attack on Pearl Harbor, a book with the term "Asian cinema" in its title was published. It was Ichikawa Sai's *Ajia eiga no sōzō to kensetsu* (The Creation and Construction of Asian Cinema, 1941) published by the International Film News Agency (Kokusai Eiga Tsūshinsha), Ichikawa's own company. Ichikawa coined the concept of "Asian cinema" to distinguish his idea from the discourse of "continent films." His conception of Asia was not limited to China but Southeast Asia and beyond. Ichikawa attempted to define Asian cinema as an export market, a Japanese film territory for a form of capitalist imperialism. Moreover, he also imagined Asian cinema as a form of cultural imperialism where the content of the films that would be produced in Asia beyond Japan would correspond to the capitalist expansion of Imperial Japan. The notion of "Asian cinema" that Ichikawa coined in his book, however, was yet to be shared by broader readers, including critics.

The Empire of Japan invaded French Indochina in September 1940 and attacked Hong Kong, the Philippines, Thailand, Singapore, and British Malaya in December 1941. The major purpose was to explore natural resources and to establish military bases in Southeast Asia. Under the military occupation, however, the Japanese colonial force adopted a pan-Asian rhetoric of co-prosperity and coexistence by claiming the so-called Greater East Asian Co-Prosperity Sphere (*Dai Tōa Kyōeiken*). A universal Asian brotherhood based on regional nationalisms was stressed by the Japanese military so that European colonial influence would be pushed back. Japanese film critics now started heated discussions on the film culture in newly acquired colonies in Southeast Asia. The words that they selected, such as "Greater East Asian cinema" (*Dai Tōa eiga*) and cinema's "Southern operation" (*Nanpō kōsaku*), clearly indicated their shared interests with the Japanese occupation force. "Greater East Asian cinema" was meant as a rhetoric to "eliminate Euro-American culture that was forced on East Asian people for several centuries" and "to construct unique East Asian culture" (Yamane 1942, 4–5). Obviously, the emphasis on co-prosperity was to justify Japanese colonialism there.

Still, as Japanese film historian Sasagawa Keiko argues, the project of "Greater East Asian cinema" was "not to mono-directionally distribute Japanese-made films to other countries" but "to coproduce films among several countries under the leadership and guidance of the Japanese military and then distribute those films to the entire Greater East Asian Co-Prosperity Sphere" (2010, 60). Beyond its propaganda purpose for the Greater East Asian Co-Prosperity Sphere, the colonial film policy was meant to stabilize the regional economy as well. The Japanese military, which led the policy, forced structural changes in Southeast Asian regions that they occupied. According to Sasagawa, the notion of "Greater East Asian cinema" was a result of a compromise: critics thought that it would be impossible to make Japanese films understood by all the people in the Sphere immediately and it was necessary first to produce films that would be easily acceptable to them but still contain ideas of Japanese supremacy (2010, 60). The ultimate question for the critics in Japan was the future of "Japanese" cinema and not the formation of "Asian" cinema. In the March 1942 issue of *Eiga Hyōron*, one of the most influential film journals of the time, four critics wrote about "the new direction" of Japanese cinema. The editorial prompt they received was this:

> How should Japanese cinema work in Malaya, Thailand, the Philippines, and other people that have newly come under the wing of Japan? How should Japanese cinema change its characteristics to develop further? Since these are the issues that Japanese cinema has not faced in the past, there will be various difficulties. Could you think about these issues?
>
> (Iijima 1942, 22)

Iijima Tadashi criticized the "island-ish isolation" (*shimaguni teki ni koritsu*) of Japanese cinema and said that it should be their "duty" to let the people in Greater East Asia Co-Prosperity Sphere know about Japan by producing culture films (documentary films) and news films (1942, 18). Noborikawa Naosuke called the Southern operation not an international but "an internal problem" (*tainai mondai*) of Japanese cinema and emphasized that it would be essential to domestically produce "excellent" films that could be exportable (1942, 20).

Some people had the idea that the "Southern operation" should be asking Japanese filmmakers to "instruct" the people in the Southeast Asian regions to make "something new" that would be comprehensible to them (Takatsu, Kaeriyama, Tamura, Hori, Chiba, Yamamoto, Taguchi 1943, 37). Scientist Takatsu Hiroshi, who made a research trip on natural resources to Southeast Asia in 1943, for instance, strongly supported this idea when it was suggested by critic Kaeriyama Norimasa, who was the central figure of the Pure Film Movement (*jun eigageki undō*) in the 1910s–'20s and had been the advocate of exploring methods of exporting Japanese cinema. But both agreed that the basic aim of the Japanese

Army, Navy, and the Ministry of Information (Naikaku Jōhōkyoku), which established the Association for Southern Sea Cinema (Nanyō Eiga Kyōkai) for its Southern operation, with support from the major Japanese film companies, Shōchiku, Tōhō, Tōwa Shōji, and Chūka Denei, was to simply bring popular Japanese films to the South (Takatsu, Kaeriyama, Tamura, Hori, Chiba, Yamamoto, Taguchi 1943, 39).

Yet, even if it was a result of a compromise, it is important to note that the term "(Greater East) Asian cinema" officially appeared for the first time in this project. When he used the term "Asian cinema" in the title of his book, Ichikawa's main gesture was undoubtedly toward China. After the 1937 China Incident, according to Nornes, Ichikawa spent a third of his time on the continent (2013, 177). After briefly overviewing the history of the overseas activities of the Japanese film industry, Ichikawa spent the core of *The Creation and Construction of Asian Cinema*, 168 pages out of 378 pages, focused on close analysis of the film industries, film politics, and film economy of Manchuria and China (including Hong Kong).

But it is noteworthy that he also included 82 pages of detailed analyses of other regions of Asia: French Indochina, the Philippines, Siam, British Malaya, Dutch East Indies, India, Burma, Ceylon, and even Hawai'i, Australia, and New Zealand. In contrast to the chapters on Manchuria and China, Ichikawa's arguments and data were not limited to the film industries of these regions. He spent equal numbers of pages describing their politics, economy, imports, exports, transportation, culture, population, and major cities. In other words, Ichikawa provides the contextual information needed to develop the film business there.

Ichikawa's notion of "Asian cinema" was not limited to the film-critical discourse of exporting Japanese cinema to Southeast Asia. Instead, his project had a much broader scope of political economy that corresponded to the changing trends in Asian studies in Japan. The focus of the Japanese intellectual conception of Asia was transitioning from East Asia to Southeast Asia. According to economist Kobayashi Hideo, "new Asian studies" (*shin ajia gaku*), which distinguished itself from "traditional Asian studies" (*dentō teki ajia gaku*), emerged in the 1940s when Japanese imperialism turned its gaze to Southeast Asia. Traditional Asian studies started in 1908 right after the end of the Russo-Japanese War with the formation of the Research Bureau of Manchurian and Korean History and Geography (Manshū oyobi Chōsen Rekishi Chiri Chōsabu). Influenced by Marxism, scholars of traditional Asian studies discussed the impact of capitalism on feudalism in China, Korea, and Japan (Kobayashi 2012, 1–5).

By early 1942, the Japanese Army had occupied the Philippines, British Malaya, the Dutch East Indies, and Burma. Scholars from Japanese universities and research centers were sent to these occupied areas to serve in colonial policymaking. According to Kobayashi, the resulting fieldwork was strongly influenced by the work of British-born historian John Sydenham Furnivall and his concept of the "plural society," in which different ethnic groups would depend on each other economically but maintain ecological specialization. Contrary to the scholars of traditional Asian studies on China and Korea, new Asian studies by these scholars in Southeast Asia had a double standard: embracing the idea of independence and nationalism in each region of Southeast Asia under the leadership and guidance of Japanese militarist occupation, whose goal was to replace the European power with Japanese power without causing strong resistance. In other words, in traditional Asian studies, the binary between East (Asia) and West was clear. Japan was a part of Asia even though, despite Kobayashi's naming of traditional "Asian" studies, I doubt those scholars called themselves "Asianists." In new Asian studies, there were three different levels: the West, Japan, and Southeast Asia.

115

Ichikawa's notion of Asian cinema reflected this doubleness. In the conclusion of his book, Ichikawa insisted that the Japanese and Chinese film industries, "which have led film productions in the Asian cultural sphere," need to "become the axis to produce films for all Asian races" (2003, 427–28). At the same time as emphasizing Japan and China's co-leadership (separation of Japan and China from the rest of Asia), Ichikawa suggested the unity of Asia, urging:

With the Greater East Asia Co-Prosperity Sphere taking root and liberating people from the national groupings of the past, we must grasp the future qualities of a racial consciousness built on a shared cultural basis. This is precisely the greatest of productive powers in Asian culture. Asian culture is not the mere transmission of Chinese and Indian culture, nor is it an imitation of the cultures of Europe and America. It is a new *combination* of the two, a glorious culture only in the cultural sphere of Asia

(Ichikawa 2003, 423; Nornes 2013, 179–80).

As Nornes points out, "this first attempt to define Asian cinema, or imagine that there was such a thing, was a regionalism" that materialized during Japan's war effort as its "new markets [for exports] in Southeast Asia and the Pacific" (2013, 180–81). In this regard, Ichikawa's idea of "Asian cinema" was not very different from the notion of "Greater East Asian cinema," which dominated the discursive field at that time.

Yet, in retrospect, Ichikawa's claim of regionalism toward the formation of "Asian culture" shared much in common with "Asia as method." His idea about the "shared cultural basis" in Asia could have easily been contained by the ideology of the Greater East Asia Co-Prosperity Sphere. But in contrast to "Greater East Asian cinema," Ichikawa's "Asian cinema" did not presuppose the elimination of Euro-American culture or its influence on it. It was geared more toward the "new *combination*" of East and West (Ichikawa 2003, 423). Moreover, Ichikawa's belief in cinema being "the prime medium for constructing the interregional cultural sphere" (Nornes 2013, 180) is what Olivia Khoo has recently suggested when she theorizes about "Asian cinema as a regional cinema" (2021, 3). Khoo argues,

Conceiving of the region Asia as not just a geographical space but also as a particular imaginary that nevertheless has a material/economic basis to it is a way of understanding how cinematic productions are constructed within capitalist structures and on cultural grounds.

(2021, 3)

Thus, while Ichikawa's notion of "Asian cinema" shared the political economy of Japanese colonialism in Southeast Asia, it also suggested the possible formation of a new regional film culture that would overcome the East-West dichotomy.

2. Continuity of the Wartime Notion of "Asian Cinema" into the Cold War: Ozu Yasujirō's *Banshun* (*Late Spring,* 1949) and Itagaki Yoichi's Southeast Asian Studies

Nornes claims that any pan-Asianism during the Cold War "was tempered by the legacy of Japanese imperialism and the overwhelming power of bilateral relationships with the United States" (Nornes 2013, 181). What exactly did this look like?

Near the opening of Ozu Yasujirō's postwar film *Banshun*, there is a conversation between the elderly professor Somiya (Ryū Chishū) and his assistant Hattori (Usami Jun):

Hattori:	"Friedrich List." It's spelled without a "z." "L-I-S-T."
Somiya:	I thought so. Liszt with a "z" was the musician.
Hattori:	1811 to 1886 . . .
Electrician (from off-screen):	I'm from the electricity company. I'm here to check your meter.
Somiya:	Please come in.
Electrician (from off-screen):	May I borrow a stool to stand on?
Somiya:	Yes . . .
Hattori:	Where is it?
Somiya:	In the corridor, under the stairs. Thanks.
Hattori:	Not at all.
Electrician:	Thanks.
Hattori:	Professor, List taught himself economics, didn't he?
Somiya:	Yes, and he became an excellent economist of the (German) Historical School. He detested bureaucracy . . .
Electrician (from off-screen):	It's 3 kilowatts over!

Banshun was released in 1949 during the Allied Occupation of Japan which continued until 1952. It was the third film that Ozu directed after he was repatriated to Japan from Singapore at the end of the Pacific War in August 1945. With its critical and financial success, *Banshun* is considered to have revived Ozu as a master filmmaker and renewed his career for him after a period of relative anonymity.

Figure 9.1   Somiya and Hattori discuss Friedrich List. *Banshun* (Late Spring, 1949).

But what I want to stress here, in the context of the idea of Asian cinema, is not renewal but continuity. The reference to Friedrich List in *Banshun* is, in fact, an interesting indication of the continuity of Japanese people's everyday experiences and their conception of time from wartime to the postwar era.

List's theory of national economy was influential in the "new Asian studies" in Japan that emerged in the early 1940s. Itagaki Yoichi, Hitotsubashi University professor, a leading member of new Asian studies and the founding father of Southeast Asian studies in Japan, was a major advocate of List's theory. "The core of the colonial issue is the ethnic issue so that colonial policy is nothing but ethnic policy," wrote Itagaki (1978, 104). Believing that "without experiences and observations of actual places, you are not qualified to conduct colonial studies," Itagaki spent his own money and went to Dutch East India from November 1940 to February 1941. Then he spent three months in the islands of Java, Madura, Bali, Sumatra, and Sulabes to "witness the ethnic movement of independence in Indonesia" (1968, 131). He also purchased more than 1,100 books on ethnic issues at used bookstores before he moved to Bangkok (1968, 141). After he went back to Japan, he made many presentations on colonial policy at the Integrated Research Group (Sōgō Kenkyūkai) for the Imperial Army and Navy.

Itagaki's first monograph, based on his research in Dutch East India, was *Seiji keizaigaku no hōhō* (The Methods of Political Economy), published in February 1942. Itagaki regarded the state as the subject of the national economy and rising anti-colonial ethnic nationalism as the primary object of Japan's imperial policy (Karashima 2018, 60). List's theory of nation-state and "Stufentheorie," or the theory dividing economic evolutions into historical stages, gave Itagaki the theoretical framework for his idea of establishing state-controlled capitalism in colonial Southeast Asia. According to Masato Karashima, Itagaki aligned with Prime Minister Konoe Fumimaro's "New Order Movement," which planned to reform capitalism and co-opt Asian nationalism (mainly in Southeast Asia) into Japan's wartime empire (2018, 61).

A new edition of *The Methods of Political Economy* was published in 1951 during the Allied Occupation of Japan. Its introduction, in which Itagaki advocated for Japanese imperialism, was removed. But he added a new appendix, an annotated bibliography of the Historical School. In the same year, Itagaki published his second monograph, *Sekai seiji keizai ron* (*The Political Economy of the World*). He historically analyzed the formation of nation-states, colonialism, and ethnic nationalism in colonies. He concluded that nationalism in Southeast Asia would need to be realized with financial support and investments by the West. Itagaki's postwar work reflected his imperialist experiences in Southeast Asia as well as the international policy of the US, including the IMF system, during the Cold War.

Considering the timing of the release of *Banshun* and the publication of Itagaki's volumes, it is interesting to imagine that Itagaki is the model for the character Somiya because, in *Banshun*, Japan's wartime past and democratic and capitalist future in the Cold War coexist in a complicated manner.[1] Ozu was sent to British Malaya in June 1943 "to observe" the condition of ethnic nationalism there and "to make a documentary film" about an independence movement by the India National Army led by Subhas Chandra Bose (Tanaka 1989, 16, 427).[2] Ozu was most likely familiar with Itagaki's work on colonial policy in Southeast Asia because Ozu's mission given by the Shochiku company followed Prime Minister Konoe's "New Order Movement." But it is known that Ozu demonstrated an ambivalent position against such colonial policy. He decided not to make any film and stayed in Singapore just to watch Hollywood films that had not been released in Japan.

The electrician's intrusion into the conversation between Somiya and Hattori is noteworthy as well. His presence does not contribute anything to *Banshun*'s narrative. On the one hand, he embodies the "bureaucracy" that List detested because he interrupts the supposedly more meaningful scholarly discussion. But on the other hand, his claim about the overuse of electricity in Somiya's household indicates the ongoing reconstruction of the Japanese economy. If Somiya's was a typical example of a Japanese family in 1949, all Japanese households were overconsuming electricity, which would have led to more demands for production, then further industrialization, and eventually to larger markets beyond the domestic. Thus, despite the apparent disparity, the presence of the electrician connects smoothly to the two scholars' dialogue on List and his political economy.

As I have discussed elsewhere, Ozu's postwar films emphasize the notion of "duration," or the continuity of Japanese people's everyday experiences from the wartime to the postwar era (Miyao 2021). Films like *Banshun* show that there was no discontinuity in Japanese people's conception of time between the two periods. The dominant mode of filmmaking under the Occupation was to create a dichotomized image of Japan, between bad militarism and feudalistic despotism in wartime versus good democracy and new beginnings in the postwar period, for the victimized ordinary people (especially women). The Occupation policy was forcefully fabricating the sense of a temporal gap before and after 15 August 1945. But the "nostalgia" or "repression" of the present in Ozu's postwar films demonstrate what the German social historian Reinhart Koselleck calls "historical times." Koselleck writes, "historical times consist of several layers that refer to each other reciprocally without being entirely dependent on one another" (translated and quoted in Zammito 2004, 130). Ozu's postwar films made the coexistence of two temporalities visible, revealing continuity between the prewar, wartime, and postwar periods.

Under such conditions of continuity in political economy between the wartime and the postwar period, in April 1954, the Japan Asian Association (Ajia Kyōkai) was established. The Association's major activity was to facilitate Japan's war reparations to Southeast Asian countries and build economic cooperation with them. Reparations projects became crucial avenues by which Japanese companies could gain access to Southeast Asian markets (Karashima 2018, 60). One of the executive directors of the Japanese Association of Asian Studies (Ajia Seikei Gakkai 1953–present), the founding organization of the Japan Asian Association, was Itagaki. He then helped create the Institute of Asian Economic Affairs (Ajia Keizai Kenkyūjo, aka Ajiken) in 1958 under the Ministry of International Trade and Industry (MITI). According to Karashima, the establishment of Ajiken as a "quasi-governmental corporation" was an important part of "Japan's efforts to find a place in postcolonial Asia where the rise of independent nation-states intersected with the Cold War geopolitics" (2018, 60). As Itagaki's presence indicates, postwar Japan's political imagination of Asia had strong connections with the wartime period in terms of people and research institutions. Itagaki's wartime idea of managing ethnic nationalism and promoting state-controlled economic development continued, and the decolonization of Southeast Asian countries turned into the primary object of Japan's international policy in the Cold War. Karashima argues, "State-led economic development was also critical to establishing the postwar regional order under Japan's dominance and subsequently to rebuilding Japan's relations with [Southeast] Asia based on anti-communism" (Karashima 2018, 61–62).

Karashima's omission of the word "Southeast" in his argument on Itagaki's idea indicates that "Asia" in postwar Japan meant Southeast Asia, just as it did in wartime. China and Korea had lost their status as the major fields of study in Asian studies in Japan because of the establishment of the People's Republic of China (1949) and the beginning of the Korean War (1950).

The most prominent "Asian cinema" project in the years that followed was the Asian Film Festival, organized by the Federation of Motion Picture Producers in Southeast Asia (FPA), "the first postwar pan-Asian film organization" founded in 1953, according to Sangjoon Lee (2020, 4). A year later, its annual event, the Southeast Asian Film Festival (renamed the Asian Film Festival in 1957), was held in Tokyo. Lee has conducted substantial research on the pan-Asian film network after the 1950s and convincingly argued that the postwar imagination of "Asian cinema" was carried over from the wartime idea that had been initiated by Japanese imperialist expansion to Southeast Asia. What Lee implies in his work is also multiple layers of continuity in colonialist ideology between the wartime and the period of the Cold War.

Epilogue

Following the period of war reparations led by the Japan Asian Association, the economic relations between Japan and Southeast Asia strengthened throughout the 1960s, '70s, and '80s by way of loans and investments from Japanese governments and private companies (Kobayashi 2012, 16). Again, as in the 1940s, Japan's economically (and politically) hierarchized position was repeated there so that Japan did not fully position itself as a part of Asia.

Alongside such an economic relationship between Japan and Southeast Asia, the notion of "Asian cinema" has become a well-circulated commercial term among popular cinemagoers in Japan. This renewed notion of "Asian cinema" is not oriented toward Southeast Asia but has a rather politically unconscious and historically amnesiac nature. The Focus on Asia Fukuoka International Film Festival initiated the renewal of the notion of "Asian cinema" from its foundation in 1991 until its final installment in 2020. Festival director, the prominent and prolific film critic Satō Tadao, programmed films from different regions in Asia. He also published several books that had "Ajia eiga" in their titles, right through the 1990s: *Ajia eiga* (*Asian cinema* 1993), *Ajia eiga shōjiten* (A *small encyclopedia of Asian cinema* 1995), *Shinseiki Ajia eiga: Ajia fōkasu Fukuoka eiga sai kara 21 seiki e* (*New millennium Asian cinema: Focus on Asia Fukuoka International Film Festival to the 21st century* 2000). As seen on his website as of 30 May 2022, Satō often used terms such as "naïve" and "pure" when he described films from Asian regions. Satō's paternalistic and pedagogical attitude ironically revived a colonialist perspective on Southeast Asia and "Asian cinema," in which Japan would not belong but play a leadership role. Thus, the renewed concept of "Asian cinema" in this commercial movement once again implied its collective otherness from the films of Japan, harkening back to the racial and cultural hierarchy that had become entrenched in Japan during the Cold War.

Notes

1 Or Somiya's model could be Kobayashi Noboru, the acclaimed economist whose initial works focused on List. Kobayashi claimed that he was influenced by Itagaki and his interpretation of List's "Stufentheorie" (Tamura 2011, 66).
2 According to Shoma A Chatterji (2020) though, Ozu was sent to Singapore instead, to make *Deruhi e, Deruhi e* (To Delhi, To Delhi) with Bose. The subject of the film was the struggle of the INA for freedom from British rule. The actors were drawn from India or Indians settled in Singapore. But

when Japan's loss became certain, Ozu claimed he destroyed the reels of the said film. However, Singapore-based visual artist and researcher Toh Hun Ping has claimed that Ozu's film on Netaji was preserved by Singapore-based Indians. They handed over the reels of the film to Pandit Jawaharlal Nehru when he was touring Singapore and Malaya in 1946. Then, Sardar Vallabhbhai Patel completed the film under the banner of the INA and the ads stated that it was "reproduced" by Patel. The title of the film was changed to *Netaji Subhas* and was released in Calcutta on 23 January 1948. The source for Chatterji is a 2019 article in *Ananda Bazar Patrika* in Bengali. https://www.academia.edu/40629375/Destroyed_and_Survived_Ozus_Film_on_INA_and_Subhash_Chandra_Bose. Accessed on 4 October 2022. The author would like to acknowledge Debashree Mukherjee for this fascinating reference. No book or essay on Ozu in Japanese has included this valuable information.

References

An, Ni. 2004. "'Dai Tōa eiga' e no kaidan: 'Tairiku eiga' shiron [Stairway to the 'Great East Asian Cinema': An Experimental Theory on 'Continent Films']." In *Eiga to "Dai Tōa kyōei ken"* [Cinema and the "Greater East Asia Co-Prosperity Sphere"], edited by Iwamoto Kenji, 129–56. Tokyo: Shinwa sha.

Chatterji, Shoma A. 2020. "Netaji Subhas Chandra Bose on Celluloid." *Upperstall: A Better View of Cinema*, 4 January. Accessed October 4, 2022. https://upperstall.com/features/netaji-subhas-chandra-bose-on-celluloid/.

Chen, Kuan-Hsing. 2012. "Takeuchi Yoshimi's 1960 'Asia as Method' Lecture." *Inter-Asia Cultural Studies* 13 (2): 317–24.

Chong, Gladys Pak Lei, Yiu Fai Chow, and Jeroen de Kloet. 2020. "Introduction: Toward Trans-Asia: Objects, Possibilities, Paradoxes." In *Trans-Asia as Method: Theory and Practices*, edited by Jeroen de Kloet, Yiu Fai Chow, and Gladys Pak Lei Chong, 1–24. London: Rowan & Littlefield.

Ichikawa, Sai. 2003. *Ajia eiga no sōzō to kensetsu* [The Creation and Construction of Asian Cinema]. Tokyo: Yumani shobō.

Iijima, Tadashi. 1942. "Nihon eiga no seikaku ni tsuite: Dai Tōa sensō ni kanren shite" [On the Characteristics of Japanese Cinema: Concerning the Greater East Asian War]." *Eiga Hyōron* 2, no. 3 (March): 16–19.

Itagaki, Yoichi. 1968. *Ajia tono taiwa* [Dialogue with Asia]. Tokyo: Shinkigen sha.

———. 1978. *Zoku Ajia tono taiwa* [Dialgue with Asia Continues]. Tokyo: Ronsō sha.

Karashima, Masato. 2018. "Itagaki Yoichi and the Formation of the Postwar Knowledge Infrastructure for Japan's Overseas Development Aid in Asia." In *Engineering Asia: Technology, Colonial Development, and the Cold War Order*, edited by Hiromi Mizuno, Aaron S. Moore, and John DiMoia, 59–82. New York: Bloomsbury.

Khoo, Olivia. 2021. *Asian Cinema: A Regional View*. Edinburgh: Edinburgh University Press.

Kobayashi, Hideo. 2012. *Nihonjin no Ajia kan no hensen: Mantetsu Chōsabu kara kaigai shinshutsu kigyō made* [The Transformation of Japanese People's Image of Asia: From the South Manchuria Railway's Research Bureau to Japanese Overseas Investment]. Tokyo: Bensei shuppan.

Lee, Sangjoon. 2020. *Cinema and the Cultural Cold War*. Ithaca, NY: Cornell University Press.

Miyao, Daisuke. 2021. "The Melodrama of Ozu: *Tokyo Story* and Its Time." *Journal of Japanese and Korean Cinema* 13 (2): 58–79.

Noborikawa, Naosuke. 1942. "Nihon eiga no shin dōkō: Sono geigōteki konmei [Japanese Cinema's New Trend: Its Compromising Chaos]." *Eiga Hyōron* 2, no. 3 (March): 19–21.

Nornes, Abé Mark. 2013. "The Creation and Construction of Asian Cinema Redux." *Film History: An International Journal* 25 (1–2): 175–87.

Sasagawa, Keiko. 2010. "Nichihi gassaku eiga *Ano hata o ute* no genei: Senryō ka firipin ni okeru Nichibei eiga sen wa ikanishite tatakawaretaka [The Illusion of *Liwayway ng Kalayaan*: Japanese Cinema's War Against Hollywood in Japan-occupied Philippines]." *Kansai Daigaku Bungaku Ronshū* 60, no. 1 (July 30): 57–85.

Takatsu, Hiroshi, Kaeriyama Norimasa, Tamura Yukihiko, Hori Kumasaburō, Chiba Shigetarō, Yamamoto Kakuzo, and Taguchi Ryūzaburō. 1943. "Saikō noetfliu gijutsu o dōin seyo!: Nanpō bunka kōsaku ni tsuite [Mobilize the Best Science Technology!: On the Southern Cultural Operation]." *Eiga Gijutsu* 3, no 4 (April): 30–41.

Takeuchi, Yoshimi. 2005. "Asia as Method." In *What Is Modernity? Writings of Takeuchi Yoshimi*, edited by Richard F. Calichman, 149–65. New York: Columbia University Press.

Tamura, Shinichi. 2011. "Kobayashi Noboru to Doitsu Keizai shisōshi kenkyū [Kobayashi Noboru and the Study of German Economist Thoughts]." *Rikkyō Keizaigaku Kenkyū* 65 (2): 57–77.

Tanaka, Masasumi, ed. 1989. *Ozu Yasujirō sengo goroku shusei* [Ozu Yasujirō, Compilation of His Utterances]. Tokyo: Firumuāto sha.

Yamane, Shōkichi. 1942. "Dai Tōa eiga ken kakuritsu no kyūmu [The Imminent Need to Establish Greater East Asian Cinema Sphere]." *Eiga Junpō* 42 (February 21): 4–5.

Yoshimoto, Mitsuhiro. 2006. "National/International/Transnational: The Concept of Trans-Asian Cinema and the Cultural Politics of Film Criticism." In *Theorising National Cinema*, edited by Valentina Vitali and Paul Willemen, 254–61. London: British Film Institute.

Zammito, John. 2004. "Koselleck's Philosophy of Historical Time(s) and the Practice of History." *History and Theory* 43 (2): 124–35.

10

FILMING TAIWAN BETWEEN A QUEST FOR ARTISTIC PURITY AND PROPAGANDA IN THE PEOPLE'S REPUBLIC OF CHINA

The Case of *Taiwan Wangshi* (*My Bittersweet Taiwan*, 2004)

Zhuoyi Wang

In 1949, the Chinese Civil War between the Chinese Communist Party (CCP) and the Kuomintang (KMT, or the Nationalist Party) resulted in a mutually closed border along the Taiwan Strait. The People's Republic of China (PRC), established by the victorious CCP on mainland China, and the KMT-ruled Republic of China (ROC), which retreated to the island of Taiwan, stood on opposite sides in the global Cold War. The two parties regarded each other's land as both the enemy's territory and an essential part of their national homeland.

Three decades later, the PRC officially departed from its Cold War Taiwan policy. Its Standing Committee of the National People's Congress (NPCSC) issued a "Message to the Compatriots in Taiwan" (henceforth the Message) on New Year's Day of 1979. The Message draws a nationalistic common ground for cross-strait unification. Part of it reads:

> Taiwan has been an inalienable part of China since ancient times . . . Throughout its history, foreign invasions and internal strife have failed to split our nation permanently . . . Every Chinese, in Taiwan or on the mainland, has a compelling responsibility for the survival, growth, and prosperity of the Chinese nation . . . If we do not quickly set about ending this disunity so that our motherland is reunified at an early date, how can we answer our ancestors and explain to our descendants? This sentiment is shared by all.
>
> *(NPCSC 1979)*

Following the publication of the Message, the PRC made a number of films featuring romantic or familial melodramas set in both Taiwan and mainland China, attempting to illustrate on the silver screen an affective cross-strait connection for the Chinese nation to

DOI: 10.4324/9781003266952-15

resist "foreign invasions" and survive "internal strife." The cross-strait hostile separation in reality, however, meant that mainland filmmakers had to fabricate such stories out of thin air. These films, including *Qingtian Henhai* (Love and Regret, 1980), *Qinyuan* (The Family, 1980), *Haiwang* (Awakening, 1981), and *Taidao yihen* (Eternal Regret of Taiwan, 1982), only produced underwhelming and easily forgettable Taiwan stories. Their negative reception in mainland China was one reason for the ensuing long-term dearth of PRC-made films set in Taiwan. Quite tellingly, the 1989 PRC film *Daihao Meizhoubao* (*Code Name: Cougar*), which is partly set in Taiwan, condenses that part as much as possible and shows it not even in moving images, but in still photos with a narratorial voice-over.

This cinematic void was filled in 2004 by *Taiwan Wangshi* (*My Bittersweet Taiwan*, henceforth *Wangshi*), the focus of this chapter.[1] In the history of cinematic representations of Taiwan in the PRC, *Wangshi* is an important transitional film as it both ended an era and began a new one. *Wangshi* ended an era because it was the last completely state-funded major PRC film set in Taiwan. Beginning with the 2006 film *Yunshui Yao* (The Knot), co-investments from private companies, including those in Taiwan and Hong Kong, would add significant commercial considerations to the pursuits and the intentions of PRC state-sponsored Taiwan subject films. In terms of political and artistic pursuits and intentions, however, it was *Wangshi* that brought the PRC's Taiwan films to a new era of sophistication. This chapter analyzes *Wangshi* as a product caught between a quest for artistic purity and political propaganda, exploring its nuances and contradictions as a window into the tensions between PRC artists' increasingly complex understanding of Taiwan and the simplistic political framework to which they had to adhere. It focuses on the cooperation and *douzheng* (struggles, conflicts) among three key members of its creative team, director Zheng Dongtian, scriptwriter and executive director Huang Dan, and original scriptwriter Zhang Kehui.

Qiyun

For the most part, *Wangshi* is a bildungsroman set in Taiwan under Japanese rule. Growing up, the film's protagonist Lin Qingwen experiences and witnesses a series of conflicts between his family and the ruling Japanese, including his father's imprisonment for being critical of Japanese rule. At the same time, he learns about his Chinese identity from his grandfather and mother, who emphasize their ancestral and cultural roots in mainland China. The bildungsroman seems to reach a happy ending when Qingwen finally survives the Japanese occupation and goes to mainland China for higher education. However, this is also the beginning of his decades-long separation from his family in Taiwan due to the 1949 divide. The film then fast forwards to the 1980s, ending with Qingwen finally reuniting with his mother and sister, quite ironically in Japan, thanks to an old-time Japanese schoolmate's help.

The film may easily remind viewers of Taiwan New Cinema director Hou Hsiao-Hsien. The title *Wangshi* bears obvious similarity to that of Hou's first internationally successful film, *Tongnian Wangshi* (*A Time to Live, A Time to Die* 1985). Similarly, the name of Lin Qingwen resembles that of Lin Wenqing (or Lin Wen-ching in Taiwanese spelling), the protagonist in Hou's universally acclaimed *Beiqing Chengshi* (A City of Sadness 1989, henceforth *Chengshi*). The similarities go far beyond just the titles and the names. Resemblance to Hou's works, especially *Chengshi*, can be found extensively in *Wangshi*'s style and narrative.

Such likeness is not coincidental and can be traced back to a 1990 article on *Chengshi* published by Zheng Dongtian, director of *Wangshi*. Thanks to the post–Cold War thawing of the cross-strait relationship, the PRC began to see an influx of Taiwanese cultural products, including films, through official and unofficial channels during the 1980s. As a professor at the most prestigious film institution in China, the Beijing Film Academy, Zheng built a comprehensive understanding of the imported Taiwanese films with better-than-usual access to them. His article features a meticulous close reading of *Chengshi*, arguing that the film sets an excellent example for applying the Chinese traditional aesthetics of *qiyun* (lit. "flowing energy and lasting charm") into filmmaking (Zheng 1990).

Zheng does not clearly define his use of *qiyun*, which is a notion that has a long history of diverse and highly context-dependent interpretations and applications in Chinese art and literature. But this notion does embody a general philosophical consistency constituted of such Confucian doctrines as *zhen* (truth) and *cheng* (sincerity), as well as such Daoist ideals as *wuhua* (spiritual fusion of self with object) and *wuwei* (acting without conscious intention or effort). As analyzed by the contemporary scholar Xiaoyan Hu, an artist creating *qiyun* is usually expected to first capture the *zhen* of the depicted object in a way of *cheng*. With insight and sincerity, they can then fuse their perception and feelings with the captured *zhen* through spiritual fusion (*wuhua*), avoid distorting it affectedly or artificially (*wuwei*), allow it to freely flow into the artwork as *qiyun*, and create spiritual resonance among artist, object, audience, and work (Hu 2021, 8, 9, 46–54, 214).

Zheng detects *Chengshi*'s *qiyun* in Hou Hsiao-Hsien's signature cinematographic style comprising *chang* (long takes), *ding* (static shots), and *kuan* (or medium to extreme long framing), as well as the mise-en-scene, sound, and editing arrangements used in conjunction with this style (Zheng 1990, 29). He dissects the sequence of Wenqing's political prison experience as a primary example. The sequence primarily consists of one nearly three-minute-long and largely static shot. The shot begins in complete darkness with the sound of several prison guards' approaching footsteps. After the guards open a cell door and summon two prisoners "to court" (in fact for immediate execution), Wenqing and his cellmates, including the two summoned prisoners, become visible sitting in the cell. The camera is low, at the knee level of the prisoners, and placed at a distance outside the cell door. The barely moving camera and the narrow door render much of the figures invisible. What can be seen is Wenqing, who is helplessly surrounded by darkness and heavy shadows. He obviously cannot bear to part from the cellmates who are soon to be executed, but nor can he do or even say anything (he is deaf and hard-of-speaking). His sad face remains the focus of the next shot, which includes the sound of two gunshots but does not show the execution.

Given the fact that Zheng does not explicitly define cinematic *qiyun* in his essay on *Chengshi*, one may speculate that Zheng may have felt *qiyun* in this sequence's aesthetic combination echoing *zhen*, *cheng*, *wuhua*, and *wuwei*. Wenqing and his cellmates are imprisoned for being involved in the 28 February Incident of 1947, which was a mass protest in Taiwan as a result of the KMT's dictatorial and corrupt rule after its takeover of the island from Japan in 1945. In response to the incident, the KMT massacred tens of thousands of Taiwanese people, placed Taiwan under martial law from 1949 to 1987, and brought the island into a period known as the White Terror. As Hou himself described, *Chengshi* made "a daring move" to depict the incident at a time when it had been under the code of silence for four decades (Assayas 1996; all Hou's quotes here are from this documentary film). As a courageous representation of the still-ruling KMT's atrocities, the sequence manifests a Confucian sense of *zhen* and *cheng* in its sincere attempt to faithfully represent the suppressed truth of history.

Such scenes showing political atrocities, though central to the plot, are few in number. They showcase *Chengshi*'s usual cinematographic pattern of presenting violence only indirectly with little active camera engagement, either off-screen or from afar through static framing. Despite this oblique treatment, *Chengshi* is by no means short of critical power as it was made with the intention, in Hou's own words, "to honor Taiwanese people's dignity under harsh suppression." What Hou actually meant can be understood through the concepts in *qiyun*. An aesthetic approach echoing the Daoist sense of *wuwei* can help avoid superfluously adding emotions and judgments to *Chengshi*'s spiritual fusion (*wuhua*) with the heavy truth (*zhen*) that the film sincerely (*cheng*) attempts to capture. In cases like the sequence mentioned, this aesthetic approach also closely connects the barely moving camera to the restrained and powerless Wenqing. It provides the audience members, who are also passive witnesses unable to change anything about the atrocities, with a deep space to find resonance with the film.

Having closely studied *Chengshi*'s style as a scholar, Zheng also attempted to create a similar kind of *qiyun* in his directorial works, including *Renzhichu* (The Beginning of Life, 1992), *Guyuan Qiuse* (Autumn Scenery in Hometown, 1998), and *Liu Tianhua* (2000), all of which are recognized as a unique kind of *wenren dianying* (lit. "[traditional] literati film") for their combination of Confucian and Daoist moral and aesthetic values (Lu 2003). *Wangshi* continues this auteurist approach and bears even more similarities to *Chengshi* for their shared subject: a Taiwanese family's losses and struggles taking place in the island's complex political history. It is not surprising that Zheng uses the word *qiyun* again in his own description of the film's artistic pursuit. Telling a story that "lasts for decades [. . .] without a continuous dramatic conflict," *Wangshi* resorts to creating "a prosaic narrative that is *xing san shen bu san*" (an established Chinese prose writing strategy that literally means "scrambled in appearance but united in spirit") with "a consistent inner *qiyun* of audiovisual figurations" (Zheng 2004, 50–51).

Stylistically, *Wangshi* is similar to *Chengshi* in that it also avoids an active camera engagement in its representations of atrocities. For example, the film chooses not to visualize the imprisonment and the torture of Qingwen's father by Japanese police but focuses on the consequences of torture on the family in delicate cinematic language. One carefully arranged detail is the two trips Qingwen and his father take in the film, passing the same railway crossing to the same fishing spot. One trip happens before the imprisonment, and the other after. During the first trip, the father sees an approaching train at the crossing, impetuously picks up the little Qingwen, and runs across the tracks. The next shot shows him looking back at the passing train with an excited face. There is also an approaching train during the second trip, but the father does not seem to notice it at all until stopped by Qingwen. He then waits at the crossing, looking at the train passing in front of him with dull eyes. The two scenes are also contrasted in terms of lighting and sound. As described by the film's cinematographer and sound mixer, the former scene features a "bright sunny day" as well as "lighthearted, cheerful, and pleasant" sound effects, while the latter scene features a "depressive" "overcast sky" as well as "ear-piercing" and "pounding" sound effects (Ma 2004, 59, Li 2004, 65). All the contrasts in performance, lighting, and sound accentuate the father's loss of his spirit after the traumatic torture.

Undoubtedly central in *Wangshi*'s creative team, Zheng was however not the only one who made important contributions to *Wangshi*'s *qiyun* aesthetics. The next section

126

discusses Huang Dan, scriptwriter and executive director of *Wangshi*, and his *zhen* and *cheng* intention to represent a more sophisticated Taiwan than that in a propagandist film.

Qingzhenyiqie and Intention

In 1999 Huang Dan was assigned to work on the original script of *Wangshi* (under another title at the time), which was written by an amateur writer Zhang Kehui, and in need of professional rewriting. Huang and the cinematographer Ma Ning conducted extensive interviews with people of Taiwanese origin all over the PRC, and they also visited Taiwan for interviews and research. Having rewritten the script, Huang decided to produce *Wangshi* himself. He initiated the project with Ma in 2001, invited Zheng to be the director, and worked as an executive director throughout the production of the film (Huang 2004).

Like Zheng, Huang is also a film studies professor and his publications demonstrate a passion for *zhen* and *cheng*, or what he terms *qingzhenyiqie* (genuine feelings and sincere attitude). In a 2002 article titled "Making Chinese Films with Genuine Feelings and Sincere Attitude," Huang criticizes many PRC-made films for dishonestly fabricating stories, emotions, and themes, implicitly including those so-called leitmotif (*zhu xuanlü*) propagandist films that he sees as uninspiring "compositions with assigned themes" or "the state's outsourced products" (Huang 2002, 140–41).[2] In a reflection article about his participation in the production of *Wangshi*, Huang recalls the 2002 article and further stresses that genuine feelings are crucial for character creation, which would fail if driven by preconceived political notions and fabricated emotions (Huang 2004, 54).

Applying this artistic vision, Huang wrote a farewell scene that takes place at a train station after the Japanese surrender. A group of Taiwanese students are seeing off their Japanese teachers. The Japanese teachers and their family members are sorrowful because many of them were born and grew up in Taiwan rather than "the mainland" (Japan), where they are "returning" but have never been. The well-respected Japanese principal of the school makes a 90-degree bow to the flag of the school. Led by Qingwen, the Taiwanese students follow suit. To Huang, this scene is a typical example of "heartfelt emotional communications driven by human nature beyond ideology, nationality, identity, as well as race and ethnicity" (Huang 2004, 54).

This scene would make *Wangshi* bear still more resemblance to *Chengshi*, which also features complex identities and emotions beyond straightforward nationalism. *Chengshi* also features a Japanese school principal who has deep emotional connections to the Taiwanese, as does his family. Probably suffering from Alzheimer's disease, the aging principal insists on visiting his Taiwanese friend, who has actually long passed away, rather than boarding the repatriation boat. The film also represents Taiwanese youth as deeply connected to Japanese culture. In the prison scene mentioned previously, the two executed prisoners' last trip is accompanied by their cellmates singing the Japanese folk song "Song of the Covered Wagon" ("Horobasha no uta"). Based on a historical record of the Taiwanese activist Chung Hao-tung's execution in 1950 during the White Terror, this scene is layered with complexities beyond simple political concepts. In his life, Chung first fought Japanese imperialism as a supporter of the KMT and then resisted the KMT as a CCP member. "Song of the Covered Wagon" was Chung's favorite song because it reminded him of his hometown in southern Taiwan (Lan 2012, 1–3). At the same time, it was also "a folk song that supported Japanese aggression in Manchuria by invoking a frontier landscape to be conquered" (Chen 2019, 87). Thus, the song is an ambivalent marker of Chung's political position and Taiwan's identity at the very center of conflicting claims over this island by Japan, the KMT, and the CCP. It begs the question: What is the homeland that Chung sacrifices himself for? Is it a Japanese colony, a part of the KMT's Republic of China, a part of the "old China" awaiting Communist revolution and unification, or an island that has developed its own identity precisely in this particular in-between position?

In his article on *Wangshi*, Zheng makes a criticism of PRC-made films that echoes Huang. He believes that "the most fundamental deficiency" of PRC-made films is that their stories and characters are "always driven by preconceived notions, messages to propagate, or ideas to preach," while a true artistic creation should rather be driven by "human characters themselves," or their "personality traits and differences." Based on this shared position, Zheng and Huang considered changing *Wangshi* into a "purer story between a mother and a son." In their ideal version of *Wangshi*, all the dramatic conflicts should derive from the mother and the son's complex "personality clashes," and the conflicts would end in the son's too-late understanding after they are separated by the 1949 divide. It would be "purer" in the sense of being more *zhen* and *cheng* for representing genuine human feelings and at the same time more *wuwei* for containing less political preaching. Together with other members of the creative team, they made much effort in this direction (Zheng 2004, 52).

But *Wangshi* ultimately was not a "purer story between a mother and a son." Both Zheng and Huang acknowledged their failure to reach their idealistic artistic purity. Zheng writes that the film "fails to create original characters," although it does manage to "avoid making characters into impersonal purveyors of concepts" (Zheng 2004, 52). Huang writes in a still more direct and sincere, or *qingzhenyiqie* manner:

> In reality, when you make a Chinese film, especially if it is of such a "sensitive" subject, you cannot make it as pure as you wish or completely for art's sake. [. . .] Sometimes I [. . .] tried to strike a compromised balance and probably lost much that I should not have. Such losses occurred throughout the process from script writing to shooting.
>
> *(Huang 2004, 55, 57)*

As reflected in both Zheng's and Huang's articles, *Wangshi* was a film made between a quest for artistic purity and propaganda. Due to the high stakes the state had in the Taiwan subject, *Wangshi*'s intended sincerity and *qiyun* encountered significant interferences and constraints.

Douzheng and Compromise

Though Huang devoted much effort to *Wangshi*, it was precisely of the type that he criticized as the opposite of his *qingzhenyiqie* ideal: a "leitmotif film" with a state-assigned theme. The author of the original script, Zhang Kehui, was the chairperson of the Taiwan Democratic Self-Government League (also known by its Chinese abbreviation *Taimeng*), a political group that was pro-unification, and the highest-level political figure among people of Taiwanese origin in the PRC.[3] Funds for the film came entirely from Chinese state organizations and institutions (Huang 2004, 55–56).[4]

Probably not coincidentally, *Wangshi* was initiated in 2000, the year that the Democratic Progressive Party (DPP) won the presidency in Taiwan for the first time. The DPP was founded in 1986 and rooted in the *Tangwai* (outside the KMT) movement against the

KMT's dictatorship in the mid-1970s and early 1980s. After the democratization of Taiwan in 1987, the DPP became the most notable party in a major political coalition favoring Taiwanese nationalism and independence over Chinese unification. It posed a fundamental threat to the PRC's Taiwan policy set by the Message, which asserted that people in the PRC and Taiwan naturally share the same Chinese nationalistic sentiment as descendants from the same ancestral family.

In response, the PRC continuously claimed that an overwhelming majority of Taiwanese people would disapprove of calls for Taiwan's independence because of their "inalienable" national bond to Chinese "since ancient times." Zhang's original script served to echo this idea from a supposedly authentic Taiwanese perspective. In Zhang's own words, he wrote the script based on his own experiences as a "Taiwan native" to "let compatriots on both sides of the Taiwan strait, especially Taiwanese compatriots, understand that we the Taiwanese love our home country, will never forget that we are Chinese, and will strive to unify our home country" (Huang et al. 2004, 5).

When describing his three-year collaboration with Huang, Zhang half-jokingly uses a highly charged word: *douzheng* (fight, struggle) (Huang 2004, 55). *Douzheng* can mean a fight against an external enemy, but in the CCP's and the PRC's history external *douzheng* is almost always connected to fierce internal *douzheng* to purge traitors, deviators, or erroneous ideas. This internal purge blurs the boundary between enemies and comrades, friends, family, and self, rendering everyone's political ideas and identification susceptible to dramatic changes. The word *douzheng*, therefore, is simultaneously associated with a "pure" political identity and the practical impossibility of maintaining it.

Many conflicts seen in the production of *Wangshi* might be seen as a kind of internal *douzheng*. When making political statements in writing, both Zheng and Huang appear to support cross-strait unification as strongly as Zhang does. For pursuing *qiyun* and *qingzhenyiqie* in filmmaking, however, they attempt to avoid propagandistic preaching, feature genuine human feelings, and represent complex situations that may not be easily explained with standard political vocabulary. There is, therefore, a distance between the artists' political positions and the politics evident in their films which opens the films to multiple interpretations. *Chengshi*, the film that artistically inspired *Wangshi*, is a good example of this kind of distance. Although Hou Hsiao-Hsien is often regarded as pro-unification, the distance between his own position and *Chengshi*'s *qiyun* allows for diverse interpretations, many of which challenge the rhetoric of Chinese nationalism and the legitimacy of cross-strait unification. Such an open space for interpretations, however, is fundamentally incompatible with the political "purity" expected from *Wangshi*, which was tasked to propagate the PRC's Taiwan policy, similar to the Taiwan stories filmed in the PRC in the early 1980s. However, I would argue that the internal *douzheng* between a propagandistic purpose and an artistic quest for *qiyun* and *qingzhenyiqie* results in a series of compromises which make *Wangshi* more ambiguous and nuanced than its 1980s counterparts.

Some compromises were relatively easy to reach. For example, Zhang's script originally covered his experiences during the Japanese occupation era, the 28 February Incident, and the beginning of the White Terror (he left Taiwan in 1948, one year into the 40-year regime). In his eyes, these are three "unavoidable" elements of the stories of his generation of Taiwanese people. But Zhang and his team found it difficult to represent the latter two elements in an artistically convincing way without damaging the intended clarity of the film's political message about the "inalienable" cross-strait Chinese identity. They agreed on an easy solution: avoiding these two "unavoidable" elements altogether (Huang et al.

2004, 5, Zhang 2001, 12). As a result, the film's plot mostly stays in the Japanese occupation era and jumps all the way to the 1980s shortly after the Japanese surrender. Nonetheless, the very avoidance of the unavoidable still produces ambiguity in the film's political message.

Other compromises were trickier to reach. Take, for example, the repeated railway crossing sequences analyzed earlier. In Zhang's original script, Qingwen's father takes only one trip by train, and that happens after he is released from the Japanese prison. The purpose of the trip, in the father's words, is to "take one more look at the beautiful scenery of my hometown." At the railway crossing, the father sees an armament train with a Japanese flag waving. Immediately angered, he curses and runs toward the train (Huang et al. 2004, 22–23). Highlighting the script's nationalistic theme, this scene characterizes the father almost as a charging soldier fighting the hateful Japanese invaders for his beloved Taiwanese/Chinese hometown. While the filmmakers adhered to the political leitmotif, they made a series of artistic changes for a more credible and relatable representation of human feelings. The purpose of the father's trip was changed to fishing with his son, an activity of family fun rather than nationalistic emotions. In the final film, the trains carry no Japanese signage, and the father's reactions to the trains, first playful and then dull, are much more personal than political. Interestingly, the film retains a moment where the father curses at the Japanese flag but moves it to another scene where he runs away from the flag rather than toward it. Moreover, the cursing takes place amid other contradictory and frantic actions, such as saluting the flag and marching, which reflects the father's formative Japanese education. Maintaining a delicate balance between the political task and the artistic pursuit, these changes subtly but significantly shifted the father from a patriotic exemplar to a human being rendered vulnerable, traumatized, and disoriented by larger political forces.

Figure 10.1 The father salutes the Japanese flag in the film *Taiwan Wangshi.*

Conclusion

Perhaps the most ironic twist of the *douzheng* and its resulting compromises took place after the film was released: Zhang Kehui, who advocated for the Chinese nationalistic story, was forced to defend it on charges of not being nationalist enough, or not pure enough. Although *Taiwan Wangshi*, primarily due to Zhang's insistence, depicts the Japanese mostly as the hateful enemy, it strikes a Sino-Japanese reconciliation note at the end through Qingwen's Japanese classmate Matsumura Takeo, who bullied Qingwen at school but becomes regretful of his behavior after the Japanese surrender. It is Takeo who helps the estranged mother and son reconnect and arranges their secret reunion in Japan at a time when the KMT still forbade cross-strait contact. Partially based upon Zhang's own experience, this ending reflects some complexities of his feelings about Japan as a person who received Japanese education until the age of 17. Such complexities, however, invited criticism of a "too soft" representation of the Japanese (Ni 2003, 8). Critics, including many on the 2003 committee for the most prestigious Chinese film awards, the Golden Rooster, considered this a major problem that "damages the film's nationalistic feelings, especially at a time that the Japanese right-wing force is reckless." They asked why Qingwen cannot meet his mother in Hong Kong (Tan 2003, 34–35). Zhang, ironically with Huang's help, had to repeatedly explain that the historical complexities were beyond these critics' imagination: the secret reunion could not have happened in Hong Kong because the KMT had an intense presence there (e.g., Huang et al. 2004, 6; Huang 2004, 56–57).

Despite these criticisms, *Wangshi* still earned artistic acclaim and political praise in the PRC. But the film was a box office failure (Gao 2003, 93). Neither the artistic nor the political pursuit for purity seemed to help attract viewers. As the Independence Movement thrived in Taiwan, the PRC needed to create a more popular appeal for its call for nationalist unification. The 2006 film *Yunshui Yao*, which also features a Taiwan story by Zhang Kehui, differs from Zheng Dongtian's *wenren dianying* in that it is a *dapian* (lit. "mega-production"), or a commercially produced blockbuster. A significant portion of the film's investments came from private companies, including those in Taiwan and Hong Kong, and the film features a cross-strait all-star cast. Later developments in this *dapian* and co-production trend even recruited John Woo, an internationally recognized Hong Kong and Hollywood director, to direct one of the PRC's leitmotif Taiwan subject films, *Taiping Lun* (The Crossing, 2014).

Wangshi, therefore, initiated an era in which the PRC's cinematic representations of Taiwan have become increasingly complex. The complexity derives from a multipartite tension among the state, the filmmakers, and the market. On the one hand, the state must insistently propagate its simple and rigid Taiwan policy. On the other hand, the state must also rely on the artists and the market for the quality and effectiveness of the propaganda. As I have shown, both filmmakers and markets constantly deviate from rigid state policies for various reasons, producing complexities and compromises. As a result, the cinematic leitmotif of Taiwan has never really created the spiritual resonance of a sentiment "shared by all."

Notes

1 As Taiwan was not open to PRC filmmakers, *Wangshi* was mostly shot in the Fujian province of the PRC. Had the filmmakers had the choice to shoot in Taiwan, however, they might still have chosen the rural areas of Fujian as a main shooting site. These areas actually offer more visual likeness to the Japanese occupied Taiwan, where the film story is set, than does today's Taiwan, which

has transformed significantly during its modernization process. Some Taiwanese directors made the same choice for their Taiwan stories, including Hou Hsiao-Hsien, whose works as discussed in this chapter greatly influenced *Wangshi*.

2 As defined by Yipeng Shen, the so-called Chinese "leitmotif films" refer to "a state-sponsored genre of mainland Chinese national cinema that is produced by state-affiliated film-makers and promotes official ideologies," such as, in the context of Huang's criticism, party-centric patriotism and nationalism (Shen 2015, 104).

3 The *Taimeng* is the smallest of the eight minor parties in the PRC. All these minor parties must accept the leading role of the CCP and hence are essentially parts of the one-party state.

4 To be precise, Huang does mention that he invested his script royalties into the film as well. Private funds like this, however, would be insignificant.

References

Assayas, Olivier. 1996. *HHH, portrait de Hou Hsiao-hsien*. Paris: An AMIP (Paris)/Hsu Hsiao Ming Film Corp. (Taipei) Co-Production, in Association with La Sept/Arte, INA, Chinese Public Television (Taiwan), Arc Light Films, PTS (Paris: International sales: Doc & Co.).

Chen, Po-hsi. 2019. ""Chanting Slogans with Muted Voice": Lan Bozhou's "Song of the Covered Wagon" and Untimely Leftist Reportage in Taiwan." *Modern Chinese Literature and Culture* 31 (2): 81–128.

Gao, Qiao. 2003. "Taiwan wangshi vs. Beiqing chengshi [My Bittersweet Taiwan vs. A City of Sadness]." *Wenhua yuekan [Culture]* (11): 92–93.

Hu, Xiaoyan. 2021. *The Aesthetics of Qiyun and Genius: Spirit Consonance in Chinese Landscape Painting and Some Kantian Echoes*. Lanham: Lexington Books.

Huang, Dan. 2002. ""Qingzhenyiqie" de zhongguo dianying [Making Chinese films with Genuine and Sincere Feelings]." In *WTO yu zhongguo dianying* [WTO and Chinese Cinema], edited by Zhenqin Zhang and Yuanying Yang, 139–42. Beijing: Zhongguo dianying chubanshe.

———. 2004. "Xinshouyichu, dishuichuanshi [A Single-Hearted Devotion Can Make Drops of Water Wear a Hole in Stone]." *Beijing dianying xueyuan xuebao [Journal of Beijing Film Academy]* (1): 53–57.

———, Zongguo An, Yin Liang, and Jinzhu Gong, eds. 2004. *Taiwan wangshi: yi bu dianying de dansheng* [My Bittersweet Taiwan: The Birth of a Film]. Beijing: Taihai chubanshe.

Lan, Bozhou. 2012. *Huangmache zhi ge* [Song of the Covered Wagon]. Beijing, China: falü chubanshe.

Li, Wei. 2004. "Wangshi zhi sheng: yingpian Taiwan wangshi luyin chuangzuo tihui [Sound of the Past: Reflections on [My] Sound Mixing Work for the Film My Bittersweet Taiwan]." *Beijing dianying xueyuan xuebao [Journal of Beijing Film Academy]* (1): 62–66.

Lu, Shaoyang. 2003. "Pingshi pusu de 'wenren dianying' [Plain and No-Nonsense 'Literati Films']." *Dangdai dianying [Contemporary Cinema]* 6: 9–12.

Ma, Ning. 2004. "*Taiwan wangshi sheying qiantan* (A Brief Discussion of the Cinematography of My Bittersweet Taiwan)." *Beijing dianying xueyuan xuebao [Journal of Beijing Film Academy]* (1): 58–61.

Ni, Zhen. 2003. "Jiaguo chunqiu qingsi bujue [The Endless Feelings about One's Home Country]." *Dangdai dianying [Contemporary Cinema]* (6): 7–9.

NPCSC. 1979. "Message to the Compatriots in Taiwan." January 1, 1979. Accessed March 5, 2022. https://en.wikisource.org/wiki/Message_to_the_Compatriots_in_Taiwan.

Shen, Yipeng. 2015. *Public Discourses of Contemporary China: The Narration of the Nation in Popular Literatures, Film, and Television*. New York, NY: Palgrave Macmillan.

Tan, Zheng. 2003. "Di 23 jie zhongguon dianying jinjijiang chuping ceji [A Report on the First-Round Reviews for the 23rd Chinese Film Golden Rooster Awards]." *Dianying yishu [Film Art]* (6): 34–38, 98.

Zhang, Kehui. 2001. *Yige Taiwan ren de lianganqing* [Cross-Strait Feelings of a Taiwanese]. Beijing: Taihai chubanshe.

Zheng, Dongtian. 1990. "Beiqing chengshi de dianying xingtai [The Filmic Formation of A City of Sadness]." *Beijing dianying xueyuan xuebao [Journal of Beijing Film Academy]* (2): 28–44.

———. 2004. "Taiwan wangshi daoyan chanshu [Director's Interpretation of My Bittersweet Taiwan]." *Beijing dianying xueyuan xuebao [Journal of Beijing Film Academy]* (1): 50–52.

11

IN THE NAME OF LOVE

Screen Representations of Taiwan Indigenous Peoples (1920s–1940s)

Ting-Wu Cho

In 2017, Professor Dan Streible at New York University invited me to investigate a newsreel listed in the University of South Carolina's Moving Image Research Collections (MIRC) catalogue. It was titled *Wild Men of Formosa* (1921) and had not yet been published online. Months later, I developed my research into a curatorial project of four film clips about the historical representations of Taiwanese Indigenous peoples and presented it at the 11th Orphan Film Symposium at the Museum of the Moving Image in Queens, New York.

"Orphan films" is a term that emerged in the 1990s within the moving image archival community. It was coined to call attention to the precarious condition and risk of irreversible loss of certain noncommercial films that deserved preservation and archival attention (Lukow 1999; Zimmermann 2008, 12). It covers a broad category of films produced "outside of commercial venues and without copyright," including home movies, amateur films, experimental works, educational films, newsreels, and documentaries (Zimmermann 2008, 12). In 1999, as part of the simultaneous efforts of international and regional film archives to refocus film history and archiving efforts on such "subaltern cinemas," film historian Dan Streible and other interdisciplinary colleagues at the University of South Carolina initiated the Orphan Film Symposium, a biennial event that brings together archivists, historians, collectors, and curators of different regions in the world to screen and discuss films that may be considered "at-risk" and are usually underseen (Zimmermann 2008, 12–13).

The theme of the 11th Orphan Film Symposium was "love." Participants were encouraged to show films that invoked creative interpretations and definitions of love, from unseen footage of Albert Einstein and his wife Elsa's joyous visit to Hollywood, restoration of the oldest surviving Chinese film, *Laborer's Love* (1922), Yugoslav newsreels of the Non-Aligned Movement, to the first African American on-screen kiss. With support from Professor Dan Streible, Professor Ray Jiing, MIRC's curator Greg Wilsbacher, and researchers at Taiwan Film Institute (TFI; now Taiwan Film and Audiovisual Institute, TFAI), I curated "Love: A Colonial Project." The screening showcased four Indigenous-themed film clips from 1920s to late 1940s Taiwan, a period when the colonial regimes in Taiwan were in transition from Japan to China, and then to the Republic of China (ROC). This chapter recapitulates and expands on my presentation at the Orphan Film Symposium by historicizing the films and examining their romanticized and exoticized representations of Taiwan

DOI: 10.4324/9781003266952-16

Figure 11.1 Hayun Usaw, the Atayal youth in *Wild Men of Formosa – Outtakes* (1921).

Indigenous people, questioning the pedagogical intentions in these colonial projects produced *in the name of love*.

Colonial Projects in the Name of Love

Taiwan, marked as "Fremosa/Fermosa" in mid-16th-century Portuguese maps, and later
known as "Formosa" by the European maritime empires, had a long history of encounters
with colonizers from the Dutch Republic, Spanish Empire, and China (Kua 2020, 340).
For explorers and missionaries from the West and bureaucrats from the Qing dynasty, the
Indigenous peoples on the island had always been observed with a sense of detached wonder – a "living tableau of queerness" as Edward Said puts it (1979, 103; Huang 2005, 440).

After its defeat in the First Sino-Japanese War, the Qing government ceded Taiwan to
Japan in 1895. At the time, Taiwan was described by Li Hongzhang, the viceroy of Zhili
and minister of Beiyang of the Qing dynasty, as a wild land with "Indigenous peoples whose
headhunting practices threatens the economic development" (Yanaihara 2022, 61–62). The
incoming government-general of Taiwan (GGT) was seriously concerned about the viability of retaining administrative control over Taiwan; unceasing anti-Japanese uprisings
in Taiwan, combined with unrest in the mainland and financial distress, led to a debate
in the Japanese Diet about selling Taiwan to another country (Yanaihara 2022, 56–57).
Eventually, Taiwan was kept for its military significance in Japan's southern expansion
operation (Ido 2000, 205). Taiwan's uncultivated state was also a perfect proving ground:
successful colonial rule over Taiwan would demonstrate that Japan had become one of the
most potent modern nation-states equal to the Western powers (Chen and Hsiao 2009,
113; Yanaihara 2022, 61). To exert full control over Taiwan's mountain areas, the GGT

combined aggressive military oppression with policies that emphasized the government's "parental love" toward its "less enlightened children" (Chen and Hsiao 2009, 120; Wu 2021, 94–112). This approach was intended to develop a loving, harmonious, and nurturing relationship between the Japanese and the Indigenous peoples.

Film, a revolutionary technology arising from the 20th-century modern experience, was the most effective medium for colonial empires to disseminate political messages and to showcase the successful administration of their colonies. For example, as discussed in Daw-Ming Lee's seminal works on early film cultures in Taiwan, the earliest film about Taiwanese society and culture is *Taiwan jikkyō shōkai* (Introducing Current Situations of Taiwan, 1907), a propaganda documentary made by Takamatsu Toyojiro upon the invitation of the GGT in 1907 to introduce Taiwan as a "model colony of the world" to the Japanese mainland (Lee 2012, 4). The film was shot in 206 locations around Taiwan, and the presence of Taiwan's Indigenous peoples is significant, seen in sections showing Indigenous trading posts, power stations, and dam constructions in the Indigenous territories, and reenactments of the process of the Japanese government's pacification of the Indigenous tribes.

Since then, the Indigenous peoples in Taiwan have not been able to escape being portrayed in documentaries and narrative films as the subject of the colonial government's civilizing mission or an exotic Other that enriches the romantic imagination of the southern island (Lee 2012, 4; 80–93; Misawa 2002). However, when the Taiwanese Indigenous peoples began to construct their own histories with the rise of Indigenous movements in the 1980s, these same moving images produced by the colonizers became historical evidence that helped remap their migration and family histories and to understand how they were governed, controlled, and imagined in ways that legitimized the colonial processes.

In the following paragraphs, I will analyze the four clips I selected for my Orphan Film presentation. These rarely seen clips were produced before, during, and after the World War II and by different modern empires: the US, Japan, and the Republic of China (ROC). The first clip is a silent newsreel from Fox News shot in 1921. The second is a sound newsreel from Fox Movietone News made in 1930. The two Fox newsreels were produced to understand Japan as a rising imperial power in the East. The third clip is a part of the propaganda film series, *Nanshin Taiwan* (Southward Expansion to Taiwan 1937–45), produced during the Imperialization (Japanization) period to promote Taiwan as a base for military advancement toward Southeast Asia. The fourth clip contains fragments from *Alishan Fengyun* (Happenings in Ali Shan 1950), one of the earliest Chinese-language feature films made in Taiwan after the Kuomintang (KMT) government reclaimed Taiwan.

The four clips demonstrate how the US, Japan, and the ROC used news films, propaganda films, and commercial feature films to collect information and secure their own versions of colonial discourse. In these films the Indigenous peoples of Taiwan are explored, re-named, re-imagined, and exhibited through curious and supposedly loving "imperial eyes" (Pratt 2007, 9; Tsai 2012, 100). They are devoid of their own voices and complicated cultures, and their representations are deeply involved in the competing narratives of the imperial powers.

1. Wild Men of Formosa – Outtakes *(USA, Fox News 1921, 4:10 Mins.)*

Wild Men of Formosa – Outtakes is Fox News' travelogue-style footage about the news team's early investigation of the so-called Wild Men of Formosa – the Atayals in the Jiaoban Mountain area in northern Taiwan.

Since the final newsreel is lost, it is unclear whether these "outtakes" were screened in public. However, according to the description from the MIRC Digital Collections, the silent footage was filmed in December 1921, plausibly for Fox News' major news beat, "Face to Face With Japan," to inform the American public about the rising Pacific empire and, more importantly, to help assess if Japan's expansion would threaten American interests (*Motion Picture News* 1922, 1255).[1] In an article in the *Motion Picture News* about the release of "Face to Face With Japan," Japan is observed as a mysterious oriental civilization, about to be unveiled for its ambition and preparation for war. Representation of Indigenous peoples in Japan's colony, Taiwan, is particularly effective in creating such a narrative. The production of this news project took months, sending Fox's star cameraperson Al Brick on a journey of "more than 6,000 miles over stretches of land inhabited in many sections of [*sic*] barbarous tribes under the military control of Japan, and into portions of the world never before photographed or entered by civilized white men" (*Motion Picture News* 1922, 1255).

The newsreel was shot in the Jiaoban Mountain area in northwest Taiwan, where the Atayal communities were located. This was an area of rich natural resources and military importance, leading the Japanese to build military bases nearby to suppress the fierce resistance of the Atayal people and introduce education, medical facilities, and new trading systems to assimilate the Indigenous peoples. Soon, the area became the "model Indigenous community" for official visits, tourism, and the foreign press (Chang 2017, 98–105).

The footage contains several shots in different locations, in which the Atayal people can be seen standing next to their primitive huts in traditional clothing, working as guides for Japanese anthropologists, studying in the Japanese school and classroom, and learning to work in the paddy fields under the guidance of a Japanese police officer. On the paper record (known as the "dope sheet") regarding this footage, Al Brick had kept detailed notes about each shot including the lifestyle of the "headhunters" and the Japanese government's policies to "civilize" them through farming and education (Brick 1921a). The camera lingers on the exotic clothing and facial tattoos of the Indigenous people, fulfilling the Westerner's curiosity about the barbaric islanders of the Far East while displaying Japan's modernization and imperial ambition.

As historian Harry Liebersohn notes, "the concern with clothing was a longstanding one in the history of European-Indigenous relations . . . In the nineteenth century, observers regularly signaled approval or disapproval by describing the Western or non-Western attire of native peoples" (2016, 385). The reform of clothing as evidence of civilization is demonstrated at the end of the film; we see a shot of two Atayal "headhunters" with facial tattoos, looking into the camera, both in their traditional garb and carrying large hunting knives, one smoking a bamboo tobacco pipe. This shot gradually dissolves into that of an Atayal youth with short slicked-back hair wearing a three-piece suit complete with a bowtie and starched collar. Upon what seems to be the request of the cameraman, the young Atayal nods and puts his fedora hat on, looking stiffly into the camera. A simple visual binary of primitive versus civilized is thus constructed through this montage. Considering the montage belongs to a series of "outtakes," it might be a pre-conceived plan by cameraman Al Brick, executed in an in-camera dissolve.

According to Al Brick's notes, the Atayal youth wearing the suit was leaving for Japan for higher education (Brick 1921a). With the assistance of the Atayal people living in the same region, I identified the name of this young man in suit: Hayun Usaw. He was one of the few Indigenous elites in Taiwan who graduated from the Taiwan Governor's Medical School and later became a community doctor (Chang 2009, 3–18). The scene was perhaps shot before he embarked on the "aborigines sightseeing tour" – an assimilation program designed by the Japanese government wherein Indigenous peoples from different tribes, usually tribal leaders or intellectuals, were selected to visit Japan's mainland or other parts of Taiwan. Besides education and the civilizing mission, the main purpose of the sightseeing tours was for deterrence against any potential uprising by displaying Japan's modern infrastructures, culture, naval industry, and most importantly, advanced arsenal (Chen, n.d.).

The series of "outtakes" as a whole demonstrates a modern Japan with political and military prowess on par with the leading Western nations in the world; its successful civilizing project of Taiwan's Indigenous peoples – the barbaric and warlike headhunters – marks the rise of an Asian empire with cultural and military dominance, making them a potential threat not to be underestimated. The montage in the end is an extremely powerful device, especially when the image of Atayal men in traditional apparel dissolves into the modern look of young Hayun Usaw in full Western formal attire. The temporary overlapping of the two images creates a haunting effect, as if the ghostly figure of the past is clinging onto a future generation erased of its own culture and history.

2. Formosa Aborigines *(USA, Fox Movietone News 1930, 17:50 Mins.)*

The second clip, named in the MIRC collection as *Formosa Aborigines*, is from a sound newsreel by Fox Movietone News released on 12 March 1930 with the title *Movietone Invades Wilds of Far East*. The Fox Movietone News team was introduced by Tanaka Kinshi, or Edward "Eddie" Tanaka, to make sound newsreels about the development of Taiwan (Lee 2013, 337–38).

In the first part of the film one can see the local Atayal people, referred to as the "newly civilized aborigines," bringing bamboo and textiles to the trading post to exchange for manufactured goods. One thing to be noted is that the music accompanying the title card is not the Atayal traditional music. The four-beat *"thump*-thump-thump-thump" (heavy accent on the first beat) rhythm and the dissonant tritone sounds used here fit the musical schemes used in American cinema to signal the appearance of the Indigenous Americans, which is a combination of misconception and aural stereotyping of Indigenous Americans that facilitates the construction of an unsettling Other (Yang 2015, 25–31). By assigning the same stereotypical aural notes as the hint for Taiwan's Indigenous people, the soundtrack does not bring the moving images closer to reality but amplifies the clichéd representation of a mysterious and savage Otherness from the perspective of a Western empire: the imperial gaze of Fox Movietone is indeed "invading" the "wilds of Far East."

In the second scene, a Japanese policeman is giving a speech to a group of Atayal people. The title card explains: "Japanese officer lectures the former head-hunters on hygiene and thrift through boy interpreter." However, this is inaccurate and a mistranslation of the Japanese spoken in the footage. The speech is actually about the need to systemize local sericulture farming. The speech, which is clearly rehearsed and staged, compares the traditional sericulture of the Indigenous peoples with the modernized facilities and methods instructed by the Japanese, which they must follow in order to yield good results for the following season.

3. Nanshin Taiwan: Taitō chō *(Japan, 1937–45)*

The third clip I screened at Orphans is a section from a seven-volume propaganda documentary series titled *Nanshin Taiwan*. The series shot on 35 mm film was discovered in 2003 together with a group of old films from a private collector in southern Taiwan (Chiu 2016, 13). In order to preserve the already deteriorated films, the National Museum of Taiwan History bought them and worked with Professor Ray Jiing from Tainan National University of the Arts to restore these films (Jiing 2006).

Nanshin Taiwan was supported by the GGT and produced during the Imperialization period (1937–1945) (Tsai 2012, 114–15). The series takes the audience on a "round island tour," introducing the landscape, natural resources, infrastructure, agricultural and industrial development, and people's daily lives in seven regions of Taiwan (Jiing 2006, 44). It was made to promote imperial Japan's "South Advancing Policy" – a strategic plan to modernize Taiwan as the military and economic base for Japan to expand control over Southeast Asia in the Pacific War (Tsai 2012, 114–15).

The part I selected for screening is from volume 7, which largely focuses on *Taitō chō* (now Taitung City), a region on the east coast of Taiwan. The first scene that introduces the Indigenous peoples in Taitung is the traditional circle dance. The dance, usually performed during sacrificial ceremonies or harvest celebrations, has long been a part of the conventional iconography of Taiwan's Indigenous cultures. However, the scene is devoid of any sense of celebration or festivity. While the women are dancing on the screen, there is only monotonous percussion sound and the narrator's voice in the background. The narrator acknowledges the performativity of the documentary by noting that the girls dancing are members of Indigenous youth groups who originally declined the request to perform because they did not want to be stereotyped and because "they had to stop working for one day, which might impair their village's prosperity."

Compared to the Fox newsreels in 1921 and 1930, this footage of *Nanshin Taiwan* suggests a new phase of the GGT's Indigenous policies, with more drastic changes in the Indigenous youths' lifestyle and identification. The Second Sino-Japanese War had led to an acceleration of Taiwan' industrialization, exploitation of resources in the areas originally preserved for Indigenous tribes, and a shortage in agricultural manpower (Kondo 2019, 289). To further utilize the natural resources and redistribute the labor force, the GGT relocated the Indigenous peoples from their original highland areas to lowland regions with high demands of manpower, forcing them to abandon their traditional hunting and shifting cultivation practices for intensive wet rice farming and providing labor for corporate plantations (Li 2001, 202). Since 1940, more than 2,000 Indigenous people were relocated from Takao chō (now Kaohsiung City) to Taitō chō (Kondo 2019, 278–79).

Since 1937, the GGT's Indigenous policies had turned from interventionism and protectionism to developing self-reliance and autonomy of the Indigenous peoples (Kondo 2019, 307). The GGT began to withdraw subsidies for the relocation projects, imposing taxes and encouraging donations and volunteers to the Japanese military (Kondo 2019, 289–90; Fu 2014). Indigenous self-support groups and youth groups were established to gradually replace the tribal leaders, helping their people get used to the Japanese lifestyle in the lowlands and more importantly, to train them to be useful citizens and be mobilized as members of the Japanese empire (Chang 2007, 4–5; Gusing 2021). As the narrator in the *Nanshin Taiwan* clip reports,

> The Indigenous peoples now have a clear tendency to escape their primitive lifestyle and move towards a life of economic prosperity. They put all their hard work in preserving the paddy fields; they are happy to engage in various types of labor work and have learned the virtue of diligence and frugality. Many of them are graduates from colleges or universities; some have become policemen or teachers.
>
> *(Translated from Japanese by the author)*

As historian Masami Kondo notes, the GGT's assimilation policies transformed Indigenous peoples into obedient farmers and fundamentally destroyed their social and economic structures (2019, 312). While for the Indigenous, their only hope for survival was to live as Japanese citizens; for the Japanese government the promotion of "self-reliance and autonomy" was a way to let the Indigenous peoples destroy their own cultures, identities, and values, replacing them with those of the ruling authority (Kondo 2019, 312). To illustrate, in a scene where Indigenous girls are wearing kimonos, the narrator explains that Indigenous youths identify themselves as "Japanese" now.

4. Alishan Fengyun *(ROC 1950)*

The last part of my curated screening program presented excerpts from *Alishan Fengyun*, a film made in another watershed moment of the Chinese Civil War, when the Nationalist government relocated to Taiwan. After Taiwan's handover from Japan to China in 1945, there was a "Taiwan fever" in Shanghai – the production center of Chinese-language cinema. Film companies were curious about the newly recovered, exotic island. Films such as *Chang Xiang Si* (Woman Without a Face 1947), *Jiamian Nülang* (Girl's Mask 1947), and *Hualian Gang* (The Hualien Port 1948), all include scenes from location shooting in Taiwan (Chen 2014). In January 1949, Cathay Film in Shanghai sent Zhang Ying and a location shooting team to Taiwan for the shooting of *Alishan Fengyun*. They were on a ship crammed with refugees fleeing Shanghai (Taiwan Film and Audiovisual Institute n.d.; Lan 2007, 60–71). However, in April, the People's Liberation Army arrived in Shanghai, leading to the postponement of the shooting of the film, and the crew that was already in Taiwan were *orphaned* on the island (Taiwan Film and Audiovisual Institute n.d.; Lan 2007, 60–71). Eventually, producer Hsu Hsin-Fu and director Zhang Ying and Chang Cheh shot the film with the Cathay Film crew left in Taiwan and members from the KMT's military drama troupes (Chen 2014).

Alishan Fengyun, originally titled *Wu Feng Chuan* (The Legend of Wu Feng), is based on the myth of Wu Feng. Little is documented about the real life of Wu Feng, a Qing official liaison in charge of affairs regarding the "barbarians" in Taiwan, who was killed in a conflict with the Tsou people. Under Japanese colonial rule, the myth of Wu Feng was intentionally constructed by Japanese officials to justify governance by foreign colonizers with their "civilizing" intention and to pacify the Indigenous resistance movement in Alishan for access to cypress wood and water resources (Chen 1991; Fu 2005, 507). In the pedagogical tale, Wu Feng was a benevolent, selfless Han Chinese who sacrificed himself to dissuade the Tsou people from their headhunting custom. The story was included in elementary school textbooks in Japan, Taiwan, and Korea and turned into monuments, songs, plays, and a Japanese feature film (*Gijin Gohō* 1932). In *Alishan Fengyun*, the story of Wu Feng is made more entertaining by introducing the struggles between two lovers from different Indigenous tribes and adding catchy melodies and songs performed by Taiwan's Indigenous peoples. Interestingly, impeded by the lingering fog and dense forest in Alishan, the film crew moved from Central to East Taiwan – Taroko, Hualien – for most of the shooting. The Indigenous dances in the film were performed by the Amis in Hualien, rather than the Tsou in Alishan (Chen 2014).

Alishan Fengyun is not preserved in its entirety. In 2014, TFI curated a retrospective of Zhang Ying and edited the fragmented parts of the film together according to the step outline of the original film. The total running time of this version is only about 46 minutes, with 19 minutes of Cantonese soundtrack. The 4-minute clip I screened contains a musical segment with a famous love song "Gao Shan Qing" ("Mountains Are Green"). It is one of the most well-known pieces of music associated with Taiwan's Indigenous culture, but the creation of the song has little to do with Taiwan's Indigenous people. According to film historian Edward W. Chen, the song, written specifically for the film, is a collaborative work of Chang Cheh, Zhang Ying, Deng Yu-Ping, and Chou Lan-Ping, all of whom were Han Chinese who had just arrived in Taiwan in 1949 (Chen 2014). There are many controversies around the true author of the song; some scholars even suggest that the lyrics written by Deng Yu-Ping were inspired not by Alishan and the Tsou people but by the scenery in his hometown, Sichuan. Whether the speculations are true, one thing is certain: the song is the beginning of the entangled relationship between Indigenous performance and KMT's nation-building project in postwar Taiwan.

Although the original soundtrack of this part of the film is lost, the song "Gao Shan Qing" became so popular that it has been re-recorded and performed by artists of different generations. To recreate the experience of watching *Alishan Fengyun* while screening this clip at the Orphan Film Symposium, I replaced the lost soundtrack with an old recording of the song released in 1950, which might be the closest version to the original film soundtrack.

The scene in which the song is used depicts the encounter of two Indigenous youths in the mountain streams. In many films about Taiwan's Indigenous peoples, especially in the Japanese colonial period and during the Cold War, such as *Sayon No Kane* (1943), *Alishan Zhi Ying* (The Nightingale of Alishan, 1957), and *Lanyu Zhi Ge* (Song of Orchard Island, 1965), Indigenous women are romanticized and exoticized, yet in *Alishan Fengyun*, it is the strong, masculine body of the Indigenous man that is accentuated. This is a signature of Chang Cheh, who later entered Shaw Brothers and revolutionized the martial arts genre by introducing a new masculine paradigm that celebrates staunch male bodies and male-comradeship.

According to recollections of actors who participated in *Alishan Fengyun* and the news advertisement of *Alishan Fengyun*, the traditional circle dance was one of the most anticipated spectacles of the film. In 1951, Chiang Ching-Kuo, then director of political warfare at the Ministry of National Defense, went to Kinmen for inspection and enjoyed the troop's performance of a circle dance to the song "Gao Shan Qing" – a dance inspired by the Amis people in Hualien, who participated in or were influenced by the production of *Alishan Fengyun*. Thinking that the group circle dance was a good way to build solidarity in the army and to boost morale, Chiang demanded more emphasis on dance activities in the troops. The officials started to organize performances and workshops to collect, modify, and promote Indigenous dances for political interests (Huang 2016, 4–6). Since then, the traditional dances of the Indigenous peoples have been appropriated to construct a cultural history dominated by the Han Chinese and to generate nationalist momentum in the Cold War era.

Restoring Imperial Memories as a Decolonizing Method

When viewed collectively, the four orphan films provide a glimpse of the development of colonial rhetoric at different stages of global geopolitical rivalries. The colonial rhetoric works as a key component of the implementation of different, even conflicting, regimes' policies toward Indigenous peoples, policies that systematically destroyed Indigenous cultures in exchange for the colonizers' nationalist aspirations.

In the two Fox News clips, Indigenous peoples are displayed as anthropological subjects, serving the Japanese government's colonial agendas and Fox News' exotic imaginations about a mysterious Asia. However, as demonstrated in the clip of *Nanshin Taiwan*, the discourse of a civilizing mission is malleable and can be developed into a more aggressive form of assimilation that aims at eradicating Indigenous cultures and identifications. After the KMT government reclaimed and retreated to Taiwan, the film *Alishan Fengyun* and its theme song, "Gao Shan Qing," commercialized and popularized the romantic southern imagination and civilizing narrative to solidify and militarize Taiwan for the exiled Chiang Kai-shek regime.

As film historian Ray Jiing asserts, colonized regions often had little or no means to preserve their own moving images. Therefore, in order to see themselves in history and reconstruct their subjectivity, the colonized must first restore the "imperial memories" of the colonizers (Jiing 2006, 47). Besides going into the archives of the colonizers, restoration and preservation of the deteriorated footages are crucial in reconstructing an archive, and finally, subjectivity, that resists the colonial discourse (Jiing 2015).

My orphan film project would not have been possible without these efforts of the archivists and historians, as well as the memories of Indigenous communities to identify lost historical sites, traditions, sounds, and individuals. In other words, the research process of this project is a decolonizing process that inserts *Indigenous memories* into imperial moving images and invites further insights into the persistent colonial rhetoric that permeates Indigenous representations even today.

Note

1 This is before "Fox Movietone News" – newsreels with sound – was introduced in 1928.

References

Brick, Al. 1921a. Dope Sheet Files of A1214. Manuscript. Fox Movietone News Collection. Moving Image Research Collections. University of South Carolina.

Chang, Meng-Hsuan. 2017. "Appeasement, Monitoring to Autonomy – The Formation and Transformation of the System of Mountain Trading from the Early Japanese Colonial Period to the Postwar Period." Master diss., National Taiwan Normal University.

Chang, Yao-Chung. 2007. "Educational Elites vs. Traditional Elites: The Transformation of Taiwan Aboriginal Leadership Institution under the Colonial Education in Japanese Colonial Period." *Taiwan Journal of Sociology of Education* 7, no. 1 (June): 1–27.

———. 2009. "The Indigenous Elites and Tribal Development in the Japanese Colonial Period." *Bulletin of Educational Research* 55 (4): 1–28.

Chen, Chu-Jen. 1991. "Shenhua yingxiong wufeng [Legendary Hero Wu Feng]." In *Wajie de diguo* [The Crumbling Empire], edited by Cho-Shui Lin, 57–104. Taipei: Avangard.

Chen, Chun-Tung. N.d. "Rizhi shiqi shouci fanrenguanguang guishi hou zhuiaong baogao [Report after Returning from the First 'Aborigines Sightseeing Tour' in the Japanese Colonial Period]." *Taiwan Historica*. Accessed March 1, 2023. https://www.th.gov.tw/epaper/site/page/224/3093.

Chen, Edwin W. 2014. "Zatan Alishan Fengyun yu qi chaqu gaoshanqing [On *Alishan fengyun* and the Song Gao Shan Qing]." *Funscreen*, no. 454 (April 14). http://www.funscreen.com.tw/feature.asp?FE_NO=388.

Chen, Kuo-chieh and Wen-chuen Hsiao. 2009. "Aboriginal Images in Taiwanese Visual Art during the Japanese Colonial Period." *Academic Journal of Kang-Ning* (11): 107–26.

Chen, Yi-Hung. 2008. "Guankan de jiaodu: nanjin taiwan jilupian lishi jiexi [Perspectives of Looking: Historicizing Documentary Southward Expansion to Taiwan]." In *Pian ge zhuan dong jian de taiwan xianying: guoli taiwan lishi bowuguan xiufu guan cang ri zhi shiqi jilu yingpian cheng quo* [Image of Taiwan in the Rolling Frames: Restoration of Documents in the Japanese Colonial Period by the National Museum of Taiwan History], edited by Mi-Cha Wu and Ray Jiing, 76–93. Tainan: Museum of Taiwan History.

Chiu, Kuei-fen. 2016. *Kanjian Taiwan: Taiwan xin jilupian yanjiu* [Regarding Taiwan: The New Taiwan Documentary]. Taipei: National Taiwan University Press.

Fu, Chi-Yi. 2014. *Taiwan yuanzhuminzu de jindai riben guojia renting* [Taiwan Indigenous Peoples' Japanese National Identification in Modern Era (1935–1945)]. Taiwan: Japan Research Institute. Accessed March 1, 2023. http://www.japanresearch.org.tw/Column/Column_Fujii_110.html.

Fu, Sue-Chun. 2005. "Ri ju shiqi yianzhumin tuxiang de shengchang ji qi pipanxing ningshi de keneng – yi renleixue shying, wufeng guhsi, shayong zhi zhong wei tanlun duixiang [The Production and the Possibility of Critical Gaze in Indigenous Images in the Japanese Colonial Period]." In *Di wu jie tongsu wenxue yi yazheng wenxue: wenxue yu tuxiang yantaohui lunwenji* [Conference Proceeding of the 5th Conference on Popular and Classic Literature: Literature and Images], 481–523. Department of Chinese Literature, National Chung Hsing University, Taichung City.

Gusing, Pa'elravang. 2021. "You guan gaoshazu zizhuhui huize biaozhun zhi jian [Regarding the Standards for Takasago-zoku Self-Support Groups]." *Newsletter of Taiwan Historica*, no. 213 (December). Accessed March 1, 2022. https://www.th.gov.tw/epaper/site/page/213/2949.

Huang, Guo-Chao. 2016. "Fan gong jiou guo mo wang shan di ge wu [Fighting Communism with Aboriginal Dancing]." *Yuanzhuminzu wenxian [Indigenous Peoples Historica]* (30): 4–10.

Huang, Kuo-Chao. 2005. "Zaixian de zhengzhi – cong zhimin yayi dai zhuti dikang de yuanzhumin xingxiang [Politics of Representation – Indigenous Images from Colonial Oppression to Resisting Subjectivity]." *5th Popular and Classical Literature Conference Proceeding* (5): 437–78.

Ido, Kinjiro. 2000. *Truthful Records of Taiwan*. Translated by Japan Culture Education Foundation. Taipei: Wenyingtang.

Jiing, Ray. 2006. "Zhimin keti yu diguo jiyi: cong xiufu yingpian nanjintaiwan tan jiyi de zhengzhi xue [Colonial Object and Imperial Memory: Politics of Memory in the Restoration of Southward Expansion to Taiwan]." In *Pian ge zhuan dong jian de taiwan xianying: guoli taiwan lishi bowuguan xiufu guan cang ri zhi shiqi jilu yingpian cheng quo* [Image of Taiwan in the Rolling Frames: Restoration of Documents in the Japanese Colonial Period by the National Museum of Taiwan History], edited by Mi-Cha Wu and Ray Jiing, 40–49. Tainan: Museum of Taiwan History.

———. 2015. "Houzhimin fangfa lun: yi yingxiang xiufu chongjian yuanzhu minzu de lishi jiyi [Decolonization Method: Moving Image Restoration to Reconstruct Historical Memories of the Indigenous Peoples]." Transcript of Speech Delivered at the Documentary Festival of Village and Tribes Across the Strait and Conference of Material, Culture, and Industry at Hualien, Tzu Chi University, December, 9–12.

Kondo, Masami. 2019. *Zonglizhan yu Taiwan: riben zhimindi de bengkui* [Total War and Taiwan: Research in the Collapse of Japan's Colonies]. Vol. 1, 3rd ed. Translated by Shih-Ting Lin. Taipei: National Taiwan University Press.

Kua, Paul. 2020. "Portuguese 'Discovery' and 'Naming' of the Formosa Island, 1510–1624: A History Based on Maps, Rutters and Other Documents." *Anais De História De Além-Mar* (21): 307–47.

Lan, Tian-Hong. 2007. *Ba shi zai cangsang hua jiu* [Nostalgic Talk of Vicissitudes in Eighty Years]. Taipei: Sanyi Publishing.

———. 2012. "Representations of Indigenous Peoples in Taiwan in Films and on Television in the Past One Hundred Years." *Yuanzhuminzu wenxian [Indigenous Peoples Historica]*, no. 4 (August): 3–14.

———. 2013. *Historical Dictionary of Taiwan Cinema*. Lanham: The Scarecrow Press.

Li, Wen-liang. 2001. "Diguo de shanlin – rizhi shiqi taiwan shanlin zhengceshi yanjiu [The Empire's Forest: A Research on the History of Taiwan Forest Policies Under the Japanese Rule]." PhD diss., National University of Taiwan.

Liebersohn, Harry. 2016. "Introduction: The Civilizing Mission." *Journal of World History* 27 (3): 383–87. http://www.jstor.org/stable/44631471.

Lukow, Gregory. 1999. "The Politics of Orphanage: The Rise and Impact of the 'Orphan Film' Metaphor on Contemporary Preservation Practice." Delivered at Orphan Film Symposium: Orphans of the Storm: Saving Orphan Films in the Digital Age, University of South Carolina, September 23, 1999. https://www.academia.edu/747012/_The_Politics_of_Orphanage_The_Rise_and_Impact_of_the_Orphan_Film_Metaphor_on_Contemporary_Preservation_Practice_.

Misawa, Mamie. 2002. *Zhimindi xia de yinmu: Taiwan zongdufu dianying zhengce zhi yanjiu* [The Colonial Silver Screen: Studies on the Policy of the Government-General in Taiwan]. Taipei: Avanguard.

Pratt, Mary Louise. 2007. *Imperial Eyes: Travel Writing and Transculturation*. 2nd ed. London: Routledge. https://doi-org.proxy.library.nyu.edu/10.4324/9780203932933.

"Remarkable Beat for Fox News." *Motion Picture News*, February 25, 1922, 1255.

Said, Edward. 1979. *Orientalism*. New York: Vintage Books.

Taiwan Film and Audiovisual Institute. N.d. "Dianying da shi ji 1949–1950 [Taiwan Film History 1949–1950]." Accessed March 1, 2023. https://openmuseum.tw/muse/exhibition/31433c802eea1 8dc519230a84065e24f#basic-to3vn68pbh.

Tsai, Chin-Tong. 2012. "Going Southward to Taiwan: Documentary as Imperial Eyes." *Taiwan, A Radical Quarterly in Social Studies*, no. 86 (March): 99–132. https://doi.org/10.29816/TARQSS.201203.0004.

Wu, Cheng-hsien. 2021. "Between a Constable and a Section Chief: Uno Hidekazu's Recipe for Aboriginal Administration (1896–1923)." *Chung Hsing Journal of Humanities*, no. 66 (March): 81–144.

Yanaihara, Tadao. 2022. *Diguo zhuyi xia de taiwan* [Taiwan Under Imperialism]. Translated by Huang Shaw-Herng. New Taipei City: Common Master Press/Walkers Cultural Enterprise.

Yang, Kaiyuan. 2015. "Savages and Romantics: How Hollywood Soundtracks Construct Native Americans." *Folio* 12: 25–31. https://foliojournal.wordpress.com/2015/01/21/savages-and-romantics-how-hollywood-soundtracks-construct-native-americans-by-yang-kaiyuan/.

Zhang, Ying, and Cheh Chang. 1950. *Alishan fengyun*. Wan Xiang Motion Picture, Taiwan Film and Audiovisual Institute, 4K Scan.

Zimmermann, Patricia R. 2008. "Introduction: The Home Movie Movement: Excavations, Artifacts, Minings." In *Mining the Home Movie: Excavations in Histories and Memories*. 1st ed., edited by Patricia R. Zimmermann and Karen L. Ishizuka, 1–28. University of California Press. http://www.jstor.org/stable/10.1525/j.ctt1pp9gx.6.

12

DESIRING NANYANG, NATION, AND HOME

Fictions of Belonging in Two Rediscovered Postwar Films from Singapore

Elizabeth Wijaya

Before they were located in 2016 by the Asian Film Archive (AFA) in the China Film Archive (CFA), *Huaqiao xuelei* (Blood and Tears of the Overseas Chinese, dir. Tsai Wen-chin 1946), and *Haiwai zhenghun* (Spirit of the Overseas Chinese, dir. Wan Hoi-ling 1946), were believed to be lost. Produced by *Zhong hua dianying zhi pian chang* (Zhong Hua Film), *Huaqiao xuelei* and *Haiwai zhenghun* are Singapore's earliest post-war Chinese-language feature films from an understudied time in the island nation's film history. According to Chew Tee Pao, archivist at the AFA, the archive had "put out several calls for film elements during the AFA's Lost Films Search (2006) and Save Our Film campaign (2010) to the public and through the AFA's professional networks but to no avail" (Chew Tee Pao, email to author, March 9, 2021). It was only when Chew attended a training course at the British Film Institute and connected with members of the CFA, that the prints of the two films were finally located. Both films were then restored by the CFA and subtitled by the AFA.

Independent of the AFA's efforts, the CFA provided the Hong Kong Film Archive (HKFA) with a reference disc copy of *Haiwai zhenghun* in November 2013 and the HKFA screened the film on March 15th, 2014 in a program titled "Re-discovering Pioneering Females in Early Chinese Cinema." Frank Bren cites Wan Hoi-ling as "the territory's first-known homegrown female film director," of whom much remains unknown (2014, 173). Within this claim of "homegrown" status lie Wan Hoi-ling's contributions to cinema and a transnational trajectory across China, Hong Kong, and Singapore. A key concern of this chapter is the possibility of thinking "home" capaciously, beyond the index of national cinema. Bren notes that while most of Wan Hoi-ling's filmography is lost, a collection of her film scripts remain at the New York State Archives (NYSA) in Albany, New York (2014, 175–83). Narratives of Wan Hoi-ling's life are often traced through her work and life with the groundbreaking film theorist, novelist, and director Hou Yao. In 1940, Hou and Wan, partners in work and life, moved to Singapore from Hong Kong and produced seven Malay-language films for the Singapore-based Shaw Brothers Limited. They were in captivity from 1942 to 1945 during the Japanese occupation of Singapore. Hou was executed during that period. After her release, Wan made *Haiwai zhenghun* (1946) and *Nanyang xiaojie* (Miss Nanyang, 1947), and the latter film remains to be found.

DOI: 10.4324/9781003266952-17

HKFA's "rediscovery" and screening of *Haiwai zhenghun* show that the unsettled narratives and gendered dimension of Wan Hoi-ling's transnational legacies transcend national cinema frameworks, recalling Jean Ma's observation on "the constitutive impurity and seriality of the concept of national cinema" (2010, 82). Frank Bren has done significant work in reclaiming Wan Hoi-ling's pioneering status as a woman filmmaker. With the restoration of Wan's work, there is time yet for more scholarship on this topic. My focus here is the alluring ambiguity of the nation at the heart of both films. Scholars such as Chris Berry (2021), Yingjin Zhang (2010), and Sheldon Lu (1997) have done field-defining work on Chinese cinemas from a transnational standpoint. Recent years have seen increased interest in remapping and retheorizing the local and the regional. Two notable works are Sangjoon Lee's *Cinema and the Cultural Cold War* (2020) and Rosalind Galt's *Alluring Monsters* (2021). Galt engages Malaysian and Singapore visual cultures "in a way that is politically located without being limited to the local" (2021, 198). Yet, in qualification criteria for film funding, in announcements of film exhibitions such as film festivals, and even in some course syllabi, the nation form frequently returns to haunt like an undying ghost, as if it was an eternal spirit rather than a contingent, historically determined entity with internal instabilities. This chapter seeks to shine light on the nation form's forceful illusions in moments of historical transition.

Alluring Fictions

In the 1930s, a film movement in China known as "national defense cinema" responded to the Second Sino-Japanese war by making state-sponsored films to provoke anti-Japanese sentiment, resistance, and mass mobilization (Bao 2015, 276). The inaugural film of this movement is generally regarded as Fei Mu's *Lang shan die xue ji* (Blood on Wolf Mountain, 1936). Wan Hoi-ling worked as assistant director and screenwriter for Hou Yao's national defense film, *Taipingyang shang de fengyun* (Storm Over the Pacific, 1938). The ideological influence of national defense cinema and the trauma of the recent war are discernible in *Haiwai zhenghun* and *Huaqiao xuelei*, which both end with images of tombstones of the heroically deceased.

Even if the film reels, the exchanges that made the film restorations possible, and the rights to access the filmic material, are housed within film archives as networks of national and nation-linked institutions, must a film belong as if it has quasi-citizenship within a nation-state? While film restoration projects are often transnational collaborations, collaborations between national archives with clearly delimited responsibilities and rights could perpetuate rather than question the primacy of the nation form. What then of the transgressive possibilities of transnational exchange, beyond that of collaborative relations between nations? Certainly, transnational film restorations are usually the work of multiple institutions that could be private or public entities. The non-profit organization, Film Foundation, that runs the World Cinema Project led by Martin Scorsese, and the privately held company, Criterion Collection, are two examples of prominent institutions that collaborate with archives around the world and film laboratories such as L'Immagine Ritrovata in Italy, for film restoration projects that could be auteur or theme-based. The geopolitics and poetics of the selection criteria, budget, and practice of transnational film restorations with respect to the entanglements of national, historical, and aesthetic interests deserve closer study. The question I focus on here: could the renewed lives of *Huaqiao xuelai* and *Haiwai zhenghun* and a re-examination of both films' affective engagement with the nation form, and ways of figuring commonality and differences reveal the porosity of the physical and symbolic borders of the modern nation-state? From regional to transnational and diaspora analysis, a decades-long debate has taken place over the definition and significance of "overseas Chinese" in the context of Chinese migration in modern times (Purcell 1951; Suryadinata 1997; Kuhn 2008; Wang 2001; McKeown 2001; Chan 2018). Taomo Zhou counts the "overseas Chinese" as those who lived outside the contemporary territories of the PRC, Taiwan, Hong Kong, and Macau, which includes "Chinese nationals (in Chinese, *huaqiao*), foreign citizens who are ethnically Chinese (*huaren*), as well as those whose citizenship status was uncertain" (2019, 5). Each definition of "Chinese" is traceable to contestations over the scope and sovereignties of a nation. What appear to be taxonomic concerns reveal the frictions between life captured under inscribed, conditional boundaries and the non-identitarian possibilities of life. Rather than argue for a new definition of overseas Chinese that would be relevant to these two films, my interest is in the encounters within the films' diegeses between groups of people identified through the co-implication of race and nation. Insofar as the colonial racial identities of Chinese, Malay, Indian, and "others" in Singapore persist in the state management of race today, the problematics of racialization underpin the films' focus on the overseas Chinese and nation-making in Nanyang. We see this in *Huaqiao Xuelei*'s antagonist Zhao Da Ma's racist attempt to distinguish between categories of people based on physiognomy, including the Nanyang people and the Chinese. It is also latent in *Haiwai Zhenghun*'s settler dream of an idyllic Nanyang as a desirable second home, with no interest in the presence and significance of the non-Chinese in Singapore. In other words, race is salient precisely because non-Chinese considerations are absent and also because the contested category of the overseas Chinese within Singapore forms part of broader categories of racial management (Hirschman 1987).

One path to thinking cinema beyond the nation is exemplified by Ariella Azoulay's proposal that forms of co-citizenship can be untethered from the modern concept of citizenship within the nation-state. In her provocative work, visual citizenship under the civil contract of photography becomes an alternative possibility for "becoming a citizen in the citizenry of photography" (Azoulay 2008, 110). In Azoulay's rehabilitation of modern citizenship's failures, photography must be "watched" in a manner that activates the "dimensions of time and movement," thus creating a cinema-like durational space of appearance in which the excluded could appear or be addressed (Azoulay 2008, 14). Among others, Gil Hochberg has questioned the extent to which Azoulay's belief in the political promise of the photographic event and the watchful citizen relies on an exchange of gazes that presumes the possibility of recognition and ethical obligation between the photographed and spectator, while understating the unequal power dynamics of witnessing when it comes to who has access to the camera that produces the photographic scene and who gets to become a witness of the photograph (2015, 104). Hannah Arendt warns us that those who are excluded from citizenship in nation-states fall into a fundamental exclusion of invisibility in which the stateless have nowhere to politically appear and claim the protection of human rights (Arendt 1973, 299). Like Wan, Arendt wrote in the aftermath of World War II; the shadow of recent wars and the question of home and homelessness loom large in their works. If photographic or cinematic events, with their respective reliance on inequalities and invisibilities, cannot guarantee the existence of an alternative, democratic space of citizenship between equals, could they still do more than critique the inadequacies of the existing order?

Both films were produced in a period of decolonization and nation-forming. The changes in legalized relations to a country are accompanied by shifting senses of affective relations to its imagined pasts and futures. We see in *Haiwai zhenghun* and *Huaqiao xue-lei* encounters between floating signifiers who remain haunted by colonial-racial categories or phantasies of ethnic or geopolitical co-belonging. The repeat invocation of the nation in the dialogue of both films suggest ritualistic desires to call the nation into being while the forms of the nation being invoked were still in flux. Over-the-top patriotic speeches in both films can be seen as performances of chasing after a slippery object of desire that was always disjunctive even from its incipient moments (and also in the inherent contradictions between nationalism that relies on fundamental forms of exclusion in order to promote structures and feelings of inclusion). It is precisely the non-sustainable fictions of the nation that demand careful maintenance through regular invocation as well as very real bodily sacrifice.

On a chronological timeline, *Huaqiao xuelei* and *Haiwai zhenghun* were made in the gap between the end of World War II in 1945 and the official start of the Cold War in 1947, with 1947 being the year that the Marshall Plan was proposed by the United States with the aim of preventing the spread of communism, and the launch of Pax Americana, a period where the military and economic power of America would guarantee "international peace." Naoki Sakai has reminded us that despite its name and stated intentions, Pax Americana was "exceptionally bloody even after World War II and succeeded in prolonging the basic colonial-imperial order of the modern international world" (2022, 2). On an existential timeline, what these films from 1946 show is the durational continuity and messiness that belie beginnings and endings.

When both films were released in 1946, China was on the cusp of a sea change with intense civil war prior to the shift from Republican China (1911–49) to Communist China (1949). Through the principle of *jus sanguinis*, the nationality law created by the Qing government in 1909 claimed the children of Chinese citizens (mainly through patrilineal lineage) as Chinese citizens (Zhou 2019, 25; Carnell 1952, 505; Purcell 1951, 150). Postwar Singapore was also at the beginning of multiple shifts in governance with the British Military Administration governing the island until March 1946, the dissolving of the Straits Settlement in April 1946, and Singapore becoming a separate Crown colony with the gradual transition to self-governance in the 1950s. F.G. Carnell writes on the evolution of Malayan citizenship in the postwar administrative disarray where the British colonial administration wanted to unify and foster loyalty to Malaya (1952, 505). It was in 1946 that all Malayan territories were brought under a unified administration, while "Singapore, with its three quarters of a million Chinese, was kept apart as a Colony in order to give the Malays a majority in the Union" (1952, 507). In June 1948, the British administration declared the Malayan Emergency, which extended to Singapore. Suspected communist sympathizers of Chinese ethnicity could be detained and repatriated to China without right of appeal. The repatriations started during intense civil war between the Nationalists and the Communists. The repatriates were frequently neither welcomed by the Nationalists nor the Communists. Choo Chin Low notes that Singapore enquired about "the possibility of using Hong Kong as a transit point for Malayan deportees en route either to Formosa (Taiwan) or Canton" but the governor of Hong Kong refused "on the grounds of political uncertainty" (Low 2014, 374).

1. Haiwai Zhenghun *and the Nanyang Dream*

Haiwai zhenghun begins in the period just before the Japanese Occupation of Malaya and Singapore (1941–45) and ends in its immediate aftermath. Two cousins, Zhong Guo Cai and Zhong Ai Hua, flee the ongoing Second Sino-Japanese War in China and travel to Singapore by ship in order to take refuge in the home of their uncle Xu Weng. As they approach their uncle's house by rickshaw, the newly arrived migrants witness unnamed young men leaving the bungalow. The young men, who have been disappointed in their attempts to solicit donations from Xu Weng, who we later find out was born and raised in Nanyang, remark that Xu Weng has forgotten that he is a *Zhongguo ren* (person from China).[1] Upon hearing the complaints of the unnamed young men who are soliciting donations, the rickshaw puller donates all his money of $6.50 to the men (significantly more than uncle Xu who had reluctantly given $5). This scene alludes to the Anti-Japanese National Salvation Movement (also known as the Nanyang Chinese National Salvation Movement) and related Singapore China Relief Fund Committee's efforts by the overseas Chinese from 1937 to 1941 (Lim 2019, 659; Zhou 2019, 25). The cousins remark that they, too, will contribute to these efforts, but the film does not dwell on these initiatives.

Haiwai zhenghun's attention is on Xu Weng's son, Xu Wei Sheng's transformative encounter with his China-born cousins. At first, Wei Sheng is portrayed as a cosmopolitan dilettante bound for London whose first line of dialogue "Hello Cousins" is in English, followed by an apology that his Mandarin is not good. The local Chinese elites in the prewar scenes are depicted as politically apathetic and willfully oblivious to the war and the looming threat to Malaya. Inspired by his cousins, Wei Sheng becomes a politically conscious person with a heightened sense of patriotism toward China. With his newfound patriotism for a *zuguo* (ancestral homeland) that he has never been to, Wei Sheng forgoes migrating to London with his fiancée Li Na, and joins Guo Cai in the journey to return to China to fight against the Japanese. They leave on 8 December 1941, but on that very day, the Japanese invade Malaya and Singapore and their steamship to China is sunk. The cousins end up in Kelantan and walk along railroad tracks in their attempt to reach China but Guo Cai is attacked by a Japanese spy and his last words are *"Zhongguo wansui"* ("Long live China"). Wei Sheng is only seen again at the end of the film, speaking of having returned from China. In the ellipsis of Wei Sheng's narrative, there is another history of asymmetrical or non-reciprocal affective relations between the overseas Chinese and the *zuguo* (Tiang 2017).

Early on in *Haiwai zhenghun*, during a visit to a coastal club in the lull before the Japanese Occupation, Ai Hua sings the song "Nanyang Ge" ("The Song of Nanyang"). In the montage, we see Li Na, the club owner, wearing a suit against the backdrop of the club's modernist architecture. The next shot is of a coconut tree swaying in the breeze. As the song progresses, the camera pans from left to right and then from right to left, luxuriating in glimpses of the coastline and a pagoda set amid lush tropical trees. The shots conjure an imaginary of Nanyang, a trope that Brian Bernards reads as "crossing colonial, national, and linguistic borders" (2015, 8). In this idyllic setting, we see a picturesque ideal of Nanyang's welcome to migrants, punctuated with shots of the appreciative faces of the well-dressed audience, altogether affirming Singapore as the promised second home for the overseas Chinese, while China remains a remembered homeland:

Nanyang, Nanyang

Ni shi women di er guxiang | You are our second home
Women yongyuan wang buliao ni | We can never forget you
Women geng wang buliao jiaxiang | And even more so, our homeland
Jinxiu de he, shan | The beautiful rivers and mountains
Jue bu rang taren wangxiang | No wishful thinking for others

Nanyang, Nanyang

Likai ni zhe xingfu tiantang | To leave such a blissful heaven

Nanyang, Nanyang

Women yao qu jianshe jiaxiang | We are going to build our home

Tessa Dwyer argues for the "productive power of translation" in subtitling (2017, 64). In my analysis of the bilingual subtitles of *Haiwai zhenghun* and *Huaqiao xuelei*, I focus on how these moments of translation carry traces of compressed histories and rich interlingual ambiguities. The rendition of "Nanyang Ge" is the only scene in the film with subtitles in traditional Chinese characters that are burned into the film stock, suggesting the intention of inviting the audience to sing along or learn the lyrics. Since the traditional characters are on the film print, they were probably done during the post-production of the film in the 1940s. It was only decades later that a set of simplified Chinese and English subtitles were added to the film by the AFA. Each line of subtitles, whether in English, traditional, or simplified characters, evokes different histories of colonial or otherwise contested national formations. Even though character simplification was already a point of discussion during

Figure 12.1 Ai Hua sings "Nanyang Ge" in *Haiwai Zhenghun* (1946). Courtesy of China Film Archive.

149

Republican China (1911–49), the Chinese Character Simplification Scheme was promoted by Communist China from the 1950s. As Jing Tsu observes: "The two orthographies, associated with the communist and nationalist script in the 1940s, have come to symbolize more than a half-century of political unease" (2011, 4). Beyond the communist and nationalist divide, simplified characters also marked China's desire for recognition in the modern international world (Tsu 2022).

Simplified characters remain the official standardized Chinese characters used in contemporary China and Singapore. Furthermore, the convention in Singapore to have dual-language subtitles in cinemas for Chinese-language films is traceable to its commitments to bilingualism, with English as an official language, while Mandarin is known as the "mother tongue" of the majority population. As Naoki Sakai (2022) has emphasized since the 1990s, a national language is part of historically contingent efforts to demarcate a unified internality to produce a national population, and "the modern regime of translation is part and parcel of the biopolitical technology of internationality whereby the identification and individuation of a national community is accomplished together with a subjectivation of an individual as a native speaker of a language" (18). This triply subtitled scene contains within it still-contentious politics of nation and language, marking the moment of messiness between an anticipated nation and memories of a left-behind nation.

The metaphor of the nation as home is not new. Both imaginaries depend on the limits of an inside and an outside, be it the walls of a home or the borders of a nation. In its two occurrences in the song, both *guxiang* and *jiaxiang* are subtitled as "home," while *jiaxiang* is subtitled first as "homeland" and then as "home." In this slippage, the missing "land" is precisely the site of contention and desire for people who are carrying the notion of a nation from one land to another since "a nation also signifies a collectivity of people who are geographically bound, who are distinguished from the rest of humanity by the fact of their residency within a determinate territory insulated from the outside world" (Sakai 2022, 32). The temporal tension between the left behind *jiaxiang* (homeland) that is not to be forgotten and the longing for a future *jiaxiang* (home) that is yet to be built is magnified in the passage of time by the linguistic inscription on the scene through the three sets of subtitles in the restored film. By the time the simplified characters and English subtitles were added to the restored film, the futural longing for a second home had become a retrospective gaze shadowed by contemporary politics and problematics of Chinese migration and the question of legal and affective affiliations.

Within the frames of *Haiwai zhenghun*, newlyarrived migrants from China are envisioned to have thicker affective relations to China than Singapore-born Chinese. The film's fantasy is that the pull towards China can be awakened by reminders of kinship ties. It is a curiosity that Wei Sheng, the Singapore-born patriot who seeks to fight for China, returns to Singapore but the film provides no explanation for what happened to him in China, if he indeed made it there, and why he returns. Wei Sheng's presence at the end of the film contributes to the film's ambiguity in its desires for an expansive notion of *zuguo* that can be spread through the diaspora and a Nanyang that resists this assimilation. *Huaqiao xuelei* is likewise marked by moments of resistant localization that cannot be subsumed by Chinese ethnonationalism. Though the geographical space of China is never seen, through frequent invocations of *zuguo*, it remains the ideological and affective center of the film and the promised unitary force of Chinese ethnicity. In both films, this unitary force is an alluring fiction, an unfulfilled promise that is strong enough to send men and women to their deaths.

2. Huaqiao Xuelei *and the Disorientations of* Guojia

Two common ways of translating the word "Chinese" are *zhong* or *hua*. The former, as center, forms part of the "Middle Kingdom" term for China and the latter often refers to *huaren* or *huayu*, that is, people or language of Chinese descent. It is thus not coincidental that the newly arrived Chinese siblings in *Haiwai zhenghun* are named Zhong Guo Cai, which homonymously sounds like "China" and uses the same character that could be translated as "nation" and Zhong Ai Hua, in which we can hear the call to "love the Hua people." In *Huaqiao xuelei*, the distinction between Nanyang as a second home and China as a motherland is more nebulous, with the inchoate beginnings of an emerging sense of localization. *Huaqiao xuelei* is the only directorial work by Tsai Wen-chin. According to Hee Wai Siam, Tsai "was one of the foremost advocates of the Mahua theater movement and one of the professional directors of the Chinese Theatre Society" (Hee 2019, 61). *Huaqiao xuelei* begins during the Japanese occupation with a multilingual scene of inspection reminiscent of the 1942 Operation Sook Ching where Japanese Kempeitai forces massacred the Chinese that were perceived to be threats. In the first four minutes, we hear Mandarin, Hokkien, Malay, and English. Young men are asked by a Hokkien-speaking man and a Japanese soldier to identify themselves before being allowed to leave or be detained. The film's first sense of a contingent community of shared precarity is invoked in a line by the male lead, Yang: "Look, all the young men are here," or literally translated as, "Look, we are all young people." It is revealed in the next shot that Yang is standing on a truck along with the other young men who did not pass the inspection. Shortly after, we see a scene of execution but Yang survives.

In my discussion of the imagination of Nanyang in *Haiwai zhenghun* as a matter of difference in affective relations to China, it might appear that race is not the relevant term and it is the dream of a nation that is at stake. However, in the titles and narratives of both films, the spirit, blood, and tears of ethnonationalism haunts this dream of a nation to be at home in. In *Huaqiao xuelei*, it is only the mercenary antagonist Zhao Da Ma who subscribes to racial differences according to nationality, regionality, and physiognomy. In a speech persuading Miss Ding to marry a Japanese colonel, Zhao Da Ma distinguishes between the Japanese, Chinese, Westerners, and those in Nanyang based on similarity in physique:

Wo congqian meiyou kanguo dongyang ren | I'd never met a Japanese

Ye bu zhidao zheyang de | And had no idea what they were like

Xianzai kanjianle | Now that I've seen them

Hai bushi gen women zhongguo ren yiyang de ma? | They are just like us Chinese

Dongyang ren bi qi xiyang ren/he Nanyang ren hao duo le | They are better than/ The Westerners and those in Nanyang.

[. . .]

Dongyang ren a | Well, the Japanese . . .

Changduan daxiao he women zhongguo ren chabuduo | They have about the same physique as the Chinese.

151

The terms *Dongyang ren* (literally "Eastern Ocean person"), *Xiyang ren* ("Western Ocean person"), and *Nanyang ren* ("Southern Ocean person") are all words of oceanic orientation with connotations of racialization as well as center-periphery relations. Like the fluid ocean within the terms, their connotations are by no means stable. In the English subtitles added for the re-release of the film, *Dongyang* is translated as "Japanese" rather than "East Asian," since in the comparison Zhao Da Ma identifies as "*women zhongguo ren*" (we, people from China). Naoki Sakai points out that the term "*xiyang*," which now refers to the "West," shifted in connotation in the late 19th and early 20th centuries, and the shift indexed a "collapse in the Sinocentric worlding: *xiyang* no longer indexed a periphery with the Middle Kingdom in the center of the world. The Middle Kingdom was now located in the Far Eastern periphery of the world" (2022, 16). The ethnonational implication in Zhao Da Ma's speech resonates across the term subtitled as "us Chinese" and its literal translation, "we, people from China." Unlike *Haiwai zhenghun*, there's no mention of *zuguo*, the ancestral homeland and China is only named once early in the film when Yang agrees to join the anti-Japanese resistance and has his spirit affirmed as *Zhe cai shi Zhonghua Minguo de guomin* (subtitled as "That's how a citizen of the Republic of China should think"). In contrast, when an undercover resistance fighter makes a speech affirming sacrifice, "*na women de shengmin xian gei guojia*" (subtitled as "We must be ready to give our lives to the country"), there is no clarification as to the extent and limits of this *guojia*, whether as country, home, nation, or state, or in China, or in Nanyang. The melodramatic mix of survival and sacrifice in *Huaqiao xuelei* under shared precarity and vulnerability occurs under an inchoate, messy sense of *guojia* that the dramatic turns of the plot avoid circumscribing. The speech ends with the call that "Our spirit will never die." While the parameters of this "Our" is not defined, this image of solidarity is shored up by the temporal threat of a common enemy and does not escape the entanglement of patriotism and ethnonationalism.

In *Huaqiao xuelei* and *Haiwai zhenghun*, the briefly appearing bodies and expository speech of the visibly non-Chinese are excluded from the dramatic, heroic action of both films. *Haiwai zhenghun* has a token Malay character referred to as Encik who informs Wei Sheng that they are in Kelantan. *Huaqiao xuelei* shows a Sikh man who appears twice in his role as a guard at the gate of a house. In a scene set in Haw Par Villa, a park with a Chinese mythology and Confucian theme, there is a mention of co-resistance with people in north Malaya. While there are scatterings of the multilingual and glimpses of an emerging locality, the films' overwhelming affective patriotism remains, as their titles indicate, concerned with the agencies of those identified as Chinese who are navigating the space of the national in transitional times. In one scene showing a clandestine meeting of anti-Japanese resistance fighters, there is a partially hidden portrait of Sun Yat-sen hanging in the background. Jessica Tan sees the portrait as a "vague gesture to China" (2019). The image is also a vestige of Sun Yat-sen's notability in Nanyang, where his revolutionary plans received support from local Chinese merchants in the early 20th century, including the establishment of the headquarters of the Tongmenghui (United Group) in 1905–06 Singapore. The truncated portrait in the background, where only the lower half of Sun's body is visible, suggests both a continuity and a break in wartime Singapore where the exigencies of local fights reduced the references to a distant land. This ambiguity harbors a productive multivalence that has been long inscribed in the debate over what it means to be "Chinese."

3. Cinema Lost and Found in Transitional Times

By 2016, when the AFA and CFA located *Haiwai zhenghun* and *Huaqiao xuelei*, along with the legacy of the fraught ambiguity of the Chinese in Singapore, the term "Chinese" has also accrued different pressures and associations. Examining Singapore's demographic changes since 1990, Hong Liu identifies intra-diasporic conflicts within and across diasporic generations and concludes that "shared cultural heritage and co-ethnicity have not led to solidarity between Singaporeans and new Chinese immigrants" (2014, 1231). A short film *Last Trip Home* (2013) by Han Fengyu, who migrated with his parents from China to Singapore as a child, premiered at the Cannes Cinéfondation competition for film students. The 26-minute film, in which homeless immigrants in Singapore decide to drive back to China, captures the affective and material alienation of being considered new migrants from China despite, or perhaps because of, those identified as ethnic Chinese being the majority population in Singapore. With continuing academic debate over the status of the Sinophone and the diaspora paradigm, and the wider, rising palpability of anti-Chinese and entangled anti-Asian racism, the renewed lives of these two restored films have entered another extended time of conflict between competing notions of "home."

When I first watched the films on a computer in the AFA office in 2018, it was painfully evident that restoration efforts can never return us to the material condition of the past. Perhaps even more so, with the deteriorated and lost visual and auditory frames, the films demand the imagination and committed attention of the audience. Following Azoulay's call in *Potential History* (2019) to unlearn the past by making its violence and imperialism present for refusal in the here and now – in rewatching these ghostly scenes where songs and dreams of Nanyang, nation, and home are all too soon and too late, where affective nationalisms have outlasted the shapes, maps, and governments of nation-states in-the-making – could we discern the dangers of affective ethnonationalism and consider non-national modes of thinking commonality? Is it necessary to understand the transitional time between nations in terms of a transition between one patriotic, ethnically weighted affiliation and another? Or was there ever a possibility of dwelling in the interstitial, beyond the binaristic, ideological, or affective bond to one governing structure of existence?[2]

Notes

1 In another instance in the film, the subtitles translate *Zhongguo* (China) as "his roots."
2 I am grateful to the Asian Film Archive and the China Film Archive for providing access to *Huaqiao xuelei* and *Haiwai zhenghun* and to Chew Tee Pao in particular for answering my questions tirelessly. I am also grateful to Thong Kay Wee and the Asian Film Archive's Reframe initiative for the opportunity in 2018 to curate a series of Chinese-language films showing transitional times in Southeast and East Asia. I am thankful for the generous, inspiring participation of Chan Cheow Thia, Ma Shaoling, Shelly Chan, Hong Guo-Juin, Shih Chun, Jessica Tan, Yeo Min Hui, and the audience members in the event. Thank you too to Weihsin Gui for the invitation to present this work in 2021 at the University of California (Riverside) and to Ruochen Bo for research assistance.

References

Arendt, Hannah. 1973. *The Origins of Totalitarianism*. New York: Harcourt, Brace and Company.
Azoulay, Ariella. 2008. *The Civil Contract of Photography*. New York: Zone Books.
———. 2019. *Potential History: Unlearning Imperialism*. New York: Verso.

Elizabeth Wijaya

Bao, Weihong. 2015. *Fiery Cinema: The Emergence of an Affective Medium in China, 1915–1945*. Minneapolis, MN: Minnesota University Press.

Bernards, Brian. 2015. *Writing the South Seas; Imagining the Nanyang in Chinese and Southeast Asian Postcolonial Literature*. Seattle: University of Washington Press.

Berry, Chris. 2021. "What is Transnational Cinema Today? Or, Welcome to the Sinosphere." *Transnational Screens* 12 (3): 193–98.

Bren, Frank. 2014. "Woman in White: The Unbelievable Wan Hoi-ling." In *Transcending Space and Time: Early Cinematic Experience of Hong Kong, Book III, Re-discovering Pioneering Females in Early Chinese Cinema and Grandview's Cross-border Productions*, edited by Hong Kong Film Archive. Hong Kong: Hong Kong Film Archive. https://www.filmarchive.gov.hk/documents/18995340/19057015/ebrochure_03.pdf

Carnell, F. G. 1952. "Malayan Citizenship Legislation." *The International and Comparative Law Quarterly* 1 (4): 504–18.

Chan, Shelly. 2018. *Diaspora's Homeland: Modern China in the Age of Global Migration*. Durham: Duke University Press.

Dwyer, Tessa. 2017. *Speaking in Subtitles: Revaluing Screen Translation*. Edinburgh: Edinburgh University Press.

Galt, Rosalind. 2021. *Alluring Monsters: The Pontianak and the Cinemas of Decolonization*. New York: Columbia University Press.

Hee, Wai Siam. 2019. *Remapping the Sinophone: The Cultural Production of Chinese-Language Cinema in Singapore and Malaya before and during the Cold War*. Hong Kong: Hong Kong University Press.

Hirschman, Charles. 1987. "The Meaning and Measurement of Ethnicity in Malaysia: An Analysis of Census Classifications." *The Journal of Asian Studies* 46 (3): 555–82.

Hochberg, Gil Z. 2015. *Visual Occupations: Violence and Visibility in a Conflict Zone*. Durham: Duke University Press.

Kuhn, Philip A. 2008. *Chinese among Others: Emigration in Modern Times*. Singapore: National University Press.

Lee, Sangjoon. 2020. *Cinema and the Cultural Cold War*. Ithaca: Cornell University Press.

Lim, How Seng. 2019. "The Anti-Japanese National Salvation Movement." In *A General History of the Chinese in Singapore*, edited by Chong Guan Kwa and Bak Lim Kua. 655–67. Singapore: World Scientific.

Liu, Hong. 2014. "Beyond Co-Ethnicity: The Politics of Differentiating and Integrating New Immigrants in Singapore." *Ethnic and Racial Studies* 37 (7): 1225–38.

Low, Choo Chin. 2014. "The Repatriation of the Chinese as a Counterinsurgency Policy during the Malayan Emergency." *Journal of Southeast Asian Studies* 45 (3): 363–92.

Lu, Sheldon, ed. 1997. *Transnational Chinese Cinemas: Identity, Nationhood, Gender*. Honolulu: University of Hawaii Press.

Ma, Jean. 2010. *Melancholy Drift: Marking Time in Chinese Cinema*. Hong Kong: Hong Kong University Press.

McKeown, Adam. 2001. *Chinese Migrant Networks and Cultural Change: Peru, Chicago, Hawaii, 1900–1936*. Chicago: University of Chicago Press.

Purcell, Victor. 1951. *The Chinese in South-East Asia*. New York: Oxford University Press.

Sakai, Naoki. 2022. *The End of Pax Americana: The Loss of Empire and Hikikomori Nationalism*. Durham: Duke University Press.

Suryadinata, Leo. Ed. 1997. *Ethnic Chinese as Southeast Asians*. Singapore: Institute of Southeast Asian Studies.

Tan, Jessica. 2019. "Migratory Times, Diaspora Moments: Films as Archives of Migration and Memories." *Asian Film Archive*, September 17, 2019. https://www.asianfilmarchive.org/migratory-times-diaspora-moments/.

Tiang, Jeremy. 2017. *State of Emergency*. Singapore: Epigram Books.

Tsu, Jing. 2011. *Sound and Script in the Chinese Diaspora*. Boston: Harvard University Press.

———. 2022. *Kingdom of Characters: The Language Revolution That Made China Modern*. New York: Riverhead Books.

Wang, Gungwu. 2001. *Don't Leave Home: Migration and the Chinese*. Singapore: Times Academic Press.

Zhang, Yingjin. 2010. "Transnationalism and Translocality in Chinese Cinema." *Cinema Journal* 49 (3): 135–39.

Zhou, Taomo. 2019. *Migration in the Time of Revolution: China, Indonesia, and the Cold War*. Ithaca: Cornell University Press.

13

WHERE IS SHANGRI-LA? IMAGINING KATHMANDU IN FILM

Dikshya Karki

In the 2016 Marvel film *Doctor Strange*, Christine Palmer, an emergency neurosurgeon, meets her injured colleague Stephen Strange and asks where he has been. He tells her he went East and landed in Kathmandu. "Like the Bob Seger song?" she asks. "Nineteen seventy-five, *Beautiful Loser*, side A. Yeah," he answers. Their conversation centers Kathmandu, the national capital of Nepal, in the "east," identifies it with American pop culture, and alludes to a geographical imaginary in the narrative and visual traditions of Orientalism. The stories, motifs, and tropes that continue to emerge and circulate in film form a part of a transnational, and in this case a trans-Asian, imaginary orient. Matthew Bernstein suggests that Orientalism in film appears "as expressions of colonialist and imperialist cultures; as reworking time-honored genre conventions and psychoanalytic scenarios; as allegories of contemporary politics" (Bernstein and Studlar 1997, 5). Orientalist geographies are often fantasy spaces depicted with beautiful and mysterious landscapes and unusual customs and habits, a magnificent spectacle for visual consumption. Shangri-La in film is one such Orientalist imaginary of sacred mountains, where mystics reside, a space of spirituality, magic, and wonder. Primitive landscapes of deserts, jungles, and mountains provide topographical specificity to a fictional Middle Eastern and Asian world.

This chapter analyzes two American films, *Doctor Strange* (2016) and *The Night Train to Kathmandu* (1988), which reference the fantasyland of John Hilton's Shangri-La by using the location of Kathmandu. Given the popularity of this idyllic paradise, the Shangri-La brand name has become a part of popular culture, used to refer to a chain of international hotels and restaurants around the world, curio shops, and even a song by a British band, the Kinks. Many Himalayan countries, however, are eager to claim themselves as the source of inspiration for Hilton's imagination. Although it was Tibet and practitioners of Tibetan Buddhism who were initially associated with the myth, Nepal, via Kathmandu, has offered a viable alternative. I focus on the narratives, motifs, and characters connected to urban histories of place-making conjured to situate Shangri-La in Nepal via Kathmandu. Films referencing Shangri-La, when located in Kathmandu, offer a strong transnational visual appeal based on the idealization of its architecture and connections to the Himalayas. This fantastical world, with its magical qualities with scope for spectacle and sorcery,

DOI: 10.4324/9781003266952-18

is not secluded and beyond reach like the Tibetan mountains. Rather, it is affordable and accommodating as a mass tourism destination. I argue that Kathmandu offers a home to the utopia of Shangri-La in film, generating a composite relationship between an imagined and real territory.

Beginnings of the Myth

John Hilton first used the term "Shangri-La" in his novel *Lost Horizon* (Hilton 1933) to refer to a place in the Tibetan mountains located in the valley of the Blue Moon, with a lamasery.[1] When Hilton – who had never been to Tibet – was writing his novel, the country was shielded from travelers. There were only a handful of Euro-American explorers who received official entry and permission to study the Tibetan language and Buddhism in "the navel of the earth" and were able to photograph its people and terrain. In the subsequent decades, with China's invasion of Tibet and the exile of the 14th Dalai Lama to India in 1959, complications were added to travel to Tibet. "Shangri-La" thus became associated with other accessible regions in the Himalayas like Sikkim and Ladakh in India, as well as Nepal and Bhutan. Shangri-La is now a global myth, a utopia built by spiritual communities, without any geographical specificity beyond Tibet (Bishop 1989). Its link to the Himalayas, which cover the territories of Nepal, China, Bhutan, India, and Pakistan, however, remains strong as travelers, writers, and filmmakers continue their search for Hilton's Shangri-La.

Governments around the Himalayan region are eager to associate themselves with Shangri-La owing to the prospects of tourism. In 2002, The People's Republic of China (PRC) renamed Zhongdian county in Yunan province to Shangri-La (Xianggelila in pinyin). The province has been sacralized, ethnicized, and exoticized by promoting it as a pilgrimage site for Tibetan Buddhism that is also inhabited by ethnic minorities living in harmony with their natural surroundings of lakes, forests, and mountains (Kolås 2008). These three place-making strategies used by the Chinese government to construct a new Shangri-La are also seen in Hollywood films fixated on the idea of Shangri-La. In *The Night Train to Kathmandu* (1988) and *Doctor Strange* (2016), Kathmandu, defined as the path to fictional Shangri-Las such as "Shar-Loon" and "Kamar-Taj," is a holy land of mystics where locals live in the company of deities, surrounded by majestic mountains.

Spiritual Encounters

Both films are journey narratives with east-west encounters. In *Doctor Strange* (2016), Doctor Stephen Strange, a British neurosurgeon who suffers nerve damage in his hands after a fatal car accident, is in search of a cure. He hears of Jonathan Pangborn, a paraplegic who has regained the use of his legs, and goes to consult him. Pangborn tells Strange of a place called Kamar-Taj where he healed his body. It is not to be found on any map, known only to a select few. Strange then takes a trip to Kathmandu to find it. Similarly, Professor Hardley Smith and Johar in *The Night Train to Kathmandu* (1988) are in search of Shar-Loon, "the city that never was" (as described in the film). Johar meets the McLeods, an American family, and travels with them to Kathmandu.

In order to emphasize the spiritual journey that characters are about to undertake, a special encounter with "a holy one" is staged in both films. In *Night Train to Kathmandu*,

Figure 13.1   Stephen Strange stands outside the door of Kamar-Taj in *Doctor Strange* (2016).

Lily, an American teenager upset about moving with her parents to Nepal, meets a Brahmin on the train. He advises her to examine the source of her unhappiness. Similarly, Dr. Strange is also asked to reimagine his life. "Forget everything you think you know," says Karl Mordo, his guide and mentor, before allowing him to enter Kamar-Taj. He will need to believe in magic, sorcery, and alternate dimensions, which can be entered and controlled by spiritual practice. Strange's search for healing and meaning in his life beyond his western medical practice in New York through a visit to Kathmandu is an example of how "Nepal [Kathmandu] serves as an enchanted, exotic destination in which to find, experience, and even heal the selves that (visitors believe) the modern West has constrained or even sickened" (Liechty 2017, 366). After spending all his money to cure himself, Strange, in one last desperate attempt, buys a one-way ticket to Kathmandu. He comes to experience the powers of eastern mysticism. Meanwhile, the McLeods, two American professors, finally realize their dream of visiting Nepal where myths may be facts. Mystery and magic are mirrored in the exotic terrain of Kathmandu requiring the attention of Euro-American explorers to comprehend it.

Filming Kathmandu

These imaginary narratives and perspectives of filming Nepal are driven by the access to and knowledge about the country and its capital. Although Nepal opened up for tourism only after a democratic uprising in 1951, the Kathmandu Valley[2] had been a religious meeting point for Buddhist and Hindu pilgrims from India and Tibet for centuries. There were missionaries from the 16th century onward, and later British colonial personnel, who were permitted to stay and work in Nepal and chronicled their experiences through journals, sketches, and photographs. The collections of British ethnologist and naturalist Brian Houghton Hodgson and Swiss geologist Toni Hagen are examples of early visual testaments of living in Kathmandu and traveling around Nepal. Indologist Hodgson was stationed in Kathmandu from 1821 to 1843, and the drawings he commissioned to artist Raj Man Singh Chitrakar are now archived at the Royal Asiatic Society of Great Britain and Ireland.[3] They depict the daily life and architecture of medieval Kathmandu. Hagen arrived in Nepal more than a century later, in 1950, and trekked across the country taking photographs and recording his journey in the documentary *Uhileko Nepal*.[4] In the decades of the 1960s and 1970s, Nepal further attracted young Euro-American tourists who wanted to tour Asia on a budget or gain a spiritual experience. Kathmandu was often the last destination point on the "hippie trail," an overland tour around Asia made popular by the "flower power" generation.

Despite various photographic, touristic, and scholarly accounts about travels to Nepal and Kathmandu, its people, cultures, and linguistic diversities, its image, however, has always been of a secluded land, home to Shangri-La. Mary Des Chene (2007) argues that the Shangri-La image of Nepal emerges from travel literature and conditioned early research on Nepal. Anthropologists were attracted to studying Nepal's mountains and its people as a pristine exotic terrain, rather than other locations of the country like its southern plains with deep cultural and linguistic ties and geographical proximity to India. "Shangri-La was not to be found at sea level or among Hindi speakers, and neither was Nepali-ness" (Des Chene 2007, 213). Nepal was its mountains and was represented through them. What attracted early scholars to Nepal is equally manifest in its continuing visual representations on film, a deep desire to maintain and build on the narrative possibilities provided by the Orientalist myth of Shangri-La. As Edward Said emphasizes, Orientalism is a way to create and, "in some cases to control, manipulate, even to incorporate, what is a manifestly different (or alternative and novel) world" (Said 2003, 12). The fascination with Nepal's mountains, its supposed medieval way of life, its assorted cultures and people, and its unexplored stories of practitioners of mystical arts are pursued by Euro-American filmmakers irrespective of the nation's geopolitical realities. "Nepal has a certain peace and tranquility. It's very difficult to describe. It's a magical place. I wanted to capture that magic," shared Robert Weimer, the director, and writer of *The Night Train* (The Disney Channel Magazine 1988, 18). His remark associates Nepal with Kathmandu in particular where the film is shot as a dwelling place of magic and mystery, where anything can happen. The film depicts Kathmandu as an exotic locale with lost talismans, holy men, a prince in hiding, old temples, and cobbled streets. This imagery permeates the myth of a mystic east located in Kathmandu fueling the imagination of Euro-American filmmakers who continue to see it as a place lost in time filled with sensual wonders and extraordinary mysteries. Charles Newirth, the executive producer of *Doctor Strange* (2016), amazed by the crowd gathered in Kathmandu to watch actor Benedict Cumberbatch, who plays Strange in the film, expressed, "It was like the Beatles showed up after *The Ed Sullivan Show*" (Collis 2015). His comment reveals an expectation to work anonymously in the country, despite the global popularity of Marvel films and the regular presence of Hollywood actors. Kathmandu was supposed to be secluded, spiritual, isolated, and untouched by modernity, whereas in fact Nepal's national capital is one of the fastest urbanizing cities in South Asia. Kathmandu has been a nodal point in the global circulation of magazines, music, and world cinema since the 1960s with young and middle-class consumers formulating their ideas on class, gender, and identity based on interaction with such media forms (Liechty 2010).

The attractions of location filming in Nepal lie in visualizing an imaginary that can be marked off from its historical and political histories to correspond to the needs of Shangri-La. James R. Curtis (1992) lists the five requirements of Hilton's fantasy land as a secluded mountainous place of rugged beauty, with promises of good health and longevity, unworldly with a dark side, and too good to last forever. The medieval Newar architecture of the Kathmandu Valley provides a spectrum of cinematic possibilities to explore the unknown through the familiar. Shangri-La is thus created through compositional style, objects, architecture, and landscape by using Kathmandu as a geographical and metaphorical background. The visual similarities between Hilton's imagination, Kathmandu's medieval palaces, and Nepal's mountains make it a plausible location to create a Shangri-La that is also aided by the low cost of filming. Marvel Studios' decision to shoot *Doctor Strange* in Kathmandu was part of its diversification strategy to use destinations around the world, such as Seoul and Johannesburg as background for its films (Goundy 2016). The undertaking was also seen as a message of solidarity by the Hollywood team with Nepal's tourism industry since the country had just witnessed a massive earthquake that took the lives of more than 8,000 people and damaged thousands of monuments in the same year.

The Gateway to Shangri-La

Kathmandu holds the key to Shangri-La, which is renamed "Kamar-Taj" and "Shar-Loon," respectively, in *Doctor Strange* (2016) and *The Night Train to Kathmandu* (1988). The architecture of stupas, pagoda-style monuments, wooden latticed windows, and cobbled streets, which are unique to the Kathmandu valley illustrate the visual markers of these fictional cities. In both the Marvel universe and in *Night Train*, Kamar-Taj and Shar-Loon are located in Kathmandu.

By locating Shar-Loon or Shangri-La in Kathmandu, *Night Train* coordinates with the presence of a well-settled exiled Tibetan Buddhist population in various areas of Kathmandu. After the 14th Dalai Lama took exile in Dharmasala (India), a large number of Tibetan monks settled in the Baudha and Svayambhu areas of Kathmandu, which became Buddhist meditation and preaching centers (Moran 2004). The arrival of the McLeods to Kathmandu is marked with a view of the Svayambhu stupa[5] emerging from a mist of clouds. There are thousands of stupas in the Kathmandu valley, but Svayambhu's monumental size, location on a hillock with a panoramic view of the city, and association with myths about the origins of the first settlement in the valley make it a tourist attraction. The heritage complex includes temples dating back to the fourth century and holds deep religious significance for Buddhists and Hindus alike. The name of the stupa, Svayambhu (self-existent), is based on local accounts chronicled in the *Svayambhu Puran* about Bodhisattva Manjushree who cut a gorge in the rim of a pristine lake to drain out the water and make it habitable after noticing a bejeweled lotus with a flame in the middle (Slusser 1982; Michael 1994; Owens 2002). The stupa in the film signifies entry to an enchanted world of mystics and magic for the characters. The pagoda[6] architecture of the Kathmandu Valley differs from other Asian countries such as Japan, China, and Thailand, creating a visual distinction for Kamar-Taj in the Marvel film. Interactions between Dr. Strange and the Ancient One are framed inside courtyards and rooms with ornate latticed wooden windows, a unique feature of Newar architecture. The effort is to materialize a Marvel cinematic world based on the architecture of the Kathmandu valley, without revealing the source of its particularities.

Mark B. Sandberg (2014) writes about the "erasure of site specificity" to refer to the production of films with a conscious effort to rid themselves of cultural signifiers from their shooting locations so that the fictional worlds can become placeless and marketable products. In films produced by Marvel and Disney, the locations of Kathmandu are used to assist the storyline of the films; the real is to stand in for the imaginary, a placeless place, where actual locations may be familiar to some viewers but not explicitly identified. There is a friction in doing so, which comes through as viewers mistake real for unreal and vice versa. A reviewer on TripAdvisor, a consumer website that includes user-generated reviews, confuses the Svayambhu stupa for Kamar-Taj and another visitor reviews Hotel Siddhi Manakamana on the outskirts of Kathmandu as a place that will give you the complete experience of Kamar-Taj (Alam 2017; Arum 2018). The real substitutes for the imaginary as Marvel fans from around the world describe their experience of visiting the stupa and other architectural sites in Kathmandu as an encounter with Kamar-Taj.[7]

In *The Night Train to Kathmandu*, the McLeods and their children take a train to the Nepal-India border in Janakpur and travel via road to Kathmandu. As they get off the train, Maureen McLeod exclaims: "Except for the cars and buses we could have stepped back a hundred years." The scene is that of a curated fair on an open field with elephants, buffaloes, chickens, goats, street vendors, carts, rickshaws, tempos, and packed buses. Nepal in miniature is inching toward modernity but still set in its village ways where buses are adjusting to elephants. Then Professor Hadley, who has come to receive the family, says, "Welcome to Kathmandu," and offers to give them a lift to town. The journey from Janakpur to the Kathmandu Valley is more than 100 kilometers and around six hours on road. In this entire cinematic itinerary, there is an evident "violence to geography," which is described by Rachel Dwyer as the liberties taken by films and filmmakers to manipulate

Figure 13.2   Doctor Strange (2016) filmed at Patan Durbar Square, Kathmandu.

the accuracy of distance between locations through editing (Dwyer 2014, 67). There is no train service to Kathmandu, as the title of *Night Train* suggests. Likewise, in *Doctor Strange*, Strange arrives in Kathmandu and goes in search of Kamar-Taj walking from the streets of Ason, then the New Road to the Pashupatinath temple complex, then Thamel, then Svayambhu, and finally in the alleys of Patan. These are localities in different parts of Kathmandu and walking seamlessly on foot from one shot to another is improbable.

Adding to the disjunction of geography are stereotypical characters modeled on the oriental imagery of explorers, seekers, and princes. These characters can easily pass for royals as well as mendicants, devoid of any ethnic, racial, cultural, or social markers. The actors themselves are implanted in the cityscape of Kathmandu, ambivalent to local histories, authorizing their Euro-American presence among Nepalis seen only as crowds and passersby in traditional wear. In *Night Train*, Johar is introduced as a Shakya prince who can speak Hindi, Urdu, French, German, Italian, and the 13 languages of Nepali. Actually, there are no variants of the Nepali language and an American actor, Eddie Castrodad, plays the role of the prince. In order to prepare for the part, he shared: "I pretended to walk on streets of gold. That was fun because I felt like I owned a lot. But I am really from Queens and I don't have anything made of gold" (The Disney Channel Magazine 1988, 17). His preparation for navigating an imagined geography relies on a perceived excess that the location of Kathmandu offers, the pathways of its core palaces fit for royals and mystics alike.

Names such as "Johar" and the "Ancient One" are rootless but pronounceable for the American filmmakers and the film's global audience. Johar is the prince of Shar-Loon serving an American family in Kathmandu, while the Ancient One is an androgynous female of an unknown age who helps protect the sanctums of London, New York, and Hong Kong. She is similar to Perrault, the High Lama from Hilton's *Lost Horizon*, a Luxembourger who has lived for more than 200 years and is now seeking a successor to take forward his legacy, while the Ancient One passes away by handing over the duties of protecting Kamar-Taj to Strange. Although Perrault is the head of a Tibetan lamasery, he is not Tibetan or Chinese, and the Ancient One is not Nepali and has no connection to Kathmandu, where Kamar-Taj is located.

Despite these repetitive narratives of seekers arriving in Kathmandu to experience spirituality, the films have also held appeal for Nepali audiences. Businesses, tourism entrepreneurs, and the media in Nepal encourage and celebrate Kathmandu's representation as a sacred, mystical city (*The Kathmandu Post* 2016; Pande 2016). Nakim Uddin, the owner of QFX Cinemas, a chain of cinema halls in Nepal stated his enthusiasm about ticket sales from *Doctor Strange* and added:

> The movie has portrayed Kathmandu so beautifully that you feel so proud just to be a resident of this beautiful land of eastern mysticism. I could tell I shared the pride with the rest of the audience because as soon as Kathmandu came onto the screen, everybody instantly began cheering.
>
> *(The Kathmandu Post 2016)*

His experience of watching the Marvel film in Kathmandu and the excitement of audiences endorses a touristic gaze of the city as a center of eastern mysticism. The collective effort is directed to encourage tourists and filmmakers to visit Kathmandu by generating media publicity around films exploiting its various locations since tourism remains an essential contributor to Nepal's economy. Since the 1950s locals have contributed to the branding of different parts of Kathmandu based on their understanding of the needs of tourists (Thapa 2016; Linder 2017). The way to commodify Kathmandu as an attractive location for global film industries and a cosmopolitan audience is to offer a stylized and marketable version of mysticism built on the myth of Shangri-La.

Conclusion

Doctor Strange (2016) and *The Night Train to Kathmandu* (1988), though released decades apart, represent an idealized embodiment of the fantasyland of Shangri-La by locating it in Nepal's national capital, Kathmandu. The representations of Kathmandu in the films as a gateway to Shangri-La are deeply rooted in colonial fantasies of travel to sacred Himalayan communities and quests for spiritual transformation and healing. There are recurrent tropes of encounters with holy men, gurus, magic, and exotic landscapes of mountains in the films, which indicate the enduring relevance of Nepal's image as one of the last Shangri-Las in the world. Even with Nepal's popularity as a tourist destination and the considerable research on Kathmandu's architectural heritage, there is a recurring desire to exoticize its landscapes, people, and monuments in film. Literary and photographic representations of Kathmandu as a mystical, strange, spiritual city are internalized and reproduced by filmmakers who see it as a contribution to the celebration of eastern spirituality and mysticism. A fixation on a romanticized account of the pagoda-scapes of Kathmandu continues in popular imagination fueled by music, travel literature, and films as the last chance for an alternate spiritual life.

Notes

1 A Tibetan Buddhist monastery.
2 The Kathmandu Valley includes the three cities of Kathmandu, Bhaktapur, and Lalitpur, and until the 19th century, the name Nepal was used primarily to refer to the Valley.
3 See https://royalasiaticcollections.org/collection/artwork/hodgson-drawings/ (accessed on 10.04.2022).
4 The documentary can be viewed in parts at https://www.youtube.com/watch?v=hBUnSqWJihk/ (accessed 10 April 2022).
5 A mound-like structure said to host the relics of the Buddha found particularly in South and Southeast Asia.
6 A pyramid structure that refers to diminished tiered roofing.
7 See, for example, https://marvel.fandom.com/wiki/Kamar-Taj (accessed 10 December 2019).

References

Alam, Shah. 2017. "Hotel Siddhi Manakmana on the Trail of Dr Strange to Find Kamar-Taj in Kathmandu." *Review of Hotel Siddhi Manakamana*. https://www.tripadvisor.co.nz/ShowUser-Reviews-g293890-d4876891-r467100429-Hotel_Siddhi_Manakamana-Kathmandu_Kathmandu_Valley_Bagmati_Zone_Central_Region.html.
Arum, Farida. 2018. "I Thought It Was Kamar Taj." *Review of Swayambhunath Temple*. https://www.tripadvisor.com/ShowUserReviews-g293890-d2018892-r552351919-Swayambhunath_Temple-Kathmandu_Kathmandu_Valley_Bagmati_Zone_Central_Region.html.
Bernstein, Matthew and Gaylyn Studlar. 1997. *Visions of the East: Orientalism in Film*. New Brunswick, NJ: Rutgers University Press.
Bishop, Peter. 1989. *The Myth of Shangri-La: Tibet, Travel Writing, and the Western Creation of Sacred Landscape*. Berkeley: University of California Press.
Collis, Clark. 2015. "Doctor Strange Star Inspired Cumberbatch-Mania in Kathmandu." *Entertainment Weekly*, December 30, 2015.

Curtis, James R. 1992. "Shangri-La and Pakistan's Hunza River Valley." Journal of Cultural Geography 13 (1), 55–67.

Des Chene, Mary. 2007. "Is Nepal in South Asia? The Condition of Non-Postcoloniality." *Studies in Nepali History and Society* 12: 207–23.

The Disney Channel Magazine. "The Night Train to Kathmandu." July 1988.

Dwyer, Rachel. 2014. *Bollywood's India: Hindi Cinema as a Guide to Contemporary India*. 37–78. London: Reaktion Books.

Goundy, Nick. 2016. "Marvel Filmed Doctor Strange in the UK and Nepal." *Kemps Film Tv Video*, October 26, 2016.

Hilton, James. 1933. *Lost Horizon*. London: Macmillan and Co. Limited.

The Kathmandu Post. 2016. "Doctor Strange Casts a Spell on Kathmandu." *The Kathmandu Post*, November 8, 2016.

Kolås, Åshild. 2008. *Tourism and Tibetan Culture in Transition: A Place Called Shangrila*. London: Routledge.

Liechty, Mark. 2010. *Out Here in Kathmandu: Modernity on the Global Periphery*. Kathmandu: Martin Chautari Press.

———. 2017. *Far Out: Countercultural Seekers and the Tourist Encounter in Nepal*.Chicago, IL: University of Chicago Press. https://doi.org/10.7208/chicago/9780226429137.003.0012

Linder, Benjamin. 2017. "Of 'Tourist' Places: The Cultural Politics of Narrating Space in Thamel." *HIMALAYA, the Journal of the Association for Nepal and Himalayan Studies* 37 (1): 41–56.

Michael, Hutt. 1994. *Nepal, A Guide to The Art and Architecture of the Kathmandu Valley*. New Delhi: Adroit Publishers.

Moran, Peter Kevin. 2004. *Buddhism Observed: Travelers, Exiles and Tibetan Dharma in Kathmandu*. London: New York: Routledge.

Owens, Bruce McCoy. 2002. "Monumentality, Identity, and the State: Local Practice, World Heritage, and Heterotopia at Swayambhu, Nepal." *Anthropological Quarterly* 75 (2): 269–316.

Pande, Sophia. 2016. "Doctor Strange." *Nepali Times*, November 11, 2016.

Said, Edward W. 2003. *Orientalism*. London, England: Penguin Classics.

Sandberg, Mark B. 2014. "Location, 'Location': On the Plausibility of Place Substitution." In *Silent Cinema and the Politics of Space*, 346. Bloomington: Indiana University Press.

Slusser, Mary Shepherd. 1982. *Nepal Mandala: A Cultural Study of the Kathmandu Valley*. Princeton, NJ: Princeton University Press.

Thapa, Rabi. 2016. *Thamel: Dark Star of Kathmandu*. New Delhi, India: Speaking Tiger.

14

AFFECTIVE-SCAPE/ING IN ZHANG LU'S INTER-ASIAN QUARTET

Ran Ma

This chapter highlights ethnic Korean Chinese (*chaoxianzu*) filmmaker Zhang Lu (b. 1962), who was born in Yanbian Korean Autonomous Prefecture (*Yanbian chaoxianzu zizhizhou*) in Jilin Province, the People's Republic of China.[1] After he moved to Seoul in 2012 upon a job offer from Yonsei University, Zhang directed Korean-language films, such as *Gyeongju* (Gyeongju 2014), *Chunmong* (A Quiet Dream 2016), *Gunsan: Geowireul Noraehada* (Ode to the Goose 2018), and *Hukuoka* (Fukuoka 2019), among others. This study focuses on these four widely circulated and critically acclaimed works lauded on the global film festival network, and investigates them as a "quartet."

Interrogating Korean trans/national cinema, JungBong Choi suggests how "any cartographic effort to chart a national cinema has to take into consideration the dispersed, archipelagic, checkered and networked nature of [. . .] nationhood," specifically given how "the 'national' has become a space increasingly populated by the diasporic, transnational, foreign, and global" (2011, 188). Zhang's inter-Asian diasporic cinema, particularly with this quartet, offers significant insights to the "multivalent connections and disconnections" between "Korean (national) and the transnational" (Choi 2012, 3). The idea of translocality is especially relevant to this study with its dual emphasis on locality and mobility (see Oakes and Schein 2006). Scrutinizing Zhang's oeuvre reveals how the films interweave with the filmmaker's own diasporic trajectory, connecting his "ancestral homeland" on the peninsula, his native place of Yanbian in the PRC, and other Asian locales such as Fukuoka and Yanagawa in Japan and Ulaanbaatar in Mongolia.

The inter-Asian quartet maps out the interconnections between the subject(s), (urban) spatiality, and affects and emotions. The films prompt us to consider how a "transed" national space – one "traversed and transformed by forces previously exterior to national territories" (Choi 2012, 6) – is engaged with and experienced cinematically. I approach affective-scape as a cinematic-discursive configuration onto which the correlations between the subjects and places are being registered and constantly reinscribed; as such, it constitutes an affective infrastructure that generates and circulates flows of affects and emotions. Importantly, I use the verb form, affective-scape/*ing*, to emphasize its performativity in *doing* things, mainly by means of drifting and journeying.

DOI: 10.4324/9781003266952-19

This chapter firstly grounds affective-scape/ing in Zhang's engagement with inter-Asian places through location shooting, wherein the filmmaker's articulations tease out the affective, non-representational dimensions pertaining to spatiality and drifting. Next, I unpack the quartet by illustrating how affective-scape/ing enables and performs "translocal *dis*-attachment" as an affective event. However oxymoronic, translocal *dis*-attachment points to how translocal movements – actual and virtual (being imagined, dreamed of, or remembered) – could potentially disturb and reconfigure the discursive and emotive affiliations normatively associated with national or diasporic identities. For instance, although the film characters in the quartet are often designed to depict the interactions between South Korean nationals and various diasporic Korean subjects from Asia, such as *Joseonjok* migrants, *zainichi* Korean or Koreans in Japan, and North Korean defectors, the films frequently problematize any essentialized understanding of national or diasporic identity. This is achieved through moments of encounter, misunderstanding, and playfulness, often utilizing minor objects to reveal what has been made invisible or marginalized. With visions from affect theory and human geography, this research highlights how Zhang Lu's inter-Asian diasporic filmmaking sheds light on the entwined issues of translocal mobility and identity in contemporary (East) Asia while also contributing to critical transnational cinema studies.

Affective-scape/ing as Method: Working with Location

Affective-scape/ing is deployed here as a critical framing to consider a cinematic-affective infrastructure linking the subject and the place. I concur with Lily Wong that affect and emotion are interconnected in terms of "a spiralling feedback loop" (2018, 10), wherein "as a mobilization of emotion, affect provides the language of movement, desire, and becoming that privileges the *potentiality* of meaning over fixed interpretive paths of signs and representation" (2018, 6; italics in original). With the quartet, Zhang and his team traveled to and filmed in various locations, including Gyeongju, Seoul (specifically Susaek), Gunsan, and Fukuoka. I argue location shooting not only unfolds and performs affective-scape/ing, it also yields conceptual insights that shed light on affective-scape/ing as method. The filmmaker for instance often captures the film locations by turning to a set of affective lexica (in Chinese) such as *qingxu* (mood), *jiezou* (rhythm), *zhigan* (texture), and so forth, reinforcing the non-representational underpinning of his methodology, which does not necessarily take representations as "reflections of some a priori order waiting to be unveiled, decoded, or revealed" (Anderson and Harrison 2010, 19). Zhang specifically illustrates how, even after the subjects, objects, and ways of life have disappeared from sight (the frame), their *traces* (*henji*) could still be sensed on the spot (Totoro 2019). For him, the "traces of time" are as much affective as they are material – they are what lingers and "haunts" the place.

Zhang's location shooting, on the one hand, works with and contributes to a mode of knowing that embraces uncertainties and heterogeneous temporalities related to a place such as a neighborhood, city, or region, and how the place entwines with inter-Asian geopolitics. Such a place-based epistemology correlates with the content of expression, concerning the narrative and its site-specific, historical context. On the other, location shooting lays crucial grounds for affective-scaping through which the auteur, the protagonists, and the viewers see, feel, and make sense of what remains invisible, forgotten, and subdued in the urban space and its history. Associated with the form of expression or film style, this underpinning constantly negotiates with and reorients the significance of location shooting as a way of knowing. Since Zhang's relocation to his "ancestral land," location shooting enables him to approach the national space as a fluid ethnoscape that not only intersects with other Asian locales but is also opened up to temporal heterogeneities. Talking about the quartet, for example, Zhang has foregrounded how he *feels* about Gyeongju, Gunsan, and Susaek, leveraging affective registers in Chinese, such as *aimei* (ambiguity) and *huanghu* (in/trance). Specifically, as Zhang vividly enumerates, such affective engagements correlate with Gyeongju as an urban space that incorporates the spectacular ancient tomb groups as part of its everyday life, Susaek which is distinguished by its incommensurability with its surrounding urban environment, and Gunsan with its historical baggage as one of the most important ports for rice trade between the Korean peninsula and Japan under Japan's colonial rule, where the American air force base is now located (Totoro 2019). I suggest that both *aimei* and *huanghu* highlight the affectivities evoked by the temporal-spatial hybridity and liminality, regarding how each locale *feels* to the filmmaker as the boundaries between reality, memory, and various media representations about the place become muddied. These terms have underscored that the auteur is fully aware of his lack of a holistic view or epistemological grasp of spatiality, and how Zhang's diasporic filmmaking creatively works with this limitation.

Drifting in the City

With the quartet, affective-scape is enacted and (re)configured through the acts of roaming and drifting in the everyday milieu. Dwelling on Chinese independent films, Linda Lai has helpfully differentiated "flânerie" from "drifting" despite the fact that, for her, both terms register the position(ing) of an epistemic subject walking the city. Although in the slightly different context of Chinese independent films, her analysis, partially inspired by Situation Internationalist's discussions on *dérive* or drifting, views drifting as a mode of walking or spatial practice that emphasizes the walker/filmmaker's "full presence and her here-and-now engagement with events and happenings that emerge along the way" (Lai 2007, 225). Through drifting, therefore, the filmmaker/walker is not privileged with the pre-established epistemic clairvoyance or total vision in interpreting the urban space, and the city is turned instead into "a space of chance encounter, whereby the 'participant' discovers" (Lai 2007, 225). Meanwhile, seemingly expecting what would be scrutinized under the umbrella term/ discourse of "slow cinema" (see Lee 2021), Lai has indicated how drifting as a narrative strategy necessarily aligns with cinematic temporality. In approaching the stylistic mannerism, such as the use of long takes in Chinese works, specifically, she underscores how cinematic drifting enacts "the moments of roaming and unproductivity" in registering a "negative poetics," namely, one of "(non)actions" (2007, 227). I agree with Lai that the (non)actions and unproductiveness are in themselves generative of affects, an idea that is relevant to the analysis I make here with its attention toward the interconnections between cinematic temporality and affects.

Furthermore, for the quartet and Zhang's oeuvre as a whole, my question concerns whether similar stylistic preferences such as the deployment of long takes would necessarily evoke the same emotions, feelings, and assemblages of affects, especially when one refers to the filmmaker's nuanced theory of spatiality. An examination of Zhang's affective-scaping cannot afford losing sight of the modes, directions, and even velocities of the transborder, translocal trips taken by the auteur as well as by his protagonists. Additionally, issues such as at *which* specific site or side (of the border) the inaction is staged and *how* do matter.

I have examined three of Zhang Lu's earlier works elsewhere as his "border-crossing trilogy" (hereafter "trilogy"), namely, *Desert Dream* (2007), *Dooman River* (2010), and *Scenery* (2013), a documentary (see Ma 2019). This "trilogy" has been mostly associated with the cinematic representations of border-crossing and refugeeism (specifically the North Korean defectors), wherein the translocal subjects are entrapped in their Sisyphean task of transgressing geopolitical border(s) and/or contesting the overwhelming changes brought by modernity and globalism. *Dooman River*, for instance, was shot in an ethnic Korean village in Yanbian, which shares its border with North Korea. In the film, an ethnic Korean boy, Chang-ho, befriends a North Korean boy, Jeong-ji, who frequently crosses the river to visit the Chinese village in search of food for his starved family. With the trilogy, the affective-scape implicates a tension-filled temporal framework for arrival and departure. The condition, underpinned by a delimited duration of stay, can be partially attributed to the historical displacement of the Korean diaspora in Yanbian and the current geopolitical realities on the Korean peninsula, particularly the situation of defectors/refugees from North Korea. It also intersects with contemporary Korea's ethnoscape under global neoliberalism, specifically in the case of the multinational migrant workers in *Scenery*. Often registering the senses of precarity and desperation, it is far from a lineup of "happy" films.

Zhang's later films cannot be completely disassociated from his earlier works. However, it is crucial to see how Zhang's status as a *Joseonjok* resident in Seoul has given the auteur more possibilities to observe and reflect upon contemporary Korean society from *within*.[2] While the quartet is populated by a similar spectrum of translocal subjects such as North Korean defectors, returnees from Japan, *Joseonjok* migrant workers, and so forth, their border-crossing movements of migration and refugeeism are no longer foregrounded as the key narrative. Their translocal trips, or those of their families and friends, often serve as the backdrop and the details of these journeys can only be accessed through conversations, objects, flashes of memories, or dreams. The four films have not only taken a more delightful and humorous stance to canvass the issues of (national) identities and senses of belonging with highly self-reflexive touches as I shall elaborate on shortly. Also, each film navigates through and is populated by aimless flaneurs, drifters who are usually nowhere closer to being the active producers and participants in the neoliberal economy. The translocal subjects, despite their diverse backgrounds, seem to have been liberated from the pressure of impending departures and arrivals. They have redeemed themselves by indulging in nothing but time, which they squander by aimlessly roaming the city.

Gyeongju, for instance, is a partial re-enactment of Zhang's first trip to South Korea back in 1995. In the film, Choi Hyeon (Park Hae-il), a history scholar, now living in Beijing, briefly returns to his home city of Daegu for a friend's funeral. Recalling his previous visit to a teahouse, Choi then decides to take a trip to the nearby city of Gyeongju. Soon he is seen wandering around Gyeongju as a tourist: he rents a bike, stops by the picturesque ancient tomb groups, engages in random conversations with strangers, and also manages to revisit the teahouse that is now owned by Yoon-hee (Shin Min-a). The squandering of time by Choi and his fellow drifters in *Gyeongju* generates a sense of lightness and eroticism. Choi does not differ significantly from Zhang's other protagonists in the quartet who, to borrow the insights of Lai, "wander around the city aimlessly doing very little, or digress into unplanned encounters by letting whatever comes by take them on the spot" (Lai 2007, 220). It is also intriguing that throughout his roaming, Choi shows little interest in leveraging his multilingual ability to facilitate cross-cultural communication. The film entertains audiences with scenarios where translation creates moments of miscommunication and humor. For instance, after a Japanese tourist apologizes to Choi about Japan's historical wrongdoings in Korea, Choi playfully responds by saying, "Actually I like *natto*." Yoon-hee, however, offers a serious statement about Korea-Japan relations in her Japanese interpretation of Choi's responses.

Arguably serving as a cross-border extension of *Ode to the Goose*, *Fukuoka* both starts and ends in a basement in Seoul, where a second-hand bookshop owned by Jae-moon (Yun Jae-moon) is located. Soon after audiences learn from Jae-moon's young, quirky female customer So-dam (Park So-dam) about their planning of a trip for two to Fukuoka, the film shows the two walking around the streets of the Japanese city. Their Fukuoka trip might have actually taken place, but the ending sequence also strongly suggests that the journey itself may have unfolded as an episode of dream or fantasy. Nevertheless, on the surface, the protagonists do not seem to be bothered by their trip to a foreign location, nor are they troubled by the barriers of languages themselves. Without any translation aids, people can simply speak their own language(s) – Korean, Chinese, and Japanese – and be understood smoothly. In contrast with the use of silence in *Desert Dream*, which for Irene Lee has registered Zhang Lu's realist consideration to portray "people living on the margin" (2021, 131), the characters in *Fukuoka*, who are by no means mainstream but are not particularly burdened in life either, are talkative and expressive. In one surprising example, a customer who frequents the pub run by Jae-moon's old schoolmate Hae-hyo (Kwon Hae-hyo) in Fukuoka even opens his mouth for the first time in ten years.

Translocal Dis-attachment

In the quartet, random encounters between the protagonists (their bodies), places and sites, as well as other minor objects such as anecdotes, jokes and poems, happenings, and daily items engender an assemblage of affects that I call "translocal *dis*-attachment." In a different critical take, Sarah Ahmed illustrates that attachment concerns "what connects us to this or that" and "what moves us, what makes us feel, is also which holds us in place, or gives us a dwelling place" (11). The idea that attachment not only can be perceived in terms of bodily and affective connections but is also productive of a "dwelling place" is important to my analysis. Affective-scape/ing enacts and performs translocal *dis*-attachment as a central affective event. Not canceling the attachment, *dis*-attachment closely associates with Zhang's narrative mechanisms, working *with* and *through* creating incongruences, ruptures, and mismatches. It also often concerns how the protagonists' attachment(s) to their places, such as homes, native places, homelands, are mixed up, disrupted, and reassembled through drifting and encounters. Throughout these processes, names, faces and places, languages, accents, and personal histories no longer correlate coherently with any essentialized, pre-given identities or imagined community. Mainly set and shot in contemporary South Korea, the inter-Asian quartet prompts us to consider "the underlying tension, contingent collision, persistent discord, and unresolvable disconnection" that the "nomadic or diasporic subjects" are living in and through (Lee 2021, 121). As diasporic subjects in the quartet constantly negotiate their senses of belonging in relation to South Korean society, translocal *dis*-attachment realigns the interconnections between a "host society," "ancestral land," and "native place" and creates instead a dwelling place in liminality, however contingent.

Writing on epistemology and subculture, Mini Nguyen explores a "minor object" as "those marginal forms, persons, and worlds that are mobilized in narrative (including archival) constructions to designate moments of crisis" (2015, 12). For Nguyen, "by way of a minor object, exclusion and normativity might be laid bare (though perhaps in no straightforward manner), and the contingent quality of knowledge or other claims fold under scrutiny" (2015, 12). Here I modify Nguyen's conceptualization to consider minor objects as the very objects of translocal *dis*-attachment. Though rarely leveraged to dominate the narrative or the emotional core of the film, minor objects emerge alongside the roaming and encounters and unobtrusively draw attention to what has remained invisible, inaudible, "out of place," and even "out of time" pertaining to the ethnoscape, while funneling with the "liminal space between the national and the transnational" (Lee 2021, 121).

In the rest of the chapter, I shall focus on two works from the quartet. Arguably, Zhang's use of narrative devices creates incongruencies and mismatches often through minor objects, which complicate the correlations between translocal subjects and their attachments to inter-Asian places. This is evident in his aesthetics of *dis*-attachment that manifest in the cinematic temporality enacted on screen.

Quietly Dreaming in Susaek

A Quiet Dream was inspired by Zhang's personal experience living in a local neighborhood called Susaek, a commercial-residential quarter where Zhang's university assigned him to stay located on the opposite side of Seoul's Digital Media City (DMC). Given how the disorder, noise, and human bonds of Susaek have particularly fascinated Zhang, the qualities of which have distinguished the neighborhood as "very unlike Seoul," it is not hard to imagine how Susaek could become the habitat for a band of outsiders. Ye-ri came from Yanbian at a young age to live with her South Korean father but now finds herself caring for him after he falls into a vegetative state. Running a small pub annexed to her house called Hometown Tavern, Ye-ri is seen hanging out with Jung-bum (Park Jung-bum), a North Korean defector, Jong-bin (Yoon Jong-bin), the son of Ye-ri's landlord, and Ik-june (Yang Ik-june), an orphaned small-time gangster. In this black-and-white film (except for the ending), the trio of idle young men fall in love with Ye-ri, while she too has become the crush of a tomboyish girl, Joo-young (Lee Joo-young). The affective-scape in *A Quiet Dream* comes into being as the gang drifts around their own turf. The use of long takes is interlaced with different shooting angles and brisk editing, and the actresses and actors deliver performances that are rhythmic yet avoid any sense of lethargy. The affective-aesthetic configuration foregrounds, playfully, the group's blatant lack of productivity and their zero commitment to work. Meanwhile, it is quite telling that Jung-bum and Jong-bin, not quite unlike the parentless Ik-june, are never seen being together with their families or talking about home; instead, the trio appears to feel "at home" wandering around Susaek and spending time together at Ye-ri's pub, an attachment and also a dwelling place for the drifters.

So far as the protagonists are attached to Susaek, an area "awaiting demolition and redevelopment" (Lee 2021, 126), their strolling and encounters underpin a pattern of repetition and temporal loop as if the band is entrapped by the territory, as they get habituated to its rhythm and tempo of inaction and unproductivity. As the gang of four gathers at the rooftop of one of the neighborhood's buildings and overlooks the impressive high-rise complex in the direction of the DMC, it is quite telling how they view Susaek as being incommensurate with the world on the other side. Arguably, what has separated the two areas has also concerned their disparate temporalities. If the DMC represents Seoul's "new future" that the metropolitan government designated at the turn of the millennium, then the gang is viewed as being stuck in a block of time that hardly progresses forward. What has seemingly disrupted the temporal loop of drifting is the shocking, yet not unexpected news about Ye-ri's death that is revealed in the last few minutes of the film. At this point, the monochrome film switches to color, with dream-like segments featuring hand-held tracking shots that simulate the point of view of nothing other than a wandering ghost. After showing a glimpse at the three male friends mourning and solemnly sitting at the pub's table by the side of Ye-ri's funeral portrait, the camera takes off and floats out of the tavern in a long take. It then witnesses Ye-ri's unconscious father standing up, leaving his wheelchair, and setting his feet on the ground in a slow tempo. The camera proceeds to hover along the familiar walking route of the gang, passing by Joo-young on the way, but in the next shot, the perspective shifts, as if we have not only traveled through space but also time, witnessing Ik-june (who in a previous shot is seen inside the pub) meeting Jong-bin around the corner. Here the viewers see the two decide to search for Jung-bum and take off together, setting in motion another day of drifting. This finale in color is both revealing and confusing – it pushes the audiences to view the monochrome part retrospectively as an assemblage of realities and imaginations where Ye-ri's roaming trajectory intertwines with the gang's reminiscing about her. The ending seemingly suggests her presence "on the spot," in the very affective-scape of liminality.

The appearance of minor objects at the "Hometown Tavern" such as the novel read by Ye-ri, and the famous Tang Poetry, "Thoughts on a Silent Night" (*Jingyesi*) by Li Bai interweaves various layers of actual and virtual experiences about inter-Asian displacement and migration. The novel, An Sugil's *Pukkando* (literally meaning "North Kando"),[3] is one of Ye-ri's few possessions left to the world (Figure 14.1). The area of Kando (Jiandao in Chinese), which used to be part of Jilin Province in Manchuria, is the present-day location

Figure 14.1   Ye-ri reading *Pukkando*.

of Yanbian. In the film, Ye-ri's unhappy family and migratory history, underpinned with her translocal identities configured between Yanbian and Seoul, are only brought up casually in their daily conversations. These experiences not only are relevant to a character like Ye-ri but also connect with the personal and creative trajectories of An Sugil and Zhang Lu. However, both the minor objects and the stories they carry remain in the backdrop. As an object of translocal *dis*-attachment, *Pukkando* specifically hints at how Ye-ri and her migrant identity cannot be fully grasped without considering the historical and geopolitical complexities surrounding Yanbian (Kando) in relation to some of the most turbulent chapters in modern East Asia. The sense(s) of belonging for the ethnic Korean people from Yanbian can be hardly integrated into any singular, transhistorical category of imagined community, either. Hence, so far as Ye-ri's roaming and daily encounters at Susaek have configured a dwelling place for her (the band gathers at her home, after all), moments of her reading and reciting, however briefly, also correlate with other places and temporalities that she could have belonged to. Crucially, Zhang is fully aware that not necessarily every spectator can fathom the significance of *Pukkando* and its nuanced use of the Korean language.[4] What remains marginal and untranslatable with the minor objects connects with Zhang's emphasis on heterogeneities and ambiguities pertaining to his affective-scape/ing. Objects as such remind us of what stays incongruent and inconsistent within Korea's national ethnoscape and cannot be conveniently contained by the state's policies of assimilationist multiculturalism today (see Rhee 2016).

To and Fro Yanbian: As Epilogue

Ode to the Goose, the well-structured and arguably most complicated work in the quartet, can be divided into two parts: the trip of Yoon-young (Park Hae-il) and Song-hyun (Moon So-ri) to Gunsan, and their uneventful roaming in Seoul. In the film, city ruins, preserved and repurposed colonial buildings in Gunsan, and the everyday landscapes in Seoul configure the backdrop for whimsical trips, random encounters, and aimless drifting (Figure 14.2). I will examine translocal *dis*-attachment by turning to the recurring instances of (mis)recognition, which unfold via unexpected encounters, particularly those revolving around Yun Dong-ju (1917–45). Born in Longjing, Kando in 1917, Yun "has been widely regarded as a national poet and a resister of imperialism" in South Korea posthumously (J. Kim 2012, 203). His life trajectory and works have intersected the socio-cultural spheres of Korea, Japan, and China.[5] As a minor object in the film, however, Yun only has his name and life story lightheartedly mentioned.

In Gunsan, while resting by the street together with Yoon-young, Song-hyun is suddenly hailed as "Sooni" (a name that also appears in Yun's verse) by a lady who claims to be her acquaintance from Yanbian, an incident that annoys Song-hyun and has obviously ruined her mood. However, in Seoul (presumably before the Gunsan trip), while dining at a restaurant together with Yoon-young, already half-drunk, Song-hyun grabs a middle-aged waitress and wants to confirm whether she is a *Joseonjok*, but the woman instead asks her, "Aren't you from China, too?" It is hard to tell whether Song-hyun's sullen reaction in Gunsan is triggered by her being recognized *wrongly* or her being mistaken as a *Joseonjok*. Interestingly, it is also at the restaurant that Song-hyun shares with Yoon-young a story about his grandpa's older brother, who migrated to and stayed in Manchuria. She then wonders, "If my grandpa stayed in Manchuria, I would be a *Joseonjok* now as well, right?" The same question is repeated when the duo visit the Yoon Dong-ju Literature Museum in

Figure 14.2   Wandering in Gunsan, where the cityscape bears marks of Japan's colonial rule.

Seoul, wherein Song-hyun turns to Yoon-young to ask, "What if Yun stayed [in China]?" This event of (mis)recognition further relates to an episode with Yoon-young's conservative father (a veteran soldier), who is seen arrogantly teaching their *Joseonjok* house-helper a lesson by telling her, "You people have no rights complaining about how you are being treated unequally on this soil!" The father is embarrassed to find later that the house helper comes from Yun's home village and is a distant relative of the poet, which also problematizes his division of "you people" versus "we people."

The episodes of (mis)recognition loosen and disturb the centrality favorably associated with the postcolonial discourse in South Korean mainstream society pre-assigned to Yun Dong-ju. This (mis)recognition connects the fraught translocal trajectories of Yun, as well as other ethnic Korean migrants like him and their communities from/to Kando under colonial rule, with those of *Joseonjok* migrants in multicultural Korea today. For instance, the popular media representations of *Joseonjok* in South Korea have been caught up paradoxically in "a nostalgic imagination of the 'shared bloodline'" with the South Koreans and "charges of disloyalty toward Korea" (Rhee 2016, 2–3). Here Zhang Lu is not necessarily seeking to "reclaim" Yun (and in that case, An Sugil) exclusively for the *Joseonjok* community so as to foreground an essentialist understanding of the diasporic identity vis-à-vis Koreanness. In the quartet, Yanbian (Kando) remains absent from sight as the object of translocal *dis*-attachment. Nevertheless, as a place, Yanbian is carried away and around by Yeri and other (female) migrant workers as they embark on their journeys, evoking an assemblage of place-based imagination: Yanbian is read, imagined, and circulated through literary works, personal episodes (such as Yeri's), and life stories (such as An and Yun's) with accents and tones. Perhaps due to its virtuality in the quartet, Yanbian also intersects with multiple locales and temporalities as well as senses of belonging. Here, attachments, such as "origin," "native place," and even "homeland," apropos the *Chaoxianzu/Joseonjok*, are constantly folded, *trans*ed, and reassembled and are always in a state of becoming. This may explain why Zhang, while reflecting upon his own diasporic experiences, laments, "Perhaps the sentiment of migrants (*yimin qingxu*) is similar all over the world. In a way, it can even be said that all of us now have lost our native places (*guxiang*), and only have the alien land (*taxiang*) to go" (Totoro 2019).

Notes

1 Zhang's grandparents and mother's generations, who migrated to what is now Yanbian at the turn of the 20th century, were originally from North Gyeongsang Province in what is now southeast South Korea. In the PRC, ethnic Koreans are referred to as *Chaoxianzu*, while in Korean language, they are called *Joseonjok* or *Chosŏnjok*. This chapter follows the official Korean language romanization system.
2 *Scenery*, presumably a transitional work, contrasts the everyday work life environments of multinational migrant workers with the alienating, dystopian urban landscape of Seoul. As of 2021, Chinese nationals accounted for 43% of foreign residents in South Korea, with a total of 840,000 people, including 614,000 ethnic Koreans (Yonhap News Agency 2022).
3 Available in the Korean-language but never published in the PRC, the five-volume *Pukkando* was "written between 1959 and 1967 in South Korea," which offered "the epic of Korean migration to Manchuria from the 1860s to 1945 and lives caught between Chinese nationalism and Japanese imperialism" (Park 2005, 25). After studying in Seoul and Tokyo for years, An returned to Kando and pursued his career as a writer. After the liberation, An settled down in South Korea (see Park 2005, 25).
4 Interview with the author on 10 March 2019.
5 Yun studied in Seoul (today's Yonsei University) and Japan and was put in jail in Fukuoka where he perished months before Japan's surrender.

References

Anderson, Ben, and Paul Harrison. 2010. "The Promise of Non-Representational Theories." In *Taking-Place: Non-Representational Theories and Geography*, edited by Ben Anderson and Paul Harrison, 1–34. Farnham, England/Burlington, USA: Ashgate Publishing.
Choi, JungBong. 2011. "National Cinema: An Anachronistic Delirium?" *The Journal of Korean Studies* 16 (2): 173–92. https://doi.org/10.1353/jks.2011.0012.
———. 2012. "Of Transnational-Korean Cinematrix." *Transnational Cinemas* 3 (1): 3–18. https://doi.org/10.1386/trac.3.1.3.
Kim, Jinhee. 2012. "The Understanding of Yun Dong-Ju in Three East Asian Countries." *Korea Journal* 52 (3): 201–25. https://doi.org/10.25024/kj.2012.52.3.201.
Lai, Linda Chiu-han. 2007. "Whither the Walker Goes: Spatial Practices and Negative Poetics in 1990s Chinese Urban Cinema." In *The Urban Generation: Chinese Cinema and Society at the Turn of the Twenty-First Century*, edited by Zhen Zhang, 205–37. Durham, London: Duke University Press.
Lee, Hee Seung Irene. 2021. "In Search of Korean Dream: Zhang Lu's Cinema of Inaction." *Korean Studies* 45 (1): 117–40. https://doi.org/10.1353/KS.2021.0006.
Ma, Ran. 2019. "Independent Filmmaking across Borders in Contemporary Asia." *Independent Filmmaking Across Borders in Contemporary Asia*. https://doi.org/10.5117/9789462986640.
Nguyen, Mimi Thi. 2015. "Minor Threats." *Radical History Review*, no. 122 (May): 11–24. https://doi.org/10.1215/01636545-2849495.
"Number of Foreigners Staying in S. Korea Decreased 3.9 Pct in 2021 Amid Pandemic." 2022. *Yonhap News Agency*, January 26, 2022. https://en.yna.co.kr/view/AEN20220126005000315.
Oakes, Tim, and Louisa Schein. 2006. "Translocal China: An Introduction." In *Translocal China: Linkages, Identities, and the Reimagining of Space*, edited by Tim Oakes and Louisa Schein, 1–35. London/New York: Routledge. https://doi.org/10.2307/20066191.

Park, Hyun Ok. 2005. *Two Dreams in One Bed: Empire, Social Life, and the Origins of the North Korean Revolution in Manchuria*. Durham, London: Duke University Press. https://doi.org/10.2307/j.ctv11312bs.

Rhee, Jooyeon. 2016. "Gendering Multiculturalism: Representation of Migrant Workers and Foreign Brides in Korean Popular Films." *The Asia-Pacific Journal* 14 (7): 1–16.

Totoro. 2019. "DeepFocus x Zhang Lu: Taxiangren Tangshi Weisheiyong [Interview: For Whom the Diaspora's Tang Poetry is For]." *DeepFocus*, January 18, 2019. https://www.sohu.com/a/289849456_758090.

Wong, Lily. 2018. *Transpacific Attachments: Sex Work, Media Networks, and Affective Histories of Chineseness*. New York: Columbia University Press.

15

POSTCARDS FROM RUSSIA

Left Discourse and Telugu Cinema

C. Yamini Krishna

Amid the renewed scholarly fascination with the Cold War era, including its enduring impacts, this chapter examines the intricate interplay between Telugu cinema and leftist ideologies, focusing specifically on industrial exchanges with Soviet Russia. I study key figures of the Telugu film industry, their ideological commitments, and the resultant creative work, thereby constructing an alternate intellectual history for Telugu cinema. While most studies on the influence of Soviet Russia and socialism on Indian films are limited to Bombay cinema, this essay views Cold War politics from the vantage point of a "regional" film industry. Through this lens we start to see interwoven connections between the Telugu film industry and Russia, thereby highlighting an understudied and intricate web of trans-Asian exchanges.

The Telugu film industry produces more than 200 films every year and is one of the most prolific media industries in India. Its linguistic address extends to the Telugu-speaking populace across the southern states of Andhra Pradesh and Telangana and beyond, to the global Telugu diaspora. This outreach is further amplified by the translation of Telugu films into Hindi, broadening their viewership on television as well as online. In recent times, the Telugu film industry has commanded international attention due to the unprecedented box office success of cinematic spectacles like *Bahubali 1* (2015), *Bahubali 2* (2017), and *RRR* (2022) around the world. Embarking on a temporal journey spanning from the 1920s to the present day, this chapter traces the interflows between left discourse and Telugu cinema.

The Telugu speaking regions have been very significant in the left movement in India. Until the late 1940s, the regions of Andhra Pradesh were under British colonial rule, and Telangana was under the rule of the Nizam of Hyderabad. The Nizam was a feudal monarch who governed the largest princely state in India. Land in Telangana was distributed in several *jagirs*, ruled by landlords. The region also had a practice of bonded labor called *Vetti*. The conditions of feudal exploitation became fertile ground for soaking in leftist cultural thought and the ideas of the Russian Revolution. Between 1946 and 1951 there was an armed rebellion by farmers and the farm laborers against the landlords in Telangana, led by local communists. Almost 3,000 villages managed to establish self-rule. This Telangana peasant rebellion is one of the key movements in the history of leftist struggle in India. In fact, Joseph Stalin was directly contacted by the Community Party of India for

DOI: 10.4324/9781003266952-20

discussion and advice on the Telangana movement (Sundarayya 1972). Telugu poet Dasar-athi Krishnamacharya, who also wrote the lyrics of more than two thousand Telugu film songs, compared the Telangana Rebellion with the Russian Revolution. He wrote, "When I remember the Telangana revolutionary stories which are comparable to those of Russian Revolution, my heart is distraught" (Dasarathi 2011, 229).

The history of interlinkages between international leftist thought, Russia, and the Telugu film industry, which I narrate in this chapter, enables us to think about the Cold War beyond the frame of nation-states. It also allows us to think about the internationalist char-acter of "regional" Telugu film. Geographically, it complicates the understanding of the region from being solely rooted in nationalist politics to being a part of transnational and intercontinental flows of ideas and objects. In this chapter I first discuss some exchanges between Telugu literary and cultural movements and Russian socialism through the work of key Telugu intellectuals and institutions. I then trace the movement of these progressive Telugu intellectuals into the Telugu film industry. Finally, I end the essay with the move-ment of Telugu films and people between the Telugu film industry and Russia, during the Cold War.

Soviet Socialism and Its Cultural Influence

The October Revolution, or the Bolshevik Revolution, led by Vladimir Lenin in 1917, was an event of great significance for the entire world. It marked the beginning of a new promise of equality and social justice. The fall of the tsarist regime represented hope for farmers, laborers, and the working class around the world. It was also seen as Marxist theory in action. The Russian Revolution had its influence across the political spectrum; it was an "experiment" that everyone was closely watching. Indian leaders, such as M.K. Gandhi, Jawaharlal Nehru, Rabindranath Tagore, and Bhagat Singh, were all closely following the developments in Russia (Komarov 2021).

Lenin emphasized the need for cultural revolution along with the political revolution (A.I. Piskunov 1981). Lenin's focus on culture inspired a wide variety of responses in the Indian subcontinent, and the Progressive Writers' Association (PWA) was one of the most prominent of these. Formed in 1934 by a group of Indian students in London, the PWA pub-lished its manifesto in 1936 in London's *Left Review* journal. It outlined goals such as "the new literature of India must deal with the basic problems of our existence today – the prob-lem of hunger and poverty, social backwardness and political subjection," and reflected the spirit of enabling people's participation in culture as outlined by Russian socialism (Allana 2018, 122). It is worth noting that prior to drafting the manifesto, one of the co-founders of the PWA, Mulk Raj Anand had attended the First International Congress for the Defense of Culture held in Paris in 1935. This important conference aimed to establish a people's front of writers to campaign against fascism. It was attended by artists from 38 countries, including stalwarts such as Maxim Gorky, Bertolt Brecht, and E.M. Forster.

The ideas of the PWA spread into many Indian languages, and several branches devel-oped across the subcontinent. The progressive cultural movement in the south-eastern region of Andhra had direct linkages with the all-India Progressive Writers Movement. It was anti-colonial, anti-fascist, and also anti-feudal. *Abhyudaya Rachayitala Sangham* (ARASAM), which was the Telugu-language branch of the Progressive Writers Associa-tion, had its first conference in 1943 in Tenali and was attended by prominent writers and poets such as Tapi Dharma Rao, Anisetti Subbarao, Bellamkonda Ramadasu, Elchuri

Subramaniam, Kundurti, Maqdoom, Somasundar, Kodavatiganti, Dasharathi, and Arudra. This was directly connected to the central leadership of the PWA.

The Indian People's Theatre Association (IPTA), a cultural organization associated with the PWA, was founded in Bombay in 1943 at the national conference of theater artists. Film director and producer Garikapati Raja Rao from Andhra attended the conference. In the Telugu-speaking regions, a local IPTA branch was created, and named Praja Natya Mandali (PNM). The artists at PNM drew on varied forms like the *veedhinatakam* (street theater), *burrakatha* (folk recital), and *harikatha* (Hindu mythological theater). Even before the formation of IPTA, a certain kind of people's theater was already popular in Andhra, such as *Raithu Bidda* (Farmer's Son), a street play about the struggles of farmers. PNM was very active during the Telangana armed struggle between 1946 and 1951, and the play *Maa Bhoomi* (Motherland) is said to have been staged more than a thousand times and reached two million people during these years (Ramakrishna 1993). The play was written and performed in support of the peasants' rebellion; it narrated the atrocities of the landlords and exhorted people to rebel against them.

On 4 July 1970, a section of Telugu writers broke away from the PWA and formed the Revolutionary Writer's Association, or VIRASAM (Viplava Rachaitala Sangham), with the poet Srirangam Srinivasa Rao (Sri Sri) as the founding president. It was formed in response to the Naxalbari movement of 1967 and the Srikakulam peasant uprising where peasant guerilla squads were formed and systematic resistance was carried out against the landlords and moneylenders. The Srikakulam uprising was crushed with an iron fist by the Indian government and the leaders of the movement were murdered. VIRASAM pledged its commitment toward armed revolution (Venugopal 2019).

I locate the left discourse and socialist ideas in Telugu cinema within this literary and cultural milieu. Film played a central role in the popularization of socialist ideas among the common people. Cinema can thus be thought of as an extension to the revolutionary theater I discussed earlier. In fact, as I illustrate in the next section, several people who were part of the revolutionary literary and theater movements moved into Telugu cinema.

Socialist Themes in Telugu Cinema

I trace socialist themes in Telugu cinema through biographies of film practitioners who were also involved in leftist literary and cultural movements and through the representation of left discourse on screen. However, I focus only on illustrating the themes and not evaluating the politics of each of the films.

Garikapati Raja Rao who started the PNM (Telugu IPTA) also produced and directed a film named *Puttilu* (Birth-place/Home, 1953). The film's writer Vasireddy, the composer Chalapathi, and the actor Jamuna were all associated with the PNM. While the film itself was a family drama with little interest in socialist ideas, it is significant to this discussion because it points out how Telugu cinema drew a lot of its crew from the left movement. Tapi Dharma Rao, Dasharathi and Arudra, members of ARASAM were also prolific film writers. Tapi Dharma Rao was one of the dialogue writers of *Raithu Bidda* (Farmer's Son, 1939), a film against the Zamindari system, where agricultural land was owned by colonially deputed Zamindars who collected cash revenues from farmers who were reduced to the status of tenants. He also wrote dialogues for *Malapilla* (Untouchable Girl, 1938), which presented a love story between an upper caste man and a Dalit girl and advocated against untouchability. *Rojulu Marayi* (Times Have Changed, 1952), which was written by Tapi

178

Dharma Rao and directed by his son Tapi Chanakya is an example of the agrarian social-ist theme in Telugu cinema. The film starts with a farm song "Oli ro poli," which presents collective farming and critiques the feudal system of theft of labor and revenue. The local elite and the documentary regimes of land titling conspire against farmers. The *zamindar* or feudal landlord takes over all the common land with the help of the local revenue official (*karanam*). The zamindar, who is also the principal money lender of the village, controls the farm workers by controlling farm financing. The title *Rojulu Marayi* gestures to the shift from the age of oppression by zamindars to the age of people's collective revolt.

Agrarian socialism had some specific industrial features in Telugu cinema. While the films themselves challenged the zamindari system, in reality they were often funded by agrarian capitalists. For instance, both *Raithu Bidda* and *Rojulu Marayi* were produced by Sarathi Studios, which was funded by Charlapalli Zamindar. This might explain why while talking about the struggle for workers' rights, these films also spoke of God's grace in the same breath.

Srirangam Srinivasa Rao (Sri Sri), commonly referred to as Mahakavi (Great Poet), one of the founding members of VIRASAM, was also a prolific film writer and wrote more than 1,000 film songs. Sri Sri was a committed leftist and visited Russia as the recipient of the Soviet Land Nehru Award.[1] In his autobiography Sri Sri recounts his joy at the prospect of visiting Russia and being impressed that Russia did not have "unemployment, begging (poverty) and sex work" (1986, 194). He visited Lenin's memorial and compared the experience to that of visiting the deity at the famous Tirupati temple. He was awed by the grandeur of Leningrad and St. Petersburg. In a poem titled "Garjinchu Russia" ("Roar Russia"), written in 1941, Sri Sri described Russia as a "land which dreamt a worker para-dise." He named "Pushkin, Gogol, Chekov, Tolstoy, Dostoevsky, Gorki, Kuprin and Marx, Engels, Bukharin, Bakunin, Kropotkin, Lenin, Stalin" as the makers of Russia who worked toward achieving freedom and equality. In the context of growing capitalism, he wrote that the world was ready, waiting, and calling for Russia (1981, 135). Sr Sri's ideology is also reflected in some of the songs he penned. In a poem titled "Maha Prasthanam," meaning the great journey, he refers to the great transformation in society that a communist revolu-tion will bring. Sri Sri writes: "A new world beckons. Let us march together and go higher" (1981, 26).

This poem was adapted into a song for the film *Rana Bheri* (War Cry, 1968). The filmed version shows the protagonists holding sickles, hammers, and swords, calling for change and inviting the rule of the people. Though the film was set in the time of the kings, queens, and princes, this song spoke to the contemporary issues of class exploitation in the 1960s. The same poem was adapted once again for the eponymous film *Maha Prasthanam* (The Great Journey, 1982), made by Madala Rangarao (whom I discuss later), where the song is filmed as a culmination of the narrative where the protagonist and all the villagers come together calling for the establishment of a new world socialist order; it is an armed insur-rection where all the common people come out with hammers, sickles and sticks against the oppressor class. The film featured Sri Sri reading the poem in the opening sequence. Sri Sri was also the dialogue writer and lyricist of the film.

Another poem of Sri Sri titled "Jayabheri" talks of the individual's contribution to the world. It talks of addressing the anguish of the people of the world and the individual becoming one with the rhythm of the world. Written in 1933, this poem was adapted into film songs multiple times. For example, in the 1988 film *Rudraveena* the filmed song reflects the anguish of a young upper caste man going against his caste and family traditions to do his bit for the world, i.e., to work for the marginalized communities and the caste oppressed. The same song was adapted again in the film *Tagore* (2003) where a vigilante college teacher takes it upon himself to cleanse society of corruption. The changing social contexts of this song indicate that the socialist poetry of Sri Sri continues to be in circulation in new filmic reincarnations.

The literary figure of Sri Sri himself has become representative of the socialist vision and rebellion for the Telugu public sphere. In the film *Aakali Rajyam* (Hungry Kingdom, 1980), the protagonist refuses to conform to the norms of society. The protagonist, an educated unemployed youth, constantly recites Sri Sri's poetry as moral ammunition to handle the systemic violence of the society. Sri Sri's poetry is therefore the conscience keeper of the protagonist and does not allow him to succumb to the pressures of the capitalist system.

Another strand of the agrarian socialist theme in Telugu cinema pertains to the Telangana peasant rebellion in pre-independence India. Some writers, such as the poet and film lyricist Dasarathi Krishnamacharya, made direct comparisons of the Telangana movement with the Bolshevik Revolution, as I have mentioned already. The Telangana peasant rebellion was represented on screen in *Maa Bhoomi* (Motherland 1979), directed by Gautam Ghose and based on Krishan Chander's novel *Jab Khet Jage* (When the Fields Awaken, 1952). Gaddar, the legendary balladeer of Jana Natya Mandali (JNM, or People's Theatre Troupe), a cultural wing of CPI (Marxist-Leninist), made his entry into cinema through this film. The screenplay of the film was written by B. Narsing Rao, also a JNM member. The exploitation by the landlords in Telangana is also presented in another film directed by B. Narsing Rao, *Daasi* (Bonded Woman, 1988). The film presents the story of bonded labor (*Vetti*) and sexual exploitation practiced by the landlords in Telangana villages in the early twentieth century.

T. Krishna and Madala Ranga Rao were two other prominent artists from PNM (Telugu IPTA) who made Telugu films. T. Krishna made films like *Neti Bharatam* (Today's India, 1983), *Desham lo Dongalu Paddaru* (There Are Thieves in the Nation, 1985), *Pratighatana* (Protest, 1985), *Repati Pourulu* (Tomorrow's Citizens, 1986). Krishna's films focused on questioning the corruption in the political and social system. For example, in his film *Repati Pourulu*, a school teacher and her fiancé attempt to challenge political corruption and as a result she is raped and he is murdered. Her students then struggle for justice for her. The film presents the moral corruption in the country, which for Krishna is marked by themes like sex work, bribes, and dishonesty. Krishna's films did not feature collective action but often presented one righteous individual questioning the exploitative nature of the system. Krishna's films can be termed as "patriotic" and "nationalist," and socialist only in the sense of talking about exploitation of the poor and women, in spite of his PNM connection. Madala Ranga Rao, another PNM member was popularly called the Red Star (*The Hindu* 3 May 2011) because he acted in and directed revolutionary films: *Erra Mallelu* (Red Jasmine, 1981), *Maha Prasthanam* (The Great Journey, 1982), *Viplava Sankham* (Revolutionary Bugle, 1982), *Navodayam* (New Dawn, 1983), *Praja Sakthi* (People Power, 1983), *Erra Sooryudu* (Red Sun, 1995), and *Nenu Saitham* (Me Too, 2004) are some of his prominent films. These films spoke about revolution, often violent, a rebellion from the bottom in factories, and among the villages.

Erra Mallelu, directed by Dhavala Satyam, was produced by Rangarao. In the opening scene we see a man reading out the news to a washerman, announcing that it was Independence Day. The washerman (belonging to Dhobi caste) drops his laundry and asks the newspaper reader if he could go to the stream and wash the clothes instead of him because independence means that the educated and the washerman are equal. The educated man says that it can never be, the hierarchy does not change, and mocks the washerman for talking about equality. Then one of the protagonists, Suribabu, arrives in his factory uniform and says it is not Independence Day but May Day, a festival for the working classes. Suribabu is referred to as "the communist," and we see him carrying the red flag with hammer and sickle alongside other factory workers carrying hammers and sickles. The film released on 1 May 1981 and had an entire song dedicated to May Day. The village is plagued by the atrocities of the panchayat president, Pedda Kapu (a caste name used to refer to landowning caste), and Karanam (a Brahmin caste name usually referring to scribes and revenue officers). The three of them torment the laborers and lower castes, take over their lands, and rape women. The film ends with the workers, farmers and the villagers together burning down the oppressors – the factory owner and three village elite. Rangarao's films thus did not hesitate to propose a violent red revolution.

R. Narayana Murthy is another important Telugu film personality associated with communist thought. He has acted in/directed films such as *Ardharathri Swatantram* (Freedom at Midnight, 1986), *Laal Salam* (Red Salute, 1992), *Erra Sainyam* (Red Army, 1994), *Errodu* (Red Person, 1995), and *Orey Rikshaw* (Hey Rikshaw, 1995). *Ardharathri Swatantram* was dedicated to T. Krishna and cast him in a prominent role as a doctor turned Naxalite who is given the death penalty. Four of his friends are inspired to carry out the revolution themselves and start working among the tribes as *annalu* (brothers), a synonym for Naxalites. One of the songs of the film refers to the Srikakulam armed rebellion of 1967. The climax of the film is the killing of the tribals by police in a scene seemingly inspired from the real incident of Indravelli of 1981, where the police opened fire at a gathering of Gonds organized by Girijana Rythu Coolie Sangham. Interestingly the film also presents a good policeman who argues with the Naxals throughout the film that change needs to be through a democratic process. However, after the massacre of the tribals, he also takes up arms and fires at the power elite responsible for the massacre. In retaliation he is killed by another policeman. The film ends with a tribal boy draped in a blood red cloth, thereby saying that the rebellion continues. The film takes a clear stance that armed rebellion is inevitable. This film is indicative of R. Narayana Murthy's themes, which can be termed as a "Naxal film." This lineage of leftist revolutionary thought continues in more recent Telangana films such as *Veera Telangana* (Valiant Telangana, 2010), *Poru Telangana* (Battle Telangana, 2011; by R. Narayana Murthy), and *Jai Bolo Telangana* (Hail Telangana, 2011), where Gaddar gave music.

What I have discussed until now are artists and intellectuals who were directly involved in left cultural movements in Telugu-speaking regions. However, socialist thought was so popular that even others without explicit political connections with the left movements professed and advocated socialism. In fact, Russia was an example to learn from. In the next section I present an archive of memoirs of artists from the Telugu film industry about their visits to Russia. These memoirs garner additional importance in the context of the Cold War.

Film and Cold War

Film was an important diplomatic tool in the Cold War politics. For example, Sangjoon Lee (2020) describes the tussle between the two superpowers during the International Film Festival of India (IFFI) held in 1952 in Bombay, which was the first film festival anywhere in

Asia. IFFI featured films from the US and the USSR along with those from other European and Asian countries.

Sudha Rajagopalan (2005) discusses the popularity of Bombay cinema in Russia: about 210 Indian films were screened in Russia between 1954 and 1991. Russian audiences loved Hindi cinema as a welcome break from the onslaught of the socialist realism of Soviet cinema. However, the Soviet state's response to Indian film was not uniform. It was dismissed as bourgeois in the Stalin era but was lauded for its socialist leanings in the post-Stalinist era (Rajagopalan 2006). Two years after IFFI the first Indian film festival opened in Moscow in 1954 (Rajagopalan 2006, 13). The films were provided with wide and favorable publicity. *Soveksportfilm*, an organization responsible for export and distribution of Soviet films ran a Bombay office since the 1949. *Soveksportfilm* studied Indian audiences to combat the growing popularity of American cinema. It also considered dubbing films into Indian languages. However, it was not successful due to various reasons of budget and even resistance from the Indian officials, as they wanted to safeguard the local market. Rajagopalan writes that many Bombay film personalities like Dev Anand, Nirupa Roy, Nargis, K.A. Abbas, and Raj Kapoor made mandatory stops in Moscow. Rajagopalan and most other research on engagement of film with the USSR focuses on Bombay cinema. However, "regional" cinemas, such as Telugu cinema, also had longstanding ideological as well as material exchanges with Soviet Russia.

The Tashkent Festival of African and Asian Cinema, set up in October 1968, was a "cinematic contact zone" that engaged filmmakers, actors, critics, governments, and business figures from 49 countries in Asia and Africa (Djagalov and Salazkina 2016). It later expanded to include Latin American countries. It was one of the major showcases of Third World cinema. Djagalov and Salazkina describe it as the now-forgotten effort to create a platform for the Third World cinemas to compete with the Hollywood. It is important to note that this festival was unaffected by the quelling of the Prague spring in the same year and despite the call to boycott issued by International Federation of Film Critics (FIPRESCI), one month before. The Telugu film industry (and other Indian industries) had exchanges with the USSR even prior to the Tashkent Film Festival. The film *Padandi Munduku* (Let's Move Forward, 1962) was exhibited in Russia in the Indian Film Festival in Moscow in 1966, the Fifth Moscow International Film Festival held in 1967, and later in the Tashkent Film Festival. In 1966, some members of the crew traveled to Russia.

The Telugu film star Gummadi along with the director Madhusudhan Rao and the actor Jamuna traveled to Moscow during the 1966 exhibition of *Padandi Munduku*. Crew members from the Hindi and Malayalam films *Arzoo* (Desire, 1965), *Shaheed* (Martyr, 1965), *Phool aur Patthar* (Flower and Stone, 1966), and *Chemmeen* (The Prawn, 1965) were also part of the contingent. Gummadi wrote a diary of the account of their travel which was published in the magazine *Vijaya Chitra*. He was very enthusiastic to see a socialist nation and marveled at it (January 1967, 42). He noted that the Moscow University had a separate focus on camera, sound, film processing, direction, scriptwriting, screenplay writing, and acting, depending on the interest of the students, and hoped that the government of India also gave such importance to the film industry (January 1967, 47). Gummadi wrote about the Pioneer Centers where students were encouraged to learn various arts. He wondered "how long it would be for us to achieve this state" where students were studying without any differentiation of race, and class with so much equality (February 1967, 22). During their visit, they interacted with Telugu students studying in Russia and the translators Uppala Lakshmana Rao and Kolachala Seetaramayya, who were responsible for constant exchange of literature between Russia and Telugu sphere (May 1967, 46).

Gummadi was impressed by the state's rejection of private property, particularly in the sphere of housing. He noted that need-based housing was allocated by the government, with minimal rents alongside pensions and maternity benefits. He reflected that it was because of private property that in India we think about saving things for "my family" and security, which leads to corruption (June 1967, 27). Gummadi also visited the Tashkent Film Festival in 1982 and wrote that the most impressive aspect of Tashkent was that the everyday groceries were kept at minimum prices so that they were accessible to everyone and there would not be any hunger (July 1982, 52). This understanding of socialism as an answer to hunger and inequality is seen in most popular Telugu cinema, some of which I have discussed earlier.

Gummadi's views on adopting a state socialist approach to filmmaking in India were significantly different. When a journalist questioned him on his views on nationalizing the film industry, Gummadi responded that nationalization could destroy identity and creativity as the government gets the power to dictate terms. Reflecting on the Russian film industry, he agreed that Indian government ought to financially support local cinema. In this, he hoped that the Indian government would learn from their Soviet counterparts and assist filmmakers (June 1967, 27). He also noted, favorably, that the USSR film market seemed to be more interested in realistic portrayals and of narratives of peasants and workers. But the ideal scenario, in his view, would entail the Indian government bearing the financial burdens of the film industry, while allowing creative freedom to the artists (May 1967, 47). More Telugu films should also be promoted and exhibited internationally, as opposed to the dominance of Hindi films. In a speech at the 1982 Tashkent Film Festival, Gummadi pointed out that if Russians truly wanted to understand the regional cultures of India they should be importing films in languages other than Hindi (July 1982, 53). Such industrial

Figure 15.1 Series image for *Padandimunduku tho Russia Yatra* (Travel to Russia with Padandi-munduku). 1 February 1967.

comparisons and cultural exposure were reciprocated when Russian film personalities visited India in 1967, 1981, and 1988.

While Gummadi said that the nationalization of the film industry was impractical, there definitely was a high moral value attributed to films with no added commercial elements. The USSR was the most accessible alternative film industry model, and hence, it often became a canvas for comparison. Specifically in the immediate decades of independence, post-1947, the socialist promise also meant "value-led" cinema as opposed to commercial cinema.

Vishwanath Reddy, the editor of the Telugu film magazine *Vijayachitra*, also traveled to the USSR on the invitation of Novosci Press Agency to understand the film production techniques there. In a *Vijayachitra* article he discussed the importance of women directors in the Soviet Union and the respect that was accorded to artists. Among the several things he was impressed with, he specifically mentioned encouragement for new experimental cinema and the non-hierarchical collective work environment. He wrote that unlike assumptions in India that the world of film is a dreamland, in the Soviet Union film work was understood to be about discipline, commitment and effort; this work culture was reflected in their films (*Vijayachitra* 1983).

Conclusion

Such minute discussions on Russia and socialism in the Telugu literary and cinematic sphere demonstrate (1) how Telugu cinema engaged with socialism as a cultural and ideological force, (2) how the Cold War played out in regional cultures, and (3) how Telugu cinema had global exchanges much before the recent "*Bahubali* moment" and exports directed at NRI (non-resident Indian, or diasporic) audience. Stars, directors, and technicians from the USSR visited the Telugu film industry, and these trips were reciprocated through the 1960s–'80s, influencing ideas about best practices in film production as well as on narrative and stylistics. These exchanges emphasize the movement of ideas, people, and films in a larger Asiatic context.

For all the Telugu literary and cultural figures I have discussed, Russia symbolized the October Revolution and socialism; they did not respond to it becoming an imperialist force even after the occupation of Czechoslovakia. In that sense, the influence of the Bolshevik Revolution was timeless up until the 1980s. It is this reference that is constantly seen in Telugu literary and film cultures. For the Telugu film industry, more specifically, the USSR set the moral compass for working culture. Russian working culture was considered to be more artistic, devoid of selfish motivations and in service of the people. These values were aspirational for some sections of the Telugu film industry. As geographically and culturally more proximate, the film industry in Russia was the yardstick against which the Telugu film industry measured itself.

Acknowledgment

The author would like to thank MaNaSu Foundation in Bangalore for access to their collection, and Professor S.V. Srinivas for enabling it.

Note

1 The Soviet Land Nehru Award was instituted in memory of Jawaharlal Nehru, India's first prime minister, after his death in 1965. The award was in the fields of literature and art and was a diplomatic venue to foster friendly relations between Russia and India. Along with a monetary reward the award included a two-week trip to Russia. Hindi poets Sumitranandan Pant and Harivansh Rai Bacchan were some of the other recipients of the award.

References

Allana, Amal. 2018. "Released into the Future: (Re)Claiming Brecht in India." *The Brecht Yearbook/DasBrecht-Jahrbuch* 42: 121–36.

Dasarathi, K. 2011. *Yaatra Smruti*. Hyderabad: Emesco Books.

Djagalov, R., and M. Salazkina. 2016. "Tashkent '68: A Cinematic Contact Zone." *Slavic Review* 75 (2): 279–98.

Gummadi. 1967. *Padandi Munduku tho Russia Yatra. Vijayachitra,* January 1, 1967: 42–43, February 1, 1967: 21–23, March 1, 1967: 46–49, May 1, 1967: 45–47, June 1, 1967: 24–27. Vijayawada: Vijaya Publications.

———. 1982. *Tashkent Chalanachitrotsavam. Vijayachitra,* July 1, 1982: 51.

The Hindu. 2011. "Red Star Madala Ranga Rao Shines." May 3, 2011. Accessed July 25, 2023. https://www.thehindu.com/todays-paper/tp-national/tp-andhrapradesh/red-star-madala-ranga-rao-shines/article1987482.ece

Komarov, E. 2021. "Progressive Indians and Our Country." In *The Russian Revolution and India,* edited by Ilsai Manian and V. Rajesh, 83–92. Oxon/New York: Routledge.

Lee, S. 2020. *Cinema and the Cultural Cold War: US Diplomacy and the Origins of the Asian Cinema Network.* New York: Cornell University Press.

Piskunov, A. I. 1981. "Lenin's Concept of Cultural Revolution and the Creation of the Soviet School." *Soviet Education* 23 (4): 63–73.

Rajagopalan, S. 2005. *A Taste for Indian Films: Negotiating Cultural Boundaries in Post-Stalinist Soviet Society.* Bloomington: Indiana University.

———. 2006. "Emblematic of the Thaw: Early Indian Films in Soviet Cinemas." *South Asian Popular Culture* 4 (2): 83–100.

Ramakrishna, V. 1993. "Left Cultural Movement in Andhra Pradesh: 1930s to 1950s." *Social Scientist* 40 (1–2): 21–30.

Sri Sri. 1981. *Mahaprasthanam*. Hyderabad: Visalandhra Publishers.

———. 1986. *Anantham. Atma charitratmaka charitratmaka navala.* Hyderabad: Virasam.

Sundarayya, P. 1972. *Telangana People's Struggles and its Lessons.* Calcutta: Communist Party of India (Marxist).

Venugopal, N. 2019. "Arunaksharavishkaraniki Ardhashatabdi." July 2019. https://kolimi.org.

SECTION III

Trans-Border Connections
Infrastructures and Desires

INTRODUCTION

Debashree Mukherjee

We envisioned this section as a call for new writing on Asian media industries, and as you will see, the resulting array of voices and methods gives us fresh insights into the scope of situated studies of technologies, sites of production, and audiences. All the chapters consider trans-border processes: from the industrial and infrastructural crossing of national borders, to cross-medial transfers and borrowings, to diasporic dreams of a cinema culture that can repair broken relationships. We also discern new trends in film and media studies that stretch the possibilities of industry studies. Production ethnography still remains the preferred mode of studying media industries today, but it does not allow ready access to the past. It seems clear that for industrial *histories* one will have to look at other methods and sites.

Two emerging axes of research bridge the gap between past and present, and embrace multiple methods. First, we have a focus on histories of communication and infrastructure that facilitate and often are coterminous with film production. Grounded in film studies, these chapters do not eschew film analysis and playfully weave representation into their material excavations of media systems and supply chains. Second, diasporic desire emerges as an underrecognized industrial engine that propels promiscuous film exchanges across borders considered hostile or impassable. For example, the two films analyzed by Hyangjin Lee were made by diasporic filmmakers occupying an ambivalent position within their chosen countries of residence (US and Japan) as ethnic minorities. This positionality has its own generative affordances, including a certain degree of creative and imaginative freedom. The diaspora thus films its own stories, crafting alternative trajectories for the story of the nation.

In "Media Topographies of East Asia," Alexander Zahlten reads a history of communications and representational infrastructures as a history of imperial ambition and conquest. The chapter traces the growth of media connectivity in East Asia along the pathways of Japan's imperial projects of the twentieth century. Zahlten presents a transmedial tale of crisscrossing wires and networks that connected railways with electrical grids, radio sets with telegraph lines, and movie theaters with amusement parks. The resulting "network of networks" constituted a media topography at the same time as it produced imaginaries of territory and region. By rethinking the relationship of media and empire in Asia via Japanese imperialism, the chapter poses an important corrective to the current predominance

DOI: 10.4324/9781003266952-22

of histories of British communications systems in postcolonial studies, as also universalist understandings of electricity within Canadian and broader North American media theory. In terms of method, Zahlten opens up a thought-space between infrastructure studies, communication studies, and media ecology, drawing equally on traditional tools of the humanities such as textual analysis alongside social histories of built forms and political economies of communication technologies. This opening chapter thus furthers our editorial commitment to thinking and reading *between* and *across* Asian histories of cinema and technology.

Infrastructure is the central analytic in Gerald Sim's chapter, "Looking Out and On the Move: Aesthetics of Infrastructure in Recent Singapore Cinema." Singaporean cinema started to gain international recognition in the late 1990s, in parallel with a marked trend in the films of the time toward abject, passive characters and bleak urban milieus verging on the claustrophobic. Sim contrasts this narrative mood with a shift in the last decade toward themes of connectedness and global mobility and argues that this cinematic change is a representation of the altered status of Singapore itself within a global system of supply chain capitalism. A case in point is K. Rajagopal's *A Yellow Bird* (2016). The film centers on the relationship between an Indian-Singaporean ex-con and an undocumented Chinese sex worker, characters who, in Sim's analysis, not only complicate the "national cinema" status of 21st-century Singapore films but also indicate a globalization from below. Of central interest here is an epistemic and narrative shift in how Singapore is viewed and framed, not as an insular nation with bounded edges but as an infrastructural hub that is fundamentally outward-facing. The chapter describes an emerging infrastructural aesthetics that can be noticed across fiction and documentary films such as Tan Pin Pin's *A Time to Come* (2017) or Anthony Chen's *Ilo Ilo* (2013), and connects this with Singapore's renewed status as a "hub." Sim employs a "world cinema" rubric alongside critical infrastructure studies, to reiterate that global trends in cinema or capitalism do not erase the particularities of the local.

Hyangjin Lee's essay harkens back to Section II by underlining the ways in which cinema was instrumentalized in Korea after World War II by the US and Soviet occupation governments in order to manufacture an ideological polarization between North and South. Lee prefers to enter this story through a reparative lens, narrating how cinema might also be used to thaw these hostilities through all three spheres of film production, distribution, and exhibition. Starting with television broadcasts of North Korean films in South Korea in the 1990s, to the theatrical premiere of *Arirang* in Pyongyang in 2002, to film festivals that showcase films from both countries, the chapter moves to its central subject: North Korean co-productions with Japan, South Korea, China, Belgium, England, and the United States, which create new spaces that defy isolationism. As filmmakers started to explore collaborative possibilities across borders in the 1990s, a new genre of the "division drama" emerged and became hugely popular with local and diasporic audiences. Lee gives us glimpses into new framings around diasporic production and address – such as the "*zainichi* film," which refers to films made by Koreans in Japan and screenings that cater to these communities. The *zainichi* also poses an interesting affective audience, with a longing for homecoming and national unification. Lee thus uses textual analysis to move beyond a reflectionist reading of films as representing state policy, to a cultural studies approach where cinematic meaning is produced between the screen and the viewer. Crucially, the diasporic filmmaker is also implicated in the same desires as the diasporic viewer, where both dream of a unified homeland and pursue that dream through cinema.

Olivia Khoo picks up the thread on transnational film traffic by moving us further east toward Australia. The essay provides a radical rethinking of the possibilities of "trans-Asia" as an imaginary and as a geographic signifier, one that can and must include Australia. Khoo presents three different orders of Chinese Australian film collaborations, from official co-productions under the China-Australia Co-production Treaty signed in 2007, to runaway productions where Australia is simply an affordable location for big-budget Hollywood films with an eye on Chinese diasporic audiences, and finally an independent production by an all-Asian Australian creative team. These categories help us think about film imaginations moving between Asia and Australia along the different axes of production, location, and on-screen representation. Once again, it is a "diasporic consciousness" that is key to these cinematic exchanges as Asian-Australian filmmakers seek to represent their own experience on screen. These moves are buoyed, on the one hand, by the global success of films like *Crazy Rich Asians* centered on Chinese characters and, on the other hand, by transnational film studios vying for Asian audiences for blockbuster "multiverse" franchises. Khoo ends the chapter with a provocative suggestion: Might we think of a possible trans-Asia as a multiverse? Not a geographic space but an imaginative space crisscrossed by affect and memory?

"Exile at the Edges: Donald Richie at the Pinch Point Between Japan and the World," is Markus Nornes' ambitious reframing of the life and career of Donald Richie. We move from the diasporic subject to the exilic subject, as Nornes narrativizes Richie's understudied role as a writer, composer, programmer, filmmaker, and cultural catalyst in 1960s Tokyo. Nornes stitches together a fascinating atmospheric portrait of Richie around the formation of *Firumu Andepandan (Film Independent)* in 1964. The figure of the exile problematizes the category of national cinema by showcasing individuals on the fringes of national-canonic film production. Though not a political exile in the standard use of the term, Richie was nevertheless escaping everyday forms of trauma in the United States, one that had dogged his childhood and adolescence as a closeted gay man. As an American in postwar Japan, Richie found himself "politely stigmatized" but also in the midst of an artistic ferment. His enthusiasm for cinema led him to occupy a significant place within this ferment as he brought together young local filmmakers and served as a cultural diplomat and translator, carrying films and film news back and forth across New York and Tokyo.

Dal Yong Jin discusses a recent phenomenon in South Korean entertainment industries – webtoons that are being adapted into film and OTT content – and chooses the mediatic framework of "transmedial storytelling" to unpack the significance of these adaptations. One of the features of transmedia storytelling is that it doesn't mean a simple adaptation but rather a narrative expansion or compression and that, further, the transmedia storytelling world is like an assemblage with circulating characters that weave in and out of different platforms. Jin shows how audiovisual media industries in Korea have successfully capitalized on the success of web-based comics and their fanbases to produce spin-off feature films, such as *Moss* (2010), *Secretly, Greatly* (2013), and *Along with the Gods* (2017) or popular OTT series such as Netflix's *Kingdom* (2019).

In "Global Stories, Local Audiences: Dubbing Netflix in India," we stay with Netflix but return to an older film technique – dubbing – that has new implications in an era of digital streaming. Tejaswini Ganti explores the complex negotiations that are required in translating content for audiences, imagined and known. Drawing on her own fieldwork in Mumbai at a prominent dubbing studio, Ganti considers the ways in which Hollywood films and Netflix originals choose to "localize" content through translation. The ethnographic approach brings great nuance to the question of translation as it maps onto producers' assumptions and the actually existing material realities of class, education, English-language fluency, and geographical location. Moving between subtitling and dubbing, Indian content translated into English and US content translated for India, the chapter skillfully draws out the many "audience fictions" that are mobilized across national/industry borders to "manage" the uncertainties of target audiences. The piece is bookended by the element of uncertainty that dogs the entire chain of distribution, from the offices of Netflix USA to Netflix India to the dubbing studios where local writers, actors, and translators improvise for an unseen "global" viewer. "Who is this dub for?" ask all the big and little players in this streaming network, a question that highlights the impossibility of "lossless" translation in an era of supposedly lossless digital streaming.

We round out our focus on trans-border connections with a conversation with Jimena Mora and Talia Vidal who founded an initiative called Futari Proyectos in 2020 with the aim to research and promote films made by Nikkei filmmakers in Peru, particularly women. The term "Nikkei" refers to Japanese emigrants and their descendants. Japanese migration to Peru dates back to 1899, with several waves of arrival necessitated by political or economic exigencies, but the category of a "Nikkei cinema" is still relatively unknown in Peru. Latin American film scholars regularly discuss a Cine Nikkei as it pertains to Brazil or Argentina, but the existence and significance of a Cine Nikkei in Peru has largely been overlooked. It is this knowledge gap that Futari Proyectos seeks to address, with a commitment to community-building as well. In as little as three years, the duo has managed to identify a starting corpus of films that can be called Peruvian Cine Nikkei, organized screenings, and also held workshops for women who want to practice documentary filmmaking. In this conversation, Zhang Zhen talks to Mora and Vidal about their vision for Futari Proyectos, their process, and what it means to create new categories for film research and programming from a feminist perspective.

16

MEDIA TOPOGRAPHIES OF EAST ASIA

Cinema, Cables, Wirelessness, and the (Somewhat) Material Imaginaries of Territory

Alexander Zahlten

On 1 September 1923 the incarnation of a centuries-old demonic figure transmits explosive tremors from an underground military construction site in the continental outpost Dairen across the sea, triggering the Great Kanto Earthquake. This supernatural mastermind's name is Katō; he wears the uniform of the Japanese imperial army and, harboring a hundreds-of-years-old grudge against the capital, has sworn to destroy it. This specific attempt fails – Tokyo succeeds in re-emerging from the devastation of the earthquake – but Katō will continue to wreak havoc throughout the 20th century. In fact, almost every major occurrence in Japan's modern history is linked to Katō's quest and the brave few waging an unseen war to prevent it from being successful.

This transmission of an earthquake across a vast distance is one occurrence in the epic *Teito Monogatari* (Tales of the Imperial Capital) media mix of films, manga, and anime based on a series of wildly successful 1980s novels by Aramata Hiroshi. The series presents an alternative and occult history of (mostly) the 20th century that is deeply influenced by the imaginary of the 1980s information society. The transmission of tremors from Dairen (now called Dalian and located in the PRC's Liaoning Province, but historically a crucial center for Japan's imperial expansion onto the Asian continent)[1] to Tokyo in a self-aware way mirrors the encroaching media network that the Japanese empire was building in Asia. It proposes that the empire's media network was not unidirectional, from "center" to "periphery." Instead, it points to the unruliness of a network, to its multidirectional force. It also hints at its connection to empire, conquest, and destruction.

This essay will trace one phase in the spread of media connectivity in East Asia, with a focus on the Japanese imperial project and its interactions with various actors on the continent. It makes the point that a number of different imaginaries of connectivity compete and negotiate with each other, at times even overlapping. These imaginaries are connected to networks such as railways, film distribution/exhibition networks, electrification, radio, telegraphy, and wireless transmission. While each of these appear at slightly different times and move at different speeds, they also all interact – a network of networks, all gaining shape and defining themselves against each other around roughly the same time. In terms of their diffusion in the popular imagination, they all, in slightly different ways, negotiate

DOI: 10.4324/9781003266952-23

the tension between the material and the immaterial, the sensible and the mysteriously ungraspable.

Cinema played an important role in this network of networks in East Asia and thereby co-created its territorial and regional imaginaries. Film helped popularize visions of the Japanese colonial empire, Cold War "free Asia," and the post-Wall negotiation of more fine-tuned trade relations, and not only through narratives in single works of film. It did so prominently on the levels of circulation of films, of creating spaces dedicated to film, of using filmic spaces to map out territory. Cinema framed these visions in specific ways, and these framings were negotiated in relation to those of other media technologies and channels. This essay will put the shifting imaginaries of these respective media technologies into relation, to understand how they formed a larger constellation that defined the specific limits and possibilities of a mediated and mediatized East Asia and co-shaped the imaginary of empire.

This raises the question of how to best frame this project methodologically. It obviously speaks to infrastructure studies and its concern with the "poetics" of "built networks that facilitate the flow of goods, people or ideas and allow for their exchange over space" (Larkin 2013, 328). The media studies inflected version of infrastructure studies – which has picked up much speed and significantly developed throughout the 2010s (see Anand, Appel, and Gupta 2018 for an excellent overview) – often extends the statistical and quantitative accounts of communication studies into a more speculative mapping of the semiotics of the material structure and the forces it entails. This essay similarly finds overlaps with discussions of media ecologies, which at times stand in subtle tension to infrastructure studies and tend to emphasize the complex entanglements and overlaps of the different actors in a media system, including humans, technological functions, and the representational "content" itself, rather than as a set of relations between separate acting entities (e.g., Lamarre 2018). Drawing on both these modes of inquiry, this essay, however, aims for tracing the poetics and force of a network that is both material and imagined, and that traffics in representations that are expressed by media objects, such as films, but also the material infrastructure itself. The ideas about and the experience of these networks themselves shifted depending on the historical moment, arguably between vernacular models corresponding to infrastructural or media-ecological perspectives.

Along with the railways, electricity provided one of the earliest templates for the modern network that tied bodies into nations and eventually empires. However, electricity retained a mysterious intangibility that made it flexible in terms of the attached imaginary. Anchored by the materiality of cables, it also seemed able to flow as an almost abstract force. In one of the Teito Monogatari franchise's films, *Teito Taisen* (Tokyo: The Last War, 1989) the Japanese government hatches a desperate plan to assassinate Roosevelt in the final stage of the Pacific war by means of a curse transmitted via a high-voltage radio tower. In the first filmic adaptation, *Teito Monogatari* (Tokyo: The Last Megalopolis, 1988), a young girl's spiritual powers are short-circuited by the electrical grid that powers Tokyo's street lights and tram system. The triangular connection of the body's spiritual energy, electric currents, and the urban-technological space is made obvious throughout the franchise; as such, it is a self-aware retrojection of the sense of corporeal entanglement of the embodied self, media technologies, and surrounding spaces that is already completely naturalized by the 1980s.

Electricity and its imaginary play a huge role in the early imaginary around media technologies, as it underlies technologies such as the telegraph, the telephone, and cinema. Early cinema's attraction beyond the thrill of moving images can be understood as, maybe more fundamentally, a way to experience electricity, a technology so abstract it seemed to defy representation. The first dedicated film theater space in Japan, founded in 1903, was called the Asakusa Denki-kan, or the Asakusa Electricity Hall. Originally a space intended for showcasing interesting electronic gadgets, it retained the name when it switched to showing films, and several other early film theaters all over Japan took on the "denki-kan" naming as well – as did the first dedicated film theater space in Dalian/Dairen in 1910 – the same year that Japan annexed Korea – which similarly was set up in the Denki Yûenchi Engei-kan (Electric Amusement Park Performance Hall). The theater's electricity was supplied by the first power plant in Dairen, set up in 1907 by Mantetsu, the South Manchuria Railway company (Sunaga 2005). Dairen/Dalian at the time was a Japanese outpost on the continent, ceded to Japan following the Russo-Japanese war of 1904/05. As we will see in a moment, film theaters were an important aspect of early Japanese imperial extensions into Asia.

The association of cinema with electricity is not incidental, then, and with it comes an imaginary that involves cables and territorial mapping – a specific model of space, of time, and of the body. As Daqing Yang has pointed out, Fukuzawa Yukichi prefigured Marshall McLuhan's claims of media as "extensions of man" when he in 1875 proclaimed, "When the telegraph serves as the nerve system of a country, the Central Telegraph office is like the brain, and branch offices elsewhere are like nerve ends. As Japan sharpens its new nerve system, its body gains a new vitality" (quoted in Yang 2010, 15). Fukuzawa was probably not thinking of imperial expansion when he made that statement, but the line of thinking was influential and similar ideas were common; Yuriko Furuhata has pointed to the biopolitical conceptions of governance put forward by Gotō Shinpei when he was head of civilian affairs in the colonial government of Taiwan (Furuhata 2019). Gotō later became the first director of the South Manchuria Railway (Mantetsu) which later founded the mentioned Denki-kan film theater in Dairen, and returned to Tokyo as Minister of Communications and eventually governor of Tokyo, where Gotō was tasked with reconstruction when the 1923 earthquake struck.

In a sense, then, the idea of telegraph lines and other communication media as extensions of the body already suggests an extension beyond the *national* body. The state, in other words, is nudged toward empire by the metaphorics of the media technology. The role of early cinema in the new electric/telecommunicational territory of nation and empire – now defined by the cables traversing it – is one of making the network tangible and experiential. In a famous 1879 woodblock print, Kobayashi Kiyochika depicts the road alongside the Yushima Seidō, an old neo-Confucian school that until the mid-19th century trained elite bureaucrats of the Tokugawa government. By the time the woodblock print is made the school has been closed and is only hinted at by the title and the walled off, monolithic block of trees on the left side of the image. On the right side of the image, it is not the road that leads into a new future; it is the telegraph poles lining it. These telegraph lines, transforming the landscape and pointing to the coming new world, also reposition the people below. They are not simply walking on a road but alongside a new communication technology that collapses space and reduces them – relatively – to a painfully slow pace, to relics of the past. Forty-five years later, in 1924, Miyazawa Kenji's short story *Telegraph Poles on a Moonlit Night* (Tsukiyo no Denshinbashira) makes the implications of the technology very clear when it describes a young man's late-night encounter with a regiment of marching telegraph poles, commandeered by a (telegraph pole) general. The regiment of poles is clearly worried about being seen – and the story thus makes the indefinite visibility of the media technology's military/imperial undertow part of its theme.

The question of visibility/tangibility of the new cable-secured network of electricity and its offshoot networks of cabled (and electrically powered) transportation and communication then finds an interim solution in cinema. Film has widely been read as an extension of photography and *gentô* (magic lantern performances), and the theaters as extensions of performance/exhibition/*misemono* spaces (see, for example, Iwamoto 2002, or Ueda 2012). But again, in another sense film is a way to represent electricity itself, to make experiential the quintessentially modern technology and the network principles essential to it – one for which as Novalis proclaimed, "We are lacking electric, magnetic, galvanic, caloric thoughts and fantasies along with the appropriate senses." Film and its theaters presented what Michael Gamper has called an "electropoetology" (Gamper 2009, 8).[2] They supplied a poetology of electrified space and the new world it mapped out. That not all cabled, communicational infrastructures did so is important to note; telegraphy transformed the landscape but stayed abstract, with its coded messages. Ocean cables, which became increasingly important after the early 1870s, were extensive but, by definition, out of sight, even if they demanded intense resources and political trade-offs. Film was a modern space that physically manifested as a node in distribution networks – of electricity, of photochemical technologies, of national cinemas. It made the network sensible.

For the national and the imperial project of Japan, communication technologies played an immensely central role. The story of Commodore William Perry's second visit to Japan in 1854 has long been a standard part in the narrative of the development of the Japanese government's intense focus on technology acquisition as an avenue for avoiding colonization, and eventually as a tool for empire. The visit entailed a demonstration of railway technology and telegraphy, and both would become a main axis of the Meiji government's vision for Japan's race to "catch up," to close the suggested temporal gap the empires of Europe and North America justified themselves with. To become "modern" through technology – and to a large degree through communication technology – was seen as a matter of survival, and it justified, even necessitated, conquest. Technology became so central that Yang has emphasized that imperialism needs to be seen as techno-imperialism (Yang 2010, 8).[3] Similarly, Janet Mimura has suggested that Japanese fascism of the 1930s is better termed "techno-fascism," as it was more of a convenient tool for technology-fixated bureaucrats (Mimura 2011). We might add that the techno in techno-fascism understands media technology as its nervous system.

For the development of empire, we find this on display in the dynamics of film networks in Japan's early imperial efforts, especially between the urban centers of Dairen and Harbin.[4] Harbin, where films were first shown in 1906, while located in Qing territory and later the Republic of China, was initially built largely with capital from the Russian empire and was home to an almost-majority Russian population. It was also an early film center with many Russian-owned theaters, showing a large number of international films in state-of-the-art theaters. The imperial contest between Russia and Japan was then also played out via cinema. Dairen initially had fewer theaters that were markedly less "modern," with tatami floors and an architectural design oriented toward live performance spaces. Distribution networks were messy, with films sometimes entering both cities from Shanghai and Japan simultaneously, leading to frictions about distribution territories – a symptom of the contested territory these distribution networks were being mapped onto. It was Mantetsu's 1925 Dairen Mantetsu Shain Kurabu (Dairen Club of Mantetsu Employees) that kick-started the modernization of film theaters in the city; it was even eventually outfitted with a motor generator to adjust the electric current – a move Ni Yan sees as stemming from a feeling of competition with Harbin and the need to put Japan's modernity on display (Yan 2015). By this time Mantetsu was a huge corporation that was also heavily invested in electricity production, and by 1923 Mantetsu had additionally started a film production division. It not only became a prolific producer but also one of the primary facilitators for Japanese major studios interested in incorporating the formal and informal imperial extensions into their works, such as Shochiku's *Minzoku no Sakebi* (Cry of the Race, 1928) (See Kurihara Kramer 2012). Mantetsu's production would have enormous ripple effects in the 1930s, eventually creating a through line to the founding of the Manchurian Film Association, or Man'ei, in 1937.

After the establishment of the puppet state of Manchukuo in 1932, calls for a strong expansion of Japanese-owned theaters in the region and a ramping up of film production grew louder. In 1934, Manchukuo had 20 Japanese-owned film theaters (that showed primarily Japanese films), but only 11 of them had sound film technology – this was widely seen as falling behind Harbin's still more technologically advanced theaters – where according to censorship records only 4.8% of films shown in the same year were Japanese (Yan 2015, 119). A film theater building boom ensued in Manchukuo, and in 1937 Man'ei was founded as one of the largest film studios in Asia with capital jointly supplied by the state of Manchukuo and Mantetsu.

To disentangle these dynamics somewhat, it is useful to consider Thomas Lamarre's formulations on what he calls the "feeling of media regionalism." Invoking Raymond Williams, along with Deleuze and Guattari, Lamarre explains that "producing distribution (technologies and infrastructures) precedes and exceeds the production of contents or programmes" (Lamarre 2015, 4). Distribution, importantly, is produced, and in turn distribution itself also produces. Among other things, it produces a sense of region. But it can also suggest a region, or an expansion into becoming one. While Lamarre is focusing on television in East Asia in this context, the dynamics in Manchuria from the 1910s through the 1930s are exactly about the production of distribution. In the context of a competition for performing modernity, of making the "modernizing" networks of hidden cables (submerged in the ocean), mysterious cables (for electricity), and encoded cables (for telegraphy) – and their specific distributive forces – visible and tangibly experiential, the Japanese empire was heavily invested in film, and by extension so was Manchukuo.

However, this also entailed demonstrating the management of that performative network. Just months after the founding of Man'ei, Manchukuo passed a film law that took effect almost two years before the 1939 film law (*eiga hô*) issued by Japan. It consolidated distribution in Manchukuo to systematize the chaotic competition of distribution territories of earlier years, and to better position Japanese cinema (and thereby strengthen cinemas specialized on Japanese films), which was still comparatively unpopular with Manchukuo's population. Man'ei was located in Shinkyô (renamed from Changchun), which was one of the centers of Japan's "informal empire" from 1907, and from 1932 it was the capital of the newly founded Manchukuo. The creation of Man'ei moved Manchukuo's film capital away from Dairen into a city that was itself a symbol – architecturally, technologically, in terms of governance – of designing modernity from scratch and that functioned as a laboratory for a new empire and its deliberately produced and controlled distributive networks and forces. Shinkyô also housed, on its central square, the headquarters of the Manchurian Telegraph and Telephone Company (MTT, founded in 1933), an impressively grand and modern building that Daqing Yang sees as representing the foundational centrality of telecommunications for Manchukuo (Yang 2010, 87). Design (however experimental), order, and boundedness fit the model of cabled networks. Cables were an external and hermetic transmission pipeline. They were visible and delineated territory; they signified an ordered and intentional network. Similarly, film theaters, as nodes of the electric network and the now consolidated, territorially exclusive distribution networks, were now purified modern spaces. While pointing to the orderly imperial network they experientialized it in a focused and bounded manner. At the same time, however, a more unruly network and a technology with a slightly different imaginary was expanding and negotiating its place: wirelessness.

Wireless technology had to position itself in relation to the very established and material imaginary of cables. These had made quick inroads on the landscape, on urban spaces, and the ocean. The Meiji government introduced the first telegraph line in 1870 – between Tokyo and Yokohama – just two years after it had been formed. The Ministry of Communication was formed in 1885, but even before that, the government was in a cable frenzy.[5] While submarine telegraph cable activities had started more than a decade before, in 1883 Japan contracted the Danish Great Northern Telegraph Company to connect Nagasaki and Busan, allowing for the first international telegraph communication from Japan. Japan simultaneously extracted a 25-year monopoly for Korea's international telecommunications activity – 27 years later Korea would be formally annexed. In 1897 a submarine cable connected Japan and Taiwan (which had been ceded to Japan two years earlier following the first Sino-Japanese War). Cables were part of prefiguring and consolidating imperial territorial gains.

Wireless technology entered the world stage from Guglielmo Marconi's demonstrations to the British government in 1896, the same year of the first public screening of a film in Japan. By the 1904/05 Russo-Japanese War it was successfully being deployed by the Japanese Navy, and in 1915 the Japanese government passed the Wireless Communication Law. While amateur radio activity was already well in place in Japan earlier, in 1925 official radio broadcast began under state control. These two aspects of wireless technology promised two slightly different things – though with much overlap – and posed slightly different problems for the quickly expanding imperial project.

Wireless telegraphy was an opportunity to slash through the complicated network of financial agreements, monopolies, and dependencies that communication cables had created in East Asia. The 1883 agreement with Great Northern had brought with it monopoly and Danish control of the cable for 25 years; it was one of many concessions Japan had to play along with to acquire the technology. While frequencies had their own politics of scarcity, wireless presented the chance for reordering the until now cabled telecommunications sphere of East Asia and the attached power relations that much favored US and European powers. It was also faster and reached further, and it carried the promise of simultaneous communication. The latter was a huge promise indeed for Japan in terms of its temporal politics, as being synchronized with "the world" stood in opposition to being locked into a relationship that defined the country (and even more so the rest of East Asia) as eternally "behind." At the same time Satō Takumi has proposed that radio presented the opportunity for a fascist public sphere in a way that telegraphy – in its unruly multitude of transmissions – did not (Satō also proposes that the subject of radio, or rather the historical trajectory of wireless communication in East Asia, allows us to periodize the history of modern Japan differently, beyond conventionally established periods such as the 15-year war or events like the Mukden incident; see Satō 2015).

However, wireless technology also introduced challenges for the idea of a territorially oriented network that cable made so tangible. The relative ease of creating overlapping transmission territories meant potential commingling of different parties on the same airwaves and worked against clear territorial delineation. China especially was seen as a chaotic space, characterized by broadcasting competition between the US, the European powers, and Japan. Unauthorized wireless telegraphy (and cabled telegraphy as well) abounded, and Japan's attempt to establish a monopoly via the Mitsui Bussan corporation and an enormous broadcasting station built near Beijing in 1923 failed in the long run (Yang 2010, 71; Ariyama 2013, 84). By the late 1920s, with a new Chinese government and intensifying wireless competition especially with France and the US in China, negotiations around bringing order to that space were agreed upon in 1930. Yang Daqing claims that the negotiations were purposefully stalled from the Japanese side to allow for the long-anticipated takeover (in 1931) of what from 1932 was to become Manchukuo with Japanese telecommunication systems intact (Yang 2010, 73). The Japanese government acted fast, and on New Year's Day 1932 the use of the Mukden Radio Station provided exchange broadcasts of speeches by military leaders from both Mukden and Tokyo (Yang 2010, 78). Two years before, as mentioned, Japanese film theaters in Manchukuo had been seen as technologically behind on sound technology and not sufficiently "modern." Radio, however, had already begun to synchronize Japanese imperial modernity across its formal and informal territories. The eventual expansion of wireless and cabled telecommunications from Manchukuo into China just a few years later would prefigure the imperial army's takeover of those very same territories.

There is much missing from this account; telephony and radar are additional technologies that shaped territorial imaginaries, each in slightly different ways. But what we see from this small excerpt is a constantly shifting negotiation of more and of less materially defined networks. Cables and wireless technologies changed their relationship to each other at various points and involved a variety of pushes, pulls, and variations of territorial imaginaries. Cinema was always squarely in the cabled, more material corner, and though immensely central in translating the telecommunicational cable network into a representable and directly experienced space, it at times struggled with fulfilling the promise of the imperial modern. It did, however, link directly into the spatialized territorial order that cables suggested. Radio, on the other hand, temporalized that order into a national and then an (at least suggested) imperial synchronicity. The attempts at the homogenization and total control over the content of media transmissions that eventually affected film, print, and telegraphy was much more modeled on the fascist imaginary attached to radio that Takumi Satō has pointed out.[6]

It is not so surprising, then, that the emperor's radio broadcast declaration on 15 August has been narrated and re-narrated as ending the war. Still, such a narrative tends toward framing that history as (synchronic) rupture. The legacy of the complex constellation of imperial networks and their territorial imaginaries however has innumerable through lines to postwar media history. When Umesao Tadao, who coined the term "information industry" long before similar terms were in circulation in English, wrote about TV in 1961, he described it in the following terms:

Very roughly speaking, for contemporary Japan the broadcast industry is a frontier industry. It is a new land for cultivation. On top of that, it is a fertile and abundant land for cultivation. People working in broadcasting are pioneers establishing a unique culture on that land for cultivation . . . Relatively speaking radio has been, quantitatively and qualitatively, fully cultivated (exploited), but in the middle of things the new land expanse of TV was added. The frontier hasn't disappeared yet.

(Umesao 2011, 34)[7]

Television is here framed in explicitly colonial terms, using the English terms "frontier" and "pioneer" to make his point (a complex operation about which there is much more to be said). Cabled networks of telegraphy and film theaters suggested territorial expansion, and wireless broadcasting suggested temporal synchronization on top of that expansion. TV and the airwaves it entails later still suggest expansion and "cultivation," but it is now the colonization of the airwaves themselves – a utopian mediaspace that will never run out. It is a turn inward and toward virtual spaces as the new territories for the expansionist drive of postwar capitalism and the spectral traces of imperialism. It is then not that surprising that the imagery and the setting of empire plays such a huge role for *Teito Monogatari* in the scene we began this essay with. The 1980s franchise simply makes explicit the legacies of the imperial mediasphere, cabled and wireless, that lived on in the imaginary around TV and eventually the information society.

Notes

1 Dalian was leased in 1905 by Japan from Qing China and later from the Japanese puppet state of Manchukuo.
2 Gamper borrows the characterization of electricity as an "epistemic thing" from Hans-Jörg Rheinberger. Novalis is quoted in Gamper 2009, 135.
3 Yang draws on the rising popularity of the term and mentions Tak Yoshihisa Matsusaka or David Wittner as others employing the term.
4 Much of the following account relies on the pioneering work of Ni Yan, see especially Yan 2015.
5 For the best and most comprehensive history of the building of the early cable network in English that much of this account draws on, see Yang 2010. For an even more detailed history in Japanese that looks at the connection to the news industry see Ariyama 2013.
6 Though it had its challenges too, as the history of multilingual broadcasting in the empire shows.
7 My translation from the 2011 republished version.

References

Anand, Nikhil, Hannah Appel, and Akhil Gupta. 2018. "Temporality, Politics, and the Promise of Infrastructure." In *The Promise of Infrastructure*, edited by Nikhil Anand, Akhil Gupta, and Hannah Appel, 1–38. Durham: Duke University Press.

Ariyama, Tetsuo. 2013. *Jōhō Haken to Teikoku Nihon: Tsûshin Gijutsu no Kakudai to Senden-sen.* Tokyo: Yoshikawa Kôbunkan.

Furuhata, Yuriko. 2019. "Tange Lab and Biopolitics: From the Geopolitics of the Living Sphere to the Nervous System of the Nation." In *Beyond Imperial Aesthetics: Theories of Art and Politics in East Asia*, edited by Mayumo Inoue and Steve Choe, 221–42. Hong Kong: Hong Kong University Press.

Gamper, Michael. 2009. *Elektropoetologie: Fiktionen der Elektrizität 1740–1870.* Göttingen: Wallstein Verlag.

Iwamoto, Kenji. 2002. *Gentō no Seiki: Eiga Zenya no Shikaku Bunka-shi.* Tokyo: Shinwa-sha.

Kurihara Kramer, Hanae. 2012. "Film Forays of the South Manchuria Film Company." *Film History: An International Journal* 24 (1): 97–113.

Lamarre, Thomas. 2015. "Regional TV: Affective Media Technologies." *Asiascape: Digital Asia* 2: 93–126.

———. 2018. *The Anime Ecology: A Genealogy of Television, Animation, and Game Media.* Minneapolis: University of Minnesota Press.

Larkin, Brian. 2013. "The Politics and Poetics of Infrastructure." *Annual Review of Anthropology* 42: 327–43.

Mimura, Janice. 2011. *Planning for Empire: Japanese Bureaucrats and the Wartime State.* Ithaca: Cornell University Press.

Satō, Takumi. 2015. "Rajio Bunmei to Fashisuto-teki Kōkyōsei." In *Sensō, Rajio, Kioku*, edited by Toshihiko Kishi, Shin Kawashima, and Ansoku Son, 2–25. Tokyo: Bensei Shuppan.

Sunaga, Noritaka. 2005. "Manshū ni Okeru Denryoku Jigyō." *Rikkyō Keizaigaku Kenkyû 59* (2): 67–100.

Ueda, Manabu. 2012. *Nihon Eiga Sōsōki no Kōgyō to Kankyaku*. Tokyo: Waseda Daigaku Shuppan-bu.

Umesao, Tadao. 2011. "*Hōsōnin no Tanjô to Seichô.*" In *Jōhō no Bunmeigaku*, 15–36. Tokyo: Chuo Kôron.

Yan, Ni. 2015. "Manshū ni Okeru Nihon Eiga ni Shinshutsu to Eigakan no Henyō." In *Nihon Eiga no Kaigai Shinshutu – Bunka Senryaku no Rekishi*, edited by Kenji Iwamoto, 111–34. Tokyo: Shinwa-sha.

Yang, Daqing. 2010. *Technology of Empire: Telecommunications and Japanese Expansion in Asia, 1883–1945*. Cambridge: Harvard University Asia Center.

17

LOOKING OUT AND ON THE MOVE

Aesthetics of Infrastructure in Recent Singapore Cinema

Gerald Sim

From the late 1990s on, films from Singapore started to gain traction at international festivals such as Cannes and Berlin. These independent productions representing the city-state's renaissance in world cinema were replete with tales about subjects undergoing psychotic breaks, who are victimized by both an authoritarian nanny state and unforgiving capitalism. They projected on screen the external effects and internal aftermaths of rigid socio-economic policies exerting pervasive pressure and exacting irreversible psychological costs. Filmmakers looked inward for insight and emerged from self-analysis rehearsing a prevalent set of themes in a spate of films that were considered, explicitly as well as implicitly, as constituting Singapore's national cinema (Chua and Yeo 2003; Berry and Farquhar 2006, 215). Looking back upon the narratives led by Eric Khoo's trailblazing features *Mee Pok Man* (1995) and *12 Storeys* (1997), for example, we meet alienated and isolated characters, frequently unmoored if not unhinged. Visually, their afflictions are traced to the overbearing verticality of urban structures, bland brutalist public housing especially that signify the inhabitants' permanent immobility imposed by the prevalent power of the state (Sim 2020, 99–100; Chua and Yeo 2003, 118; Wee 2012, 983–84). Chua Beng Huat and Meisen Wong (2012) elaborate poetically on this "aesthetic of the pathetic," with which these abject figures can be interpreted either through pathos as victims, or alternatively as resilient embodiments of neoliberal individualism. That is to say, these Janus-faced characters are socio-political critiques on behalf of victims, as well as validations of a triumphal national ideology. The point is, both exegeses reach for internal local conditions to find explanatory context.

But something new has appeared in the last decade. This national cinema broke free from phenomenological limitations earlier circumscribed by traditional notions of how local identity is to be expressed through filmmaking. One discerns a locational openness, effectuated in part by prominent displays of transportation and economic infrastructure that connote mobility and connectedness, and of greater a propensity if not willingness to gaze outward, often embodied by subjects standing at the outskirts of the island's social and geographical imaginary. These characters and narratives evince a more open and willing curiosity about how the world beyond informs the national self. They adopt an updated

DOI: 10.4324/9781003266952-24

view of Singapore's place in the world system, particularly within global networks that comprise supply chain capitalism.

Anna Tsing's trenchant article "Supply Chains and the Human Condition" conceptualizes an uncommonly generative schema that grasps global capitalism as a system in which "labor, nature, and capital are mobilized in fragmented but linked economic niches" (2009, 149). Film scholar Kay Dickinson has demonstrated the argument's utility for apprehending cinema's often international division of creative labor (2021, 174), particularly applicable to cinemas of small nations reliant on foreign financing and markets. But it is Tsing's particular attention to the "human condition" that truly illuminates Singapore cinema. Having doubled down on longstanding economic investments in the services sector, the city-state's bona fides as an infrastructure hub inflect social relations and cultural expression ever so deeply. Via the Marxian definition of infrastructure's determinative relationship to the superstructure, much can be read into recent work emerging from Singapore's modest filmmaking tradition, prominently represented in what follows by a handful of both fiction and non-fiction films. More often than not, they underline Tsing's emphasis on the nature of exploitation that supply chain capitalism subtends.

Among these works, K. Rajagopal's *A Yellow Bird* (2016) instantiates the trend most incisively. Despite receiving recognition during International Critics Week at the Cannes Film Festival, the neorealist drama remains oddly understudied. It tells the story of Siva, an itinerant Indian-Singaporean ex-convict who bonds with an undocumented Chinese sex worker, Chen Chen, on the social, economic, and geographical margins of the island. *A Yellow Bird* continues the habit observable since the 1990s of local productions to feature the marginalized or members of Singapore's underclass, except for its move to highlight precarious workers and migrant laborers. Rajagopal was among several filmmakers to decenter national subjectivity in this way. The documentaries *Sementara* (2020) and *IN TIME TO COME* (2017), both inspired by the occasion of Singapore's 50th anniversary celebrations, made similar pivots. By centering the presence of temporary residents, the films reconceive what it means to be *from* and *of* Singapore. *A Yellow Bird* in particular uses actor Sivakumar Palakrishnan's physical performance of Siva, a visceral character not given to introspection and dwelling within the infrastructural interstices of urban landscape, to defamiliarize the city-state's more familiar postcard-friendly vistas. Its images serve more than unvarnished realism; they revise local iconography.

The denouement of Singapore's initial decade-long cycle of national cinema may have come about through a combination of creative redirection or simply emotional fatigue. Audiences and critics tire of wretched pessimism. Films can only wallow in abjection for so long before thematic exhaustion. Recent films, including the cluster of works highlighted here, continue to harbor healthy levels of cynicism within languid stories expressed in social realist style; they sometimes persist with handy tropes that make films intelligible to international audiences, namely, alienated protagonists subsisting at the margins (Khoo 2006, 92–93). But whereas those characters' incessant navel-gazing exacerbated psychological damage in the past, we now see a collective decision to step back from the abyss, sometimes literally so. Before, it was common to see characters in despair jumping to their deaths from atop the very buildings that symbolize their plight. This would happen onscreen and off, in the narrative foreground and its backdrop as in *12 Storeys*, *Eating Air* (1999), *15* (2003), and *Be With Me* (2005) (Sim 2020, 125–27). Even when the incidents occurred in subplots, these tragedies only magnified the horror by fomenting the implication that the grisly spectacles were commonplace.

The humdrum recurrence of those suicides makes what happens during a key scene in *Ilo Ilo* (2013) feel like a significant moment of inflection. Writer-director Anthony Chen's celebrated first feature about an adolescent's bond with his family's Filipina domestic helper set during the Asian financial crisis won the Caméra d'Or, making it the country's first entrant to win an award at Cannes. The relationship between young Jiale and Terry, who hails from the city named in the title, is initially fraught. The maladjusted boy tests his minder incessantly. One day, Terry witnesses a suicide jump – someone driven to it by the economic calamity spreading throughout the continent. Soon after, Jiale takes Terry to the roof of the adjacent block and flippantly muses about the nice view at the rumored spot from which the victim decided to end it all. Terry jerks him back from the edge, rebukes his insouciance with a tight slap, and says, "You think killing yourself is so funny, huh?" The strike freezes Jiale, who looks back holding his face in stunned silence. Chen's camera lingers on them with a pair of two shots, just long enough for us to realize that at this juncture between the first and second acts, the insolent boy fails to react in the way we expect. Terry's hand jars Jiale from his morbid indifference to the death and suffering of others, confronting him with a view that is not his own of the world below. Can I prove that this is the juncture at which thematic or perspectival change occurred within a film cycle? No. But the scene stands out, I argue, as an important moment of cinematic reflexivity. Within *Ilo Ilo*, the transformational gesture marks a turning point in Jiale's relationship with Terry. The more she becomes a part of his life, the more he understands their shared existence. Compared to the earlier films with a death drive, the incident signals a phenomenological U-turn.

When Terry arrives via a well-traveled route from a valued Southeast Asian neighbor to deliver an admonishment about what it means to be of Singapore, she recapitulates the actual irony that Singaporean productions are less likely to attract a local audience without first earning recognition abroad (Yun 2018). In that respect, to even exist, the films have to be meaningful to people beyond its shores. This rooftop scene also provides the film with its most well-circulated image, that of Terry and Jiale looking happily into the distance where the boy is pointing. The production still does not appear in the film but was used for the film poster. Above the photograph the title is layered over what appears to be the landmasses of an archipelago floating among the white and gray clouds in a Singaporean sky. We are asked to reckon that they are looking in the geographical direction of Ilo Ilo, the Philippine city from which many migrants find their way to Singapore for work as domestic helpers. Indeed, in accordance with a thematic pivot away from solipsism, Singapore cinema navigates its way toward the peripheral, liminal, and exterior. Over the course of artistic maturation, films come to terms with the contingency and instability that constitute the national condition – a state of being perpetually defined by externalities.

A Transnational Infrastructural Hub

Modern Singapore's geopolitical identity was grafted by the British, who saw the island at the tip of the Malay peninsula as a strategically located trading settlement and port, a base on which to challenge Dutch dominance of maritime shipping lanes. After gaining independence in 1965, the city-state continued to press its geographic advantage. The Port of Singapore has been among the two busiest in the world for decades. The country has also leveraged its locational asset with substantial outlays for its world-class airport, a vital node for international cargo and passenger travel. Since operations began in 1981, Changi International Airport has opened a new terminal every decade and will vie, like the Port, to be the world's busiest when the fifth terminal is completed in 2030. Singapore's rapid transformation from a Third to First World economy in a single generation was driven by manufacturing and services. Although manufacturing remains an important but diminishing part of the local economy, the services sector now contributes more than 70% to Singapore's gross domestic product. To that end, the state has underwritten infrastructure construction of all kinds. A massive petrochemical refining complex sitting on reclaimed land off the island's western coast is responsible for the economy's second biggest export, refined petroleum. A deregulatory regime of financial policy helped to turn Singapore into a regional leader in financial services, a position unachievable without digital communications infrastructure. Do not be surprised that Singapore is one of the most connected countries in the world with twice as many submarine cable landing stations as China. This has facilitated the country's rising market position in media, marketing, e-commerce, and data colocation.

On financial media and global news sites like *CNBC*, *Forbes*, and *Wired*, state agencies place snazzy advertorials touting the island's infrastructural facilities and as a welcoming destination for business and investment. Singapore also positions itself as a platform for infrastructural investments throughout Asia: the place with the financial, industrial, and regulatory systems to help strike those deals (Rajah 2016). Over and over, we regularly come across two terms in these policy statements and branding exercises: infrastructure and hub. The latter, in particular, has burrowed into local vernacular. On websites, mission statements, and other forms of public messaging, "hub" denotes well-located retail, service, and transportation centers. Hubs refer to physical places offering one-stop convenience but also to virtual sites that we used to call homepages or sitemaps. These words peppering local speech demonstrate that the calculated decision to lean into the growing services sector has redefined more than the economic base. Doubling down on being an infrastructural hub has trickled down to the quotidian experiences of people, who eventually take on those aspirations themselves, of being a center of regional activity, a vital node within a network, an advantageously situated common space serving multiple communities, markets, transactions, and routes. As Brian Larkin writes, infrastructure can "address and constitute subjects" (2013, 329). Hubs are gateways, points of convergence, connectivity, and accessibility. They are material objects of utility – assets and systems that support, connect, communicate, mediate, and store. But eventually, they translate into a notional existence, an idea, an identity that people and societies inhabit.

Themes of movement, travel, and exchange with people and places outside oneself echo throughout this discourse. The idea is that Singapore today is not simply a country with world-class infrastructure, or a place for infrastructure. Rather it's *of* infrastructure, or rather, it *is* infrastructure.[1] It is a part of its character and has reified in important films of the last decade, a cinematic trend that coincides with greater scholarly attention originating both within film studies (Leow 2020) and without (Comaroff 2014; Chua 2020) to the policy and practice of land reclamation. Sand is imported from neighboring states, transported in barges, then emptied onto the shoreline to expand Singapore's landmass. Its geological reality originates elsewhere, and is not its own. Charmaine Chua raises the crucial point that the disruptive effects of geological displacement on regional socio-economic ecosystems and migratory flows rehearses the historical circumstances behind Singapore's "colonial nationhood and the global trade it would facilitate" (244). By and large, writers believe that sand and thus land – the scarce, precious, highly politicized resource that is definitional to Singapore – is therefore a referent that is epistemologically unstable and, in fact, contingent. They present yet another way in which the country itself takes on the transitory character of infrastructure (Chua, 239; Comaroff; Leow, 171).

Gerald Sim

When the rate of film production sprang to life in Singapore during the mid-'90s, the screens were populated with obverse, antithetical themes like disconnection, stasis, and vacuity. The social immobility of the working class and underclass were expressed in characters experiencing sensorimotor paralysis within Deleuzean time-images (Sim 2020, 121–23), wherein relief could be accessed by turning oneself over to gravity, then into the ground. But a decade or so onward, I sense a daring to imagine the prospect of movement, and an increasing acknowledgment of others when constituting that self. Earlier, scholars and critics privileged authenticity within debates of postcolonial hybridity and subaltern agency (116–17). These days, as a de facto project in national cinema-making, films are relinquishing the notion that identity is something essential and unique, something discoverable, negotiable, and resolvable by looking inward.

An Aesthetic of Infrastructure and Supply Chains

As if in the process of reconciling itself with the prospect that authenticity and identity are impossible for a piece of infrastructure, recent films seem willing or intent on defining them with a different tack. The purest grade of that aesthetic purpose can be found in documentarian Tan Pin Pin's *IN TIME TO COME*, a non-narrative excursion of Singapore's vaunted infrastructure: local pavements, gleaming elevator foyers, train stations, public housing void decks, mall walkways, pedestrian crossings, underpasses, and pristine, freshly built underground highways. Tan's camera seeks and finds beauty in these anonymous interstitial spaces, enacting an understated but bold redefinition of national culture. Also prompted by the nation's 50th anniversary milestone to reflect on national identity, Joant Úbeda and Chew Chia Shao Min's documentary *Sementara* adopts a different tack by curating a set of interviews. It too is fascinated with Singapore's relationship to its infrastructure. The film's observational gazes, B-roll footage, and visual transitions seek out port cranes in the foggy distance, migrant construction laborers and worksites, and the curious sight of a couple posing for wedding snapshots at Changi Airport. The camera drifts to highways, drainage canals, footpaths, and alleyways; rolls through the subway's tunnels, tracks, and trains; and is captivated by the hypnotic vision of underground expressway lighting streaming overhead. "Sementara" is the Malay word for transience, akin to the people, goods, vessels, and cultures on the move through an infrastructural hub.

In addition to mise-en-scène, films also take on an infrastructural perspective by opening their visual and narrative gazes outward, as if animated by systems thinking, which emphasizes the interrelationships of parts within a whole. These sightlines occur along pathways established by infrastructural edges and transportation routes. One way or another, they turn toward other nodes in the logistical network to which Singapore is inextricably and economically connected through supply chain capitalism. These neighboring lands, peoples and cultures are increasingly recognized as part of Singapore's social constitution. Earlier films portrayed one tormented denizen after another. Subjects now encompass marginalized outsiders and racial Others on whom modern Singapore depends but still often effaces when imagining national identity. The impetus for change probably originated in filmmakers' desire to counter xenophobia against new immigrants and nonresident workers particularly from China, India, and Bangladesh.[2] In doing so, their films follow Tsing's lead in seeking to highlight the depths of economic exploitation within supply chains.

IN TIME TO COME partakes in the respite of South Asian laborers eating and napping on the grass. *Sementara* humanizes immigrants by interviewing a homesick Bangladeshi construction worker living in a cramped dormitory, the young Chinese proprietor of a small boutique, and a Filipina domestic helper lamenting about condo rules forbidding her from swimming in the pool. Women like Terry in *Ilo Ilo* enabled significant numbers of local women to enter the workforce (Hui 1997, 118). They were followed by unskilled Chinese laborers, just like Chen Chen in *A Yellow Bird*. Siva's solidarity with her spotlights his countervailing conflict with the Chinese men renting a room in his mother's cramped flat. The battles that he wages with the tenants read like an irresistible metaphor for actual hostilities that arose from the Sinicization of retail spaces and public soundscapes. "Fuck off from my house!" Siva snarls at one of the men. But by not asking audiences to identify with the local Indian's misdirected aggression, Rajagopal stymies hostility toward the foreigners. *A Yellow Bird* had a hometown companion at Cannes that same year. Boo Junfeng's *Apprentice* (2016) offered restorative justice for Singapore's other dark-complexioned minority with a cast and screenplay that are mostly Malay.

These films swivel to face the outside while perched on the fringes of the national imagination. Storylines often observe this 180-degree rotation through scenes in which characters gaze out from the island's edges. Evicted by his mother, Siva begins sleeping at a dank shoreline encampment where Chen Chen begins working for a pimp. The vegetation looks dispirited but at this liminal place on the island's periphery, he emotionally regroups. The couple bathe in the water, bond on the shore, and eventually consummate their relationship. The film later takes Siva to an embankment under an expressway, a spot unclaimed by Singapore's need to salvage every bit of buildable land. He squats on a stretch of mud, rocks, and driftwood and stares pensively out at the water. We only observe him traveling toward those banks, never in the opposite direction. A border affinity can explain why *A Yellow Bird* keeps a distance by merely circling historical events such as the 2013 Little India riots, Singapore's first incident of mass racial violence in five decades. When a private bus ferrying Indian migrant workers killed a pedestrian in the ethnic enclave, bystanders swelled into a mob that rioted for two hours. *A Yellow Bird* uses the event to situate itself locally but only alludes to the episode tangentially. We traipse with Siva when he happens upon a group of rioters dashing past. He scuffles with a policeman, extricates himself, jumps a barrier, and finds refuge underground in a canal, taking us into another interstitial space. He sleeps on the floor of the cavernous drain, and rises in the morning to the rumble of a passing subway. In long shot, he spots daylight peeping through grates overhead (Figure 17.1). He looks around, then scales a steel ladder embedded in the wall, not searching for an exit, but surveying and orienting. It is an odd, surreal narrative pause, in a film whose mise-en-scène returns often to infrastructural architecture and concrete: canals, drains, alleys, highways, paved sidewalks, corridors, stairwells. In sum, after stumbling upon the riots, readable to local eyes as an unmistakable historical reference, the film stays decidedly on the periphery, where Siva's contemplative interregnum prompts reflection on, I would argue, the national character. Here, anonymous infrastructure that signifies not locations but the means to reach destinations, connote transportation, movement, and transience, prevalent themes of Singapore cinema's infrastructural cycle.

Ilo Ilo, set in the urban heartland, conspires to reach the water's edge on multiple occasions. When Terry has to leave due to the family's dwindling finances, Jiale looks away from Singapore as the family returns from the airport along its southeastern coast. The protagonist in *Perth* (2004), a middle-aged former merchant mariner, narrates his backstory at the docks while staring wistfully at passing ships. The film also looks asea by engaging in symbolic irony. Its title frame superimposes the name of the Australian city over

Figure 17.1   Siva finds refuge in a canal (*A Yellow Bird* 2016. Director: K. Rajagopal).

Singapore's iconic waterfront skyline. *Ilo Ilo*'s title rehearses the same semantic trick. Thus, as these two stories about the national condition commence, the words prompt spectators to glance southeast toward Australia, or northeast toward the Philippines. *Ilo Ilo* even inserts an additional layer of multilingual polysemy. The film's Chinese titles read, "Father and Mother are not home." They too beckon us to redirect our vision, to look elsewhere, outside. Irresistibly, *Ilo Ilo* joins *Perth* in referencing the long durée of Singapore's maritime history. At the start of this Oedipal drama between Jiale, his mother (Hwee Leng), and the Filipino woman who cared for him, the very first thing we are told about the matriarch is that she works at a shipping company. Hence, by the time we watch Hwee Leng typing up a termination notice addressed to a colleague and victim of the Asian financial crisis, our awareness of migratory flows and interconnected economies is thoroughly activated.

The same two actors were cast in the director's next film, *Wet Season* (2019), this time playing a student and an unhappily married school teacher who have an affair. Commenting on the 30th Singapore International Film Festival's choice of *Wet Season* for opening night, executive director Yuni Hadi cited the event's historical importance to local filmmaking "anchored on resonating stories of home, or steadfast tales with Singaporean sensibilities at their core" (Sindie 2019). No wonder then, that when the woman divorces her husband and ends the illicit relationship, she reaches closure in her hometown . . . semirural Taiping in northwest Malaysia. This Singaporean irony recurs once more in Sundance award-winner *Shirkers* (2018), Los Angeles–based author Sandi Tan's self-reflexive documentary. When they were teenage cinephiles in Singapore, Tan shot an unfinished film with Vassar film professor Sophia Siddique and filmmaker Jasmine Ng. Part autobiography, part exploration of the cinematic imagination, Tan weaves their memories with the life of Georges Cardona, their filmmaking mentor who absconded to Louisiana with the unfinished film. Cutting between Singapore in the past and America in the present, the emigrant's odyssey takes Tan home only to inevitably draw her out.

The cultural logic of supply chain capitalism's thematic mobility and transnational flows occasionally expresses itself through referential realism in the form of images shot at the island's edges as they were in *A Yellow Bird*, *Perth*, and *Ilo Ilo*. In this regard, the liminal border preoccupations of Tan Pin Pin and Charles Lim's work in art and documentary video stand out as well. When the goal is psychological realism, the logic manifests in intimate stories shot elsewhere; *Apprentice*, for example, outsourced the locations for its prison scenes to Australia. Correctional facilities are of course another type of infrastructure. While locational stand-ins are not uncommon in filmmaking, and international co-productions especially, the practice carries added importance in Singapore cinema where infrastructure is an idea that spills from the referent into the signifier and signified.

Singapore's cinema can't help but return to it. The films are of infrastructure, the thing Singapore embodies, having fashioned all the ways to patch itself into the global supply chain. Still, do not be deceived by infrastructure's stereotype as anonymous architecture, devoid of color and texture, or risk failing to recognize local specificities both social and cinematic through which people express autonomy. As Tsing puts it, the basic units of supply chain capitalism are "commodity chains based on subcontracting, outsourcing, and allied arrangements in which the autonomy of component enterprises is legally established even as the enterprises are disciplined with the chain as a whole" (148). She discourages us from thinking that global capitalism standardizes or homogenizes. The call resonates with voices in world cinema studies counseling the same (Hjort 2010, 15). Dudley Andrew's grammar in "An Atlas of World Cinema" is particularly striking for its lexical intersections with concepts of travel and movement between complex ecologies (2004, 10, 21). These thinkers obligate us to understand the world's cultural tapestry in full. For Tsing, we would then appreciate how supply chain capitalism uses "diverse social-economic niches" for production efficiency. Within these niches, workers are encouraged to fashion themselves as entrepreneurial subcontractors, laboring in actuality by performing the cultural differences that end up subjugating them further. "These figurations blur the lines between self-exploitation and superexploitation" (171).

Tsing's argument steers me back toward *A Yellow Bird*'s expression of these tendencies. The film begins by foregrounding the very social relations that Tsing believes define labor within supply chains. Rajagopal parachutes us into the middle of Siva's workday. When the camera recedes from the initial closeup, we see him marching in line, curiously the lone Indian among a group of Chinese men, all clad in uniforms that include black hats with red furry trim. After a beat or two, we decipher that he is marching in a Taoist funeral procession. Among the outsourced mourners is an undocumented woman from mainland China (Chen Chen), marked as such by her non–Southeast Asian accent. Compelled to secure a better paying gig to support her child back home, she turns to sex work, but not before hiring Siva as private muscle. By what must be coincidence, these two entrepreneurial figures – a manual laborer and a sex worker – were cited by Tsing as examples of supply chain labor that produces value in part by performing the differences "that establish their superexploitation: gender, race, ethnicity, and so forth. [I]t is a familiar feature of independent contracting. A day laborer must perform brawn and availability; a prostitute must perform sexual charm" (158–59). Moreover, when Siva agrees to be Chen's protector, he actually becomes doubly exploited.

If this is a fluke, then it should not be a surprise, given the degree to which the syntax behind this dilemma of supply chain capitalism is refracted and rehearsed in Singapore. By way of a conclusion, consider its instantiation within a sociological phenomenon that has vexed the state for most of its existence. Educated and socio-economically mobile people who use their means and opportunities to emigrate with their labor, skills, and tax dollars were branded as "quitters" by Singapore's first two prime ministers at National Day speeches more than 32 years apart. In 2002, with the Asian financial crisis fresh in the memory, the quitters were derided as "fair-weather citizens" over "stayers," who remain committed to the country and, more importantly, *in* it, "rain or shine" (Goh 2002). Interpreted as judgmental and moralizing, the address triggered months of public debate. That larger reaction to the speech obscures the fact that emigrants had already been marked using the same formulation in 1969 and 1970. It occurred in the context of a graduate brain drain, an exodus triggered by the institution of national military service in 1967 (Lim 2007, 123–24; Lee 1970). Sandi Tan may find a somewhat familiar ring in the language even back then:

> Whether we are shirkers or quitters, or stayers and fighters, will determine whether we live in peace or not. If people believe that we are stayers and fighters, we are more likely to live peacefully.
>
> *(Lee 1970)*

Such are the inexorable conundrums of both a state and its citizens integrally reliant on the outside, on global flows, and on supply chains. It is the dilemma of success, because national aspiration is tautologically conflated with geographical portability and economic mobility. By default, excelling at infrastructure confers anonymity, while being a hub normalizes transition and transience. Consider the irony of stamping foreign workers as temporary, a status codified in state policy no less (Yeoh, Huang, and Gonzalez 1999, 117), when mobility and leaving are imbricated in the national ideal to quit. This cycle of Singaporean films presents the symptoms of that condition, in poignant acknowledgment of its history and purpose as a gateway, conduit, and transnational service hub. They also coincide with the rise of media infrastructure studies as a discipline, where scholars at least since Larkin (2013) have grappled with questions about the text's relevance in comparison to the infrastructures behind it. At this opportune moment, these films step forward from a context that is infrastructural all the way down, in myriad ways that these passages have only begun to consider. They raise world cinema as a useful platform for those debates, and volunteer themselves as affective purveyors of infrastructural style, or supply chain aesthetics – Gesamtkunstwerks of an infrastructural age.

Notes

1 The concept was distilled into the 2022 multimedia art exhibition, *Lonely Vectors*, hosted by the Singapore Art Museum at its new space, a repurposed warehouse at a historic shipping terminal. The artwork's purpose was to "draw our attention to the fault lines, choke points, exclusive zonings and infrastructural politics that characterize our global economy. Agricultural and irrigation channels, trade and shipping routes, economic zonings and migratory patterns are engraved across the surface of the earth, and are integral to our contemporary lives" (Lonely Vectors 2022).
2 Liberalized immigration policies in the 2000s led to rapid population growth that strained infrastructure and stiffened competition for jobs and housing. Locals directed ire at arrivals who were both high-earning professionals and unskilled laborers who populated service positions and construction sites.

References

Andrew, Dudley. 2004. "An Atlas of World Cinema." *Framework: The Journal of Cinema and Media* 45, no. 2 (Fall): 9–23.

Berry, Christopher, and Mary Farquhar. 2006. *China on Screen: Cinema and Nation*. New York: Columbia University Press.

Chua, Beng Huat, and Meisen Wong. 2012. "Aesthetics of the Pathetic: The Portrayal of the Abject in Singaporean Cinema." *Access: Contemporary Issues in Education* 31 (2): 138–47.

———, and Wei-Wei Yeo. 2003. "Singapore Cinema: Eric Khoo and Jack Neo – Critique from the Margins and the Mainstream." *Inter-Asia Cultural Studies* 4 (1): 117–25.

Chua, Charmaine. 2020. "Sunny Island Set in the." In *Digital Life in the Global City: Contesting Infrastructures*, edited by Deborah Cowen, Alexis Mitchell, Emily Paradis, and Brett Story, 238–47. Vancouver: UBC Press.

Comaroff, Joshua. 2014. "Built on Sand: Singapore and the New State of Risk." *Harvard Design Magazine: Architecture, Landscape Architecture, Urban Design and Planning* 39: 138.

Dickinson, Kay. 2021. "Supply Chain Cinema, Supply Chain Education." In *Assembly Codes: The Logistics of Media*, edited by Matthew Hockenberry, Nicole Starosielski, and Susan Zieger, 171–87. Durham: Duke University Press.

Goh, Chok Tong. 2002. "Remaking Singapore – Changing Mindsets." *National Day Rally Address*. Singapore: Ministry of Information, Communications and the Arts, August 18.

Hjort, Mette. 2010. "On the Plurality of Cinematic Transnationalism." In *World Cinemas, Transnational Perspectives*, edited by Nataša Ďurovičová and Kathleen Newman, 12–33. New York: Routledge.

Hui, Weng-Tat. 1997. "Regionalization, Economic Restructuring and Labour Migration in Singapore." *International Migration* 35 (1): 109–30.

Khoo, Olivia. 2006. "Slang Images: On the 'Foreignness' of Contemporary Singaporean Films." *Inter-Asia Cultural Studies* 7 (1): 81–98.

Larkin, Brian. 2013. "The Politics and Poetics of Infrastructure." *Annual Review of Anthropology* 42 (1): 327–43.

Lee, Kuan Yew. 1970. "Summary of Speech by the Prime Minister at the 5th National Day Celebrations." *National Archives of Singapore*, August 16. Accessed April 27, 2022. https://www.nas.gov.sg/archivesonline/data/pdfdoc/lky19700816.pdf.

Leow, Joanne. 2020. "'this land was the sea': The Intimacies and Ruins of Transnational Sand in Singapore." *Verge: Studies in Global Asias* 6 (2): 167–89.

Lim, Selina Sher Ling. 2007. "Rethinking Albert O. Hirschman's 'Exit, Voice, and Loyalty': The Case of Singapore." PhD diss., The Ohio State University.

Lonely Vectors. 2022. Singapore Art Museum, Singapore. June 3–September 4.

Rajah, Indranee. 2016. "Keynote Speech." *Asia Pacific Energy and Infrastructure Finance Forum*. Singapore: Marriott Tang Plaza Hotel, March 3.

Sim, Gerald. 2020. *Postcolonial Hangups in Southeast Asian Cinema: Poetics of Space, Sound, and Stability*. Amsterdam: Amsterdam University Press.

Sindie. 2019. "ShoutOUT! 'Wet Season' to Open the 30th SGIFF." *Sindie*, October. Accessed April 25, 2022. https://www.sindie.sg/2019/10/shoutout-wet-season-to-open-30th-sgiff.html

Tsing, Anna. 2009. "Supply Chains and the Human Condition." *Rethinking Marxism: A Journal of Economics, Culture & Society* 21 (2): 148–76.

Wee, C. J. W.-L. 2012. "The Suppressed in the Modern Urbanscape: Cultural Difference and Film in Singapore." *Positions: Asia Critique* 20, no. 4 (Fall): 983–1007.

Yeoh, Brenda S. A., Shirlena Huang, and Joaquin Gonzalez. 1999. "Migrant Female Domestic Workers: Debating the Economic, Social and Political Impacts in Singapore." *The International Migration Review* 33 (1): 114–36.

Yun, Daniel. 2018. "Getting Singaporeans to Take Pride in Homegrown Films." *Today*, June 7. Accessed April 22, 2022. https://www.todayonline.com/commentary/taking-pride-singapore-films.

18

NORTH KOREA'S INTERNATIONAL CO-PRODUCTION VENTURES

Nation and the Post-national

Hyangjin Lee

Korean cinema emerged during the Japanese forced occupation period (1910–45), and was divided into two national cinemas after a settlement of Japan's defeat in World War II by the Allies. The politics of division enforced by the US and Soviet military occupation governments (1945–48) deepened the conceptual discrepancy between notions of the nation as an ethnic entity and of the state as a political entity. The discrepancy is arguably the most conflicting ideological dimension to North and South Korean cinemas, which resulted in their contrasting and marked differences in style and content (Lee 2018). This chapter engages with a question about how North Korean cinema could heal the rupture from the politics of Cold War and communicate across its borders. In this way, it is possible to break away from such deep division and isolation to overcome the boundary between the North and the South and share their works with a wider range of global audiences.

International co-production can dismantle the nation-state's monopoly of North Korean cinema and revitalize it as a significant global force crossing national borders. To investigate a quest for the post-national, I first investigate North Korea's international co-production ventures from a historical perspective. I then analyze two North Korea's international ventures as an attempt to break down the national boundary; the first North Korea–Japan co-production, *Sae* (Birds, 1992), produced by a *zainichi* (Korean residents in Japan) Lee Bong-woo, and a North and South Korea–America co-production animation *Wanghu Shim Chŏng* (Empress Chung, 2005), produced by a Korean-American, Nelson Shin.

The textual analysis of the two North Korea's international co-productions articulates the post-national positioning of the creators, Lee and Shin, in reconstructing the screen images of "one" nation. The in-between ethnic identity and cultural hybridity working in Japanese and American film industries, respectively were ingrained during the filmmaking and their multiple sense of belonging marked the production process. The two films minimize commentaries on politics of division and instead engage with the transnational aesthetic of breaking boundaries. The aim is to simultaneously satisfy the needs of disparate audiences. Aesthetic hybridization may also make viewers uncomfortable due to the mixture of heterogeneous elements informed by North Korea's *juche* (i.e., self-reliance) ideology and Western capitalism. The textual analysis aims to illustrate the limits of the

DOI: 10.4324/9781003266952-25

political-determination approach, which can be found in many existing North Korean film studies. This approach tends to treat films as a continuity of public propaganda and political education policies, revealing the oppressive reality of a closed society controlled by public power (Han 2018). This study explores the significance of audience-oriented filmmaking and the role of the audience in completing the textual meaning in the pursuit of viewing pleasure (Sulieman 1980). The intentions of film authorities cannot entirely control the autonomy and subjectivity of cultural practices. The interpretation of textual meaning is often endlessly renewed and generated by multiple individuals who have diverse social and historical backgrounds, as well as worldviews and emotional motives. Furthermore, the diversity of investment destinations and expected audiences in international co-production works serves to emphasize the post-national aesthetics of North Korean cinema.

Division as Ideological Rupture of Korean National Cinema

Under the United States and Soviet Union military administrations, both the USAMGIK (United States Army Military Government in Korea) in the South and the SCA (Soviet Civil Administration) in the North actively used film to legitimate the hostile state-controlled ideologies of anticommunism versus communism (Kim 1994; Kang 1995; Ryu 2016). The Department of Public Information was formed in March 1946 to operate the Central Film Distributor within the USAMGIK to exclusively distribute Hollywood films to theaters in the South (Cho 2011; Cho 2018). SCA distributed Soviet films to theaters in Pyongyang through Sovexportfilm and Joseon-Soviet Union Cultural Association which was established on November 11, 1945. The cultural intervention of the US and Soviet Union through the distribution of their films was expanded after the withdrawal of troops and the emergence of the two Korean governments in 1948 (Kang and Cho 2006). The Korean War (1950–53) then erupted along the lines of ideological conflict; it was the first hot war of the Cold War. Film on both sides has served to remind the people of the fear of war, amplifying hatred and hostility toward the enemy, the communist North or the capitalist South.

The Soviet Union played an important role in the development of color technology for North Korean films. The first North Korean color film, *1950 nyŏn 5.1 chŏl* (May Day, 1950) was produced with the support of the Soviet Union, and the first North Korea–Soviet Union co-production, *Tongbang-ŭi Achim* (Eastern Morning, also known as *Hyŏngje* or Brothers, and *Bratya* in Russian), was made in 1957. Kim Jong-il used cinema as the most significant means of cultural governance. He graduated from university in 1964 to work at Propaganda and Agitation Department, and published the most authoritative textbook for North Korean cinema, *On the Art of Cinema*, in 1973. Subsequently, three North Korea–Soviet co-productions, namely, *Yŏngwŏnhan chŏnu* (One Second for a Feat, 1985), *Pombutŏ kaŭl-kkaji* (Spring to Autumn, 1987), and *Kuwŏn-ŭi kisŭk* (The Shore of Salvation, 1990) were made in an effort to internationalize the film industry. These films frequently portrayed the Japanese invasion of the Korean peninsula, and they sought to emphasize the strong military solidarity and longstanding friendship between the two countries.

North Korean cinema under Kim Jong-il's rule dramatically expanded and vigorously engaged in international co-production. In the 1990s and 2000s, international co-production and collaboration were expanded to Asia and Europe. Through international collaboration and co-production projects with Japan, China, the UK, and other European countries, Western capitalism and consumer culture were introduced to those hoping for the gradual opening-up of North Korean society.

Inter-Korean and Japan–North Korea Co-productions

From South Korea's point of view, the growing public interest in inter-Korean relations since the 1987 democratization is most clearly illustrated by the popularity of division dramas starting with Kang Je-gyu's *Shiri* in the 2000s. With the first meeting of the inter-Korean summit between Kim Dae-jung and Kim Jong-il in 1998, South Korean broadcasting companies started to air North Korean films. The Seoul Broadcasting System (SBS) aired *Anjunggŭn idŭngbangmun-ŭl ssoda* (Ahn Jung-geun, Shooting Ito Hirobumi), and the Korean Broadcasting System (KBS) did *Lim Kkeok-jeong* I–V (1987–89), and then Munhwa Broadcasting Corporation (MBC) followed them to broadcast *Ondal* (1986) in 1998 and 1999. Discussions on co-production and exchanges between South and North Korean filmmakers began with the 2000 inter-Korean summit. *Arirang* (2002) directed by Lee Doo-yong became the first South Korean film to premiere in Pyongyang. On the occasion of the 100th anniversary of Korean film history, inter-Korean co-production has emerged as a new project for filmmakers in Korea. Starting with the Busan International Film Festival, local film festivals are also popular venues attracting audience participation in inter-Korean film exchanges.

Overseas Koreans were also actively engaged in the breaking down of boundaries between South and North Korean films. The South-North Korean Film Festival was held in New York in 1990. In Japan, North Korean film screenings were held centering around *zainichi* communities. A special filming team of Toho, a major Japanese film company participated in the production of a North Korean film *Bulgasari* (1985) produced by South Korean director Shin Sang-ok, who was kidnapped by Kim Jong-il in 1978. Although the escape of Shin from North Korea in 1986 postponed its Japanese release until 1998, its commercial success far surpassed the Hollywood film *Godzilla* (1998) which was screened in the same year. Finally, the film was released as a DVD in 2004 in Japan. It was the first North Korean film released in a form of DVD in the global market.

In the 1990s, mainstream Japanese films began breaking the border between North and South Korea. *All Under the Moon* (1993), by Sai Yoichi (Korean named Choi Yang-il), is the first commercially successful and critically acclaimed "*zainichi* film" (Lee 2021). The satirical comedy articulates the absurdity of the division politics between two Koreas deepened in the *zainichi* community. Unlike the previous tragic portrayals of ethnic Koreans in Japan based on colonial rule, forced mobilization, and discrimination in Japanese society, it ridicules the dominant discourse and representation of the *zainichi* by incorporating the carnival spirit along with the activity of laughter as depicted in the Bahktin's carnivalesque discourse (Bakhtin 1984; Lee 2021). Subsequently, *Go* (2001), *Break Through!* (2004), and *Blood and Bones* (2004) continued to be acclaimed by critics for their stunning box office records and cinematic performance. In 2006, director Yang Yong-hi's documentary *Dear Pyongyang* won the Netpac Award at the Berlin International Film Festival and the Special Jury Prize at the Sundance Film Festival.

The role of *zainichi* in the history of North Korea's international cooperation is crucial (Chong 2014).[1] Starting with Kang Hong-shik, the director of the first North Korean narrative film *Nae Koyhyang* (My Hometown, 1947), a number of directors and actors representing colonial Korean cinema chose the North after the liberation (Jang 2008; Lee 2017; Han 2019). Several of them remained in Japan, collaborating with those who went to the North to create an aesthetic and industrial base for North Korean cinema. The politics of division forced them to choose between North and South Korea. However, they were the first agents to break down the inter-Korean border with their national identity, which was not exclusive to both. They made decisive contributions to the formation of the North Korean film industry by supporting equipment and manpower. They later became central figures for co-production projects and exchanges, and supported the production and distribution of North Korean films under the prevailing difficult circumstances at that time (Lee 2021; Chong 2014; Itagaki 2019; Ahn 2018). Furthermore, by crossing the boundaries between the North and the South, overseas Korean audiences were allowed an important opportunity to view North Korean films. In a sense, this has become a "window" for inter-Korean integration and communication.

Shin Sang-ok and North Korean International Co-production

A discussion of Shin Sang-ok's films can make a critical contribution to the study of breaking the boundaries between North Korean films from the perspective of the post-national. In "The Postnational Constellation and the Future of Democracy," Habermas stated that the dynamics of globalization would put an end to the global domination models of nation-states as political organizations (Habermas 2001). Bloemraad elaborated further that "the dynamics of globalization, especially international migration, challenge traditional frameworks of citizenship and promoted scholars to develop new models of membership: transnationalism and postnationalism" (Bloemaraad 2004: 389). Indeed, globalization of production and distribution processes, changes and trends in markets, modes of communication and commerce, and cultural hybridization all put an end to the classical form of nation-states based on exclusive sovereignty.

On the other hand, the notion of post-national as a global phenomenon evolved in the West is limited in identifying it as a local phenomenon as conveyed in North Korean international co-production ventures. The nation as an imaginary community developed by Anderson (1998) remains valid for Koreans to dismantle the historical trauma of Japanese colonial rule and build a nation-state for the nation. However, Japan's forced occupation ultimately resulted in the fixation of the national division to be responsible for exploiting the notion of nation as a dominant signifier remodeling the exclusive boundary of a nation-state and deepening enmity between members of a nation located outside the borders of a nation-state (Shin 2011; Jeon 2018). In the North, nationalism is identified with Kimilsungism, the ruling ideology that seeks to isolate the people from the dynamics of Western-led globalization. From this point of view, Shin's international co-production ventures provided an important clue to dismantle the North Korean concepts of nation, and led to integration with Western-led globalization for post-national construction.

According to Kim Jong il's *On the Art of Cinema* (1973), a film director is considered "the commander" who should be actively involved in everything from film literature to acting, art, music to filming on-site. The collective authorship and interpretation informed by Kim Il Sung's *juche* (i.e., self-reliance) idea are the basic principle of filmmaking in North Korea. However, the international co-production process cannot be performed within this hierarchical, top-down command system as imposed by Kim Jong-il. The style, taste, and intention of foreign investors, directors, and producers informed by different cinematic experiences, and the different expectations between heterogeneous sectors of audiences intervene in the process of production and might resist political coercion. In short, producers and directors, who participated from outside, tended to make films for global audiences' consumption.

Shin was able to make films since 1983 after five years of detainment in a political prison camp. Kim Jong-il sought to use him to transform North Korean film into a hybridized form with a capitalist entertainment mode (Shin 2007; Lee 2005). Most of the films he made in North Korea were produced in a form of international co-production, and the aim was to present the works at international festivals. Shin was relatively free from the Kim Il Sung's *juche* ideology system, and effectively supported by the party. The director himself was more concerned with audience criticism and not the collective interpretation required by Kim's film theory. He brought up a new crevice into North Korean cinema by engaging in South Korean cinematic mode of representation and thematic concerns (Chung 2014). According to Shin, *Sarang Sarang Nae Sarang* (Love, Love and My Love, 1985), his North Korean version of *Sŏng Chunhyang* (1961), a South Korean film based on the traditional *Pansori* text of interclass marriage offered North Koreans their biggest cultural shock (Lee 2000). Kim Il Sung specifically pointed out the story of Chunhyang as harmful to young North Koreans. On top of this, the word "love," which had not ever been used as a title or even in the dialogue, was also a novel and unexpected surprise for them. Another example is the rape scene in *Sogŭm* (Salt, 1985), which had never been shown in any North Korean film. *Bulgasari* and *Shimchŏngjŏn* (The Story of Shim Chung, 1985) are the first monster and fantasy genre films that the socialist realism tradition of North Korean film had never allowed before. Kim Jong-il gave Shin exceptional freedom to innovate North Korean films and communicate with the outside world. He had to prevent himself from imposing his command system of filmmaking, which he often adamantly insisted on (Lee 2005).

International collaboration can stimulate the interest and fascination of North Korean audiences regarding capitalist society. Shin is the master of the 1960s South Korean melodrama genre. Most of Shin's works in North Korea were produced in the facilities of the Joseon Film Studios, but some were completed through international cooperation including the participation of overseas production teams and partial studio and location shooting overseas. *T'alchulgi* (The Story of Escape, 1984) and *Salt* were shot in China and *The Story of Shim Chung* in Munich, Germany. The foreign characters and exotic scenery stimulated North Korean audiences' curiosity and gave them much entertainment pleasure. Shin presented North Korean audiences with a cinematic fantasy of crossing boundaries to satisfy their curiosity about capitalist society, a taboo in the isolated society. Shin's films provided a glimpse across the borders and provided audiences with new forms of entertainment as they did not propagate the regime or give explicit praise to its supreme leader. They allowed audiences to have a free scope for ambiguous interpretation and demonstrated themselves with cultural hybridity. Although he tried to avoid the political propaganda of North Korea by making historical dramas, Shin was actively engaged in the political mobilization through cinema in support of Park Chong-hee's authoritarian military rule (1961–79) in South Korea. His film world has given us a chance to reflect on how the politics of division, regardless of system or region, defines the relationship between film and politics (Lee and Han 2018).

To a greater extent, the collaboration with the General Association of Korean Residents in Japan takes place within the North Korean film production system, but some filming took place in Japan. *Bomnal-ŭi nunsŏgi* (Thaw of Spring Day, 1985), *Ŭnbit pinyŏ* (A Silver Hairpin, 1985), *Sarang-ŭi taeji* (Land of Love, 1999), *Ŏmŏni-ŭi sowŏn* (The Mother's Wish, 2000), and *Tonghae-ŭi norae* (Song of the East Sea, 2009) are some of most representative films, portraying the *zainichi*'s aspiration of homecoming and devotion to the national unification. They can satisfy the North Korean audience's viewing pleasure of the landscapes and everyday lifestyle in Japan, an advanced Western capitalist society. At the same time, however, the works can be subject to censorship for being sensational and anti-people. *Thaw of Spring Day* was banned in 2016 by the film authority due to the portrayals of "decadent lifestyle and human rights in foreign countries," (Hong 2016).

The international co-production has continued after the death of Kim Jong-il. Some of most recent international co-production, for example, a Chinese–North Korean co-production film titled *Pyongyang-esŏ mannayo* (Meet in Pyongyang, 2012), English-Belgian co-production *Kim dongmu hanŭl-ŭl nalda* (Comrade Kim Goes Flying, 2012), and a North Korean–American co-production *Sannŏmŏ maŭl* (The Village over the Hill, 2012) were produced during Kim Jong-un's era. They have been screened in various international film festivals including the Busan International Film Festival.

The project of *Meet in Pyongyang* was planned to improve relations between North Korea and China and was filmed with Chinese equipment. Investment was made from the Chinese side, and shooting was done by the North Korean side. Most of the characters were North Korean actors except for Chinese dancers and extras around them. The film was screened at the Gwangju International Film Festival in 2012 in South Korea. In North Korea, it began airing again in 2018 after Kim Jong-un's visit to China since its first airing in 2014. Similar to *Meet in Pyongyang*, which integrates the stories of dance, mass gymnastics, and artistic performances of *Arirang* festival, *Comrade Kim Goes Flying* is about aerial acrobatics. Belgium and Britain production companies invested funds in the film and composed its background music. Delivering North Korea's unique sound through their musical instruments and the lyrics of explicit regime praise, the film provides more accurate messages, whereby it embodies collectivistic North Korean film art theory. The two films also combine not only music but stage performances and collective dance together in order to maximize the collective creative effects by socialist art form. There were scenes showing banners and street views so as to deliver messages of praise for the regime. *The Village over the Hill* produced by a Korean American producer Bae Byeong-jun portrays a love story set in the Korean War of a South Korean soldier and a North Korean nurse. It took a long time to complete this film. The film contains the classic message of wishing for a national unification of Koreas, instead of showing cultural hybridity or experimenting with removing the border. In a sense, the films are still compliant politically.

Birds and *Empress Chung*, chosen for the textual analysis, can be seen as an alternative form of international co-production to express the resistance and negotiation of the filmmakers from outside of the North Korean production system. The cinematic hybridization articulates their sense of Koreanness as ethnic minorities living in the United States and Japan. It affirms that their filmmaking process can challenge the collective production and interpretation system monitored by the party.

Birds (Lim Chang-beom 1992)

Co-projected by three Japanese companies including Tokuma Japan Communications, Hakuhodo, and FM Tokyo, *Birds* is the first North Korea–Japan co-production film with a production investment of 100 million yen. This film is based on a true story. A North Korean ornithologist, Dr. Won Hong-gu (a former professor of Kim Il Sung University), who was separated from his two sons during the Korean War, lived alone in North Korea.

One of his sons is Won Byung-hwi, a former biology professor at Dongkuk University, and the other is Won Byung-oh, a former biology professor at Kyung Hee University. One day, Dr. Won Hong-gu finds a Japanese identification ring on a bird that Byung-oh sent to North Korea and realizes that his two sons are alive in South Korea. Their story was originally featured in the North Korean newspaper *Rodong Shinmun* in 1965, the Soviet Union's *Pravda*, and American, Japanese, and South Korean newspapers in later years.

Birds was a project with a purpose of finding new global talent.[2] There was the worldwide screenplay competition open to anyone in five different regions: five of the screenplays from the United States, France, Britain, and others have been selected and adapted to films. Kim Se-ryun wrote the screenplay adapted from the original novel that a North Korean writer Rim Jong-sang published in *Josŏn Munhak* (Joseon Literature) in March 1990. The entire production, except for the Japanese dubbing, took place in North Korea and was completed by North Korean crew and actors. Yang Yong-hi, the Korean Japanese director of *Dear Pyongyang*, stars in the film as a Japanese character. After the film was screened once at the fifth Tokyo International Film Festival for the section of Best Asian Film Week, it was not even known of its existence. However, it premiered to a South Korean audience at the first Pyeongchang International Peace Film Festival in 2019. It has not been confirmed whether it has also been screened in North Korea.

Unlike other previously known North Korean co-production films, *Birds* was created with the producer deeply involved in the production process and with decision-making rights. He chose the screenplay and casted the director and actors, being more concerned with the audience in Japan. Lee chose Lim Chang-beom as the director, whose filmography

Figure 18.1   *Birds* (1992) is a work based on the true story of a father and son, Dr. Won Hong-gu and Dr. Won Byeong-oh, who worked as ornithologists in the North and the South, respectively, after separating during the Korean War. The black-and-white photo of the father and son taken before their breakup and the images of birds crossing the military demarcation line suggest a post-national approach to confront division through their memories. Courtesy of PyeongChang International Peace Film Festival.

includes *I Will Play the Drum* (1977) *Thaw of Spring Day* and *The Problem of My In-Laws*, among the series of *The Problem of My House* (1983–88). Lim's portrayal of characters through satire and humor in family dramas is warmer and suggestive rather than directly addressing or emotionally appealing thematic concerns. The comic and warmhearted father's image in *The Problem of My In-Laws* had an important influence on choosing Lim. Lee revised the screenplay several times for removing political content and phrases praising the social system and the current ruling ideology. For example, Kim Il Sung's name appears only once in a slogan written on a wall in a lab scene.

Birds does not address political messages in an explicit way. The scenes showing beautiful nature continue, which make resonance of the pain of separated families who cannot fly like birds and cross the military demarcation line. This sentiment is reflected and sung in the theme music, *Imjin River*, a North Korean pop song which was very popular as a folk song with guitar accompaniment in the 1970s in Japan. In the film, instead, the song is sung by a chorus with orchestral music, a typical North Korean style. The music aims to evoke nostalgia for the era when civil society movements were active and compassion for the suffering of *zainichi* and communicate the *zainichi*'s role as an intermediary between not only the North and the South but also Japan and Korea. The warmhearted characterization of Japanese colleagues and neighbors assisting the family reunion also supports this observation, which is unprecedented in the North Korean film language. Furthermore, Lee created the reunion scenes of the father and the son in Japan, different from the original story. He chose Mun Ye-bong as the mother's role to convey his idea of the undivided Korea and a sense of home he felt about Japan. Mun is the representative actress of colonial Joseon cinema. She disappears from the screen during the period of the party's purge until the early 1980s.

A co-production film made with active involvement by outside investors may help break the boundaries imposed by the division politics. In particular, overseas Korean investors, whose collective historical memories and resistances against the oppression of the division politics, are often involved in the textual composition of co-production films from the very earlier stage. Significantly, they can reject the collective interpretation of North Korean film authority. Indeed, the post-editing may weaken the resistance of producers and investors outside the national boundary. According to Lee, for instance, the scene of a father-to-son reunion in a father's dream, a climax in *Birds*, was deleted from the North Korean version. However, the message of the film still conveys the absurdity of the division politics denying freedom of movement and family reunions. The hybridization of Japanese and North Korean cinematic traditions is also a significant achievement as international co-production work. Some scenes remind us of melodramas or romantic comedies in mainstream Japanese films at the time: the male protagonist, who peeps at the female protagonist in a bath, and a couple's bedroom scene shot at a hotel in Pyongyang, not at a regular house. Three decades later, the film evokes nostalgia and laughter for South Korean audiences. They illustrate the transboundary aesthetic, which is the hybridity of tastes and cinematic imagination of heterogeneous audiences.

Empress Chung (Nelson Shin 2005)

Made by COAA Film Seoul, COAA Film (America) and Choseon April 26 Children's Studio (North Korea) over seven years, *Empress Chung* is the first film simultaneously released in South and North Korea. It is an animated adaptation of the classic novel *Shimchŏngjŏn* portraying a filial piety. Shin directed and supervised the entire production process.[3] Shin had no intention of collaborating with North Korea but met a North Korean animation artist team coincidently in China to work with them. A collaboration process led *Empress Chung* to denounce the politics of national division.

Empress Chung shows the hybridization of typical character setting and visual characteristics of films across the borders between North and South Korea and the United States. It visualized Shin's longing for home coming on the screen with a milestone showing the name "Hwanghae-do," his hometown located in the North Korean territory above the military demarcation border. In the film, several blind men come to a feast at the royal palace. They speak Gyeongsang and Jeolla dialects of the South, thus emphasizing a lack of national division. It also features his shaggy dog, Tanchu, a breed from the South. It literally means a button for Western clothes. This use of the word as well as the creation of a dog as a main character not well fit in a traditional story subtly suggests Shin's transnational film careers in South Korea and America. He is a creator of numerous famous American animations such as *Pink Panther* (1974), *Star Wars* (1976), *Transformers the Movie* (1986), and *The Simpsons* (1989).

Chung is both smart and vivacious in creating the image of Ariel in *The Little Mermaid* (1989), for example, but has no rebellious spirit like a good kid in North Korean animation. In addition, her stepmother, Ppaengdeok, is described as a greedy, cunning, and manipulative woman with a glamorous, sensual body, who often appears in Western cartoons and movies. Also, Chung is sold as a sacrifice to a sea monster, not to calm the wind. The episode with cute and active fish that she meets under the sea also reminds the audience of Disney's *Little Mermaid* or *Finding Nemo* (2004), demonstrating the hybridization of Disney with Korean local animation tradition.

Meanwhile, the characterization of Chung's father, Shim Hak-kyu, is a kind of cliché in North Korean film tradition, embodying the virtues of loyalty and filial piety. In Shin's reinterpretation, Shim is a loyal servant of the highest power, not a poor blind man as in the original story. He was accused of treason and ousted from his public office. Risking his life to save the baby Chung from the fire, he became blind to complete the image of unwavering loyalty to the supreme leader and of the self-sacrificing, omnipotent, and generous father of the people. Chung's characterization can be discussed in a similar way. Chung is a diligent and filial daughter. Her sacrificing image reminds the audience of a good daughter and wife, Chunhyang, in the North Korean version of *The Story of Chunhyang* (1980), who shows camaraderie working hard like her servant Hynagdan to serve her mother together and keep her chastity against the tyranny of governors (Lee 2000). Chung is a model worker who works day and night to serve her father. She ultimately sacrifices herself in order to open her father's eyes.

According to Shin, the North Korean version uses North Korean actors recording the voices, but the South Korean version uses South Korean actors, dubbing it with high-pitched sounds and with an accurate Seoul dialect. However, the music played by the North Korea orchestral band and the female ensemble clearly shows the locality of North Korean animation. In short, the film has experimented with the way of co-producing with North Korea beyond the border and how it is possible for heterogeneous audiences to enjoy co-production films simultaneously.

Conclusion

This chapter examined the aesthetics of crossing boundaries and cultural hybridity in North Korean cinema from a post-national perspective. It aimed to underscore the autonomy of an interactive communication between creators and audiences generated by international co-production ventures. The limited space does not allow an in-depth discussion of "foreign" films produced by the collaboration with North Korea, but it should be noted that there are a series of films making a significant contribution to the historical evolution of North Korean cinema. Among them *Moranbong, a Korea Adventure* (1959) directed by Claude Jean Bonnardot, in particular, manifests the post-national aesthetic and cultural hybridity of the early North Korean cinema, highlighting the political openness and confidence of the then society (Morris 2015). Furthermore, it offers unique insights into the postwar North Korean society and cultural formation as a nation state.

In 2022, Cho Syung-hyung, the director of a German film titled *Brothers and Sisters in the North* in 2016, is working on the co-production project of the first North Korea–Germany drama series despite a strong national lockdown of North Korea owing to COVID-19.[4] Under Kim Jong-un's rule, the number of films produced has been significantly reduced, and the produced works are also less prominent. On the other hand, the production of TV dramas has become more active than before, and the boundaries between drama and film have become more blurred in recent years. The North Korean–German drama co-production project can be seen as an effort to find a new resurgence of the national cinema for a global audience.

On the other hand, these international collaboration efforts still face a dilemma. They must try to satisfy the viewing pleasure of the audience in capitalist societies and, at the same time, attempt to accommodate the North Korean government's need for the political indoctrination of its people. In this respect, *Birds* and *Empress Chung* communicate the creators' efforts to keep a distance from the North Korean film authority's expectation and pursue to satisfy the audiences' viewing pleasure informed by the cinematic tradition of Western societies.

Thanks to the radically changed global media environment in the digital age, the global audience can easily access North Korean films at various online sites in more recent years. On the other hand, even in the 2020s, there are the videos trying to expose the "inhumane life conditions" of North Korea with a hidden camera, for example, using the clips of *kkotchebi*, i.e., homeless or street children who suffer from famine during the years of the Arduous March (1994–99). Also, some of the North Korean co-production films are not available at home whereas they were produced in cooperation with North Korean authorities for the audience outside (Valentino 2020). Sony Pictures' *The Interview* (2004), depicting the assassination of Kim Jong-un, was a huge commercial success, but North Korean audiences were unable to view it in cinemas (McCarter 2020).

In a sense, "North Korea" became a commodity in the present global media environment. Amid the flood of North Korean films, the international co-productions may be considered a methodological framework which serves to reduce the barriers existing in North Korean cinema. They have the potential to heal the rupture from the division politics informed by the Cold War confrontation in the region.

Acknowledgment

This study was supported by the National Research Foundation of Korea Grant funded by the Korean government (NRF-2017S1A3A2065782). This chapter is based on a public lecture I gave at the 2019 Busan International Film Festival Forum celebrating the One Hundred Years of Korean Cinema. That lecture was published as a journal article in Japanese by Nagoya University in *JunCture* 13 in 2022.

Notes

1 Interviews with Yo Ungak, the adviser of Chongryon Film Production between 2006 and 2009.
2 Interviews with Lee Bong-woo, 16 and 20 August 2019.
3 Interview with Nelson Shin, 17 August 2019.
4 Interview with Cho Sung Hyung, 13 May 2022.

References

Ahn, Minhwa. 2018. "Taljŏmnyŏng-ŭi 'kŭpchinjŏk tongshidaesŏng'-ŭrosŏ-ŭi chaeilchosŏnyŏnghwain jiptan-ŭi hapchak tak'yument'ŏri-migunjŏng hanil munhwayŏnghwa-ŭi chayujuŭi riŏllijŭm-ŭl nŏmŏsŏ ['Radical Contemporary' as the De-occupation of Co-produced Documentary Film by *Zainichi* Korean Filmmaker's Collective-Beyond Liberal Realism of Cultural Documentaries of U.S Military Occupation in South Korea and Japan]." *Journal of Popular Narrative* 24 (1): 9–56.
Anderson, Benedict. 1998. *Imagined Communities: Reflections on the Origin and Spread of Nationalism*. London and New York: Verso.
Bakhtin, Mikhail. 1984. *Problems of Dostoevsky's Poetics*. Minneapolis: University of Minnesota Press.
Bloemaraad, Irene. 2004. "Who Claims Dual Citizenship? The Limits of Postnationalism, the Possibility of Transnationalism, and the Persistence of Traditional Citizenship." *IMR* 38 (2): 389–426.
Cho, Hye-jung. 2011. "Migunjŏnggi nyusŭ yŏnghwa-ŭi kwanjŏm-gwa inyŏmjŏk kiban yŏngu [A Study on the Viewpoint and the Ideological Basis of the Newsreels Under the USAMGIK]." *Han'guk minjŏk undongsa yŏn'gu* [Study of Korean National Movement] 68: 323–256.
Cho, Jun-hyoung. 2018. "Pulanhan Tongmaeng: chŏnhu miguk-ŭi p'ijŏmryŏngji yŏnghwa jŏngch'aek-kwa migunjŏnggi han'guk yŏnghwagye [Unstable Alliance between US Government and Hollywood-Post-war US Film Policy in Occupied Territories and Korean Cinema-]." *The Journal of Korean Studies* 48: 11–48.
Chong, Young-hwan. 2014. "Intabyū gendaishi o chōsen eigajin toshite ikite : sōren eiga seisakusho ryo ungak ko toi ni kiku [Interview Survivor in Contemporary History as a Korean Cineaste: Talk with The General Association of Korean Residents in Japan Corporate Advisor Yo Ungak]." *Jinken to seikatsu* [Human Rights and Life] 38: 32–41.
Chung, Steven. 2014. *Split Screen Korea: Shin Sang-ok and Postwar Cinema*. Minneapolis: University of Minnesota Press.
Habermas, Jǔrgen. 2001. "The Postnational Constellation and the Future of Democracy." In *The Postnational Constellation: Political Essays*, edited by Max Pensky, 58–113. Cambridge: Polity Press.
Han, Seungho. 2018. *Pukan-ŭi chosŏn yesul yŏnghwa* [North Korea's Chosun Feature Film]. Seoul: Communication Books.
Han, Sangheon. 2019. *Kang Hongshik-chŏn* [A Story of Kang Hongshik]. Seoul: Hang Sangheon Film Research Center.
Itagaki, Ryuta. (1955) 2019. "Eiga *Chosen no ko* no seisaku puroresu wo megutte [The Production Process of Children of Korea]." *The Review of Social Science* 128: 39–65.
Jang, Moon-seok. 2008. "Wŏlbukchakka-ŭi haegŭm-gwa chakp'umjip ch'ulp'an (1)-1985-1989 nyŏn shigi-rŭl chungshim-ŭro-[The De-prohibition of Writers Who Went to North and Publication of Anthology (1): Focused on the Period of 1985-1989]." *Kubohak'oe* [The Society of Kubo] 19: 39–111.
Jeon, Jaeho. 2018. "2000 nyŏndae han'guk-ŭi 'talminjokjuŭi nonjaeng yŏn'gu: Chuyo Jaengjŏm-gwa Kiyŏ [The 'Post-Nationalism' Debate in Korea During the 2000s: Its Main Arguments and Contribution]." *Han'guk-kwa kugje jŏngchi* [Korea and International Politics] 34–43: 33–64.
Kang, Inn-Goo. 1995. "1948 nyŏn pyŏngyang soryŏn munhwawŏn-ŭi sŏllip-kwa soryŏn-ŭi joso munwa kyoryu hwalttong [A Historical Study of Soviet Cultural Palace (Дом Сов етской Культуры) for North Korea in 1948]." *Han'guksa yŏngu* [Study of Korean History] 90: 403–26.
———, and Han Bum Cho. 2006. "Han'guk jŏnjaenggi pukan-e taehan soryŏn-ŭi munwajŏk gaeip: rŏsiachŭk-ŭi charyŏ-rŭl chungshim-ŭro [Cultural Intervention by the Soviet Union toward North Korea during the Korean War: Focus on Russian Data]." *International Journal of Korean Unification Studies* 15 (2): 247–265.

Kim, Ilsung. 1994. *Kimilsŏng jŏnjip je 8 kwŏn* [Kim Il Sung: Selected Works 8]. Pyongyang: Chosun Labor Party Publication.

Kim, Jong-il. 1973. *On the Art of Cinema*. Pyongyang: Chosun Labor Party Publication.

Lee, Bong Beom. 2017. "Naengjŏn-gwa wŏlbuk, (nap)wŏlbuk ŭije-ŭi munhwa chŏngchi [The Cold War and the Defects to North Korea, Cultural Politics of Agendas on the Kidnapped by North Korea and defects to North Korea]." *Korean Historical Studies* 2 1 (1): 229–294.

Lee, Hyangjin. 2000. *Contemporary Korean Cinema: Culture, Identity and Politics*. Manchester: Manchester University Press.

———. 2018. *Korian shinemā –kankoku·kitachōsen·toransu nashonaru–* [Korean Cinema – South and North Koreas, the Transnational–]. Tokyo: Misuzu.

———. 2021. "Choi yangil kamdok-ŭi talgukkajuŭi yŏngsang chŏngchihak [Politics of Post-national Cinema by Choi Yangil]." In *Tongil gŭ ihu-rŭl saenggakada* [Think about after the Unification], edited by Woo Young Lee and others, 107-137. Seoul: Hanul.

Lee, Junyeop, and Sangeon Han. 2018. "Pukan ch'ogi kalla yŏnghwa-ŭi hyŏngsŏng-gwa tŭkch'ing (1950 – 1057) [Characteristics and Formation Process of Early North Korean Color Film]." *Contemporary Film Studies* 14 (4): 111–140.

Lee, Myung-ja. 2005. "Shinsangok yŏnghwa-rŭl tonghae pon pukan-ŭi chakkajuŭi [Auteurism in North Korea-Concentrating on Shin Films]." *Review of North Korean Studies* 8 (2): 125–156.

McCarter, Reid. 2020. "Read this: Behind the scenes of North Korean action." *AVCLUB*, August 25, 2020. https://www. Avclub.com/read-this-behind-thescenes-of-north-korean-actionmov-1844840561

Morris, Mark. 2015. "Ch'unhyang at War: Rediscovering Franco-North Korean Film *Moranbong* 1959). In *Korean Screen Culture: Interrogating Cinema, TV, Music and Online Games*, edited by Andrew Davide Jackson and Colette Balmain, 199–218. Oxford: Peter Lang.

Ryu, KeeHyun. 2016. "1945–1950 nyŏn choso munhwa hyŏphoe-ŭi jojik-kwa hwalttong [Korea-Soviet Cultural Association 1945–1950: Organization and Activities]." MA thesis, Seoul National University Graduate School.

Shin, Hyong-gi. 2011. "Ilguk munhak·munhwa-ŭi talgyŏnggye – posŭtŭ-naesyŏnŏllijŭmjŏk kwanjŏm-ŭi sŏnggwa-wa jŏnmang [Out of Boundary of National Literature·Culture – Accomplishment and Prospects of the Post-nationalistic Perspective]." *The Journal of Modern Korean Literature* 45: 7–33.

Shin, Sang-ok. 2007. *Na-nŭn yŏnghwayeŏtta* [I was the Cinema]. Seoul: Random House Korea.

Sulieman, Susan R. 1980. "Introduction: Varieties of Audience-Oriented Criticism." In *The Reader in the Text: Essays on Audience and Interpretation*, edited by Susan R. Suleiman and Inge Cosman, 3–45. Princeton: Princeton University Press.

Valentino, Andrea. 2020. "'Ten Zan': The Disastrous Italian Action Movie Filmed Entirely in North Korea." *NK News*, June 11, 2020. https://www.nknews.org/2020/06/ten-zan-the-disastrous-italian-actionmovie-filmed-entirely-in-north-korea/.

19

TRANS-ASIAN CIRCUITS OF CINEMA AND MEDIA EXCHANGE BETWEEN AUSTRALIA AND ASIA

Olivia Khoo

Described as "the biggest Australian film you've never heard of" (Quinn 2019), *The Whistleblower* (Xue Xiaolu 2019) appeared on Australian screens to a dismal opening of AU$20,857. From an estimated AU$50 million budget, the film grossed only $7.5 million worldwide, more than half of that from China.[1] While the film attempted to capitalize on the large Chinese diaspora in Australia, it did little to appeal to this audience, with its vision of a globalized China at home in Australia remarkably devoid of Chinese Australians. Two years later one of the biggest opening weekends ($71.4 million) was achieved by *Shang-Chi and the Legend of the Ten Rings* (Destin Daniel Cretton 2021). Eschewing simultaneous release on streaming platforms by other Marvel features such as *Black Widow* (Cate Shortland 2021), *Shang-Chi* broke theatrical box office records (Lang 2021). Directed by Destin Daniel Cretton, a Japanese-American filmmaker born in Hawaii, the film was shot at Fox Studios in Sydney, Australia. *Shang-Chi* is a rare blockbuster featuring diasporic Asian characters in lead roles. But while it depicts "the Asian-American experience through the eyes of a budding superhero" (Travis 2021), Asian Australians are also absent from this runaway production. These big budget films can be considered alongside an independent Asian Australian romantic comedy, *Rhapsody of Love* (Joy Hopwood 2021). Described by the director Hopwood as "crazy middle-aged Asians," *Rhapsody of Love* received a limited theatrical release in Australia, without the glitz and glamour of the high-profile film, *Crazy Rich Asians* (Jon M. Chu 2018), it ostensibly references. These three very different films map out the terrain of contemporary Asian Australian film relations: the official co-production, the runaway production, and the independent production. While these filmmaking practices are not new, these recent films exemplify an intensification of these practices in the past decade.[2] They are noteworthy for how they construct an imaginary between Australia and (East) Asia that exceeds a diasporic framework and can more accurately be described by the term trans-Asian cinema.

Trans-Asian film movements emphasize cross-border connections among countries in Asia. In this chapter I make a case for including Australia within trans-Asian media flows. The rise of streaming platforms has meant a steady supply of East Asian media (particularly from South Korea) readily accessible in Australia on platforms such as Netflix. At the same

DOI: 10.4324/9781003266952-26

time, greater transnational collaborations with Asian film partners have also impacted on the cultural identity of screen media content being made by Australian producers (Khoo 2019). In this landscape, the so-called boundaries of East Asian media culture have been transnationalized beyond the boundaries of East Asia as a geographic territory. Australia has a particular and significant role to play in rethinking regional relationships between East Asia and the media cultures it increasingly reaches.

Situating Australia within East Asian media flows and as part of a trans-Asian imaginary shifts the dominant framing of Asian Australian cinema away from a discourse of marginality to one of connection, flow, and exchange. A diasporic framework does not take into account the broad range of transnational film practices that characterize Asian Australian film collaborations today, from big-budget co-productions to runaway productions. Nor does it not account for the mainstreaming of "minority" filmmakers within, and beyond, the national film culture. It also fails to adequately acknowledge that the balance in transnational exchanges has shifted with the economic development of Asia since the late 1990s. Trans-Asia becomes a useful concept, and a method, that bridges diasporic cinema and transnational cinema to capture the cross-border movements between Australia and Asia.

The idea of trans-Asia as method has been developed by Koichi Iwabuchi to understand Asia as "an affective and imagined framework" that resists drawing fixed boundaries since these are a barrier to flow and exchange (Chong, Chow and de Kloet 2020, 6). The "trans" in trans-Asia highlights movement and connection but also going "beyond" to create change and transformation (Chong, Chow and de Kloet 2020, 6). As Iwabuchi (2020) puts it, "the intensification of cross-border cultural flows and human mobilities have been newly engendering trans-local dialogues, connections, association, rivalry, and antagonism in Asian (mostly East Asia . . .) contexts" (27). Oakes and Schein (2006) define the related term translocality as "being identified with more than one location" (xiii). In the context of (trans-)Asia, translocality is used to comprehend the tension between mobility and locality and, unlike transnationalism, is not limited by a focus on the nation state. In the case of Asian Australian cinema, translocality and trans-Asia are not entirely new methods but rather ways to historicize a new wave of intensifying cross-border interactions between Australia and Asia. Trans-Asia also foregrounds the regional context that for Australia has shifted over time; earlier descriptions of Australia's "internationalizing" film strategies tended to privilege Euro-American sites of filmmaking that have dominated Australian cinema studies to date.

The following sections will outline three trans-Asian film practices in turn – the co-production, the runaway production, and the independent production – to examine how a rich network of media exchange has formed between and across Australia and Asia to form a nascent trans-Asian imaginary.

The Co-production: *The Whistleblower* (Xue Xiaolu 2019)

Film co-production is one of the most significant developments in Australia's film policy in the past two decades (Walsh 2012). It has allowed Australia, which has a limited domestic market, to gain access to larger audiences elsewhere. Australia has now signed 14 co-production treaties, five of those with countries in Asia (China, Malaysia, Singapore, South Korea, and most recently, with India). These Asia-focused treaties are designed to enhance the Australian screen industry by supporting new business partnerships with key Asian territories. The most significant of these regional markets, in terms of new resources, audiences, and opportunities, is with China. The China-Australia co-production treaty was signed in 2007. Seven films have since been made under that treaty with a combined total budget of AU$177 million.[3]

From China's perspective, co-producing with Australia can be an attractive proposition for a number of reasons: to develop creative and technical skills, especially in the postproduction and digital effects sector (Yecies, Shim, and Goldsmith 2011), to learn from the professionalism of Australian practitioners (Peng 2016), and to increase China's soft power influence (Peng and Keane 2019). Nevertheless, despite mutually beneficial reasons to pursue co-production on both sides, the film co-productions that have been made between Australia and China have not nearly been as commercially successful as anticipated. Analyzing the lackluster reception of three Australia-China co-productions – *The Children of the Silk Road* (*The Children of Huang Shi*) (Roger Spottiswoode 2008), *33 Postcards* (Pauline Chan 2011), and *The Dragon Pearl* (Mario Andreacchio 2011) – Audrey Yue (2014) points to the films' lack of cultural specificity, with Australia as a "free-floating signifier" (194), and the "accented uses of Mandarin" (200) as confusing to audiences on both sides. A consideration of these earlier failures should have, as Weiying Peng notes, "provide[d] the Australian film industry with some useful lessons" (80). A decade later with *The Whistleblower*, at the height of this filmmaking strategy, and as the most expensive Australia-China co-production produced to date, it would appear these lessons have not been learnt.

The Whistleblower opens in Malawi, Africa, where a devastating earthquake has wiped out an entire village.[4] It later unfolds that this earthquake was caused by new gas extraction technology being developed by an Australian mining company, aimed at ridding China of its air pollution problems. The film stars well-known Chinese actors Tang Wei and Lei Jiayin as lovers harboring the secrets of this company. Lei Jiayin plays Mark, a Chinese expat and senior executive in the mining company. Mark has been in Australia for more than a decade, but he still has not applied for his Australian citizenship. This is somehow linked to a bigger cultural issue perceived by Mark: "As a Chinese working for a foreign company, there is always a glass ceiling." This seemingly throwaway line about a refusal to be naturalized is revealing. The line between the "Chinese" and the "Australians" is never completely lowered or crossed, and Chinese Australians do not seem to exist in the world of the film except as minor figures. The film is made to appeal to mainland Chinese audiences, signaled from the beginning by the lavish opening scenes at popular tourist landmark "The Twelve Apostles" on the Great Ocean Road, (over)developed, using computer generated imagery, into a mammoth resort that the fragile coastline could never in reality withstand. A disclaimer placed at the end of the film states that the imaginary resort "does not reflect the future development intentions of this iconic and protected area."

At the same time, the premise of the film – the idea of whistleblowing – apparently caused confusion among Chinese audiences. Whistleblowing, which means to inform on an individual, company, or organization, not for personal gain but for wider public interest such as anti-corruption, is not a concept well-known in China, particularly as it puts the whistleblower at personal risk. Bill Kong, president of Edko Films (one of the film's producers), recalls that there was a misunderstanding of the film's title by audiences. "In China, no one knows what a whistleblower is. People were asking, 'Is this a sports movie?'" (cit. Quinn 2019).

The film imagines China in Australia, but it does not see Australia in China, or in Chinese Australians. Nor, indeed, does it recognize China's influence in Africa. On China's soft power strategy through film co-production, Peng and Keane (2019) comment:

The failure of China's film culture to resonate with international audiences is a critical indictment of China's government-led soft power strategy, which censors and approves outgoing messages. Success is mixed; some content escapes the heavy censorial hand and finds critical success, often in film festivals; and of course, multiple online channels now exist to access and share Chinese content, which in turn brings the Chinese Diaspora into a closer cultural connection. The narratives, however, remain very Chinese, mostly inflected towards the Mainland, which raises the problem of how to engage with new audiences, unfamiliar with Chinese cultural and linguistic idioms.

(905)

With *The Whistleblower*, Australia remains peripheral in on-screen representation, despite the fact that 95% of the 200 crew members were local Australians (Kong 2019). Australia's integration into a dialogic space of the trans-Asian media sphere remains marred and uneven.

The Runaway: *Shang-Chi and the Legend of the Ten Rings* (Destin Daniel Cretton 2021)

A vastly more successful film that was shot at Sydney's Fox Studios is *Shang-Chi and the Legend of the Ten Rings*. Australia has invested heavily in global film studios in Sydney, the Gold Coast, and Melbourne. These film studios have allowed some of the biggest Hollywood films to be made in Australia, leading to economic benefits on both sides: lower costs of production for the overseas partner and income generation for local crew in Australia.

Shang-Chi received AU$24 million in funding from the Australian government, with an additional AU$10 million from the NSW state government. Filming began at Fox Studios and throughout New South Wales in February 2020 but was put on hold in March due to the COVID-19 pandemic. Sue Chan, *Shang-Chi*'s production designer, explains that the village of Ta-Lo was a special set built on a hillside outside Sydney at Prospect Reservoir: "It was basically just an empty field and we built the entire village there and it was surrounded by a bluescreen . . . We built the bamboo dome. We built all the buildings, we built the temple. We probably used all the bamboo in all of Australia" (Swanson 2021). The scale of these so-called "runaways" is immense; however, the films are regarded as contentious because they are often devoid of any local cultural content and are perceived as diverting resources away from local productions and local communities.

From a cultural perspective, while *Shang-Chi* does not explicitly feature Australia or Asian Australians, it does centralize the diasporic Asian perspective, albeit an Asian American perspective. Indeed, *Shang-Chi* has been praised as being the first Marvel Studios film with an Asian director and a predominantly Asian cast. From a representation point of view, this is ground-breaking. Li (2021) writes:

A Marvel film quickly topping the box office isn't surprising, but *Shang-Chi*'s consistent viewership is noteworthy. Its persistence indicates the importance of an attentiveness to innovation that's often clear to artists but neglected by risk-averse studios . . . *Shang-Chi*, without including a single pioneering Avenger in its main cast, confidently introduced its viewers to a new set of lead characters and a new corner of the Marvel universe.

Shang-Chi is the first film in the Marvel franchise to feature an Asian lead superhero. The film stars Tony Leung, Simian Liu, Michelle Yeoh, and Awkwafina, with a screenplay written by Chinese American writer Dave Callaham. Cretton, the director, is Japanese American. The film's opening begins with narration entirely in Mandarin, which is a bold move for Marvel to feature a language other than English in this way. The film also features influences from Japanese (including anime), Chinese, and South Korean cinemas.

The broader transmedia context of the Marvel Cinematic Universe is relevant if we remember that trans-Asia, like transmedia, is marked by boundary crossing but also by connection. The term "transmedia" was first used by Marsha Kinder in her book *Playing with Power in Movies, Television, and Video Games* in 1991. It was reintroduced by Henry Jenkins to describe the multiplatform expansion of media content in the digital era. Jenkins (2007) defined transmedia storytelling as "a process where integral elements of a fiction get dispersed systematically across multiple delivery channels for the purpose of creating a unified and coordinated entertainment experience" (1). Transmediality suggests using multiple media technologies and forms to unify content and narrative strains. With the increasing ubiquity of digital technologies, this has become a common commercial practice, enabling "multiple revenue streams and numerous sites of engagement" (Freeman and Gambarato 2019, 1). Although Jenkins' model of transmedia is one of an intertwined story world across different media platforms, transmedia as a concept has been used more recently to develop a brand, or a kind of franchising, for commercial gain. Benjamin Birkinbine, Rodrigo Gómez, and Janet Wasko (2017) refer to transmedia as an example of how large media conglomerates, such as Disney and Time-Warner, "take advantage of globalization to expand abroad and diversify" (15).

If we consider the term "transmediality" in the context of a trans-Asian media sphere, we can gain a better understanding of transmedia distribution across the region, in terms of not only online platforms or cross media but also geographical shifts tied to the development of digital media technologies in Asia. In relation to film specifically, transmediality is used "to facilitate the spread of content, discourse, and discussion about the film across platforms to both extend audiences and deepen their engagements" (Atkinson 2019, 19). Beyond Jenkins' idea of storytelling, this might more accurately be akin to a concept of world-building (Boni 2017).

Shang-Chi builds a very different world (or universe) where trans-Asian connections are centralized, rather than marginalized. The film rewrites earlier Marvel storyworlds where Asian characters are minor or peripheral, or sometimes entirely absent and whitewashed. Some of these examples include *Doctor Strange* (Scott Derrickson 2016), where actress Tilda Swinton appears as the Ancient One, a figure who in the original comics is portrayed as an East Asian man (Browne 2021). Marvel is also responsible for the Netflix series *Iron Fist*, which features a white American man, Daniel Rand, who returns to New York with secret kung fu skills after being presumed dead when his family's plane crashes over China. In *Iron Man 3* (Shane Black 2013), Ben Kingsley plays a Chinese supervillain, the Mandarin, who is Iron Man's archnemesis. In *Shang-Chi*, Kingsley reprises the role he played nearly a decade ago in *Iron Man 3* as Trevor Slattery, exposed as a drunken actor masquerading as the Mandarin. As Li (2021) notes, "*Shang-Chi* tackled Marvel's legacy head-on, immersing the action in martial arts and addressing the fake Mandarin story, positioning Wenwu as the true Mandarin and bringing Kingsley back as comic relief." These references across the comic books, films, and television series in the Marvel Cinematic Universe are transmedial not because they "involve the telling of the same events on different platforms [but because] they involve the telling of new events from the same storyworld" (Evans 2011, 27).

The storyworld of the Marvel films is expansive enough to incorporate new trans-Asian and transmedial connections. Writer Dave Callaham has stated that there is "no single Asian American voice" in *Shang-Chi* and that the film was meant to speak to "the wider Asian diaspora" (Yu 2021). This is a storyworld broad enough to include the Asian Australian diaspora through its expansive incorporation of diverse Asian myths and folklore, language, and characters.

Against these big budget films, we can consider a very "local" film, *Rhapsody of Love*, which uses a globally popular genre – the romantic comedy – to connect it to a wider trans-Asian imaginary by reference to *Crazy Rich Asians*.

The Independent: *Rhapsody of Love* (Joy Hopwood 2020)

Rhapsody of Love is an independently funded and self-distributed feature released on 24 June 2021 at Dendy Theatres in New South Wales, Australia. The film centers around four couples and their relationship trials and tribulations. The main story revolves around events planner Jess (played by Kathy Luu) who meets photographer Justin (played by Damien Sato) at a wedding. Although there is a mutual attraction, Justin is in a relationship with one of Jess's new clients.

The film has been dubbed the "first Asian-Australian romantic comedy" (Kappos 2021). Diverse representation is central not only on screen but also behind the camera. Producer Ana Tiwary, cinematographer Goldie Soetianto, and production designer Jessie Singh are all Asian Australian creatives.

Hopwood has said that she hoped to ride the momentum of success brought on by *Crazy Rich Asians* with her self-described take on "Crazy Middle-Class Asians" (Trieu 2021). The film Hopwood references, *Crazy Rich Asians*, was a standout hit, the highest-grossing romantic comedy in a decade. It is also significant for being the first US studio-released film with an all-Asian cast since *The Joy Luck Club* (Wayne Wang 1993) 25 years earlier. For this reason, *Crazy Rich Asians* was tasked with a heavy representational burden. Its cast was criticized for not being "Asian enough," presumably an attack on the casting of biracial actor, Henry Golding (of Malaysian Iban and English descent), in the lead role of a Chinese Singaporean. Nevertheless, the symbolism of having a theatrically released film with the backing of a major studio, in this case Warner Brothers, was important enough for the producers of *Crazy Rich Asians* to famously turn down a lucrative deal with Netflix (including a greenlighted trilogy) in favor of a theatrical release with aspirations toward blockbuster status (Sun and Ford 2018). Releasing the film in theaters also created a venue for communal viewing among Asian (and non-Asian) audiences.

Rhapsody of Love was released theatrically in this same spirit, albeit with a much more limited (two week) theatrical run and box office takings.[5] Hopwood has remained focused on making films for release in the cinema, despite the difficulty of releasing culturally diverse, independent features. Her production company, Joy House Productions, has supported a number of local productions with limited theatrical release, from Pearl

Tan's feature film *The Casting Game* (2018) to Hopwood's own first feature, *The Script of Life* (2019). Hopwood's latest feature, *Get a Life, Alright!*, a musical romantic comedy co-written with Shamini Singhal and lensed by Linda Ung, premieres theatrically in 2022. Hopwood remarks, "It's the first indie rom-com musical led by diverse female key creatives." (Kappos 2021). This preoccupation with being "the first" and yet being derivative of *Crazy Rich Asians* reflects a tension in Australia's place in the trans-Asian media sphere, in this case through a translocalization of the popular global genre of the romantic comedy to Asian Australia. Through its self-asserted connection to the success of *Crazy Rich Asians*, *Rhapsody of Love* extends the boundaries of the trans-Asian media sphere to incorporate this local, independent production. Appealing both to local markets as "the first" but also through savvy marketing as "coming after" and in dialogue with a global Asian blockbuster, *Rhapsody of Love* straddles its place in the trans-Asian media sphere through its boundary crossing minor locality.

Conclusion

As I was writing this chapter, one of the most talked about films on the screen at the time was *Everything Everywhere All at Once* (2022), directed by Daniel Kwan and Daniel Scheinert, known collectively as Daniels. In discussing the concepts of translocality and trans-Asia, it would be remiss not to consider one of the most used cinematic tropes in recent years, that of the multiverse. The concept of the multiverse is probably most well known in connection to the Marvel Cinematic Universe, taking center stage across several recent films including *Spider-Man: No Way Home* (Jon Watts 2021) and *Doctor Strange in the Multiverse of Madness* (Sam Raimi 2022). In *Everything Everywhere All at Once*, the multiverse becomes a platform on which to stage a new diasporic consciousness.

Everything Everywhere All at Once places the diasporic experience at the center of its narrative. Set in Simi Valley, California, it chronicles the mundane existence, and parallel adventures, of Evelyn Wang (Michelle Yeoh) and Waymond Wang (Ke Huy Quan), immigrants from China who have raised their daughter Joy (Stephanie Hsu) in the United States. The Wangs run a struggling laundromat and are being audited by the Internal Revenue Service. Evelyn's father, referred to as Gong Gong (James Hong), has come to visit and Evelyn tries to hide from him the fact that Joy is gay, introducing Joy's girlfriend Becky (Tallie Medel) as a "good friend." This potted summary does not do the film justice. What transpires over the next two hours is a roller coaster ride of alternative lives in a multiverse. Yeoh plays multiple versions of Evelyn, including as a famous movie star, a hibachi chef, a rock (of the geological variety), and a lesbian with hot dog fingers. Despite some more successful versions of Evelyn than others, we are told that the first Evelyn we were introduced to in the laundromat in California, "the most unsuccessful version" of herself, who is "bad at everything," is the one that will succeed in healing a huge rift with her daughter Joy that is causing the fracturing of the multiverse system. Evelyn manages to connect to Joy and others through simple acts of (far-reaching) kindness, telling Joy truthfully that there is nowhere else she would rather be but at home with her family.

I set out to write this chapter with the intention of examining the importance of locality but as the film's title makes clear, our lives are intertwined in an experience that is simultaneous and connected. If we consider the diasporic immigrant experience to be like a "multiverse" of coincident, parallel, and sometimes unexplainable interrelationships, trans-Asia, as a way of understanding this "multiverse," becomes a productive concept to frame this shared imaginary.

The examples I have focused on in this chapter demonstrate the different filmmaking practices that mark Australia's intensifying cinematic engagements with Asia in recent years. These Asian Australian films circulate as part of a broader trans-Asian media sphere in which films like *Everything, Everywhere All at Once* and *Crazy Rich Asians* have become important points of reference. As these points of reference continue to grow, so too will the points of connection, and dialogue, between them.

Notes

1 https://www.imdb.com/title/tt8971476/; https://www.boxofficemojo.com/title/tt8971476/.
2 For an extended survey of historical Asian Australian cinema connections, see Khoo, Smaill, and Yue 2013.
3 Screen Australia, October 2022, https://www.screenaustralia.gov.au/funding-and-support/co-production-program/partner-countries/china.
4 The varied landscapes of Melbourne and Victoria stand in for China as well as for Malawi (Wilson 2019).
5 Box office takings: $9,414 (https://www.boxofficemojo.com/releasegroup/gr3015463429/).

References

Atkinson, Sarah. 2019. *The Routledge Companion to Transmedia Studies*, edited by Matthew Freeman and Renira Rampazzo Gambarato, 15–24. London/New York: Routledge.

Birkinbine, Benjamin, Rodrigo Gómez, and Janet Wasko. 2017. *Global Media Giants*. London/New York: Routledge.

Boni, Marta. 2017. *World Building: Transmedia, Fans, Industries*. Amsterdam: Amsterdam University Press.

Browne, Kesewaa. 2021. "Why Asian superhero *Shang-Chi* Could Truly Change the World." *BBC*, September 7. https://www.bbc.com/culture/article/20210906-why-asian-superhero-shang-chi-could-truly-change-the-world.

Chong, Gladys Pak Lei, Yiu Fai Chow, and Jeroen de Kloet. 2020. "Introduction: Toward Trans-Asia: Projects, Possibilities, Paradoxes." In *Trans-Asia as Method: Theory and Practices,* edited by Jeroen de Kloet, Yiu Fai Chow, and Gladys Pak Lei Chong, 1–24. Lanham, MD/London: Rowman and Littlefield.

Evans, Elizabeth. 2011. *Transmedia Television: Audiences, New Media, and Daily Life*. London/New York: Routledge.

Freeman, Matthew, and Renira Rampazzo Gambarato. 2019. "Introduction: Transmedia Studies – Where Now?" In *The Routledge Companion to Transmedia Studies*, edited by Matthew Freeman and Renira Rampazzo Gambarato, 1–12. London/New York: Routledge.

Iwabuchi, Koichi. 2020. "Trans-Asia as Method: A Collaborative and Dialogic Project in a Globalized World." In *Trans-Asia as Method: Theory and Practices,* edited by Jeroen de Kloet, Yiu Fai Chow, and Gladys Pak Lei Chong, 25–41. Lanham, MD/London: Rowman and Littlefield.

Jenkins, Henry. 2007. "Transmedia Storytelling 101." *Confessions of an Aca-Fan*, March 21, 2007. http://henryjenkins.org/2007/03/transmedia_storytelling_101.html.

Kappos, Matthew. 2021. "For Joy Hopwood, Diversity is a 'Rhapsody of Love.'" *IF Magazine*, June 9. https://if.com.au/for-joy-hopwood-diversity-is-a-rhapsody-of-love/.

Khoo, Olivia. 2019. "Not Kidding Around: Australian-Asian Children's Television Co-productions." *Metro* 202: 44–47.

———, Belinda Smaill, and Audrey Yue. 2013. *Transnational Australian Cinema: Ethics in the Asian Diasporas*. Lanham, MD: Lexington.

Kinder, Marsha. 1991. *Playing with Power in Movies, Television, and Video Games: From Muppet Babies to Teenage Mutant Ninja Turtles*. Berkeley, Los Angeles: University of California Press.

Kong, Bill. 2019. "Partner up with Australia: Film Victoria, Edko Films & Village Roadshow Entertainment Group." https://www.ausfilm.com.au/what-we-do/campaigns/partnerships/film-vic-edko-village/.

Lang, Brent. 2021. "Box Office: *Shang-Chi* Dazzles with Mighty $71.4 Million Opening Weekend." *Variety*, September 5, 2021. https://variety.com/2021/film/news/shang-chi-marvel-box-office-opening-weekend-simu-liu-1235056782/.

Li, Shirley. 2021. "The Movie That's Reminding Studios What Audiences Want." *The Atlantic*, September 14, 2021. https://www.theatlantic.com/culture/archive/2021/09/shang-chi-box-office-success/620060/

Oakes, Tim and Louisa Schein. 2006. *Translocal China: Linkages, Identities and the Re-Imagining of Space*. London/New York: Routledge.

Peng, Weiying. 2016. "Chasing the Dragon's Tail: Sino-Australian Film Co-productions." *Media International Australia* 159 (1): 73–82.

———, and Michael Keane. 2019. "China's Soft Power Conundrum, Film Coproduction, and Visions of Shared Prosperity." *International Journal of Cultural Policy* 25 (7): 904–16.

Quinn, Karl. 2019. "*The Whistleblower* is 2019's Biggest Australian Film You've Never Heard of." *Sydney Morning Herald*, December 14, 2019. https://www.smh.com.au/culture/movies/the-whistleblower-is-2019-s-biggest-australian-film-you-ve-never-heard-of-20191212-p53jhe.html.

Sun, Rebecca, and Rebecca Ford, "The Stakes are High for *Crazy Rich Asians* – And that's the Point," *Hollywood Reporter*, August 1, 2018, https://www.hollywoodreporter.com/features/crazy-rich-asians-story-behind-rom-com-1130965.

Swanson, Larry. 2021. 'Shang-Chi Production Designer Recalls How Ta Lo Village Was Built', *CBR.com*, September 3. https://www.cbr.com/shang-chi-buliding-ta-lo-village/.

Travis, Ben. 2021. "Shang-Chi Portrays 'The Asian-American Experience Through the Eyes of A Superhero.'" *Empire*, October 2, 2021. https://www.empireonline.com/movies/news/shang-chi-asian-american-experience-superhero-exclusive/

Trieu, Andy. 2021. "Joy Hopwood's 'Crazy Middle-Class Asians' Bridges a Big Gap in the Industry." *Screen Hub*, June 24. https://www.screenhub.com.au/news-article/reviews/film/andy-trieu/film-review-rhapsody-of-love-is-a-warm-and-diverse-rom-com-262413.

Walsh, Mike. 2012. "At the Edge of Asia: The Prospects for Australia-China Film Co-Production." *Studies in Australasian Cinema* 6 (3): 301–16.

Wilson, Jake. 2019. "Chinese-Australian Co-Pro is All Over the Map." *Sydney Morning Herald*, December 11, 2019. https://www.smh.com.au/culture/movies/chinese-australian-co-pro-is-all-over-the-map-20191211-p53ivm.html.

Yecies, Brian, Ae-Gyung Shim, and Ben Goldsmith. 2011. "Digital Intermediary: Korean Transnational Cinema." *Media International Australia* 141: 137–45.

Yu, Phil. 2021. "Simu Liu is Hitting New Heights with *Shang-Chi and the Legend of the Ten Rings*." *Entertainment Weekly*, July 6. https://ew.com/movies/simu-liu-cover-shang-chi-legend-ten-rings/.

Yue, Audrey. 2014. "Contemporary Sinophone Cinema: Australia-China Co-Productions." In *Sinophone Cinemas*, edited by Audrey Yue and Olivia Khoo, 185–202. London and New York: Palgrave Macmillan.

20

GLOBAL STORIES, LOCAL AUDIENCES

Dubbing Netflix in India

Tejaswini Ganti

With over 220 million paid subscribers spanning hundreds of countries, Netflix is a behemoth in terms of global streaming platforms. In their public statements and interviews, Netflix executives credit themselves with "making local stories global," by pointing to their significant investments in local language content production across the world in Asia, Europe, and Latin America (Chopra 2021). These investments can be seen as a continuation of the localizing initiatives of the Hollywood majors such as local-language production (LLP) strategies that began in the late 1990s when Hollywood studios began to partner with local producers to produce and circulate local-language films in sites as diverse as Brazil, China, and Germany (Donoghue 2017). However, by enabling films and web series from a wide range of non-English-speaking media industries such as France, Germany, India, Spain, South Korea, and Turkey to be distributed across wide geographical distances – allowing these industries to garner audiences in nontraditional markets – Netflix executives also assert that they are countering the cultural imperialism associated with American produced film and television (Chopra 2021). Central to these circulations and border crossings is translation, as the majority of entertainment media in the world is consumed in a translated form either through dubbing or subtitling.

Netflix understands the importance of translation for its continued growth and has been investing significantly in these efforts, translating more content into more languages at an unprecedented scale, making it perhaps the "most multilingual television service that has ever existed" (Lobato 2019, 121). While all of its content is subtitled, Netflix has been paying more attention to dubbing as a form of translation, a move that many mainstream news outlets covered in 2019 (The Economist 2019; Goldsmith 2019; Lee 2019) with one asserting that Netflix was sparking a "dubbing revolution" (Roxborough 2019) by trying to make foreign shows "less dubby" (Goldsmith 2019). A major impetus for its efforts to improve the quality of dubbing was that Netflix discovered from its viewing data that a significant majority of viewers in the US watched non-English language content in their dubbed rather than subtitled forms (Goldsmith 2019).

While some scholars have acknowledged the immense contributions made by the hundreds of translators all over the world required to circulate content through Netflix

DOI: 10.4324/9781003266952-27

(Lobato 2019), others have written about the alterations and discrepancies between translated media content from their originals (Brezolin and da Silva Medeiros 2021; Hayes 2021, Hayes 2022; Sanchez-Mompean 2021; Santos 2019; Spiteri Miggiani 2021a, 2021b), or studied the difference in viewer response to dubbed vs subtitled content (Ghia and Pavesi 2021; Riniolo and Capuana 2020; Sandrelli 2018). Very little, however, has been written about the production process of audiovisual translation. It should not be surprising that differences will exist between a media text and its translated version because of grammatical and semantic differences between languages (Gal 2015). The production of dubbed media content, however, involves much more than translating dialogues from one language to another. Examining *how* a media text is dubbed – the choices and decisions made by the "small army of translators" hired by Netflix (Lobato 2019, 118) – offers insights into the gatekeeping and evaluative logics that govern the translation and circulation of global media texts. These logics are crucially tied up with questions of the audience, which as scholars of media production have pointed out, are always prefigured in the production process (Ang 1991; Cantor 1988; Crawford and Hafsteinsson 1993; Dornfeld 1998; Espinosa 1982; Gans 1957; Ganti 2012; Kapsis 1986; Ohmann 1996; Zafirau 2009a, 2009b). Scholars have argued that "audience fictions" generated by producers to manage the inherent unpredictability of audience response are an integral part of the media production process (Allor 1996; Anderson 1996; Ang 1991; Bennett 1996; Blumler 1996; Ganti 2012; Ohmann 1996; Traube 1996). What happens if media producers are unable to imagine or ascertain who the audiences are for their productions, which in this case are the translated media texts? How does this uncertainty affect the translation and dubbing process?

Based on ethnographic fieldwork in a dubbing studio in Mumbai observing Hollywood films being dubbed into Hindi and Netflix originals being dubbed into Hindi and English, this chapter examines the challenges and dilemmas that emerge from trying to translate media content when the target audience is unknown and details the choices and decisions made by dubbing professionals despite this uncertainty. I focus on the scripting and dubbing into English of Netflix's first Hindi original series, *Sacred Games* (season 1), for which I translated and co-wrote the English dub script, and discuss how the original dialogue and socio-cultural context or a combination of both posed particular difficulties for dubbing professionals. The uncertainty about the target audience initially resulted in a greater concern with social and linguistic verisimilitude rather than with intelligibility or localization. Once the target audience became clearer, decisions about translation were frequently dictated by this imagined audience. Examining the dubbing of *Sacred Games* into English illustrates how audience imaginaries are central to the translation and adaptation process of media texts.

Before delving into a discussion of the adaptation and dubbing of *Sacred Games*, I first offer some background about the dubbing of American content and Netflix's presence in India. Then, I discuss dubbing professionals' audience imaginaries, which are the discursive constructions of the vast filmgoing public as opposed to actual socially and historically located viewers. Such audience imaginaries shape how dubbing professionals try to localize content in a manner that displays their cultural and linguistic expertise. Finally, to illustrate how being certain about one's audience impacts the translation and dubbing process, I briefly describe the dubbing of Hollywood films and season 5 of *House of Cards* into Hindi as a point of contrast to *Sacred Games*.

Dubbing American English Content into Hindi

While the practice of dubbing films across various Indian languages has been taking place in India since the arrival of sound in the 1930s, it is in the 1990s that inter-lingual dubbing became more prevalent with the expansion of satellite television, a resurgence in theatrical attendance, and the desire on the part of mainstream filmmakers to tap new markets. The 1990s also marked the beginning of a consistent presence of dubbed Hollywood films in India with the unparalleled commercial success of the Hindi dub of *Jurassic Park* in 1994. All of the major animated, action, superhero, creature, and science fiction films are now released theatrically in India in dubbed Hindi, Telugu, and Tamil versions. Since 2012, Hindi dubbed Hollywood films have been steadily making a mark at the domestic box office and earning profits for their Indian distributors.

The entry of Netflix into the Indian media landscape in 2016 raised the profile of dubbing significantly as Netflix's initial strategy in the Indian market was to dub its signature series, such as *Narcos, House of Cards, The Crown*, and *Stranger Things*, into Hindi. Netflix also expanded the practice of dubbing considerably since Netflix originals produced in India in Hindi are now dubbed into English for a global market. The English-language dubbing of the Indian Netflix shows takes place in India, usually in Mumbai, which is a contrast from shows produced in France (*Lupin*), Spain (*Casa de Papel*), South Korea (*Squid Game*), and Turkey (*The Protector*), where the English dubbing takes place in the US. Generally, films and television shows are dubbed in the country or region where they circulate rather than from where they originate. Netflix's decision to have its Hindi content be dubbed into English in India rather than the US is a result of two factors: its efforts to make the dubbed content appear more natural or "less dubby" and the high levels of English proficiency among media professionals in India. These factors, however, as I will demonstrate later, can raise certain obstacles during the dubbing process.

Overall, when taking into account Hollywood films, American television programs, and Netflix shows, more media content in India is dubbed into Hindi than into English. When dubbing professionals spoke about the challenges of translating Hollywood films into Hindi, they represented the audiences for such films as working class with very little understanding of English, which was highly reminiscent of Bollywood filmmakers' descriptions up until the mid-2000s of the "masses" as the main audiences for Hindi cinema (Ganti 2012). A central assumption governing dubbing professionals' practice is that viewers who are fully bilingual in both English and Hindi would never see the dubbed version of a Hollywood film; and that watching a dubbed film is out of necessity, rather than a choice or preference for Hindi.

Dubbing professionals emphasize that their job is to simplify concepts and language so that the "Hindi audience" can comprehend these films. Making the content easier or simpler, however, is not a straightforward task but a difficult one. Dubbing professionals describe their work as a "transcreation" rather than "translation," as scriptwriters assert that a literal translation can never be successful, either linguistically or culturally.[1] Scholars of audiovisual translation have argued that dubbing films or television shows always involves more than an inter-lingual transfer (Ascheid 1997; Bernabo 2017; Ferrari 2011). When Indian dubbing professionals describe their process as "transcreation," they are referring primarily to their efforts to make Hollywood films appear less alien and more familiar to Indian audiences. However, unlike the European contexts where Hollywood circulates,

Indian dubbing professionals speculate that white faces speaking in Hindi is inherently alienating and constantly calls attention to the foreignness of Hollywood films. Dubbing professionals attempt to reduce this disjuncture as much as possible, so while the faces may remain foreign, the slang, dialect, stereotypes, and pop culture references are resolutely local and familiar. Transcreation, therefore, is a process of domesticating and erasing difference in the audio track, even as difference remains in the image track (Ganti 2022).

Taking liberties in terms of localization is highly dependent on the genre that is being dubbed, however. Dubbing professionals point out that superhero films or animated films offered much greater creative freedom for localization and translation than dramas or thrillers such as *The Martian* (2015), *Gifted* (2017), or *Unsane* (2018), which have also been dubbed into Hindi. Therefore, a show like *House of Cards* is not localized to an Indian context when being dubbed into Hindi. All of the references and terms about the American political system, such as the Senate and the House of Representatives are kept intact and frequently remain in English. I noticed during the dubbing of season 5 of *House of Cards*, that the voice actors were attempting to pronounce the names of the US states in an American style. The dubbing director of *House of Cards*, Divya Acharya, explained that was because they were not trying to "Indianize" the show in the way that they do with Hollywood films. She also pointed out that they did not change the way proper names were pronounced in the show and tried to retain the original pronunciation even if an Indian pronunciation existed – for example, the name "Ahmad," which they kept saying as "Aakhmed," as it was said in the original, rather than "Ehmad," as it would be pronounced in India. Acharya said that their goal in the dubbing process was to make unfamiliar concepts or terms, such as "ticket" (referring to running for political office) or "acting president," clearer for Indian audiences.

Acharya asserted that it was much easier to dub a Hollywood film because dubbing professionals had more flexibility to adapt and play with the content whereas in a political drama like *House of Cards*, they had to maintain the gravitas of the topic. For example, in season 5, episode 7, a character comes upon the aide of Claire Underwood (who is the acting president) lying on a bed in a room in the White House, and he sarcastically remarks, "Are you sure you should be in there, Goldilocks?" The dubbing team decided that the Goldilocks reference was unfamiliar for Indian viewers and did not communicate the intended intent in Hindi. Rather than trying to come up with a suitable local reference, the team decided to translate it as "I didn't realize that you had a room in the White House also."[2] A crucial contrast between Hollywood films or *House of Cards* and *Sacred Games* was that while dubbing professionals were very confident of their intended audience when dubbing such content into Hindi, when it came to *Sacred Games*, they were completely flummoxed as to who the audience was for the English dub.

Sacred Games and Challenges of English Translation[3]

A significant challenge faced during the translation and dubbing of *Sacred Games*, which was in stark contrast with Hollywood films or even other Netflix series, was that Netflix never sent the dubbing studio any sort of concept brief or instructions. When dubbing studios work on Hollywood projects to dub into Hindi, they are accompanied by a concept briefing and the original script comes heavily annotated with explanations about grammar, slang, idioms, humor, pop culture, and historical and cultural references to help the writer in the translation process. In the case of *Sacred Games*, the dubbing studio was first informed that they would receive the English scripts from Los Angeles, indicating the work of adaptation and translation would happen in the US. However, when the first adapted script arrived, one of the senior dubbing directors at the studio started comparing the script with the show. After a few minutes of watching the video, she said, "This is completely useless! They've just sent us the subtitles. We can't use this – nothing will sync!" Despite having "English Adapted Script" printed on the first page, it was quite obvious that the third-party vendor that had prepared the script basically provided a transcript of the subtitles as a dub script. Subtitles and dubs follow very different logics, which are actually diametrically opposed. While subtitles, because of their visual placement, have to follow a logic of verbal economy since they have to communicate with the least number of words, dubbing is the exact opposite. Dubbing follows a logic of verbal plenitude where one has to make sure to replace all of the speech along with numerous other nonverbal sounds, like sighs, breaths, sobs, groans, grunts, screams, chuckles, and laughter.

Once it was apparent that the scripts would have to be redone and Netflix gave the go-ahead for the dubbing studio to do the scripting itself, I was recruited for the task since as an Indian American anthropologist, the head of the dubbing studio felt that my knowledge of English and India would be useful in the adaptation process. Although *Sacred Games* was helmed by two prominent directors of the Bombay film industry – Anurag Kashyap and Vikramaditya Motwane – and the original English novel written by Vikram Chandra was adapted by well-known Hindi screenwriter and lyricist Varun Grover, with the exception of the original actors who dubbed their own parts in English, none of the members of the writing, direction, or production team played a part in the English dubbing of the series.[4] Not having a clear brief from Netflix as to who the audience was for the English dub led members of the studio to constantly keep asking "Who is this dub for? What sort of English do they want? Indian? American? British?" and wondering aloud "Why is this even being dubbed in English?"

Not knowing who the target audience was for the English dub of *Sacred Games* led to some ambiguous instructions for me, which included being told to write in "neutral" or "simple" English. Part of that mandate was to avoid any obvious American conventions, such as contractions like "how'd ya" ("how did you"), "did'ja" ("did you"), "should'ja" ("should you"), "could'ja" ("could you"), or "would'ja" ("would you")." However, what I was struck most by was the tremendous recourse to social stereotyping that was articulated through a discourse of linguistic authenticity and verisimilitude. Since the dubbing professionals were unclear about the target audience for *Sacred Games* and thus could not translate accordingly, they focused an immense amount of attention on how the class of people being indexed by the characters – many of them representing poor and working-class slum dwellers – would speak English in a real-world context. One of the main characters of the series is Ganesh Gaitonde, a Marathi-speaking gangster with little formal education who makes his fortunes from controlling the garbage trade from a particular neighborhood in the outskirts of Mumbai. The very first day that I started scripting with a senior dubbing director, when I suggested the use of the word ASAP – to translate the sentence, "*Mereko sardar mangta aaj abhi*" ("I want the sardar today ASAP") – her response was, "Someone from the gutter wouldn't speak like that."

As I continued scripting, I constantly encountered statements such as "These people (as in slum dwellers or Maharashtrians) won't say . . ."[5] One afternoon Tara, a young dubbing director in training who was helping me out, and I were working in the conference room on the laptop, watching episode 2 and scripting the dialogues. A dubbing director walked in and was working at her computer. At one point, while we were working on a particular dialogue – because she could hear us saying the lines as we were trying to match the length of the original Hindi – she casually remarked, "Ladies, remember a slum dweller will not speak very proper English. It can't be proper. It has to be very simple." Her statement was in response to me looking up synonyms for taunting – as I was trying to translate the sentence – "*Woh laal gaadi mujhe chubta tha.*" I was initially going to write, "That red car used to really bug me," but then I was told, "These people won't say 'bug.'" When the dubbing of episode one was underway, the voice actor voicing for the gangster Gaitonde, asked at one point, "Will a person of his class say 'yeah?'" – as opposed to "yes." What is noticeable in these comments is a lack of acknowledgment of the artifice that accompanies the project of audiovisual translation and a desire for a form of social realism. The fidelity being argued for is not to the media text that needs to be translated, but instead to the social context, and more importantly to dubbing professionals' language ideologies about English and social class.[6] The "suspension of linguistic disbelief" (Romero 2009) is part and parcel of dubbing: very poor people from a slum in Mumbai will not be conversing in English, but neither would an American superhero be speaking in Hindi. However, when translating from English to Hindi, the discussions over register and vocabulary were more commonly posed as an issue of intelligibility for audiences, rather than of verisimilitude within the diegesis, and about making sure the film reflected contemporary spoken Hindi.

Once Kevin, the dubbing producer from Netflix's main office in Los Angeles, arrived in Mumbai to check in on how the dub was proceeding, some of the mystery about the target audience was solved when he informed us that the English dub was primarily for the North American market, followed by the UK, Australia, and New Zealand, and that in all of these countries, the dubbed English version of *Sacred Games* would play automatically unless the Hindi audio was selected. In his words, he felt the target audience in the US were young men who liked gangster films and web series like *Narcos*. If "these people/slum dwellers" operated as a form of disciplining during the writing process, Kevin introduced another figure that further disciplined the translation and dubbing process: "the kid, person, and people in Ohio." These viewers represented the target one had to reach through the dub and were the prism through which Kevin evaluated its intelligibility both in terms of the English and of cultural references.

On Kevin's first day at the studio, when he was shown the dubbed version of episode 1, there were a number of places where he invoked the imaginary viewer from Ohio as a way to rationalize his requests for changes. Some examples had to do with him not understanding the pronunciation of a word because of the actor's accent: when a police constable asks, "Want me to track him?" Kevin said, "I don't want to be so picky, but the way he says 'track' is not clear. I'm trying to think of the kid in Ohio." Other examples had to do with cultural references to legendary cricket players such as Sunil Gavaskar and Sachin Tendulkar and iconic Hindi film stars like Amitabh Bachchan and Parveen Babi. In the first instance, Kevin said, "If I can't understand it, then that person in Ohio definitely won't understand it. They pay my bills; they keep me employed." Regarding the names of the actors, Kevin said, "If I can't understand it, Ohio, forget it." At one point Kevin was perplexed as to why a Hindi swearword, "*choot,*" was used in combination with the English "fucking" in a particular scene, especially since he heard the word as "shoot." This particular profane combination was the brainchild of one of the voice actors who was dubbing for the character of the police officer Sartaj Singh, the other main lead in the series. During that earlier moment, the dubbing director, Aarti, approved of the neologism thinking it was both edgy and rustic. After Aarti explained her rationale, Kevin said, "That's so cool, but I'm thinking about the millions of people in Ohio who'll be watching." To which Aarti quizzically asked, "These people in the Midwest are really cut off aren't they? They're like our villagers?" After a while "Ohio" simply operated as a type of shorthand; when Kevin did not approve of something, he could just make a face and say "Ohio," and the dubbing team knew to tag that point in the show, known as placing a marker, for redubbing.

The removal of specific cultural references and contextual elements in order to make the English dub of *Sacred Games* intelligible to the "person in Ohio" belies the statements made by Netflix executives about how they are not sacrificing cultural specificity for the sake of global circulation. For example, in Netflix's Q1 2018 Earnings Interview, the chief executive officer, Reed Hastings, and the chief content officer, Ted Sarandos, discussed Netflix's investments in non-English language programming along with their dubbing and subtitling. Sarandos asserted,

> What's been really great is that we can bring our technology know-how to bring a great story from anywhere in the world to the rest of the world and using our ability to subtitle and dub, and getting better and better at doing that quickly, and accurately, and artfully can make a very local show at least pan-regional, and at best global . . . One of the nice things is that we're not trading off, we're not watering down the local aspect of the show at all to make it travel. These are local storytellers, telling stories for local audiences that are so good they travel globally.
>
> *(Netflix Investor Relations 2018)*

Sarandos' statements put forth a vision of narrative and storytelling as somehow distinct and separate from language. Such an idea rests on the assumption of language as a transparent medium – rather than a symbolic system – and that translation is simply a matter of finding the corresponding words in another language (Delaney 2004, 138). However, as illustrated in this chapter (and by many other scholars already cited), dubbing is a form of cultural production, which transforms existing media texts as media producers attempt to adapt them for new markets, i.e., new social and cultural contexts. Audience imaginaries such as the "masses" who do not know English or "the person in Ohio" are central to this process. While the team who dubbed *House of Cards* into Hindi were not very familiar with the American political, historical, or social context depicted in the show, they were confident of their target audience and made decisions accordingly; in the case of *Sacred Games* the dubbing professionals were familiar with the show's social and cultural milieu, but not of their target audience. Even after being told that Americans were the intended audience for the English dub, members of the dubbing team were constantly asking me whether I thought Americans would actually understand the show.

Despite detailed viewing data at their disposal, online streaming platforms, such as Netflix and Amazon Prime, rarely share this data with the content creators, and almost never with dubbing professionals. Therefore, the uncertainty that marks media production for large-scale audiences is ironically heightened in the online streaming space, as there are no external feedback mechanisms – however flawed – such as box-office grosses, television ratings, DVD sales, or number of views, with which to gauge response. This uncertainty is intensified further when content has to be adapted, translated, and dubbed for a "global" English-speaking audience as in the case of *Sacred Games*.

Conclusions

Paying serious analytical attention to the process of dubbing leads us to interrogate which sorts of differences (that inhere in the category "local") in a media text are valued, versus those that are regarded as impediments to broader, i.e., "global," circulation. In the case of *Sacred Games*, in addition to the narrative content and mise-en-scène of the series, what appeared to be valued as a sign of the "local" was the fact that the dubbing was taking place in Mumbai using either the original actors or Indian voice actors. However, other differences – such as heavily Indian-accented English, Indian English, or Indian pop culture references – were characterized as potential obstacles to circulation. In this instance, the "global," by way of the Midwestern United States and American English, appears highly provincial. Rather than making "local" stories "global," what Netflix's dubbing projects do – as all dubbing projects do – is to actually make global stories local.

Acknowledgments

Fieldwork in Mumbai in 2018 was supported by an American Institute of Indian Studies Senior Short-Term Fellowship. I would like to thank Mona Shetty, Divya Acharya, and all of the other dubbing professionals with whom I conducted research, who have made this article possible. I am really grateful to Anupama Chopra, Datta Dave, Amit Khanna, Anjum Rajabali, Siddharth Roy Kapur, and Shyam Shroff, who helped to facilitate crucial introductions and contacts within the dubbing world.

Notes

1 The term "transcreation" is also used by Indian scholars in their discussions of theories of literary translation that exist in Indian languages, which is beyond the scope of this article.
2 The Hindi dialogue was "*Mujhe nahi pata tha tumhara White House mein bhi kamra hai.*"
3 All of the names of people in this section are pseudonyms.
4 The three principal actors – Radhika Apte, Saif Ali Khan, and Nawazuddin Siddiqui – ended up being dubbed by voice actors because of scheduling difficulties. In terms of the lack of input by the original production team, this was a concerted choice on the part of the Netflix producer who felt that having the original directors and writers usually slowed down and impeded the dubbing process.
5 I compiled a list and some of the words included: *avenge, busting, elite, delicious, dessert, destroyed, occurring, screwed, scum, sissy, thrashing, truly, wimp.*
6 Linguistic anthropologists define language ideologies broadly as "shared bodies of common-sense notions about the nature of language in the world," and more specifically as "sets of beliefs about language articulated by users as a rationalization or justification of perceived language structure and use" (Woolard and Schieffelin 1994, 56). Elsewhere I have argued that dubbing is a language ideological project where discussions of linguistic difference, intelligibility, and skill are deeply entangled with assertions of social difference (Ganti 2021).

References

Allor, Martin. 1996. "The Politics of Producing Audiences." In *The Audience and Its Landscape*, edited by J. Hay, L. Grossberg, and E. Wartella, 209–47. Boulder: Westview.
Anderson, James A. 1996. "The Pragmatics of Audience in Research and Theory." In *The Audience and Its Landscape*, edited by J. Hay, L. Grossberg, and E. Wartella, 75–93. Boulder: Westview.
Ang, Ien. 1991. *Desperately Seeking the Audience*. London: Routledge.

Ascheid, A. 1997. "Speaking Tongues: Cinema as Cultural Ventriloquism." *The Velvet Light Trap* (40): 32–41.

Bennett, Tony. 1996. "Figuring Audiences and Readers." In *The Audience and Its Landscape*, edited by J. Hay, L. Grossberg, and E. Wartella, 145–60. Boulder: Westview.

Bernabo, L. E. N. 2017. "Translating Identity: Norms and Industrial Constraints in Adapting Glee for Latin America." PhD diss., University of Iowa.

Blumler, Jay G. 1996. "Recasting the Audience in the New Television Marketplace?" In *The Audience and Its Landscape*, edited by J. Hay, L. Grossberg, and E. Wartella, 97–112. Boulder: Westview.

Brezolin, Adauri, and Fernanda da Silva Medeiros. 2021. "Bad Words in the *The Good Place*: Analyzing the Euphemistic Function of Wordplays in Subtitling and Dubbing – A Case of English and Portuguese Language Pair." *European Journal of Literature, Language and Linguistic Studies* 5 (1): 14–29.

Cantor, Muriel G. 1988. *The Hollywood TV Producer: His Work and His Audience*. New Brunswick: Transaction Books.

Chopra, Anupama. 2021. "Our Work in India has just Begun: Netflix Co-CEO Ted Sarandos." *Film Companion*, July 25. https://www.filmcompanion.in/interviews/hollywood-interview/netflix-movies-sacred-games-delhi-crime-ted-sarandos-our-work-in-india-has-just-begun/.

Crawford, Peter I., and Sigurjon Baldur Hafsteinsson, eds. 1993. *The Construction of the Viewer*. Aarhus: Intervention Press.

Delaney, Carol. 2004. *Investigating Culture: An Experiential Introduction to Anthropology*. Hoboken: Blackwell Publishing.

Donoghue, Courtney Brannon. 2017. *Localising Hollywood*. London: BFI, Palgrave.

Dornfeld, Barry. 1998. *Producing Public Television, Producing Public Culture*. Princeton: Princeton University Press.

The Economist. 2019. "Dubbing is Coming to a Small Screen Near You." December 21. https://www.economist.com/christmas-specials/2019/12/21/dubbing-is-coming-to-a-small-screen-near-you.

Espinosa, Paul. 1982. "The Audience in the Text: Ethnographic Observations of a Hollywood Story Conference." *Media, Culture and Society* 4: 77–86.

Ferrari, C. F. 2011. *Since When is Fran Drescher Jewish? Dubbing Stereotypes in The Nanny, The Simpsons, and The Sopranos*. Austin: University of Texas Press.

Gal, Susan. 2015. "Politics of Translation." *Annual Review of Anthropology* 44: 225–40.

Gans, Herbert J. 1957. "The Creator-Audience Relationship in the Mass Media: An Analysis of Movie-Making." In *Mass Culture: The Popular Arts in America*, edited by B. Rosenberg and D. M. White, 315–24. New York: Free Press.

Ganti, Tejaswini. 2012. *Producing Bollywood: Inside the Contemporary Hindi Film Industry*. Durham, NC: Duke University Press.

———. 2021. " 'English is so Precise and Hindi Can be so Heavy!:' Language Ideologies and Audience Imaginaries in a Dubbing Studio in Mumbai." In *Anthropology, Film Industries, Modularity*, edited by Steven C. Caton and Ramyar Rossoukh, 41–61. Durham, NC: Duke University.

———. 2022. "Creating that 'Local Connect': The Dubbing of Hollywood Films in India." In *Routledge Companion to Media Industries*, edited by Paul McDonald, 329–39. London: Routledge.

Ghia, Elisa, and Maria Pavesi. 2021. "Choosing Between Dubbing and Subtitling in a Changing Landscape." *Lingue e Linguaggi* 46: 161–77.

Goldsmith, J. 2019. "Netflix Wants to Make Its Dubbed Foreign Shows Less Dubby." *The New York Times*, July 19. https://www.nytimes.com/2019/07/19/arts/television/netflix-money-heist.html.

Hayes, Lydia. 2021. "Netflix Disrupting Dubbing: English Dubs and British Accents." *Journal of Audiovisual Translation* 4 (1): 1–26.

———. 2022. "Linguistic Variation in Netflix's English Dubs: Memetic Translation of Galician-Spanish series Farina (Cocaine Coast)." In *New Perspectives in Audiovisual Translation: Towards Future Research Trends*, 185–210. Valencia: Publicacions Universitat Valencia.

Kapsis, Robert. 1986. "Hollywood Filmmaking and Audience Image." In *Media, Audience, and Social Structure*, edited by S. J. Ball-Rokeach and M. G. Cantor, 161–73. London: Sage.

Lee, W. 2019. "Netflix and SAG-AFTRA Sign Contract That Includes Dubbing Work." *Los Angeles Times*, July 20. https://www.latimes.com/entertainment-arts/business/story/2019-07-20/netflix-and-sag-aftra-sign-contract-that-includes-dubbing-work.

Lobato, Ramon. 2019. *Netflix Nations: The Geography of Digital Distribution*. New York: NYU Press.

Netflix Investor Relations. 2018. "Q1 Earnings Interview." https://www.youtube.com/watch?v= A9S1jeqbBY0

Ohmann, Richard, ed. 1996. *Making and Selling Culture*. Middletown: Wesleyan University Press.

Riniolo, Todd C., and Lesley J. Capuana. 2020. "Directly Comparing Subtitling and Dubbing Using Netflix: Examining Enjoyment Issues in the Natural Setting." *Current Psychology*. https://doi. org/10.1007/s12144-020-00948-1.

Romero, Pablo F. 2009. "Naturalness in the Spanish Dubbing Language: A Case of Not-so-Close Friends." *Meta* 54 (1): 49–72.

Roxborough, S. 2019. "Netflix's Global Reach Sparks Dubbing Revolution." *The Hollywood Reporter*, August 13. https://www.hollywoodreporter.com/news/netflix-s-global-reach-sparks-dubbing-revolution-public-demands-it-1229761.

Sanchez-Mompean, Sofía. 2021. "Netflix Likes It Dubbed: Taking on the Challenge of Dubbing into English." *Language & Communication* 80: 180–90.

Sandrelli, Annalisa. 2018. "An Italian Crime Series in English: The Dubbing and Subtitling of Suburra." *Status Quaestionis* 15: 161–89.

Santos, P. S. S. 2019. "AVT Solutions for the Linguistic Variety of English in the Netflix Show *Dear White People*." *Curitiba* 7 (12): 298–318.

Spiteri, Miggiani. 2021a. "Exploring Applied Strategies for English-Language Dubbing." *Journal of Audiovisual Translation* 4 (1): 137–56.

———. 2021b. "English-Language Dubbing: Challenges and Quality Standards of an Emerging Localisation Trend." *Journal of Specialised Translation* 36: 2–25.

Traube, Elizabeth. 1996. "Introduction." In *Making and Selling Culture*, edited by Richard Ohmann, xi–xxiii. Middletown: Wesleyan University Press.

Woolard, Kathryn, and Bambi G. Schieffelin. 1994. "Language Ideology." *Annual Review of Anthropology* 23: 55–82.

Zafirau, Stephen. 2009a. "Imagined Audiences: Intuitive and Technical Knowledge in Hollywood." PhD diss., University of Southern California.

———. 2009b. "Audience Knowledge and the Everyday Lives of Cultural Producers in Hollywood." In *Production Studies: Cultural Studies of Media Industries*, edited by Vicki Mayer, Miranda J. Banks, and John Thornton Caldwell, 190–202. New York: Routledge.

21
WEBTOON-BASED KOREAN FILMS ON NETFLIX

Shifting Media Ecology in the Digital Platform Era

Dal Yong Jin

Korean cinema has witnessed several new developments in the early 21st century. Korean cinema, which is also part of the "Korean Wave" – referring to the rapid growth of local cultural industries and the global expansion of Korean popular culture and digital technologies, which started in the mid-1990s – has become one of the largest box offices around the globe, ranked fifth in 2020 while producing more than 800 films during the same year (Motion Picture Association of America 2021; Korean Film Council 2022). From independent films to hit series streaming on OTT (over-the-top) platforms, South Korean movies are also capturing audiences worldwide on Netflix. The success of Korean cinema abroad took off in the 1990s – after the last vestiges of its repressive military regimes ended. Censorship laws were eased, and investment started trickling into the film business by large Korean companies, known as chaebols. Investments through conglomerates like Samsung, Daewoo, and Hyundai all played a major role in the country's film industry. Following the 1997 financial crisis, new conglomerates like CJ Entertainment, the Orion Group (Showbox), and Lotte Entertainment emerged to become the most prominent players in the Korean film industry (*DW* 2022). Korean cinema has also been earning global critical recognition. Lee Chang-dong's *Burning* won numerous accolades from international film festivals in 2019, and Bong Joon-ho's *Parasite* won Oscars in 2020.

More importantly, Korean screen culture has experienced a significant shift since the mid-2000s when webtoons, known as webcomics in the US, started to become source materials for movies and dramas. Webtoons are an art form based in the more traditional comic, or *manhwa* format, but transformed by digital technology, including smartphones. For example, unlike traditional manhwa or Japanese manga that people read horizontally, people enjoy webtoons vertically on their smartphones as the vertical format fits in the smartphone. Reading webtoons has become popular among Korean youth and young adults partially because the nation is number one worldwide in smartphone ownership and Internet usage (MacDonald 2019). It is also very common in the Korean cultural sphere to enjoy webtoon-based movies. Several successful movies, such as *Secretly, Greatly* (2013), *Misaeng* (2013), *Inside Men* (2015), *Along with the Gods: The Two Worlds* (2017), *Along with the Gods: The Last 49 Days* (2018), and *Start-Up* (2019) were adapted from famous webtoons. Due

DOI: 10.4324/9781003266952-28

to the success of these movies, many filmmakers started to develop webtoon-based films. Only a decade ago, film directors attempted to transform popular books and manhwas into films; however, mainly starting in the early 2010s, Korean film production companies have developed webtoon-based films.

Consequently, Korea has developed a new type of transmedia storytelling. Webtoon is a neologism that combines *web* and *cartoon*. A webtoon is a manhwa-style webcomic that is typically published in episodes online (Kwon, O. S., 2014). Unlike traditional manhwa, which is usually in black-and-white, webtoons are mostly in full color. Due to several unique characteristics of webtoons, including fresh and visual images alongside diverse subjects and genres, they become source materials for movies and dramas. When they turn into big screen culture, cultural creators expand webtoon's original stories and visual images while maintaining basic storylines due to differences between webtoon audiences and moviegoers. As transmedia storytelling is not only copying the original stories but also expanding them (Atarama-Rojas 2019) to fit into the new cultural content, it is common for cultural creators to modify webtoons for their big cultural content. In Korea, the rapid growth of webtoons has created a unique youth culture, and the local entertainment industries and global OTT platforms have been depending on webtoons as new sources for their cultural forms, as I discussed elsewhere (Jin 2019a, 2019b, 2022a).

By employing transmedia storytelling as a theoretical framework, this chapter discusses significant dimensions of the contemporary Korean film industries. It analyzes the recent process of webtoon-based films, which means that it addresses the ways in which film production companies have utilized webtoons as a source of transmedia storytelling for cultural production. It investigates how webtoon-based transmedia storytelling takes a primary role in local cultural production for both the local film industry and the global cultural markets.

Transmedia Storytelling in Cultural Production

Transmedia storytelling refers to a widespread technique in cultural production wherein "a project's contents [are made] available on different technological platforms, without causing any overlaps or interferences, while managing the story experienced by different audiences" (Giovagnoli 2011, 17). As Lamarre (2022, 124) points out, transmedia storytelling can be explained as transmedia serialization, which is also often "described in terms of media convergence or media mix." Webtoon-based transmedia storytelling particularly relies on existing webtoon fans as they used to enjoy webtoon-turned into movies and dramas, which means that cultural creators have to consider both existing fanbases as potential big-screen audiences and new audiences who did not read webtoons yet during the adaptation process. While transmedia storytelling is not new, webtoon-based transmedia storytelling has gradually become popular in Korea in recent years. Previously, various novels and Japanese manga were significant sources for transmedia storytelling. In the early 21st century, webtoons have become the new source materials of big screen culture, such as television dramas and films (Jin 2019b). When film directors and television producers seek new transcripts for their cultural production, webtoons attract these cultural creators.

Webtoon-based adaptation has changed the scope of contemporary transmedia storytelling, as transmedia storytelling "needs to be understood not only as the flow of story from the original text to several different platforms but also as the expansion or compression of the original story to fit into platforms' unique attributes" (Jin 2019b, 2096). As Jenkins (2012, 150) points out, "a transmedia story represents the integration of entertainment experiences across a range of different media platforms." While "the process of adapting a story from one medium to another does involve some variation on sameness," transmedia storytelling needs "to change in order to work within the medium it is presented in" (Freeman 2017, 21). In other words, transmedia storytelling as stories told across multiple media "is not just an adaptation from one media to another: it is a narrative expansion" (Scolari 2017, 125). Cultural creators can develop different stories by adding new characters and texts to appeal to big screen audiences. As can be seen in a few successful cases like *Along with the Gods: The Two Worlds* (2017), *Itaewon Class* (2020), and *Moving* (2023), which are webtoon-based big screen contents, film directors and television producers add new characters who did not exist in the original webtoons.

More importantly, in the 21st century, transmedia storytelling certainly involves not only text but also characters (Shige 2018; Steinberg 2012) and visual images. This new direction demands that we comprehend the limitation of the current focus on the adaptation of textual stories. The future of transmedia storytelling seems "contingent on acknowledging the very multiplicity of transmediality and its many possible potentials," and it is critical to "broadening our understandings of the transmedia phenomenon" as the webtoon-based transmedia storytelling becomes a new trend (Freeman 2017, 199).

As webtoons have become one of the unique digital youth cultures in the early 21st century, local cultural creators utilize webtoons. Webtoons are the latest and one of the most noteworthy cultural forms of Korean transmedia storytelling, which itself is becoming part of the global cultural sphere. In the digital platform era, webtoons have played a key role in transmedia storytelling, both nationally and globally.

Webtoon-Based Korean Films

The adaptation of webtoons into film goes back to the early 2000s. When Korea started to develop webtoons mainly by a few mega webtoon platforms that started their service in the early 2000s like Daum (2003) and Naver (2004), numerous cultural creators, both television producers and film directors, paid attention to webtoons as their sources. Kakao, another mega digital platform, also launched KakaoPage – a new webtoon platform – in 2013, and therefore, a handful of mega platforms also play major roles in the webtoon sector, including transmedia storytelling. The Korean film industry was suffering from a lack of new ideas, and filmmakers began to consider this new cultural genre as potential source material. While television dramas are the primary cultural products into which webtoons are adapted, a few early webtoons, such as Kang Full's *Apt* (2006) and B Class Dal-gung's *Dasepo Naughty Girls* (2006), were turned into films, although they were not successful.

The turning point arrived in 2010 when *Moss,* the movie adaptation of *Ikki* – Yoon Tae Ho's webtoon – achieved success. As Young-jae Jeon (2021, 432–33) aptly puts it, *Moss* (2010) is a feature-length film based on the webtoon *Ikki* (2007). While *Ikki* raised tension at once through omissions and blanks, *Moss* raised the tension slowly by informing the audience of the reality of the threat in advance. Webtoons and films are similar in that they are narrative-based mediums, however, there is an important difference between them. While audiovisual media like movies and television dramas can emphasize the situation more directly with camera movement and background music, webtoons fill frames and blank spaces with the imagination of the reader. *Ikki* took the strategy of hiding information from the reader and then popping it out at once, while *Moss* took the strategy of building up tension by following the movement of the characters (See Table 21.1).

Table 21.1 Webtoon-Based Films in the Early 21st Century

Released	Webtoon Title	Movie Title	Genre
2006	A.P.T.	A.P.T.	Thriller/Horror
2008	Ba:Bo	Ba:Bo	Drama
	Sunjeong Manhwa	Hello, Schoolgirl	Melo/Romance
2010	Ikki	Moss	Drama
2011	Geudaeleul Salanghabnida	Late Blossom	Drama
2012	26 Years	26 Years	Action
	The Neighbors	The Neighbors	Thriller
2013	The Fives	The Fives	Thriller
	Secretly, Greatly	Secretly, Greatly	Action
	Fist of Legend	Fist of Legend	Action/Drama
2014	Gat Funeral	Cat Funeral	Melo/Romance
	Fashion King	Fashion King	Comedy
2015	Timing	Timing	Animation
	Inside Men	Inside Men	Crime
2017	Ban-deu-si Jab-neun-da	The Chase	Thriller
	Cheese In the Trap	Cheese In the Trap	Melo/Romance
	Steel Rain	Steel Rain	Action
	Along With the Gods	Along with the Gods: The Two Worlds	Fantasy
2018	Student A	Student A	Drama
	0.0MHz	0.0MHz	Thriller/Horror
	Along With the Gods	Along with the Gods: the Last 49 Days	Fantasy
2019	Sidong	Start-up	Drama
	Haechijianha	Secret Zoo	Comedy
	Long Live the King	Long Live the King	Action
	Anaereul Jukyessda	Killed My Wife	Thriller
2020	Secret Zoo	I Don't Bully You	Comedy/Drama
2021	Shark: The Beginning	Shark	Action/Drama
	Seungriho	Space Sweepers	SF/Action

See: Jin 2022a.

The film version of *Ikki*, a crime thriller, is significant because

it skillfully blends the Hollywood-influenced thriller genre with a social-activist approach characteristic of Korean fiction produced during the period of military dictatorship in Korea (1961–1988). The stronger role accorded Yŏngji in the film is consistent with the increased visibility of women in Korean literature in the new millennium as well as in Korean politics and society in general. The film's portrayal of prosecutor Pak Minuk as an activist is likewise salutary in the context of Korean history, both traditional and modern, in which literary representations of the bureaucracy are rife with images of inaction, incompetence, and lack of integrity.

(Fulton 2019, 2234)

Since the commercial success of *Moss* in Korea, film adaptations of webtoons have been thriving.

A handful of webtoon-based films that followed have been successful in Korea. *Secretly, Greatly* was very successful at the box office in 2013 as the story translated to the big screen. The movie is about three North Korean spies who are dispatched to South Korea on a mission to disguise themselves as a fool, a rock star wannabe, and a high school student to monitor Koreans. *Steel Rain* (2017) – another action thriller film portraying a secret mission between North and South Korean intelligence agencies to prevent the breakout of a nuclear war on the Korean peninsula – was moderately successful. While the webtoon version – directed by Yang Woo-suk, based on his 2011 webtoon of the same name – could be categorized as a drama-thriller, the movie version was categorized as an action-thriller to appeal to moviegoers. *Inside Men* (2015) became a national sensation due to its focus on corruption in Korean society. It is a political action film based on Yoon Tae Ho's webtoon, and more than seven million Koreans watched the movie (Korean Film Council 2015).

Among these, *Along with the Gods: The Two Worlds* (2017), which was developed from Joo Ho-min's webtoon, was one of the highest-grossing webtoon-based movies. *Along With the Gods* was released in December 2017 and became a massive hit at the box office. Directed by Kim Yong-hwa, the blockbuster had a production cost of $40 million because two films were produced simultaneously. The second film was screened in August 2018. Together, these two films earned as much as $170 million (Korean Film Council 2018; Cho 2018). Webtoon-based films have grown in both the number of films and their market share in Korean cinema. In the early 21st century, moviegoers want to enjoy fresh and unusual genre films like *il-sang* (daily chores) and *hagwon* (school issues), which are very popular webtoon genres, and webtoons have worked as one of the most significant source materials in contemporary transmedia storytelling in Korean cinema.

Webtoon-Based Cultural Programs in the Netflix Era

Once Netflix entered the Korean cultural market in 2016, the situation surrounding transmedia storytelling rapidly changed. Netflix is for everything, from television dramas to film to reality shows, and it blurs the boundary between movies and dramas. The number of subscribers were relatively small unlike Netflix's expectation in the first two years due to the lack of original content; however, since funding Bong Joon-ho's *Okja* in 2017, Netflix became a significant player in Korea. Netflix invested $50 million in *Okja*, as it planned to stand out in Korea (Kang 2017) and has advanced its business model by expanding its original programs. In 2019, Netflix released its original Korean drama series, *Kingdom* – a genre-defining six-episode zombie mystery thriller – which was adapted from a webtoon series *Land of the Gods,* which was published by Kim Eun-hee in 2014. The webtoon series is unique series that combines the politics of the Joseon era and the modern-day concept of zombies. Netflix has continued to increase its financial support for several cultural programs to produce original series, including *Squid Game* (2021) and *All of Us Are Dead* (2022), which were global sensations. As a global distributor of Korean cultural content, Netflix has been the largest OTT platform to control cultural production and Netflix Korean originals have achieved remarkable performances across the globe in recent years. In 2021, for example, *Hellbound* ranked number 1 on the top 10 global TV series chart and the latest high school zombie gore show, *All of Us Are Dead* (2022), ranked number 5 on Netflix's most popular non-English series chart (Burt 2021; Maas 2022; Kim 2022).

Netflix is able to create its original programs in Korea because of a few major reasons, including the growth of webtoon culture, skilled talents and know-how accumulated through the Korean Wave, and cheaper production costs compared to other countries. In other words, Korea can provide high-quality stories based on webtoons, as well as talented producers and crew members. The production cost is a focal point as well. As *Squid Game* proves, production costs in the Korean cultural market are much cheaper than the US. Netflix spent only $21.4 million for the whole show, or $2.4 million per episode (O'Rourke 2021). This is "10 to 100 times more than Korean producers usually work with but is still considered cheaper than other Netflix originals. *The Witcher*, the second-most-watched Netflix original, received $15 million per episode" (Yoon 2022).

Netflix's business model works out in Korea. Netflix guarantees as much freedom as it can to its creators, which allowed *Squid Game, Hellbound*, and *All of Us Are Dead* to be as dark and gory as they wanted to be (Jin 2022b). According to the Broadcasting Act, Korean shows cannot "promote crimes, immoral conduct or speculative spirits" or "promote lewdness, decadence or violence which has a negative influence on a sound family life." Under this circumstance, "*Squid Game* director Hwang Dong-hyuk had his script turned down by every local studio he submitted it to 10 years ago when he first finished it. Broadcasters are naturally more restricted than online streaming services because people can't choose what they want to see on a specific channel" (Yoon 2022). Netflix's journey in Korea has been unremitting. Netflix has announced that it would spend $500 million in 2022 as part of efforts to expand Korean content (Saxena 2022). Furthermore, in April 2023, Netflix pledged to spend $2.5 billion over the next four years in Korea, seeking a few Squid Game successes (Kim 2023).

Webtoons are expected to grow due in large part to their soaring popularity beyond Korean youth, and it goes beyond the national boundary. Mega webtoon platforms like Line Webtoon and KakaoPage have heavily invested in both non-Western markets and Western markets, and global *manhwa* fans have started to pay attention to webtoons. With the increasing number of global webtoon fans, cultural creators in these countries will adapt and transform well-made and popular webtoons into big screen culture, as can be seen in the case of Netflix. The global cultural industries are interested in Korean webtoons mainly because of the possibilities of the adaptation of webtoons to make big screen cultures. For example, in 2016, Line Webtoon released one of its most extensive global blockbuster digital comic series, *Noblesse: Awakening,* as a 30-minute animated film, which marked Line Webtoon's first entry into video content in the US. *Noblesse: Awakening* is an animated adaptation of the popular comic that offers fans a new way to relive the series' original story arc (Line Webtoon 2016).

Global OTT platforms are keen on webtoon-based transmedia storytelling, and it is undeniable that Netflix has played a vital role in this new cultural milieu. There are a few local OTT platforms, including Wavve, Tving, and Watcha; however, they do not have enough money to compete with Netflix. Most of all, their distribution power is minimal as they cannot circulate cultural content globally. In September 2023, Netflix had 247.2 million paid subscribers across 190 countries around the world. When a new original hits, it is simultaneously distributed in regions across the globe (Netflix 2022, 2023). As global OTT platforms, including Netflix, seek new stories and, therefore, new original programs, webtoons are set to play a crucial role in their transmedia storytelling strategy. Webtoons in Korea are rapidly growing in terms of the number of webtoonists and viewership, and OTT platforms continue to adapt and transform them into big screen culture.

Interpretation of Webtoon-Based Transmedia Storytelling

There are several primary reasons why webtoons have become such popular sources for adaptation in cultural production. To begin with, webtoon's creativity plays a crucial role in attracting film directors and television producers. "Webtoons have been a boon for novice writers who have innovative ideas and previously had a limited platform. Because they don't have any limitations on imagination, webtoons can deliver interesting and unusual stories. A drama or film may benefit from a good story that does not initially consider cost as a deciding factor" (MacDonald 2019). The stories featured in webtoons are fresh, vivid, and amusing and, therefore, provide the possibility of a transformation into big screen culture. In other words, unlike written texts like novels, webtoons consist of visual images and texts at the same time; therefore, they provide visual images, which are enjoyable, while providing new stories that cannot be found in novels, which are text-based materials. The remediation of webtoons has become popular.

Second, the existing fan base plays a significant role. It is common to change the storyline when webtoons are made into big screen culture (Jin 2019b). However,

> webtoons' core parts, which the fan base is created on, such as its charming characters and their lines, remains the same. For example, Naver Webtoon, launched in 2004, attracts more than eight million readers daily and two of their most popular webtoons *Cheese in the Trap* and *Along with the Gods*, both became films and dramas. Recent drama adaptations include *My ID is Gangnam Beauty* and *Mama Fairy and the Woodcutters*. The mass popularity of webtoons makes it easier to attract a ready audience for an adaptation. Loyal fans are excited long before the first day of filming.
> *(MacDonald 2019)*

As briefly explained in the early part of this chapter, webtoon-based transmedia storytelling is unique partially because many webtoon fans also enjoy movies and dramas adapted from webtoons. However, since some loyal fans don't want dramatic changes, cultural creators have to be very careful in the adaptation process.

In fact, webtoon fandom has become a primary reason for webtoon's use as a transmedia storytelling product. Transmedia storytelling of webtoons is highly appealing, especially since cultural creators know there is a fan base out there. More importantly, webtoons are original sources, with strong genre-specific narratives (Lee 2017), which means that there are many new genres differentiating webtoons from other cultural forms. Again, Korean webtoons show various genres and themes that traditional cultural forms could not touch on. Webtoons focus on *il-sang* (people's daily activities), *hagwon* (school issues), and BL genres, which were not dealt with in the realms of Korean movies and dramas. As one of the latest cultural forms in the Korean cultural industries, webtoons attract many readers who become part of the fandoms of particular webtoons and webtoonists. In the 21st century, Korean youth and young adults enjoy webtoons, and some popular webtoons have a few million views. When they read their favorite webtoons, they post their opinions on webtoon platforms, including KakaoPage, Naver Webtoon, and Daum Webtoon, share episodes on social media, and recommend them to new users. They also express their best-loved tastes and demands through various mechanisms. These fan activities eventually persuaded webtoonists to develop new genres (Hwang 2018; Jin 2022a). Webtoons have become a popular medium among younger generations. When television producers and film directors turn these webtoons into big screen culture, they can immediately attract webtoon fans as audiences.

Last but not least, webtoons are limitless in their textual and visual expressions, which attract many cultural creators. Novels are traditionally good sources for big screen culture; however, they are limited in terms of the number of novels produced per year. They could not develop various genres due to several socio-cultural restrictions; however, webtoons are different. There are so many talented webtoonists who create new genres on a daily basis and storylines with no limitations as they create all kinds of webtoons based on various themes and genres. Sometimes, writers and drawers work together to create one webtoon, which means that the webtoon world has attracted many young talents. Cultural creators used to stick to their own preferred genres; however, with webtoons, they are able to develop new genre movies.

There are some concerns with the increasing role of global OTT platforms. Most of all, due to Netflix's impact, local cultural creators are concerned that filmmakers and production firms only flock to Netflix. This may seem like an opportunity for the production industry to grow a bigger pie, but it's only in the short term. Although Netflix pays good money to its producers and doesn't demand compensation if the show turns out to be a flop, it doesn't offer any bonuses if a show becomes a hit. Content diversity also has to be taken into account. If all producers want to make monster flicks or zombie action dramas, there will be less content to fulfill the needs of audiences looking to consume other types of content (Yoon 2022)

Meanwhile, the Korean film industry – in particular, production companies – has lost its intellectual property (IP) rights to Netflix. As can be seen in *Squid Game*, Netflix's investment limits the intellectual property rights of Korean creators as it demands the entire IP of the show Netflix invests in. As discussed, Netflix spent $21.4 million on *Squid Game* but earned an estimated $900 million in profit from an increase in subscribers (*The Korea Times* 2021). However, as Netflix holds the IP right of local cultural content, cultural creators cannot secure additional income and incentives. Netflix holds the copyright of *Squid Game*, and this business model is not a boon but a disaster for local cultural creators in the long run. Although local cultural creators currently need global OTT platforms, including Netflix, they have to make more efforts to ask for their IP rights. Otherwise, the entire value chain, in this case, from the creation of webtoons to the adaptation of webtoons into movies and dramas to copyright, cannot secure its critical value.

Conclusion

This chapter has analyzed Korean cinema, focusing on webtoon-based transmedia storytelling. Korean cinema has become one of the significant non-Western film industries in the early 21st century. Amid the conflicts and collaborations between the government and the film sector, Korean cinema has increased its presence in the global cultural market. Korean cinema has especially developed a new form of transmedia storytelling based on the growth of webtoons, which are new source materials for adaptation and transformation. Many local cultural producers, including film directors, have paid attention to webtoons and adapted various famous webtoons into movies. Several webtoons have also become globally popular, and a few foreign directors are also keen on webtoons as their transmedia cultural products, and therefore, webtoon-based films have gradually expanded their infiltration into global markets. The Korean film industry has been considerably influenced by webtoons, as many webtoonists develop their creative works for several cultural forms, including films, while both domestic and foreign cultural producers pay attention to webtoons.

Transmedia storytelling based on the growth of Korean webtoons has become a new model for both local cultural creators and global cultural creators. In particular, webtoons are playing a vital role in the digital platform era. As a global OTT platform, Netflix plans to advance new cultural programs, and it finds several original scripts from webtoons. Netflix has become a new player to adapt and transform webtoons into its own original programs, both films and television dramas, which makes the boundaries blurring. In the digital platform era, Korean cinema has shifted its attention to webtoons as primary resources, and webtoon-driven transmedia storytelling has gained a milestone in the early 21st century.

Overall, the Koran film industry has advanced webtoon-based films, and this new cultural trend will likely continue because "webtoons are a treasure trove of original stories. They come with an established fanbase and the format itself is a narrative and visual map that the producers can use as a foundation" (You and Kang 2016). Webtoon-based transmedia storytelling has become a symbol of the convergence of digital culture and popular culture over the past twenty years. When media convergence between digital technologies and popular culture has become a norm in the contemporary cultural sphere, Korea's webtoon-based transmedia storytelling shown in the realm of local cinema is getting its momentum.

References

Atarama-Rojas, T. 2019. "Transmedia Storytelling and Construction of Fictional Worlds: Aliados Series as Case Study." *Correspondencias & Análisis* 9 (2): 1–14.

Burt, K. 2021. "From Hellbound to Itaewon Class – Best K-Dramas Based on Webtoons." *Den of Geek*, November 4. https://www.denofgeek.com/tv/best-k-dramas-based-on-webtoons/.

Cho, J. Y. 2018. "Along with the Gods Made 12 Million Viewers – Recovered Production Cost for the Sequel." *Yonhap News*, November 9. https://www.yna.co.kr/view/AKR20180111053900005

Freeman, M. 2017. *Historicising Transmedia Storytelling: Early Twentieth-Century Transmedia Story Worlds*. London: Routledge.

Fulton, B. 2019. "The Multimedia Life of a Korean Graphic Novel: A Case Study of Yoon Taeho's Ikki." *International Journal of Communication* 13: 2231–38.

Giovagnoli, M. 2011. *Transmedia Storytelling: Imagery, Shapes and Techniques*. Pittsburgh, PA: Carnegie Mellon University ETC Press.

Hwang, S. T. 2018. *Crowdsourcing Webtoon Storytelling*. Seoul: Communication Books.

Jenkins, H. 2012. "Transmedia Storytelling and Entertainment: An Annotated Syllabus." In *Entertainment Industries: Entertainment as a Cultural System*, edited by A. McKee, C. Collis, and B. Hamley, 145–60. London: Routledge.

Jeon, Y. J. 2021. "A Comparative Study on the Directing of Tension through the Webtoon <Moss> and the movie <Moss>." *Cartoon and Animation Studies* 64: 397–433.

Jin, D. Y. 2019a. *Transnational Korean Cinema: Cultural Politics, Film Genres, and Digital Technologies*. New Brunswick, NJ: Rutgers University Press.

———. 2019b. "Snack Culture's Dream of Big-Screen Culture: Korean Webtoons' Transmedia Storytelling." *International Journal of Communication* 13: 2094–115.

———. 2022a. *Understanding Korean Webtoon Culture: Transmedia Storytelling, Digital Platforms, and Genres*. Cambridge, MA: Harvard Asia Center/Harvard University Press.

———. 2022b. "Transnational Proximity and Universality in Korean Culture: Analysis of *Squid Game* and BTS." *Seoul Journal of Korean Studies* 35 (1): 5–28.

Kang, J. S. 2017. "Okja, Netflix, and the Future of Film." *Culture Science* 9: 248–68.

Kim, S. 2022. "How Korean Webtoons are Taking Over the K-Drama and Streaming Worlds." *Newsweek*, January 14. https://www.newsweek.com/k-drama-korean-webtoons-netflix-streaming-television-south-korea-1669402

———. 2023. "Here's How Netflix Is Betting $2.5 Billion on South Korea as K-Drama Mania Grows." *Time*, June 22. https://time.com/6289170/netflix-invests-south-korea-content-k-dramas/

The Korea Times. 2021. "Global Success of 'Squid Game' Sparks Controversy Over IP Rights." October 27. https://www.koreatimes.co.kr/www/art/2021/10/398_317719.html

Korean Film Council. 2015. *Annual Box Office*. Busan: KOFIC.

———. 2018. *Annual Box Office*. Busan: KOFIC.

———. 2022. *2021 Korean Film Industry Report*. Busan: KOFIC.

Kwon, O. S. 2014. "Korean Webtoons Go Global with LINE." *Medium*, March 6. https://medium.com/the-headline/korean-webtoons-go-global-with-line-b82f3920580e.

Lamarre, T. 2022. "Transmedia-genre: Non-continuity, Discontinuity, and Continuity in the Global 80s." *New Review of Film and Television Studies* 20 (1): 119–131.

Lee, H. W. 2017. "Why South Korean Filmmakers are Adapting Local Webtoons into Movies and TV Shows." *Variety*, December 3. https://www.hollywoodreporter.com/news/general-news/why-south-korean-filmmakers-are-adapting-local-webtoons-movies-tv-shows-1054466/.

Line Webtoon. 2016. "Line Webtoon Adapts Global Sensation Noblesse for First Animated Movie." *Press Release*, February 4.

Maas, J. 2022. "All of Us Are Dead' Scores Netflix's 5th Most Popular Non-English Series Debut." *Variety*, February 8. https://variety.com/2022/tv/news/all-of-us-are-dead-netflix-top-10-ratings-1235174812/.

MacDonald, J. 2019. "Webtoons Provide Abundant Storylines for Korean Film and Drama Adaptations." *Forbes*, February 12. https://www.forbes.com/sites/joanmacdonald/2019/02/12/webtoons-provide-abundant-storylines-for-korean-film-and-drama-adaptations/?sh=1046aac05dc4.

Motion Picture Association of America. 2021. *2020 Theme Report*. Washington, DC: MPAA.

Netflix. 2022. *Letter to Shareholders*. Los Gatos, CA: Netflix, January 20.

———. 2023. *Letter to Shareholders*. Los Gatos, CA: Netflix, October 18.

O'Rourke, R. 2021. "Squid Game' Reportedly Only Cost Netflix $21.4 Million From Their Massive Piggy Bank." *Collider*, October 13. https://collider.com/squid-game-budget-cost-netflix/.

Saxena, A. 2022. "How South Korean Movies are Dominating World Cinema." *Deutsche Welle*, February 3.

Scolari, C. 2017. "Transmedia Storytelling as a Narrative Expansion Interview with Carlos Scolari." In *Young & Creative. Digital Technologies Empowering Children in Everyday Life*, edited by L. Eleá and L. Mikos, 125–29. Gothenburg: Nordicom.

Shige, S. 2018. "Yokai Monsters at Large: Mizuki Shigeru's Manga, Transmedia, and (the Absence of) Cultural Politics." Paper Presented at the Asian Transmedia Storytelling in the Age of Digital Media Conference, Vancouver, Canada, June.

Steinberg, M. 2012. *Anime's Media Mix: Anime's Media Mix: Franchising Toys and Characters in Japan*. Minneapolis, MN: University of Minnesota Press.

Yoon, S. Y. 2022. "[WHY] Is Netflix the Only Reason Korean Originals are Gaining Attention?" *Korea JoongAng Daily*, February 21. https://koreajoongangdaily.joins.com/2022/02/21/business/tech/Netflix-Korea-original/20220221173218682.html.

You, E., and C. Kang 2016. "Webtoons as the New Trend for Korean Dramas and Films." *Korea.com*, January 18. http://www1.korea.com/bbs/board.php?bo_table=SHOW&wr_id=1501

22

EXILE AT THE EDGES

Donald Richie at the Pinch Point Between Japan and the World

Markus Nornes

It's on the edges of national cinemas that single actors or small efforts can make a difference. The inaugural issue of *Transnational Cinemas* had a nice essay by Will Higbee and Song Hwee Lim titled "Concepts of Transnational Cinema: Towards a Critical Transnationalism in Film." They parse transnational cinema studies into three subfields: The first is built on a national/transnational binary, with the former found lacking and the second presented as more "subtle" or "complex" in an age of globalization and new media. The second focuses on regionalism and the third on exile and diaspora. In this essay, I explore the third arena through the example of Donald Richie in postwar Japan. On the face of it, exploring exile through a white American man arriving in Asia as part of a conquering force would seem to fly in the face of conventional definitions of exile as an escape from political violence. However, as we shall see, Richie had good reasons to flee his native Ohio. No doubt, he enjoyed great privileges as an American in Japan, and his journals and writings make it clear he was self-conscious about his positioning. That position was at the nexus of Japan and the world, and he leveraged it to both nurture his adopted country's cultural scene while promoting it abroad. Curiously, he often concentrated his energies on the margins of the culture industry – the avant-garde, and most intensely in the late 1950s and early 1960s, just as artists in every area of practice were overturning the conventions of old. This constitutes one of Richie's overlooked contributions to Japanese cinema.

There are only a few instances where exiled filmmakers have made a historical impact on a mainstream cinema, the most notable being the German filmmakers that fled fascism for Hollywood. It's an amazing crowd: William Wyler, F. W. Murnau, Billy Wilder, Joseph von Sternberg, Erich von Stroheim, Otto Preminger, Ernst Lubitsch, Fritz Lang, Douglas Sirk, and others. To this we can add Luis Buñuel, who is often claimed for the national cinemas of Spain, Mexico, and France. These figures automatically problematize a given film's "origin"; they force us to think about the country of the production company or studio, the language on the soundtrack, the sources of funding, the nationalities of the staff (director, producer, screenwriter, cinematographer, stars, and so on), the cultural source for subject matter and thematics – and all this against the increasing complexities of international co-production and multi-platform distribution. There are also a few momentous examples

DOI: 10.4324/9781003266952-29

of exile in Asian cinema history, particularly the bifurcation of the Shanghai film industry in the years during and after World War II.

However, the work of most diasporic or exiled filmmakers is less consequential. The scale of film industries and the inertia of convention mean a single figure's impact is minimal by default. In contrast to these mass movements, I'd like to explore the more impactful exile at the edges through the figure of Donald Richie, focusing on a key period between 1958 and 1967, roughly his second decade in Japan. While Richie is mainly known for his erudite film criticism and essayistic work, he also participated in a wide array of cultural production – painting, writing novels, teaching literature, composing music, writing and directing theater, and directing dozens of experimental shorts. This essay explores the power of individual actors in the *edges of the transnational* by focusing on Richie's activities as writer, programmer, and filmmaker around the formation of *Firumu Andepandan* (Film Independent) in 1964, which kicked off an era of transnational interaction and movement between the edges of the industry of Japan and the art cinemas of the West.

Donald Richie was born in 1924 in Lima, Ohio of a loving mother and a brutal father, who berated his wife for raising a "sissy." Toward the end of his life, Richie produced a novelistic memoir of his childhood, as yet unpublished, titled *Sections of a Child*. In addition to portraits of his homelife, he writes of his discovery of desires he couldn't admit to and which ultimately drove him out of the country. There's attractive Uncle Kenneth with his motorcycle, aromatic dirty underwear, and his exciting swimming lessons – and dark Manuel from school, a "gypsy" classmate who young Donald would stand next to at the urinals to get a look at "his most secret part." Literature and cinema provided escape from both his frightening father and secret desires, and it also pointed him to the world outside of little Lima. In *Sections of a Child* he writes,

> Escape. I do not remember a time when I was not considering it. Even several years later when the Lindbergh baby was kidnapped, taken from its little bed, vanishing without a trace into the night, only a ladder and an open window left behind, I showed concern along with everyone else, but all I felt was envy. Here was one child who had gotten out. There was not as yet a way out of these varying differences for me, but there were many happy periods of my forgetting about them.
>
> *(Richie n.d., 6)*

Upon graduation from high school, Richie moved 90 miles south to Antioch College. Pearl Harbor broke out his senior year and he ended up in the US Maritime Service. Now he crossed oceans on Liberty Ships transporting cargo to the fronts – exotic places like Algeria, Italy, France, England, China, and Pacific islands. In his unpublished journals from the period, he wrote about his fascination for the utter darkness out at sea. It was a seductive and safe space where anonymous crewmembers would wait at the prow of the ship, searching for the companionship forbidden in the bright light of day.

When the war ended, Richie faced the prospect of returning home to Lima. He had good reasons to think twice after seeing so much of the world. For one thing, racism was woven into daily life. For example, just eight years before Richie's birth, Lima was home to Ohio's last lynching. The event involved a sympathetic sheriff hiding a black man from a mob of over 50 white men, making national news. W.E.B Du Bois' *The Crisis* followed the subsequent trials of the white instigators closely, dubbing it "This Ohio Frenzy" (Fauset 1916,

284; Bush 2021). Ohio was also a dangerous place for queer people. Essentially, homosexuality was rendered illegal through longstanding anti-sodomy laws. A wartime revision of these laws enabled courts to label someone convicted of sodomy as "psychopathic" and convert a 1-to-20-year prison sentence to indefinite commitment to a mental health institution. Just such a scenario played out precisely when Richie was contemplating life after World War II: Lima was embroiled in scandal after three local men were rounded up for sodomy and sent to Lima State Hospital for the Criminally Insane. Before their sentencing the court forced them to hand over a list of all the gay men they knew in Lima, a list of "150 men and boys" that police immediately suppressed (Painter 2004).

Richie opted for exile. He explored his options with the military, capitalizing on his typing ability to apply for work as a clerk. The *Lima News* announced that, while his first two choices were Berlin and Paris, Richie was assigned to Tokyo (Wilbur 1963). On New Years of 1946, he stepped out onto the land of Japan. Okinawa, to be specific, but he swiftly found himself in Tokyo as part of the Occupation. He started as a typist until they found he could write, and he became a feature writer for the military's *Stars and Stripes*. His first creative job.

Japan was revelatory. And liberatory. Full of fascinations. And it was relatively tolerant of male homosexuality – and other kinds of sexuality, all of which deeply interested Richie. He had traveled about as far as he could from rural Lima, Ohio; however, this radically different place was far more comfortable than his threatening homeland, even welcoming. He chose to stay. While Richie hardly hid his attractions to the locals in later books like *Inland Sea* (1971a), it's unclear how he grasped the racial dimensions of his life in Japan. Nevertheless, in 1948 as he decided to return to America for graduate school, Richie wrote a touching letter to his mother to accept – yet ignore – the side of her son she could never know. He signed off with the following thought:

> I shouldn't be surprised if I came back to Japan [after Columbia], not to lead the life I'm leading now but simply to lead a comfortable one. I am more at home in Japan than I've been in America and I like the Japanese better than I do the Americans. My difficulties here, that is the superficial mode of life, are not the fault of the Japanese upon me, simply my job and its necessities as well as the Americans I'm with constantly. I've several excellent opportunities for employment after this damned occupation is over.
>
> *(Richie 1948)*

Indeed, aside from grad school at Columbia during 1949–53 and a stint as the first Curator of Film at MOMA during 1968–73, Richie settled in Japan for the rest of his life. He settled into his modest life of voluntary exile. In *Minima Moralia,* Theodor Adorno thought of exile as a "damaged life." He wrote,

> Every intellectual in emigration is, without exception, mutilated, and does well to acknowledge it to himself, if he wishes to avoid being cruelly apprised of it behind the tightly-closed doors of his self-esteem. He lives in an environment that must remain incomprehensible to him . . . he is always astray. His language has been expropriated, and the historical dimension that nourished his knowledge, sapped.
>
> *(Adorno 2005, 33)*

Said began his "Reflections on Exile" with a similar sentiment: "Exile is strangely compelling to think about but terrible to experience" (Said 2000b, 137). However, unlike Adorno, he recuperated exile as a productive space – in both physical *and* metaphorical senses – marked by "restlessness, movement, constantly being unsettled and unsettling others" (Said 2000a, 373). He asserted this most forcefully in *Cultural and Imperialism,* where he wrote,

> Exile, far from being the fate of nearly forgotten unfortunates who are dispossessed and expatriated, becomes something closer to a norm, an experience of crossing boundaries and charting new territories in defiance of the classic canonic enclosures, however much its loss and sadness should be acknowledged and registered.
>
> *(Said 2012, 313)*

Said often argued for counterpoint as a principle, a working against the grain and the univocality of national pedagogies, especially those linked explicitly or implicitly to empire and nationalism. This can come easy to the exilic intellectual or artist. In *Continental Strangers,* Gemünden pits Adorno's notion of exile as the stuff of "anguish and suffering" against Edward Said's "plurality of vision" affected by the life of exile, to cross a national border to find a new home and to "break barriers of thought and experience" (Gemünden 2014, 192). Hamid Naficy compellingly called the exilic life a "slipzone of indeterminacy [that] involves an ambivalence about both the original and the host cultures" (Naficy 1998, 4). At the same time, he importantly cautioned not to use the word too expansively:

> Thanks to the globalization of travel, media and capital, exile appears to have become a postmodern condition. But exile must not be thought of as a generalized condition of alienation and difference, or as one of the items on the diversity-chic menu. All displaced people do not experience exile equally or uniformly. Exile discourse thrives on detail, specificity, and locality. There is a there *there* in exile.
>
> *(Naficy 1998, 4)*

While Lima, Ohio, was hardly fascist Germany or the Nakba, there is no question it was an unwelcoming and even dangerous place. In contrast, Richie found the lack of generalized Christian mores in Japan refreshing and attractive. Japan liberated him of America's oppressive pressures, thanks to its relative tolerance of sexual difference, Richie's lack of familial ties that can often provoke discrimination and, most especially, his skin. As a white American man arriving with a victorious occupying force, he was afforded a privileged space in Japan. At the same time, I argue that he earned a place in the Japanese film world as a very specific kind of displaced intellectual, artist, and collaborator. He instinctively tuned into Said's "plurality of vision," learning the swiftly contrapuntal point of view of the exile. In a late summer 1947 journal entry, only months after his arrival, he wrote,

> Another country, I am discovering, is another self. I am regarded as different, and so I become different – two people at once. I am a native of Ohio who really knew the streets of little Lima, and I am also a foreigner who is coming to know the streets of Tokyo, largest city in the world. Consequently, I can compare them, and since comparison is creation, I am able to learn about both . . . So, I remain in a state of surprise, and this leads to heightened interest and hence perception. Like a child with

a puzzle, I am forever putting pieces together and saying, Of course. Or, *naruhodo,* as
I am trying somehow to learn Japanese.

(Richie 2005, 25–26)

After four decades of thinking and writing about his not-quite-home, Richie came to characterize this vantage point as his "lateral view." In a September 26, 1998 journal entry he
wrote,

Smilingly excluded here in Japan, politely stigmatized, I can from my angle attempt
only objectivity, since my subjective self will not fit the space I am allotted . . . how
fortunate I am to occupy this niche with its lateral view. In America I would be denied
this place. I would live on the flat surface of a plain. In Japan, from where I am sitting, the light falls just right – I can see the peaks and valleys, the crags and crevasses.

(Richie 2005, 424–25)

Here the exile's lateral view is literally magic hour. After returning to Japan from Columbia
in 1954, Richie capitalized on this exilic perspective through his many creative pursuits and
was astoundingly productive. He became the film critic for *The Japan Times* and lectured
on American literature at Waseda University. On the side, he wrote a novel about the American occupation, publishing it as *Where are the Victors?* in 1956 (translated into Japanese
the following year), along with *Eight American Authors* and the Japanese book *Gendai
Amerika Bungaku Shucho* (The Main Tide of American Literature). After this began his
decade of productivity – both in terms of sheer numbers and also that activity's manifold
impact.

While he is best known for his writings on Japanese cinema, Richie pursued a varied
publishing program. In 1958, he published *Eiga Geijutsu no Kakumei* (The Cinematographic View, lit. The Revolution of Film Art) and *Strata of Japanese Literature,* following
it up with *American Humor: The 19th Century* in 1959. Accompanying the Grand Kabuki
to America as a simultaneous interpreter in 1960, he converted his scripts into book form
for *Six Kabuki Plays* (1963). This was followed by two collections of letters from Japan
by Henry Adams (in 1960) and Rudyard Kipling (in 1962). He also contributed to books
on Japanese design in 1963, Japanese tattooing and ikebana in 1966, followed by what he
affectionately called "my ochin-chin book," *The Erotic Gods: Phallicism in Japan* (1967).
On the side, he even collaborated with George Bluestone (of *Novels into Film* [1957] fame)
and director Irving Lerner on an adaptation of *Where Are the Victors?*

However, by the end of this decade-long push, he was primarily known for his writings
on cinema. In 1958 an acquaintance, Joseph Anderson, invited him to co-write a general history of Japanese cinema. Anderson had finished a stint in military intelligence, and
was now devoting himself fulltime to this project. Organizing a film history book through
a national rubric was a new, postwar phenomenon, mainly represented by Falcon Press'
"national cinema series." It was also a Cold War phenomenon, and both Richie and Anderson were resolutely anticommunist at the time. These were some of the few books in English using the nation state as an organizing principle. By the time Anderson got serious,
the series ended, so he took as his model one of the other unusual books organized as a
"national cinema," Lewis Jacob's 1929 classic, *The Rise of the American Film: A Critical
History* (Anderson 1996/1997, 33). All those books are now forgotten, but the astonishing

The Japanese Film: Art and Industry (1959) has proven to be one of the most durable books from the era before disciplinary film studies.

Curiosity about Japanese cinema had become intense after years of festival successes, and the book was greeted with great enthusiasm. Richie was immediately tapped for programming retrospectives. In the few years after *The Japanese Film* appeared, he organized programs on Mizoguchi Kenji at Cannes (1961), Ichikawa Kon at MOMA (1961) and later in Denmark (1967), Kurosawa Akira at Berlin (1961), Ozu Yasujiro in Berlin (1963), Japanese underground films for a US tour (1966), and recent Japanese films for another US tour (1967). Some of these packages toured around Europe, and there were published catalogs for the Ozu and Ichikawa exhibitions. The end of this period is punctuated by an invitation from MOMA's Willard van Dyke to become their first visiting film curator in 1969, which turned into the first official curator the following year (he quit and returned permanently to Japan in 1973). By the end of the decade, Donald Richie was firmly positioned as the conduit through which the world learned about Japanese cinema. He sat at the pinch point of Japan and the world.

As Mitsuhiro Yoshimoto points out in his powerful historiography of Japanese cinema in the introduction to *Kurosawa: Film Studies and Japanese Cinema* (2000), Richie's writings are paradigmatic for a humanist approach to film criticism. Films are valued to the degree that they embody universal values through particular cultural examples – here the (film) culture of Japan. "The best films," Yoshimoto writes, "can teach audiences, without overtly being didactic, important moral lessons regarding human dignity, freedom, and the unity of the human race" (Yoshimoto 2000, 10). And they do so through a slippage between the universal and particular, often by suppressing difference in the latter. In this way, a filmmaker as unique as Ozu becomes a paragon of human value. Richie and Anderson's book has endured the way it has because of its prescient focus on industrial underpinnings. Richie's subsequent books from this period too often lapse into vast generalizations, a tendency culminating in his 1971 book with the revealing title *Japanese Cinema: Film Style and National Character* (Richie 1971b).

As time went on, Richie stayed in tune with the critiques of national cinema studies. Although he would occasionally deploy audience-pleasing caricatures of Japanese culture, he firmly rejected the notion of a "national character" and effectively replaced his previous general histories with *A Hundred Years of Japanese Cinema* in 2001 (Richie 2001). This and other later work exhibit Said's contrapuntal approach of the exile, leveraging his lateral view to search for a way to write about the difference of Japanese cinema without collapsing everything into an essentialized other. This effort particularly centers on the history of film form, a project inaugurated by Noël Burch's *To the Distant Observer* (1979), which has yet to be adequately resolved to the present day.

Up to now, I have concentrated on Richie's commanding influence over foreign knowledge of the Japanese feature film – in effect one edge of world cinema. In the remainder of this essay, I turn to his impactful presence in his provisional yet permanent home in Tokyo. This would be his lively participation in the emergence of postwar experimental cinema. In her typologies of national cinema study, Susan Hayward speaks compellingly of a set of oppositions between centers and edges: between Hollywood and the "indigenous" film, between the homogeneity of equipment and the heterogeneity of productions methods and mode of narration and style, between the central indigenous cinema and the artisanal film, and finally between fiction and non-fiction (Hayward 1993, 13–14). The emergent experimental cinema of the early 1960s sat at the nexus of these intertwining binaries, and Richie was on the spot as both observer and agitator.

Figure 22.1 Richie was a regular speaker at film discussions and screenings in the 1960s. This was at Ginza's Lunami Gallery, one of the first venues for experimental film screenings. It is most likely an appearance with director Jonouchi Motoharu on 14 February 1967 after the screening of Richie's *Atami Blues* (1962). Photo courtesy of Namikawa Emiko, Lunami Gallery.

Richie was something of a dilettante. Throughout this period, he was writing music; for example, "The Room" (1951) was an eight-piece suite he called "true *musique d'ameublement*" (furniture music), as each piece was named after a feature of his home (Lerner 2004, 10). He painted in oil, having studied with Maurice Grosser (longtime companion of Virgil Thompson). He was remarkably capacious, getting to know the likes of novelists Kawabata Yasunari and Mishima Yukio alongside filmmakers like Ozu and Kurosawa, all the while agitating for a community of experimental filmmakers still in their 20s. Richie's most productive decade coincided with the appearance of Neo-Dada, pop art, butoh dance, and experimental music. While many people hold a rather stodgy image of Richie, he was an enthusiastic participant in this heady art scene.

Richie had started making films back in high school, but in Japan he was in the heart of the avant-garde and making shorts on 8 mm, 16 mm, and even 35 mm. He collaborated with the likes of butoh dancer Hijikata and musician Takemitsu Toru, towering figures in postwar Japanese performing arts. They were perverse, scatological, intelligent works. In 1963, he even enjoyed a retrospective of his films at the Cinémateque Française. Adachi Masao, who had just directed his first experimental films – *Wan* (Bowl, 1962) and *Sain* (Closed Vagina, aka Holeless Vagina, 1963) – recalls Richie playing an important role in connecting people, and feels grateful for that to this day. He said,

Richie had his own tastes, but brought people together with great enthusiasm. The idea was to bring together people, professional or amateur it didn't matter, and do something interesting together. Richie just wanted to bring people together, like a *matsuri*. He was living in an old, borrowed house in the middle of the city. He invited people over to show their work and talk about it every week. Everyone was very different, so he had an audacious plan to make something like a library. It was a time when people who were into film weren't thinking like that.

(Adachi 2003, 136)

His collaboration with these young filmmakers mirrored his role on the international feature film scene, funneling information about the outside world of experimental film to the young artists around him. Iimura Takahiko has explained that he and others learned about what was going on – especially in New York – from Richie, who showed them clippings from *Life* and other magazines. This happened to be a turning point in the history of experimental film in the United States; P. Adams Sitney memorialized 1963 as the "high point of the mythopoeic development within the American avant-garde" (Sitney 2002, 135). Stan Brakhage had just finished the first two parts of *Dog Star Man* (1962–63), and audiences were also bowled over by Kenneth Anger's *Scorpio Rising* (1963), Gregory Markopoulous' *Twice a Man*, Stan Vanderbeek's *Breathdeath* (1963), and Jack Smith's *Flaming Creatures* (1963).

These films were all shown at the EXPRMNTL, a film festival organized by Jacques Ledoux through the Cinémathèque Royale de Belgique and taking place in the seaside resort of Knokke Le Zoute from Christmas Day 1963 until New Year's. This was only the third edition after its 1949 start. Although there were 107 films in the program, the festival is remembered mostly for the uproar caused by *Flaming Creatures*, which was accepted and then rejected on censorship grounds. Jonas Mekas smuggled a print inside a can labeled *Dog Star Man* and surreptitiously showed the film in hotel rooms before invading the main venue. The other surprise of the festival was a juror's special prize bestowed on the package of Japanese films put together by Richie and others.[1] The films included Yoshida Naoya's *Nihon no monya* (The Patterns of Japan, 1963), Fujino Kazumoto and Obayashi Nobuhiko's *Tabeta hito* (An Eater, 1963), Hirata Sakio's *Ie* (A House, 1963), Iimura Takahiko's *Onan* (1963), and Richie's own *War Games* (1962). The list embodies the vivacious interactions going on across the Japanese art scene: *Nihon no monyo* had art design by graphic designer Awazu Kiyoshi and music by Takemitsu Toru, this just a few years before the New York Philharmonic commissioned "November Steps," Richie collaborated with butoh dancer Hijikata, and Iimura used a score by experimental musician Tone Yasunao.

The EXPRMNTL award was energizing, and this led to a celebratory reprise of the program at Sogetsu Art Centre on 10 June 1964, followed by the formation of Film Independent that fall. This was a group modeled on the openness of the Yomiuri Independent, a non-juried, open art exhibition – i.e., "independent" – that helped give rise to new anti-art groups like the Neo-Dada Organizers, the Kyushu-ha, Zero Jigen, and Group Ongaku. As the exciting late-'50s art became increasingly anarchic, Yomiuri pulled out after 1963. The filmmakers around Richie picked up where Yomiuri left off, deciding the time was ripe for these avant-garde energies to explore the art of film. They issued a manifesto in September 1964 under the signatures of Donald Richie, Obayashi Nobuhiro, Iimura Takahiko, Sato Jushin, Kanesaka Kenji, and Ishizaki Koichiro, proclaiming:

Through the process of eliminating of all the constraint, the Film Independent aims to release film from the limitations imposed by commercial and political ideologies and to return cinema to the truly creative artist. Whilst before we could have only imagined totally free cinema, now on the other hand the filmmaking has become possible for everybody due to the wide spread of (small) camera. In such [a] situation indolence is the only excuse of the filmmaker who could be not able to work creatively . . . This will most definitely generate a change in the nature of film.

(Richie et al. 1964/2014, 71–72)

Their manifesto contained a call for 2.5-minute shorts on 16 mm – 100 feet of film. Taking a hint from the recent publication of Norman Mailer's experimental autobiography (Mailer 1959), the theme was to be "An Advertisement for Myself" – as opposed to the consumer products of capital. They held their first screening of 23 films at Kinokuniya Hall on 16–17 December. And they followed this up with a screening in Kyoto the following June. The loose group met to watch and discuss films, talk about cinema itself and make plans for the future. They were united by a desire to find places to collect films, show films, mount a festival, and give awards. Richie's old house in Yanaka was often the venue for these gatherings.

According to Adachi, Richie emphasized that this was a *ba* (place or space) where they could better express their philosophy and thinking (Adachi 2003, 136). Richie gave them energy. It was a movement birthed from a manifesto. However, in the end, Adachi found that no one talked about philosophy and it began to devolve into people simply describing what they made. They were interested in Film Independent to the degree there was something in it for them. So Adachi, ever the movement cinema filmmaker, pulled out without having made anything or shown anything. Richie continued, even staging a MOMA retrospective of their work in 1966: Experimental Films from Japan for MOMA, featuring Iimura's collaboration with Neo-Dada performance artist Kazakura Sho, *A Dance Party in the Kingdom of Lilliput* (1964), Fujino and Obayashi's *Tabeta hito*, Adachi Masao et al.'s *Wan* (Rice Bowl, 1962), Takabayashi Yoichi's *Musashino* (1965), Obayashi's Pop Art montage film *Complexe* (1964), Tomita Katsuhiro's *The Martyr* (1963), and *Jinsei* (Life, 1964) by Richie.

Film Independent dissolved after this, giving way to the initial institutionalization of the experimental film scene with the establishment of Japan Filmmakers' Cooperative by Sato Jushin in 1968, then Kawanaka Nobuhiro's Japan Underground Centre (the progenitor of Image Forum) the following year. Despite its ephemerality, Film Independent most definitely kicked off an era of transnational interaction and movement between the edges of the industries of Japan and the West. Shortly after this Iimura, Oe Masanori and others moved to New York, along with Ono Yoko, Kusama Yayoi, and many other fine artists.

Quite the opposite of Adorno, from the very beginning Richie's exile was marked by liberation and play. At this decisive moment, with his lateral view on the Japanese film and art scenes, he framed mainstream Japanese cinema for the world while having a significant impact at the mainstream's periphery by sharing information these monolingual filmmakers couldn't glean otherwise – bringing people together to learn, debate, and create.

Before concluding, it's important to note how race figures into the transnational node of Richie's exile. To some very real but inestimable degree, Richie's liberatory experience was predicated on his skin and the privilege conferred upon it. He surely enjoyed what later became known as the *gaijin pasu* (foreigner pass), where rules fall away and doors magically open simply because of the foreigner's otherness. By the late 1950s – a short 15 years since the Japanese and Americans were trying to annihilate each other – the enthusiasm of a capacious intellectual like Richie's was deeply attractive to equally vivacious artists and filmmakers with an eye on the world.

Race also played an equally important part as the world eyed Japan. While it embraced the artful features of the 1950s, Burch would have us recognize how those films were valued to the degree that they looked like *our* films – effectively containing the difference of Japanese cinema at the edge of world cinema with Hollywood at its center (Burch 1979). At the same time, even the edges have hegemonizing and homogenizing centers, as evidenced in the posthumous publication of letters of another famous exile, Jonas Mekas.

In the wake of EXPRMTL in Belgium, Mekas put together a package of American experimental films and shopped it to venues in Europe. He wrote a 22 January 1964 letter to Yoko Ono, then in Japan and circulating in the same crowds as Richie, Adachi, and Iimura (Adachi even babysat for her). Mekas' letter betrays quite the imperial attitude: "I saw the Japanese entries at the Brussels Film Exposition [EXPRMNTL] and they were BAD, really BAD, Sorry to say. Good intensions, but so derivative, and so heavy heavy heavy, and endddlessssss. The more reason to bring our Exposition to Tokyo [*sic*]" (Mekas 2020, 408). One senses the same dynamic a few years earlier on August 19, 1962, when Ono wrote to Mekas wondering why he's ignoring her and pleading for an answer. She tells him about a symposium of Japanese experimental filmmakers and their plan to translate the proceedings and publish it in "some American film magazine" (hint hint). "I do not know just how you feel about it. I do know that Japanese filmmakers are eager to have this symposium since they want to reach the American filmmakers and others who are interested in knowing the conditions of filmmakers in Japan" (Mekas 2017, 101). Here we can abundantly recognize how an exile at the edge like Mekas can exhibit the arrogance of the cinema of the center.

Looking back at his collaboration with Richie on *The Japanese Film*, Anderson wrote this cringeworthy reminiscence: "From the beginning, we saw our joint undertaking as a kind of Lewis and Clark job. Two white men journeying through territory uncharted by their kind even though it was territory thoroughly familiar to the indigenous. Our objective was to broadly map this *cinema incognita* and provide a few paths for those who might follow. End of metaphor" (Anderson 1996/1997, 36). It remains unclear how Richie understood the racial dynamics of his own sexual exile. We can say he did play an important role in introducing the developments in America and Europe to that heady intermingling of pop art, Neo-Dada experimentation, and intermedia experimentation in Japan. It wasn't until members of Film Independent and others moved to North America and Europe that they were recognized as peers. But Richie, staying behind, continued to inflect the world's understanding of Japanese feature filmmaking through essays, books, programming, and gatekeeping. The pinch point at which he stood relaxed and gave way in the 1990s when a new generation of bilingual film scholars appeared, international travel intensified, and the Internet made information about far-flung film cultures instantly available. He remained a cogent observer and generous interlocutor until his death in 2013, in Tokyo.

Note

1 It is unclear who else organized the program, but probably Iimura Takahiko and Obayashi Nobuhiko.

References

Adachi, Masao. 2003. *Eiga/Kakumei* [Cinema/Revolution]. Tokyo: Kawade Shobo Shinsha.
Adams, Henry. 1960. *Letters from Japan*. Edited by Donald Richie and Harashima Yoshimori. Tokyo: Kudansha.

Adorno, Theodor. (1951) 2005. *Minima Moralia: Reflections on a Damaged Life*. Translated by E. F. N. Jephcott. London: Verso.

Anderson, Joseph. (1996) 1997. "Tales from Peripheries: Why Write about Japanese Movies?" *Asian Cinema* 8, no. 2 (Winter): 9–43.

Anderson, Joseph, and Donald Richie. 1959. *The Japanese Film: Art and Industry*. Tokyo: Charles E. Tuttle.

Bluestone, George. 1957. *Novels into Film*. Berkeley: University of California Press.

Burch, Noël. 1979 *To the Distant Observer: Form and Meaning in the Japanese Cinema*. Berkeley: University of California Press. [Ann Arbor: Center for Japanese Studies Publication Program Online Reprint. https://quod.lib.umich.edu/c/cjfs/distant-observer.html].

Bush, Perry. 2021. "We Have Them Whipped Here": Lynching and the Rule of Law in Lima, Ohio." *Ohio History* 128, no. 2 (Fall): 7–41.

Fauset, Jessie. 1916. "Our Lynching Culture." *The Crisis* 12, no. 16 (September): 282–84, 289–91.

Gemünden, Gerd. 2014. *Continental Strangers: German Exile Cinema, 1933–1951*. New York: Columbia University Press.

Hayward, Susan. 1993. *French National Cinema*. New York: Routledge.

Kipling, Rudyard. 1962. *Letters from Japan*. Edited by Donald Richie and Harashima Yoshimori. Tokyo: Kudansha.

Lerner, Bennett. 2004. "The Room." In *Music by My Friends*. Hong Kong: Naxos Digital Services, Streaming Music. Accessed June 4, 2022.

Mailer, Norman. 1959. *Advertisements for Myself*. New York: Puttnam.

Mekas, Jonas. 2017. *A Dance With Fred Astaire*. New York: Anthology Editions.

———. 2020. *I Seem to Live: The New York Diaries 1950–1969*. Vol. 1. New York: Spector Books.

Naficy, Hamid. 1998. "Framing Exile: From Homeland to Homepage." In *Home, Exile, Homeland: Film, Media and the Politics of Place*, edited by Hamid Naficy and Homi K. Bhabha. New York: Routledge.

Painter, George. 2004. "The Sensibilities of Our Forefathers: The History of Sodomy Laws in the United States: Ohio." *Sodomy Laws*. Accessed May 1, 2023. https://www.glapn.org/sodomylaws/sensibilities/ohio.htm.

Richie, Donald. 1948. *Letter to His Mother. Donald Richie Collection*. Boston University Special Collections.

———. 1956a. *Eight American Authors*. Tokyo: Kenkyusha Jiji Eigo Raiburarii.

———. 1956b. *Gendai Amerika Bungaku Shucho* [The Main Tide of American Literature]. Translated by Kashima Sho. Tokyo: Eihosha.

———. 1958a. *Eiga Geijutsu no Kakumei* [The Revolution of Film Art]. Translated by Kashima Sho and Mushiake Aromu. Tokyo: Shoshinsha.

———. 1958b. *Where are the Victors?* Tokyo: Tuttle.

———. 1967. *Erotic Gods: Phallicism in Japan*. Tokyo: Shufushinsha.

———. 1971a. *The Inland Sea*. New York: Weatherhill.

———. 1971b. *Japanese Cinema: Film Style and National Character*. Garden City: Doubleday. [Ann Arbor: Center for Japanese Studies Publication Program Online Reprint. https://quod.lib.umich.edu/c/cjfs/japanese-cinema.html].

———. 2001. *A Hundred Years of Japanese Cinema: A Concise History, With a Selective Guide to DVDs and Videos*. New York: Kodansha USA.

———. 2005. *The Japan Journals: 1947–2004*. Edited by Leza Lowitz. Berkeley, CA: Stone Bridge Press.

Richie, Donald. George Bluestone and Irving Lerner. 196? *The Blue Eyed Wonder: A Film Scenario*. Unproduced Screenplay. UC Berkeley Library.

Richie, Donald, and Ito Ken'ichi. 1967. *The Erotic Gods: Phallicism in Japan*. Tokyo: Zufushinsha.

Richie, Donald, and Watanabe Miyoko. 1963. *Six Kabuki Plays*. Tokyo: Hokuseido Press.

Richie, Donald, Iimura Takahiko, Ishizaki Koichiro, Obayashi Nobuhiko, Sato Jushin, Kanasaka Kenji. (1964) 2014. "Film Andepandan [Independents] Manifesto (Japan, 1964)." In *Film Manifestos and Global Cinema Cultures*, translated by Julian Ross, edited by Scott MacKenzie, 70–72. Berkeley, CA: University of California Press.

Richie, Donald, and Harashima Yoshimori. 1959. *American Humor: The 19th Century*. Tokyo: Hokuseido Press.

Said, Edward. 2000a. "Intellectual Exile: Expatriates and Marginals." In *The Edward Said Reader*, edited by Moustafa Bayoumi and Andrew Rubin, 368–81. New York: Vintage.

———. 2000b. "Reflections on Exile." In *Reflections on Exile and Other Literary and Cultural Essays*, 137–49. Cambridge, MA: Harvard University Press.

———. 2012. *Culture and Imperialism*. New York: Knopf Doubleday Publishing Group.

Sitney, P. Adams. 2002. *Visionary Film: The American Avant-garde, 1943–2000*. Oxford: Oxford University Press.

Wilbur, Bob. 1963. "Ex-Sailor Turns Film Editor: Richie's Art, Writing Praised by Japanese." *Lima News*, December 15, n.a.

Yoshimoto, Mitsuhiro. 2000. *Kurosawa: Film Studies and Japanese Cinema*. Durham, NC: Duke University Press.

23

TRANS-PACIFIC CONNECTION AND *CINE NIKKEI* IN PERU

A Conversation

Zhen Zhang, Jimena Mora, and Talia Vidal

Zhang: In 2020, you two founded Futari Proyectos, an initiative devoted to the promotion and study of Asian cinema, especially Peruvian Nikkei filmmakers' works in Peru,[1] and Asian female directors. Can you tell me the meaning of the project's name, your motivation and objectives?

Vidal and Mora: Our project began to take shape in 2018, when Nikkei director Hideki Nakazaki introduced us because we both shared the same interest in Japanese cinema. We agreed that our path in researching Asian cinema had been quite lonely, meeting each other gave us the motivation to create our own space to share, with more people, these films that we enjoyed.

In addition to the exhibition, we were also interested in conducting workshops to disseminate the films we both admired. Another affinity we found in common is that we are both feminists and share many interests and questions about Japanese cinema, like why there are so few Japanese women directors that we know of, and why their films have hardly been distributed in Latin America. Is it because the canonical history of Japanese cinema is written without a gender perspective? In addition, we felt it was important to reflect on this in Spanish, as there is not much information in our language on Asian cinemas, exacerbated by the fact that it's very hard to find Asian films with Spanish subtitles.

We started mapping Nikkei films made in Peru because several colleagues involved in Asian studies were researching Nikkei literature and visual art. The tradition of Nikkei artists in Peru is quite broad. The poet José Watanabe is one of the greatest exponents of Peruvian poetry and in the canon of Peruvian plastic arts, the painters Tilsa Tsuchiya, Venancio Shinki, and Eduardo Tokeshi stand out. The debate was mostly about those two artistic fields. And what about cinema? Was there any Nikkei cinema? We asked ourselves these questions together just a year before the pandemic started and then we began researching Nikkei films.

When the pandemic came in March and time seemed to stand still, we decided to take refuge [in] issues for which we felt a deep motivation. That's why on 4 April 2020 we created Futari Projects ("futari" [二人] is a Japanese word that can be translated as "the two of us"). To date we have two main lines of research: Cinema made by female Asian directors and Peruvian Nikkei Cinema. Our project is not only dedicated to deepening our and public

DOI: 10.4324/9781003266952-30

knowledge on both topics, but also to be able to screen the films and create workshops to share the films with a wider audience.

We carried out research about Nikkei cinema that was translated into a film curatorship and thus our first exhibition "A Regard at Nikkei Cinema" was born. We gathered twenty-two short films and one medium-length film, which we divided into four day-long programs. Our curatorship continues to grow as we find more films. The first time we organized a screening was through Facebook Live in December 2020. Since then, we have been able to take the show to different spaces on site, such as screenings at the Cine Club of Lambayeque in Chiclayo in 2021 and at the Nikkei Cultural Festival of the Japanese Peruvian Association in 2022 and 2023.

Zhang: **I am aware of the existence of a large Nikkei population and their literary and media production in Brazil, which has received considerable attention in Euro-American academia.** *Cine Nikkei* **in Peru is in comparison much less known. Why has it become a central research and programming focus for** *Futari Proyectos***?**

Mora and Vidal: Peru was the first country in Latin America to build diplomatic relationships with Japan and is also home to the second largest Japanese community in South America (after Brazil) and the third largest in the world, according to the Japanese Cooperation Agency (JICA). This story began on 3 April 1899, when the first Japanese immigrants arrived in Peru aboard the ship Sakura Maru, giving rise to the Nikkei community in our country. Since then, there have been five generations of Nikkei in Peru, according to the website of the Japanese Peruvian Association.[2] Four events that marked the history of the Peruvian-Japanese community are vital to take into account because they are reflected in Nikkei cinema: (1) the beginning of migration at the end of the 19th century, (2) Peru's involvement in the deportation of Japanese to concentration camps in the United States during World War II,[3] (3) the *dekasegi* phenomenon (for better employment in Japan after reverse immigration) in the 1980s, and (4) the regime of President Alberto Fujimori during the 1990s.

The first migrants traveled as laborers to work in coastal plantations of Lima and northern Peru.[4] The Nikkei community still has an important presence on the northern coast of the country. It is also important to note that most of the Japanese migration to Peru came from Okinawa, and several of the Nikkei filmmakers have rescued this Uchinānchu (Okinawan descent) legacy in their productions. To this day, the Peruvian Japanese community does not usually comment much about the deportations and later generations grew up with this wound since many parents and grandparents, in saving themselves from being deported, had to hide their identity. The repercussions are felt to this day and are explored in Nikkei cinema by the younger generations. Older ones stopped teaching their children the Japanese language, changed their names to Spanish ones, or simply never discussed this historical episode at home. In this way, many young people feel that they have grown up with this silence that they now want to heal through film. Younger generations are seeking to reconnect with the identity that their grandparents once had to hide to survive.

The *dekasegi* phenomenon represents the "return" of members of the Nikkei community to Japan in the 1980s during Peru's hyperinflation period, in search for better working opportunities. In Peru they were not considered fully Peruvian, and they found out that in Japan they were not considered fully Japanese. This has resulted in an identity crisis that has been explored in literature by authors such as Augusto Higa in his book *Japan Gives No Second Chances*. Cinema has been used specially by young Nikkei women filmmakers to explore this feeling, since several of their parents are *dekasegi*.

Finally, the 1990s were marked by the dictatorship of Peruvian president Alberto Fujimori, an engineer who claimed to be Nikkei. Again, the Peruvian Nikkei community became a political target, but in a different way. Racism toward this community increased when the Fujimori regime began to face allegations of human rights violation. A reflection of this period can be seen in a documentary film called *Against the Grain* (2008) about art and politics in Peru made by Nikkei American film director Ann Kaneko. It documents the testimonies of four artists during this period. One of them is the Nikkei artist Eduardo Tokeshi, who recounts the discrimination he suffered, which extended to anyone with Asian features, during the two consecutive presidential terms of Fujimori.

The history of the Nikkei community that we have just presented is an important chapter in the history of Peru, and we felt that it needed to be more widely disseminated at a national level. This interest in the history of the Nikkei community immediately met with our motivation to research Japanese cinema, so we decided to start from home. We were surprised to find that there was a large group of Nikkei films that reflected upon these topics.

When we started the idea of screening them, we questioned ourselves a lot, because why would two non-Nikkei Peruvian women be the organizers of this exhibition? Was it possible to do it? Could we talk about Nikkei identity and expression without being Nikkei? We discovered that more than giving answers to these questions, we wanted to learn more because there was no previous study on Nikkei identity and film in Peru. That is why we sought the support of Nikkei collectives when we began to shape our curatorship. Our research is ongoing, and we hope to continue finding more Nikkei films.

Our curatorship and our research are intimately connected. Our aim is to contribute to building a space where memory and identity can be kept and shared with a wide Peruvian audience. However, we are aware that we do not belong to the community and from our place, somewhat distant, we look with deep interest, appreciation and respect to the community and its cinema. For this reason, we decided to conduct our research based on questions and try to answer them together with Nikkei filmmakers.

Zhang: Can you provide a brief genealogy of *Cine Nikkei* in Peru? What are some of the main themes and characteristics?

Vidal and Mora: Nikkei artist Eulogio Nishiyama had an important role in Peruvian cinema since the 1950s. Nishiyama was a photographer, photojournalist, and filmmaker from Cusco, and together with Manuel Chambi, Luis Figueroa, and César Villanueva, formed the Cine Club Cusco. This collective began to produce mainly ethnographic works with touches of visual poetry. In 1961 they directed *Kukuli*, the first film entirely spoken in Quechua language and a landmark in Peruvian cinema. Neither *Kukuli* nor Eulogio Nishiyama's other works, as far as we know, reflected on his Nikkei identity. This led us to ask ourselves a series of questions: does Nikkei cinema necessarily have to be one that dialogues with identity? Just because a film is directed by a Nikkei filmmaker does it qualify as Nikkei cinema? After Eulogio Nishiyama, we have not been able to find any film directed by a Nikkei person until the 2004 medium-length film *The Wait of Ryowa*, directed by Cyntia Inamine and Raúl del Busto.

All the films in our curatorship were produced from 2017 to 2022, and the exceptions are *The Wait of Ryowa* (2004) and *Ame* (2011) by Juan Carlos Yanaura and Pauchi Sasaki.

About the themes and characteristic of Peruvian Nikkei Cinema, we would like to mention that our curated program "A Regard to Nikkei Cinema" was divided into four days that reflect three thematic axes: "Cinema made by Nikkei women," "Experimental cut," and "Identity and Nikkei protagonists." The first day of the exhibition was titled "Cinema made by Nikkei women directors," because during our research, we were pleasantly surprised to find that around 40% of the films were directed or co-directed by women.

Since the conceptualization of the project, we decided to invite Nikkei youth collectives to hold film forums after the screenings, to reflect on the themes addressed in their cinema. Thus, we had the presence of the Bugeisha Collective, an initiative created by Nikkei women Harumi López Higa, Adriana Miyagusuku, and Tomiko Takagi in 2019. They seek to make visible the role of Nikkei women throughout the history of Japanese immigration to Peru. The three of them are artists. Tomiko mentions that they wanted to honor the actions of their women ancestors and highlight the role they played in society, either by choice or imposed, and how it has had an impact until now. Adriana says that the driving force to create Bugeisha was because it was the 120th anniversary of Japanese immigration to Peru and they wondered how this history has been constructed and about the place of women in that construction.

Together with Bugeisha, we reflected on female identity and the relationship between different generations of women within the same family and how they were represented in the films screened. A strong characteristic of Peruvian Nikkei Cinema made by women is rescuing the life stories of their grandmothers (*obāchan*) who break with tradition and appear as agents of preservation of memories. Another characteristic is that most of these films have an autobiographical nature and belong to the documentary field. There is also a shared tendency to use found footage such as old photographs and VHS tapes. In addition, the stories are historically contextualized, such as representing the *dekasegi* phenomenon in the 1980s.

Two films that summarize these concepts well are *Yonsei* (2021) by Harumi López Higa, an autobiographical documentary that explores the four generations of Nikkei women in her family that highlights the strengths and different struggles of each one of them. And then there is *Ubicua* (2022), by Narumi Ogusuku Higa, where she reflects about her Nikkei identity. Her parents belong to the *dekasegi* phenomenon, a fact that forced her to rethink her identity as a fluid one, because she was born in Japan and emigrated to Peru in her teenage years.

The second day of screening was called "Experimental cut." In our search for Nikkei films, we found three pieces that proposed narrative ruptures, such as *Hanabi* (2019), by Julio Mora, with the performance of Javier Ormeño; *K'uKu* (2020), by Juan Carlos Yanaura and Pauchi Sasaki (*k'uKu* means "green fruit" in Quechua); and *The Wait of Ryowa* (2004), by Cyntia Inamine and Raúl del Busto, a medium-length film that follows the everyday life of Mr. Ryowa who migrated to Peru several years ago and has kept his house and lifestyle as back in Japan. Performance plays an important role in the films presented on this day. In the case of *The Wait of Ryowa*, the slow pace challenges the viewer and breaks with the conventions of mass cinema, or movies from the film industry. In other words, they are visually daring works.

日系映画を巡る
Una Mirada al Cine Nikkei

18
DICIEMBRE
8:30 pm

Yonsei
Harumi López Higa

Ojiisan
Hiroko Beraún

Soy
Daniela Goto

Inori
Hideki Nakazaki

Hatsuko
Sofía López

Realizado por:

En colaboración con:

Figure 23.1 Futari Proyectos – first Nikkei Film showcase poster (2020).

The third day of our program was titled "Identity and Nikkei Protagonists." A characteristic we found is that directors rescue emblematic figures and places of the Nikkei community. Another feature is that in most cases they do not have a family link with the protagonists of their films, unlike the films made by women. As in previous days, most of these films belong to the documentary genre.

Some movie examples from the third day are *Takehara* (2017), by Jarot Mansilla, about a Peruvian Nikkei bonsai master (produced at DOCUPERU's[5] EOD documentary workshop in 2017 and selected for the Doc Fortnight festival at MoMA [Museum of Modern Art] in New York in 2019). Also, we found *Chancay Nikko, Chapter 1* (2017), by Ruben Sugano, a documentary about the first school created by Japanese migrants in Peru, located on a coastal plantation of Lima city. It ceased to exist due to political persecution during World War II. Another example is *El Trapiche* (2020) produced by the House of Peruvian Literature, a stop motion piece inspired [by] a short story written by José Watanabe (1945–2007), published in 1966 and set in the Laredo sugar plantation in northern Peru.

At the first exhibition, on the third day, we invited Sin Retorno Collective (No Return). In their own words, *"No Return seeks to be a space to share, in different ways, our identity as children, grandchildren, great-grandchildren of migrants . . . More than a century after the arrival of the first Japanese immigrants, we, their descendants, undertake this task of rethinking our identity. However, not with our eyes set on the lands our ancestors left behind, but with our feet set on the place where they arrived . . . we are going to build something new. Something uncertain. Something shared. Something personal. Something for us. Something for everyone who wants to join us."* The collective was created during the pandemic and is formed by Adriana Miyagusuku, Satoshi Arakaki and Alessandra Oshiro who decided to open a space on Discord, a free voice, video, and text communication service where you can create communities, in their case they used this platform to discuss Nikkei identity in a secure space.

From the conversation with Sin Retorno we were able to conclude that our research was on the right track and seemed valid for the Peruvian Nikkei community. The starting point of the members of the collective was to position themselves as a young Nikkei generation, seeking to integrate into Peruvian canonical history and not to confine themselves to its own ethnic community. It was important for them that the history of their ancestors was shared with other Peruvians. In the words of Satoshi Arakaki, "Our stories also matter."

Our fourth day of screening did not have a specific theme, that is why we called it "Miscellaneous," because it gathered the latest films we found. The program includes *Inori* (2019), by Hideki Nakazaki, which tells the story of a Nikkei girl who can see the ghost of her grandmother; "Spring Sea" (2019), by Harumi López Higa, who explores the director's personal history in her process of independence as a person with a disability, learning to listen to both her body and her memories (selected among the 50 best short films of the 12th International Inter University Short Film Festival Bangladesh 2020); *Té por la memoria (Tea for Memory)* (2021) and *Qampiq* (2021), by Trimedia Films (Julio Mora and Javier Ormeño), which concern the period of the Internal Armed Conflict during the 1980s in the city of Ayacucho, Peru. It is important to note that the latter's title is a Quechua word meaning doctor. *Tea for Memory* belongs to a saga of projects that show the offering of Japanese tea ceremony to either a person or place that commemorates the horrors experienced by Peruvians during this violent conflict in our history. This offering is a way of healing our past. The last film incorporated in the fourth day of screening is *La luz de Masao*

Nakagawa (2021), by Hideki Nakazaki, originally filmed in 16 mm, about Nakagawa, founder of the first photographic studio in northern Peru in early 20th century.

In one of our screenings, we invited directors Harumi López Higa, Julio Mora, and Javier Ormeño for discussion. The conversation with them allowed us to reach some conclusions about Peruvian Nikkei Cinema characteristics. Harumi López Higa mentioned that one particular feature was silence. The Nikkei community went through a period of violence in the 1940s due to post–World War II political persecution in Peru which meant that to survive, many Japanese descendants were forced to hide their origins, their language, and their customs. Harumi feels that this secrecy was passed down from generation to generation. Only recently, new groups of young Nikkei are daring to talk about their past. That is why many of the films in the exhibition are autobiographical in nature. It is through audiovisual means, that they could express themselves. We would like to emphasize the power of this medium to make visible fragments of hidden history. We believe that these stories that belong to the Peruvian Nikkei community [also] have a universal appeal.

It seems that the short films included in our exhibition are not isolated creations, but could be included in a single movement, which we could call Contemporary Nikkei Cinema. For example, 21 out of 23 films were produced in the same period, between 2017 and 2022, and they also share similar themes and characteristics.

There is still a lot of research to be done on contemporary Nikkei cinema, for example, whether it is possible to speak of an aesthetic of its own. We would like to continue the quest for new films, motivated by the desire to support the personal and collective reflections on the past and the present by the Japanese community in Peru.

Zhang: In July 2022 I was very fortunate to meet Jimena in Cusco and attend an exhibition of short films made by Peruvian women, which you and your colleagues at DOCU-PERU organized in a nice event space at a local hotel. I recall seeing several films by Nikkei filmmakers. My Spanish was very limited back then, so I could not really follow the voice-over or dialogues, but the themes of family history and cultural identity articulated through riveting images and sounds left a deep impression on me. Please share the background and program of the event in some detail.

Mora and Vidal: In 2022, DOCUPERU carried out one of its latest projects called Mochila Documental (Documentary Backpack) XX+ aimed at training women in the audiovisual industry in three cities: Cusco, Arequipa, and Pucallpa. The workshops were intended to provide tools for young women directors to get advice on documentary filmmaking. As part of these workshops, documentary film screenings were organized at the end of each day. One of the films shown in this exhibition of Peruvian women directors was the abovementioned short film *Yonsei* directed by Harumi López Higa.

Zhang: **How have these Nikkei films been received, both within the Nikkei community and outside? It appears to be a rather recent and marginal movement so far. In addition to workshops and cineclub programs, do these films have other exposures such as public television and domestic or international film festivals?**

Mora and Vidal: We would like to mention that the term Nikkei Cinema is almost unknown in Peru. In other South American countries such as Brazil and Argentina, this film category has been analyzed for some time now, and there is more research regarding the subject. Latin American scholars still use this label, which doesn't mean that the term has not been exempt from being questioned. We are very eager to join this debate. We are very thankful to Nikkei associations, institutions and collectives that have welcomed and supported our research.

Regarding the exhibition of Nikkei cinema in commercial theaters or film festivals, we must mention and explain several points:

1. The multiplexes in Peru, as in many parts of the world, exhibit mostly big-budget and commercial films. Formerly in Peru there was a policy of promotion and protection of Peruvian cinema, through the so-called screen quota. In other words, theaters had to show Peruvian short films before each screening. Unfortunately, this measure was abolished. Therefore, it is very difficult for our national cinema to have access to these commercial or more popular spaces.
2. Many of the films we found have been made in training spaces, for example, in documentary filmmaking courses at universities and institutes or in private workshops for learning the documentary genre. In other words, many of them are student films.
3. Some of the short films in our curated programs, despite having been made in training spaces, have participated in international festivals with very good results, for example, *Yonsei, Spring Sea* and *Takehara*.
4. Other short films produced professionally have had access to film festivals, such as *Hanabi*, by Trimedia Films, that was screened in Festival Al Este de Lima, or *La Luz de Masao Nakagawa* (*The Light of Masao Nakagawa*), by Hideki Nakazaki, that won the IDFA Bertha Fund and was premiered at the Malaga Film Festival and toured in different festivals around the world, like Biarritz Festival in France. It won the National Documentary Production Contest of the Peruvian Ministry of Culture in 2021, as well as the Work in Progress (WIP) award of the Mar del Plata International Film Festival (Argentina).

Zhang: **Do you have connections with Nikkei filmmakers or other Asian-descendent film/ media networks in South America, say, Brazil and Chile? Also, do you have any plans to bring Cine Nikkei to Japan and elsewhere?**

Mora and Vidal: The year 2022 was a fruitful year for Futari Proyectos in which we were able to share our Nikkei film research with fellow researchers from Brazil, Argentina, and Chile in venues outside of Peru. We met Marina Kodato, a Brazilian Nikkei researcher, who approached us because she is working on her doctoral thesis at the University of Tsukuba on the self-representation of Nikkei women in Latin American cinema and was interested in knowing what the situation was like in Peru, since there is still nothing written on the subject and there is no place where the films are archived. Her master's thesis was dedicated to two Brazilian Nikkei women directors. She has directed an audiovisual work that reflects on her Nikkei identity, but she is more dedicated to academic research for the moment. We talked with her about the need to show Brazilian and Peruvian Nikkei film productions in Japan, both for a Japanese audience and for the Nikkei South Americans living there. We hope that this project will come to fruition soon.

One of our dreams is to continue to make Peruvian Nikkei cinema visible. We would also love to take the exhibition outside of Lima, because it could motivate more people to collect family memories or reflect on their identity.

Regarding Argentina, last June we traveled virtually to Buenos Aires to share our Nikkei Cinema research at the Nichia Gakuin Institute, thanks to the kind invitation of Professor Marcela Canizo. She is an Argentinean researcher specialized in Japanese cinema and Argentinean and Brazilian Nikkei cinema. She has lived many years in Brazil studying the local Nikkei diaspora. She teaches a course on Japanese cinema at the institute and invited us to screen *Yonsei*, by Harumi López Higa, and *Qampiq* and *Tea for Memory*, by Trimedia Films (Julio Mora and Javier Ormeño). Together we reflected on the particularities of Peruvian Nikkei cinema. It was interesting to talk with young Argentineans, who for the first time, saw and heard testimonies about the repercussions of the internal armed conflict in Peru and the persecution of Japanese people by the Peruvian state in the 1940s.

Meeting Marcela was also very interesting because the three of us agreed that there are very few people who are dedicated to researching Japanese cinema in Latin America and, above all, Nikkei cinema. Like us, she is probably the only one who is researching this topic in her country. It was nice to know that little by little networks are being woven and it will be less of a solitary act. Knowing more about other countries can help us to see our own particularities by contrast.

In Mexico we are in contact with Jessica Conejo, who wrote a doctoral thesis on Japanese cinema and is researching Brazilian Nikkei cinema. We met her because of our mutual interest in Japanese women directors and we have already collaborated a couple of times on this topic. We found it amazing that she is also interested in Latin American Nikkei cinema, and we have plans in the near future to carry out a joint activity.

Finally, in November 2022, in Chile, we made a presentation called "Cinema Made by Nikkei Women Directors in Peru" as part of the VI Conference of Japanese Studies of the Club Cultura Japonesa Concepción, whose theme was Japan and Latin America in Dialogue. There was a diverse body of research presented on the impact of Japanese cultural products in Latin America and on Nikkei artists. We will continue to create spaces to promote contemporary Peruvian Nikkei cinema.

Notes

1 Nikkei refers to the Japanese emigrant descendants.
2 https://www.apj.org.pe/los-nikkei-en-el-peru.
3 Regarding political persecution during the 1940s, see sociologist Luis Rocca Torres's *Los desterrados: la communidad japonesa en el Peru y la Segunda Guerra Mundial* (The Exiled: The Japanese Community in Peru and the Second World War) (Lima: Pontificia Universidad Católica del Perú, 2022). He mentions that as early as the 1930s "the anti-Japanese campaign in Peru intensified, which grew until it reached its highest level of tension and conflict during World War II" (p. 23). Then began the deportations in the 1940s, with help of the Peruvian state, when Japanese men and women and their children born in Peru were taken to concentration camps in the United States, especially to one called Crystal City.
4 The book, *Japanese Immigration to Peru, 75th Anniversary, 1899–1974* tells this story well. Edited and published by Perú Shimpo (1974).
5 DOCUPERU is a non-profit organization that promotes, disseminates, and produces multi-format documentary materials, as tools of expression and empowerment to encourage the democratization of communication and the development of national and international communities.

References

Perú Shimpo, S. A. 1974. *Japanese Immigration to Peru, 75th Anniversary, 1899–1974*. Lima, Peru.

Torres, Luis Rocca. 2022. *Los desterrados: la communidad japonesa en el Peru y la Segunda Guerra Mundial* (The Exiled: The Japanese Community in Peru and the Second World War). Lima: Pontificia Universidad Católica del Perú.

SECTION IV

Beyond Genre
Modes, Motifs, Memories

INTRODUCTION

Intan Paramaditha

"Asian cinema" is often associated with specific genres from Asia that travel globally via screen media and festivals, recognized through categories such as martial arts films, Asian extreme, Asian horror, Bollywood musicals, anime, and yakuza films. However, as we have learned from the films of Satyajit Ray, Apichatpong Weerasethakul, Hou-Hsiao-Hsien, and many others who might not have received the same level of visibility in the global festival circuits, Asian filmmakers have crossed genre boundaries and reworked genres to offer new aesthetics and ways of seeing. Titled "Beyond Genre," this section refers to the creative processes of the filmmakers in finding references by activating transnational imagination and revisiting history and tradition to disrupt genres and borders, which can be seen through authors' discussions of the melodramatic mode, the action film genre, and animated films from East and Southeast Asia, from post-WWII to the contemporary period. "Beyond Genre" also means thinking beyond familiar Asian genres due to their global commercial presence through, for instance, sound and memory in experimental films or the connection between the motif of the face veil and the gaze in Islamic film genre. Further, "Beyond Genre" is also an invitation to reconsider Asian cinema and film and media studies through Asian philosophical frameworks as well as screen cultures that influence film style, genre, and screen performance in the region.

Two chapters in this section, Stephen Teo's "The Melodramatic Mode in Asian Cinema: Usmar Ismail's *Lewat Djam Malam* (*After the Curfew*)" and "Christina Klein's Bong Joon Ho's *Parasite* as a Remake of Kim Ki-Young's *The Housemaid*: Creating an Aesthetic Genealogy Within South Korean Cinema," offer new insights to the study of Asian melodrama and provokes a discussion of influences and genealogy. As the films discussed deploy various styles from melodrama to noir, melodrama here is better understood as a mode rather than a genre category. Both chapters indicate that Asian postwar melodrama, while always transnational in influences, is a dynamic and fluid site that reveals how modern subjects navigate the capitalist structures, emphasizing Wimal Dissanayake's (cited in Teo's article in this volume) description of Asian melodrama as a reflection of "the fabric of life and cultural contours of the society." Teo investigates the melodramatic mode of storytelling of an Indonesian classic, *Lewat Djam Malam* (1954), by Usmar Ismail. While the styles of Western world cinemas can be traced in the film through the motifs of music, representation

DOI: 10.4324/9781003266952-32

of leisure, and noir imagery, *Lewat Djam Malam* also shows discontinuities between the Western melodrama traditions and the melodrama in a specific Indonesian context. Focusing on the implications of local/traditional music and song, Teo demonstrates that these elements are significant in accentuating the crisis faced by the protagonist, whose ideas of revolution are challenged by postwar socio-economic realities, thus compelling him to seek a resolution to his moral dilemma. *Lewat Djam Malam*, Teo suggests, is both a social and political melodrama that helps us better understand the impact of modernization in Asia.

Christina Klein's chapter proposes new perspectives of Korean cinema as a transnational cinema by indicating a link between two films that depart from and push the limits of melodrama: Bong Joon-Ho's *Parasite* (2019) and Kim Ki-Young's *The Housemaid* (1960). Klein makes a case of *Parasite* as a makeover of *The Housemaid* because it alludes to as well as expands elements of the source material particularly in style, set design, and the use of space while toning down the psychosexual motif and amplifying the class conflict. *The Housemaid* itself cannot be pinned down easily into one genre category; as a gothic noir domestic melodrama with a horror bent, it is a playful approach to genres in the period of Korea's Golden Age. Klein's chapter acknowledges the transnational influences that shape contemporary Korean cinema, mainly Hollywood films, but it reminds us that allusions to local sources and film history are some of the ways to think about trans-Asian cinemas. Crossing borders also means rediscovering (*The Housemaid* was not easily available when Bong grew up) and re-signifying the works of one's film history. Highlighting the active effort of Bong Joon-Ho to align with Korean history by revisiting and remaking a film from the Golden Age period, Klein shows the possibility of revisiting history and creating an aesthetic genealogy in Asia as an intervention in trans-Asian cinema.

Films such as *Lewat Djam Malam* and *The Housemaid* provide a look into how individuals, family structures, and relationships are shaped by the Cold War. In this section, some other chapters also situate cultural production within the Cold War context and explore how filmmakers use genres to transcend the limits of imagination. Daisy Yan Du asks what it means to imagine the West from Asia during a period in which information between communist and capitalist blocks was considered delayed or isolated. Her chapter, "Melting the Iron Curtain: Political Immediacy, Metal-Morphosis, and the Caricatured Western Leaders in Agitprop Animation in Socialist China, 1949–65," indicates that certain genres have opened up possibilities to transcend barriers of imagination. Du examines animated films in socialist China (1949–65) to trace how the capitalist West was imagined and visualized. While the West was almost absent in live-action cinema, it appeared more prominently in animated films, a medium that allowed the representation of what was unrepresentable by live-action films due to the limitation of technology. Focusing on international-motif agitprop animation, Du argues that the Cold War which shaped these films triggered a "heated" imagination of the West that "melted" the Iron Curtain.

Also informed by the Cold War politics, Raymond Tsang's "The 'Mirrored' Cultural Revolution: The Geopolitical Making of Apolitical Hero in Chang-Cheh's *The Assassin*" delves into Hong Kong action films, a well-recognized global genre, by focusing on the figure of Chang Cheh, known as a director who revolutionized the genre of action movies in the late 1960s. While acknowledging Chang as someone who has pushed the limits of genre, moving away from highly staged choreography in the genre to his own style of "aesthetic of violence," Tsang offers a reading that asks what this motif of violence means by revisiting Chang's film *The Assassin*. Tsang's analysis goes against scholars who build their argument on aesthetics as a mirror to reality, linking Chang's style of violence to the rebellious mid-'60s youth culture, counterculture movement in the West, and student movements all over the world. On the contrary, Tsang situates violence as a site for Chang to retrieve traditional Chinese virtue that was presumed to be lost in the face of the Cultural Revolution.

Moving away from the Cold War context and a more popular genre, we delve into "memory film" as a form explored in Southeast Asian experimental cinema. Focusing on prominent Southeast Asian artist filmmakers, Apichatpong Weerasethakul and Shireen Seno, Philippa Lovatt's "The Vernacular Sonorities of the Memory Film in Southeast Asia" underlines their similar interest in personal and social memory. Through their "memory films," Weerasethakul's *Mysterious Object at Noon* and Seno's *Big Boy*, Lovatt analyzes how vernacular inflections of historical memory are conveyed through sound and non-linear, experimental modes of storytelling. She argues that in both films, traces of the past appear through sounds and images that demand the active acts of listening, imagining, and interpreting. In her discussion of two distinctive artist-filmmakers, Lovatt also shows the rich and often unexplored film cultures and genres in Southeast Asia. While Apichatpong and Seno have both produced internationally known short and feature films and moving image installations in the global art circuit, other filmmakers working with the limits of official histories in the region need to be further discussed.

Rachel Harrison's contribution in this section provides a larger context for the transnational trajectories of Thai directors. Her chapter, "Global Aspirations/Local Affiliations: Exploring the Tensions of 'Post-Crisis' Thai Cinema, 1997–2004," focuses on the works of the "new wave" directors who emerged in the late 1990s and changed the cinematic landscape in Thailand: Pen-Ek Ratanaruang, Nonzee Nimibutr, and Wisit Sasanatieng (Apichatpong Weerasethakul, the fourth member of the "New Wave," has been discussed in the previous chapter) were known for their quirky, experimental, genre-bending and stylized visual aesthetics that challenged the commonly known Thai low-brow comedy, romance, and horror genres in the 1980s. Harrison argues that the aspirations of Thai filmmakers to succeed on the world cinema stage ambivalently coexist with their rejection of the global through various textures of representations of the local. Harrison unpacks the significance of the rural by tracing it to the colonial processes of Siam's modernity project in the late 19th to early 20th century. The chapter echoes Klein's analysis of Korean cinema in demonstrating how historical legacies – as conscious or deep-seated ideas– continue to inform and reshape film aesthetics in Asia amid the constantly expanding transnational imaginary.

Alicia Izharuddin's chapter offers another view from Southeast Asia and contributes to the discourse of film and religion through the Asian lens in this section. Although not all chapters in this rubric focus on a particular genre, it responds to "film and religion" as a growing field in film studies that explores the political, economic, spiritual, and philosophical aspects of religion and/in cinema. Izharuddin's "Revisiting the Face Veil in Post-Pandemic Times: The Humane Visual Ethics of Indonesian Islamic Filmmaking" focuses on three Indonesian short and feature films shaped by the important contexts of global Islamic modernity: post-9/11 and the COVID-19 pandemic. Drawing on the work of Emmanuel Levinas to consider the meaning of the face and the motif of the face veil, the chapter explores the potential for humane visual ethics through Islamic filmmaking and visual culture in Indonesia.

While Alicia Izharuddin's chapter discusses films that fit into, and at the same time rede-fines, the Islamic film genre (*film Islami*), a major genre in Indonesia as a country with the world's largest Muslim population, Victor Fan's chapter rethinks film, religion, and phi-losophy by showing how Buddhism can provide a framework for contemporary film and media philosophy while addressing the universal-particular debates in thinking about Asia as method. In "Karma-Image; Insight-Image: on Buddhism and the Cinema," Fan argues that Buddhism enables us to see "a process of interbecoming" between different layers of reality that constitute images and spectators. He uses the 1931 film *Love and Duty* by Richard Poh (Bu Wancang) to discuss how film can be considered as an "insight-image" in a Buddhist frame, allowing the spectator to become mindful of an assemblage of personal, socio-political, historical, and cultural conditions. Fan also states that due to these inter-dependent conditions, Buddhism cannot be considered the sole interpretative framework but one of the many agents in the making of image-consciousness. Fan's chapter brings philosophical frameworks from Asian and Euro-American traditions into a dialogue, thus proposing alternatives for our ongoing discussion of the trans-Asian method in film and media studies.

The last chapter in this section invites us to think about the genre of film magazines while reminding us that film genres, style, and acting are shaped by film cultures and ideas shared between critics and audiences. Enoch Yee-lok Tam's chapter, "Personality and Morality in Screen Performance: Hong Kong Film Criticism and Social Reform of the 1920s," examines how 1920s film publication *Yinguang* (*Silver Light*) contributed to shaping the discourse around cinema in Hong Kong and elevated the social status of films from low brow to serious art. Although it shared some similarities with American film magazines in the same period in its preoccupation with movie stars and their lives, it goes beyond the genre by placing an in-depth discussion of acting and performance, linking the actors' lived experi-ences to the quality of their acting. Highlighting authenticity as a value, the writers of *Silver Light* believed that actors' exemplary personality and self-cultivation had a direct connec-tion to screen performances that were real and authentic. In creating film discourse that was centered around morality and artistic quality, transcending themes such as celebrity gossip commonly found in the film magazine genre, *Silver Light* created a bridge between cinema, actors, and the audience's active participation to engage in moral reflection, thus re-emphasizing the critical role of film publications and film cultures in film production and reception.

24

THE MELODRAMATIC MODE IN ASIAN CINEMA

Usmar Ismail's *Lewat Djam Malam* (After the Curfew)

Stephen Teo

Melodrama, as a generic mode of expression in the cinema, is wide open to "differing levels of genericity," following Rick Altman's semantic/syntactic principle toward genre (Altman 1984, 12). Disparities between Asian expressions and the Western postulation of the genre are therefore to be expected. These may be based on different understandings of what constitutes melodrama. For example, in Chinese cinema, the term for melodrama is *wenyi*, meaning the literary and the artistic, which are far different from the original root terms of *melos*, a Greek word meaning song or melody, and *drame*, the French word for drama. According to Peter Brooks, the word and the genre were invented by the French and were established in France "at the dawn of the nineteenth century [. . .] in the aftermath of the Revolution" (Brooks 1995, xvi). Brooks defines melodrama as "a dramaturgy of hyperbole, excess, excitement, and 'acting out'" (Brooks 1995, viii). The Chinese term *wenyi* conveys entirely different meanings and seems far from the standard melodramatic qualities as Brooks has defined them. They denote the essence of Chinese melodrama, which is based on literariness and artiness, but these characteristics do not necessarily exclude the excessive and exaggerated style which is usually thought of as "melodramatic."

It is not within the scope of this chapter to analyze *wenyi* nor is it my intention to present it as an archetypal form of Asian melodrama. The intention is rather to show how melodrama relates to Asian cinema, in an effort to re-endorse Dissanayake's observation that melodrama "also constitutes an important area of creative expression in many Asian cultures" (Dissanayake 1993, 2). Furthermore, an examination of culture and society is implicit in the process since Asian melodramas signify a "relation to the fabric of life and cultural contours of the society from which they emerge" (Dissanayake 1993, 3). The task in this chapter is to define a distinctive *Asian* mode of melodrama. One might call it an Asian *idiom* of melodrama based on the idiomatic expressions of both *melos* and *drame* components of melodrama. In Asian cinema, we can hold up Bollywood cinema as the classic paradigm of this mode. Contrast Bollywood melodramas, which are filled with songs and drama, with Western film melodrama, and we can see a vast difference. Our case study in this chapter is not Bollywood but the Indonesian classic, *Lewat Djam Malam* (After the Curfew, 1954), directed by Usmar Ismail. The choice of this film bears up Dissanayake's

DOI: 10.4324/9781003266952-33

insightful pronouncement on melodrama in relation to Asian cinema, which is that it "enables us to understand better the dynamics of modernization taking place in Asia," and that it "helps us to appreciate some vital dimensions of social modernization in terms of cultural differences" (Dissanayake 1993, 4). This a melodrama that has been culturally modulated from the Western tradition, and it is political in substance, told from the perspectives of nationalist Indonesian filmmakers including the director Usmar Ismail and the screenwriter Asrul Sani. Our purpose is to examine its melodramatic expression based on an analysis of the characters and their reactions to the social and political conditions of its setting, Bandung, Indonesia. The film takes place in 1949 as the War of Independence concludes (this is the war against the Dutch colonizers from 1945 to 1949) but the country is still under emergency and a state of curfew has been imposed. The setting and the performances are key to the work's status as a melodrama. From our reading of the melodramatic mode of expression, we may of course look at the film as a model of generic practice in world melodrama. However, the task of this volume is to distinguish the film's generic practice as a more unique form of melodramatic expression within the scope of Asian cinema.

Lewat Djam Malam can first be designated a melodrama purely from the notion of the social melodrama as expounded by Cawelti in his article "The Evolution of Social Melodrama" (1991). Significantly, Cawelti begins his definition of social melodrama by citing the Dickensian formula wherein the writer "synthesized social criticism with the archetype of melodrama and thereby gave readers the pleasure of seeing the follies of men and institutions combined with the satisfaction of witnessing the triumph of virtue and the punishment of evil" (Cawelti 1991, 33). This seems to me to typify the kind of melodrama at play in *Lewat Djam Malam*. However, in terms of how the film may be taken as a classic model of the social melodrama within the concept of Asian cinema, I would define it as a mode of storytelling that is influenced by the structural and cultural features of social lifestyles under historical-materialistic conditions of development in Indonesia in 1949 following the war of independence. Krishna Sen has referred to this era as one that accentuated the historical and nationalist circumstances of melodrama. She writes:

> In every one of his earlier films, the narrative progressed along the lines of the pro-
> tagonists' effort to change their lives and conditions of the society around them.
> These were texts that, imbued with the confidence of a nation that had just won its
> independence from the colonial Dutch, registered the transformative possibilities of
> human action. These texts constructed heroes who acted in and upon history and
> moved it along. Textually the spectator was positioned to identify himself or herself
> with the hero, the historical agent of nation building.
>
> *(Sen 1993, 208)*

Given the historical context of his melodrama, Usmar Ismail transmutes *Lewat Djam Malam* into a political melodrama that reeks of noir-like suspense and moral conflict. As a result, it is fair to call *Lewat Djam Malam* both a social and political melodrama. However, its political content seems to distinguish the film more so than the social. Usmar Ismail is in fact somewhat of a specialist in political melodramas. His best films are all underpinned by large political events, primarily the struggle against the Dutch for independence, as evidenced in *Darah dan Doa* (The Long March, 1950), *Enam Djam di Djogja* (Six Hours in Jogjakarta, 1951), and *Pejuang* (Warriors for Freedom, 1960). At the same time, all of them deal with social anxieties and civilian trepidations on war and sacrifice. Indeed, the film seems to present the hero as a "caricatural revolutionary," as Adrian Jonathan Pasaribu has described him, with a flawed political vision for social change driving his rage towards society: "As much as it is political, his rage could also easily be seen as hysterical" (Pasaribu 2020).

The political drama of *Lewat Djam Malam* is focused on the hero, Iskandar. The film begins as the emergency curfew kicks in at the stipulated time of 10:00 p.m., and we see a closeup of the hero's legs striding the streets trying to reach the home of his fiancée (the hero breaking curfew is a motif that Usmar repeats from his earlier film *Enam Djam di Djogja*). Later, we see that the hero experiences classical post-traumatic stress arising from an incident in which he was ordered by his commander to kill a family of innocents. At the same time, he perceives the inherent injustices of the new order to which he instinctively knows that he cannot belong. He takes it upon himself to deliver justice to his ex-commander, Gunawan, now a businessman who seeks to prevail in peacetime by using the same ruthless strongarm tactics he employed during wartime (more on him shortly). The social and political implications of the film are naturally of great significance, obvious to any casual viewer of the film, and a great part of the significance lies in how these implications reveal the foundations of Indonesia's uncertain development from its inception as an independent state to its destiny as a modern, democratic society in the new millennium. It is particularly resonant when we remember the tragic consequences of this development particularly throughout the mid-1960s as the country underwent a crisis of political transition from the regime of its first president Sukarno to the military dictatorship that followed under the strongman Suharto.

The socio-political and historical implications are undoubtedly the most important nuances that we can gather from the film. Essentially, these implications are didactic and moral in substance even if they are also political. Here, it is necessary to expound briefly on the importance of didacticism and its correlation with Asian melodrama. In fact, it is integral to any discourse on Asian melodrama. How often have I heard it said, pejoratively, at least in Chinese melodramas dealing with family relationships that they are didactic, implying that they are not so subtle and sophisticated, a low form of picture-making. In fact, didacticism traditionally points to a pedagogical strain that has long been associated with Asian cinema implying that such dramas are intrinsically of a high artistic and moral order (this was true in China, for example, when film became an industrial mode of production and came to be regarded as a "tool of didacticism and enlightenment [*qimeng*]": see Huang 2014, 4). If didacticism contains political messages and moral implications, the better we may then recognize the melodramatic impact of the work. *Lewat Djam Malam* is indeed very political with a didactic strain that serves to shore up the political impact of its content and we need to recognize that the political content is part of the film's distinction – after all, Usmar has made other films that are merely "melodramatic" entertainments, such as the musical *Tiga Dara* (1956), with little or no political effect but are highly didactic (a typical work of this nature is his Singaporean film *Korban Fitnah* [1959], which he directed under the Indian-sounding pseudonym of P. L. Kapur). *Lewat Djam Malam* is perhaps the one work of Usmar Ismail in which we feel that the didacticism implicit in melodrama is auspiciously factored into the narrative and the fusion is transparent. Such transparency can be taken as a mark of distinctiveness in Asian melodrama and may be put in contrast with what Peter Brooks calls "the moral occult." The concept of "moral occult" is "the domain of operative spiritual values which is both indicated within and masked by the surface of reality," "the repository of the fragmentary and desacralized remnants of sacred myth," "a realm which in quotidian existence may appear closed off from us" – and to Brooks, the melodramatic mode "in large measure exists to locate and to articulate the moral occult" (Brooks 1995, 5). In Asian cinema, the melodramatic mode is in large measure intrinsically a didactic mode in which moral or spiritual values are driving forces of heroic action. Asian didacticism implies that there is no such thing as a "moral occult" (a rather clumsy term to my mind) but a moral clarity of purpose.

The achievement of Usmar is that he gives us layers of meaning in the narrative that we need to uncover without feeling that we are given a lesson in social morals or political ethics. These layers function as structural latticework supporting the cultural and political substance of the screenplay. Thus, we may talk of a melodramatic structure in the film that is built upon the aesthetic interrelationship between melodrama and realism as well as on the political and historical events that have been mentioned. To proceed, we must excavate and appraise the formative layers of this melodramatic structure. I will first demonstrate how the film displays the purely expressive form of melodrama in terms of excess and exaggerated gestures of drama. Second, I will dwell on the impact of this drama denoted through the classic form of *melos*, or song, which is strikingly illustrated in key scenes as diegetic components of the drama (as opposed to non-diegetic music heard on the soundtrack). Diegetic song sequences may be seen as part of an Indonesian tradition (primarily under the influence of Indian films) that is culturally repeated in the films of Usmar Ismail such that it is part of his melodramatic style. I will seek to delineate examples of these two aspects below. To begin with, I will denote certain key scenes in the film showing how the social-political element and the melodrama are integrated as a complete whole under Usmar's approach.

The melodramatic dimension easily pervades the narrative of the political plot, which concentrates on Iskandar's plight as an ex-revolutionary trying to fit into a normal postbellum existence and contribute to rebuilding society in peacetime based on honor and justice. At first, he tries to reintegrate himself into a life of domesticity with his fiancée, Norma. As the film begins, we see him returning to the home of Norma from the war, which signifies at the very least his desire for domesticity. In the opening scene, the hero is violating the curfew; we see him running away from soldiers when he is ordered to stop, and they fire a warning shot. But he manages to evade the soldiers and is safely ensconced in the fiancée's home. In the subsequent scenes, he seems made to order for the domestic life of a middle-class family, and the next day, he shows his willingness to appease his prospective father-in-law's misgivings of his character by following up on his recommendation that he work in the governor's department through the good offices of a friend. This short domestic sequence and the subsequent scene of Iskandar working in the governor's office are the groundwork for a classic hero's dilemma in Asian melodrama – the hero is torn between settling down and settling scores. The hero has unfinished business to settle, which will interfere with his longing for domesticity. Just what the unfinished business is will be made clear shortly, but first we need to consider the sequence of the governor's office, which shows how the social realities of the workplace operate to break down the hero's propensity toward domesticity as portrayed in Norma's home.

The job turns out to be a disaster for Iskandar when the staff gives him the cold shoulder and he gets into a scrap with the supervisor. The scene's realist aesthetics (in an austere stage-bound manner) demonstrates the apparent discontinuity between the nationalistic fervor of the independence struggle and the modern realities of development in which people must protect their jobs and not to give them away to ex-revolutionaries at the whim of those at the top. In turn, it demonstrates the problematic existence of the ex-revolutionary who must adjust his idealism to suit reality in peacetime and the sad fact that he is not mentally or intellectually equipped for the task. In this failure to reconcile idealism with practical materialism, we have a glimpse of the tragedy that will unfold in the melodrama – and an indication of the national tragedy of Indonesia from that historical moment onward. This is, no doubt, one of the great signs of the film's significance, offering some points of contestation. The fact that it deals with a tragic revolutionary hero with intimations of a tragic fate for the country has been interpreted by Yngvesson and Alarilla as a viewpoint (one shared by other films and filmmakers) that is "paradoxically distinguished by its consistently apprehensive view of nationalism and the nation" (Yngvesson and Alarilla 2020, 38). However, I doubt that nationalistic filmmakers of that era would harbor an "apprehensive view of nationalism and the nation." Objectively speaking, nationalism is an outcome of the struggle for independence from the Dutch colonizers. I would say that filmmakers in that era would generally hold a positive view of nationalism and the nation, but it does not mean that they would not be critical of certain internal aspects of the nation and its development. Its nationalism reflects the strong anti-colonialist currents of the independence struggle but does not offer easy solutions to the corruption and cynicism inherent in the nation once independence is won. In my view, *After the Curfew* is not less nationalistic for its critical view of the nation.

Another scene of great melodramatic impact is the meeting between Iskandar and his ex-commander, Gunawan. Having walked out of his job, Iskandar drifts in the streets, and he ends up paying a visit to the business office of Gunawan's private company. The moment he steps in, it is apparent that his presence is an awkward one, and we are given a scene of the unequal and unpleasant relationship between the protagonist and Gunawan – and indeed, it is with Gunawan that the hero must settle his "unfinished business," referred to earlier. Gunawan appears as an archetypally strident and overemphatic villain; therefore, he is the fitting model of an Asian melodramatic villain. There is an element of inevitability in this meeting; it performs as a kind of moral compass and gives the reasons for the hero's troubled state of existence and what motivates his actions and behavior (the "unfinished business"). Gunawan is in the middle of a business phone call during which he is threatening the other party. Gunawan has become a businessman whose revolutionary fervor in peacetime is just as strident as it was during the war, and he resorts to intimidation and threats against his economic competitors. He tries to recruit Iskandar to his side, offering him money to threaten a company director. "The revolution isn't over," he says, "as ex-freedom fighters we must still be revolutionaries." During the war, Iskandar had previously followed Gunawan's orders to kill a family of rich refugees from Jakarta whose fortune Gunawan had then appropriated to start his own business. Should the hero follow his commander once again as though the war is still going on? Indeed, Gunawan tells Iskandar as much: "The economic struggle is even more intense than fighting with guns and bayonets. What's the point of freedom if our rice pot is still dependent on the pity of foreigners? We must also become economically independent. We must remove all obstacles."[1]

A key aspect of Gunawan's villainy is his militarized nature and crude persona. In contrast, Iskandar is more like the cultured man of letters. As such, he is the man of virtue, or rather the hero who must follow the path of virtue. Gunawan follows the path of evil, persecuting the good and denying justice to the virtuous. We may recognize here the devices of an Indonesian cultural form known as *wayang*, a traditional Javanese puppet theater. From this perspective, the apparent refinement of the hero, as typified by Iskandar, and the archetypal villainy as embodied in the figure of Gunawan, can be related to characters in *wayang*, or to be more specific, the *wayang golek menak*, which is based on Islamic legends. It shows the character of the *kafir* as an evil prototype "who customarily display a way of acting in the world that is in sharp contrast to accepted modes of Javanese behavior" (Petersen 1994, 267). Iskandar embodies the home-grown "Javanese" character. "Whereas the 'Javanese' characters in the performance display a preference for personal restraint, described as *halus* or refined, the *kafir* indulge in their animal appetites, desiring every type of worldly pleasure in a way that is described as *kasar*: coarse and vulgar" (Petersen 1994, 267).

An interesting point from this *wayang* tradition is "the contrast between good and evil is so complete that the identity of evil is in many ways hinged upon the identity of good" (Petersen 1994: 268). This aptly explains Iskandar's relationship with Gunawan, which has the ring of an obsessive-compulsive disorder. Certainly, we already have indications of psychological anxiety in Iskandar's character in previous scenes, but it is his encounter with Gunawan that puts his character's anxiety in perspective, following the idea that his identity and that of Gunawan are inextricably linked together. They are completely bound together in a play of, to quote Peter Brooks writing about Henry James,

> heightened moral alternatives, where every gesture [. . .] is charged with the conflict between light and darkness, salvation and damnation, and where people's destinies and choices of life seem finally to have little to do with the surface realities of a situation, and much more to do with an intense inner drama in which consciousness must purge itself and assume the burden of moral sainthood.
>
> *(Brooks 1995, 5)*

This is also "the theme of renunciation which sounds through James's novels" (Brooks 1995, 5). We hear it resounding in Usmar's film through the plot of Iskandar's preoccupation with Gunawan, who plagues the most inner and darkest recesses of Iskandar's mind.

Finally, I come to another hugely symbolic figure in the melodramatic mode, one that bears a great psychic impact on the hero although in a different way from that exerted by Gunawan. This is the character of the female prostitute, Laila – and she brings me to the second aspect of the melodramatic expression that I seek to expound on in this chapter – namely, song, or *melos*. While still on the streets after his encounter with Gunawan, Iskandar meets his ex-comrade Puja, who has become a gambler and a pimp. Puja takes him to his house and there Iskandar meets Laila, who lives in the house together with Puja. When Iskandar first meets Laila, she is in the middle of singing a song, "Nasibku Yang Malang," which translates as "My Miserable Fate," and we get the sense that the song, integrated diegetically into the drama, is highly significant from the point of view of the story. The song is repeated, again diegetically, several times in other scenes and it contains more significance each time when sung by Laila in connection with the hero, who is always present in these scenes. We sense that Laila's song and Laila herself offer support for the hero, about which I will have more to say. Thus, the first time we see Laila singing is a deceptive moment, for we might regard her singing as a trifling piece of business of no consequence to the narrative, but apart from being the first plank of the film's melodic structure, it is part of Usmar's melodramatic style, song and dance being featured in almost every Usmar film. (Such song sequences in Indonesian films are an influence of Indian cinema, which was highly popular with local audiences at the time. Their use in Indonesian films was part of a strategy to compete with Indian films, which were imported in large numbers and shown in second-run theaters, the very venues mandated to show local productions; the imported Indian films "thus directly competed with local films" [Suwardi 2000, 27]).

Here we must first point out that the film's portrayal of the crisis engulfing the life of Iskandar is done uniquely using music and song sequences. Such sequences convey a quality of softness, even of femininity, which informs Iskandar's character and his troubled reintegration into the social world. As a social melodrama there are several sides to the "social" that the film delineates. We have examined that side in which the hero is ostracized from the workplace, and then a more personal side in which the hero must face up to the moral implications in his relationship with a corrupt senior associate (Gunawan). Now the film shows Iskandar unable to fit into the social circle of friends and well-wishers: the scene of Laila in Puja's home is of this nature, and later, Iskandar is the center of attention in a welcoming home party that Norma has organized in her home, but his presence strikes a completely discordant note in the party atmosphere. The *melos* component of the melodrama appears to accentuate the hero's social predicament. It brings him into a sort of psychic-aesthetic realm where song and dance become symbolically relevant to the hero's decision making about settling the score with Gunawan. Song is used to denote the social as a dialectic of hardship and recreation as first represented by Laila's song. Later, there are some key scenes in which we see a process of the hero's struggle of action and inaction as he contemplates the killing of Gunawan; these scenes take place amid song and dance as if the artistic performances represent his thought processes.

Figure 24.1   The songstress Laila singing "My Miserable Fate."

287

Because of their striking interpositions, I will briefly describe and analyze these scenes. After an ensemble performance by all the partygoers of the popular folk song "Rasa Sayange," in which everyone contributes a self-composed *pantun* or quatrain, the hero, mentally out of sync with the harmony of the song, slips out with his army pistol and sets out to kill his nemesis. As he stops outside the home of Gunawan, he sees Gunawan's shadow at the window but does not shoot him, being plagued by second thoughts. He then drifts into the streets and comes across a festive event going on, its main attraction being a traditional *tayuban* dance. We hear the voice of a singer singing in a folk style under the tones of gamelan music, and the crowds are watching people dance. This is an erotic dance form in which the male and female partners make certain risqué gestures, such as when the man mimics the act of kissing by pecking the cheek of the female. As Iskandar pushes through the crowd, a *taledhek* (female dancer) looks at him suggestively but he ignores her and leaves the site.

This *tayuban* song and dance sequence is a culturally specific moment that is briefly denoted in the film and should leave a touristy kind of impression on the viewer (on the *tayuban* and *taledhek*, see Hefner 1987, 75–94). However, it plays a significant role in the hero's crisis by impressing a sexual-cum-psychic effect on his mind process. It also repeats the hero's dilemma during the previous musical sequence (the "Rasa Sayange" sequence), but it offers a stronger cultural contrast for its traditional folk elements. The traditional element is perhaps incidental to the hero's dilemma, but the sexual connotation in the dance and the *taledhek*'s look appear to drive him back into the home of Laila. Laila invites him in, and she repeats the song "Nasibku Yang Malang," with Iskandar sitting by as if dutifully listening and pondering further on the meanings and implications of the song and all the song and dance sequences that have occurred prior to Laila's scene beginning from the "Rasa Sayange" sequence to the striking *tayuban* sequence.

These sequences emit sensual and cultural sentiments and atmospherics adding to the social world in which Iskandar finds himself implanted beyond his choice. For all his awkwardness, Iskandar is an indispensable signifier of the social underlining of the melodrama; he becomes embedded into the *melos* sequences which gently push the narrative into a coil of cognitive signs. The *taledhek*'s gesture is one of these signs and so is Laila's song, both working as driving forces that compel Iskandar toward his final action to rid society of one of its corrupt agents, and the resolution of his moral dilemma. Sequences like the *tayuban* dance and Laila's vocal performances are particularly memorable due not only to their cultural resonance, but their super-structural effect of dialectical counterpointing against the drama of the hero. We gain a fascinating perspective from the entanglement of song (and dance) with drama. The *melos* motif operates as a kind of aesthetic varnish casting a "pink" verdigris, as it were, over the drama of the hero's red-hot emotions brewing inside him. It may also illustrate the hero's existentialist crisis in a world of illusion, exemplified in a line spoken earlier to Norma: "I am surrounded by people who don't live in the real world. They don't take anything seriously. I feel like a foreigner when I am with them." The songs, ironically, push the hero back into the real world and he becomes embedded in the reality of real-world suffering. The gestures of the *taledhek* and Laila, who not only sings sad laments of her fate but also collects clippings of middle-class lifestyle images from *Life* magazine, touch the hero and drive him toward his final act of killing.

The last point I wish to make is that of class difference. This class factor highlights, to my mind, a socialistic theme in the drama which supplements the political and the nationalistic strands of the story. This socialistic theme emphasizes two things: first, the inequality of social classes as laid out in the tableau of song and dance scenes (Norma's household and her party guests representing the Indonesian bourgeoisie, and the *taledhek* and Laila representing the lumpen proletariat), and, second, the aspiration of the lower classes to attain the good life (Laila's album of *Life* magazine cuttings being a representation of this), which fundamentally brings out the class sympathy of Iskandar, solidifying his sense of social justice and driving him to his final action. The class theme, with its concomitant theme of democratic social justice and equality, is in the background during the film's final sequences where Iskandar returns to the party at Norma's home but then flees again after being made aware that the police are on the heels of Gunawan's killer. He goes out into the streets just as the curfew once again kicks in, closing the circle on the hero and ultimately reinforcing the point that it is the militarized ruling class that will prevail. It is the theme that reveals the hero's tragedy, which, by extension is the nation's tragedy.

To conclude, this chapter has sought to explicate the melodramatic mode of expression in the Indonesian classic *After the Curfew* essentially by analyzing both *melos* and *drame* components. The contribution of its director Usmar Ismail is crucial. Fundamentally, melodrama's tendency of excess and overstatement is mitigated through personal *mise-en-scène*, Usmar's masterly infusion of the social and the political into the drama of ordinary lives as the protagonists struggle to fit into a society thrown askew by war and internal conflict. Usmar's handling of the material, his depictions of characters, and his measured process of outlining excess and overstatement are outstanding, but he reaches up to the next level with his calculated employment of song and dance. This *melos* material is sublimely laid out in the film, accentuating the role of song as an intrinsic part of melodrama. In doing so, Usmar may have demonstrated the original spirit of melodrama when its evolution in the cinema has generally transfigured *melos* into what Brooks calls "the pervasive exploitation of background music" (Brooks 1995, 48) rather than being an active and radical part of drama. His achievement is worthy of our respect and recognition.

Note

1 The English translations of the dialogue quoted are taken from the Criterion Collection disc in "Martin Scorsese's World Cinema Project No. 3."

References

Altman, Rick. 1984. "A Semantic/Syntactic Approach to Film Genre." *Cinema Journal* 23 (3): 6–18.
Brooks, Peter. 1995. *The Melodramatic Imagination: Balzac, Henry James, Melodrama, and the Mode of Excess.* New Haven: Yale University Press.
Cawelti, John G. 1991. "The Evolution of Social Melodrama." In *Imitations of Life: A Reader on Film and Television Melodrama,* edited by M. Landy. Detroit: Wayne State University Press.
Dissanayake, Wimal. 1993. "Introduction." In *Melodrama and Asian Cinema,* edited by W. Dissanayake, 1–8. Cambridge: Cambridge University Press.
Hefner, Robert W. 1987. "The Politics of Popular Art: *Tayuban* Dance and Culture Change in East Java." *Indonesia* 43: 75–94.
Huang, Xuelei. 2014. *Shanghai Filmmaking: Crossing Borders, Connecting to the Globe, 1922–1938.* Leiden/Boston: Brill.
Pasaribu, Adrian Jonathan. 2020. "*After the Curfew*: A Nation of Dead Ends." *Current,* September 20. Accessed August 11, 2023. https://www.criterion.com/current/posts/7116-after-the-curfew-a-nation-of-dead-ends.
Petersen, Robert. 1994. "The Character of the Kafir: Domains of Evil in the *Wayang Golek Menak* of Central Java." *Asian Theatre Journal* 11 (2): 267–74.

Sen, Krishna. 1993. "Politics of Melodrama in Indonesian Cinema." In *Melodrama and Asian Cinema*, edited by W. Dissanayake, 205–17. Cambridge: Cambridge University Press.

Suwardi, H. 2000. "Indonesia." In *The Films of Asean*, edited by J. F. Lacaba, 17–47. Quezon City: Asean Committee on Culture and Information.

Yngvesson, Dag, and Adrian Alarilla. 2020. "A Nation Imagined Differently: The Critical Impulse of 1950s Indonesian Cinema." In *Southeast Asia on Screen: From Independence to Financial Crisis (1945–1998)*, edited by G. C. Khoo, T. Barker, and M. J. Ainslie, 37–57. Amsterdam: Amsterdam University Press.

25

BONG JOON-HO'S *PARASITE* AS A REMAKE OF KIM KI-YOUNG'S *THE HOUSEMAID*

Creating an Aesthetic Genealogy Within South Korean Cinema

Christina Klein

Bong Joon-ho's *Gisaengchung* (Parasite, 2019) is one of the most important Asian films of recent years. It won the prestigious Palme d'Or at the Cannes Film Festival and broke records at the 2020 Academy Awards, where it was the first South Korean film to receive a nomination and the first non-English-language film to win Best Picture. It garnered tremendous attention around the world and almost universal critical acclaim, appearing on over one hundred year-end top-ten lists.

When Spike Lee announced Bong as the winner of the award for Best Director, the audience erupted into a standing ovation that seemed to express genuine affection for the director and whole-hearted support for his big win. Up on stage, Bong's excitement was palpable: he smiled and laughed, and also covered his mouth and wiped his brow in unfeigned gestures of emotional overwhelm (Oscars n.d.). Bong's acceptance speech suggested his unique position as a filmmaker who straddles the boundaries of national and transnational cinema. On the one hand, he spoke almost entirely in Korean, a choice that communicated a sense of national pride amid an otherwise all-English evening and that recalled his gently mocking comments at the Golden Globe Awards, where he observed of Americans that "Once you overcome the 1-inch-tall barrier of subtitles, you will be introduced to so many more amazing films" (Chang 2020). On the other hand, Bong used his time not to thank the Korean members of his production team but to acknowledge graciously the other, American, nominees for Best Director in ways that demonstrated his intimate knowledge of and affection for Hollywood cinema. He referenced a quotation from "the great Martin Scorsese" that had been important to him during film school, thanked Quentin Tarantino for his years of support – "Quentin, I love you" – and made knowing reference to the cult film *The Texas Chainsaw Massacre* (1974) as he expressed a desire to share his trophy with Todd Philipps and Sam Mendes. He wrapped up his remarks with a humorous comment in English – "Thank you – I will drink until next morning!" – that demonstrated his familiarity with the ritual of Oscar after-parties while also indicating, through its slight grammatical imperfection, that he was still something of an outsider ("Bong Joon Ho," n.d.).

DOI: 10.4324/9781003266952-34

Bong's status as a simultaneously national and transnational filmmaker is evident across his body of work. He directed six feature films before *Parasite*. Four of them explore Korean history and locally resonant social issues. The other two are set largely outside the country's borders, explore global issues of climate change and industrial food production, and include non-Korean actors and English dialogue. Most of his films were made with Korean production resources. Most of them also draw on genre conventions and stylistic patterns imported from Hollywood. With *Parasite*, Bong is doing something different. Like other of his films, it grapples with social issues that bedevil contemporary Korea. Unlike his other films, however, its aesthetic genealogy lies primarily in a single Korean movie, the classic *Hanyeo* (The Housemaid, 1960), directed by Kim Ki-young. By remaking – or "making-over" – Kim Ki-young's masterpiece, Bong creates an explicit link between the nation's two great periods of cinematic creativity: the Golden Age of the postwar period and the Korean Wave of the neoliberal era.

Parasite tells the story of a poor family, the Kims, who scheme to get themselves hired as servants for the rich Park family by exaggerating their credentials and passing themselves off as unrelated strangers. When the Parks leave for a camping trip, the Kims celebrate their good fortune by making themselves at home in the Parks' living room, only to be interrupted by the return of the previous housekeeper, Moon-gwang, who claims to have left something in the basement. That "something" turns out to be her husband, Geun-se, who has been hiding out in a secret bunker for four years. A violent conflict ensues after Moon-gwang discovers and threatens to reveal the Kims' deception, which culminates in her death. When a rainstorm causes the Parks to return unexpectedly, three of the Kims – father Ki-taek, daughter Ki-jung, and son Ki-woo – sneak out of the house and return to their own apartment. The next day, when all four Kims are back at work, Geun-se escapes the bunker and kills Ki-jung with a kitchen knife during a party. In the mayhem that follows, Geun-se is killed by Ki-jung's mother, Chung-sook, and Mr. Park is killed by Ki-taek, who then retreats to the secret bunker to escape arrest. The film ends with Ki-woo drafting a letter to his father promising to free him by earning enough money to buy the Parks' house, a prospect that the film makes clear is unlikely to happen. Despite the eruption of violence rooted in class rage and resentment, the working-class characters remain impoverished and symbolically entombed.

Parasite has most often been interpreted as a critique of life in capitalist South Korea today. From this perspective, *Parasite* depicts the social consequences of the neoliberal reforms launched in the early 1990s and furthered by the economic restructuring demanded by the IMF in the wake of the 1997 financial crisis. These consequences include an increase in income inequality (as seen in the contrast between the Kims and the Parks), the collapse of the middle class (the Kim family was previously more financially secure), the rise of irregular gig work (before becoming servants, the Kims eke out a bare living folding pizza boxes), and the rise of crippling personal debt (Geun-se is hiding from creditors). The Kim children, Ki-woo and Ki-jung, inhabit what Korean millennials have dubbed "Hell Joseon." This phrase refers to the difficulties faced by young people in particular, including high unemployment rates, intense pressure to get into prestigious universities, a mania for learning English, a lack of upward mobility despite hard work, and a pervasive sense that social and economic rewards go only to those who have connections. Ki-woo can't pass the college entrance exam, despite years of studying, and Ki-jung can't get a job despite her sharp intelligence, creativity, and charisma. All of the poor characters are willing to work hard and, once hired by the Parks, do their jobs diligently and well. The film makes clear that their economic precarity is not their own fault. While the film depicts the specific economic and social conditions within South Korea, the film has resonated with audiences across Asia and the West. When asked to explain this seeming contradiction, Bong pointed to the transnational nature of the problem he depicts: "We all live in the same country now: that of capitalism" (Mintzer 2019).

For all Bong's interest in social critique, however, he is not a sociologist. He is a filmmaker, and he believes that the way a fiction film deals with the "structural problems" caused by capitalism should not be as direct as is done in "social science books or documentaries." Instead, a commercial film must show "how calamities stemming from the structure are tragically transferred to individuals" (Sohn and Jung 2021, 292). Bong's job as a filmmaker, as he understands it, is to show how ordinary people are living the consequences of structural economic change. So how does a filmmaker depict an abstraction as large as the structure of capitalism in a way that is both entertaining and meaningful? One way is by looking to other films for inspiration.

Bong describes himself as a member of Korea's first cinephile generation of directors, which is to say that he learned how movies work by watching a lot of them, rather than by working his way up through the film industry. Bong fell in love with movies as a child in the 1970s and '80s. He didn't, however, fall in love with Korean movies. His favorite films were the Hollywood pictures that dominated the Korean film market in those years and that aired on TV, movies by directors such as Alfred Hitchcock, Francis Ford Coppola, and William Friedkin. He continued his informal film education at Yonsei University, where he spent most of his time watching movies at the university film club and obsessively managing its collection of VHS tapes. After graduating, he enrolled in the Korean Academy of Film Arts, the country's top film school. At Yonsei and the Academy, he discovered the great masters of Asian cinema, such as Akira Kurosawa and Hou Hsiao-hsien. Bong still has a voracious appetite for films, including those from Europe and other parts of the world, and he admits to owning a collection of more than 6,000 DVDs (Raup 2019).

Bong has openly discussed the many films that served as inspiration for *Parasite*. These include Joseph Losey's *The Servant* (1963), Claude Chabrol's *La Cérémonie* (1995), Akira Kurosawa's *Tengoku to Jigoku* (High and Low, 1963), George Miller's *Mad Max* (1979), and Alfred Hitchcock's *Psycho* (1960). The film Bong has discussed most often in relation to *Parasite*, however, is Kim Ki-young's *The Housemaid*. Kim, whose career extended from the 1950s through the mid-1980s, is regarded as one of Korea's greatest and most original directors. He made highly idiosyncratic films characterized by their focus on sexual obsession, social taboos, and horror, and he is known for his gothic melodramas and expressionistic, often surreal style. Kim's films were rediscovered in the 1990s by the cinephile generation of filmmakers who, like Bong, collected them on VHS. Bong has frequently said that he admires Kim for his deeply original vision and artistic integrity and that he regards him as a mentor. *The Housemaid*, which Bong has characterized as "Korea's *Citizen Kane*" (Bong 2009), is among his favorite films and says that he watches it regularly, especially when he feels depressed.

Bong has described *Parasite* as an homage to *The Housemaid*, but I think it makes more sense to see it as a "makeover" of Kim's film. Andrew Horton defines a makeover as "a particular form of remake that purposely sets out to make significant changes in what is either acknowledged or perceived as a prototype or important precursor to the film in question" (Horton 1998, 174). The concept of a makeover highlights the strategies of difference and continuity that connect a film to its progenitor. When the Korean Film Archive digitally restored *The Housemaid* with the help of Martin Scorsese's World Cinema Project and released it on DVD in 2009, Bong recorded the audio commentary (accompanied by film critic Kim Young-jin). I want to suggest that Bong's careful dissection of Kim's film created a template that he would use ten years later to craft his own film's story, themes, and expressive use of film form. In what follows I trace out the ways in which *Parasite* reproduces and gestures toward specific elements of *The Housemaid*, and also the ways in which it expands and elaborates upon its source material.

Parasite has strong narrative continuities with *The Housemaid*: both films tell a story about an affluent family that hires domestic help, only to have things go terribly wrong. *The Housemaid* is a gothic-noir domestic melodrama that tips into horror. It depicts the rise and fall of a family that moves from a cramped apartment into a spacious two-story house. While the husband gives piano lessons to young female factory workers, his pregnant wife sews piece-work at home so they can afford the new house and the accompanying comforts of middle-class life. When the wife falls ill, the husband hires a young woman to do the housework. The housemaid soon seduces the husband and becomes pregnant, creating a scandalous situation that threatens the family's upward mobility. After the housemaid is pressured by the wife to abort her child, she extracts revenge by killing the family's son and seizing control of the household. In the end, the husband is so anguished about what his behavior has wrought that he poisons himself in a double suicide with the maid.

Bong appropriates and modifies many of *The Housemaid*'s story elements. Alongside the psychosexual dynamics of obsession, jealousy, shame, and revenge, Bong sees class anxiety as a central concern in Kim's film. In his DVD commentary, he observes that "the theme of survival of a middle-class family is a very important issue." The family members are "obsessed" with money and status, which they express through their dialogue, because they "haven't been middle class for long" and are intimately aware of how easy, and how "terrible," it would be to "degenerate into the lower class." In the wake of the Korean War (1950–53) Korea was one of the poorest countries in the world, with widespread unemployment, high rates of inflation, and pervasive corruption. Earning enough money to rise out of poverty and stay there was very difficult for ordinary workers. For Bong, Kim's expressionistic style unveils an ugly truth about postwar Korean society: "It's like a nightmare to become middle class." In *Parasite*, Bong strips away the psychosexual dimension entirely in order to sharpen the focus on class. He expands the lone housemaid into a family of four, elevates them into the role of protagonists, and transforms them into sympathetic characters complete with backstories. He displaces the struggle for upward mobility onto the servants while maintaining *The Housemaid*'s rise-and-fall plot structure, with the first half charting the family's rise to a position of financial security and the second half charting their collapse. Bong replicates the pivot point in Kim's plot: in both films, the sudden appearance at the door of a wet housekeeper during a torrential rainstorm halts the characters' upward trajectory and redirects the film's tone toward horror. By the end of *Parasite*, as in *The Housemaid*, the families of the employer and the servants have been destroyed by the effort to rise within the class hierarchy.

In his commentary, Bong remarks upon how Kim Ki-young created an ambiguous morality in *The Housemaid* through the creation of "monstrous" characters. Initially, the femme fatale housemaid appears as "a foreign substance or monster" because she is a "lower-class woman" who "threatens this middle-aged man who wants to become middle class"; she becomes more fully monstrous when she kills the family's son. The housemaid is not the only such character, however. The demure "wife is monstrous" when she pressures the housemaid to abort her fetus. Women become monstrous, and thus not fully human, when their desires – for sex, for revenge, for status– lead them to violate the norms of submissiveness, chastity, and maternal instinct. Bong sees Kim ascribing the quality of monstrosity only to women: while the husband is "weak," "indecisive," "incapable," and emasculated by the two strong-willed women, he never loses his humanity.

In *Parasite*, Bong translates Kim Ki-young's monstrous women into a verminous family, who appear less than fully human due to their position at the bottom of the class hierarchy. The equation of the Kims with pests begins in the opening scene, when a fumigator inundates their dingy apartment with a cloud of pesticide. Their verminous nature becomes explicit when they celebrate their employment by getting drunk in the Parks' living room. Chung-sook, responding to her husband's boasting, accuses him of being a coward who would "run and hide like a cockroach" if the Parks were to return. When they do return unexpectedly, Ki-taek scuttles under the large coffee table along with his children, where they all lie rigidly flat on their backs. When the Park parents settle into the couch they discuss Ki-taek's body odor, comparing it to the smells of an old radish, a boiled rag, and the subway, thus reinforcing his association with the subterranean and the unclean. Like cockroaches, the Kims share a space with the Parks but remain unseen, physically so in this scene and metaphorically as members of the precariat. Ki-taek eventually crawls out from under the table, only to freeze like an insect in the shadows when the Parks awaken and turn on a light. The film's central verminous metaphor is, of course, its title. Who exactly is the parasite? The Kims clearly are, in that they latch on to the Parks and derive their livelihood from them while deceiving them about their true identities. So is Geun-se, who secretly inhabits the Park's basement for years and eats their food. However, the Parks also engage in parasitical behavior, living comfortably off the labor of the Kims and Moon-gwang, who meet all their domestic needs. As Kim Ki-young does in *The Housemaid*, Bong creates a slippery morality that implicates all the characters and causes the viewer's sympathy to ricochet among them.

Bong expresses admiration for how Kim employed the house as *The Housemaid*'s primary setting and used its "very limited range of places" to conduct a social experiment in which "people from different classes live together." Bong is fascinated by the way Kim created a spatial system that identified different characters with distinct parts of the house, and then destabilized that system by having characters invade spaces not their own. "There are many occasions," Bong notes, "when a character invades some place or other improperly." The husband enters the women's locker room at the factory, the factory workers enter the house uninvited, and the housemaid enters the off-limits piano room and the conjugal bedroom. "Invasion of territory," observes Bong, "is an important theme" and an emotionally unsettling one: "it provides the strongest tension and suspense." Invasion is linked to class, as working-class people violate middle-class spaces, and also to sexuality, as the maid pursues the husband. The theme of invasion is also linked to the idea of the monstrous and the tonal shift toward horror, all of which are visible in the nighttime shots of the housemaid looming outside the glass door of the piano room and frightening the children inside. Ultimately, these acts of invasion across the boundaries of class and normative sexuality erode the foundations of the middle-class family and trigger its collapse.

In *Parasite*, Bong takes up this same challenge of restricted space. He expands Kim's spatial system by splitting his setting across two homes, the design of which visualizes the class divide. The Parks' house, where most of the film is set, echoes that in *The Housemaid*. It is a modern two-story structure with Western-style furniture and modern appliances, updated into a high-modernist mansion. The furnishings are streamlined and elegant, giving the space an uncluttered look, and the polished floors reflect the abundant sunlight streaming in; a lush green yard is visible through a floor-to-ceiling rectangular window in the living room. The Kim family, in contrast, lives in a tiny semi-basement apartment whose cramped and cluttered rooms are suffused with a dim greenish light. A lone window echoes the rectangular shape of the one in the Parks' living room but offers a ground-level view onto a crowded street where drunks urinate. The basement bunker in the Parks' house functions as a third "home." It exaggerates the conditions of the Kims' apartment – it is further underground, smaller in size, receives no daylight at all, and is suffused with an even greener gloom – in keeping with Geun-se's position further down the class hierarchy as an unemployed debtor.

Bong expands *The Housemaid*'s acts of invasion. The Parks' home is invaded not just by one housemaid but by an entire family, whose members disperse themselves into the kitchen, pantry, bedrooms, bathroom, and even the sauna. Because Bong wanted the pivotal scene of Moon-gwang's return to occur at the exact mid-point of the film, he had "to make the poor family . . . complete their invasion in sixty minutes" (Bong 2020). While Ki-woo's and Ki-jung's invasion happens leisurely, the "third invasion for the driver [and the] fourth invasion for the housekeeper goes very quick." The "invasion of the house snatchers," as Bong calls it, culminates in the living room scene, where it takes on a darker tone. As they make free with the Parks' liquor and snacks, the Kims claim the house as their own and fantasize about Ki-woo marrying the Parks' daughter. They become less sympathetic as they get sloppy drunk, breaking a glass and spreading their mess across the pristine room. This scene provokes "tension" in audiences and "makes them nervous," says Bong, "because it's not their house," and he extends the scene's duration to allow the audience's discomfort to grow. As it does, it becomes clear that the "story of this movie is invading other people's private life" through "the erasing of the borderline of privacy and private life between two classes." As in *The Housemaid*, crossing the class line leads to disaster.

Kim Ki-young created a vertical set design for *The Housemaid* whose most prominent feature is the staircase. Bong regards the staircase, which Kim used in over 20 scenes, as "another protagonist" because of its centrality to the film's expressive vocabulary. "The staircase is an exquisite establishment for me," he notes, because it visualizes both the family's desire to ascend the class hierarchy and the ever-changing power relations among the characters. Initially the staircase is "a place of id," because it leads to the second floor where adultery takes place. Later, the "many shots of climbing stairs" become a way to make apparent who has "the upper hand" in the household. For example, the wife climbs the stairs to assert her domestic authority and to demand that the maid abort the baby, which she does by throwing herself down the stairs, while a shot of the maid standing atop the stairs after poisoning the son, who tumbles down them to his death, "describes well that dominating power has moved to the housemaid." Kim heightened the sense of verticality, and the social relations it expressed, through his cinematography. When characters stood at the top or bottom of the stairs, he used an extremely high or low camera angle to increase the sense of height; when characters ascended or descended the stairs, he used a tracking shot combined with an upward or downward tilt to emphasize the sense of movement. For Bong, this combination of staircase and cinematography "is very cinematic" because each successive ascent and descent accrues to create "layers" of meaning. As characters' relationships to each other change, they ascend and descend the stairs. "That," observes Bong, "is the drama of the film."

The set design of *Parasite* owes a good deal to *The Housemaid*, especially its expressive use of stairs. "I really wanted to make a movie very vertical," says Bong. "I called *Housemaid* a 'staircase movie' – *Parasite* is also definitely a movie about stairs." There are about 13 different sets of stairs in Bong's film, at least one of which appears in almost every scene. In the Kims' apartment, steps lead to the toilet and up to the street; in the Parks' house, there are stairs from the street to the front door, from the front door to the yard, from the garage to the first floor, from the living room to the dining/kitchen area, from the first floor to the second floor, from the kitchen to the basement pantry, and from the pantry down to the bunker; there are also four long staircases separating the Parks' hilltop mansion from the Kims' below-ground apartment. *Parasite* is constructed along a vertical axis, which expresses its core ideas of class hierarchy and inequality. Bong uses his staircases in a more binary fashion than did Kim Ki-young. In the first half of the film, the Kims generally climb up stairs as their economic fortunes improve, beginning with Ki-woo's departure from the semi-basement apartment for his job interview and culminating in the arrival of all the Kims on the second floor of the Parks' house. In the second half of the film, the Kims generally go down the stairs, starting with their descent into the basement bunker when they discover Geun-se and culminating in their return to the semi-basement at the film's conclusion.

The most celebrated use of staircases in *Parasite* comes with Ki-taek, Ki-woo, and Ki-jung's nighttime journey back to their apartment during the torrential downpour. In a spectacular ten-minute sequence that launches the film's third act, they go down, down, down – reversing their previous upward climb. The sequence begins when, after scuttling out from underneath the coffee table, they descend the hill outside the Parks' house, their movement captured in a low-angle shot that emphasizes the steepness of the street and reverses an earlier shot that captured Ki-joon's initial ascent for his interview. A series of static shots track their movement through the city as they descend sloping streets, a tunnel, and three long sets of stairs. The rain accentuates their downward movement as it flows down the stairs, falls in sheets from above, inundates their street, and finally pours into their apartment through an open window. As they make their downward journey, they cross a series of "lines" on the ground – a drainage grate, a stair step – that mark their return across the class divide and back into a space of poverty they believed they had escaped. Here, in the bottom of Seoul, all the qualities of the Parks' hilltop home are reversed: sunshine is replaced by night, dry comfort by wet misery, and private interior space by public exterior space. The descent returns them to their verminous selves, as Bong captures them in extreme long shots that render them like tiny insects scurrying for cover. It is Bong's more elaborate version of the final scene of *The Housemaid*, in which the dying maid is slowly, painfully dragged headfirst down the stairs by the staggering, poisoned husband. The descent visualizes the Kims' social and economic debasement, as they are expelled from their temporary habitation in the land of the rich.

Bong reproduces and modifies Kim Ki-young's expressive cinematography. *The Housemaid* deploys two signature camera movements: a lateral tracking shot that follows the maid and the husband as they move along the balcony connecting the husband's piano room and the maid's bedroom and that suggests their sexual relationship, and a forward/backward tracking shot that accentuates characters' movement up and down the staircase. *Parasite* features two similar camera movements. Bong uses a bold lateral pan in place of a cut to follow a character's movement or to link two characters in a dialogue scene. He uses a more subtle descending crane/boom shot as the equivalent of Kim's tracking shots to emphasize verticality. Bong introduces this movement in the opening shot. The shot begins with the camera looking out the window of the Kims' semi-basement apartment onto a cluttered alley; after a few moments the camera slowly descends to reveal Ki-woo staring at his cell phone as he discovers that they have lost access to their neighbor's Wi-Fi. As the camera moves downward, it crosses a strong horizontal line created by the alignment of the window frame with the surface of the road. This downward motion across a static horizontal line powerfully expresses the film's core ideas. It conveys a sense of both hierarchy and descent, as the camera moves from one clearly demarcated space above the line, which is suffused with sunlight, to a second demarcated space that is considerably darker. Ki-woo is entirely contained within this bottom space, which introduces the idea that the Kims occupy a social and economic space "below" others. Bong repeats this distinctive shot at least six more times, all of them after the pivot point of Mon-gwang's return that redirects the Kims' movement from ascent to descent. We see it, for instance, in the living room scene: the shot begins centered on the Parks as they sit on the couch in their spacious living room, then drops across the horizontal line formed by the top of the coffee table, and settles on Ki-taek as he lies rigid in the tiny space underneath. The combination is repeated when the Kims descend the stairs into their neighborhood during the rain storm, as they try to sleep in the public shelter after the flood, as Ki-taek and Mr. Park crouch behind the bushes in their Indian headdresses at the birthday party, and in the final shot of the film, which duplicates the opening shot and reveals Ki-woo once again sitting in the semi-basement, with the same hanger of socks cluttering the frame. This vertical drop across a horizontal line is an essential pattern in the film's cinematography and visual design, and more than any other camera movement in the film it communicates the sense of rigid class hierarchy that forms the intellectual heart of the film.

What is at stake in seeing *Parasite* as a makeover of *The Housemaid*? In an essay about Hollywood filmmakers of the 1960s and 1970s, many of whom Bong greatly admires, Robert Kolker makes some observations that apply equally well to *Parasite*. Kolker observes that post-classical directors – such as Martin Scorsese, founder of the World Cinema Project, which helped restore *The Housemaid* – had a highly developed awareness of film history that they manifested in their own work "by alluding to and quoting from other films" (Kolker 1998, 35). While all artists "learn from, copy from, and expand upon the work of their predecessors," those who identify as modernists to one degree or another take this a step further: for them, "a 'new' text is built from the appropriation and accretion of other texts" (Kolker 1998, 37). Post-classical directors were in this sense modernists: rejecting the invisible style of classical Hollywood, they "did not want to hide the genesis of their films or suppress the fact that films come not from life or from an abstract convention of 'reality' but from other films." In other words, their films announced that movies come from other movies. Two things follow from this. First, it increased the pleasures of spectatorship. These directors sought "to provoke the audience into recognizing film history, and in doing so pleased the viewer by asking for her response and her knowledge." Second, this awareness of film history changed the viewer's understanding of the film's style. For Kolker, this "cinema of allusion" serves to "inscribe the markings of an individual style by recalling the style of an admired predecessor." This is "a subtle means of giving depth to a film, broadening its base, adding resonance to its narrative and a sense of play, and, through all of this, increasing narrative pleasure" (Kolker 1998, 36). In other words, these gestures toward film history deepened viewers' appreciation of a film's narrative and cinematic form by allowing them to recognize a set of associations carried over from earlier films. As a cinephile director himself, Bong's allusions to and quotations of *The Housemaid* work similarly, inviting the audience into Korean film history and allowing them to expand their own mental VHS libraries.

Parasite's allusive style also helps to reconstruct Korean film history. John Biguenet writes that "the function of allusion has most often served the essential task of investing a work of literature with a lineage, a tradition, quite literally a context, within which an interpretation may be grounded" (Biguenet 1998, 131). By claiming Kim Ki-young as his mentor and "making over" his most celebrated film, Bong is strengthening a lineage within Korean film history. Korea has a somewhat discontinuous film history in which today's commercial auteurs have often looked outward for inspiration to other cinemas, typically Hollywood, rather than mining previous eras of their own national cinema, such as the Golden Age of the mid-1950s to early 1970s. With *Parasite,* Bong is establishing a creative genealogy that ostentatiously connects the Korean Wave cinema to the Golden Age. He is creating a lineage, an aesthetic tradition, that is based not just on recurring stories and characters, but also on the evolution of film style, including plot structure, set design, the use of space, and cinematography.

Seeing *Parasite* as a makeover of *The Housemaid* also highlights the role of film preservation in the construction of a national film tradition. Kolker asserts that "in a basic, material way, modernism demands that the works of imagination remain viable and usable, that they exist as the seeds of other works" (Kolker 1998, 39). Until it was restored by KOFIC and the World Cinema Project, *The Housemaid* did not exist as part of a "usable" past "in a basic, material way": it was not easily accessible as a complete and legible film. This was the case with many Golden Age films prior to the creation by the Korean Film Archive of the Korean Movie Database in 2006, which has a VOD streaming service, and the Korean Classic Film YouTube channel in 2011. *The Housemaid* only became fully available for Bong to remake, and for audiences to recognize Bong's film as a remake, once it had been restored and made widely available. This is why Bong's DVD commentary on the film is so important: it reveals an early step in his creative process whereby he breaks down an existing film in order to make its parts available to himself for appropriation and allusion in a new creative work. Through this process of breakdown and reconstruction, Bong is able to update Kim's formal inventiveness in a way that creates a stylistic continuity across a gap of six decades and that links together the two most important periods in Korean film history. *Parasite* demonstrates that *hallyu* can learn from Golden Age cinema, as well as from Hollywood.

References

Biguenet, John. 1998. "Double Takes." In *Play It Again, Sam: Retakes on Remakes*, edited by Andrew Horton and Stuart Y. McDougal, 131–43. Berkeley: University of California Press.

Bong, Joon-ho. 2009. "Commentary." *The Housemaid*. DVD. Directed by Kim Ki-young. KOFIC and Bluekino.

———. 2020. "Commentary." *Parasite*. DVD. Directed by Bong Joon-ho. Criterion Collection.

Chang, Justin. 2020. "Golden Globes; A Night for Revelry as Well as Reflection; 'Parasite' Filmmaker Bong Joon Ho Calls Out Hollywood's Stubborn Myopia." *Los Angeles Times,* January 7, 2020. *ProQuest*. Web.

Horton, Andrew. 1998. "Cinematic Makeovers and Cultural Border Crossings." In *Play It Again, Sam: Retakes on Remakes*, edited by Andrew Horton and Stuart Y. McDougal, 172–90. Berkeley: University of California Press.

Kolker, Robert. 1998. "Algebraic Figures." In *Play It Again, Sam: Retakes on Remakes*, edited by Andrew Horton and Stuart Y. McDougal, 34–51. Berkeley: University of California Press.

Mintzer, Jordan. 2019. "Bong Joon-ho Talks True Crime, Steve Buscemi, Unlikely Success of 'Parasite'." *The Hollywood Reporter*, October 18, 2019. https://www.hollywoodreporter.com/news/general-news/bong-joon-ho-parasite-success-true-crime-steve-buscemi-1248655/.

Oscars. n.d. "Bong Joon Ho Wins Best Director." *YouTube Video*. https://www.youtube.com/watch?v=ekMl5VHBH4I.

Raup, Jordan. 2019. *Bong Joon Ho on Family and Class in Parasite, Collecting Films, and Memories of Murder*. Film at Lincoln Center. https://www.filmlinc.org/daily/bong-joon-ho-on-family-and-class-in-parasite-collecting-films-and-memories-of-murder/.

Sohn, Hee-jeong, and Jung Yijung. 2021. "Gender in 'Korean Reality'." *Azalea: Journal of Korean Literature & Culture* 14: 289–310.

26

MELTING THE IRON CURTAIN

Political Immediacy, Metal-morphosis, and
the Caricatured Western Leaders in Agitprop
Animation in Socialist China, 1949–65

Daisy Yan Du

Socialist China under the leadership of Chairman Mao was often regarded as a period of closure, isolated from the rest of the world due to Cold War ideologies. As Michael Berry observes, the West (mainly America) almost acted like an absence in socialist live-action cinema after the eruption of the Korean War (1950–53). In films like *Shanggan ling* (Shanggan Ridge, 1956) and *Yingxiong ernü* (Heroic Sons and Daughters, 1964), American soldiers only assume a phantom existence, appearing and disappearing quickly without uttering a word on the battlefields. In the model opera film *Qixi Baihu tuan* (Raid on the White Tiger Regiment, 1972), American officials, played by Chinese actors with heavy makeup, are more visible, but their characterization is very flat due to anti-imperialism discourse at that time. Even after China began its cultural interactions with America in the late 1970s and early 1980s, America was still framed by "tropes of absence, distance, and invisibility" in Chinese films like *Lushan lian* (Love on Lushan, 1980) and *Muma ren* (The Herdsman, 1982) (Berry 2012, 553). Berry suggests a practical and ideological reason for this strategy of absence: (1) Chinese filmmakers could not afford to pay the high cost of American actors and location shooting in America, and (2) America was regarded as the imperialist enemy in socialist China and there was reluctance to acknowledge its presence (Berry 2012, 569).

When live-action films failed to represent the significant Other, animation seized the opportunity, represented the unrepresentable, and even dramatized it on screen. Prior, there had never been so many Chinese animated films portraying the capitalist West (especially America), which led to the rise of the international motif film genre (*guoji ticai pian*). As such, animation returned to its primitive role as special effects to achieve what live-action films could not do at the time.[1] The animated films that dared to show the Other allowed us to see how the capitalist West was imagined and visualized and to understand the Cold War culture from the unique perspective of animated cartoons.

Interestingly, the international motif film emerged almost simultaneously with the National Style in the late 1950s and early 1960s, when Chinese animation returned to traditional Chinese arts, folklore, and literature after emulating the Soviet style in the 1950s. While the National Style film featured folklore and legends rooted in the past, the international motif film captured contemporary international affairs like a snapshot. In terms of formal style, the National Style beheld a painterly quality, with elaborate background

DOI: 10.4324/9781003266952-35

and meticulously designed characters inspired by traditional Chinese arts and aesthetics, while the international motif exhibited a modernist style, with minimal to no background, simplified and abstract cartoonish characters with just a few lines, and even still images, tables, and charts. Whereas the National Style film demonstrated a Chineseness, the international motif film tended to be de-Sinicized and exotic in both form and content (Du 2019, 125–28).

The international motif film has long been neglected in Chinese animation studies, which are preoccupied with National Style films, such as those done in ink-painting and papercutting animation that articulated a distinct Chinese aesthetics and identity. Foregrounding the genre of international motif film and the frequent caricature of Western leaders represented in these films, this chapter argues that the coldness of the Cold War ironically triggered an unprecedented, heated imagination of the West that melted the Iron Curtain, generating a Cold War Occidentalism, or the over-presence of the West in socialist animation.

Agitprop Animation

Many international motif films were agitprop animation, made quickly as propaganda in response to proximate international affairs. Animated filmmaking is labor-intensive and time-consuming; thousands of drawings with slight variations need to be photographed and animated frame by frame. As such, animation is often regarded as an unsuitable medium for portraying recent news and events as it takes too long to produce. In addition, animation is usually regarded as an art form of fantasy and thus a poor fit to portray pressing nonfiction events. Due to those factors, many Chinese animated films were about folklore, legends, fables, parables, and fairytales, fantastic and timeless stories that could be made without any urgency.

Chinese animation took on a new life in socialist China when animators began making many animated films in immediate response to current domestic and international political events, with the purpose of mobilizing the masses to participate in political campaigns and internalize communist ideologies. They called this new type of animation *zhengzhi gudong pian* (political agitprop animated film), *xuanchuan gudong pian* (propaganda agitprop animated film), or *manhua xuanchuan pian* (cartoon/caricature propaganda animated film). Often made with political urgency, these films usually adopted a minimalist style with simplified outlines and backgrounds. They frequently drew on the visual style of cartoons, caricatures, and posters and used many still pictures, photos, images, and even tables and charts to save time. Passionate voice-over narrations, slogans, mood music, and other sound effects were used to reinforce the direct political message. Although the contents, such as the characters, stories, and backgrounds, were based on recent events, they were frequently represented as exaggerated and distorted to such a degree that they became highly fantastic, magic, and satirical – a perfect combination of realism and fantasy. Collaged this way, many films lacked a coherent and well-crafted tight storyline, seeming more fragmentary and improvisatory. Likewise, commonly without clearly defined protagonists and antagonists, these films did not have the in-depth characterization that could lead to audience identification. Unlike the ordinary socialist animated films that targeted children, the target audience for agitprop animated films was adults who could understand the sophisticated political messages.

Agitprop animation was often regarded as a new genre that was born during the Great Leap Forward (1958–60), especially as the form emphasized speedy production, or a great leap forward, in animated filmmaking. With the making of a cel-animated film titled *Gan Yingguo* (Overtaking England, 1958), animators inaugurated a new genre in Chinese animation, including but not limited to *Bayue shiwu qing fengshou* (Celebrating the Harvest during the Mid-Autumn Festival, 1958), *Gechang zong luxian* (Praising the General Line, 1958), and *Da yuejin wansui* (Long Live the Great Leap Forward, 1959).

Departing from the agitprop animated films of the late 1950s about domestic matters (the Great Leap Forward in particular), agitprop animation of the early 1960s revolved around international issues (international motif film), especially American imperialism. Some of these films include *Yuanxing bilu* (Showing True Colors, 1960), *Yazhou renmin nuzhu wenshen* (The Asian People Expelling the God of Plague in Anger, 1961), *Zhichi Duomi'nijia renmin fandui wuqi qinlue* (Support Dominicans' Struggle against Military Invasion, 1965), *Zhichi Yuenan renmin dadao meiguo qinlue zhe* (Support Vietnamese's Struggle against American Imperialists, 1965), *Jiechuan Meidi hetan pianju* (Exposing the Peace Talk Swindle of American Imperialism, 1965), and *Weida de shengming* (A Great Statement, 1968).

In China in the early 1960s, a fantastic art form (animation) was used in a realistic way to document immediate political events and feature the capitalist West. At this same time, in America, a realist art form (television documentary) was used in a fantastic way (the adoption of Hollywood narrative and filmmaking strategies) to portray the communist Other (Curtin 1995, 177–96). In both cases, the ideological Other existed not only as a material and political reality, but also as a construct manipulated by different representational mechanisms.

Metamorphosis and Metal-morphosis in Early Agitprop Animation

Although international-motif agitprop animation flourished in the late 1950s and early 1960s, there were already early experiments of it in the late 1940s – when the Communist Party started its own film industry at the Northeast Film Studio in Changchun. To mobilize the masses, especially the People's Liberation Army, to fight against the Nationalist troops under the leadership of Chiang Kai-shek, Chinese animators made *Huangdi meng* (Dreaming to Be an Emperor, November 1947) and *Wengzhong zhuobie* (Capturing the Turtle in the Jar, December 1948), which were based on Hua Junwu's political caricature. *Dreaming to Be an Emperor* was a puppet animated film that criticized Chiang Kai-shek for bartering away the sovereignty of China to obtain weapons and support from the American government. *Capturing the Turtle in the Jar* portrays how Chiang Kai-shek, empowered by American weapons, is finally captured like a turtle by the triumphant People's Liberation Army (PLA) during the Civil War. These films were often screened for the PLA soldiers to marshal their fighting spirits right before they launched the battles against the Nationalists.[2]

Both *Dreaming to Be an Emperor* and *Capturing the Turtle in the Jar* frame America as the evil backstage manipulator of Chiang Kai-shek and the Civil War in China. They severely criticize America for its military support of the Nationalist Party in annihilating the communists. The American leaders are always depicted in military uniforms, stamped with words like "Marshall" and "US" or the symbol of an eagle, which clearly marks them as American. They are usually fat and robust, dwarfing the thin and small-figured Chiang Kai-shek. Aggressive, arrogant, condescending, and greedy, they often dominate the timorous Chiang Kai-shek and usurp the sovereignty of China. Based on cartoonist Hua Junwu's drawings, the images of these American leaders are caricatured, exaggerated, and distorted with a comic twist.

The American leaders are often metonymically associated with metals and machines, thereby giving them a privileged hard edge in international relations. In *Dreaming to Be an Emperor*, when Chiang Kai-shek is in the dressing room, Marshall brings him a gift basket filled with metal weapons (military aircraft, tanks, and cannons) and gold coins. In exchange, Chiang Kai-shek gives Marshall the Sino-US Friendship and Mutual Assistance Treaty, signed by him on November 4, 1946. The treaty grants the US many privileges and benefits at the cost of China's sovereignty and dignity. When the transaction is done, Marshall assists Chiang to dress up as an emperor. Marshall sprays a special perfume (Democracy Brand, made in USA) on Chiang and gives him a smiling mask, which has a metal quality as well. Masqueraded by George Marshall, Chiang Kai-shek is transformed into a Peking opera emperor who is to perform on stage.

It is in the cel-animated *Capturing the Turtle in the Jar* that American leaders transform themselves into metals and achieve metal-morphosis during the Cold War. The film begins with an American military leader smoking a pipe in front of the iron gated military camp, stamped with a "Sino-American Cooperative Organization" sign. He is obese, tall, and robust, with a murderous look. Chiang Kai-shek, who is overshadowed by the American leader, wears a black cloak and approaches him cautiously. He bows to the American official and presents a scroll of paper to him with both of his hands. The American leader grabs the paper condescendingly and impatiently. The paper is a map of China, written with the words "the sovereignty of China." The American leader happily shakes hands with Chiang Kai-shek and opens the gate for him. Chiang Kai-shek takes off his hat, bows to him, and squeezes himself into the military camp. Later when Chiang Kai-shek is about to be defeated by the People's Liberation Army, the American leader watches with his telescope, transforms himself into a transport aircraft (Figure 26.1), and drops military supplies with parachutes to the Nationalists. His metal-morphosis represents America's shift to an iron fist diplomacy to coerce communism in the world.

In Chinese agitprop animated films of the Cold War, only men and powerful countries can achieve such metal-morphosis. Gender and nation interlock with each other in the discourse of power and domination. In a different context, Rosi Braidotti observes that in mainstream culture, the man is privileged to meta(l)morphoses into a machine, but "the woman seldom if ever metamorphoses into a machine," even in texts written by women themselves (Braidotti 2002, 234). This kind of literal and symbolic metal-morphosis can be

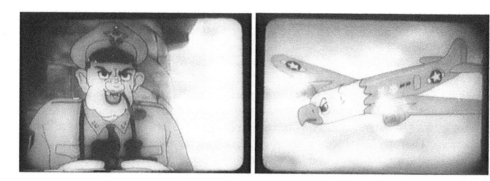

Figure 26.1 The American leader transforms into a transport aircraft, *Capturing the Turtle in the Jar*, 1948.

dramatized in cel animation, a form that indulges in the violent transformation of outlines and body forms.

While the American leader's metal-morphosis suggests the hegemonic power of the American state, Chiang Kai-shek's metamorphosis into a degrading animal indicates the decline of the Nationalist Party. Metals and animals are thus positioned in a hierarchy of power relations. After the American leader, in the form of a transport aircraft, drops military supplies, Chiang Kai-shek and his soldiers eagerly grab these American weapons and try to fight back, but only to be defeated by the PLA soldiers. Chiang Kai-shek diminishes and transforms himself into a turtle, while the pillbox where he is hiding shrinks into his shell. A PLA soldier, whose size is now magnified and looks monumental, steps on the shell, and grabs him by the neck. By becoming a turtle, Chiang Kai-shek and the Nationalist Party are devalued into lesser beings. Only the PLA soldiers, what I call the "sublime figure of (in)animation," remain human and intact throughout the film. They cannot be over-animated with the animation principle of movement and plasmaticness, because to be animated means to be depowered. In contrast, America is becoming metal (metal-morphosis) and the Nationalist Party is becoming animal (metamorphosis). The violent bodily changes, whether elevating (metal-morphosis) or degrading (metamorphosis), are frequently channeled to the dehumanized and inhuman Other, whose political agency and power decrease with their increased physical movements and emotions (Du 2022).

The Metal-morphosis of American Presidents

American presidents frequently appeared in agitprop animated films in the first half of the 1960s. They were criticized for the oppression of their own people and their military aggression in the so-called Third World. They assumed unprecedented visibility in Chinese animated films, albeit, in reality, they were absent in China until President Richard Nixon's official visit in 1972. Among these international motif agitprop animated films, *Showing True Colors* (1960) was probably the most representative one. It was made in immediate response to President Dwight Eisenhower's Far East Trip (12–26 June 1960), which was conducted before he resigned in January 1961. Eisenhower planned to visit Japan, South Korea, the Philippines, and Taiwan, but he canceled his travel to Japan at the last minute due to the anti-American riots led by the Communist Party there. Eisenhower's Far East Trip, especially his state visit to Taiwan on 18–19 June, aroused great indignation in socialist China. *The People's Daily*, the mouthpiece of the Chinese communist government, published numerous essays to criticize Eisenhower's infringement of the sovereignty of China. As a special way to "welcome" and "see off" Eisenhower, dubbed by the Chinese Communist Party as the "God of Plague," Chairman Mao even ordered his armies in Fujian province to bombard Kinmen in Taiwan on the days when the American president came and left.

In this film, the American leader is again associated with metals and machines. At the beginning of the film, TV assumes a very prominent role for Eisenhower. In his office, Eisenhower is examining his military bases that surround the red communist areas on a world map. He then turns on the TV and sees footage from Asia in which many Asians are chasing an American soldier. He is soon surrounded by many red hands and cries for help. In Africa, local people are shown carrying two Western colonizers like pigs. Eisenhower turns off the TV in anger, and his face turns blue. He goes to sleep but is soon awoken, only to turn the TV on again and see the local people throwing tomatoes at Americans in Latin America. Eisenhower faints and collapses.

Eisenhower's connection with TV comes as no surprise because his presidency witnessed the greatest growth of television in American history. When he became the president in 1953, the percentage of Americans who had TVs was around 30%; the number increased to almost 70% when he was reelected in 1956 and to around 90% when he resigned in 1961. Eisenhower regarded TV as a breakthrough in American enterprise and was deeply aware of the societal transformations being brought about by TV. Labeled as a "TV president," TV became Eisenhower's most important means of communication (Allen 1993, 189). In the animated film, it is through TV that Eisenhower learns what is happening in the Communist world. Although at that time, the Soviet Union surpassed America in terms of rocket technology with the launch of Sputnik in 1957, it lagged far behind America in TV technology and industry (Allen 1993, 167). Fascinated by it, TV was the new machine that Americans took pride in. Across the way, socialist China largely used sound and radio to disseminate its messages to the whole world.

In *Showing True Colors*, China is represented by a monumental radio tower with a shining red star on its top, shown in the background of Tiananmen Square brightened by glamorous firework displays. With its radiating light, the disembodied voice of China reaches the White House and shocks Eisenhower. Eisenhower then begins his metamorphosis in the restroom, the place where women apply makeup. Realizing that overt military coercion of communism with military bases might fail, he decides to change himself and his foreign policies. He picks up a brush and bottle of paint (Peace Brand) and paints himself until he is covered in white paint from head to toe. Like a woman, he powders his face and sprays perfume on his body. He examines himself in the mirror and learns that his face has become a blank sheet of paper without features, so, like a geisha, he picks up a pencil and draws his eyes, nose, wrinkles, hair, and a smile. Crying *"heping"* ("peace") with a high-pitched feminine voice, he happily dances in the restroom until he is disrupted by the China "we want real peace" broadcast by the red star on top of the radio tower.

Eisenhower metamorphoses into a lesser being, a peaceful womanish figure, similar to Chiang Kai-shek's transformation into a degraded Peking opera emperor in the dressing room in *Dreaming to Be an Emperor*. The difference is that while Eisenhower makes the transformation all by himself, Chiang Kai-shek achieves his metamorphosis only through the assistance of America. With this new face and identity, Eisenhower's foreign policy also changes into "fake peace, true war preparation" and becomes de-metalized and de-militarized. With an olive branch in hand, he flies gracefully like a dove over the White House and Wall Street and ties the olive branch with a white ribbon on American cannons (Figure 26.2). When he sees American tanks marching on the ground, he scatters white powder and they become immobile. He touches American ships and submarines and cries "peace," and they soon disappear and hide underwater.

However, Eisenhower's cries for peace soon end when he becomes "metal" again. Riding on an American plane with a telescope, he sees the red star on top of the tower radiating with white lights. He transforms himself into a black U-2 spy plane and keeps taking photos with his camera until he is intercepted by a red plane. This alludes to a historical event in which an American U-2 spy plane briefly and successfully invaded Soviet airspace, and was later shot down and the pilot was captured alive by the Soviet Air Defense Forces on 1 May 1960. Eisenhower falls to the ground and becomes a savage, ripping his shirt to reveal a skull on his chest and begins to fight back. At the same time, Soviet, Japanese, and African people are roaring and shouting, "Down with American imperialism." Eisenhower is then forced to flee back to his office, right in front of the world map. The film then ends

Figure 26.2   Eisenhower ties the olive branch with a white ribbon on American cannons, *Showing True Colors*, 1960.

with the red star radiating with white light, while the people in the world, such as Africans and Latin Americans, march forward arm in arm.

Unlike America which is often portrayed as a metalized threat, Great Britain is imagined with contempt and ridicule. The agitprop animated film *Catching up with England* (1958) was made by a group of young and relatively inexperienced animators in immediate response to the communist government's slogan of "Catching up with England in Fifteen Years" during the Great Leap Forward. To better capture the spirit of the age, animators watched numerous news documentaries about the Great Leap Forward (Xu, Yan, and Qu 1958, 28). The film begins with a young, robust, and energetic male giant worker, who wears a white shirt and a red overall, with the characters "China" written on his chest. He represents the Chinese people, who are roaring a song collectively and passionately: "Let high mountains lower their heads; let the seas make way; let iron and steel obey; let England lag behind! Let's catch up with England in 15 years!" John Bull, a fat and short English gentleman wearing a bowler hat printed with the national flag of England, enters the scene riding a cow. John Bull is old and extremely slow, even portrayed with gray, a color associated with sunset and decline, while the young Chinese giant is depicted mainly in red, a color linked with the rising sun and youth. When he hears the collective and passionate slogan sung by the Chinese people, John Bull panics but soon composes himself by humming a song to himself: "My industry has a hundred years' history; my products have both quality and quantity; if others want to catch up with me, they need at least 100 years!"

In comparison to how America is linked with metals and machines capable of metal-morphosis, Great Britain is associated with an animal, the bull, and is portrayed as incapable of metal-morphosis. The film depicts a fierce competition between the Chinese giant and John Bull, with the Chinese giant winning the game. John Bull first shows off some industrial products such as reactive dyes and tires, and challenges the Chinese giant, "Do you have this?" In the end, John Bull admits, "Oh, they have them all." He then shows off a map of coal production in England, and the Chinese giant responds by extracting coal, which piles up quickly and buries John Bull. After more arguing, a fearful John Bull sees the Chinese giant riding a big red horse and marching toward him. He packs up his stuff and slowly rides on his cow to escape. While shouting, "China is marching forward," the Chinese giant's horse is transformed into a motorcycle and then a rocket. Holding a red flag, he soon catches up with John Bull and leaves him far behind.

Here, China achieves metal-morphosis for its rapid progress in industries. Contrary to the American leaders who undergo metal-morphosis, the Chinese leader (the giant worker) does not change his human body form, because as a "sublime figure of (in)animation," he must keep his bodily inviolability, which stands for socialist integrity and dignity. It is his transportation vehicles that undergo metal-morphosis. While metal-morphosis is generally associated with empowerment, the American metal-morphosis is portrayed as a threat while the Chinese one as a positive and celebratory force. In sharp contrast, the British leader John Bull, metonymically associated with the extremely slow, old, and feminized cow, is incapable of metal-morphosis, suggesting the conservatism, inflexibility, and the stagnation of industrial progress in England.

A Feast of Metal: Cannibalistic Imperialism

In addition to the types of animated films discussed earlier, there emerged a new subgenre called *zhengzhi fengci pian* (politically satirical animated film) during the socialist decades. This new subgenre held similarities to agitprop animation except rather than depicting real political events and historical figures, it was more focused on fictional characters and stories, albeit they were set against the backdrop of current affairs. Consequently, the latter type of film, due to its fictionality, usually had a more coherent and complete storyline and clearly defined protagonists and antagonists and in-depth characterization that led to audience identification. While the former type of film demonstrated a political immediacy and was often made quickly, the latter indeed referred to current political events as well but was made with careful artistic and thematic planning and deliberation. This is because the functions of the two kinds of films were different: political agitprop animation aimed to create direct propaganda messaging to mobilize the masses into action using elements like slogan voice over narrators, and politically satirical animation focused more on exposure, satire, and criticism with veiled political messages. The two types of films both mainly targeted an adult audience. Many animated films featuring the capitalist West, such as *Longxia* (Lobsters, 1959), *Huangjin meng* (The Dream of Gold, 1963), *Gezi* (The Pigeon, 1960), and *Shei chang de zuihao* (Who Sings the Best, 1958), belong to the category of *zhengzhi fengci pian*.

The Dream of Gold (1963) is about international relations during the Cold War. The first half of the film is about the relations among capitalist countries in the West, while the second half is about the relations between the biggest five capitalist countries and the rest of the world. Based on the caricature style of Hua Junwu's political cartoons, *The Dream of Gold* was often called *manhua shi de donghua pian* (cartoon-like animated film), characterized by plasmaticness, exaggeration, distortion, and satire. It was cel-animated and therefore demonstrated much greater fluidity in terms of outlines, character images, the transformation of body forms, and storylines, with minimalized backgrounds.

The relationship among Western capitalist countries is characterized by fierce monetary competition, which is portrayed through violent metal-morphosis. The film takes place in the Empire of Gold Coins – the capitalist West. The beginning of the film shows a bag full of gold coins, which gradually metamorphoses into a fat gentleman, who wears black suit, a high bowler hat, and sunglasses, with a walking cane and a cigar in his mouth. He is the persona of the United States. Each capitalist country is represented by a gentleman who transforms from a bag of gold coins. They all drive a car and arrive at the Club of the Empire of Gold Coins, which is the life-or-death arena for them. They politely greet each other by patting their own stomachs, which are full of gold coins and thus produce a metal sound. To become a member of the club, they need to be of or over a certain weight, that is, if they have enough gold coins. If not, they will be thrown out immediately. The fattest and the heaviest one is the persona of the United States, who is so heavy that he breaks the scale. When these qualified gentlemen/capitalist countries enter the club in order, they begin to do warm-up exercises in the club's gym. When the clock strikes noon, Manager Egg (a caricature of President Kennedy), the boss of the club, blows the whistle and kicks off the duels among these gentlemen. This fighting sequence, although bloodless, is very violent. Using all kinds of weapons, such as swords, scissors, and boxing gloves, these gentlemen exert themselves in killing each other. If a gentleman is wounded and defeated by his rival, he dies and is transformed into metals, or a pile of gold coins in this case. Manager Egg throws away the victims' clothes and collects all the corpses/gold coins. When time is up at 6:00 p.m., only the five strongest kings remain. They are then qualified to have a sumptuous dinner, feasting on the dead gentlemen's bodies, or gold coins (Figure 26.3).

The cannibalistic metal dinner sequence depicts the greed of Western capitalist countries and the internal competition, strife, annexation, and uneven distribution of wealth and interests among them. The five strongest kings are served gold coins stir-fried by General Cannon and blood wine prepared by Mr. Mosquito in the kitchen. The gentleman in the middle, the persona of the US, has a lion's share of the food. The gentleman on the right corner of the table is served with the smallest amount of gold coins. He tries to steal some metal food from the plate of his neighbor but is intercepted in time by his vigilant neighbor. Although they are all gluttonous, they still have different table manners. One eats slowly and chews carefully, followed by a sip of blood wine, while others eat more quickly and

Figure 26.3 The winners are eating the gold coins, transformed from the killed ones, *The Dream of Gold*, 1963.

greedily. The most impatient and wolfish eater is the king of the United States, who, not even bothering to use utensils, holds the plate with his hands and pours the gold coins directly into his big mouth. His voracious appetite symbolizes the super metal virility of the country he represents.

The five strongest kings/countries still feel hungry after devouring all the metals and blood wines, so they embark on the journey of colonization outside the Western world to acquire more metals and blood to gratify their gluttonous appetite. Manager Egg orders General Cannon to look for diamonds and Mr. Mosquito to collect more human blood. He also orders a scientist, Dr. Fuddle, to calculate the total number of stars so that they can be divided up by the five kings. Following this, the film becomes a journey of imperialism and colonization on earth and in the sky. The various missions demonstrate the wolfish greed of capitalist countries to colonize the earth and the sky with overt military aggression, secret schemes and exploitation, knowledge, and advanced science and technology; however, their imperialist agendas are doomed to fail. Mr. Cannon is frozen and buried by the snow while digging native land for diamonds. Mr. Mosquito is discovered by the native people and wounded. Dr. Fuddle flees. The five kings' cannibalistic desire to devour the diamonds/stars and gold coin/the moon turns out to be a dream.

Conclusion: Cold War Occidentalism

The Cold War did not mean the freezing, isolation, or delay of information between communist and capitalist blocks. Rather, the "cold" relationship ironically sped up the flow of information and heated up the imagination between the two camps. In the late 1940s and 1950s, there was a tremendous fascination with Asia in American middlebrow cultural productions, generating a kind of "Cold War Orientalism" (Klein 2003, 4). In the early 1960s, the "golden age" of American television documentaries emerged, featuring the communist Other prominently to promote Cold War ideology and awaken Americans to their "global responsibilities," ironically at a time when they turned inward by paying more attention to their immediate domestic surroundings (Curtin 1995, 2–3). In the other hemisphere across the Iron Curtain, indeed, the capitalist West seemed to be a remote, invisible, and abstract enemy far away from people's daily lives. When the West was almost absent in live-action cinema, it saturated socialist animation and imposed its over-presence in socialist China, generating a socialist Occidentalism, even as Chinese animation, conversely, turned inward by promoting the National Style in the late 1950s and early 1960s. The Iron Curtain during the Cold War was melted in socialist animation.

Acknowledgment

The writing and revision of this chapter were funded by the Research Grants Council of Hong Kong (ECS 26400114 and GRF 16601823).

Notes

1 In *Huoshao honglian si* (*The Burning of the Red-Lotus Temple*, Mingxing 1928–31), animation was used to portray swords automatically fighting with each other in the sky, which live-action film could not portray due to the technological limitations. See Zhang (2005). A similar case took place in wartime Japanese live-action film, in which Western enemies were almost absent due to practical and political reasons. When live-action film failed to portray the wartime Other directly, animation,

indeed, represented the unrepresentable more directly. As a result, the West became more visible and prominent in wartime Japanese animated films such as *Momotarō's Sea Eagles* (1943) and *Momotarō's Divine Sea Warriors* (1945).

2 The two films were made by a Japanese animator named Mochinaga Tadahito. For discussions of this Japanese animator and the animation industry in early socialist China, see Du, *Animated Encounters*, 68–113.

References

Allen, Craig. 1993. *Eisenhower and the Mass Media: Peace, Prosperity, and Prime-Time TV*. Chapel Hill/London: The University of North Carolina Press.

Berry, Michael. 2012. "The Absent American: Figuring the United States in Chinese Cinema of the Reform Era." In *A Companion to Chinese Cinema*, edited by Yingjin Zhang, 552–74. Malden, MA: Wiley-Blackwell.

Braidotti, Rosi. 2002. *Metamorphosis: Towards a Materialist Theory of Becoming*. Cambridge: Polity Press.

Curtin, Michael. 1995. *Redeeming the Wasteland: Television Documentary and Cold War Politics*. New Brunswick: Rutgers University Press.

Du, Daisy Yan. 2019. *Animated Encounters: Transnational Movements of Chinese Animation, 1940s–1970s*. Honolulu: University of Hawai'i Press.

———. 2022. "A Theory of Suspended Animation: The Aesthetics and Politics of (E)motion and Stillness." *Discourse: Journal for Theoretical Studies in Media and Culture* 44.1 (Spring): 42–77.

Klein, Christina. 2003. *Cold War Orientalism: Asia in the Middlebrow Imagination, 1945–1961*. Berkeley, Los Angeles, CA/London: University of California Press.

Xu, Jingda, Dingxian Yan, and Jianfang Qu. 1958. "Donghuapian gan yingguo shi zenyang chuang-zuo de [How the Animated Film Catching up With the United Kingdom Was Made]." *Dazhong dianying* [Popular Cinema] (22): 28.

Zhang, Zhen. 2005. "Bodies in the Air: The Magic of Science and the Fate of the Early 'Martial Arts' Film in China." In *Chinese-Language Film: Historiography, Poetics, Politics*, edited by Sheldon Lu and Emilie Yueh-yu Yeh, 52–75. Honolulu: University of Hawai'i Press.

27

THE "MIRRORED" CULTURAL REVOLUTION – THE GEOPOLITICAL MAKING OF APOLITICAL HERO IN CHANG CHEH'S *THE ASSASSIN*

Raymond Tsang

In Hong Kong film historiography, Chang Cheh, as a master of action movies, revolutionized the genre of action movies during the late 1960s. Chang's films broke away from traditional stagy choreography and female-centered cinematic traditions and instead introduced a new sense of masculinity on the screen. Chang's use of violent action sequences developed his own signature "aesthetics of violence" called *yanggang*, or hard masculinity, that captivated the youth culture of Hong Kong at the time. Scholars have studied Chang's films and identified various factors that contributed to their success. David Bordwell's formal analysis (2003) illustrates how Chang's use of the zoom and narrative strategies generates a pulsating effect in response to the turbulent student movements. Other scholars (Lo 2003; Desser 2005; Teo 2009) attribute the success of Chang's heroes to the mid-'60s youth culture, initiated by the counterculture movement in the West, the Cultural Revolution in China and the leftist riots in 1967 Hong Kong. These scholars believe that the aesthetics of violence in Chang's films reflect the violence that was prevalent in the real world. They argue that there is a direct identification relationship between the aesthetics of Chang's films and the world they represent. Young people related their "spirit of rebellion in the territory" to the one on the screen (Desser 2005, 24). The specular framework used by these scholars implies there is an indexical relationship between the aesthetics and the world. Cinema is like a mirror, reflecting what is happening in real life.

Recently, scholars like Man-Fung Yip and Luke White have suggested that the blatant muscular prowess and violence in Chang's films represent "the capitalist subjectivity grounded in the values of individualism, competition and conquest, and ascetic discipline" (Yip 2017, 17). They argue that these themes satisfy the audience with desires, whose origins can be traced back to the Boxer Rebellion of 1900 (White 2015, 94). However, the specular framework used by these scholars oversimplifies the relationship between the reality and aesthetics. In his memoir, Chang expressed no sympathies with the Boxer, demonized as the Boxer bandits (*quan fei*) associated with the Chinese Communists in the Kuomintang historiography.[1]

DOI: 10.4324/9781003266952-36

In the preface of Chang's memoir, Hong Kong film critic Sek Kei provides a different perspective on the relationship between reality and the aesthetic in Chang's films. Sek Kei suggests that the relationship is like a mirrored image, where Chang's films serve not only as a reflection of reality but also as a plane mirror that reverses left to right. According to Sek Kei, Chang launched a "militaristic revolution" (*wu ge*) that aimed to rescue traditional Chinese virtue and culture from the Cultural Revolution (*wen ge*) through masculine heroes on the Hong Kong silver screen (Sek 2002, 12). This indicates that Chang's films do not merely reflect reality but have different ideological workings. Chang's works do not promote youthful rebellion or class struggle in mainland China but rather aim to protect the lost virtue in the face of the Cultural Revolution. For Chang, it was high time to replace Communist culture with traditional Chinese virtues, as he stated, "Now, for heaven's sake, the films in the mainland are going to be extinct because of the Cultural Revolution; it is time for us to replace them" (Chang 1968, 35).

The specular framework used by film scholars attempts to establish a correlation between the film form and sense and the brutal reality. The relationship between cinema and reality is akin to a concentric circle, where the fourth wall of cinema tries to find its reflection in reality. Sek Kei's mirrored image fails to take into account the brutal reality of the Cultural Revolution, which was just as violent as the imagery portrayed in Chang's films. The simplistic correlation between the film aesthetic and reality is insufficient to fully comprehend the complexity of the geopolitical context in which Chang's films were produced. In this paper, I will use my term the "mirrored" cultural revolution to demonstrate the complex nature of the specular formation and its geopolitical structure, particularly in the Cold War context. I will illustrate that the "mirror" is more than a reflection but a site of defensive mechanism of negotiation and battle, orchestrated by Chang, the Shaw Brothers Studio, the colonial government, and the US during the Cold War. The "mirror" is understood within a framework of interrelated power dynamics rather than solely in relation to cinema and its referents. More important, I will demonstrate that the "mirror" is structured from a specific perspective, as a response to the Cultural Revolution taking place in mainland China at the time.

This paper will focus on Chang's 1967 film *Da Ci Ke* or *The Assassin*, which is based on Sima Qian's *Cike liezhuang* (Biographies of Assassins), completed around 94 BC, and is also a direct response to Guo Moruo's play, *Tang di zhi hua* (The Flower of Blood). The latter shares a similar story of assassination and was written by Guo, a Communist archaeologist, historian, politician, poet, and writer. During the War of Resistance against Japan (1937–45), *Tang di zhi hua* was a cultural work aimed at calling for national unification in opposition to Japanese imperialism. Before being a film director, Chang had a political career that involved working with Pan Gongzhan of the CC clique, a powerful fascist faction, and Zhang Dao-fan, an officer of propaganda in the Kuomintang government. He later became a political adviser at the National Defense and an instructor at the Political Warfare Cadres Academy in Taiwan. During his time in Shanghai, Chang saw Guo's play and criticized its portrayal of female-crossing in the play and strongly opposed any emasculated heroes. He waited until the success of his film *The One-armed Swordsman* (1967), to direct his first historical martial arts film, *The Assassin*. The film not only served as a personal response to Guo Moruo's play but also worked as a strategy of cultural containment during the Cold War. However, Chang did not politicize the film, promote the Republic of China, or espouse US imperialism to achieve cultural containment. Instead, the film's heroes are apolitical, distancing away from any kind of collectives, such as family, royal court, government officials, or ministers. The film showcases traditional Chinese virtue through impaired bodies rather than patriotic bodies, action rather than words, now-or-never passion and sacrifice rather than calculation and planning, and film form rather than content.

Collaborative Powers and the 1967 Leftist Riots

Despite Chang's assertion that his films are inherently apolitical and his decision to distance himself away from politics after turning 30 (Chang 1988, 135), his criticism of Guo's play *Tang di zhi hua* and historical costume pictures appears to be rooted in both political and aesthetic concerns. In one of his articles published in Shaw Brothers Studio magazine *Southern Screen*, he claimed that his *yanggang* heroes serve as effective vehicles for promoting the idea of "counter-attacking the Communists and restoring the country" (*fan gong fu guo*) (Chang 1968, 34). These heroes are for combating the Cultural Revolution, which he believed was a continuation of the Westernization of Chinese culture that began during the May Fourth movement (1919). The specular framework provided by Yip Man-fung ignores the biographical and geopolitical concerns mentioned. Yip suggests that the success of Chang's films and the rise of Shaw Brothers Studio can be attributed solely to their willingness to capture "the changing tastes of viewers by producing a string of flashy, youth-oriented musicals" (Yip 2017, 61). The framework ignores the significant fact that the rise of the Shaw Brothers Studio and Chang Cheh's movies is based upon the colonial government–KMT–film industry collaboration.

Prior to the leftist riot in 1967, Shaw Brothers faced stiff competition in Southeast Asia from leftist film studios in Hong Kong. However, the failure of the riots caused the leftist theaters to lose tens of thousands of fans, resulting in five left-wing cinemas incurring heavy losses. Due to the public offensive against labor strikes, workers and leftists' organizations, some top stars, producers and directors from the leftist film studios defected to the pro-Nationalist Hong Kong and Kowloon Free Filmmakers General Association (HKFFGA) ("Now Red Film Stars May Quit" 1969). Additionally, the two main distribution-production companies, Cathay and Shaw Brothers, stopped distributing any films produced by leftist film studios in Malaysia and Singapore (Wong 1969). The decline of rivals allowed Run Run Shaw to expand his movie empire. During the 1967 leftist riots, he suppressed a labor strike and fired more than a hundred workers who participated in it. One of the laborers was allegedly killed brutally by a police officer ("Fearless Shaws Employees" 1967; "No Room" 1967; "Shaws Fired" 1967; "Two Labors" 1967). After the riots, Shaw capitalized on the failure of leftists' unions and labor strikes, and secured exclusive contracts with his artists and workers, as well as exclusive rights to his films.[2] In an interview, he overtly admitted,

> We have no anti-trust law . . . To start with, labor here was in a much better position for our work, while in Singapore there were unions and in our business, it's very difficult to follow the union laws, to make pictures . . . We are making forty pictures a year, and if there is a union the working hours are limited, you know, and with union conditions, we would not be able to make so many pictures.
>
> *(Barnouw 2000, 26)*

Following the 1967 riots, the governor of Hong Kong, Sir David Trench, visited Shaw's Movietown and officiated at a foundation stone laying ceremony. The governor was proud of the expanding film business in Hong Kong and called for modernization of ideas and technology. With the governor's approval, Run Run Shaw stated, "Under the leadership of our Hong Kong governor, we need to build a peaceful, ordered and prosperous Hong Kong; because of this, we will try our best in the film business to expand our highest efforts and carry out our responsibilities" ("Hong Kong Governor" 1968, 7). This highlights the idea that the film business was not just about entertainment business, but it was seen as integral to creating a safe and prosperous Hong Kong. Even though the colonial government did censor Shaw's films, Run Run Shaw always worked closely with the colonial government. As cultural diplomats, Run Run Shaw and Tan Sri Runme Shaw escorted Queen Elizabeth II during her three-day visit to Singapore in 1972. All the cultural, industrial, and phil-anthropic contributions made by the Shaw brothers paid off when Run Run Shaw was appointed Commander of the Order of the British Empire (CBE) in 1974 and was knighted in 1978 by Queen Elizabeth II.

After the leftist riots in 1967, Run Run Shaw collaborated closely with the Kuom-intang government in Taiwan to further the strategy of "counter-attacking Communist and restoring the country." As part of the Chinese Cultural Renaissance (*zhonghua wenhua fuxing yundong*),[3] Shaw Brothers, as the primary convener of supporting the Chinese cul-tural renaissance movement, signed the "Joint Convention for the Support of the Chinese Cultural Renaissance Movement" with the Cathay Organization/MP & GI, Hong Kong Rong Hua Company, and Kong Ngee Company in June 1968. This covenant aimed to aid production from free and independent film companies supported by the Kuomintang government while promising not to buy and distribute films from leftist studios and not to employ any leftist artists who did not claim that they had defected. In August 1967. During the peak of the leftist riots, Run Run Shaw left Singapore for Eastern Europe in August as a member of the Singapore commerce investigation program. Out of the need for the Free World alliance, the program aimed to investigate the economy and lives under Communist authoritarian regimes. He visited the Soviet Union, Denmark, East and West Germany, Czechoslovakia, Austria, Hungary, Yugoslavia, and Bulgaria. Run Run Shaw reported that there was only poverty in Communist countries. "If more people from the Free World visited [behind] the Iron Curtain, the Communist propaganda would never suc-ceed outside the Curtain," he exclaimed ("Understanding the Progressive" 1968, 36–37). As a diplomat-capitalist, Run Run Shaw secured his entertainment empire by collaborating with the colonial government and playing an important role in the Cold War crusade. The Cultural Revolution and the 1967 riots in Hong Kong actually "helped" expand the Shaws' empire. It is not solely because the films can reflect the aesthetics of violence in Hong Kong, but during the Cultural Revolution, the directors, capitalists in Hong Kong, colonizers, reactionary regimes in the region, and the Cold War hegemons ensured their own "cultural revolution" as part of the strategy of containment.

Sacrifice and Apolitical Heroism

Although Chang's films were part of the strategy of containment and the Chinese Cultural Renaissance Movement, his heroes are never grand historical figures, such as emperors, statesmen, or Confucius. Instead, his heroes distance themselves from engaging in politics and they are often portrayed as physically impaired individuals who have lost their limbs, had their eyes gouged, or have been disemboweled. The story of *The Assassin* centers on Nie Zheng, a young swordsman who is approached by Yan Zhongzi, a statesman in the

Han state, to assassinate his rival, Han Kuei. Despite knowing that this is a suicide mission, Nie Zheng agrees to carry out the assassination, as he prefers sacrificing himself to working as a butcher and attending to his mother. In order to protect his girlfriend, who is pregnant with his child, and his sister, Nie Zheng kills himself by gouging his eyes and disemboweling himself, to avoid being recognized.

From the differences between Chang's film, Guo Murou's play and Sima Qian's original story of the assassin, we can see how Chang creates his apolitical Nie Zheng. In his memoir, he directly responded to Guo's.

> I chose the story of Nie Zheng with the intention to challenge Guo Moruo's *Tang Di Zhi Hua*! Guo was a "master" playwright of his time who took great pride in mimicking his lines on translation of Shakespearean plays. Reminiscent of regional operas, cross-dressing roles and mistaken identities run through Guo's play like a seam of gold. But how credible is a story that portrays a woman cross-dressing as a man wooed by another woman?
>
> *(Chang 2002, 85–86)*

His acrimonious disputes about Guo's use of cross-dressing roles in his play led him to place the emphasis on the individual masculine hero. In Guo's play,[4] the heroes are not just Nie Zheng but also his older sister Nie Ying, his girlfriend Chun Gu, and his friend Han Shan Jian, who all commit suicidal assassinations. Chang's *The Assassin* focuses only on Nie Zheng as the sole hero. Guo's play strengthens the collective heroes and agency of female power, and the female cross-dressing scene is for the heroine to take up the role of her twin brother and show her bravery and independence. Nie's sister never gets married, and his girlfriend criticizes the poverty and the collaborative government in front of the military guards. In Chang's film, the assassination is exclusive to the individual young man.

In Sima Qian's original narrative, Nie Zheng's sister Nie Ying kills herself and earns a reputation of *lienü* (heroic woman). Chang's female characters are a burden for Nie Zheng, who needs to wait for his mother's death and his sister's marriage before going to carry out the suicide mission. Singing prostitutes are playthings of rich men or people with high social status in the film. Only if women are serving the heroes are they considered good women. The ending shot that slowly zooms out, focusing on Nie Zheng's girlfriend Xia Ying pregnant with their child, from a high angle,[5] places her in the colorful reeds where she and Nie used to hang around. Women in the end are there simply to help carry the bloodline of men's passion and sacrifice.

The differences between the texts lie not just in gender and heroes' solidarity but the cause of action. Guo's play allegorizes the Qin state as the Japanese empire and calls for unification, as the Jin state was divided into three different states. The play focuses on the decision to assassinate the minister Han Kuei and the emperor from the Han state, who are going to collaborate with the Qin state. Chang's film shares the same thematic concern. However, much more emphasis is put on Nie Zheng's existential crisis than unification. His melancholic dialogue with his girlfriend, Xia Ying, accentuates his uselessness in history: "I am just an ordinary person, and my hope and passion are empty . . . but what should I do with such a brain and body? In the end, I was like that grass and wood, putrid and spiritless." The urge for spirit and rebellion aptly captured the zeitgeist of the late 1960s. Nie Zheng's existential crisis is emphasized by placing Yan Zhongzi, a typical patriotic character who advocates nationalism and patriotism, in the background. Nie Zheng in Chang's film is an individual martial artist. This is a departure from Sima Qian's story and Guo's play, which do not have a martial arts teacher. Nie Zheng in Chang's film has a teacher named Wu, who encourages his students to keep themselves updated on current affairs. The teacher lectures them on the fall of central China:

> We used to wear big clothes and copper-made weapons. Now we all wear short Tartar clothes (*hu fu duan zhuang*) and use steel blades. We seem to be uncomfortable with that. However, things in the world need to change. The fall of the statesmen in central China is due to their stubbornness. Now we have a big enemy, the Qin state. The Qin has the same customs as Tartars (*rong di*). We used to wear clothes with big sleeves and Qin people go to war bare chested. Why can't we be more flexible and wear their short Tartar clothes?

Luke White suggests that the Tartar clothes and the steel blades represent the Red Guards and the countercultural movement in the West. (2015, 87) However, it is just a simple allegory, as the central China-Tartar binary is typical of Chang's Han-centered ethnonationalism. The saying of "flexible" also echoes Chang's call for modernizing traditional virtues in the face of strong nations and Westernization. Later in the film, the teacher gives Nie Zheng a sacred sword, Shu Luo, which has a historical significance dating back to the Spring and Autumn Period (771 BC–476 BC). Fuchai, the emperor from the South who gave the sword to Wu Zixu, is best remembered for his war with Guojian, the king of the Yue state, and their stories revolve around revenge-seeking and suicide. All these ethnonationalistic elements (the Tartar analogy, the stories of Fuchai, and the sword) are absent in Guo's play and original story. Although the sword represents Han-centered nationalism, Nie Zheng's heroism differs from the patriotic statesman Yan Zhongzi as he does not fight for the country or particular value. Instead, he fights for himself and he rescues himself through a heroic sacrifice.

But why was a heroic sacrifice of an apolitical hero utilized in Chang's films as a response to Guo's play and as a means of illustrating the essence of traditional Chinese virtue as part of the strategy of containment during the Cold War? Scholars may argue that audiences can identify with such impaired heroes because of their resonance with the violence in the riots, the division of the nation during the Cold War, or the pulsating effect experienced in the emerging modernity in Hong Kong. However, what interests me is how Chang created a new language for heroes, a language of negativity. Heroes are not defined by political ideas, patriotism, or protection of the weak but solely by their passion. However, the passion or heroism is void in content and reduced to the form of action. The negation is taken to the extreme that the form of sacrifice becomes an exhibition itself and stops the narration.

The film form of *The Assassin* denies Nie Zheng from engaging with history, which is not the place for him to exhibit his passion. Inspired by Fei Mu's *Confucius* (1940), Chang shot the entire film from a low angle with a static 40 mm lens (Chang 2002, 66). To present the grandness of history, he uses 40 medium and long shots throughout the film (1989, 219) to show the symmetry of the settings like the opening scene of the palace and the sword-training school. Put in the middle ground or background, individuals in the face of history are blocked by the things in the foreground. Nie Zheng is visually "blocked" in the middle and background. When Nie Zheng works as a butcher and his sister asks him about the invitation of Yan Zhongzi, he is blocked by the wooden door blinds in the background. Even in the portrait shot of Nie, a shadow of the blind is cast on his face. Wooden door

Figure 27.1   Wooden door blinds put Nie Zheng in the background.

blinds, big columns, and silkscreens are recurring motifs of the grandness of history in the film. The columns, blinds, and screens, which are articulated with the static low camera angle, register the coldness and solemnity in history out of which the film forms capture the death of the hero Nie Zheng.

The concept of apolitical heroism is positioned on the periphery of history. Heroes, driven solely by their passions, often find themselves outside the boundaries of historical narratives. In the case of Nie Zheng, a representative of a passionate, existentially conflicted and irrational young man, he attempts to locate himself within the rational and inevitable progression of history. The distance and distinction between an individual hero and history assume the hero's lack of power and political engagement. History is too big to fail and he can only express himself to the extreme through the violent disembowelment. Leaning on a black column, Nie Zheng, after several quick zooms, cuts his abdomen. After his last fight, in order to protect his identity from being known, he disembowels himself and cuts his eyes out.

In this violent scene, Nie Zheng slashes his eyes, the shot becomes a black screen – a non-diegetic insert of a stage performance. Showing the sword sliding rightward, signifying he is slashing the eyes, a medium black screen highlights the blood spraying on the screen. No sooner, a wide shot shows Nie Zheng, who is barely lit and standing in the dark background, dropping his sword and falling down. The music of string ensemble and Chinese gong reaches a high pitch and accentuates his fall, while the screen remains dark.

Jerry Liu argues that that scene elevates Nie Zheng's death into transcendence. History is halted by the death of the hero since he swiftly ascends to the realm of myth (Liu 1981, 160–61). Yip Man-Fung also states that this death "leads not to nothingness but to immortality . . . Nie can only attain ultimate liberation in the form of a brutal, but heroic, death" (Yip 2017, 39). While I agree with their points about transcendence, what did that transcendence mean for a cultural strategy of containment? In the case of Nie Zheng, his act of disembowelment and slashing his eyes serves to show victimhood and call for "to-be-look-at-edness" in the grand history. The act inverts the concept of the male gaze, as presented in Luara Mulvey's seminal work, with Chang's martial arts films showcasing the

Figure 27.2   The tragic death of Nie Zheng in a black screen.

Figure 27.3   Silkscreen is a recurring motif to block Nie Zheng.

exhibitionism of suffering as a male privilege that is political in nature. Rather than fetishiz-ing the patriotic body of counselor Yan Zhongzi, the male gaze fixates on the damaged Nie Zheng. That gaze is not structured by sexual desire but the political desire as it functions as a witness to the historical trauma to the marginal hero. Politically, this marginal position seems to contradict Chang Cheh's ideas to make masculine or *yanggang* heroes, because the bodies are damaged and emasculated. Bérénice Reynaud (2003) points out how the hero in *One-Armed Swordsman* (1967) confronts the symbolic *vagina indetata*. On the contrary, the exhibition of disembowelment accentuates the spectacle of the individual victimhood in the face of history and the distance with it. By showing the scar, heroes can elicit identifica-tion with their masculinity from the audience. The impaired heroes become such residual regions of expression in a troubled time, and one could witness these heroes in the "mir-ror" revolution calling for witness from the audience. We can see other impaired heroes in Chang's films like *The Invincible Fist* (1969) and *Vengeance!* (1970) in an arrestingly original new set of formal motifs. Chang shows how heroes suffer blindness by means of slow motion, freeze frame, non-diegetic sequence, etc. In the case of Nie Zheng, the suicidal assassination confirms the impulse to the light, with a very sober look at the possibility that the darkness will win. To Chang, it is a teaching of Chinese civilization and culture that the Chinese have forgotten and related to darkness. At the same time, the politicization of the traditional Chinese culture as part of the strategy of containment is defined by celebrating apolitical heroes and their distance away from grand narratives.

The tragic death of Nie Zheng is not one of *beiju* (tragedy), but *bei zhuang* (tragic and solemn). To Chang Cheh, *beiju* is didactic and prevalent in tear-jerkers and historical costume pictures (Chang 1989, 54), while *bei zhuang* is about aestheticizing sacrifice and virtue which is exclusive to young men. In short, it is the Chinese beautiful virtue, one that can help rescue the Chinese national essence, representative of the Orient that can challenge Western values, defined by instrumentality, commodification, and communism. Nie Zheng is a model that Chang Cheh used to battle against Guo Murou's. As part of the strategy of containment supported by the colonial government, the KMT, and the studio, Chang Cheh's heroes help counterpoise the threat brought down by the Cultural Revolution. This language of negativity to define heroism – passion-driven heroes who have no political ideas outside of history – has a great impact in the following decades. For example, the illiterate Chen Zhen in Lo Wei's *Fist of Fury* (1972) can only define Chineseness in a negative way "Chinese are not sick men of Asia;" Fly in Wong Kar Wai's *As Tears Go By* (1988) prefers to die a hero for one day than being a fly; ordinary heroes know nothing about political ideals but sacrifice themselves to protect the father of the Republic of China in Teddy Chan's *Bodyguard and Assassins* (2009).

Indeed, Chang Cheh broke a new way to create the aesthetics of violence on the screen: chops and cuts, tortures, quartering and disembowelment, wreathing in pain and blood before they finally die. (Sek 2004, 15–16) However, the meaning of violence cannot be put into a simple specular framework where the "aesthetics of violence" seem to echo the student movements all over the world, the gory Vietnam War, and other forms of physical violence. On the contrary, Chang Cheh took up and adapted the violence into a convenient conduit for youth restlessness, anger, and frustration. Violence became a site for him to restore national essence and traditional virtue, renarrate the history and create new languages for heroism. "He might even be said to be Hong Kong cinema's Mao Zedong – his martial arts films fostering a cultural revolution of Chinese cinema." (Sek 2004, 11) If Chang really fostered a cultural revolution of Chinese cinema, it might be a "mirrored" revolution, flipping ultra-left to ultra-right, making individual heroes apolitical, and distancing individuals from engaging with the grand history. Chiang Kai-shek died in 1975 while Mao died in 1976. The Great Proletarian Cultural Revolution faded out as the national spiritual campaign did in Taiwan. The inflated production budgets and poor financial performances of *Ba guo lian-jun* (Boxer Rebellion, 1967) and *Hai jun tuji dui* (The Naval Commandos, 1977) dragged Chang's company into dire financial straits. Lau Kar-leung, Chang's action choreographer, had a conflict with him and established his own name in the studio. It is no accident that Chang's films lost popularity in the late 1970s, as the "mirrored" revolution reached its end.

Notes

1 In the beginning of the Cultural Revolution (1966), Chiang Kai-shek in Taiwan gave a message to national soldiers and people in celebration of the 55th anniversary of the Republic of China. Accusing the Red Guards in mainland China of destroying 5,000-year-old traditional culture, he attributed the Maoist bandits' (*mao fei*) rebellion to the fantasy of the Boxers bandits (*quan fei*).

In his memoir, Chang says, "I don't sympathize with the Boxers, but I fully endorse the resistance movements initiated by folk heroes who were driven purely by their nationalist beliefs" (Chang 2002, 55).

2 Without legal regulations of minimum wages and maximum working hours, stuntmen's wages were paid on a daily basis. The best stuntman would earn was 150 HKD a day, while a third-tier stuntman would earn around 70 HKD a day (Liu 1970, 57).

3 The campaign included protection of authentic traditional Chinese culture, publications of classical Chinese works, attacks on communist regimes and cultures, promotion of national language as well as customs and morals, advocating Mandarin and Confucian values, and support for overseas Chinese studies and research. The renaissance faded out in the late 1970s when Chiang Kai-shek died in 1975.

4 Different from Chang Cheh, who adapted Sima Qian's *The Biographies of Assassins*, Guo Moruo based his play upon classic publications of chronicles of ancient China like Sima Qian's *Records of the Grand Historian*, *Bamboo Annals* (*zhushu ji nian*) and *Annals of the Warring States* (*zhan guo ce*).

5 The name Xia Ying (literally "summer baby") in the film probably corresponds to Chun Gu (literally "spring maiden") in Guo's play.

References

Barnouw, Erik. 2000. "Last of the Great Movie Moguls." *Asian Cinema* 11 (2): 24–31. https://doi.org/10.1386/ac.11.2.24_7.

Bordwell, David. 2003. "How to Watch a Martial Arts Movie." In *Heroic Grace: Chinese Martial Arts Film*, edited by Cheng-sim Chute and David Lim, 9–12. Los Angeles: UCLA Film and Television Archive.

Chang, Cheh. 1968. "On Wuxia Films (Tan Wuxia Pian)." *Southern Screen* (126): 34–35.

———. 1988. *Zhang Che Jinzuo Ji (1986–88): Ji Jiang Jingguo Xiansheng De Yi Ge Jieduan, Dianying Zaxie Ji Qita* [Collection of Chang Cheh's Recent Works (1986–88): The Chiang Ching-Kuo Period, Film Notes and Others]. Hong Kong: Crystal Window Books.

———. 1989. *Huigu Xianggang Dianying Sanshi Nian* [Looking Back at Thirty Years of Hong Kong Movies]. Hong Kong: Joint Publishing (H.K.) Co., Ltd.

———. 2002. *Chang Cheh A Memoir*. Edited by Wong Ai-ling. Hong Kong: Hong Kong Film Archive.

Desser, David. 2005. "Making Movies Male: Zhang Che and the Shaw Brothers Martial Arts Movies, 1965–1975." In *Masculinities and Hong Kong Cinema*, edited by Day Pang and Laikwan Wong, 17–34. Hong Kong: Hong Kong University Press.

"Hong Kong Governor Visits Movietown and Officates the Laying of Tun Ho Building Foundation Stone." 1968. *Southern Screen* (124): 6–8.

Liu, Jerry. 1981. "Chang Cheh: Aesthetics = Ideology?" In *A Study of the Hong Kong Swordplay Film (1945–1980)*, edited by Mo-ling Leng, 159–64. Hong Kong: The Urban Council.

Liu, Zhiyuan. 1970. "Fangwen Wushu Zhidao Tangjia [An Interview with Action Choreographer Tang Jia]." *Hong Kong Movie News*, no. 55 (July): 54–57.

Lo, Wai Luk. 2003. "Zhangzhe Wuda Dianying de Nanxing Baoli Yu Qingyi [Masculine Violence and Romance in Chang Cheh's Martial Arts Films]." In *Shaoshi Yingshi DiGuo Wenhua Zhongguo de Xiangxiang*, edited by Jinfeng Miao. Taipei: Maitian Chuban.

Reynaud, Bérénice. 2003. "The Book, the Goddess and the Hero: Sexual Aesthetics in the Chinese Martial Arts Film." In *Heroic Grace: The Chinese Martial Arts Film*, edited by Chute David, 18–22. Los Angeles: UCLA Film and Television Archive.

Sek, Kei. 2002. "Chang Cheh's Revolution in Masculine Violence." In *Chang Cheh A Memoir*, edited by Ain-ling Wong, Ching-ling Kwok, and May Ng. Hong Kong: Hong Kong Film Archive.

"Shao Shi Zhigong Bupa Xia; Yongtui Shi Che Canbao Dui [Fearless Shaws Employees; Bravely Taking Down Ten Cruel Riot Cars]." (Shao Shi Zhigong Bupa Xia; Yongtui Shi Che Canbao Dui), 1967. *Ta Kung Pao*, June 26.

———. 1967b. "No Room for 'Neturality' before National Causes; Filmmakers Organizing Struggle Committee (Zai Minzu Dayi Meiyou 'zhongli' Yudi; Dianying Jie Renshi Yi Pi Zu Dou Wei Hui)." 1967. *Ta Kung Pao*, June 27.

"Shaws Fired More Than 100 Strikers" (Shao Shi Kaichu Bai Yu Bagong Zhe), 1967. *Mingpao*, June 24.

———. 1967b. "Kong Shao Shi Liang Gongren Konghe Bagong; Qi Yi Pu Bi Ji Suo [Two Labors Who Accused of the Shaws Threaten People to Do Labor Strike; One of Them Gets a Sudden Dead in Detention Center]" (Kong Shao Shi Liang Gongren Konghe Bagong; Qi Yi Pu Bi Ji Suo), 1967. *Mingpao* June 27.

STAR. 1969. "Now Red Film Stars May Quit." November 8, 1969.

Teo, Stephen. 2009. *Chinese Martial Arts Cinema The Wuxia Tradition.* Edinburgh: Edinburgh University Press.

"Understanding the Progressive Development of the Home-Country Film Industry; Run Run Shaw's Trip in Home Country; Promoting Transnational Connections for Domestic Films (Liaojie Zuguo Dianying Gongye Jinbu Qingxing; Shaoyifu Zuguo Xing; Jiaqiang Zuguo Dia." 1968. *Hong Kong Movie News* (28): 36–37.

White, Luke. 2015. "A 'Narrow World, Strewn with Prohibitions': Chang Cheh's The Assassin and the 1967 Hong Kong Riots." *Asian Cinema* 26 (1): 79–98. https://doi.org/10.1386/ac.26.1.79_1.

Wong, Vincent. 1969. "Communist Film Industry in Hongkong Fights for Survival." *South China Morning Post,* June 1, 1969.

Yip, Man-Fung. 2017. *Martial Arts Cinema and Hong Kong Modernity Aesthetics, Representation, Circulation.* Hong Kong: Hong Kong University Press.

28

THE VERNACULAR SONORITIES OF THE MEMORY FILM IN SOUTHEAST ASIA

Mysterious Object at Noon (2000) and Big Boy (2012)

Philippa Lovatt

This chapter attends to the vernacular sonorities of the memory film in relation to two early works by leading contemporary Southeast Asian artist filmmakers, Apichatpong Weerasethakul's *Dokfa nai meuman* (Mysterious Object at Noon, 2000) and Shireen Seno's *Big Boy* (2012). Based in Chiang Mai in Northern Thailand and Quezon City in the Philippines, respectively, Apichatpong and Seno are somewhat distinctive in the context of the Southeast Asian film scene as they both make and exhibit work across both global film and art contexts, having produced highly acclaimed narrative feature films, shorts, and photography and moving image installations. Beyond this institutional comparison, however, the aesthetic practices of Apichatpong and Seno reveal similarities stemming from a shared interest in memory and the limits of official histories. Indeed, both *Mysterious Object at Noon* and *Big Boy* correspond with memory theorist Susannah Radstone's description of the "memory film," which she posits "complicate[s] the relations between personal and social memory, underlining the fact that memories are not simply 'ours' by drawing from and mediating a cultural memory bank of cinematic images and sounds" (Radstone 2010, 328). In tracing these connections, I mobilize the term "vernacular" because I am particularly interested in the ways that local inflections of historical memory are rendered audiovisually through non-linear and experimental modes of storytelling. My inquiry is motivated by a central question: sound is often thought of as an ephemeral and fleeting phenomenon, so how might it evoke a sense of the past, and its relation to the present, when it is (re)mediated through memory and the moving image?

As memory films, the narrative and aesthetics of both *Mysterious Object at Noon* and *Big Boy* traverse multiple registers and scales mediating a particular kind of regional affect (Gopinath 2018); one that gestures back to Southeast Asia's Cold War formation and colonial past through references to Thailand's and the Philippines' respective American eras (which in Thailand spans the post–World War II period to the 1960s and in the Philippines from 1898 to 1946) while at the same time engaging a register of "the anti-monumental, the small, the inconsequential, the micro, the irrelevant" (Halberstam cited by Gopinath

DOI: 10.4324/9781003266952-37

Figure 28.1 Big Boy (Shireen Seno 2012).

2010, 187). Correspondingly, both films were shot on small gauge film formats: *Mysterious Object at Noon* on black-and-white 16 mm stock and *Big Boy* on color Super-8; they share a grainy and fragmentary "amateur film" aesthetic evocative of moving image practices of past eras. However, both also experiment with non-synch, anachronistic sound, producing a textured audiovisual collage of embodied memories and sensory experience in which the vernacular sonorities of "small-gauge" stories unfold against a larger historical backdrop of colonialism, the Cold War, and the effects of American cultural imperialism across the region.

Oblique allusions to what feminist cultural historian Annette Kuhn refers to as the overlap of "everyday historical consciousness and collective memory" emerge through the assemblage of fragments of sounds and images; at the same time, in foregrounding the partiality of memory the films reveal a deep ambivalence about whether "collective memory" is ever possible (Kuhn 2010; Brunow 2015, 7). Making use of fragments of audio, sometimes repurposing "found" material, and deploying a modality that foregrounds the materiality and fragility of the medium, Apichatpong and Seno deploy an aesthetic strategy of "decomposition" in order to break down the dominant forms of aurality through which one can trace a lineage from the atrocities of the past to the political violence of the present. In the parallel contexts of ongoing patriarchal authoritarianism in the shadow of military dictatorships in Thailand and the Philippines (embodied by Thai prime minister Prayut Chan-o-cha in power since a coup d'état in 2014 until 2023 and the election of president

Ferdinand Marcos Jr. in the Philippines in 2022), alongside media censorship and unending waves of resistance from pro-democracy social movements, I suggest that the radical politics of *Mysterious Object at Noon* and *Big Boy* lies in the spaces they create for alternative narrative trajectories to emerge, evincing, however obliquely, the possibility to imagine otherwise.[1]

Sound and the Memory Film in Southeast Asia

According to sound theorists Jean-François Augoyard and Henry Torque, sound has the ability to span vastly different scales that are both temporal and spatial, referring to the experience of anamnesis, which they describe as "an evocation of the past" as when "a sound or a sonic context revives a situation or an atmosphere of the past" (Augoyard and Torque 1995, 22). The memory film often uses music to provide a bridge between the present and the past, a technique that has particular resonance in the absence of official archives. Examples from Southeast Asia include Davy Chou's *Golden Slumbers* (2011) and Truong Minh Quý's *Nhà cây* (The Tree House, 2019), which depict the devastation caused by the Cambodian genocide carried out by the Khmer Rouge in the late 1970s and the impact of the American-Vietnam War both on the Indigenous communities in Vietnam's Central Highlands and on Vietnamese refugees who fled overseas. In both cases, music becomes a repository for memories of historical trauma as songs affectively reduce spatial as well as temporal distance through anamnesis.

However, in other examples of Southeast Asian film, memories of place reverberate through environmental sound and more-than-human auditory perspectives. For example, Anocha Suwichakornpong's *Jai Jumlong* (Come Here, 2021) takes place in Kanchanaburi province, alongside the historical site of Death Railway, built at the time of the Japanese occupation of Thailand during World War II in order to link Thailand and Burma, resulting in the deaths of thousands of forced laborers. The dialogue is de-emphasized and ambient sound, composed of the voices of many other species who now inhabit the site, including birds and other sound-emitting beings, is heightened, suggesting that place itself holds memory, even when humans are unaware or ambivalent to it. Memories of place are also rendered through environmental sound in the Migrant Ecologies' *{If your bait can sing the wild one will come} Like Shadows Through Leaves* (2021). The film is the outcome of several years spent with the community living alongside a former railway line in one of Singapore's oldest housing estates, Tanglin Halt. Before being abandoned in 2011, the railway had been owned by the Malaysian state and was protected from development resulting in a flourishing bird population. Due to redevelopment as a biotech and media hub, the housing blocks were demolished along with tree shrines, community farms and other community spaces, leading to the loss of many species. Placing field recordings of bird songs in relation to human voices, the film explores human and more-than-human sonic memories of the site (Hsu 2021).

Historical Consciousness and an Evocation of the Past

For Kuhn, the memory film has a distinct way of rendering cinematic temporality, often having a "repetitive or cyclical quality" or fusing different events together in ways that are not always logical. As such, she suggests, these films often take the form of a montage of "remembered events [that] seem to be outside any linear time frame or may refuse to be easily anchored to 'historical' time" (Kuhn 2010, 299). *Mysterious Object at Noon* and *Big Boy* similarly reveal the act of remembering as being at once personal and social; individual and familial memories are entwined with wider cultural and political histories, through imaginative processes that are far from straightforward. The unfolding of memory is not a process of disentangling personal recollections from national myths, folktales, and other narratives. Rather, both films use fragments of sound and image to foreground the partiality of memories as they feed into the national imaginary. Their collage-like structure recalls Kuhn's description of the composition of memory texts as being made up of "vignettes, anecdotes, fragments, 'snapshots,' flashes" rather than following the linear organization of national narratives that are grounded in what she calls " 'real' historical time" (Kuhn 2002, 162). Through these aesthetic strategies, Apichatpong's and Seno's films reveal a shared interest in the role of narrative in the construction of a national imaginary as they draw attention via formal and narrative ellipses to the absences, gaps, contradictions, and collective amnesias involved in such processes. In doing so, they draw on personal memories and testimony, which may or may not be "truthful" or "authentic" and from a range of cultural references, including songs, comic books, manga, science fiction, soap operas, *likay* folk theater, radio, and television, as well as from personal audio recordings of sonic ephemera. The social memories evoked through the interweaving of different discourses are reflected in the fluid shifts across and between moments of personal recollections and direct or indirect references to the social, cultural, and historical moments in which they are imbricated.

Mysterious Object at Noon

The absences and erasures in official accounts of the past and the collective amnesia that accompanies them are recurrent themes in contemporary Thai art cinema and experimental film, which often explore the ways that social practices might begin to undo this process of forgetting. As Malinee Khumsupa and Sudarat Musikawong explain,

> Central to the Thai term for memory *khwamsongcham* = ความทรงจำ is *song*, which . . . translates as form or medium. The word *khwamsongcham*. . . forges an embodiment of the past (albeit always interpreted), and signals the capacity for the transformation of memory through various forms and mediums, including social practices and material culture. One commits to embodied remembering because there is a fear of forgetting.
>
> *(Khumsupa and Musikawong 2016)*

Historian Thongchai Winichakul argues that in the shadow of state violence there exists a space of ambivalence and liminality where one can neither remember nor forget. In *Moments of Silence: the Unforgetting of the October 6, 1976 massacre in Bangkok*, he conceptualizes the relation between national trauma and memory as an absence of sound that exists alongside passive processes of *misremembering* facilitated by the state (Winichakul 2020). In what follows, building on Malinee and Sudarat's discussion of "the transformation of memory," I show how the anachronistic layering of sound and image in *Mysterious Object at Noon* begins to unravel the monolithic linearity of state discourse and in so doing contributes, albeit ambivalently, to a collective process of unforgetting.

Mysterious Object at Noon begins silently with an inter-title – "Once Upon a Time" – signaling that what is to come will have its roots in the storytelling traditions of oral culture and the folktale. From behind the windscreen of a small fish van driving through Bangkok suburbs, glimpses of the city pass by: tower blocks, market stalls, parked cars, bicycles, pedestrians, and street vendors. The grain of the film's soundscape also emerges through a multiplicity of fleeting ambient sounds that move swiftly in and out of auditory focus. Car horns, motorbike exhausts, and voices converge at the point-of-audition within the moving vehicle, immersing us in a world of transient, vernacular sonority. The film begins by drawing the listener into the world of the imagination (a place of no particular time), before entering an environment where the threads of multiple narratives are woven into the textural ambience of everyday life. These opening moments set up a multi-layered narrative space that becomes further entangled as the film's story-worlds expand, in which a multitude of different voices represent the space of social memory and collective imagination as a dynamic heterotopia in a state of constant transformation and becoming. As the film progresses, its mood changes as the "plot" becomes secondary to the imaginative processes involved in the act of telling, and how the films' narrators/protagonists occupy and transform the spaces they inhabit through these processes. Fittingly, the film only comes to an end with the breakdown of the apparatus; narrative resolution is withheld, offering instead a radical opening to the myriad possibilities of alternative endings and beginnings.

Beginning around the time of the 1997 financial crisis, *Mysterious Object at Noon* was shot over a period of two to three years, and takes the form of a journey across Thailand starting with Bangkok and ending with Panyi Island. The film reflects on the performative nature of social memory through its playful openness to polyphonic storytelling. Adopting the surrealist method of Cadavre Exquis (Exquisite Corpse), a parlor game invented in Paris in the 1920s that involved drawing parts of a body on paper before folding over and passing on to the next player, the film mirrors the process as Apichatpong invites participants to add to a gradually unfurling narrative where each speaker continues where the previous person stopped. Disrupting hegemonic, linear modes of storytelling, the film foregrounds an assemblage of multi-regional and multi-generational perspectives through its narrators who advance the ambiguous tale of "Dogfahr and the Mysterious Object" in whichever direction they choose. Beginning with a story about a teacher and a paraplegic child, and ending with a Witch-Tiger and an alien, with each "unfolding" the Dogfahr narrative changes form: from folklore to likay folk theater, to soap opera melodrama and social realism, and eventually to manga-influenced science fiction. *Mysterious Object at Noon*, meanwhile, is itself a hybrid form of fictional road movie and experimental ethnographic documentary.

As Noah Viernes has observed in his reading of the film, the layering of different voices and sounds emphasizes plurality, creating a textured and interconnected discursive space that refuses the authority of a single voice or speaking position (Viernes 2013, 249). The sense of polyphony is foregrounded not only by the presence of so many narrators, or by the words that they say, but by how their voices are recorded, and the many non-verbal utterances, rhythms, and sonic materialities that their voices and the diegetic world of the film produce. David Teh notes that while Apichatpong "rejects documentary's claim to truth" with this film, he does not reject its aesthetic (Teh 2011, 597). I would suggest that this ambivalence is perhaps most pronounced in relation to the film's soundtrack, which often resembles that of observational documentary in that it incorporates a multitude of sighs, hesitations, repetitions, and overlaps between different voices, dialects, and sounds, as well as idiomatic forms of expression, which are themselves drawn from multiple sources – diegetic, metafictional and archival footage. The audio captures the "phatic qualities" of speech that signify "sociability" as Jeff Ruoff explains: "Speakers in everyday life typically fill in the gaps of their phrases with various exclamations and sounds that maintain the flow of verbal communication. In conversations, we interrupt one another, digress, ask questions, hem and haw . . . Dialogue in observational documentaries overlaps considerably as characters interrupt one another, speak at the same time, and affirm their listening stance" (Ruoff 1993, 27–28). Just as the human voice stutters and stumbles and occasionally runs ahead of itself, so too the narration of the Dogfahr story is shaped by the temporal instability of pauses as much as it is enlivened by digressions, overlaps and repetitions. These aural aspects mimic the ways that memory is itself inflected by moments of forgetfulness and doubt as much as it can be trapped in a cycle of traumatic return or marked by the absences and erasures in official records. It is also in these gaps in speech, however, that the film itself becomes a ludic space for renewal and invention, presenting collaborative storytelling as a form of "critical fabulation" (Hartman 2008b) that offers a radical alternative to the linearity of state discourse in Thailand. As Viernes writes, the film "makes audible what would otherwise remain silent" (Viernes 2013, 251).

A young woman begins her story in the cramped space of the back of the fish van. With her shoulders hunched over and her arms held closely to her body, her voice cracks with emotion as she tells Apichatpong, who is listening but out of the frame, about when her parents sold her to her uncle in Bangkok in exchange for the bus fare to get back to their home in northern Thailand. In a juxtaposition that James Quandt notes in his discussion of the film "insinuates a critique of patriarchal exploitation and neglect" (Quandt 2009, 34), her monologue is framed visually against election posters of three male politicians, inevitably drawing associations with what Thak Chaloemtiarana calls the "despotic paternalism" of Thailand's political structure (Chaloemtiarana 2007). Apichatpong then asks, "Now, do you have any other stories to tell us? It can be real or fiction." The woman dries her eyes on the sleeve of her T-shirt and begins the story of "Dogfahr and the Mysterious Object." As she talks, the image cuts to a scene that visually depicts her words. In a stark aural as well as visual contrast to the fluid, handheld camerawork of the noisy street scene that preceded it, this quiet mise-en-abyme is filmed mostly in silence and in a subdued, static manner. An inter-title reads: "What did you see in the outside world today?" A boy in a wheelchair speaks to his teacher, but while we might see his lips move, there is no sound. Instead, the soundtrack is composed of the booming male voice of the fish vendor trading alongside the laughter and chatter of his customers, as the image switches between the two worlds. The anachronistic layering of the silence of the metafictional world and use of inter-titles, with the asynchronous voice of the fish vendor of the film's diegesis, draws together storytelling conventions of silent cinema with those of an older, oral culture, or with the auditory experience of mobile cinema projections, in which stray ambient sounds inflect the story-world as different voices and stories overlap, flow into, and give shape both to the lived space of the present and to memory.

The "doubling" of space-time through the anachronistic layering of sound and image in this scene recalls Henri Bergson's description of the experience of time as duration – "the continuous progress of the past which gnaws into the future and . . . swells as it advances" (Bergson 1998, 4). For Bergson, "There is no perception which is not full of memories." By this he means that the process of remembering involves the coexistence of multiple time frames at the moment of recollection. He describes this as a temporal "doubling," arguing that our experience of time "is twofold at every moment, its very up-rush being in two jets exactly symmetrical, one of which falls back towards the past whilst the other springs forward towards the future" (Bergson 2002, 145). In this sense, all experience is characterized by this dualism: actual (perception) and virtual (memory). In Apichatpong's film, the method of exquisite corpse presents storytelling as a dynamic mode of mediating memory, thought, and perceptual experience in ways that I would argue closely resemble Bergson's description.

The aesthetic practice of "doubling" in *Mysterious Object at Noon* extends to the film's anachronistic use of audio alongside archive footage (which may be real or staged) and photographs. In one scene, after a sharp feedback squeal on the soundtrack (the sound of the "real" bleeding into the space of the "fictional"), the distorted acousmatic sound of the production manager's voice speaking through a walkie-talkie can be heard saying that she wants the next part of the Dogfahr story to be told in flashback. Without indicating a particular time period, she explains that in the story a woman and her son were on a plane that was shot down on its arrival at a Cambodian airport during the war. The image then cuts to a series of photographs of a young woman with a baby, and then to some (presumably staged) television footage of a family being interviewed on a talk show about the survival of the boy, followed by a montage of sun-bleached photographs of the crash scene. "This is your Thai wife?" asks the talk show host. "His mother is Chinese. The plane crashed in Cambodia, not Vietnam. We wonder . . . how this boy survived? Tell us from the beginning." Indicating a temporal wavering between past and present, the image flickers as if filmed from a television screen; as the show ends, its soundtrack enacts a further spatial-temporal leap across to the diegetic space of the Dogfahr story. Within *this* narrative space, Dogfahr tells the paraplegic child that her family "fled the war to live in an Indian temple" as the image cuts to footage of an unnamed war-ravaged city under demolition in the aftermath of the Pacific War. Against these archival images, the soundtrack remains situated in the spatial-temporal location of Dogfahr's house in the present – a soundscape dominated by the soft, rural sounds of woodpigeons cooing and a crowing cockerel. The anachronistic juxtaposition of archival images with present-day environmental sounds creates a jarring sense of temporal dislocation that destabilizes the "meaning" or the veracity of the images we have witnessed while mimicking the selective use of the past by the nation-state.

As the diegesis returns to the present, two schoolgirls use sign language to narrate their part of the story, the image then cuts back to the metafictional space of an apartment in Bangkok where Dogfahr's boyfriend attempts to sell the paraplegic boy and his friend, making an oblique reference to the 1997 economic crash. The sound source switches from the narrator's diegetic space to that of the metafictional world and as the two men talk, the faint sound of pop music can be heard on the radio, which is interrupted by an announcement from the Bureau of Communication. Again the "authenticity" of the archival radio broadcast is ambiguous – here, the uncertainty that its placement brings about disrupts the authority of auditory regimes of the nation-state, in which radio has always played a crucial role. While the radio goes in and out of focus, the broadcast is interrupted by the pop music but then returns to the announcement from the Bureau of Communication that the government had declared an end to the Pacific War. The broadcaster urges listeners to "remember the bravery of our army units that sacrificed their lives for the country and for the global army units that resisted the Japanese forces . . .[and] appreciate the good deeds of America." He then explains the new laws that have been introduced, instructing listeners to "honour the Americans" and "use American products" as well as promote "friendly relations by sending our youngsters to educate in the United States."

In an essay on Chris Marker's "fake" documentary, *Level 5* (1997), Jonathan Kear argues that primary source historical documents such as archival film footage play a crucial

role in historiographic accounts because these materials "ground retrospective interpretations of the past in the historical context to which they refer, and assert the reliability,
authenticity and authority of the narrative that is relayed to those past events. Such primary
source documents, whether visual or verbal, serve as testimony to the 'real'" (Kear 2007,
134). However, *Mysterious Object at Noon*, like Marker's film, upends this association. In
the scene described, the lack of cohesion between sound and image disrupts the notion of
this material as authentic or having any intrinsic value as evidence. Instead, woven as it is
into the temporality of the (diegetic) present, it has an uncanny resonance – although the
images, certainly those of the Pacific War, are "real," their lack of placement within a coherent narrative creates a dialectical gap where fixed meaning is lost. The disjuncture of sound
and image disrupts the apparent seamlessness of dominant narratives – like Walter Benjamin's use of allegorical juxtaposition in *The Arcades Project*, this "unruly" use of sound
and image can similarly "[rip] up the manifestly natural context of things, snapping open
the apparent continuity of nature and history and prising apart space for reinterpretation
and transformation" (Leslie 2000, 199). The duality suggested here as a "prising apart"
resonates with Bergson's temporal "splitting" of memory and perception mentioned earlier.
The interplay of sound and image in *Mysterious Object at Noon* thus evokes the experience
of history which, like memory, is inherently fragmentary and disconnected.

Big Boy

Set on the island of Mindoro in the Philippines after World War II, *Big Boy* presents a
sensory history told loosely from the perspective of Julio, the eldest of six children. Julio
is made to drink a cod liver oil mixture made by his parents – a "health tonic" that his
father and mother believe will make him grow taller. Regularly tormented by a daily ritual
of having his arms and legs pulled by his family members in order to stretch him and made
to stand for hours on end under the heat of the sun while his siblings play in the fields
and forests around their home, his parents use their son's dubious height gain to make
money by selling the homemade "miracle" cod liver oil to their neighbors. The family live
in poverty, with two of Julio's siblings being sent to live with their aunts because their
parents can't afford to feed them. *Big Boy* takes the perspective of a child, twice filtered
through Seno's recollection (as an adult) of her father's memories of his childhood, told
to her when she herself was a child growing up in Japan. Recalling hearing her father's
memories, Seno notes,

> For me it was like another world . . . When I finally started to write them down from
> memory, I asked my father to retell them, and it was so different from the way I had
> envisioned them all along. I liked the idea that memory can change spontaneously and
> doesn't always make sense.
>
> *(Seno in Hirano 2013)*

The film takes place at a moment when the Philippines was experiencing what Seno describes
as the "growing pains" of a nation at a time "when the Philippines was . . . trying to come
out of another country's image" (Seno 2021). In this way *Big Boy*'s depiction of a family's
obsession with height as an outward marker of social mobility has a broader resonance
that relates to the social and psychological effects of being a colony of the United States.
On 4 July 1946 the American colonial period ended, following a short period of occupation

by the Japanese between 1942 and 1945, the Philippines had finally achieved full independence from the United States following a ten-year period of transition that began with the Tydings-McDuffie Act of 1934. Despite gaining independence, as José B. Capino has described, American imperialism was still prevalent as it continued to dominate the country economically and culturally. Echoing the propagandist state radio broadcast in *Mysterious Object at Noon* discussed earlier, *Big Boy*'s soundtrack evokes this dominance from the outset, foregrounding its association with consumerism and the idealized body (Capino 2010).

The film begins with the use of nonsynchronous "found sound" of a crackling radio broadcast. The anachronistic use of audio, which would have been broadcast more than a decade before the film's setting, references the specter of American cultural imperialism and presents an experience of history and memory that is nonlinear and fragmentary while grounded in sensory and corporeal experience.[2] The audio is a short fragment of *The Gibson Family*, a musical comedy, sponsored by Procter & Gamble, that was broadcast in the US on NBC's Red Network for a short time between 1934 and 1935. The show regularly featured promotions for the sponsor's skin care and laundry products – Ivory Soap and Ivory Flakes – and the family's daughter, Sally Gibson, often "extolled the virtues of Ivory Soap, which she used on her face, and Ivory Flakes, which she used for her washing" (Zimmers 2021, 89). In the fragment played at the beginning of *Big Boy*, the announcer takes the listeners backstage as Sally can be heard giving skin care advice to her maid, Hilda who complains of her boyfriend losing interest in her because of having red blotches on her face. The audio then cuts to the diegetic present in 1950s Mindoro and to the sound of dripping water and the squeaking springs of Julio's parents' bed as they have sex – the three sounds interconnecting corporeal discourses of beauty, health, hygiene, and sex. Through the related themes of consumerism and the idealized "healthy" body, Seno's film places her own family history within the larger framework of the nation at a crucial juncture in its history. The difficulty of this transition is also observed at a material and sensory level; as a microcosm of the nation, Julio's family also feed and clothe themselves by making use of the detritus of American colonialism. In one scene they discover a parachute caught in a nearby tree containing canned food and other American goods. After eating the food, Julio's mother repurposes the parachute by using the fabric to make matching outfits for the family, literally draping their bodies in the material remains of empire.

In her discussion of discourses of "aspirational embodiment" in relation to the "clean, hygienic, healthy body" in Manila's film culture of the 1920s and '30s, Jasmine Nadua Trice posits that "progressivist body discourse" presented in cinema and marketing material of this period was highly racialized in the way that it connected the body of the citizen-consumer to colonial ideologies of modernity and progress (Trice 2022, 34). Prior to *Big Boy*'s postwar setting, corporeal regimes had been introduced by the American and Spanish colonial administrations to the Philippines that, according to Julius Bautista and Ma. Mercedes Planta, "imposed political, economic and social changes that encouraged a revision of people's ideas about their own corporeality" (Bautista and Planta 2009, 146). While such regimes enacted and perpetuated structures of dominance through and on the colonized body, at both an administrative and a social level, Resil Mojares posits that they also operated in the realm of the intimate and quotidian (Mojares cited in Bautista and Planta, 148). Through the small-gauge amateur film aesthetic and the juxtaposition of archival "found sounds," particularly those of the domestic sphere, *Big Boy* presents a sensory history of this period, calling attention to the sonic intimacies of everyday life in which these corporeal regimes operated. Reflecting a pivotal moment in the history of the Philippines where the nation struggled to emerge from the shadow of US imperialism, Julio's parents pin their hopes on their entrepreneurial endeavors leading to a better, more affluent, life – one that is symbolized by the "healthy" body of their eldest son. The family's aspirational body image for Julio, reveals an attitude to height and social mobility that emerged in the 1930s that Gideon Lasco describes as "modernist, eugenicist ideas of progress . . . [that] problematized shortness and treated height as something that could be improved through scientific approaches, such as better nutrition and physical education" (Lasco 2018, 377). Furthermore, he explains that during this period, children were regularly measured as height became a quantifiable measure of children's health as well as a marker of "successful governance and more broadly of the colonial project itself" (ibid., 378).

Describing her approach to making *Big Boy*, Seno has said that she wanted "to work with the materiality and immateriality of memory. A memory of a memory" (Seno in Hirano 2013). While the materiality of memory is evoked visually through the textural quality of Super-8 film stock and the film's references to photography, the use of haptic "found" sound in *Big Boy* also imbues a sense of materiality and texture. Resembling more of a personal, if abstract, family memoir than the collaborative stream-of-consciousness that is *Mysterious Object at Noon*, with *Big Boy*, Seno pieces together fragments of memory in the way one might stitch together a narrative from looking through the pages of a family photograph album, a process that often relies heavily on the imagination to help us trace connections across the gaps. While the role of photography as a technology of memory is an important theme in the film, and in Seno's practice more broadly, her use of anachronistic sound also registers a particular structure of feeling – a temporal affect that is evoked through the immaterialities of sonic memories and associations that are placed in relation to one another.

Sampling fragments of home audio recordings of her father whistling in the shower, recorded through the door on her phone a few years earlier, Seno enfolds her own auditory memories of her father into her re-imagining of *his* memories of childhood in Mindoro. In the process, she weaves the sonic textures of more recent times into the fabric of the distant past, producing a relational encounter that closes the spatio-temporal gap between these two sites of memory, not through language, which has a different familial association for Seno, but through sound. She explains,

> I wanted to capture that I grew up hearing him singing or whistling in the shower a lot. And it's something that's associated with him because my father doesn't talk very much. So things like this . . . form my memory of him. . . . [With] my father it's more about sounds rather than speech, whereas my mother was a teacher so I was always sort of being made to recite or to perform or to repeat . . . something she was saying.
> *(Seno 2021)*

The act of recording sound is itself an act of documenting and giving shape to fleeting, and seemingly incidental, moments in time. Recording the sounds of such everyday domestic routines is both an archival practice of the everyday (providing an uncanny echo of audio from *The Gibson Family* that began the film) and at the same time, an anamnestic encounter that reduces the sense of spatio-temporal dislocation between Seno's relationship to her family home (in the diaspora) and that of her father to his (in the Philippines). Through the placement of her father's whistling as a refrain that recurs across the collagist soundtrack of the film, this kind of sonic intimacy, mediated through Seno's home recording, allows the listener to affectively inhabit both sites at once. This palimpsestic practice layers different temporalities and geographical locations, from the recent past of her parent's home, to the spatial-temporal location of her father's childhood, and the embodied present in which we encounter it. The subject of the film is thus not simply Mindoro in this historical period, or her father's memories, or the "growing pains" of living through post-independence in the Philippines, but it is also about Seno's relationship to those things told from a place of distance and curiosity.

Connecting the "materiality and immateriality of memory" through sound, *Big Boy* gestures toward the affective and ephemeral nature of memory through the recurrent sonic motif of the needle stuck in the run-off groove of a record on rotation. While the music etched onto the disc might have evoked dreams of other times and places, from times past or those yet to come, its absence evokes the opposite: the repetitive crackle and rhythm of the needle circling the run-off groove seems to seep into the film's consciousness in between moments of fragmentary dialogue, song, and sometimes complete silence, evoking a sensory history that conveys the static temporal experience of living in postwar Mindoro, still under the shadow of empire, a sensation that continues to reverberate, albeit in different ways, in the present.

Conclusion

Kuhn notes that in memory work the act of narration can involve embellishments or fabrications as certain parts are given extra weight, moved into the center of the frame, obfuscating others in the telling. These imaginative trajectories are what Seno has described as the "tall tales" told across generations and within families and communities that are always open to reinvention and reinterpretation. Both *Mysterious Object at Noon* and *Big Boy* explore how traces of the past can be found in the stories we tell and the clues that emerge as sounds and images interweave private and public memories alongside the absences and erasures of official accounts of the past. In foregrounding practices of sounding and listening, these small-gauge stories suggest that memory as it is lived and felt is not static but involves active processes of interpretation and imagination, it is in these "tall tales" that the possibility to imagine otherwise emerges.

Notes

1 A variation on this theme of "vernacular" sound can be found in Benjamin Tausig's (2018) article "Sound and Movement: Vernaculars of Sonic Dissent," which discusses protest songs.
2 For an insightful discussion of anachronism in relation to Seno's later film *Shotgun Tuding* (2014), see Trice (2019), "Gendering National Histories and Regional Imaginaries: Three Southeast Asian Women Filmmakers."

References

Augoyard, Jean-François, and Henry Torque. 1995. *Sonic Experience: A Guide to Everyday Sounds*. Montreal: McGill-Queens University Press.
Bautista, Julius, and Ma. Mercedes Planta. 2009. "The Sacred and the Sanitary: The Colonial Medicalization of the Filipino Body." In *The Body in Asia*, edited by B. S. Turner and Y. Zhang, 76–102. Oxford: Berghahn Books.
Bergson, Henri. 1998. *Creative Evolution*. Translated by Arthur Mitchell. Mineola: Dover Publications.

———. 2002. "Memory of the Present and False Recognition." In *Henri Bergson: Key Writings*, edited by Keith Ansell-Pearson and John Mullarkey, 141–56. New York: Continuum.

Brunow, Dagmar. 2015. *Remediating Transcultural Memory: Documentary Filmmaking as Archival Intervention*. Berlin: Walter de Gruyter.

Capino, José B. 2010. *Dream Factories of a Former Colony: American Fantasies, Philippine Cinema*. Minneapolis: University of Minnesota Press.

Chaloemtiarana, Thak. 2007. *Thailand: The Politics of Despotic Paternalism*. Chiang Mai: Silkworm Books.

Gopinath, Gayatri. 2010. "Archive, Affect, and the Everyday: Queer Diasporic Re-Visions." In *Political Emotions: New Agendas in Communication*, edited by Janet Staiger, Ann Cvetkovich, and Ann Reyolds, 165–92. London: Routledge.

———. 2018. *Unruly Visions: The Aesthetic Practices of the Queer Diaspora*. Durham: Duke University Press.

Hartman, Saidiya V. 2008b. "Venus in Two Acts." *Small Axe: A Journal of Criticism* 66: 1–14.

Hirano, Mayumi. 2013. "Interview with Shireen Seno." *Art, Writing & Archives*, May 11. http://2050artandwriting.blogspot.com/2013/11/interview-with-shireen-seno.html

Hsu, Fang-Tze. 2021. 'Ensounding Memories: *Like Shadows Through Leaves* (2021) and Cinematic Remembrance." *Soft:Doc*, 12. https://soft-doc.com/?p=286

Kear, Jonathan. 2007. "A Game that Must be Lost: Chris Marker Replays Alain Resnais' *Hiroshima Mon Amour*." In *The Image and the Witness: Trauma, Memory and Visual Culture*, edited by Francis Guerin and Roger Hallas, 129–42. London: Wallflower.

Khumsupa, Malinee, and Sudarat Musikawong. 2016. "Counter-Memory: Replaying Political Violence in Thai Digital Cinema." *Kyoto Review of Southeast Asia* (20). https://kyotoreview.org/issue-20/counter-memory-replaying-political-violence-in-thai-digital-cinema/.

Kuhn, Annette. 2002. *Family Secrets: Acts of Memory and Imagination*. London: Verso.

———. 2010. "Memory Texts and Memory Work: Performance of Memory in and with Visual Media." *Memory Studies* 3 (4): 1–16.

Lasco, Gideon. 2018. "'Little Brown Brothers': Height and the Philippine–American Colonial Encounter (1898–1946)." *Philippine Studies: Historical & Ethnographic Viewpoints* 66, no. 3 (September): 375–406.

Leslie, Esther. 2000. *Walter Benjamin: Overpowering Conformism*. London: Pluto Press.

Quandt, James, ed. 2009. *Apichatpong Weerasethakul*. Vienna: Austrian Film Museum.

Radstone, Susannah. 2010. "Cinema and Memory." In *Memory: Histories, Theories, Debates*, edited by Susannah Radstone and Bill Scharz, 325–42. New York: Fordham University Press.

Ruoff, Jeffrey. 1993. "Conventions of Sound in Documentary." *Cinema Journal* 32, no. 3 (Spring): 24–40.

Seno, Shireen. 2021. "In Conversation with the Author at CAMPLE LINE Gallery." January 30. https://vimeo.com/506758190

Tausig, Benjamin. 2018. "Sound and Movement: Vernaculars of Sonic Dissent." *Social Text* 36, no. 3 (September): 25–45.

Teh, David. 2011. "Itinerant Cinema: The Social Surrealism of Apichatpong Weerasethakul." *Third Text* 25 (5): 595–609.

Trice, Jasmine Nadua. 2019. "Gendering National Histories and Regional Imaginaries: Three Southeast Asian Women Filmmakers." *Feminist Media Histories* 5 (1): 11–38.

———. 2022. "Haunted by the Body: Cleanliness in Colonial Manila's Film Culture." In *Uncanny Histories in Film and Media*, edited by Patrice Petri, 32–59. New Brunswick, NJ: Rutgers University Press.

Viernes, Noah. 2013. "The Geo-Body of Contemporary Thai Film." *South East Asia Research* 2 (2): 237–55.

Winichakul, Thongchai. 2020. *Moments of Silence: The Unforgetting of the October 6, 1976 Massacre in Bangkok*. Honolulu: University of Hawai'i Press.

Zimmers, Tighe E. 2021. *That's Entertainment: A Biography of Broadway Composer Arthur Schwartz*. Jefferson: McFarland.

29

GLOBAL ASPIRATIONS/LOCAL AFFILIATIONS

Exploring the Tensions of "Post-Crisis" Thai Cinema, 1997–2004

Rachel Harrison

Pen-ek Ratanaruang's turn-of-the-millennium, comic crime movie, *Rueang talok 69* (Funny Story 6ixty-Nine 1999), is set during the *Tom Yam Kung* economic crisis that befell Thailand in 1997. The film opens with the cruel ritual of a finance company lay-off in which three employees are made redundant by a process of drawing lots. Consecutive close-ups of the tense faces of the women gathered in this Bangkok board room are immediately followed by the figure of their male boss, super-imposed against the city skyline, towering, god-like, over the high-rise banks and offices, his head amid the clouds. With his back to the assembled all-female and identically uniformed personnel, he announces that economic pressures have forced him to let "fate" decide which members of his business "family" he must reluctantly let go. As the last woman shakes out her numbered spill from the container,[1] one among the group opportunistically asks if the boss will also take a turn. The answer is a firmly resounding, "No. I am the manager!" (*Mai khrap, phom pen phu borihan*).

Gender politics and the disempowerment of the subaltern are clearly central to this darkly comic cinematic engagement with the impact of economic collapse on the lives of ordinary Thais, many of whom had moved to the city from rural backgrounds to take up the white-collar jobs that had proliferated in the rapid expansion of the economy in the boom years of the early '90s. Key protagonist Tum is just such a character, having come to work in Bangkok from the southern province of Surat Thani. On selecting unlucky spill number 9 in the lottery of continuing employment, Tum is summarily made redundant.[2] She promptly packs up her office belongings, including a photograph of Princess Diana commemorating the date of her death in 1997. En route home to her dingy Bangkok condominium, Tum observes the poignant symbols of Thailand's economic demise: a laborer collapsed in deep yet precarious slumber in the mouth of a static Hitachi digger; a mangy street dog weaving its way between the traffic on a busy road. The deceased princess, the suspended laborer, the homeless dog – all stand in as markers of the tragedy of Tum's own personal predicament.

Taking the economic collapse as a turning point in Thailand's relations to globalization and to the West, this essay sets out to examine the complex cultural response of

DOI: 10.4324/9781003266952-38

contemporaneous Thai cinema to the effects of the *Tom Yam Kung* crisis. In doing so, it explores the work of Pen-ek and his contemporaries Nonzee Nimibutr, and Wisit Sasanatieng – referred to as part of Thailand's so-called "new wave" of directors who rose to prominence in the late 1990s. My particular focus rests with the tensions that exist between the desire, on the one hand, to be recognized, acknowledged, and successful on the world cinema stage, while on the other simultaneously rejecting globalization and the lure of the West in a deep-seated cultural attachment to the significance of the national, the local, and the rural.[3] In the course of this argument, I survey a range of differing representations of the texture of the Thai local in its shifting, and often double, role – as part signifier of the culturally pure and the authentic, and part bearer of the jejune and the uncivilized by comparison with the superior embodiment of Thainess by the urban elite. In this sense, the double demarcation of the rural precisely echoes the hierarchies of the internally colonizing processes of the late 19th and early 20th centuries in which Siam strove to build itself into the modern nation now known as Thailand. I refer here, in particular, to the 19th-century discourse of the "others within" (see Winichakul 2000), whereby the elite center that is Bangkok directs its colonial-style "civilizing influence" outward over a compliant provincial population. As the political upheavals of the new millennium testify, such discourses remain in place as an effective project of power.

Thailand's "New Wave" Filmmakers

Pen-ek Ratanaruang, Nonzee Nimibutr, and Wisit Sasanatieng are among a small group of avant-garde Thai filmmakers who gained recognition as a result of the experimental ideas and classy production values that they brought to a Thai film world widely considered to have been in the doldrums since the 1980s. With its predilection for low-brow comedies, teen romances, horror movies, hammy performances, and faintly ridiculous plotlines, Thai cinema's absence of quality appeal had led to the resounding dominance of Hollywood in the local market. The Thai "new wave" introduced a revivified brand of national cinema that was also attractive to the overseas market as a result of its vibrant visual aesthetics and quirky narrative arcs. For the first time in cinema history, Thai movies regularly made their way into international film festivals and were picked up by big-time art-house distributors, such as Miramax and Pathé. As Wisit Sasanatiang proudly proclaimed to the Thai media following the international success of his debut feature, the idiosyncratic, multicolor cowboy Western *Fathalayjone* (Tears of the Black Tiger, 2000): "We have gone international. We aren't strangers anymore." The Western press enthusiastically agreed. Writing in the *Financial Times* on the release of *Tears of the Black Tiger* in UK cinemas in August 2001, Nigel Andrews reported that Wisit Sasanatieng has "put a new country on the world movie map . . . even if nobody has a clue how to pronounce his name" (18 August 2001). Others, less enthusiastically, likened the film – the first ever entry from Thailand to have been screened at the Cannes Film Festival – to a two-hour advertisement for Wranglers! The criticism was not without cause, given that Wisit, like his contemporaries, Pen-ek and Nonzee, shared a previous career trajectory in advertising.

Having graduated from the Pratt Institute in New York, Pen-ek (also known by the more Western-friendly pseudonym Tom Pannet), for example, commenced work alongside Wisit at the Film Factory in Bangkok in 1993, producing television commercials for which he won numerous accolades. Notable among them was a bronze medal at the Cannes Lion Awards for a Clairol anti-dandruff shampoo. Wisit's Silpakorn University classmate in visual communication design, Nonzee Nimibutr, similarly went on to become a director of commercials and music videos, as a result of which many of the languorous shots of his early *oeuvre* – such as the visually sensuous opening sequence of *2499, anthaphan khrong mueang* (Daeng Bireley and the Young Gangsters, 1997), the almost self-exoticizing attention to flora, fauna, and custom of his 1999 ghost drama *Nang Nak* (Nang Nak), and the high aesthetics of his subsequent tale of erotic escapade *Jan Dara* (2001) – share the attributes of Tourism Authority of Thailand's signature advertising campaign *Amazing Thailand*.

Drawing on the winning formula of this slick and nostalgic beautification of visual elements, the Thai "new wave" began to gain newfound international acclaim for their feature films in the latter half of the 1990s. Initially released in Thailand in April 1997, Nonzee's *Daeng Bireley* was celebrated for meeting "international standards" in a way that largely eluded earlier works from the industry, with its predominant focus on the cheap and cheerful low-budget B movie, manufactured for a local, low-brow market and ostentatiously shunned by the educated Thai middle classes. As Thai critic Kong Rithdee (2020, page unnumbered) notes, "In film textbooks, *Daeng Bireley* (which was also a huge hit grossing 75 million baht) is regarded as the film that heralded the renaissance of Thai cinema." It went on to win awards for Best Picture and Best Director at the Thailand National Film Association Awards, as well as being nominated for a Dragons and Tigers Award at the Vancouver International Film Festival. Later the same year, it became one of the first Thai movies to be screened in the UK, along with Pen-ek's debut movie *Fun Bar Karaoke*, which enjoyed its world premiere at the 1997 Berlin Film Festival. In the Q&A session with the director, following *Fun Bar*'s screening at the Institute of Contemporary Arts in London, audience members drew attention to its resonance with the work of Quentin Tarantino, in particular to *Reservoir Dogs* (1992) and *Pulp Fiction* (1994). What is significant here is that Nonzee and Pen-ek's earliest movies display no indication of a rejection of the global, nor a particular fetishization of the local, a trend that only emerges in earnest with the collapse of the very economy that had financially supported these directors' rise to international acclaim. On the contrary, *Daeng Bireley*, a biopic of the eponymous real-life gangster set in Bangkok in 1956, arguably fetishizes Thailand's entanglement with the West in terms of both form and content. Daeng derives his very name from the imported Bireley's orange juice he and his fellow hoodlums enjoy while listening to the songs of Elvis Presley and modeling themselves on James Dean. Nostalgia with a hard edge, the film leads its audiences – Thai and Western alike – on a dizzying visual journey down Cold War memory lane. Here, for better or for worse, Thailand and the US walk firmly hand-in-cultural-hand. An about-turn in narrative thrust came, however, with the collapse of the baht in July 1997.

The Cultural Effects of Economic Crisis and the Death of the City

As the ripple effect of the *Tom Yam Kung* economic crisis made itself felt across the entire region, the International Monetary Fund (IMF) stepped in to stabilize the global economy, creating a "rescue-package" for Thailand that enabled it to avoid default and imposing requirements for reform to currency, banking, and financial systems. Although this resulted in prompt economic recovery, the negative cultural effects of IMF intervention nevertheless persisted for much longer and well into the new millennium. In a reflection of the ways in which Thailand grappled with the painful psychological experience of the forces of globalization, and with what it felt to be a neocolonial intervention into its own private affairs, movies made in the aftermath of the bail-out deal, both overtly and implicitly, with these deep-seated cultural implications. While this anti-Western turn included the work of "new wave" filmmakers, such as Pen-ek and Nonzee, it was far from limited to the avant-garde and roundly encompassed by others. This included popular genres such as action movies, exemplified by Yuthlert Sippapak's *Mue puen/loke/phra jan* (Killer Tattoo 2001) and Prachya Pinkaew's *Ong Bak* (Ong Bak, Muay Thai Warrior 2003), and historical dramas such as Thanit Jitnukul's *Bang Rajan* (2000), Chatrichalerm Yukol's *Suriyothai* (The Legend of Suriyothai 2001), and Surapong Phinijkhar's *Thawiphop* (The Siam Renaissance 2004). With passing reference to the nationalistic texture of these popular works by way of wider cultural context, the remainder of this essay will examine the particular nuance and manifestation of the anti-global turn in Thai "new wave" filmmaking. I return, therefore, to the opening discussion of *Rueang talok 69*, in which Tum's tragic experience of city life becomes central to an understanding of Thailand's "post-crisis" cultural rejection of globalization.

Set predominantly in the run-down apartment block and the claustrophobic studio flat in which she lives, Tum appears isolated and strangely disconnected from her neighbors. Aside from the avuncular gaze of a resident septuagenarian who watches the comings and goings of its idiosyncratic "community," her only human encounters come in various forms of toxic masculinity, ranging from violent gangsters and policemen to simpleton Thai kickboxers and sexually promiscuous cheaters and chancers. As the complexities of the plot unfold, leading Tum into darker and more dubious territory, the narrative concludes with her escape from the brink of criminality to the embrace of a moral order that is characterized by a return to the rural. Poised with the possibility of escaping newfound poverty through the acquisition of ill-gotten financial gains, Tum instead jettisons the stolen banknotes she has inadvertently acquired and burns her forged Thai passport to foreclose her escape abroad. In a gesture of allegiance to the (pastoral) homeland, she instead packs up her meager belongings, together with the caged bird that symbolizes her Bangkok lifestyle, and returns to the countryside.

In *Rueang talok 69* the final resolution for Tum is to therefore return "home" to the rural idyll of provincial Thailand, the locus of an "authentic" and caring (maternal) community. As such she directly enacts the words of advice issued by the then-king of Thailand, Rama IX (r. 1946–2016), in the aftermath of the nation's deep financial crisis – to renounce the material trappings of globalization and to follow a path to self-sufficiency (*setthakit pho phiang*), expressed through his metaphor of "walking backward into the canal."[4]

Tum's final journey home plays out to the song "Duang dao, duang ta, duang jai" ("The Stars, the Eyes, the Heart") by the well-known "songs for life" band Caravan, in which the melancholy, folkish tunes of lead singer Nga (Surachai Janthimathon) mourn a loss of innocence and extol the virtues of an inner road to salvation. The era to which the music refers, that of 1970s Thai radicalism, is also significant here, with its nod to the contemporaneous socialist-realist filmmaking of such veteran directors as Prince Chatrichalerm Yukol (*Rueang talok 69* is also edited by the prince's daughter, Pattamanada Yukol). Chatrichalerm's classic movie *Thongpoon Kokepho – Ratsadon tem khan* (Taxi Driver 1977), modelled on Vittorio De Sica's *Ladri di Bicicletta* (Bicycle Thieves 1948), together with its sequel *Itsaraphap khong Thongpoon Kokepho* (Citizen II 1984), paint a similar cultural picture of Thailand's capital as a den of iniquity in which the hapless migrant worker from the boondocks will inevitably meet their demise. Despite the passage of over a decade, Pen-ek's choice to conclude *Rueang talok 69* with the emblematic act of rural repatriation in rejection of modern urbanization typifies much of Thailand's "new wave" filmmaking of the *Tom Yam Kung* crisis years.

It is this positioning of the rural as the idyllic antidote to what is cast as the failed globalizing and modernizing project of the Thai metropolis that this essay now turns.

The Pervasiveness of History

As I and others (see Harrison and Jackson 2010) have argued extensively elsewhere, the processes by which Siam/Thailand has been constructed as a nation-state cannot be extracted from its entanglement with the West, in particular from the colonial dominance of Britain and France in the 19th century; and the neo-imperialist strengths of the US in the Cold War era. At key stages in this lengthy history, Siam/Thailand's concern focuses on how it has been viewed and perceived by the West, and its national cultural identity subsequently molded under this powerful gaze. A key example is provided by the way the Siamese court responded to the damning observations of moralizing Christian reprimand, whereby the royal harem was disbanded, and as Peter Jackson (2003) identifies in his detailed discussion of presentations of gender distinctions in Siam, there ensued alterations to the traditional short hairstyles and gender-neutral dress codes which Western missionaries and travelers found so illustrative of Siamese "barbarity."

In the gestation of this national parturition, the significance of appearances and the power of the visual became, and remains, an important mode in the representation of Thai cultural value. Rosalind Morris (2000) asserts as much in her observation that Thai modernity rests on the fetishism of appearances and the demand for a signifying surface. Her observations are compounded by the work of Maurizio Peleggi (2002) on the acquisition of luxury goods during King Rama V's royal visits to Europe in 1897 and 1907, which included the purchase of both still and movie cameras. The moving image soon became popular in Siam, exemplified by prompt screening of the Lumière brothers in Bangkok in 1897. The visual image in general, and the moving image in particular, became important bearers of the identification of Thainess in a world on which Siam was keen to take its place on the world stage. And, as I indicate at several junctures in this essay, the past and the present, both literally and metaphorically, are never far apart from each other in the context of Thai global aspirations and its constituent local affiliations. This persistent and dynamic tension between the aspiration to be global on the one hand, and to remain resolutely local on the other, is crucial to this reading of "post-crisis" Thai cinema between the years of 1997 and 2004.

As I noted earlier, the historical dimension is, in particular, an important one, given that understanding the complexities of Thailand's cultural response to the West post-1997 requires an attention to the texture of the Siam's relations with colonial powers from over a century before. The allure of the West was, and remains, an ambiguous one for Siam/Thailand, holding both positive and negative connotations for the characterization of its national culture. While on the one hand constituting a draw, and acting as a source of desire, status and fascination, the West conversely and simultaneously represents a threatening negation of imagined Thai moral and cultural values. Nowhere better is this articulated than in Thongchai's treatment of bifurcation as an intellectual strategy for "coming to terms with the West," wherein he observes:

> To Thais of all social strata, the relationship with the West has entailed a paradoxical set of desires: how to catch up with the West without "kissing the asses of the *farang*" (*tam kon farang*); how to be like the West yet also to remain different; how not to

love the West despite its attractions; and how not to hate it, despite its obnoxious dominance.

(Winichakul 2010, 135)

Thongchai's deployment here of the highly evocative term "obnoxious dominance" is one that most accurately describes the Thai response to Westernization in the aftermath of the *Tom Yam Kung* crisis, both in relation to what was perceived as the cultural arrogance of the IMF and, more broadly, in terms of the damaging effects of too much globalization on the "purity" of an imagined "authentic Thai culture." Movies such as *Thawiphop* explicitly refer to the perceived cultural cruelty of the IMF itself, linking it directly to the historical moment of the Paknam Crisis of 1893, the pinnacle of France's colonial threat to Siam. At a ball hosted by the crass and loathsome French consul to Siam, Manee, the time-traveling heroine of *Thawiphop*, finds herself being questioned by a young American woman on the subject of slavery – one that was central to Western disapproval of Siam on the civilizational scale: "What do you think about abolishing slavery, as they are doing right now in America?" the young woman asks. "Abolishing slavery in Siam, it's going to happen," Manee accurately predicts, with the hindsight that comes from her 21st-century persona. "I mean, it's going to happen for the sake of humanity, and not culture." The term *culture* is pointedly deployed in this English language dialogue, as the camera switches from Manee's shrewd expression to the raucous display of frilly underwear provided by the backdrop of French can-can entertainers, in an ironic visual remark on the base sexual nature of this national cultural signifier. "You must know the place – USA, new country?" the white woman continues superciliously. "Oh, we've heard of them," Manee retorts. "Have you heard of IMF? WTO? CIA? MTV?" The acronyms that Manee chooses display a tellingly sinister relationship to one another. Leaning over to whisper more tantalizingly in the American woman's ear, she educates the Westerner: "Our future generation will love them, believe me!"

Here Manee's words of warning about the fragility of "Thainess" as a pure and unadulterated cultural form reiterate the observations made in an earlier conversation when she speaks of 21st-century Thailand with the 1850s courtiers Dhep and Tri:

Manee: Our country is very modern. There are many skyscrapers. Everything has changed. We have cars, electricity, movie theaters. We dress in a Western style. We revere Westerners more than we revere one another. We have everything Westerners have. We are everything Westerners are. We eat everything Westerners eat. We like anything Westerners tell us to like. We want to be them and refuse to be ourselves.

Dhep: **But you said we were not colonized. And do we still have a king?**

Manee: This is the only thing that keeps us as ourselves . . .

This statement precisely reflects the Thai nationalist post-economic-crisis zeitgeist, which pertained long after the positive economic impact of IMF intervention. This lasting sense of trauma in relation to the corrosive effects of "too much Westernization" reverberates through the content of much Thai cinema produced during this period, echoing the dominant narratives of the 19th century. It is a version of events that, written from a Siamese nation-building perspective, vociferously argues for the significance of the deft diplomacy of the monarchy (notably Kings Rama IV and V) and the Bangkok elite, spearheaded by an innately (Buddhist) Thai penchant for compromise that directed them to "bend with the winds of change" and hence salvage the greater part of the whole by yielding to a degree of Western control. In short, this version of history heralds the important nationalist lesson that Siam was never formally colonized by the West. Were the message not clear enough from the plot and dialogue of *Thawiphop* itself, it is further substantiated by the non-fictional opening sequence of the DVD release of the film. The selection of expert talking heads who didactically inform their viewers of the cultural significance of this quasi-historical narrative includes then vice president of the Thai Parliament, Somsak Pritsanananthakun, who explains to the camera:

> The message that the director of this movie aims to present is of the utmost importance to Thai society [today]. It is something which young people should know – the techniques that our forefathers, those alive in 1893, used to fight [against imperial powers]. They used the politeness, gentleness, humility, and ability to offer a warm and friendly welcome which typify Thai society. They applied the knowledge of how and when to concede the battle in order to win the war.

That the relationship with the outside world – and in particular the West – is seen as one of conflict, struggle, and combat is evident from a number of films made in this period, and while *Thawiphop* celebrates certain putative Thai national characteristics as vehicles of the will to compromise, other movies, such as *Ong Bak* and *Bang Rajan*, instead celebrate the heroism and moral authority of outright combat. As the battlefield lies scattered with the corpses of the defiant villagers of Bang Rajan, who fought valiantly against the invading Burmese armies in 1766, the somber music of this popular collective biopic leads to a view of the modern-day monument to their bravery, and the significance of commemorating their defiance is highlighted by the following narration:

> Eight months later, Ayutthaya was destroyed. [. . .] Siam remained in disarray until its people once again were reunited into a single sovereignty by the warrior who would become King Taksin the Great. The Siamese had their freedom once again, and from that time on, the Kingdom of Siam has remained independent and has never to this very day become the colony of any other nation.

One of the key strategies by which Thai cinema reiterated this imagined continuity between the uncolonized past and the independent present was through the historical movie genre, enhanced with the lavish aesthetic pleasures of nostalgia. Whereas neither Surapong nor Thanit is considered part of the Thai avant-garde, their approaches to popular nationalist/localist narratives do not fundamentally differ from the tropes adopted by their "new wave" contemporaries, such as Pen-ek and Nonzee, as I go on to posit here.

Inventing the Rural

While the predilection for nostalgia was already evident in Nonzee's first feature film, *Daeng Bireley,* nurtured by the director's experience in the world of TV commercials, his second feature, *Nang Nak,* took up a view of history with a renewed sense of national pride. Although this depiction of Thailand's best-known female ghost, Nang Nak, did meet with a degree of global success, its dominant impact was felt both in the domestic market, and among its wider Asian neighbors. Writing for the English-language daily *The Bangkok Post*, Thai film critic Kong Rithdee (2020, page unnumbered) notes:

> Nang Nak, directed by Nonzee Nimibutr and written by Wisit Sasanatieng, unleashed an unprecedented momentum of enthusiasm and became the first Thai movie to blaze past the 100-million-baht mark at the box office. It would eventually earn 150 million baht – an astounding figure in 1999, when a cinema ticket cost 100 baht or less. At that time nobody thought it possible for a local production to prove such a massive hit. Nang Nak represented a watershed moment, ushering the Thai film industry into a new era of financial and creative possibilities; it restored audiences' confidence in Thai cinema after years in the doldrums, and also helped put Thai film on the world cinematic map after a successful international tour. It was, in many ways, a film that transformed Thai film forever.

Given the iconic status granted to *Nang Nak* in both domestic and international terms, what is of specific interest in relation to the themes of this essay is its hyper-nationalist pretensions and its deft demonstration of what Winichakul (2010) refers to as a strategy of bifurcation in "coming to terms with the West." As Kong Rithdee (2020) remarks in his review of the film, the story of the female ghost Nang Nak is one known by the entire Thai population – a mythical tale of a woman who dies in childbirth while her husband, Mak, is away at war. Transformed into a ghost, Nak resides with Mak on his return, wreaking havoc on local villagers who threaten to inform him of his delusion. The immense popularity of the story made it the subject of numerous low-brow cinematic versions in the 1960s, '70s, and '80s, combining the traditional tropes of ghostly haunting with slap-stick comedy. Widely available in cheap VCD format, they include titles such as *Mae Nak Phrakhanong* (Nak of Phrakhanong), *Mo Mae Nak* (Nak's Pot), *Mae Nak khuen chip* (Nak Returns to Life), and *Mae Nak America* (The American Nak).

Nonzee's innovative approach to this traditional tale was to cast it as a myth grounded in a quasi-authentic historical context, hence granting it the symbolic authority of a chronicle. His specific choice of historical moment is also one of deep significance, aligning it to the "scientific brilliance" of the modernizing monarch King Rama IV (r. 1851–68) that dominates nationalist mythmaking at the commencement of the Western colonial threat to Siam. The film opens with the scene of a solar eclipse, giving the precise date as 18 August 1868, the very moment of an actual eclipse correctly predicted by the monarch as a result of newly acquired knowledge from the West. As people go about their daily business on the canal, panic ensues with the gradual disappearance of the sun. Birds scatter and monks chant as the moment of total darkness arrives. As such, the sequence encapsulates the primary concerns of the narrative – the battle between darkness and light, rational knowledge versus superstition, modernity over backwardness, the assertion of the "civilized" center over a rural periphery that has spun out of control.

The marauding spirit of Nang Nak, who introduces a reign of terror among local villagers in order to prevent them from informing her battle-scarred husband that she is in fact a ghost, unfailingly challenges the capacities of rural spiritual practitioners and ghost banishers to bring her under their control. Only a visit to the village from the high dignitary Somdet To – a real historical figure in the court of King Rama IV – has sufficient spiritual clout to resolve Nak's entrapment in the karma of this life and release her into the next. Symbolic of King Rama IV's campaign to "modernize" Buddhist practice in Siam – a key element, again, of the intellectual strategy of bifurcation in coming to terms with the West – Somdet To brings an end to "uncivilized" rural superstition in his destruction of the curse of Nang Nak. While Nonzee does introduce a novel degree of sympathy for this tragic heroine's plight as an unfulfilled lover, wife, and mother, the audience nevertheless experiences the relief necessary to the horror film genre's structure that is delivered by the concluding suppression of her malevolence. Hence, the scene in which Somdet To pushes back the crowd of rural onlookers gathered around her grave and chants an incantation inviting her to bid farewell to her life in ghostly/human form is not without a certain metaphorical violence. Having finally laid her to rest as a decaying corpse, he instructs his temple boy to chip out a sizable piece of her forehead, so releasing the evil winds inside her and entrapping them in the bony relic. Calm ensues: Mak is pictured by her funeral pyre as a newly ordained Buddhist monk, and, again related in faux-historical terms, the narrator offers this closing edification:

> Since that time, no one has been haunted by ghost of Nang Nak. Somdet To made the forehead relic into a girdle brooch which he wore for the remainder of his life. Legend has it that after his passing, the brooch became the possession of HRH Prince Chumbhorn Ketudomsak, and was subsequently handed down to many others, with no knowledge of where it currently resides.

As with other films produced in this post-crisis era, the final sentence asserts a vital continuity between past and present.

The continuity implied in Nonzee's version of *Nang Nak* relates, in this instance, to the superiority it grants to the palace/center via the role of the high dignitary over the raucous supernatural misadventures of the periphery. As such, this hyper-royalist nationalist narrative serves to confirm the importance of nation/religion/king (*chat/satsana/phra maha-kasat*) – the triolet deployed as the linchpin of Thai national cultural identity from the time of King Rama VI (r. 1910–25). As in Thongchai's discussion (2000) of the suppression of "others within" as fundamental to the Bangkok elite's internally colonizing nation-building agenda, the village community among whom Nak resides is rendered pure by the intervention of the higher orders of the centralizing state. Hence, in this conservative nationalist imaginary, the spiritual superiority of the monarchy, symbolized by the figure of Somdet To, reigns supreme.

While there may appear to be something of a contrast here between Nonzee's depiction of the rural as backward, and Pen-ek's view of the provinces as a source of escape from the depravity of the city, these apparently contrasting images in fact represent two sides of the same nationalist coin: for both confirm the supremacy of Thai royal discourses in the path to cultural survival. In *Nang Nak* the threat of the colonial West is implied by the very date of the narrative and its allusion to the diplomatic brilliance of King Rama IV in his spiritual form of resistance to Western "civilization." In *Rueang talok 69* the rejection of global capitalism and materialism is more overt as Tum drives herself home to the provinces in a rusty pickup truck loaded with a meagre set of belongings. Both films, in their different ways, reiterate the warning issued by King Rama IX in his 1998 birthday speech on the merits to Thailand of self-sufficiency in the face of too much globalization. And yet both movies were made by filmmakers intensely caught up in that very project of globalization – through their professional training and their clear aspirations to the interdependent factors of commercial and international success. In achieving this success at the very point at which Thailand experienced economic crisis and a subsequent cultural withdrawal from the allure of the West, "new wave" directors such as Pen-ek Ratanaruang, Nonzee Nimibutr and Wisit Sasanathieng found themselves at a complex nexus of intersecting influences and demands, many of which are explored through their representation of the local and the rural.

Notes

1 This refers to a specific ritual practice of fortune-telling, usually in Thai Buddhist temple environ-ments, in which a round wooden container is filled with wooden spills, each with a number on it. The person seeking a prediction shakes the cask in their two hands until one spill loosens itself from the others and falls to the floor. The number on the spill corresponds to a paper with the same number in a nearby cabinet, on which the relevant prediction is written. In some cases it is difficult to encourage only one spill to separate from the others and all fall from the cask together, as we also see happen to the most nervous participants in the opening sequence of this film.

2 Pen-ek's choice of the number 9 here is arguably an interesting one, given the significance of par-ticular numbers in Thai culture. The pronunciation of the word 9 – *kao* in Thai – echoes that of the word for "progress," as a result of which it is usually considered to be lucky rather than to portend misfortune. In addition to that, the film is made and set during the reign of the highly revered King Rama IX (r. 1946–2016), which is surely a further indicator of good fortune. Given the way in which the narrative concludes, the director perhaps leads his audience to understand that the final resolution for Tum is ultimately the best outcome on both a personal and national political level.

3 The chapter deliberately omits reference to the fourth member of the Thai "new wave" – Apichatpong Weerasethakul – whose work does not fit this trajectory and about whom much has already been written.

4 The full details of the monarch's approach to the self-sufficiency economy, from which these words are taken, are provided in his birthday speech, delivered on 4 December 1998. For further details, see https://www.chaipat.or.th/eng/concepts-theories/sufficiency-economy-new-theory.html (accessed 8 June 2023).

References

Harrison Rachel, V., and Peter A. Jackson, eds. 2010. *The Ambiguous Allure of the West. Traces of the Colonial in Siam/Thailand*. Hong Kong: Hong Kong University Press.

Jackson, Peter A. 2003. Accessed June 18, 2023. https://8limbsus.com/wp-content/uploads/2014/03/Performative-Genders-and-Perverse-Desires-A-Bio-History-of-Thailands-Same-Sex-and-Trans-Gender-Cultures-Peter-Jackson.pdf.

Morris, Rosalind C. 2000. *In the Place of Origins: Modernity and Its Mediums in Modern Thailand*. Durham, NC: Duke University Press.

Peleggi, Maurizio. 2002. *Lords of Things. The Fashioning of the Siamese Monarchy's Modern Image*. Honolulu: University of Hawai'i Press.

Rithdee, Kong. 2020. "Nang Nak at 20." Accessed June 8, 2023. https://www.bangkokpost.com/life/social-and-lifestyle/1719095/nang-nak-at-20.

Winichakul, Thongchai. 2000. "The Others Within: Travel and Ethno-Spatial Differentiation of Sia-mese Subjects 1885–1910." In *Civility and Savagery: Social Identity in the Tai States*, edited by Andrew Turton, 38–62. Richmond, Surrey: Curzon.

———. 2010. "Coming to Terms with the West: Intellectual Strategies of Bifurcation and Post-Westernism in Siam." In *The Ambiguous Allure of the West. Traces of the Colonial in Siam/Thai-land*, edited by Rachel V. Harrison and Peter A. Jackson. Hong Kong: Hong Kong University Press.

Thai Filmography

Bang Rajan (dir. Thanit Jitnukul), 2000.

Citizen II (*Itsaraphap khong Thongpoon Kokepho*) (dir. Chatrichalerm Yukol), 1984.

Daeng Bireley and the Young Gangsters (2499, *anthaphan khrong mueang*) (dir. Nonzee Nimibutr), 1997.

Fun Bar Karaoke (dir. Pen-ek Ratanaruang), 1997.

Funny Story 6ixty-Nine (*Rueang talok 69*) (dir. Pen-ek Ratanaruang), 1999.

Jan Dara (dir. Nonzee Nimibutr), 2001.

Killer Tattoo (*Mue puen/loke/phra jan*) (dir. Yuthlert Sippapak), 2001.

The Legend of Suriyothai (dir. Chatrichalerm Yukol), 2001.

Monrak Transistor (dir. Pen-ek Ratanaruang), 2001.

Nang Nak (dir. Nonzee Nimibutr), 1999.

Ong Bak, Muay Thai Warrior (dir. Prachya Pinkaew), 2003.

The Siam Renaissance (*Thawiphop*) (dir. Surapong Phinijkhar), 2004.

Taxi Driver (*Thongpoon Kokepho – Ratsadon tem khan*) (dir. Chatrichalerm Yukol), 1977.

Tears of the Black Tiger (*Fathalayjone*) (dir. Wisit Sasanatieng), 1999.

30

REVISITING THE FACE VEIL IN POST-PANDEMIC TIMES

The Humane Visual Ethics of Indonesian Islamic Filmmaking

Alicia Izharuddin

Introduction

The face mask became a global symbol of protection from the spread of the COVID-19 pandemic in 2020, generating numerous commentaries on its intersubjective implications (Ricca 2020; Lee 2020; Calbi et al. 2021; Sikka 2021; Yan and Slattery 2021). Used as an effective barrier against the highly infectious airborne coronavirus, mask-wearing became compulsory across much of the world in early 2020, especially in indoor spaces where physical distancing was more difficult to maintain. Although there is a near-universal concession to the face mask on public health grounds,[1] there are arguments against it, stating that the partial concealment of the face has a deleterious effect on the fundamentally "socially reflexive" nature of humanity (Kowalik 2021). Indeed, the foregoing argument against face masking has echoes, albeit ways more philosophically considered, in the proposal to ban the niqab, which purportedly violates the spirit of "living together" in Europe and the mask bans in the United States that targeted environmental activists and Antifa (Ricca 2020; Kahn 2020). At the root of this philosophical argument is that social and ethical connection fails when the face is obscured.

The continuities between the face mask and face veil, however, have not gone unnoticed by scholars;[2] both cover the lower half of the face, revealing only the eyes. Widely interpreted as a woman's submission to ultra-conservatism and social segregation, the face veil has gained new meaning in a world where every individual must wear a face covering. Indeed, the COVID-19 pandemic has necessitated a shift in meanings and perceptions toward all manner of facial coverings worn by different groups of people for both better and worse, including some unexpected outcomes. In cultural contexts where face veiling was a minority practice, women who have adopted the face veil found themselves feeling safer and more accepted in a world that has been required to do the same.[3]

In Indonesia, the right to wear the niqab (*cadar*) takes place in a discursive struggle over religious authenticity, ideological politics, and personal piety. Subject to attempted bans and othering, the face veil is not widely practiced in a country with the largest Muslim population in the world. This chapter examines feature-length and short films from Indonesia – *Khalifah* (2011) and *Cadar* (Face Veil 2020) – and juxtaposes them against the

DOI: 10.4324/9781003266952-39

public discourse on face coverings during the pandemic to illuminate the shifting fault lines of ethics of the face. These films were released during particular moments of the geopolitics of Islamic modernity and global history of pandemics – the world after 9/11, before and after COVID-19. The niqab, or *cadar* in Indonesia, is a fabric covering worn by women who follow a more conservative interpretation of Islam. Worn with a hijab that tightly conceals the hair and a loose, enveloping garment known as the abaya, these articles of clothing are more commonly worn in countries of the Gulf states, although a smaller number of women wear them in parts of South and Southeast Asia. Women who adopt them wear the niqab as an expression of their faith, modesty, and privacy, their face belonging only to the realm of permissible intimacy. But in public social contexts where they represent a visible minority across Western and Asian societies, they are vulnerable to violent Islamophobic, xenophobic, and racist attacks (Piela 2021).

The meaning of the covered face in Indonesia has gained new meaning during a time when everyone is required to cover theirs. Is there more ethical compassion and understanding for a group of women long relegated to the category of Other in this post-COVID-19 moral landscape? Drawing on the work of Emmanuel Levinas, this chapter considers the meaning of the face and revisits the charged semiotic field of the face veil in Indonesia's Islamic filmmaking and visual culture and argues that the partially concealed face holds the potential for a humane visual ethics.

The Humane Visual Ethics of the Covered Face

For Emmanuel Levinas, ethics begins with the recognition of the other's uniqueness and without requiring seeing the other like oneself. That recognition takes place in the face-to-face encounter with the Other:

> The absolute nakedness of a face, the absolute defenseless face, without covering, clothing or mask, is what opposes my power over it, my violence and opposes it in an absolute way, with an opposition which is opposition itself.
>
> *(Cited in Bauman 1993, 73)*

From this quote, Levinas makes it clear that an ethical encounter can only occur between unconcealed faces for a face covering would only obscure one's humanity. The encounter demands the individual to take moral responsibility for the safety of the other as precedence over the security of the self. The face is crucial for Levinas. Without a face or language, we cannot feel morally compelled to protect the other, which is why he argues that plants and animals fall outside the remit of absolute moral responsibility. For Levinas, the face of the other calls upon us to submit to its vulnerability. It demands us to see its humanity (Campbell, McPhail and Slack 2009). Rather famously, Levinas asserts that the naked face and its universal humanity make an injunction, "Thou shall not kill" (Levinas 1997, 8–9). And so long as there is a "face" in our encounter with the other, we have an ethical obligation to protect them.

While Levinas's concept of the face has both literal and metaphorical meanings, its ethical implications are much more elusive than meets the eye. Crucially, as Bauman comments on Levinas's "face," the ethics of difference means confronting "the other as a face, not mask" (1995, 59). When is a face not a mask when it is partially concealed? Before the pandemic, debates about the niqab and burqa have raised similar questions but have produced different answers. Studies suggest that certain human expressions are harder to discern than others behind the niqab (Fischer et al. 2012). More concerningly, positive (happier) expressions were less perceptible because the lower half of the face is obscured, while negative emotions were more easily established from the eyes of the wearer of the niqab (Kret and de Gelder 2012; Kret and Fischer 2018).

The global mandate for face-masking, however, has undermined Levinas's prescription for moral subjecthood. Zygmunt Bauman finds that the moral responsibility commanded of the viewer is less convincing when we must face and encounter so many others. In fact, he argues that in modern society we often find ways to avoid encountering others (Campbell, McPhail, and Slack 2009). Bauman situates the face in a sociological context of difference, in an attempt to find the answer to why the moral responsibility called upon by the face of the other fails. That context is modernity whereby the face has become dehumanized by differentiation. For the face to restore its ethical claim, it has to be unmediated and liberated from social categories – race, color, gender, class, and disabilities (Tester 2002; Junge 2001). Bauman's rejection of the mediating element of social categories is inspired by Levinas's claim to the face's transcendence and irreducibility as an object. Moreover, it would seem that the opportunity for a face-to-face encounter is made much more difficult because, phenomenologically, individual experiences may unavoidably be mediated through social categories and, during the COVID-19 pandemic, higher-order biopolitical mechanisms that absorb the other into the wider populace.

The face veil as a global symbol of protection, however, is not in fact universal but "positional" (Lee 2020, 238). The COVID-19 pandemic has laid bare the differentiated terrain that determines who is able to cover their faces safely and who is not. As accounts emerge when the pandemic unfolded in the United States, racialized faces do not always feel protected by mask mandates. Due to the racist criminalization of black bodies, Black American men in particular express reluctance to don a face covering that was not explicitly medical grade. Their refusal to mask can be traced to the longer history of bans on face masks by groups that are deemed to be threatening to social order (Kahn 2020). Conversely, communities of color that are culturally conditioned to wear face masks in public are not treated as more responsible or hygienic but quite the opposite. As Lee herself found (2020), being an Asian American woman in a face covering in New York makes her an object of anxious suspicion, as commuters sit some distance away from her on a crowded subway train. In these socially distanced times, seeing people close enough is discouraged as a public health precaution. The face, of what can be seen of it, is too distanced for a close ethical encounter.

Indeed, a partially concealed face requires us to look longer, to impress our gaze to the other, and to consider it more carefully. In other words, the veiled face requires another (longer) look, a double take. Because Levinas has left open what he means by the face, others have stepped in to establish ocular-centric particularities of the encounter without necessarily needing the entire face for ethical recognition:

It is the way that someone looks us in the eye that allows us to break through the form in which the other appears. The eyes are absolutely naked and in the vulnerability of this nakedness, in its unmasked non-presence, the face gets it meaning or its expression.

(Kaulingfreks and ten Bos 2007, 305)

This quote suggests that an ethics with the other begins with the eyes can be established behind the partially concealed face, with the exception of the eyes behind the burqa. Here, we find that because alterity and unfamiliarity form the principle underpinning the other's being, the notion of the face is in fact reconfigurable. That the face is still a face insofar as it is made up of a pair of eyes, discernible facial expressions, a nose, and a mouth, though concealed, that is able to speak. The face is potentially reconfigurable because it exceeds any attempts of objectification. To be objectified, according to Levinas (1993), is to be relatable to one's stable and organizing frame of reference. The Levinasian face is singular, unique, and requires no context (Kenaan 2011). As Levinas himself asserts, "The face enters our world from an absolutely foreign sphere [. . .] from ultimate strangeness. The signifyingness of the face is, in the literal sense, extraordinary, outside of every order, outside of every world" (Levinas 1998: 96). Although Levinas makes a rather mystical claim about the face of the other, he advances an ontology that transcends familiarity and embraces the strangeness of the stranger. Does the ultimate strangeness of the partially covered face elicit moral responsibility in the viewer?

Face Veiling in Indonesian Filmmaking

The face veil has a particular historical modern resonance in Indonesian cinema. Its first appearance was in the 2008 film by Hanung Bramantyo, *Ayat-ayat Cinta* (Verses of Love). *Verses of Love* marked the film industry's convergence with the geopolitics of Islamic modernity and went on to elicit much commercial interest in the production of films about pious Indonesians living in a world remapped by 9/11. Such films loosely belong to the category of the Islamic film genre, films that deploy visible and audible symbols of Islam with an ethical agenda of transforming the spirituality and consciousness of its audiences (Izharuddin 2017). Across different Muslim-majority societies, such as Iran and Turkey, films with Islamic themes resonate with and reflect the prevailing Islamic resurgence of the public sphere. Indonesia is no different in this respect; Islamic films dominated the cinematic sphere in the years after the end of the New Order regime, a 32-year period marked by the repression of political Islam. Such films may require the legitimacy of religious authorities to be regarded formally "Islamic," although the cinematic medium allows for considerable flexibility in the spheres of interpretation (see Pak-Shiraz 2011) for the role of the clergy in "spiritual" Iranian cinema). It bears mentioning here that the Islamic film genre did not originate in the post-9/11 cinematic landscape but had existed since the beginning of the Indonesian film industry itself. The Islamic film genre engages with issues that are mainly topical and contemporary, occasionally venturing into landmark historical events, legends of holy men, and hagiographic biopics of leaders against the incursions of Dutch imperialism (Izharuddin 2017), underlining the close associations of the Islamic film genre with nation(alistic) themes. As I have argued elsewhere (Izharuddin 2020), modern Indonesian films about Islam are ethnographic and autobiographical in that they are ways of narrating the national self. The genre has gained attention often for its unambiguous mission to inspire piety in audiences who may be faced with moral choices in a relatively unfettered media landscape (Sasono 2013). However, such a mission is in tension with a less spiritual commercial imperative, an aspect that has made the genre both popular and controversial (Imanda 2012).

The films discussed in this chapter are no different in this respect. They join the many films of the Islamic genre in Indonesia since the New Order period that engage in varying degrees with the questions of nationhood, typically deploying historical, Qur'anic, and fictional protagonists as vehicles for both the nation and hegemonic interpretations of Indonesian Islam. Nurman Hakim's *Khalifah* (90 minutes), a commercial film released in 2011, takes as its point of departure a woman's embodied journey through global ideological and gendered discourses in her practice of face veiling (see Izharuddin 2015a for a detailed analysis of the film). Khalifah is a young woman married to a traveling businessman who has gone to Saudi Arabia for work. On his return, he presents to her the niqab and abaya brought back from his business travels and persuades her to wear them. Her dramatic change of daily attire disrupts her employment as a hairdresser and alienates her from the rest of society. She is brought back from the brink of social isolation after learning that wearing the niqab can land her in mortal danger posed by the trigger-happy figures of law enforcement who kill terrorists disguised as niqabi women. It is an implausible risk to her as a genuine wearer of the niqab but one that Khalifah is unwilling to take and so she removes her face veil thereafter. By discarding the niqab, she returns to the fold of the nation, blending imperceptibly into the fabric of society. Critical of Salafist Islam, the film's underlying message is that the niqab alienates its wearer from the nation and any possibility of collective embodied difference.

Other films about the face veil have a more humanistic message of conviviality, of living together in difference that *Khalifah* suggests is impossible to accomplish. *Cadar* (Face Veil 2020), by Izzul Muslimin and Zulebid, in collaboration with an Islamic school in Central Java, is a six-minute short film that makes an assertive claim to belonging to the nation. Their short film is a response to another, much-contested short film, *My Flag – Merah Putih vs Radikalisme* (Red White vs Radicalism 2020), produced by the largest Islamic organization in Southeast Asia, the Nahdlatul Ulama (NU) and released primarily for online viewership, that pits nationalism against Islamist radicalism. It is more overtly ideological than Nurman Hakim's film. Vehemently jingoistic in tenor, the short film by NU portrays a group of young women and men leading a flag-bearing campaign in their village to spread the spirit of nationalism. The film drew criticism for its battle scene between the patriotic young individuals against their antagonists, those who bear the flags of Islamist extremism. Among the latter are women who wear the *cadar*. The young nationalists defeat their antagonists but not without tearing the face veils from the vanquished women. Izzul Muslimin and Zulebid's short film utilizes the founding ideological slogan, Unity in Difference (*Bhinneka Tunggal Ika*), to make a claim on the centrality of difference as a pillar of collective nationhood. Difference here refers to gendered and religious difference as a touchstone of belonging. As its title suggests, difference is embodied by women who wear the face veil whose nationalistic fervor cannot be discounted on account of their alterity. The value of difference is cultivated in the school environment where a young teacher who wears the face veil educates her female students the virtue of national belonging, occupying the role of the Other who teaches (Todd 2003). It ends with a symbolic scene of mutual integration – from either side a group of young women in hijab holding their flag. One carries the red-and-white Indonesian flag, and the other, in a face veil, flies a white flag inscribed with the shahada, a phrase of allegiance to Islam: "There is no God but Allah, and Muhammad is his messenger" in Arabic. The two groups walk toward each other until they are face-to-face before coming together in a loving embrace.

In another short film released online also called *Cadar* made in 2020 by Dwi Putri Mawar, the notion of difference posed by the face veil is established right from the outset. Like the other short film, *Cadar*, it concerns a young woman who wears the face veil and must face overcome her otherness in school. She has moved from the more conservative state of Aceh to a new school where the practice of face veiling is much less common. Upon her arrival, she is aware of the disparaging looks she receives from fellow members of the school who do not wear the face veil; she is a literal stranger to her new surroundings. A bullying scene sets the discourses of the face veil and face masking in collision with the polysemic meanings of the "virus." Two girls attack the new student with the degrading epithet associated with the niqab, "ninja," and throw water in her face for acting as if the COVID-19 virus has arrived in their village. By linking her face veil with the infectious coronavirus, the bullies perpetuate the associations of Othered bodies with contagion. There is no information on when the short film was made, but it is likely to have been made between February 2020 and the date of its publication on YouTube in November 2020, when the global pandemic was well underway. During this short window of historical time, Indonesia was grappling with a public health crisis of misinformation and denials of the coronavirus's existence and deadly spread (Nasir, Baequni, and Nurmansyah 2020).

The three films demonstrate the powerful, often over-determining visual power and meanings of the partially covered face. They situate the discourse of face veiling within a highly charged landscape of religious authenticity and national belonging. Historically, the idea of Indonesia as a nation has had a much-contested relationship with political Islam. It had been founded on an ideologically pluralist politics that maintained the subordination of political Islam to the modern nation-state. Veiling had been banned in Indonesian schools for its associations with political Islam until the early 1990s. When the repression of overtly political expressions of Islam was fully lifted following the end of the New Order regime in 1998, face veiling became a new point of contention, a boundary for Islamic expression in the public sphere. Terrorist attacks post-9/11 and in Bali in 2002 urgently shifted the national discourse toward preserving a "peaceful" culturally indigenous Islam from the incursions of a "violent," extremist version that is both inauthentic and foreign, codewords for Arab-influenced practices and ideological beliefs. While the veil has been accepted as part of the religious fabric of the national self, the face veil remains outside of this schema.

It bears mentioning here that these three films mobilize a methodology that eludes much of the global discourse of face veiling: the woman behind the face veil as narrator-protagonist. The face of the other for Levinas is not of one who is spoken for but rather the one that does the speaking. The women at the center of the three films speak to assert their humanity and difference. They do not pursue a project of assimilation into the fabric of the self-same nation but remain other in an ethical relationship with the nation. In a similar spirit as Levinas, they demand viewers of their concealed faces to challenge their preconceptions, confront their alterity, and be provoked into moral compassion and solidarity.

Conclusion: Lowering One's Gaze?

At this juncture, one may wish to ask what the Islamic implications are for a Levinasian ethics of the face and indeed the eye-to-eye encounter. In the Qur'anic injunction to Muslim adherents, one must lower our gaze on the opposite sex as an expression of modesty to avert sinful feelings of desire[4] and prevent illicit sexual relationships. This injunction would mean that it could be difficult for pious Muslims to look deeply into another's eyes if the meaning of the face-to-face encounter can be misconstrued. Moreover, in the gendered dynamics of looking in a conservative male-dominated society, men do the looking and women can only be looked at. The Levinasian of ethical encounter with the other might fail under these circumstances.

All three films operate in a particular kind of scopic regime that strives to resolve the tension the face veil raises in what Lacan calls the field of the gaze. In Lacan's formulation, the field of the gaze refers to the gaze that sees the seer: "I see only from one point but in my existence I am looked at from all sides" (1998, 72). In the closing sequence of *Khalifah*, the central character comes to terms with herself when she faces her reflection in a mirror; she is face-to-face with herself, declaring "I am Khalifah," unifying the self and Other within herself. Via the mirror, she reclaims her feminine "spectatorial subjectivity" (Fuss 1994). The visual-ethical resolution in Dwi Putri Mawar's short film *Cadar* is triggered by a sudden change of heart; the bullies apologize for their behavior and welcome the girl in the face veil into their fold; they accept her Otherness without requiring her to look like them. Likewise, in Izzul Muslimin and Zulebid's short film *Cadar*, the young women bearing different flags confront one another face-to-face and embrace their ideological differences.

There are no men involved in these climactic moments of face-to-face encounter with the other, circumventing the Islamic prohibitions of the gaze. The women do not need to lower their gaze to see each other face-to-face. These are looks that are exchanged between veiled women, which depart from the classical model of the gaze. The veil, the face veil included, does not make the wearer invisible nor "blind" to others as they are frequently rendered in the visual-psychoanalytic writings about the veil (Ragland 2008; Copjec 2006; Alloula 1986). Rather, they are often rendered much more visible because of their difference. As Gökarıksel and Secor (2014) argue, veiled women are inserted into the scopic regime as both subject and object of the gaze. Thus, as a consequence, Othering does not always take place between the looks of veiled women. The female gaze between women operates in a different kind of politics (Izharuddin 2015b); one appeals to another kind of desire, one of mirror mutuality and identification. These films have demonstrated the continuity of othering across geopolitical and pandemic epochs and the potential of ethical encounters that embrace the Other.

The COVID-19 pandemic has brought to our attention the meaning of both the naked and covered face in unprecedented ways. It exposes the historical, gendered, racialized, and ideological fault lines that have made the covered face contentious and positional instead of universal. But as public health measures to manage the spread of infectious diseases have restored much of the freedoms in public life for most people, among which includes the ability to be in public spaces without face coverings once more, facial concealment may mark certain bodies as once again Other.

Notes

1 The mask mandate is far from uncontested. Opposition to mandatory face coverings on various political and ideological grounds has been swift.
2 The niqab, however, is insufficient as protection from the contagious coronavirus because it does not fully cover the nose and mouth from external air flow.
3 Muslim women who cover their faces find greater acceptance among coronavirus masks – "Nobody is giving me dirty looks." Anna Piela, "The Conversation," 10 April 2020, accessed 28 April 2022, https://theconversation.com/muslim-women-who-cover-their-faces-find-greater-acceptance-among-coronavirus-masks-nobody-is-giving-me-dirty-looks-136021.
4 There are types of deliberate looking that are permissible and forbidden according to Islamic theologians, such as voyeurism and looking at the contents of a secret missive (Maghen 2007).

References

Alloula, Malek. 1986. *The Colonial Harem*. Minneapolis: University of Minnesota Press.

Bauman, Zygmunt. 1993. *Postmodern Ethics*. Oxford: Blackwell.

Calbi, Marta, Nunzio Langiulli, Francesca Ferroni, Martina Montalti, Anna Kolesnikov, Vittorio Gallese, and Maria Alessandra Umilta. 2021. "The Consequences of COVID-19 on Social Interactions: An Online Study on Face Covering." *Nature Scientific Reports* 11: 2601.

Campbell, David J., Ken McPhail, and Richard Slack. 2009. "Face Work in Annual Reports: A Study of the Management of Encounter Through Annual Reports, Informed by Levinas and Bauman." *Accounting, Auditing and Accountability Journal* 22 (6): 907–32.

Copjec, Joan. 2006. "The Object-Gaze: Shame, Hejab, Cinema." *Filozofski Vestnik* 27 (2): 11–29.

Fischer, A. H., M. Gillebaart, M. Rotteveel, D. Becker, and M. Vliek. 2012. "Veiled Emotions: The Effect of Covered Faces on Emotion Perception and Attitudes." *Social Psychological and Personality Science* 3: 266–73.

Fuss, Diana. 1994. "Fashion and the Homospectorial Look." In *On Fashion*, edited by Shari Benstock and Suzanne Ferriss, 211–32. New Brunswick, NJ: Rutgers University Press.

Gökarıksel, Banu, and Anna Secor. 2014. "The Veil, Desire, and the Gaze: Turning the Inside Out." *Signs: Journal of Women in Culture and Society* 40 (1): 177–200.

Imanda, Tito. 2012. "Independent versus Mainstream Islamic Cinema in Indonesia: Religion Using the Market or Vice Versa?" In *Independent Southeast Asian Cinema: Essays, Documents, Interviews*, edited by Tilman Baumgartel. Hong Kong: Hong Kong University Press.

Izharuddin, A. 2015a. "The Muslim Woman in Indonesian Cinema and The Face Veil As 'Other'." *Indonesia and the Malay World* 43 (127): 397–412.

———. 2015b. "Pain and Pleasures of The Look: The Female Gaze in Malaysian Horror Film." *Asian Cinema* 26 (2): 135–52.

———. 2017. *Gender and Islam in Indonesian Cinema*. Singapore: Palgrave Macmillan.

———. 2020. "Cinema of Misrecognition: Gender, Islam, and the Terrorist." In *Muslims in the Movies: A Global Anthology*, edited by Kristian Petersen. Cambridge: ILEX Foundation.

Junge, Matthias. 2001. "Zygmunt Bauman's Poisoned Gift of Morality." *British Journal of Sociology* 51 (1): 105–19.

Kahn, Rob. 2020. " 'My Face, My Choice?' – Mask Mandates, Bans, and Burqas in the COVID Age." *New York University Journal of Law and Liberty* 14 (3): 651–708.

Kaulingfreks, Ruud, and René ten Bos. 2007. "On Faces and Defacement: The Case of Kate Moss." *Business Ethics: A European Review* 16 (3): 302–12.

Kenaan, Hagi. 2011. "Facing Images After Levinas." *Angelaki: Journal of Theoretical Humanities* 16 (1): 143–59.

Kowalik, Michael. 2021. "An Ontological Argument against Mandatory Face-Masks." Accessed May 1, 2022. https://philpapers.org/archive/KOWAHC.pdf.

Kret, M. E., and B. de Gelder. 2012. "Islamic Headdress Influences How Emotion is Recognized from the Eyes." *Front. Psychol.* 3: 1–13.

Kret, M. E., and A. H. Fischer. 2018. "Recognition of Facial Expressions is Moderated by Islamic Cues." *Cognition and Emotion* 32: 623–31.

Lacan, Jacques. 1998. *On Feminine Sexuality: The Limits of Love and Knowledge*. New York: Norton.

Lee, Pamela M. 2020. "Face Time, Pandemic Style." *October Magazine* 173: 230–41.

Levinas, Emmanuel. 1993. *Outside the Subject*. London: Athlone Press.

———. 1997. *Difficult Freedom*. Baltimore: Johns Hopkins University Press.

———. 1998. "Meaning and Sense." In *Collected Philosophical Papers*. Pittsburgh: Duquesne University Press.

Maghen, Ze'ev. 2007. "See No Evil: Morality and Methodology in Ibn Al-Qaṭṭān al-Fāsī's Aḥkām al-NaZar bi-Ḥāssat al-Baṣar." *Islamic Law and Society* 14 (3): 342–90.

Nasir, Narila Mutia, Baequni Baequni, and Mochamad Iqbal Nurmansyah. 2020. "Misinformation Related to COVID-19 in Indonesia." *Jurnal Administrasi Kesehatan Indonesia* 8: 51–59.

Pak-Shiraz, Nacim. 2011. *Shi'i Islam in Iranian Cinema: Religion and Spirituality in Film*. London: Bloomsbury Publishing.

Piela, Anna. 2021. *Wearing the Niqab: Muslim Women in the UK and the US*. London: Bloomsbury Publishing.

Ragland, Ellie. 2008. "The Masquerade, the Veil, and the Phallic Mask." *Psychoanalysis, Culture and Society* 13: 8–23.

Ricca, Marco. 2020. "Don't Uncover That Face! Covid-19 Masks and the Niqab: Ironic Transfigurations of the ECtHR's Intercultural Blindness." *International Journal for the Semiotics of Law* 1–25.

Sasono, Eric. 2013. "Islamic Revivalism and Religious Piety in Indonesian Cinema." In *Performance, Popular Culture, and Piety in Muslim Southeast Asia*, edited by Timothy P. Daniels. New York: Palgrave Macmillan.

Sikka, Tina. 2021. "Feminist Materialism and Covid-19: The Agential Activation of Everyday Objects." *NORA – Nordic Journal of Feminist and Gender Research* 29 (1): 4–16.

Tester, Keith. 2002. "Paths in Zygmunt Bauman's Social Thought." *Thesis Eleven* 70 (1): 55–71.

Todd, Sharon. 2003. *Learning from the Other: Levinas, Psychoanalysis, and Ethical Possibilities in Education*. Albany: State University of New York Press.

Yan, Sijin, and Patrick Slattery. 2021. "The Fearful Ethical Subject: On the Fear for the Other, Moral Education, and Levinas in the Pandemic." *Studies in Philosophy and Education* 40: 81–92.

31

KARMA-IMAGE; INSIGHT-IMAGE

On Buddhism and the Cinema

Victor Fan

Buddhism addresses many concerns in contemporary film and media theory. For example, as a philosophy that examines how consciousness is informed through the interdependencies between forms, sensations and affections, perceptions, and memories and dispositions, Buddhism offers an understanding of how the image is constituted. Meanwhile, Buddhism also scrutinizes how we can reconcile our lived experience in the perceptual-conceptual world, which is founded on the constant discrimination between subject and object, and *tathatā* (Pāli)/*tathātā* (Sanskrit) (the way it is), which is nondiscriminative. This line of investigation corresponds to contemporary film philosophers' attempt to rethink the relationship between spectator and image as an intersubjective process or a process of becoming in which intersubjective relations are constantly being inscribed and reinscribed onto an assemblage of energetic and affective flows.[1]

This chapter has a dual purpose. On the one hand, I introduce the basic principles of Buddhism and explain how it can engage in a conversation with Euro-American film and media philosophy. In this regard, I argue that the cinematographic image is informed by an assemblage of karmic relationships (karma-image), which can potentially induce wisdom or insight.

On the other hand, I also bring the readers' attention to the conundrum of any attempt to put philosophical frameworks from Asia and Euro-America into a comparative dialogue. In film and media studies, questions of perception, consciousness, and image-formation are regarded as universal. However, in the process of theorization, we often universalize observations and ideas from a particular regional or historical context and authorize it as a universal truth. If this is the case, how can we conduct this comparative discourse with a mindfulness of this pitfall? Furthermore, when we interpret a film from Asia, we often feel the need to refer to a hermeneutic framework that is specific to that region. Nonetheless, if our sensory-perceptual process is supposed to be universal, a filmic experience should then be regarded as *universally approachable*. If so, why is it necessary for us to add a context (e.g., Buddhism) to a text (e.g., a film) that would otherwise be considered universal (Lamarre 2017, 286)?

This conundrum can in fact be rethought by using Buddhist philosophy. The divides between universal and particular, text and context, and in fact, *kamma/karma* (karma) and

DOI: 10.4324/9781003266952-40

paññā/prajñā (insight) are often thought dualistically. But if we think about these ideas *relationally* and *interdependently,* we shall realize that their positions often change in a complex process of interbecoming.

Buddhism as a Philosophy

In the *Majjhima Nikāya* (Middle Collection), Buddha Śākyamuni considers his teaching as a method, not a philosophy, which is best understood not through logical reasoning, but mindfulness practice (MN63 1998). However, even during his lifetime, Buddha Śākyamuni engaged in philosophical dialogues with Brahmins and other scholars (MN98 1998). After his death, early and sectarian (later known as Theravada) Buddhists developed philosophical treatises, which are collectively known as the Abhidhamma/Abhidharma (metadiscourse) (*Kathāvatthu* 1894–97). From the second to the seventh centuries, the study of the Abhidharma flourished in India, and the debate there would then be further developed in other parts of Asia after Buddhist studies declined in India itself around the seventh century (Stcherbatsky 1993).

From the fourth to seventh centuries, Yogācāra scholars focused on the study of *viññāṇa/ vijñāna* (consciousness). They believe that the world as we know of it is a *vijñapti* (manifestation) or image of our consciousness. This is not to say that the world is not real or that everything is simply a projection of our mental formation. Rather, our sensory-perceptual reality is a manifestation based on our memories and dispositions, not *the way it is* (*Lanka-vatara Sutra* 2012). The Yogācāra understanding of the image, as I shall demonstrate, has profound implications on our understanding of what the cinematographic image is and what role a spectator plays in its formation.

For Śākyamuni, our body and its associated milieu are constituted by the five *khandhas/ skandhas* (aggregates). For him, our body and its associated milieu are an assemblage of molecules and energies, which all affect – and are affected by – one another. In fact, these molecules and energies co-arise and co-perish interdependently. One cannot exist without another. In other words, none of these molecules and energies exist on its own, and none arise out of any *sabhāva/svabhāva* (intrinsic nature). When these energies or molecules aggregate, some become the *forms* that constitute our body and other become the forms of the body's associated milieu. And when the forms of the body and the forms of its associated milieu are in contact, *vedanās* (sensations and affections) arise not only in our own body but in the bodies of all sentient beings and objects.

Sensations and affections co-arise with *saññas/samjñās* (perceptions). *Samjñās* are sometimes translated as discriminations. This is because sensations and affections arise with the differentiation between self (the subject who senses) and other (the object being sensed). Perceptions are therefore the results of a constant discrimination between the self and the other and from one being or object from another. These perceptions are informed by *saṅkhāras/samskaras* (memories and dispositions). Memories can be personal or communal, intergenerational or intermigrational, and interspecies or even cosmic.

Meanwhile, dispositions refer to afflictions such as avarice, anger and frustration, delusion, conceit, suspicion, worry, sorrow, suffering, as well as anxiety and fear. They can also be non-afflictive, such as mindfulness and diligence. These memories and dispositions have been formed for eons (without beginning) and are so strong that we often misrecognize them as our volition. In other words, on a day-to-day basis, we keep thinking that there is a *self* that compels us to live. In truth, this *self* is an aggregate of our memories and dispositions (MN109 1998).

The operation of this process of becoming is enabled by two abilities: *darśana bhāga* (the ability to sense and perceive) and *nimitta bhāga* (the ability to turn what being sensed and perceived into forms, signs, and intentions). These two abilities are collectively known as consciousness. The Yogācāra scholars never argue that what we call the *external* world is simply a projection of our mind. Rather, what we call the body and its associated milieu are aggregates of molecules and energies, but the way we perceive and conceptualize them as *sense data* is configured by memories and dispositions. This is called *parikalpitah-svabhāva* (taking what we perceive and conceptualize as the way it is). The resulting perceived-conceptualized reality follows the principle of interdependent co-arising, also known as *paratantra-svabhāva* (*Jie shenmi jing* 2010).

If André Bazin argues that the photographic image is an imprint of reality, he has not identified the ontological ground of the photographic image itself (Bazin 1958, 14–15, 18). Rather, he has identified the ontogenetic interdependency between two perceptual-conceptual realities – the lived reality of the moment at which the photograph was taken and the reality of the moment at which the photograph is beheld – and the photographic reality. In logical terms, we can say that based on the photographic technology of the 1940s, because a lived reality in the past arose, in which a photographer took a picture, a beholder in the present can now perceive and conceptualize the photographic image as an imprint of that reality. This is the *paratantra-svabhāva* of the image. This interrelation is in turn dependent on the *darśana bhāga* and *nimitta bhāga* of those people who were involved in taking that picture and the *darśana bhāga* and *nimitta bhāga* of the beholder themselves. This is the *parikalpitah-svabhāva* of the image.

The ontological ground, if any, is the assemblage of memories and dispositions that compelled the photographer and the photographed subject to capture that flitting moment on film and the assemblage of memories and dispositions that compels the beholder to form a relationship with this image. However, if the perceptual-conceptual reality is constituted out of an assemblage of interdependent relationships, memories and dispositions cannot be regarded as an ontological ground. It is because memories and dispositions are simply part of an assemblage of conditions that act on and are acted on one another (Fan 2022, 47–53). In Pāli and Sanskrit, the interdependent relationships between acting on and being acted on is called *kamma/karma*. In other words, existence has no ontological ground; instead, it is a perceptual-conceptual impression that arises out of an assemblage of karmic relationships (Yin Shun 1952, 272–307).

If we look at this example, it seems that consciousness is consciousness *of* something. For instance, when I look at a photograph, I am conscious of the reality of which it serves as an imprint. Yet if we think more carefully about the five aggregates, my body and its associated milieu are an overall assemblage of molecular and energetic flows. The so-called *I* is in fact retroactively inscribed onto a sub-assemblage of molecules and energies (the body). In other words, I may have the impression that *I* have a consciousness that belongs to me, which relates itself to the photographic image as a consciousness. However, *the way it is* is that consciousness encompasses both the body and its associated milieu. In this consciousness, the subject-object divide is constantly inscribed, reinscribed, and repositioned onto the ever-changing molecular and energetic flows. This idea corresponds to Gilles Deleuze's idea of the movement-image, which is best understood not as an image projected onto the screen, but a process of becoming of which the technical body of the cinema and the organic body of the spectator are a part (Deleuze 1983, 83–84; Bergson 1939, 1–71).[2] Thích Nhất Hạnh calls such a process *interbeing* or *interbecoming* (Thich 2006, 210–12).

In *Cinema Illuminating Reality,* I therefore argue that the cinematographic image is, first and foremost, a karma-image. However, not all our memories and dispositions are afflictive. As I mentioned earlier, memories and dispositions such as mindfulness and diligence help produce insight. An insight refers to a mindfulness of how each presence of the present or *here and now* is constituted by perception-conception and dependent originations. Historically, many East Asian painters and aesthetes have employed and discussed formal strategies in art to nurture mindfulness, and certain modes of cinematic experiences can also transform a karma-image into an insight-image (Fan 2022, 71–156).

Buddhism as Method

Before I explain how a film can be considered as an insight-image, I want to draw our attention to a rift between how media philosophers and scholars in regional studies ruminate on the same issue differently. In media philosophy, the formational process of the cinematographic image, as a sensory-perceptual process, is presumably universal. Meanwhile, in regional studies, the sensory-perceptual process is contingent on socio-political and historical differences. How do we reconcile these two positions from a Buddhist perspective?

The presupposition that the sensory-perceptual process is universal is in fact challenged in the *Śūraṅgama Sūtra*: that such a presumption fails to explain the difference between potentiality and its actualization. For the writers of the *Śūraṅgama Sūtra,* the potentialities to perceive and conceptualize are always part of a cosmic assemblage of memories and dispositions. Nonetheless, these memories and dispositions are not always actualized when some sensory-perceptual functions are *concealed* because of a physical or mental disability or because they are rendered purposeless in a meditative state (*Śūraṅgama Sūtra* 2012, 41–42).

For Buddhist philosophers, therefore, knowledge building is always an act of turning a (subjectively-)objective sensory-perceptual field into an (objectively-)subjective reality, since an episteme is constituted out of forms, signs, and intentions (Ñāṇananda 2012, 5–6). In European philosophical terms, Buddhist philosophers believe that there is no such thing as an episteme; rather, what we take for granted as an episteme is *technē*, that is, a body of knowledge built on technics such as memories and language.

Acknowledging the fact that all theoretical and philosophical frameworks speak from their respective subjective positions has serious political implication. As Gayatri Chakravorty Spivak argues, under colonialism and postcolonialism, theory has been produced either by Euro-Americans or by non-Euro-American intellectuals who employ the Euro-American critical paradigm. Therefore, the process of theorization inevitably posits an unmarked Euro-American subject, who observes other regions not only as their object of study but as an *exception*. The resulting knowledge about these regions is therefore less about what and who they are but about how they are different from the presumed Euro-American norm (Spivak 1988, 276–86).[3]

However, as Ani Maitra and Rey Chow as well as Thomas Lamarre point out recently, postcolonial studies have inadvertently produced another conundrum. On the one hand, media theorists and philosophers continue to maintain that discussions of our sensory-perceptual process, the relationship between human and technics, and media and mediation are presumably universal. On the other hand, scholars in regional studies tend to provide local contexts for both individual film and media texts and the presumably universal theoretical or philosophical frameworks themselves. In so doing, the presupposed universality of Euro-American knowledge and the universal approachability of individual film and media texts remain largely unquestioned. Moreover, Asia as a context continues to function as an exception to the Euro-American norm.

Maitra and Chow propose the use of "actant theory" to rethink the relationship between media objects and their technicity, human participants, and socio-political, cultural, and historical formations. For Maitra and Chow, instead of considering media objects and their technicity as the texts, human participants as the mediators, and the socio-political, cultural, and historical formations as the contexts, we can rethink them all as *actants*, that is, active agents who act on and are acted on one another. Lamarre concurs with this approach and further argues that as molecular, energetic, and affective energies continue to change and exchange in an assemblage, human beings, technical objects, and their associated milieus continue to be retransindividuated from one phase to another, resulting in a constant individual-milieu recoupling in which all these components are active agents (Lamarre 2017, 286–88; Maitra and Chow 2016, 212).

In *Understanding Our Mind*, a reworking of Vasubandhu's fourth-to-fifth-century treatise *Vimśatikāvijñaptimātratāsiddhi* (Twenty Verses on Consciousness Only) and *Triṃśikāvijñaptimātratā* (Thirty Verses on Consciousness Only), Thích Nhất Hạnh explains the Yogācāra's position on this issue. For the Yogācāra scholars, all *bījas* (seeds or potentialities) remain dormant in a domain of our consciousness called the *ālaya-vijñāna* (storehouse consciousness). At each given moment, an assemblage of conditions would activate some of these potentialities, which are then actualized as memories and dispositions in the conceptual domain of our consciousness or *manos-vijñāna*. These specific memories and dispositions will then configure the sensory-perceptual domains of our consciousness.

Thích further argues,

> Some seeds are innate, / handed down by our ancestors. / Some were sown while we were still in the womb, / others were sown when we were children.
>   Whether transmitted by family, friends, / society, or education, / all our seeds are, by nature, / both individual and collective
>
> (Thich 2006, 13–14)

If so, there is no division between text and context, since all the actants in a mediating process are constituted out of interdependent co-arisings, and these interdependent relationships are manifestations of personal, communal, contemporaneous, and historical potentialities. No actant in this mediating process arises from a fundamentally *universal* or *regional* nature. If we perceive a phenomenon that appears to be universal, it is because certain memories and dispositions that constitute it have been shared by so many interbeings and processes of interbecomings for generations or even eons. If we perceive a phenomenon that appears to be local or regional, it is because these memories and dispositions are shared predominantly in a specific community. Yet within the storehouse consciousness, there is no discrimination between seeds that are universal and seeds that are local. Rather, they are all parts of an assemblage of potentialities and conditions that are constantly interaffecting one another.

Toward the Insight-Image

Insight is attained through *sati/smṛti* (mindfulness). *Smṛti* generally refers to an awareness that arises at a *kṣaṇa* (moment or smallest unit of time) (DN22 1998). An awareness, for Yogācāra scholars, is a manifestation of an avalanche of interdependent memories and dispositions. When an awareness arises, we are usually not aware of its nature as a manifestation (*parikalpitah-svabhāva*) and its nature of arising out of an assemblage of interdependent conditions (*paratantra-svabhāva*). Instead, we perceive such an awareness as an interval between the past and the future. However, as second-century Buddhist philosopher Nāgārjuna argues, the past no longer exists in the present; likewise, the future has yet to exist in the present. In other words, the only moment that exists – out of dependent originations – is the here and now (Yin Shun 1952, 342–52).

Mindfulness is therefore an engagement with the here and now: the constitution of the physical body as an aggregate of molecular and energetic flows; the arising and extinction of sensations and affections; the formation of an awareness by an avalanche of memories and dispositions; and the processes of interbecoming between the body and its associated milieu *as* consciousness. Since the Six Dynasties (220 or 222–589), Chinese intellectuals have found the Buddhist understanding of mindfulness resonating with the Daoist idea of *zuowang*, which refers to a complete engagement with the here and now as a cosmic process of interbecoming, thus enabling one to surrender the discrimination between self and other. For these intellectuals, art – especially painting, poetry, and music – enables one to attain such *jing* (*dhatu/dhātu* or realm) of mindfulness (Sima 2009; Yu 1989).

In Sanskrit, *dhātu* is neither a mystical nor transcendent state of mind. Rather, it refers to the interdependent conditions and physical elements that give rise to the fleshly body (sensory-perceptual domains of the consciousness) and its embodied mind (consciousness's conceptual, volitional, and storehouse domains) (MN140 1998). In other words, the *dhātu* of mindfulness is a state of complete engagement with the body and its associated milieu here and now.

Zong Baihua, based on the aesthetic discourses from the Six Dynasties to the mid-Qing dynasty (18th century), argues that a painting engages a beholder's mindfulness by inviting the consciousness to *you* (navigate) in a constantly mobile space. This idea corresponds to Nāgārjuna's argument that *existence* is spatialized from one moment to another in a constant process of interbecoming. The resulting image-consciousness is therefore movement itself, as movement is not *something* that is added to an image but a perception-conception that informs the image itself. When someone beholds an ink wash painting, their eyes navigate from a point in the painting that forms the middle of the distance between the overall milieu and the beholder's body. Since the eyes are embodied, the beholder's body is enabled to journey to the different areas in the painting, a movement that continuously produces and reconfigures the body's relationship with its associated milieu. Such a journey enables the beholder's *xin* (heart) to be liberated, thus disconcealing the *tathātā* of the body and its associated milieu as a perceptual-conceptual manifestation and an assemblage of processes of interbecomings (Zong 1987, 246).[4] In Buddhist terms, when an assemblage of *bījas* is manifested, the ripe conditions facilitate the arising of the image as movement.

In the 1990s, the Hong Kong film scholar Lam Nin-tung borrows the Daoist notion of *qi* (energy), *yun* (essence), *sheng* (arising), and *dong* (movement) to further theorize Zong's idea in relation to the cinema. For Lam, energetic flows inform the essence from which the image-consciousness comes to exist, which is constantly in movement. In his writing,

Lam argues that since the 1920s, Chinese filmmakers have been consciously following the principles of *qi, yun, sheng,* and *dong* in their mise-en-scène, a formal strategy that he calls *jingyou* (mirroring-journeying). Even though Lam presents archival evidence to corroborate his claim, his argument is both historiographically overgeneralizing and culturally essentialist. We can at most argue that aesthetics that is inspired by a syncretism between Buddhism, Daoism, and Confucianism has indeed formed part of an assemblage of memories and dispositions of many Chinese filmmakers and spectators since the 1920s. As a result, the cinema is best understood not as a manifestation of such aesthetic syncretism; rather, such aesthetics manifests itself *with* other values taken from Euro-American thinking and modes of vernacular modernity.

For example, Lam argues that Richard Poh (Bu Wancang) was one of the filmmakers who committed himself to developing a *youdong de kongjian yishi* (mobile spatializing consciousness) (Lam 1983, 58–85). Poh started his career in 1921 when he worked as a camera operator for Benjamin Brodsky. In 1926, he joined the Star Motion Picture Company and directed Lily Yuen's (Ruan Lingyu) debut *Guaming de fuqi* (A Married Couple in Name Only, 1926) and became one of the most influential filmmakers of his time. He then joined the United Photoplay Service in 1930 and continued to work consistently during the Second Sino-Japanese War (1937–45), including productions that were probably sponsored by Japanese investors. Then, in 1948, he migrated to Hong Kong, where he made Mandarin features till 1968.

Lam argues that Poh has a tendency to use long shots in his films, in which dramatic actions would take place in the *zhongjing* (middle distance between the spectator and the background of the frame). Between the spectator's body and the action, that is, the foreground of the frame, Poh would place a *ge* (obstacle), which can be a table, window, or even small object. For aesthetes from the Six Dynasties, a *ge* either blocks the action that takes place in the *zhongjing* or emphasizes the distance between the action and the spectator. Such an obstacle arouses the spectator's desire to get closer to the action or even initiate tactile contact with it. Yet the distance between the spectator and the action and the barrier imposed by the obstacle itself and the cinematographic screen remind the spectator of the interbeing between the spectating body and the associated milieu, a process of becoming generated precisely by the desire to see, as well as other afflictions such as anger and frustration, delusion, and fear and anxiety. The image-consciousness, which is informed by this process of interbecoming, is therefore not limited to the action itself and the afflictions it generates. Rather, the sensory-perceptual and conceptual domains of the consciousness become mindful of the assemblage of interdependent conditions that is constantly in movement. When these domains are in motion, the image-consciousness effectively *spatializes* these interdependent relationships as forms.

Such aesthetic strategies are more visible and tangible in Poh's wartime works including *Mulan congjun* (Mulan Joins the Army, 1939), *Wanshi liufang* (Eternity, 1939), and *Guohun* (The Soul of China, 1948). In these films, Poh eliminates all camera movements. Instead, he uses static long shots in most of the scenes to enable the spectators to meditate on these seemingly stationary, though intra-affectively mobile, images. His earlier works, however, often employ formal strategies seen in films directed by King Vidor and F. W. Murnau. For instance, in *Lian'ai yu yiwu* (Love and Duty, 1931), when the young and handsome Li Tsu-yi (played by Raymond King, Kim Yeom, or Jin Yan) follows Yang Nai-fang (played by Yuen) down a suburban street on their way to school, Poh uses a single tracking shot reminiscent of Vidor's or Murnau's camerawork. To enable the two characters to emanate their youthfulness, Poh not only shoots this sequence on a sunny day with high exposure but also provides supplementary lights on the side of the dolly itself to create "halos" behind the characters' heads consistently. Furthermore, by limiting the focal length of the lens, the camera operator can rack the focus between the foreground and background characters in order to highlight the playfulness of these two lovers.

Poh's references to Vidor and Murnau (the film's karma-image), however, coexist with shots that are akin to the insight-image. Figure 31.1, for instance, is taken from a scene in which Nai-fang pays a visit to the film's villain, Hwang Da-jen. We can see that the key action – Nai-fang playing with her child Ping-er – is staged in the *zhongjing*. This distance between the spectator and the action arouses the spectator a desire to get closer to the action and become mindful of the interdependent relationships between the spectating body, the action, and the overall milieu. Such a process of interbecoming between the spectator and the action enables the sensory-perceptual and conceptual domains of the consciousness to navigate to the *shenyuan* (distance in depth) to appreciate the carefully designed semicolonial décor and to the front to catch a glimpse of the film's villain, Da-jen, who deliberately ignores her in favor of his own work. In fact, Da-jen's indifference to Nai-fang's financial difficulties and suffering highlights a key theme in the film: the impermanence or unpredictability of life and the karmic relationship between one's action and one's own consequences.

In *Cinema Illuminating Reality*, I suggest that the karma-image and the insight-image are two categories. However, a cinematographic image, by default, always arises out of karma, whereas an insight-image enables the spectator to become mindful of the assemblage of interdependent conditions as well as the karmic relationships that inform the image-consciousness itself. Nonetheless, in Mahayana Buddhism, karma and insight are both perceptual-conceptual categories. It is because the image is informed by karma that an insight into its formational process can be generated, and it is because an insight can be

Figure 31.1 The use of the *zhongjing* in *Lian'ai yu yiwu* (Love and Duty, Richard Poh 1931).

generated that the spectator can perceive and conceptualize karma. These categories are not dualistically opposed to each other. Rather, they are relationally *interbe*. In this light, the karma-image and the insight-image are two processes of interbecoming.

Conclusion

Buddhism addresses many concerns in contemporary film and media theory, and it enables us to rethink the cinematographic image and its embodied experience as a process of inter-becoming between the reality in which the film was shot, the reality in which the spectator forms a relationship with the image, as well as the technical intervention that forms part of the overall assemblage of interdependent conditions. This process of interbecoming is driven by memories and dispositions. Some of them are shared by many people and sentient beings, whereas others are personal. In fact, all philosophical discourses of the cinema are affected by memories and dispositions. Meanwhile, each film, as an image-consciousness, arises out of an assemblage of personal, socio-political, historical, and cultural conditions, which are all active agents in its process of becoming. Because of this, Buddhism cannot be considered the sole interpretative framework of any given film. Rather, it is one of the many actants that con-stitute the image-consciousness. In *Love and Duty,* for instance, Buddhism is one out of many *technai* that actively inform the film as an assemblage of *interbeings* and *interbecomings*.

Notes

1 Film phenomenologists regard the cinematic experience as an intersubjective process. See, for example, Sobchack (1992, 3–12). Gilles Deleuze, meanwhile, regards the cinema as a process of becoming in which intersubjective positions are inscribed onto energetic flows. This idea is elabo-rated in Deleuze and Guattari (1972, 24–25).
2 For an alternative view, see Thich (2006, 159–65).
3 See also Chen (2010).
4 The idea that image is movement can be found in Yin Shun (1952, 79–100) and Deleuze (1983, 19).

References

Bazin, André. 1958. "Ontologie de l'image photographique." In *Qu'est- ce que le cinéma? 1, Ontolo-gie et langage*, 9–17. Paris: Éditions du Cerf.

Bergson, Henri. 1939. *Matière et mémoire: Essai sur la relation du corps à l'esprit*. Paris: Presses Universitaires de France.

Chen, Kuan-Hsing. 2010. *Asia as Method: Toward Deimperialization*. Durham, NC: Duke University Press.

Deleuze, Gilles. 1983. *Cinéma 1: L'image Mouvement*. Paris: Éditions de Minuit.

Deleuze, Gilles, and Félix Guattari. 1972. *L'Anti-Œdipe: Capitalisme et schizophrénie 1*. Paris: Édi-tions de Minuit, 2012.

DN22. 1998. "The Great Establishing of Mindfulness Discourse: Mahā Satipaṭṭhāna Sutta." In *Dīgha Nikāya*, translated by Thānissaro. https://www.dhammatalks.org/suttas/DN/DN22.html.

Fan, Victor. 2022. *Cinema Illuminating Reality: Media Philosophy Through Buddhism*. Minneapolis: University of Minnesota Press.

Jie shenmi jing [Saṃdhinirmocana Sūtra or Sūtra of the Explanation of the Profound Secrets]. 2010. Translated by Xuanzang. Putian: Guanghua si.

Kathāvatthu [*Points of Controversy*, dated circa 240 BCE]. 1894–97. Edited by Arnold C. Taylor. London: Pali Text Society by H. Frowde.

Lam, Nin-Tung. 1983. "Zhongguo dianying de kongjian yishi" [The Spatializing Consciousness of Chinese Cinema]. *Zhongguo dianying yanjiu* [*An Interdisciplinary Journal of Chinese Film Stud-ies*] 1: 58–85.

Lamarre, Thomas. 2017. "Platformativity: Media Studies, Area Studies." *Asiascape: Digital Asia* 4 (3): 285–305.

The Lankavatara Sutra. 2012. Translation and commentary by Red Pine. Berkeley, CA: Counterpoint.

Maitra, Ani, and Rey Chow. 2016. "What's 'in'? Disaggregating Asia Through New Media Actants." In *Routledge Handbook of New Media in Asia*, edited by Larrisa Hjorth and Olivia Khoo. Abingdon, Oxon: Routledge.

MN63. 1998. "The Shorter Instructions to Malunkya: Cula-Malunkyovada Sutta." In *Majjhima Nikaya*, translated by Thānissaro. https://www.dhammatalks.org/suttas/MN/MN63.html.

MN98. 1998. "Vāseṭṭha." In *Majjhima Nikaya*, translated by Thānissaro. https://www.dhammatalks.org/suttas/KN/StNp/StNp3_9.html.

MN109. 1998. "Maha-Punnama Sutta: The Great Full-Moon Night Discourse." In *Majjhima Nikaya*, translated by Thānissaro. https://www.dhammatalks.org/suttas/MN/MN109.html.

MN140. 1998. "An Analysis of the Properties: Dhātu-vibhaṅga Sutta." In *Majjhima Nikaya*, translated by Thānissaro. https://www.dhammatalks.org/suttas/MN/MN140.html.

Ñaṇananda, Kañukurunde. 2012. *Concept and Reality in Early Buddhist Thought: An Essay on* Papañca *and* Papañca-Saññā-Saṅkhā [1971]. Sri Lanka: Dharma Grantha Mudrana Bhāraya.

Sima, Chengzhen. 2009. *Zuowang lun* [*On Zuowang*]. Beijing: Beijing Airusheng shuzihua jishu yanjiu zhongxin.

Sobchack, Vivian. 1992. *The Address of the Eye.* Princeton: Princeton University Press.

Spivak, Gayatri Chakravorty. 1988. "Can the Subaltern Speak?" In *Marxism and the Interpretation of Culture*, edited by Cary Nelson and Lawrence Grossberg, 276–86. Urbana: University of Illinois Press.

Stcherbatsky, Fyodor. 1993. *Buddhist Logic* [1930–32]. New Delhi: Motilal Banarsidass Publishers.

The Śūraṅgama Sūtra. 2012. Translated by Hsüan Hua. Ukiah: The Buddhist Text Translation Society.

Thich, Nhat Hanh. 2006. *Understanding Our Mind.* Berkeley: Parallax Press.

Yin Shun. 1952. *Zhongguan lunsong jiangji* [*Lectures on the Mūlamadhyamakakārikā*]. Taipei: Zhengwen chubanshe.

Yu, Anlan, ed. 1989. *Hualun congkan* [*Theories of Painting Series*]. Beijing: Renmin meishu chubanshe.

Zong, Baihua. 1987. "Zhongguo shihua zhong suo biaoxian de kongjian yishi" [The Spatial Consciousness Manifested in Chinese Poetry and Painting, 1949]. In *Meixue yu yijing* [*Aesthetics and yijing*]. Beijing: Renmin chubanshe.

32

PERSONALITY AND MORALITY IN SCREEN PERFORMANCE

Hong Kong Film Criticism and Social Reform of the 1920s

Enoch Yee-lok Tam

During the early 1920s, film production and cinema-going emerged in Hong Kong, and several publications began discursively promoting film culture. The earliest extant examples of film criticism written by Chinese writers in Hong Kong can be traced to three publications: *Xinbizhao yingxilu* (Coronet Motion Picture Bulletin 1924, six issues), *Yingxihao* ("Film Corner," a film column in the newspaper *Chinese Mail* 1924–1925), and *Yinguang* (Silver Light 1926–1927, five issues). *Silver Light*, allegedly the first film periodical in Hong Kong, was founded by Wei Chunqiu, Pan Qingxin and Yang Weiwen, with Mo Hanmei in charge of reader submissions and Chen Qiwen of art design. The magazine was inaugurated on 1 December 1926, by the Film Arts Society, a nonprofit organization for film enthusiasts, during the Hong Kong–Canton General Strike (1925–26). The strike severely impacted the local film industry in the following four years until 1929, with many film studios and production companies forced to cease operations or move to Shanghai (Chu 2003, 5–6). Nevertheless, *Silver Light* continued to be published, bearing witness to the ongoing development of film culture in Hong Kong through its discursive practices. One of the magazine's features was its comprehensive coverage of the film industry in both Hong Kong and China, including news and updates on the latest productions, directors, and actors. Additionally, *Silver Light* provided its readers with news and updates from foreign countries, allowing them to stay informed about the latest developments in the global film industry. Through in-depth analysis and critical commentary on the film industry and individual movies, *Silver Light* helped to shape the discourse around cinema in Hong Kong and fostered a greater appreciation for the art form among its readers (Yu Mowan 1996). In doing so, the magazine aimed to elevate the social status of what was then considered low-brow entertainment to the level of serious art.

Silver Light provided extensive coverage of movie stars, including interviews, profiles, and features on some of the most famous and influential actors and actresses of the time. While this coverage of movie stars was a common practice in film publications at the time – a service to subscribers and a vehicle to boost sales and circulations – *Silver Light*'s reports on movie stars were not merely trivial gossip. Rather, they served as a means to explore what constituted a productive and rewarding screen performance. This emphasis on the

DOI: 10.4324/9781003266952-41

critical elements of acting was crucial in activating the audience's sense of morality, as the relationship between actor and spectator played a significant role in the social education functions of cinema. One crucial concept that was deeply ingrained in *Silver Light*'s approach to acting was *renge*, or "personality," a notion that originated from the philosophical and political debates of the late Qing and early Republican eras in China. Personality was seen as a fundamental element of successful acting on the silver screen and was carefully examined and analyzed by the magazine's writers. Through the concept of personality, an actor's morality could be identified, as it was understood to radiate out to the audience to transform them. By exploring the nuances of personality and its impact on-screen performance, *Silver Light*'s writers reworked the idea of acting and performance in their film criticism, developing a new understanding of cinema and its role in shaping both the film industry and wider society.

Acting Authenticity

In the early 20th century, the focus on actors and acting in film writings was common in local newspapers, despite the overwhelmingly negative view of actors as mere puppets in Chinese society. The same practice was followed by Hong Kong media without exception. For instance, the critics of "Film Corner" wrote about the pivotal role of actors in cinema and covered star news while publishing many articles on acting and performance. Of nearly 290 pieces, more than 32% concerned movie stars (Cheung and Tsoi 2018, 87–88). Various aspects of performance, including facial expression (Yishi 1924a; Chen 1924; Zhang 1924), gestures and postures (Mengzhi 1924), acrobatic movement (Wozhi 1924; Yishi 1924a), and costume and makeup (Ligong 1924b), were often discussed and used to evaluate the artistic achievement of an actor (Ligong 1924a). For example, a critic of "Film Corner" compared Charlie Chaplin with Harold Lloyd, disapproving of the former's exaggerated postures and body movements while praising the latter for keeping himself within bounds (Yishi 1924b).

During this time, the performance-focused ethos of film criticism in Hong Kong placed actors at center stage, especially in *Silver Light*. As Su Chunchou (1926b) noted in the first issue of *Silver Light*, an actor's ability to express genuineness through bodily and facial expressions was unique; an artistic actor was assumed to possess the quality of authenticity, which was perceived by the authors in *Silver Light* as a means of manifesting the actor's quality. An actor with intrinsic quality has the potential to express what another *Silver Light* writer, Pan Ziping (1926), called the "spirit" of the film, in contrast to the superficial "form," or artificiality, seen in the stagecraft of a star. However, this quality was not discussed through the idea of authentic inner emotion but as the genuine form of life instead. Pan noted that many film stars learned to put on exquisite costumes and pose seductively in a Western and modern way – some "forms" that made them look like stars. The gestures and costumes, however, could not pass as authenticity, which could only be attained through genuine lived experiences. Similarly, another *Silver Light* writer, Bukuangsheng (1927), noted that the actor's authenticity could be measured by the level of verisimilitude in reflecting the real-life experiences the actor possessed. In his evaluation of the acting of the first Chinese female film stars, Bukuangsheng criticized Zhang Zhiyun's "unnatural step" as a major flaw in the performance of elegance and grace. While Yang Naimei's cunning expression was praised for having "the wonder of verisimilitude," Wang Hanlun's highly skilled technique was deemed too flawless to look real.

The discourse of acting put forth by the *Silver Light* writers concerning genuineness and authenticity is reminiscent of Zhang Zhen's and Jason McGrath's discussion of *neixin biaoyan* (interior acting) and its relationship with authenticity. Zhang's (2005) reading of the school textbook used at the Changming Correspondence Film School, established by Zhou Jianyun and Xu Hu in Shanghai in 1924, asserts that interior acting brought out the actor's hidden *qingxu* (mood), creating a direct link between actor and spectator. Similarly, Jason McGrath (2013) demonstrates that the new style of interior acting was conveyed through the actors' eyes and faces to "move" modern audiences with authenticity. However, the *Silver Light* writers did not subscribe to the method proposed by the Changming Correspondence Film School, which affirmed mood or emotion as the site of perceived authenticity. Instead, they proposed that an actor's authenticity could be observed through their capability to render real-life experiences in their acting. By telling the life stories of various actresses and actors, Yang Weiwen (1927) provided evidence for this belief: Western actor Tom Mix learned his acting skills in childhood by riding with his father in the wilderness, Hoot Gibson's hobby of driving a chariot trained him to be capable of performing dangerous acts in a movie, Mae Murray mastered her delicate movements through her enthusiasm for dancing in her childhood, and Ronald Colman's experience of serving in the army prepared him to perform masculinity and virility when he later joined the movie industry. Similarly, Su Chunchou (1926a) wrote a long article about the Italian actor Rudolph Valentino's life story, arguing for the authenticity of Valentino's romantic on-screen image as he was living an equally romantic life in reality. This correspondence between his real and imaginary images confirmed his performance's authenticity, which helped elevate him to the status of a true artist for the silver screen.

The phenomenon of revealing the private lives and secrets of movie stars was a common practice in early film culture. According to Richard deCordova (2001, 98–116), Hollywood film magazines have been describing the private lives of movie stars and revealing their secrets to readers since the emergence of the Hollywood star system in the 1910s. This phenomenon can be seen as a response to the rising public interest in the intimate details of a star's real life or true identity, which emerged with the Hollywood star system. It generated a discourse of what deCordova calls "picture personalities" that publicized tidbits about stars' acting backgrounds, personalities, and private lives, revealing layers of "behind-the-screen" truth (2001, 101). In particular, the body received unprecedented public attention, and any information that pierced the veil of secrecy surrounding the body was especially fascinating. Thus, Heather Addison (2003, 69–114) argues that physical culture gained prominence in Hollywood in the early 1910s, resulting in stars being frequently featured in relation to their physical appearance or bodily features. Star biographies that focused on weight loss, for instance, were a key part of film magazine culture. Hollywood stars of this period were perceived as proficient body shapers, and reducing weight was regarded as a means to improve professional performance. Stars functioned as ideal figures for the audience to consume and emulate.

At approximately the same time, film cultures in Asian countries, such as India and China, offered a similar physical culture with different understandings of stars and their bodies. In India, physical fitness was configured as national strength (Watt 2022), and film magazines routinely commented on the physicality of film stars as a means of promoting physical fitness and lifting feeble Indians out of physical decadence (Mukherjee 2020, 193–96). Wrestling, in particular, was seen as a site for the rejuvenation of the effete Indian male, and Indian cinema's narrative endorsements of wrestling could be viewed as an active agent generating the social capital of virility in physical culture (Mukherjee 2020, 194–95). In China, a similar type of physical culture emerged in Shanghai, particularly during the national crisis brought on by the Japanese invasion (Morris 2004, 77–140). Li Lili became a central figure of this physical fixation as her cinematic persona was long regarded as athletic, and as a film star, she was frequently shown participating in competitive sports and practicing physical exercise. This physically focused screen presentation was coupled with a sexually innocent and fervently anti-Japanese image (Gao 2010). Through her body, as argued by Zhang Zhen (2005, 78), there is an inescapable message that the individual body must be harnessed for nation-building. Thus, in both India and China, physical culture was often a way of promoting national strength and resilience in the face of colonialism and foreign invasion in their early cinema histories.

It is important to note that for this physical culture to propagate, at least three conditions needed to be fulfilled: first, a star must acquire the social status of a public figure whose charisma is confirmed to be desirable; (Alberoni 2007, 66–68; Dyer 2007, 82–84) second, a well-established star system is necessary, in which stars acquire the level of recognition typically possessed by celebrities; (Nayar 2009, 4–6) and third, a well-developed media industry is required to disseminate the names and faces of the stars for public identification (Nayar 2009, 6–10). However, in the *Silver Light* era in Hong Kong, these conditions had yet to be fulfilled. As one of the earliest film magazines published in Hong Kong and one of the few media outlets attempting to bestow a publicly recognized social status to screen actors, *Silver Light* chose instead to use authenticity to capitalize on screen actors' morality to elevate their social status, as argued in the next section. The writers of *Silver Light* believed that the "truth" of film did not lie in "a question of the 'true' identity of the actor," as argued by deCordova (2001, 112) in his discussion of the early Hollywood star system. Instead, they believed that a new style of acting was conveyed through performances informed by the actor's lived experiences to motivate modern audiences to believe that the screen performances were real and authentic. Thus, for the writers of *Silver Light*, the authenticity of an actor's performance relied on their ability to convey a genuine connection between their on-screen performance and their real-life experiences.

Theory of Screen Performance: Personality and Morality

To achieve this level of acting, *Silver Light* writers proposed the idea of self-cultivating one's personality and confirmed the contribution of morality to the degree of trustworthiness in acting. Giving weight to authenticity as a definitive quality of good performance, Shenfu (1927) added that good morality would push the actor to pursue improvement in acting, which, in turn, would lend authentic expression to their performance. Becoming a star, to him, was a transformative process of embodying morality in authentic expressions. Similarly, Luo Juemin (1926) and Taisusheng (1927) discussed acting techniques through the lens of personality, which captured the morality of the actor's personal life. To them, the authenticity that valorized an actor's performance must be supported by both virtuosity in rendering real experiences through acting and a virtuous and wholesome personality. This authenticity was rooted not only in their technical skill but also in their personal integrity.

It should be highlighted that the concept of personality as a methodology in screen performance was not novel to Chinese film criticism, and it was equaled in importance by other concepts, such as *bizhen*, or verisimilitude or approaching reality (Zhang 2005; Fan 2015), and *xinyingxiong zhuyi*, or neo-heroism (Bao 2015; Tam 2015). The idea of personality was already echoed in film articles published in the *Shen Bao*, a Shanghai-based newspaper with nationwide circulation (Chang 1924; Qianjian 1924). Some critics for the *Shen Bao* praised actors with a "complete" personality (Guanzhuo 1923; Zhaohua 1923a, 1923b; Qianjian 1924). By "complete," they meant being self-motivated to maintain high moral standards in all areas of life (Zhaohua 1923a). They believed that advocating for screen actors to develop their full personalities was a crucial step toward improving the social status of the film industry (Gu 1924). Following their Shanghai counterpart's endorsement of personality, *Silver Light* writers enriched the discourse of personality by emphasizing the role screen actors play in bridging the delicate distance between real life and the portrayal of reality on screen through a good personality.

How does a good personality bridge this delicate distance in acting? Xu Guanyu (1927a) suggested that *xiuyang*, self-cultivation, was key to achieving virtuosity. By self-cultivation, he meant that actors should abandon a "decadent lifestyle." In his treatise "On the Actor's Personality," Taisusheng (1927) used current affairs to attest to the danger of immorality in an actor's personal life. An actor who seduced a married woman was killed because of his deviation. This incident prompted many actors to exercise self-control and to "preserve one's moral integrity;" some even issued public statements to denounce "debauched performers." Taisusheng commented that regardless of gender, performers should uphold moral integrity. To him, immorality, such as promiscuity and debauchery, not only risked the actor's life but also impaired their acting technique and spoiled on-screen authenticity, which could eventually bring down the entire industry. Following the assertion of moral integrity as a crucial means to high artistic values in performances, Zui Xingsheng (1927) criticized the mundane and debased lifestyles of actresses for contributing nothing to the arts. To him, only actors with moral integrity could be qualified as true performers.

Silver Light's emphasis on the equivalence of morality and artistic quality was heavyhanded, as it created an immanent space for morality to be expressed through an actor's personality in performance. This approach upheld the well-being of individual actors and the film industry and was not uncommon in the early history of film. Similar ideas can be found in Japan, where Hideaki Fujiki's (2013, 50–88) analysis of early stardom highlights the career of Japanese actor Onoe Matsunosuke. Onoe was able to rise from a derided purveyor of low-brow entertainment to the status of a "great man" in society, thanks to the predominant social value of 1910s Japan, *shuyo* (self-cultivation) (Fujiki 2013, 76). Onoe's greatness was attributed not only to his acting virtuosity but also to his off-screen morality, which included the cultivation of character, moral rectitude, diligence, and thrift. Thus, acting was just as important as personality for Onoe. His persona was not only utilized to elevate his own status but also to distinguish the low status of motion pictures from the highbrow culture of popular educational recreation. His contemporaries recognized the potential of cinema as a medium for educating society, and they used Onoe's popularity and his emphasis on morality and character to promote the notion that cinema was a legitimate form of social education (Fujiki 2013, 79–80). Similarly, by emphasizing the importance of an actor's personality, practices of self-cultivation, and capability of rendering real-life experiences in their acting, *Silver Light* writers sought to elevate the social status of actors and cinema as a whole. By promoting a socially engaged cinema that emphasized morality and character, the writers of *Silver Light* believed that cinema itself could contribute to the education of society. In this way, both Onoe's career and *Silver Light*'s discourse on performance reflect a broader belief in the potential of cinema as a medium for social and cultural education.

Cinema and Social Education

In asserting the social function of cinema, writers in *Silver Light* repeatedly used vocabularies, such as *fenghua* ("changing manners"), *xuanchuan* ("inculcation"), and *anshi* ("implication"). Yutian (1927) termed immorality and social injustices as "life's problems" (*rensheng wenti*) and further elaborated on these problems: wealth inequality, prostitution, the concubine and slave system, and the corrupt institution of traditional marriage. He hoped that "socializing" (*shehuihua*) and "popularizing" (*pingminhua*) the cinematic arts might help alleviate these social ills. Similarly, Luo Juemin (1927a, 1927b) suggested that films could serve as a wake-up call to citizens by revealing society's dark side, such as hypocrisy and inequality. By helping to reshape customs and culture while nurturing morality and the new principles of etiquette, cinema could actualize its role in society. To achieve this, the *Silver Light* writers argued that cinema possessed the power of inculcation and implication (Pan 1927a, 1927b). Wu Baling (1927) confirmed that through its power of inculcation, cinema could catch the interest of the audience, attract them into the film world, and "implicate" the audience in the obligation to mimic the worldly wisdom they learned during the viewing process. He described this process as "imperceptible nurturing" (*qianyi mohua*). To highlight cinema's power in changing social customs and manners or even inciting political activism, Yuwen (1927) urged examining how viewers respond to social issues after watching a good film.

The recognition of imperceptible nurturing through inculcation was cultivated through the actor's personality in performance. In "The Missions of the Film in Social Education," Xu (1927b) critiqued traditional theaters as feudalistic and incapable of improving society next to modern motion pictures, which could "help people acquire pure thoughts, noble personalities, applied techniques and practical knowledge to enhance the well-being of society and maintain social order." This was where a noble personality played its part. Through the personality mediated by the actor's artistic performance, the social values of a good movie, namely, the ability to effectively reshape audience morality and reform society, were illuminated.

This understanding of personality had its roots in the early philosophical examination of the national crisis in the late Qing. The term was first introduced in the writings of Liang Qichao, a Chinese social and political activist whose thoughts significantly influenced the modernization of China. Following Johann Kaspar Bluntschli's philosophy, Liang (1936) used the term *wanquan renge*, meaning "complete and refined personality," to define the personality of the new citizens (*guomin*) – the agencies who could participate in public affairs and make real social change (Shen 2006, 11–12). This concept opened up a discursive space for later thinkers to elaborate on the concept of personality in political and ethical terms. Building on Liang's work, philosopher Zhang Dongsun examined the idea of personality in terms of morality (1920) and moral education (1918a, 1918b, 1919c) and later extended it to the legal and social realms (Gu 2005). Scholar Qu Junong continued Zhang's discussion of personality with respect to education by confirming that an outstanding education should assist people in completing their personality and contributing to a "bigger whole" – the nation (Qu 1923).

It was no surprise that the idea of personality entered the public domain of Hong Kong in the 1920s, given the political philosophy of the aforementioned thinkers and politicians, who emphasized the pedagogical potential of personality. This concept could find its support in the public submission of articles to the *Overseas Chinese Daily News* (*Huaqiao*

Ribao), in which personality was linked to proper public behavior, and education was taken as a practical means of cultivating good social manners and improving citizens' personalities or character (Boping 1924; Shaoguo 1924). In this context, the writers of *Silver Light* upheld the notion of personality in their vision of cinema as a medium that achieved missions of social reform by conveying the actor's personality. Promiscuity and debauchery emerged as symbols of a deformed personality, which was deemed unsuitable for the realm of cinema. Thus, screen actors could construct a productive site of social reform through their seemingly innocuous performances.

The concept of utilizing an actor's personality as a platform for social education, as promoted by *Silver Star* during 1926 and 1927, reflected the magazine writers' aspiration to transform modern cinema into a mechanism for moral guidance. However, the moral understanding of cinema often faced derisive commentaries from Shanghai critics, with some accusing the philosophy of embracing Chinese traditionalism at the expense of synchronizing with modern and progressive ideas (Lu 1927). Despite these criticisms, *Silver Star* remained committed to its vision of prioritizing the cultivation of personality and the promotion of moral values as a way of improving society. In this context, the Republican political philosopher Zhang Junmai's discourse on morality and the "new self" offers valuable insights. Drawing inspiration from the works of German philosophers Johann Gottlieb Fichte and Immanuel Kant, Zhang argued that a radical overhaul of morality was imperative for the nation's progress. This overhaul would facilitate the revival of morality that could overcome the mechanistic materialist view of life (Lee 2019, 288–90) and the emergence of a "new self" that could foster a newfound sense of self-respect and community spirit (Nelson 2020, 191–92). This moral reawakening would be anchored in the principles of moral autonomy and, according to Zhang (1926), could catalyze the individual and collective growth of "self-power," thereby emancipating the nation from the shackles of colonial slavery and tutelage.

Likewise, Zhang Junmai's intimate associate and another political philosopher of the era, Zhang Dongsun, supported Zhang Junmai's notion of forging a "new self" through moral transformation. Zhang Dongsun contended that morality, as a form of self-cultivation, engenders a virtuous disposition that radiates its influence on those who come into contact with the moral individual. By adopting Kant's concept of morality as self-regulation, Zhang Dongsun dismissed Karl Marx's historical materialism and the Chinese communist approach to rejuvenating the nation through class-based revolution, asserting the inherent potency of morality in destroying capitalism and enhancing the nation's progress and even the progress of humankind (1919a, 1919b, 1919d; Fung 2002). The writers of *Silver Light* shared a perspective with Zhang Junmai and Zhang Dongsun on the nature of personality, the cultivation of morality, and the virtuous influence that can be achieved through the process of inculcation and moral implication. They viewed screen actors as the conduits for this moral influence and contact, thereby transforming the moral economy surrounding the social standing of performance artists, the educational purpose of cinema, and the audience's reception of moving images at theaters.

While various political philosophers have utilized the concept of personality and its associated attributes of self-cultivation and morality as theoretical resources for national reform, there is scant evidence to suggest that *Silver Light* engaged in such discussions of national reform. Instead, they proposed social reform, primarily focusing on the cultivation of one's own personality as a representation of moral values in contrast to the pervasive corruption of Hong Kong society. The social and moral overtones in *Silver Light*'s discourse on personality may be attributed to two reasons. First, Hong Kong in the 1920s was caught between Chinese traditionalism, supported by Governor Cecil Clementi's (1925–30 in office) reform after the Hong Kong–Canton General Strike, and modernist aspirants seeking to revolutionize the entire Chinese nation (Law 2009, 103–30). The Hong Kong government collaborated, on the one hand, with local Chinese bourgeoisie who presented themselves as allies to the colonizers and, on the other, with the literati of the old Chinese tradition who aimed to maintain a Chinese identity by grasping the roots of a purportedly Confucian-based tradition (Carroll 2005, 131–58; Law 2009, 106–9). Separately, new Chinese intellectuals from the North cherished modernist ideals of revolution and reform for the nation, considering Hong Kong an adherent of an obsolete Chinese traditionalism. They depicted the city's colonization as a source of moral unpredictability and decay (Law 2009, 113–15). As a result, the *Silver Light* writers had to defend themselves from accusations of embracing Chinese traditionalism by incorporating modern thinking around personality. Meanwhile, they also had to highlight their aspirations toward a higher moral standing to distance themselves from perceived moral decay.

The second reason for these social and moral undertones might be that actors were regarded unfavorably by local audiences due to their involvement in morally questionable activities, such as promiscuity and debauchery, which lowered their social standing. In fact, the phenomenon of stardom has predominantly been concerned with imaginary identifications, whereby individual fans use stars to enhance their lives with meaning or find avenues of pleasure that are absent in real life (Stacey 1991). By cultivating charisma through name and face recognition and with the adoration they receive, stars can mobilize a devoted following and establish a relationship with fans that often assumes the characteristics of a cult, thereby wielding influence in political realms (Prasad 2014). However, the relatively low social status of screen actors in the Hong Kong film industry during that time indicates the absence of a traditionally respected star charisma, which prevented them from attaining the same exalted position typically reserved for stardom and celebrity. Therefore, the impact of film stars on the political realm, which is observable in the United States (Ross 2011), India (Prasad 2014), and other parts of the world today, was scarcely conceivable to the writers of *Silver Light* in 1920s Hong Kong. Nonetheless, their emphasis on personality as a means of social and cultural education was a significant departure from the notion of cinema as entertainment and highlighted the unique role that cinema played in shaping the cultural and social landscape of Hong Kong during that period of time.

Conclusion

Silver Light magazine illuminated the potential for motion pictures to promote self-cultivation, social education, and reform through the lens of personality. However, this space could not have been socially productive without the adherence of screen actors to the pursuit of a complete and refined personality in their off-screen lives. This performance-focused ethos was at the core of *Silver Light*'s mission to valorize the silver screen and beyond. The magazine can be best understood as a platform for promoting a cinema of social education, emphasizing the importance of portraying life on screen and showcasing the cinema's ability to inculcate moral values and implicate the audience into adopting them. The writers of *Silver Light* contended that the aim of cinema was to embody life experiences through the performance of virtuous and virtuosic actors, allowing the audience to appreciate not just the form of acting but life itself as acquired through the actor's self-cultivation. By doing so, they created a space for moral reflection and encouraged the audience to engage in this process. The screen actor became a site for radiating and promoting these values through their encounter with the audience, showcasing the personality of the actor as a source of morality and virtue. In this way, *Silver Light* hoped to transform the cultural and social landscape of Hong Kong by elevating the status of screen actors and promoting the idea that cinema could be a means of social and cultural education, contributing to the broader project of China's modernization and progress.

Although the magazine had a relatively short lifespan, its discourse on self-cultivation and social education continued to influence Hong Kong's film industry. One example of this can be found in the Cantonese Film Cleansing Movement of 1935, which aimed to "modernize" Cantonese films by promoting nationalism, morality, scientific knowledge, and Euro-American values of humanism (Cheng 2011; Fan 2018). Among these values, morality drew significant attention and discussion, with the local literary magazine *Red Bean* even dedicating a special feature to the Cleansing Movement and its advocacy of uplifting morality in films. The Cleansing Movement strongly denounced the popular film genres of the time, such as magic-and-demon flicks and martial art films, which were believed to propagate the "lower taste" that promoted obscenity and wrongdoing and had a harmful influence on young people (He 1935; Liu 1935; Xu 1935). The screen actor was an integral and inseparable part of this discourse, as Xu Juefu (1935) emphasized the role of screen actors and performance in promoting the Cleansing Movement. He noted that after the end of the Hong Kong–Canton General Strike, the Hong Kong film industry resumed production and adapted numerous Cantonese opera plays into Cantonese movies. This led to a significant integration of the business of Cantonese opera and Cantonese cinema and a widespread cinematic practice of utilizing famous Cantonese opera troupes and theater actors (*hongling*) as a way to guarantee box office success. To Xu, this phenomenon of widely adapting Cantonese opera into film made these movies "vulgar," "obscene," "superstitious," and "low taste," which he believed would have a detrimental impact on society. Along with Xu, other writers who supported the Cleansing Movement also considered these harmful films as hindrances to social education (He 1935; Liu 1935). While there is limited evidence to directly link the participants of the Cleansing Movement to *Silver Light*, one can draw parallels between *Silver Light*'s artistic belief that cinema can serve as a tool for social education and the Cleansing Movement's advocacy of cinema as a means of educating society. Thus, the legacy of *Silver Light*'s vision of cinema as a promoter of moral values and social reform continued to influence the discourse around the role of cinema in Hong Kong during the 1930s and beyond.

Acknowledgment

I would like to express my sincere gratitude to Prof. Emilie Yeh for her invaluable contributions in raising important questions and providing insightful comments for the first draft of the chapter. I would also like to extend my thanks to the editors of the anthology, particularly Prof. Zhang Zhen and Dr. Debashree Mukherjee, for their meticulous feedback and guidance, which have been instrumental in refining my argument. Their generous support and encouragement have been crucial in the completion of this work. I am truly grateful for their inspiration.

References

Addison, Heather. 2003. *Hollywood and the Rise of Physical Culture*. New York: Routledge.

Alberoni, Francesco. 2007. "The Powerless 'Elite': Theory and Sociological Research on the Phenomenon of the Stars." In *Stardom and Celebrity: A Reader*, edited by Sean Redmond and Su Holmes, 65–77. Los Angeles, CA and London: Sage.

Bao, Weihong. 2015. *Fiery Cinema: The Emergence of an Affective Medium in China, 1915–1945*. Minneapolis, MN: University of Minnesota Press.

Boping. 1924. "Personality." *Overseas Chinese Daily News*, March 9, 1.

Bukuangsheng. 1927. "On the Goods and Bads of the 'Movies' and 'Stars'." *Silver Light* 4.

Carroll, John M. 2005. *Edge of Empires: Chinese Elites and British Colonials in Hong Kong*. Cambridge, MA: Harvard University Press.

Chang. 1924. "How Other Countries Discuss American Movies (7)." *Shen Bao*, July 9, 21.

Chen, Zhuomin. 1924. "Pessimism Toward the Chinese Film Circle." *Chinese Mail*, August 16.

Cheng, Matthew. 2011. "Education, Arts, Entertainment or Business? The Discovery and Elaboration of Historical Materials on the First Film Cleansing Movement." *Literary Criticism* 15: 85–92.

Cheung, Ting-Yan, and Pablo Sze-Pang Tsoi. 2018. "From an Imported Novelty to an Indigenized Practice: Hong Kong Cinema in the 1920s." In *Kaleidoscopic Histories: Early Film Culture in Hong Kong, Taiwan and Republican China*, edited by Emilie Yueh-Yu Yeh, 71–100. Ann Arbor: University of Michigan Press.

Chu, Yingchi. 2003. *Hong Kong Cinema: Coloniser, Motherland and Self*. London and New York: Routledge.

DeCordova, Richard. 2001. *Picture Personalities: The Emergence of the Star System in America*. Urbana: University of Illinois Press, 2001.

Dyer, Richard. 2007. "Stars." In *Stardom and Celebrity: A Reader*, edited by Sean Redmond and Su Holmes, 79–84. Los Angeles: Sage.

Fan, Victor. 2015. *Cinema Approaching Reality: Locating Chinese Film Theory*. Minneapolis: University of Minnesota Press.

———. 2018. "Too Intimate to Speak: Regional Cinemas and Literatures." *Journal of Modern Literature in Chinese* 15 (2): 47–71.

Fujiki, Hideaki. 2013. *Making Personas: Transnational Film Stardom in Modern Japan*. Boston: Harvard University Asia Center.

Fung, Edmund S. K. 2002. "Socialism, Capitalism, and Democracy in Republican China: The Political Thought of Zhang Dongsun." *Modern China* 28 (4): 399–431.

Gao, Yunxiang. 2010. "Sex, Sports, and China's National Crisis, 1931–1945: The 'Athletic Movie Star' Li Lili (1915–2005)." *Modern Chinese Literature and Culture* 22 (1): 96–161.

Gu, Hongliang. 2005. "Moral Personality and Legal Personality: Liang Qichao and Zhang Dongsun on Personality and Rights." *Oriental Forum* 5: 54–58.

Gu, Kenfu. 1924. "Contribute to the Advancement of the Chinese Film Industry." *Shen Bao*, January 1, 42.

Guanzhuo. 1923. "Books About Film Artists' Stress on Personality." *Shen Bao*, September 8, p. 17.

He, Yan. 1935. "Issues of Film Education." *Red Bean* 18: 5–7.

Law, Wing Sang. 2009. *Collaborative Colonial Power: The Making of the Hong Kong Chinese*. Hong Kong: Hong Kong University Press.

Lee, Soonyi. 2019. "Revolt Against Positivism, the Discovery of Culture: The Liang Qichao Group's Cultural Conservatism in China After the First World War." *Twentieth-Century China* 44 (3): 288–304.

Liang, Qichao. 1936. *Discourse on the New Citizens*. Shanghai: Chunghwa.

Ligong. 1924a. "My Thoughts on the Chinese Film Industry." *Chinese Mail*, July 5.

———. 1924b. "Silver Screen Review." *Chinese Mail*, August 9.

Liu, Huozi. 1935. "On the Film Cleansing Movement." *Red Bean* 18: 8–10.

Lu, Mengshu. 1927. "Talking: Refute the Fifth Issue of *Silver Light*." *Art World* 15: 7–8.

Luo, Juemin. 1926. "Actor-Director." *Silver Light* 1: n.p.

———. 1927a. "Suggestions to Filmmakers." *Silver Light* 2: n.p.

———. 1927b. "My Tiny Experience with Film." *Silver Light* 3: n.p.

McGrath, Jason. 2013. "Acting Real: Cinema, Stage, and the Modernity of Performance in Chinese Silent Film." In *The Oxford Handbook of Chinese Cinemas*, edited by Carlos Rojas, 400–20. New York, NY: Oxford University Press.

Mengzhi. 1924. "On Shuan's 'Comments on the Film'." *Chinese Mail*, July 27.

Morris, Andrew D. 2004. *Marrow of the Nation: A History of Sport and Physical Culture in Republican China*. Berkeley: University of California Press.

Mukherjee, Debashree. 2020. *Bombay Hustle: Making Movies in a Colonial City*. New York: Columbia University Press.

Nayar, Pramod K. 2009. *Seeing Stars: Spectacle, Society and Celebrity Culture*. New Delhi and London: Sage.

Nelson, Eric S. 2020. "Zhang Junmai's Early Political Philosophy and the Paradoxes of Chinese Modernity." *Asian Studies* 8 (24.1): 183–208.

Pan, Ziping. 1926. "On Film Actor's Social Intercourse and Clothes." *Silver Light* 1: n.p.

———. 1927a. "Relationship Between Education and Film." *Silver Light* 2: n.p.

———. 1927b. "Random Talk on Silver Light." *Silver Light* 2: n.p.

Prasad, M. Madhava. 2014. *Cine-Politics: Film Stars and Political Existence in South India*. New Delhi: Orient Blackswan.

Qianjian. 1924. "Preview of *Good Brothers* (2)." *Shen Bao*, July 19, 21.

Qu, Junong. 1923. "Personality and Education." *Supplement of Chen Bao*, June 13–14.

Ross, Steven J. 2011. *Hollywood Left and Right: How Movie Stars Shaped American Politics*. Oxford: Oxford University Press.

Shaoguo. 1924. "Beware of Your Behaviors in the Theatre." *Overseas Chinese Daily News*, September 24, 1.

Shen, Sunchiao. 2006. "Discourse on *Guomin* ('the Citizen') in Late Qing China, 1895–1911." Translated by Hsiao Wenchien. *Inter-Asia Cultural Studies* 7 (1): 2–23.

Shenfu. 1927. "The Upward Aspiration." *Silver Light* 2: n.p.

Stacey, Jackie. 1991. "Feminine Fascinations: Forms of Identification in Star/Audience Relations." In *Stardom: Industry of Desire*, edited by Christine Gledhill, 141–63. London: Routledge.

Su, Chunchou. 1926a. "A Brief History of Rudolph Valentino." *Silver Light* 1: n.p.

———. 1926b. "The Future of the Chinese Film Industry." *Silver Light* 1: n.p.

Taisusheng. 1927. "On the Actor's Personality." *Silver Light* 4: n.p.

Tam, Enoch Yee-Lok. 2015. "The *Silver Star* Group: A First Attempt at Theorizing *Wenyi* in the 1920s." *Journal of Chinese Cinemas* 9 (1): 62–75.

Watt, Carey. 2022. "Physical Culture and the Body in Colonial India, c.1800–1947." In *Routledge Handbook of the History of Colonialism in South Asia*, edited by Harald Fischer-Tiné and Maria Framke, 345–58. New York: Routledge.

Wozhi. 1924. "Douglas Fairbanks Was Irritated to Practice Sword Movements." *Chinese Mail*, July 12.

Wu, Baling. 1927. "How to Impress a Film to Spectator's Mind." *Silver Light* 3: n.p.

Xu, Guanyu. 1927a. "The Issue of Actor's Personality." *Silver Light* 3: n.p.

———. 1927b. "The Missions of the Film in Social Education." *Silver Light* 2: n.p.

Xu, Juefu. 1935. "The Future of the Film Cleaning Movement." *Red Bean* 18: 12–17.

Yang, Weiwen. 1927. "Histories of Movie Stars." *Silver Light* 2: n.p.

Yishi. 1924a. "On *Robin Hood*." *Chinese Mail*, July 26.

———. 1924b. "Reply to Mr Lu Juefei's Commentary." *Chinese Mail*, July 5.

Yu, Mowan. 1996. *History of Hong Kong Film*, vol. 1. Hong Kong: Sub-Culture Ltd.

Yutian. 1927. "The Unexploited Land of the Chinese Film Industry." *Silver Light* 5: n.p.

Yuwen. 1927. "Values and Missions of Film." *Silver Light* 5: n.p.

Zhang, Dongsun. 1918a. "Personality and Assertion." *The China Times*, December 16, 3.

———. 1918b. "The Influencing Power of Personality." *The China Times*, March 25, 3.

———. 1919a. "Socialism and China." *Current Affairs News*, November 6.

———. 1919b. "The Third Civilization." *Liberation and Reform* 1 (1–2): 1–5.

———. 1919c. "The Power of Personality." *The China Times*, November 1, 2.

———. 1919d. "Why Shall We Talk About Socialism?" *Liberation and Reform* 1 (7): 3–14.

———. 1920. "The War Between Personality and Non-Personality, Morality and Non-Morality." *The China Times*, January 15, 1.

Zhang, Junmai. 1926. "A Patriotic Philosopher: Fichte." *The Eastern Miscellany* 23 (10): 71–77.

Zhang, Yurong. 1924. "(Review of) *Lotus Fall.*" *Chinese Mail*, August 23.

Zhang, Zhen. 2005. *An Amorous History of the Silver Screen: Shanghai Cinema, 1896–1937.* Chicago: University of Chicago Press.

Zhaohua. 1923a. "Actress Mae Marsh on 'Beauty'." *Shen Bao*, September 14, 17.

———. 1923b. "Comments on the Film." *Shen Bao*, September 26, 18.

Zhi, Xingsheng. 1927. "Reply to Mr Xianjue." *Silver Light* 2: n.p.

SECTION V

Independent Practice

Networks, Labor, and Voices at the Margins

INTRODUCTION

Intan Paramaditha

Independent cinema is generally seen as the practice of filmmaking outside an established or mainstream system that maintains an oppositional position or projects a creative vision against the dominant culture. In this section, authors explore the conditions of production, voices at the margins excluded from the mainstream imagination, and the link between film practice and the logic of care in film community spaces within Asia, often through a comparative, trans-Asian perspective. As most independent film productions discussed here need to navigate the structures of 21st-century neoliberal capitalism, reflections on labor, care work, and precarity continue to inform the creative practice in narrative feature films, animation, and documentary, as well as the ways in which filmmakers form networks and communities. With four chapters focusing on women filmmakers and their concerns with care, labor, class, and caste, this section underlines the importance of an intersectional feminist perspective in the study of independent film practice.

It is notable that the term "independent" is also elusive and unstable. The degree of independence can vary, and Southeast Asian film scholar May Adadol Ingawanij reminds us to examine "constitutive dependencies within shifting networks" (Ingawanij and McKay 2012, 2) that enable independent film practice. Independent cinemas in Asia largely depend on transnational funding networks and film festivals, state film policies, and film communities and cultures. In the late 1990s and early 2000s, with the proliferation of digital technology, new independent film movements grew in various parts of Asia. Filmmakers were able to create low-budget films with affordable cameras and editing software, which allowed them to convey alternative visions that did not find a place in mainstream, commercial film production. Two decades later, what does it mean to be independent? Decreasing opportunities for global funds, shifting viewing practice, and the rise of streaming platforms are factors to consider when we think about the diverse and amorphous shapes of independent filmmaking in the region.

The questions of what has changed and what remains the same inform the opening chapter of this section. Gaik Cheng Khoo's article, " 'Still Doing It Themselves, with a Little Help from Friends': Independent Filmmaking in Malaysia Two Decades Hence," reflects on challenges and sustainability two decades after Malaysian indie "new wave" filmmakers first emerged in the transnational film circuit. Based on her interview with several independent

DOI: 10.4324/9781003266952-43

filmmakers, Khoo indicates that the Malaysian indie scene is less vibrant and productive compared to other Southeast Asian countries, such as the Philippines, Indonesia, and Thailand, due to structural reasons. These include Malaysia's highly segmented market because of its multiracial population, inconsistent support from the government, more decentralized and elusive viewing practice, and the middle-income trap experienced by many filmmakers. With the lack of structural support, Khoo emphasizes the importance of local and transnational networks as essential aspects to sustain filmmaking.

Independent film practice expands spaces for filmmakers to explore stories about alternative or marginalized voices that do not fit easily in the dominant culture. In these spaces, women filmmakers are at the forefront, pushing feminist perspectives to interrogate restrictions of political freedom in neoliberal states or create intervention in heteronormative and capitalist ideologies. Sophia Siddique's interview with film director Tan Pin Pin reveals resistance in terms of subject matter, a critical view of the Singaporean state, and in the filmmaker's persistence to find alternative circulation and distribution channels when faced with censorship. Tan mobilized the grassroots network when her film *To Singapore with Love* was banned from public screenings, echoing Gaik Cheng Khoo's point about local and transnational networks as infrastructures for independent filmmakers. Tan's work highlights film activism as the driving force in independent filmmaking, whether in making cinema with the aim "to transform, inform, and create change," as Tan describes, or in engaging in advocacy and community building to "grow an environment where more of these works can be made."

The next two chapters focus on how women filmmakers engage with the intertwining relation between gender, labor, and the everyday life in their films. Yau Ching's 2002 film *Let's Love Hong Kong* or *Ho Yuk* is considered Hong Kong's first feature film about Hong Kong lesbians told by a woman filmmaker. In this chapter, Arnika Fuhrmann focuses on affective relations concerning labor and capital in the age of electronic capitalism. Rather than resorting to normativity or glamorizing the upward mobility of queer subjects, the film explores possibilities of intimacy under the new regime of finance capital. Fuhrmann argues that new kinds of affective expressions and desires have emerged in a world characterized by coding, finance, and transactionality. Shuting Li's "Care in Filming, Change by Love" also focuses on independent women filmmakers, Yang Lina in China and Lee Ching-hui in Taiwan, who have directed their attention to care practice in the family shaped by Confucian values. Both Yang and Lee emerged in the late 1990s when DV technology developed and opened up the opportunities to document the everyday life. They use film to tell stories of women, especially in their roles as caregivers, while complicating ideas about love in family structures. Using the concept of "matter of care" by Maria Puig de la Bellacasa, Li argues that care in the documentary is embedded in the practices of production, circulation, and consumption; in the feminist films by Yang and Lee, care practices shape the relationship between filmmakers and their subjects as well as between films and audiences.

The link between creative practice and care work is also explored in Jasmine Nadua Trice's chapter, "Domestic Temporalities and Film Practice: Los Otros, Quezon City, and Forum Lenteng, Jakarta." Examining the practice of two experimental film groups in Southeast Asia, Forum Lenteng and Los Otros, Trice discusses the space of the home that they use to build a community. Located in cities characterized by rapid urban transformation and environmental crisis, the home of both groups signifies what Trice calls "a site of temporal intervention." The home is reframed as a place for combining creative practice and care work, developing pedagogical models, and documenting the cityscape. Jinying Li's chapter continues the discussion around creativity, labor, and collectivity in her study of Chinese independent animations. In "Unstable Pixels, Modular Selves: Digital Subjectivity in Chinese Independent Animations," Li proposes a shift of perspective from spectators-as-subjects to imagine makers-as-subjects. Her analysis of three works – the *Xiao Xiao* series, the *Kuang Kuang Kuang* series, and AT Bingtanghuluer – demonstrates how Chinese independent animations provide a material condition for a digital subject in exploring aesthetic plasmaticness, semiotic pluralism, and labor precarity. The latter indicates how animators respond to the precarious conditions of creative labor, despite the rapid growth in Chinese digital media, by engaging in collaborative work and promoting plurality of knowledge. Amid China's transition to post-industrial capitalism with "Chinese characteristics," a collective ethos is emerging in China's alternative digital culture.

The last two chapters in this section focus on documentary as a site for independent practice, particularly in pushing for certain aesthetic experimentation as well as addressing the question of whose voices we do not hear in the public sphere. Eric Sasono's "Experimentation and Transnational Influences: Documentary Film in Post Authoritarian Indonesia," re-emphasizes transnational funding and circuit of exhibition – significant infrastructures that support independent film practice in general – as interconnected networks of communities and technologies that support documentary filmmaking in Indonesia. The chapter gives us a historical overview of Indonesian documentary history, particularly through the practice of Sinema 8, a student film collective during the New Order government (1965–98). By revisiting the New Order, Sasono also provides an insight into what independent practice means in the authoritarian period, in which experimental filmmakers explored the aesthetics of the documentary beyond the dominant understanding of the genre as tools for government propaganda or instructional medium.

Finally, Fatima Nizaruddin's interview with filmmaker Deepa Dhanraj demonstrates issues at stake for a feminist independent practice. As a woman documentary filmmaker who started working in the 1980s, Deepa Dhanraj addresses the question of "whose voice" in the field of documentary as well as the feminist movement, in which working-class women's political participation was often invisible: "It was impossible to see or hear rural or urban working-class women speak on film." Working collaboratively to address not only the issues of gender and politics but also class and caste, Dhanraj's films exemplify the tradition of strong political commitment in documentary as well as Asian independent film practice that refuses to conform to the dominant political and cultural views. The interview itself is an invitation for scholars to enrich the discussion of independent cinemas by seeking more traces of intersectional feminist thinking and practice across Asia.

Reference

Ingawanij, May Adadol, and Benjamin McKay, eds. 2012. *Glimpses of Freedom: Independent Cinema in Southeast Asia*. Ithaca: Cornell Southeast Asia Program Publications.

33

"STILL DOING IT THEMSELVES, WITH A LITTLE HELP FROM FRIENDS"

Independent Filmmaking in Malaysia Two Decades Hence

Gaik Cheng Khoo

Introduction

In the question and answer with director Tan Chui Mui at a Malaysian screening of her long-awaited third feature, *Barbarian Invasion* (2021), Tan thanked her producer Woo Ming Jin and actor Pete Teo.[1] Both had been key to helping her reshape her script and find its focus. She quoted fellow indie filmmaker, Amir Muhammad, who once said, "If you don't have money, it's good to have friends." Veterans from the first wave of digital independents from the 2000s, Tan, Amir Muhammad, James Lee (who acted and directed the action sequences in *Barbarian Invasion*), and Liew Seng Tat established Dahuang Pictures in 2004. Under Dahuang, they acted, produced, edited, and lensed for one another and other filmmakers before going their own ways. As if to reiterate this point, in *Barbarian Invasion*, a film about filmmaking, friendship is emphasized over love by the director (played by Pete Teo) in conversation with his actress (played by Tan herself). The film's success signaled the return of "the Malaysian indies," the wave that emerged in the early to mid-2000s. *Barbarian Invasion* emblematizes this chapter's title that independent filmmakers are "Still Doing It Themselves, with a Little Help from Friends."

But what happened to independent filmmaking in Malaysia in the intervening years just as independent filmmaking in the region was taking off? According to Woo Ming Jin, the ecosystem in Malaysia has not improved since he began (interview, 15 April 2022). While independent films were still being made each year, not many were selected for top festivals overseas. Were Malaysian films just an exotic quirk on the international festival circuit or had its stories about racial tensions and multicultural harmony worn thin over time compared to Philippine neorealism embodied by Lav Diaz and Brillante Mendoza and the Thai avant-garde as inspired by Apichatpong Weeresethakul? Mapping out the independent filmscape in Malaysia since the mid-2000s, this chapter explores the development, persistent challenges, and possibilities that enable the sustainability of independent filmmaking. Based on interviews with Malaysian filmmakers and producers, it argues that

DOI: 10.4324/9781003266952-44

Malaysian independent filmmakers face systemic and structural challenges unique to and reflecting its society, culture, and history that impede their success when compared to their counterparts in the region. These challenges signify a weak internal ecosystem in which stakeholders consisting of the state, local funders, filmmakers, and viewers are embedded: (1) Malaysia's multiculturalism being a double-edged sword: while offering a diverse range of film styles that are ethnically inclined, its linguistic diversity leads to a segmented market; (2) inconsistent film policies and lack of government understanding and support (the role of government); (3) the lack of audience for alternative films; and (4) the dilemma of a middle-income economy. These challenges are somewhat complicated by technological changes, specifically OTT streaming platforms, whose impact on sustaining indie filmmaking I will discuss. The chapter then closes by focusing on persistent challenges and questions of sustainability.

Developments Since the Mid-2000s

While the filmmakers I interviewed could explain the intricate problems connected to the film industry specifically, inevitably they would draw a macro picture contextualizing their frustrated ambitions. So, I will begin first with a brief introduction about the state of things in Malaysia. An increasingly conservative Malay Muslim-majority middle-income nation that is multiethnic, Malaysia has endured an ethnonationalist ideology that privileges Malay Muslims in affirmative action policies, politics, and national culture that uphold Malay supremacy since independence. The civil service is dominated by Malays, while most non-Malays, unable to get jobs in government, end up in the private sector. This bifurcation does not strictly adhere along racial lines, but it explains what sorts of ideological and aesthetically conforming positions indie filmmakers are "alternative" to. The government sector is regarded as not filled by the most capable or qualified actors, which partially explains the inefficiency of the National Film Development Corporation (FINAS). Further, a right-wing authoritarian government decimated multiple freedoms of expression in the 1980s through preventative acts, including the right of university and college students to protest and imprisonment without trial. While some draconian laws have been dismantled, the effects of decades of authoritarian rule continue. Critical thinking is not encouraged in an education system where affirmative action for the majority supersedes meritocracy. Through the National Cultural Policy, the film industry is regarded as a mirror of Malay culture that accepts other cultures based on assimilation.

When the Malaysian digital independents first appeared in the 2000s, the digital medium provided an alternative to mainstream studio films that were shot on 35 mm, freeing up would-be filmmakers from producing formulaic genres and stories offered by Malay films, Chinese dramas, and Kollywood. Cosmopolitan in outlook, they emulated the films of Wong Kar Wai, Hou Hsiao Hsien, Satyajit Ray, and various art cinema auteurs whom they watched on pirated DVDs. Unlike the Malay films dominating the mainstream national industry, independent films represented the spectrum of languages spoken in Malaysia and non-Malay stories and actors. Indie films were personal, low-budget, self-funded, and non-profit-oriented, often made without the thought of commercial release or screening in the mainstream cinemas. As such, indie filmmakers could make experimental features and take more risks in telling stories. But even then, the nascent rise of a new generation of filmmakers also included those who favored more commercial means of storytelling rather than slow cinema and non-acting (Khoo 2007). Today Malaysian indie filmmakers are making films that are increasingly more mainstream in narrative style and pacing, partly to survive because "the actual interest from the public never really grew" for art films or festival films (Amir Muhammad interview, 3 April 2022). There is a shift toward popular genres like horror, Emir Ezwan's *Roh* (2019), and action/thrillers – Dain Said's *Interchange* (2016), Ho Yuhang's *Mrs. K* (2017), Zahir Omar's *Fly by Night* (2018), Namron's *Crossroads: One Two Jaga* (2018), and Nadiah Hamzah's *Motif* (2019) – with fewer formalist experiments unlike in Thailand – Phuttiphong Aroonpheng's *Manta Ray* (2018) and Anocha Suwicha-karnpong's *Come Here* (2021) – or Indonesia – Yosep Anggi Noen's *The Science of Fictions* (2019) and Kamila Andini's *Before, Now and Then* (2022). Hence, this chapter defines independent films as films where the filmmaker retains creative control over projects that may be stylistically alternative to mainstream films, that challenge national agendas and may be difficult to market for mass audiences. This category includes but is not limited to art films.

In 2018, Amir Muhammad, who left filmmaking to be a successful independent publisher, returned to independent filmmaking by founding Kuman Pictures. This second time around, he wanted to make more market-driven and genre films to "stay relevant to something wider." Kuman produces cheap horror films with an average budget of RM 500,000 (USD 113,000).[2] Horror is extremely popular with Malaysian audiences and the genre most likely to recoup production costs. He explained that "the major change since the mid-2000s is that you can't just make films for the film festival circuit." The digital indie filmmakers from his batch are likely to experience burnout and fatigue because the situation "isn't changing. Unlike in other countries. Because we feed off our audience but if there's no feedback, then it just becomes writing grants to impress first-world people to give us money." Amir describes a "cannibalized" situation where the people who watch the film are the ones who worked on it, and that the earlier indie filmmaking scene becomes very "solipsistic" and untenable. Those from his generation also faced funding difficulties for their third film as available grants focus on helping first or second features only.

Nevertheless, small personal stories revolving around families continue to be produced, some with the help of funding pieced together from awards, grants and sponsors: the first Penang Hokkien film, *You Mean the World to Me*, by commercials director Saw Teong Hin (2017), and debut features like Shanjhey K. Perumal's *Jagat* (2015), Tan Seng Kiat's *Shuttle Life* (2017), Quek Shio Chuan's *Guang* (2018), Lau Kek Huat's *Buluomi* (2019), Jacky Yeap's *Sometime, Sometime* (2020), or Chong Keat Aun's *The Story of Southern Islet* (2020), and the surprise hit by Lay Jin Ong, *Abang Adik* (2023).

While more funding opportunities[3] are available to Malaysian filmmakers and producers compared to their predecessors who self-produced, worked with a small budget on their passion project and learnt on the job by doing everything themselves (Khoo 2007), yet not many filmmakers end up on this co-production/grants trail which includes building their portfolio with award-winning short films, entering film labs and workshops to develop and polish their scripts, and taking advantage of residencies (i.e., Cannes Cinefondation). Liew Seng Tat's second feature *Lelaki Harapan Dunia* (2014) took seven years to make as he wanted to go the professional route compared to his debut *Flower in the Pocket* (2007). Because pursuing grants and possible co-production funds take so long, independent filmmakers like Shanjhey Perumal may prefer to keep their budgets small so that their projects can be realized sooner, particularly if their main audience is local. Other scripts could also be considered to be too mainstream by film festivals and yet too art film for local commercial film studios to sponsor (Nandita Solomon interview, 26 April 2022), thus making them truly financially independent.

Compared to ten years ago, there are more avenues to help producers, even though they are very exclusive. Savvy producers can connect with European partners at various festivals like Udine and Singapore. *Tiger Stripes* producer and former Dahuang worker, Foo Fei Ling mentions the Asian Film School (Busan Film Commission), and EAVE (European Audiovisual Entrepreneurs), a professional training, project development and networking organization for audiovisual producers. EAVE's workshops gave Foo and Solomon, former participants of EAVE, a strong idea of what it means to be a long-term producer. Aside from EAVE, there are the European ACE Producers that accept Asian producers from time to time, the Rotterdam Producers Lab, and Locarno Open Doors, although the latter shifts geographical focus every three years (Foo Fei Ling interview, 19 April 2022).

Nevertheless, funding has been cut due to the pandemic and there is more competition nowadays from hungrier, more original, bolder creative filmmakers from Cambodia, Indonesia, Thailand, and Vietnam, such as films by the Anti-Archive in Cambodia which functions like a collective similar to Dahuang when they first started.

Regional connections are now tighter through the circulation of films at proliferating film festivals in Asia and beyond where Southeast Asian filmmakers meet. The SeaShorts Film Festival organized by Tan Chui Mui in Malaysia helps expose Malaysian audiences to high-quality alternative and experimental films from Southeast Asia that can hopefully set a high bar for upcoming filmmakers. These connections are further enhanced when film workshops in Malaysia invite regional film industry experts to run master classes or act as jury, among them Filipino indies like John Torres, Khavn de la Cruz, and Lav Diaz. Malaysian indies also look to Thailand for high quality post-production services and the trend toward a more regional outlook can be seen in *Interchange* (Dain Said 2016), *Barbarian Invasion* (2021), and *Stone Turtle* (2022). Regional co-productions are becoming common and some producers (Thai, Indonesian, Singaporean) are highly sought.

But four structural factors unique to Malaysian society explain what is holding back independent festival film production.

1. Malaysia's Multiculturalism Leads to Market Segmentation

Compared to neighboring film industries like those in Thailand, Indonesia, and the Philippines, Malaysia's smallish media industry is segmented by language and culture: Malay, Chinese (Mandarin and other dialects), Tamil/Hindi, and English.[4] Nik Amir summarizes the problem of the lack of audience for independent films:

> So [with] the market [being] segregated, the low brow taste, the economic power to care about films, we are left with a very small market. Even to compete regionally it's hard. Collection: RM100–200k ringgit. How to make a film for a million ringgit? Who are you going to get 1 million from to make only RM100,000?
>
> *(interview, 24 April 2022)*

Regardless, despite the linguistic market segmentation, younger filmmakers who are cosmopolitan in their mindsets, and open to exploring and representing each other's cultures (Khoo 2007), are skeptical of the political racial discourse of divide and conquer, and prefer to collaborate on the basis of shared common values. This gives rise to films like *Fly by Night* (Zahir Omar 2018), where an ethnic Malay director helms a story about a cast of Chinese characters with Mandarin/Cantonese dialogue and some Malay; or an ethnic Chinese Malaysian directs a military action film mainly in Malay (*P.A.S.K.A.L: The Movie*, Adrian Teh 2018); or a film that showcases the relationship between a Malay illegal taxi driver and a Chinese social escort with a backdrop of race politics to divide Chinese and Malays (*Prebet Sapu/Hail, Driver!* 2020). However, market segmentation is but one manifestation of structural racialization, fostered by years of pro-Malay policies.

2. The Role of the State

For years, FINAS, the National Film Development Corporation Malaysia, under the previous Barisan Nasional government was regarded as inept (being mainly staffed by bureaucrats with no specific knowledge about cinema or the industry), wasteful and non-transparent in awarding grants. The FINAS CEO as well as the chairperson are appointed on two-year contracts, so film policies would change depending on whoever was the new FINAS head. FINAS also sits under the Ministry of Communications and Multimedia and when governments change, policies would likely follow. CEO tenures may not get renewed if they push against a clunky bureaucracy used to the old ways of working. Moreover, years of prioritizing Malay language as the national language has entrenched its bureaucracy in a deeply ethnonationalist pro-Malay outlook despite the rhetoric of going global.

However, incremental changes were made during the tenure of Dato Kamil Othman as Director General of FINAS (2014–16). The latest progressive move is FINAS' collaboration with Asia's biggest international film festival, the Busan International Film Festival (BIFF) and Asian Contents & Film Market (ACFM) to form MyLab, an incubator program to develop early-stage scripts and film projects aiming for international grants with guidance from regional and international experts (Alhamzah 2022). Curated by Malaysian programmer/producer Lorna Tee, who has an international standing, eight film projects were selected, and the best project (*The Depth of Darkness*, dir. Gogularaajan Rajendran and prod. Kumanavannan) was awarded RM 20,000 (approx. USD 4,500) to further develop the film.

Strategic state-led activities like MyLab are long overdue when compared to what the Singapore Film Commission (SFC) and the Film Development Council of the Philippines (FDCP) have been doing. The SFC focuses on talent development, internationalization and audience cultivation as key strategies for growth. With an eye toward the burgeoning VOD market in the Asia Pacific and an already high domestic mobile penetration rate of 148.8%, it is building a next generation of content creators who are versatile storytellers on multiple platforms (https://www.imda.gov.sg/-/media/Imda/Files/Industry-Development/Sectors/Media/SFC-Review.PDF). As for the FDCP, its website lists a series of programs aimed to ensure "growth and empowerment of the Philippine film industry and the production of quality films" (https://fdcp.ph/programs). Both these state bodies have an eye toward a long-term plan for sustaining the industry, from which independents will benefit: not only technical training programs, but also film scholarships are provided for talented individuals to study at institutes of higher learning. The SFC's strategy to develop audiences through free outdoor screenings of Singaporean films, fostering young film critics and other ways of increasing film literacy and public engagement should be emulated. Cultivating young audiences to expect different ways of storytelling and to allow room for experimentation is crucial to broadening viewership for independent or alternative films. Lastly, both Singapore and the Philippines also focus on film preservation and restoration in having dedicated film archives, as compared to Malaysia which does not have one.

Aside from the comparative lack of support, Malaysian indie filmmakers also face possible censorship over racial and religious sensitivities. For example, the producer of the film *Babi/ Pig* (2020) about a race riot that breaks out at a secondary school was charged for not having a FINAS license to produce and distribute the film even though it was wholly shot and produced in Taiwan (Tee 2021). If found guilty, he could face two years imprisonment or a fine of RM 50,000. The Malaysian Artistes Association (Seniman) also lodged a police report against it for allegedly having elements of racism that tarnished Malaysia's image, and the film poster was accused of insulting Malays because beside the film title "Babi" was scribbled the tiny word "Melayu." Knowing that the topic would be too sensitive to pass the censorship board in order to be screened in local cinemas, Namewee chose to release the film in Taiwan. Contrastingly, hypocrisy is reflected when no action is taken against films like the ethnonationalist film *Mat Kilau* (2022), which provides a one-dimensional testosterone-fueled distorted account of history where Malays are anti-colonial heroes and Sikhs are blood-thirsty traitors. The film received a production grant of RM 1.5 million and RM 300,000 from the marketing Digital Content Fund. It has become the highest-grossing Malaysian film in history (Sathiabalan 2022).

Notwithstanding these barriers, perhaps the largest problem is the tendency of government and audiences to only regard film as purely entertainment and to evaluate its quality based on economic returns rather than its artistic and social merit. Hence, building audiences for alternative stories and storytelling methods is key.

3. Viewers

Interest from the wider public in indie films is restricted to a very niche audience as audiences are raised on a steady diet of Hollywood spectacles. Tellingly, the top-grossing local films in the Malaysian cinemas are horror, action, animation, and comedies. That said, Amir Muhammad explained that films made for the festival circuit are "made in a vacuum" and have no direct relevance to Malaysians' immediate circumstances (interview, 3 April 2022). Producer Nandita Solomon wonders if indie filmmakers themselves are to be blamed for not building home audiences and being busy chasing festivals (interview, 26 April 2022). Even though film programs have burgeoned, several filmmakers who have been jury on student film competitions noted that Malaysian film students lacked original ideas and mainly followed Marvel, Chris Nolan, and trends like using the latest filters and lenses rather than creating their own trends (Shanjhey Perumal interview, 15 April 2022). Story-wise, Jacky Yeap, former programer of the SeaShorts Film Festival, also noted that Malaysians, unlike Filipinos and Indonesians, seemed to be stuck on simple themes about family rather than attempt to broach harder topics like history and politics (interview, 9 April 2022). Many attribute this to the education system that discourages critical thinking. And thus, what happens with the unsustainability of independent filmmaking in Malaysia is a reflection of the larger problems facing a society which, unlike its neighbors, did not undergo dictatorship or revolutions.[5]

4. Middle-Income Trap?

One explanation for the lack of consistent international presence of Malaysian indies at film festivals is that most Malaysian filmmakers are middle-class and can find work and live off of making television commercials, corporate videos, and television work. The comfortable life can make them complacent whereby struggling to raise funds to make an independent feature, with no expectation of recouping the budget seems meaningless. This situation and sentiment can change as the costs of living and film production rise while grants and budgets for making commercials shrink. In the 2000s, a minimum project for a two-to-three-minute commercial was RM 50,000 (USD 11,238). Today, videos could be produced for as low as RM 10,000 (USD 2,247) (Ng Ken Kin interview, 3 April 2022). Moreover, despite higher living costs, television budgets have remained stagnant for two decades (Wahab Masri and Hashim 2021) and independent or freelance directors find themselves having to take on more commercial projects in order to sustain themselves. Nonetheless, passionate indie filmmakers like Nik Amir Mustapha (*KIL* 2013; *Nova/Terbaik Dari Langit* 2014), who takes commercial jobs on the side to support a family, persevere. His third feature, a sci-fi titled *Imaginur*, premiered at the New York Asian Film Festival in July 2022.

Persistent Challenges

Many Malaysian indies felt not much had changed since the 2000s. The much larger population size of Indonesia and the Philippines, the non-fragmented nature of their markets, the lack of a holistic long-term vision of film as a legitimate art form capable of conveying cultural expression that needs to be supported and preserved at a national level in Malaysia, and FINAS' limited role are factors that impede the growth of independent Malaysian filmmakers. While there are FINAS grants and some support for independent filmmakers for production, script development (in the past), and marketing, they are piecemeal efforts that do not consider the film project from beginning to end. Worthwhile schemes like *wajib tayang* (mandatory screenings https://www.finas.gov.my/en/services/wajib-tayang/), meant to guarantee that locally produced films would get two weeks' screening at the local cinemas, require enforcement to make sure that exhibitors do not circumvent the regulations (Khoo 2015, 224–25). It remains to be seen if the new unity government can affect positive changes.

Outside of film schools and universities where good taste is cultivated, cineastes can catch alternative, quality films at Wayang Budiman (programmed by film academic Norman Yusoff) and several filmmaker-run microcinemas (Next New Wave, TDSC, Cinemata) in KL, depending on organizers' busy schedules. The risk of such volunteer-run screenings is a lack of time and resources to be consistent and sustainable. Before, the Kuala Lumpur Film Appreciation Club or Kelab Seni Filem (KSF) played a key role through its regular screenings of art films and hosting of the Malaysian Shorts and Malaysian Documentaries program several times a year. It was through these events that the film community was formed across the various language and ethnic cliques and the indies learned about each other's works and found collaborators. But with the advent of DVD and then streaming platforms, viewing practices became more atomistic and decentralized. Renting a professional screening hall is expensive once KSF lost its free viewing space at HELP University. So the Malaysian indies now lack a central space that unites filmmakers, cineastes, and students.

Undoubtedly what has changed is the technoscape. Many indie directors have emigrated to make TV series on OTT streaming platforms. A proliferation of Asian OTT exists, though their viability remains to be seen once the market gets saturated with the entrance of the giants. Already Hooq (2015–20) and iFlix have closed down, the exception being the Hong Kong–based Viu. All three also create original local TV series, aside from carrying popular content like Chinese and Korean dramas, romantic dramas, horror, and animation. One might say that the demand for content creation has led to better quality

Malay-language TV series like *Jibril* (2018), *The Bridge* seasons 1 and 2 (2018, 2020), and the dark comedy *Keluarga Baha Don/Baha Don's Family*. Viu originals are carried also by Media Prima TV Networks (MPTN), which also commissions indie filmmakers to create online content for their streaming service, Tonton.

Turning to global OTT streaming platforms, other than the rather commercial Taiwanese-Malaysian TV series *The Ghost Bride*, directed by Ho Yuhang, and Quek Shio Chuan, Netflix does not commission original Malaysian content because Malaysian viewers do not watch local content on its platform, unlike, for example, Filipino audiences. Most local content are acquisitions paid at varying rates, depending on the film's box office takings and whether it is part of a package. Indie filmmakers interviewed were thankful for streaming platforms (including Viddsee, MUBI), but the low to no returns meant that such platforms cannot be the main income stream. Nevertheless, for low-budget producer Amir Muhammad, OTT platforms seem attractive especially when cinema rental is expensive and theater exhibition risky when weighed against the competition from Hollywood big-budget films and their promotion machinery: "Why go through all this hassle? We might as well use that [money] to make a movie." In dealing with contracts with OTT Amir cautions that one has "to be smart about carving out territories because Netflix may not take all territories" (interview, 3 April 2022). Indie filmmakers who previously made films with the help of studios and had no control over their licensing rights are more conscious of this going into future projects.

Digital filmmakers of varying waves acknowledge that the presence of smaller screens and newer technology ultimately affect cinema and film viewing. Some assume a more pragmatic position to engage with the medium or to embrace it, as inevitably viewers are increasingly accessing films on their mobile phones. For Amir, film is after all a means of communication and making genre films is a way to reach a wider audience, never mind whether in the cinemas or on a mobile phone. Still embodying the "just do it (yourself)" spirit (a can-do attitude that is about spontaneity), he derides filmmakers who are paralyzed when they cannot get funding from FINAS or the local TV stations. Amir crowdfunded RM 435, 203[6] for *Pendatang* (Ken-Kin Ng 2023), "a dystopian thriller set in Malaysia where the different races are not allowed to mix, by force of draconian law."[7] Scripted by Lim Boon Siang, Amir decided to crowdfund and release the film on YouTube for free because he felt its topic was too controversial to be screened in theaters. Upon upload, the film gained 1 million views in 27 days. Shanjhey Perumal, too, is optimistic about the sustainability of independent filmmaking: in the future he and his producer want to have their own online platform by building their audience and charging a small subscription (they plan to make eight films over the next eight years). Audience-building is key and it has to be developed locally, regionally, and beyond. Streaming platforms help in that regard. For example, *KL24: Zombies* (2017) was made at an estimated RM 200,000 and then released on YouTube for free, where it has garnered 8.8 million views, partly for its prescient prediction of COVID-19.

But most still aim for theatrical release and focus on making professional grade films the conventional way. Indeed, all hopes are pinned on two Malaysian festival features debuting in 2023: *Tiger Stripes* (Amanda Nell Eu) and *Oasis of Now* (Darrel Chia Chee Sum). But as Liew Seng Tat quips, "They are ten years late! We cannot have a big gap. Every year we need to have one out" (interview, 13 April 2022). Keeping up the momentum requires government grants and incubators (plans for a Malaysian Film Academy not unlike that of Busan IFF or Cinemalaya are underway) and consistent screenings planned throughout the year.

Finally, while generally important in the industry, it is even more crucial for the indies to network and cultivate friendships in a competitive hardened atmosphere: at film festivals, film labs, film academy, and workshops and while working on film projects together, opportunities for formal and informal mentoring arise. And in turn, the more experienced filmmakers/producers themselves end up guiding and nurturing younger talents (Tan Chui Mui helped produce for younger filmmakers Jacky Yeap and Lim Han Loong; Shanjhey has 12 under his wing, while producers Nandita Solomon and Bianca Balbuena help upcoming filmmakers by providing advice with script development and marketing). For shy Darrel Chia, who had been lurking in the background since the peak of the indies in the mid-2000s, it was a matter of not knowing how to access the inner circle of that first wave that partially led to his delayed journey to filmmaking. These networks also need maintenance over the years as indie directors go off to work on their individual projects but find renewed synergies when they return to collaborate together: *Turtle Stone* (premiered at Locarno in 2022) reunites the director-producer team of Woo Ming Jin and Edmund Yeo, with Liew Seng Tat taking a new role as production designer.

Returning to *Barbarian Invasion*, a scene toward the end of the film reveals the cast and crew of the film within the film viewing the dailies and then wrapping up. Unbeknownst to most viewers, they are the actual crew of *Barbarian Invasion* – and among them, besides real-life producer/director Woo Ming Jin, are the Malaysian next new wave, younger people who are worthy short filmmakers themselves: Award-winning short films maker Putri Purnama Sugua received KRW 10 million (USD 7,581) for script development and was invited to participate in the Busan Asian Contents and Film Market's Asian Project Market with her script *Life I Stole* in 2022. Location soundman and Taiwan graduate See Wee Aw's

Figure 33.1 *Barbarian Invasion* (2021) featuring filmmaker-director Tan Chui Mui as retired actor Lee Yoon Moon making a comeback after her divorce.

390

short film *Kampung Tapir* (2017) won the NETPAC (Network for the Promotion of Asia Pacific Cinema) Award at the Busan International Short Film Festival. Last, Rou Ning Teh is making her short film this year. Having worked in the trenches as volunteers for the Next New Wave Young Filmmakers' workshops, there is hope that with enough financial support and friends, they will get to make their features in the near future.

Acknowledgment

Grateful thanks to the following filmmakers and producers for their valuable time to be interviewed between 1 April and 6 June 2022: Amir Muhammad, Elise Shick Chong, Chin Yew, Amanda Nell Eu, Foo Fei Ling, Darrel Chia, Edmund Yeo, Jacky Yeap, Ng Ken Kin, Liew Seng Tat, Nandita Solomon, Nik Amir Mustapha, Shanjhey Perumal, Sidney Chan, Woo Ming Jin, and Yve Vonn Lee.

Postscript: In memory of one of the pioneers of the first wave, Deepak K. Menon (1979–2024) whose return to indie filmmaking with *The Diaspora Story* was cut short.

Notes

1 The author moderated the q and a after the afternoon screening on October 31, 2021 at LFS Coliseum Theatre, Kuala Lumpur.
2 1 USD = MYR 4.73 (2024 rate of exchange).
3 See production grants from the Singapore Film Commission (est. 2019), Bangkok-based Purin Pictures, and SEAFic (2016–April 2022).
4 While India also has linguistically diverse film industries, its much larger population attenuates this problem of having to compete for few viewers.
5 For example, political violence and unrest in neighboring countries like Indonesia become fodder for independent films like *Vania on Lima Street* (Bayu Prihantoro Filemon 2022). As if Malaysia lacks histories of student radicalism, Edmund Yeo's *River of Exploding Durians* (2014) turns to the 6 October 1976 Thai student massacre as inspiration for its characters.
6 The final amount is on the crowdfunding platform, Indiegogo: https://www.indiegogo.com/projects/pendatang-movie#/
7 This description is taken from the film company website: https://www.kumanpictures.com/pendatang

References

Alhamzah, Tahir. 2022. "#Showbiz: MyLab Partners with Busan International Film Festival, Asian Film Market." *New Straits Times*, April 26. Accessed August 15, 2023. https://www.nst.com.my/lifestyle/groove/2022/04/791977/showbiz-mylab-partners-busan-international-film-festival-asian-film.
Khoo, Gaik Cheng. 2007. " 'Just-Do-It-(Yourself)': Independent Filmmaking in Malaysia." *Inter-Asia Cultural Studies* 8 (2): 227–47.
———. 2015. "Syiok Sendiri? Independent Filmmaking in Malaysia." In *Independent Filmmaking Around the Globe*, edited by Doris Baltruschat and Mary P. Erickson, 213–35. Toronto: University of Toronto Press.
Sathiabalan, Indra. 2022. "Why the Fuss Over 'Mat Kilau: Kebangkitan Pahlawan'?" *Malaysiakini.com*, July 12. Accessed August 15, 2023. https://www.malaysiakini.com/news/627962.
Tee, Kenneth. 2021. "Producer of Namewee's 'Babi' Charged with Unauthorised Production, Promotion." *The Malay Mail*, July 21. Accessed July 6, 2022. https://www.malaymail.com/news/malaysia/2021/07/21/producer-of-namewees-babi-charged-with-unauthorised-production-promotion/1991459?utm_source=pocket_mylist.
Wahab Masri, Ahmad Fadhli Ab, and Rohani Hashim. 2021. "Pekerja Filem dan Isu Bayaran Dalam Industri Filem Malaysia" [Film Workers and Payment Issues in the Malaysian Film Industry]. *Malaysian Journal of Media Studies* 23 (2): 17–38.

34

SLIPPERS OUTSIDE THE DOOR

An Annotated Interview with Tan Pin Pin

Sophia Siddique

Situating Tan Pin Pin: Tan Pin Pin (b. 1969) is a renowned Singaporean filmmaker who works primarily within the documentary genre. According to Tan, her films interrogate how we know what we know. This epistemological impulse finds vibrant and potent expression in those films that center Singapore as their primary subject matter. One does not simply view Tan's films; one experiences them. Her films harness the full power of the senses to make material and palpable such evanescent states as memory and belonging. Tan works intuitively to express the unique voice of each film and to engage in powerful grassroots distribution campaigns.

   Situating the annotated interview: I interviewed Tan Pin Pin on 29 March and 4 May 2022 via Zoom. The editors for this volume wanted us to discuss three themes during the interview: film activism, censorship, and distribution (national and transnational). What follows is not a chronological transcript of both interviews. Rather, like a montage, I've organized the interview thematically, selecting relevant responses from both interviews and placing them within each designated theme. I've edited my questions and Tan Pin Pin's responses for clarity. Italicized paragraphs are present throughout to provide additional context for the interview. Readers may choose to read the italicized paragraphs alongside the interview or they may choose to engage with the italicized paragraphs after finishing the interview. I made Tan Pin Pin an editor on a shared Google document so that she could bring her own insights and feedback to this collaborative process.

The Ecosystem of Singapore Film Activism

SS: Can you describe your sense of Singapore activist film practice, historically and within this contemporary moment?
TPP: When I think in terms of activist film practice, I can only think of Martyn See. Everyone else wouldn't come close to what he has done. Especially with his films *Singapore Rebel* (2005) and *Zahari's 17 Years* (2006).

Directed by Martyn See, Singapore Rebel *is a documentary featuring opposition party member Chee Soon Juan. The People's Action Party, in power since Singapore's independence in 1965, claimed that the film contravened the Films Act's 1998 provision against party political films. According to the provision, See could face "a fine not exceeding $100,000 or to imprisonment for a term not exceeding 2 years or to both" (Films Act 1981). After an approximately 1.5-year investigation, See was issued a warning.*

DOI: 10.4324/9781003266952-45

Zahari's 17 Years *centers on Said Zahari, a journalist who was arrested in 1963 and subsequently detained for 17 years. The documentary was banned in Singapore. For more information about the details of the police investigation, including questions asked by the police, the questioning of Tan Pin Pin, and a surrender of all copies of* Singapore Rebel *within See's possession, please go to http://singaporerebel.blogspot.com/.*

SS: In terms of Martyn See's activist stance, he really did lay his body on the line in terms of being subjected to authorities and having his films banned. In what ways did his interventions open up a space for you?

TPP: Martyn made *Singapore Rebel*, a portrait of Dr. Chee Soon Juan, an opposition politician when there was a chance that the short film could have been banned and he himself fined or jailed for possession of the film for contravening the Films Act, which had a clause disallowing vaguely defined "party political" films. I think he made this film to also show how unfair this law was against the Opposition. True enough, when the film was submitted to the censors for a public screening (as all films have to do in Singapore), he was called up for questioning by the police. He was editing *Singapore GaGa* with me then, so by association, I was also called in for questioning – my first time being questioned by the police. Later, a group of us ten filmmakers wrote a letter to the *Straits Times* to protest against this investigation by asking the authorities to "clarify" the Films Act.

Directed by Tan Pin Pin, Singapore GaGa *(2005) is a documentary that showcases the polyphonic nature of Singaporean life (Khoo 2014). It features urban, quotidian soundscapes as well as music and other aural testimonies of Singapore as a sonic nation (Tan 2012).*

TPP: Martyn opened up the space for me in these ways: He made me aware of how unjust and self-serving the Films Act is. That it could be enforced to preserve the status quo. In order to move things forward and increase political space for different voices in films, filmmakers may have to break laws but face the consequences of breaking them. I, like many of us, was brought up in an environment where we were taught to ask permission for everything. I learned from him that some things, you just have to do. He documented each police interaction on his blog (http://singaporerebel.blogspot.com) so that everyone could see for themselves transparently what the weight of the State bearing down on one person entailed. This was a brand-new approach in 2005. Usually, once the police come into the picture, the creators, afraid of the heavy penalties, would stop whatever they were doing and surrender their cameras and footage as if they were guilty. Three Ngee Ann Polytechnic lecturers – Tan Kai Sing, Mirabelle Ang, and Christina Mok – made a film called *A Vision of Persistence* (2001), which was a portrait of J. B. Jeyaretnam (Brenez 2016). In that instance, I remember from hearsay that they gave everything to the police and never saw their footage again. The film was supposed to have been screened at the Singapore International Film Festival, but the film was quietly withdrawn. It is unclear what happened. The filmmakers did not speak to the press or document their experience.

Martyn gave a generation of filmmakers and activists a local framework to think about why we do what we do and how to negotiate when we are called up. I felt that Martyn, by shedding light on the investigation process in his blog, may have protected himself against further illegal use of force by the state. I am sure the police were reading his blog as much as we were!

Martyn gave out copies of his film on DVD by submitting it to human rights film festivals like the Amnesty International USA Film Festival and the New Zealand Human Rights Film Festival as he was being investigated. So that if he was caught, it would already be out there. People could see for themselves.

Following this "template," when I completed *TSWL*, having had an inkling that the film may ruffle some feathers based on how Martyn's films was treated, I too decided to world premiere the film at Busan IFF (who partly funded the film with their Asian Network of Documentary Fund) as well as international film festivals like the Berlinale and Dubai IFF, where it won a Best Director award. It was important that copies of the film existed outside the country in case there was a blackout of it in Singapore. I usually would world premiere my film in Singapore first.

TSWL received an NAR (Not Allowed for All Ratings) from the Media Development Authority. The NAR rating is given when a particular film is perceived to "undermine national security" (MDA Press Release 2014). Tan Pin Pin appealed the decision. According-ing to a press statement from the Films Appeal Committee (2014), twelve members were present at the deliberations. Nine members voted to uphold the NAR decision and three members voted for a Restricted 21 (R21) rating (Tan 2014). The documentary features the lived experiences of Singaporean political exiles and Tan traveled to Malaysia, the UK, and Thailand to document their stories (Leow 2020).

SS: **It's interesting you say it's kind of a template. Was that in the back of your mind with *TSWL* (2013) after it got banned?**

TPP: As I was going to appeal the ban, I decided that I was not going to release *TSWL* online, like throw it on YouTube. If I did that, it would not put any pressure on the appeal. The appeal committee could say, "Okay, why do we need to pass it? It's being circulated anyway." Part of me may have been worried that releasing the film on YouTube would jeopardize the film's chances of having the rating lifted, I was that hopeful.

In addition, I didn't release *TSWL* online when it was banned because I wanted people to watch the film together, then have a discussion about the issues raised by the film. Who are we? How did we become who we are today? Where do we want to go? So there was less of a point in releasing it online and having it being watched by persons alone in their bedrooms in the dead of the night.

This rating allowed for private screenings only, which meant I could not publicize the screenings or sell tickets for it. I just said, "Okay, if you allow for private screenings, I'll do private screenings. *TSWL* went on a private Q&A road tour in Singapore the whole of 2015. We toured living rooms, offices, civil society organizations, arts groups. We even screened it during a Christmas party at my aunt's house from her little cathode ray TV. I saw many slippers outside doorways that year. It was my way of celebrating Singapore's 50th year of independence.

The appeal for *TSWL* was unsuccessful. Unlike Martyn, I didn't write about my interactions with the authorities during the appeals process. In retrospect, I should have done it for the benefit of future creators undergoing the same process.

When I made *TSWL*, it started out as a photography project about circumnavigating Singapore. I had done *80 km/h* (2003) and I wanted to do one where I'm on a boat circumnavigating Singapore. To take a continuous video of the coastline in one take or at least take photographs. And in the process of researching this whole being outside and inside, I stumbled upon *Escape from the Lion's Paw* (Teo and Low 2012). And then from that grew *TSWL*. So it was a chance sighting of a book. Pin Pin is referring to the book mentioned earlier: *Escape from the Lion's Paw*. My starting point is very different from Martyn's. But at some point, when I was editing, I realized that I could very likely get into the same trouble that Martyn had gotten into if I had continued with editing the film then screening it. I continued because I asked myself, and this is something I said in Joanne Leow's interview, "Why am I a filmmaker if I'm going to shirk from this?" (Leow 2018). But it was a question that I never had to ask in the beginning, I was circumnavigating Singapore! In the journey as you went along, it became pertinent to ask. But I feel that that's a question that not everyone needs to ask, but when you do get asked, you have to answer it. And not to avoid the question.

80 km/h (2003) is a 38-minute long take of a journey along the Pan Island Expressway from the eastern point of the island city-state to the western point. Tan kept her speed at 80 km/h, so the film would have "cartographical value" (Tan 2015). Escape from the Lion's Paw: Reflections of Singapore's Political Exiles (2012), *edited by Teo Soh Lung and Low Yit Leng, features the narratives of six Singaporean political exiles, including Ang Swee Chai and Francis Khoo.*

SS: And speaking about Cherian George's notion of calibrated coercion, if the government had then put Martyn in jail, that would have been too extreme.
TPP: The public would have seen the film as it was on YouTube and seen for themselves how mild a film it was. It would have been obvious that it was done to penalize Chee Soon Juan, and it would not be fair even to the moderates. I feel as a result of *Singapore Rebel*, the censors did not ban *TSWL* outright but they gave it an NAR rating.

Scholar Cherian George aptly describes the State's exercise of power in Singapore as "calibrated coercion" in which "coercion is increasingly calibrated for maximum effectiveness at minimum cost" (George 2007, 133).

SS: I felt that in terms of calibrated coercion, the ban on *To Singapore, With Love* was also too extreme.
TPP: It is all relative. I felt *TSWL* was banned because it humanized the people the party wanted to condemn, because only then can they justify the illegal (in my view) use of the ISA on opposition politicians leading to the 60-year reign of one party over Singapore.
SS: I think there are gradations of Singapore activist film practice. On the one end, you have Martyn See, but I also see you as playing a role or having a presence in Singapore film activist practice.
TPP: **Of course, when *TSWL* was banned from public screenings, we took the film on the roads of Singapore. Having conversations after the screenings about Singapore and how we have come to be who we are. Do you consider this film activism?**

SS: I think this is why film activism in Singapore has to be nuanced. You cannot use the same definitions of activism in the American context and operate in Singapore. That's why even though you haven't located yourself within the activist ecosystem, I would argue that you are engaged in activism – but these are more micro-interventions because power operates in quite different ways in Singapore. Would you see yourself as participating in Singapore's film activist practice?

TPP: I get asked that question. Invariably, toward the end, someone will say, are you a filmmaker or are you an activist? As if it is two parts, and put on the spot like that, I always end up saying, I am a film director. But I am also a living, breathing, aware person who was born and bred here and has gone through enough to sense the different injustices and has come up with enough smarts to know where one can make the most difference.

I believe in the power of cinema to transform, inform, and create change. My work with the film community was to champion the making of films that do that and that may not have been of commercial value. For example, they had cultural and artistic merit. If we left it entirely to market forces, we would only have films from the Marvel Universe. We need to cultivate our own voices, to tell our stories about our specific conditions. The advocacy we have done is to grow an environment where more of these works can be made.

In a similar vein, I was on the board for the Singapore International Film Festival. It champions world cinema, especially films from Southeast Asia. I feel strongly that film is a key medium to help us understand our place in the world and also in Southeast Asia. That is why I totally jive with the idea of the festival.

Tan Pin Pin was also on the board of the Substation (2004–11) and the National Archives of Singapore (2007–09).

SS: How do you develop that acuity or that discernment about how to intervene and when to intervene? In Joanne Leow's interview with you in *Senses of Cinema,* you say "being an artist can be a political gesture" (Leow 2018). Can you elaborate on that? Do you see that as a connective thread through your work?

TPP: The mere act of pointing a camera and recording can be a political act. That's why the Films Act forbids recording devices in certain scenarios. For the longest time, I thought it was enough to ask questions in my films, showing the effects of this and that policy, but not asserting something as right or wrong in my work, preferring the viewers to make up their own mind. I think that kept me a "safe" entity, traversing the world of metaphors. However, now that I am older, less patient and less idealistic and I have also grown a thicker skin, I am calling things out more, pulling less punches in person as well as in my work.

SS: Exactly. That's why I also think what you said about being an artist can be a political gesture. You were talking about just how even pointing a camera in the context of Singapore; depending on what and how you're choosing to shoot, is already a certain intervention.

TPP: Correct.

SS: This brings me to the second keyword: censorship. In Singapore, the landscape is quite amorphous with shifting OB (out-of-bounds) markers, some that you recognize and some that you don't. How do you navigate that terrain? How do you think through the implications of censorship in your work? Does self-censorship ever enter into your creative process?

Scholars Lyons and Gomez define OB markers in Singapore as "areas where civil society activists dare not venture because they are deemed too politically sensitive and thus 'out-of-bounds' " (Lyons and Gomez 2005, 128). *Such subjects can include race and religion.*

TPP: I mean, of course, also self-censorship would come in, but I think less and less so after *TSWL*. I think that after *TSWL*, and having had a whiff of how self-serving the censorship rules were especially with regards to Singapore politics, I felt that I didn't want to play that game anymore. It was a lose-lose process, losing some and then losing more and then having nothing left. Because in my mind, if *TSWL*, which was made with so much care for both sides of the argument, was excised from the island, then for me it was just obvious that the regime would tolerate no discussion about its past acts even if most Singaporeans would understand the circumstances of those gestures today. So with that kind of experience, why does one want to have to negotiate?

Shaping Perception: The Ethics of Distribution and Exhibition

SS: It's interesting to me to link *TSWL* and how you were distributing and exhibiting the work to a dimension of activist film practice. I notice that educational institutions are spaces where your work is quite tactical as an intervention in how we understand Singapore. Singapore's historiographies are dominated by the PAP's version of history. In thinking of *TSWL*, the film was banned but you could get permission to screen the film at educational institutions.

TPP: *TSWL* is allowed to screen at tertiary institutions in Singapore, but professors have to write in to justify that it is necessary for the course and they must explain in their proposal how they are going to "balance" the views in the film.

SS: If that's not Singapore activist film practice at the grassroots level, I don't know what is.

TPP: And that has been really great for my practice as a film director because I had always imagined one way of distributing a film using cinemas and festivals, and then when I did this, I realized, this is where I belong.

SS: I'm looking at some of the phrases that describe your distribution practices for *TSWL*. Like the phrase "suitcase tours" from your interview with Olivia Khoo (2015). You came to Vassar with the film on that educational trajectory.

The suitcase tour included stops at Georgetown University, New York University, and Northwestern University (Khoo 2015). Olivia Khoo has written about TSWL *in Senses of Cinema (2015).*

TPP: I still remember the 2015 US tour. I had seven days for the tour due to family commitments. But I could have just gone on and on and on, just traveled all the university campuses across the US. There were people willing to put me up. The USA college tour was organized by Singapore students themselves. They collectively raised funds and pulled the schedule together. In each city, I was met by a different student. I would be staying in a senior's room which she had vacated for me in a dingy part of town. I loved it. This Was

Figure 34.1 Slippers outside the door: *In Time To Come* (Rumah Attap Library and Collective, Kuala Lumpur, Malaysia, 2018).

what filmmaking was all about for me. That is the way to go, people just finding a way to screen a film.

SS: I think there's a way to think about *TSWL*, but maybe your other films as well, as a kind of grassroots distribution and exhibition strategy.

TPP: Yes, I feel that for independent films, the grassroots strategy is one of the ways to get the audiences to come to see the films. Using pre-existing networks to spread news about the screenings and meetups.

SS: How did you arrive at Vimeo as your preferred online distribution platform?

TPP: Very early on in my filmmaking career, as I started making work, I realized that even though I had always been forward-looking, there was a throughline between all the different works. And the sooner I was able to lasso this way of seeing the work together, well, the better. The individual films themselves speak for themselves, but a body of work speaks even louder. And I was just trying to find out different ways of letting people see these works, because shorter films, especially, normally fall between the distribution cracks. I was looking for a host to contain all the films. At that time, Vimeo offered ease of use and they also took the smallest cut for each film sold.

SS: When you say you see a throughline in your work and that your body of work speaks even louder, what is that voice communicating?

TPP: My work tries to address how we know what we know and how we become who we are today. I also want to speak up for communities and themes that have not been spoken for. Finally, tying it all together is the act of documenting. If well organized, the footage we have in our archives is powerful. We have proof.

I also wanted to have an option for people to pay to see my films. So that's when we stumbled upon Vimeo at that time. I started using Vimeo about ten years ago. There were other options at that time, but Vimeo provided the most functionality and it took the lowest cut per film. And I've been with Vimeo ever since, even though I can't collect emails of people who sign up for these films. Now, there are more sites where when people sign up to watch, you can collect their emails, and that collection of that email is very, very important. People are voting for you by paying for your film and that act of confidence in the land of the free is valuable. You want to maintain connections with people who do that.

SS: And that can help inform the marketing and promotion of your future films.
TPP: Yes. It's a long-term relationship. I knew that for a fact when after *To Singapore, With Love*, I was thinking, how am I going to sell *IN TIME TO COME* (2017)? Because people who have seen *Singapore GaGa* and seen *TSWL* would probably be totally befuddled when they see *IN TIME TO COME*. It is a film featuring everyday scenes with no talking heads or hard information. I remember people coming up to me and saying, "I don't get it, I really think it's really brave that you did this. But whatever you make, I will come and see anyway."

IN TIME TO COME *explores the unearthing of a one-time capsule and the process of putting together a new one (Stein 2022). According to her website, the film "itself is a vessel that transports us through past, present and future, a prism through which we glimpse alternate realities" (Tan 2017).*

SS: **I'm curious about the different distribution strategies that you have between the longer films and the short films. Is there a reason for the distinction between the short films being free and available and the other films, the longer work being paid for on Vimeo.com?**
TPP: I feel that the longer films were theatrically released. Whereas the shorter films were sometimes shown as part of a film compendium for free, mostly. So I wanted to reflect on that hierarchy. But in more marketing terms, you could say that the shorts are a taster, and if you like it you can upgrade to premium. The amounts are very nominal but for me, it was important that you paid $1.99 because, it's a vote for the film and a vote for the film director and her body of work.
TPP: I think film festivals played a very important role in these longer works.

SS: **Can you talk more about that strategy? How did you decide which festivals to submit your work to? You said something along the lines of distribution shapes perception. Can you talk more about that?**
TPP: The medium is the message. For my films, the manner and location of the launch is critical to how a film can be received. Because my films are all so different, how do you signal it to people who have not seen it? That is why, there is so much weight put on getting a film into an A-list festival. But this is not the only way. Many works are launched direct to the streamers or even YouTube these days.

For my first film, *Singapore GaGa*, when I was still a relatively unknown entity, I was just grateful that SGIFF (Singapore International Film Festival) chose it for its world premiere; the festival has a long history of launching and supporting Singapore films. What was interesting for me was that SGIFF had not put it in the main program, they put it in a fringe program. Some people would have seen the allocation as kind of an insult because this was a free screening at the Goethe Institut's all-purpose hall as opposed to a cinema. In retrospect, it was the perfect sidebar for the film. I don't know if you've seen the stills from the first screening, everyone was sitting cross-legged on the floor. The film was so well received that they organized new screenings at the festival. Now, looking back 17 years later, I think the reception, with everyone sitting cross-legged on the floor having a communal experience together, watching a version of Singapore projected back at them is what some of my films are about. This is what I mean by the setting being the message. After the very successful response at SGIFF, it went to have an eight-week sold-out run at the Arts House, the first for a Singapore documentary. News about it spread through word of mouth. I wrote about its screening journey in *GaGa* tours Singapore. Independent venues and organizations championed the film and were key to its success. *Invisible City* had its world premiere organized by NUS Museum before going on to a theatrical run at the Arts House again. Given the historiographical slant to the film, I felt NUS Museum was a suitable launch pad for the film.

For *IN TIME TO COME*, the world premiere took place at Vision du Reel in Switzerland. Later back in Singapore, its premiere was co-hosted by a Singapore contemporary arts space, Center for Contemporary Art at Nanyang Technological University (NTU). This film had 5.1 sound (my first) so it needed a cinema with those speakers. I designed for the film to have a theatrical run at Filmgarde multiplex. I remember doing Q&A almost every night for one month during its run at Filmgarde. I think it is important for my films to have their world premiere in Singapore. While I hope to make my films for an international audience, my key audiences are Singapore residents.

TSWL had its world premiere outside of Singapore for reasons mentioned above. It had a very different trajectory from my other films Subsequently, all of them are available on Vimeo, together with the other shorts. *Singapore GaGa* and *IN TIME TO COME* are now on Netflix Southeast Asia too.

SS: **Why Netflix Southeast Asia? How does that work with Vimeo and what made you decide on this particular means of access?**
TPP: I felt that after the theatrical window had lapsed, putting the film in a way that people could easily access it, was important. And I was approached by an aggregator who collected works for Netflix. And I said yes. Netflix has cut the distribution pie into different regions, so that's why I've negotiated with Netflix to keep Vimeo so that viewers can access it even if they do not have Netflix.

SS: **Are you a one-person show? Are you the branding, the marketing, the strategic brain behind all of this?**
TPP: Yes, I am, but I usually run through these ideas with different people and more personnel is hired when work gets busy. I've now come to realize that there is a whole non-theatrical world of touring films at NGOs or colleges. I have been to small arts spaces in Cambodia sitting cross-legged on the floor showing *Singapore GaGa*, going to Taipei and screening in a small bookshop for migrant workers, while showing *TSWL*. Or going to an independent library in Kuala Lumpur to screen *IN TIME TO COME*.

SS: **How did you find these NGO spaces?**

TPP: The news of the ban and then the content just gets out quite quickly. Why have I been confined all these years to a very precious cinema kind of release? Certain films need that. IN TIME TO COME would need that kind of environment, but *Singapore GaGa* definitely can go out into a community center, can go out to schools, and in a way, it lived that. To *Singapore, With Love* achieved its full potential in terms of a lot of these screenings even in the US, when we went on tour, they were organized by students themselves. They have their own underground telephone system and then they organize the screenings, raise the funds, and pull it all together. That is the way to go. People just finding a way to screen the film.

As my films are now screened in different settings, I have become less fussy about the projector and audio quality of the film. I have screened in homes, in offices, in arts spaces. But I still send a note to the projectionist with films that need it. For example, in *IN TIME TO COME*, there is a snow scene in City Square Mall that does not have sound. The note would mention it in case the projectionist was worried as to why her audio has suddenly dropped.

It was never only about lights on with velvet drapes behind me. It was about all kinds of slippers just outside the door. And then when you come out, you cannot find your slippers.

SS: You cannot find where your slippers are, but your perception of Singapore has shifted. It's a monumental shift. You can't watch *Singapore GaGa* or *To Singapore, With Love* and love Singapore in the way that maybe you had before.

TPP: I would hope that that is the reaction. That means that I have won.

I thank Tan Pin Pin for taking the time to speak with me, especially given the pandemic and the time difference between Singapore and New York.

Figure 34.2 Sitting cross-legged: *To Singapore, With Love* (Brilliant Time Bookstore, Taipei, Taiwan, 2016).

Tan Pin Pin's Filmography

Lurve Me Now (1999)
Microwave (2000)
Moving House (2001)
Rogers Park (2001)
Building Dreams (2003)
Gravedigger's Luck (2003)
80 km/h (2003)
Crossings: John Woo (2004)
Singapore GaGa (2005)
Invisible City (2007)
Impossibility of Knowing (2010)
Snow City (2011)
Thesaurus (2012)
Yangtze Scribbler (2012)
To Singapore, with Love (2013)
Pineapple Town (2015)
IN TIME TO COME (2017)

Additional Resource

https://tanpinpin.com/
Tan Pin Pin's short films are available for free on her website. IN TIME TO COME, Invisible City, *and* Singapore GaGa *are available on Vimeo on Demand for rental or purchase.* IN TIME TO COME *and* Singapore GaGa *are available for streaming on Netflix Southeast Asia. Each of the longer works has its own Facebook page.*

Singapore Activist Ecosystem

Singapore Rebel, directed by Martyn See (2005). *https://www.youtube.com/watch?v= DHlu6Tt8bmk*
Said Zahari's 17 Years, directed by Martyn See (2006). *https://www.youtube.com/watch?v= lXnmN0ZcwOs*
1987: Untracing the Conspiracy, by Jason Soo (2015). https://www.youtube.com/watch?v= eBJqJroWt3E

References

Brenez, Nicole. 2016. *Tan Pin Pin: No Vacation from Politics*. Translated by Brad Stevens, April 7. https:// archive-magazine.jeudepaume.org/blogs/each-dawn-a-censor-dies-by-nicole-brenez/2016/04/ 07/tan-pin-pin-no-vacation-from-politics/index.html.
Films Act. 1981. https://sso.agc.gov.sg/Act/FA1981?ProvIds=pr33-#top.
George, Cherian. 2007. "Consolidating Authoritarian Rule: Calibrated Coercion in Singapore." *The Pacific Review* 20, no. 2 (June): 127–45.
Khoo, Olivia. 2014. "Singapore, Sinophone, Nationalism: Sounds of Language in the Films of Tan Pin Pin." In *Sinophone Cinemas*, edited by Audrey Yue and Olivia Khoo, 77–97. London: Palgrave Macmillan.

———. 2015. "On the Banning of a Film: Tan Pin Pin's *To Singapore, with Love*." *Senses of Cinema* 76. https://www.sensesofcinema.com/2015/documentary-in-asia/to-singapore-with-love-documentary/.

Leow, Joanne. 2018. "Gestures of Resistance: An Interview with Tan Pin Pin." *Senses of Cinema* 88. https://www.sensesofcinema.com/2018/feature-articles/gestures-resistance-interview-tan-pin-pin/.

———. 2020. "Circumventing the Archive: The Art of Charlie Chan Hock Chye and *To Singapore, with Love*." *Verge: Studies in Global Asias* 6, no. 1 (Spring): 58–67.

Lyons, Lenore, and James Gomez. 2005. "Moving Beyond the OB Markers: Rethinking the Space of Civil Society in Singapore." *Sojourn: Journal of Social Issues in Southeast Asia* 20, no. 2 (October): 119–31.

Media Development Authority. 2014. "The Media Development Authority (MDA) Has Classified the Film '*To Singapore, with Love*' as Not Allowed for All Ratings (NAR)." Press Release, September 10. https://www.imda.gov.sg/news-and-events/Media-Room/archived/mda/Media-Releases/2014/mda-has-classified-the-film-to-singapore-with-love-as-not-allowed-for-all-ratings-nar#:~:text=10%20September%202014%20%2D%20The%20Media,for%20All%20Ratings%20(NAR).

Stein, Erica. 2022. "Telling One Another's Stories: The City Symphony and Cine-Genre Narrative." *The New Review of Film and Television Studies: Special Issue on Cine-Genres* 20 (1): 25–36.

Tan, Boon Huat. 2014. "The Films Appeal Committee Upholds MDA's Decision to Classify '*To Singapore, with Love*' as Not Allowed for All Ratings (NAR)." Press Statement, November 12. https://www.imda.gov.sg/news-and-events/Media-Room/archived/mda/Media-Releases/2014/the-films-appeal-committee-upholds-mdas-decision-to-classify-to-singapore-with-love-as-not-allowed-for-all-ratings-nar.

Tan Pin Pin. 2012. "*Singapore GaGa* Tours Singapore." In *Southeast Asian Independent Cinema: Essays, Documents, Interviews*, edited by Tilman Baumgärtel, 131–39. Hong Kong: Hongkong University Press.

———. 2015. "80 km/h (2003)." https://tanpinpin.com/80kmh/

———. 2017. "IN TIME TO COME (2017)." https://tanpinpin.com/in-time-to-come/

Teo, Soh Lung and Low Yit Leng, eds. 2012. *Escape from the Lion's Paw: Reflections of Singapore's Political Exiles*. Function 8 Limited.

35

LET'S LOVE HONG KONG

Hyper-Density, Virtual Possibility, and Queer Women in Hong Kong Independent Film

Arnika Fuhrmann

Hong Kong has long been figured as the paradigmatic location that signals the transformation of cities into generic hubs for capital flow and electronic connectivity, factors largely thought to impede human connection. Across local and international cinemas Hong Kong's supposed hyper-urban character materializes especially in genres such as science fiction, gangster films, horror, thrillers, and other films that figure the urban as dystopic or hyperbolic.[1] *Let's Love Hong Kong* offers a particularly concentrated, critical look at the city. As Fran Martin (2002) writes, "Aside from the three women, the character most powerfully present in the film is the city itself" (46). The urban is usually imagined as a site of possibility for queerness. However, Denise Tang's critique of *Let's Love* evocatively details the ways in which Hong Kong's condition of urban density comes to hamper the possibilities of lesbian relationality. In Tang's analysis, Hong Kong emerges as an environment in which urban density tips into a too-much, an impenetrable hyper-density, that makes "one painfully reticent to act on one's same-sex desires" (Tang 2006).[2] While others have thus persuasively detailed the ways in which *Let's Love*'s physical and virtual Hong Kong constrain queer intimacy, I investigate the film as one in which cybersex and sex work, the transition to electronic capitalism and the precarity it engenders also become the domains for novel kinds of affective flows, desires, and appetites on the part of its lesbian protagonists. I read the hesitation, reticence, silence, and non-contact on the part of queer women in the cybernetic-alienated Hong Kong of *Let's Love* not only as deficits but rather as transitional affects in a period in which female embodiment and queer desires work through new relations to labor, capital, the money form, and intimate electronic communication. I contrast my analysis of *Let's Love* with another cinematic treatment of female intimacy and the city space of Hong Kong – that of Ann Hui's *Tak Haan Chao Faan* (All About Love, 2010).

Let's Love's opening scene is organized around the notions of both physical space and cyberspace in Hong Kong, juxtaposing the lives of its three main characters. Zero sits in her seat in the abandoned movie theater that is her home and reads job ads with the light from a flashlight. The circle of light creates her own space within the public theater; it appears as a space of privacy but also as one of isolation. Chan dreams about her regular

DOI: 10.4324/9781003266952-46

meetings with a sex worker. From here we cut to Nicole and the cybersex world of "Let's Love Hong Kong," a domain that Nicole frequents and in which Chan works – and which critics read as producing a distancing effect, as the two women never quite meet. Rather than only moving between physical and virtual modes of isolation, or indicating their non-intersection, however, the film's opening scene also signals a switch from analog to digital media: the cinema, which stands in for the analog, is abandoned and no longer in use, while the digital (along with shifts to finance capitalism) is becoming a part of everyone's lives.

This switch from analog to digital modalities thus also introduces questions of temporality. What happens if we turn the focus to time or to a city space infused with the temporalities of the digital and of electronic capitalism (rather than opposing physical and virtual space to each other)?[3] What if we saw *Let's Love* not only as a complaint, but as a film that enacts rifts in contemporary urban temporality and enables us to ask how queer personhood, relationality, and collectivity reinvent themselves in the context of such a rift?

To understand the presentation of queerness and city space in Hong Kong cinema, a comparative look at independent filmmaker Ann Hui's lesbian-themed film, *All About Love*, is instructive. In Hui's film, old lovers Anita and Macy are reunited in a chance meeting. What the women's romance lightly chafes against are the hostility to bisexuality, rigid feminist attitudes as well as heteronormative limits on what a family should look like. Against these constraints, the two protagonists set irreverent attitudes and eventually expand the form of the family to one that includes four mothers, two fathers, and two babies. At the same time, the film largely retains the conventional notions of commitment and the couple form at its core.

All About Love vitally roots Macy and Anita's rekindled romance in the quaint and colonial spaces of the built environment and boutique atmosphere of the privileged Midlevels neighborhood of Hong Kong's Central district. The two lovers, both pregnant from one-night stands, spend the first half hour of the film walking each other home several times in the same night. Especially the Central–Midlevels escalator, the walkway that executives ride down to work in the finance district, and the adjoining territory of SoHo furnish the backdrop to the playful romance. In *All About Love* genteel living never rubs up against anything else, and same-sex desire effortlessly maps onto beautiful urban design and the colonial-built environment as the aesthetics of the good life. The urban space that capital has built and invested with the qualities of "lifestyle-rather-than-living" never stands in the way of a female-female alliance in which both partners, despite challenges to their livelihood, remain securely ensconced in an upper-middle-class milieu and in the institutions of high finance.

As Esther Cheung (2010) has poignantly detailed, life in Hong Kong is overdetermined by real estate arbitrage, and Hong Kong cinema to a great extent reflects this a condition of struggle. *All About Love* represents a useful example of how electronic capitalism enjoins us to valorize models of personhood and collectivity that are seemingly opposed to capital, but in reality remain its anachronistic drivers (Spivak 2000). The very fact that Hui's film locates the protagonists' supposed queer oppositionality within a boutique notion of dwelling that can only be enabled by high finance illustrates these contradictions all too well.

What thus makes *Let's Love Hong Kong* worth reevaluating is that the film's figuration of same-sex desire is anything but "As Normal as Possible" (Yau 2010). Gina Marchetti (2017) argues that Yau Ching's film figures female sexuality in "expressly feminist terms"

(4) and "take[s] women's sexuality beyond the narrative tropes of romantic comedy and domestic melodrama" (6). As Marchetti further asserts, "The combination of the film's countercinematic style with its advocacy of women's rights, political participation, and social justice in relation to female sexuality made the film particularly provocative" (3).

City and Self in the Time of (Finance) Capital

In her analysis of electronic capitalism and the postcolonial megacity, Gayatri Spivak teaches us that the attachment to certain, formerly laudable, notions of self and postcolonial collectivity has become anachronistic.[4] Like Saskia Sassen, she sees the city as a service headquarters for globalization, with a new infrastructure that doesn't serve anyone but global finance. In both Sassen's and Spivak's readings, cities become hyperbolic locations (Sassen 1996). For Spivak, cities, as hubs of electronic capitalism, are more closely tied to their global counterparts than to their national or regional locations or their impoverished urban populations. She labels this tendency *secessionist* – concluding that, e.g., "Bangalore is not in India." Against this background Spivak argues that the clinging to notions and rhetorics of independent self and postcolonial nationhood disregards the resolutely secessionist character of the city and the operations of capital. At the same time, such holding fast to anachronistic notions of self and collective remains the driving force of this same secessionist, electronic capitalism.[5]

Let's Love is a film that helps us recognize such a discrepancy in the temporalities of personhood and collectivity through its juxtaposition of three distinct characters and modes of existence in an early 2000s, future-oriented Hong Kong. Instead of outlining ascendancy into normativity, valorizing couplehood, or asserting an upwardly mobile queer subject in the manner of *All About Love*, *Let's Love* resolutely details the fractures of queer existence and desire under finance capital. Zero, who lives in the abandoned movie theater, stands in for a simultaneously precarious and flexible existence. Nicole is an emotionally dissatisfied management-level worker in the transnational economies of finance and its support services. Finally, there is Chan, whose petit-bourgeois home life is contrasted by her work in cybersex. The lives of all three are organized around an economy that is continuing to transition from industrial to finance capital.

The film's three main characters' relation to urban space is indeed vexed. Zero is basically homeless, while Chan lives in cramped quarters with her parents, and Nicole's well-appointed house has a *feng shui* problem of impeded flows, so that also Chan and Nicole remain "unhoused" in some sense.[6]

Several analyses of the cyber domain in which Chan works – and in which Nicole lusts after her – conclude that this virtual space largely precludes lesbian connection. *Let's Love* would then be showcasing breakdowns of communication in a world overdetermined by problems of coding. Though Tang notes that "one cannot neglect the role that new communication technologies have played in how we have come to define intimacies," the affective state that many critics read from *Let's Love*'s cybernetic-alienated world is one of non-contact in the sense both of a lack of physical, interpersonal touch and of the possibilities of lesbian expression (Tang 2011, 130). The (almost) only domain that represents a domain of emotional plenitude is that of Chan's cramped family home, where motherly love and cooking envelop a character who often seems orphaned (Tang 2011, 138–140). At the same time that this home proffers affective and sensory plenitude, however, this space also imprisons Chan in her solitude and silence. As Tang (2006) writes, she "dwells in silence that in due course engulfs her within a sphere of lesbian invisibility." Chan's touring of apartments throughout the film becomes the search for a space in which to exist – and in which being a lesbian is possible. Ostensibly, for Chan this never becomes a reality, however, even when same-sex intimacy is offered to her.

Apartment Hunting

On the one hand, the precarity of lesbian existence and relations in this film is materially grounded in the precarity engendered by real estate arbitrage. However, this precarity does not merely designate an impasse. This is where the film is at its most perceptive. Visually, *Let's Love* obsessively details the near-ruins of industrial capital and consistently lingers on older tracts of lower-to-middle-income urban housing blocks and walk-up apartments as well as on shophouses. Here the film records in loving detail the fading vivacity of mixed-use areas where living and small commerce mix.

In contrast to *All About Love*, the cityscape in *Let's Love* – rather than anchor the accomplishment of same-sex marriage, the queer patchwork family, or even the couple form – comes to function as an evocative setting for investigating the "minor intimacies" of longing, pursuit, and commercial sex (Berlant 2000, 5). For one this is instantiated by the film's lingering on apartment details as well as by the incessant talk about real estate.

In Chan's constant apartment hunting, the closest that we come to a quintessentially lesbian space – or one that could house sustained forms of lesbian affectivity – is the old, high-ceilinged apartment, painted green, that furnishes the initial location of Chan's meeting with Zero. While Chan does not, or not yet, have the capital to buy or rent such a space, her continued visits to these transitional spaces represent an inhabiting of queer affectivity and an actualization of intimacy of sorts. Approximately 15 minutes into the film, Zero

Figure 35.1   Imagining a space for desire.

is viewing the apartment with a female client, while Chan is with her agent. Zero stands behind an iron-barred window inside the apartment looking out onto the balcony where Chan stands, with her elbows resting on the balcony railing, gazing upon the rows of shop-houses opposite. After some time, Zero steps out onto the balcony and assumes the same pose as Chan. They stand in silence for a long moment until string music starts up and we cut to a view of giraffes playfully swinging their long necks around each other. The scene on the balcony between Chan and Zero *is* an intimate scene – and the film's refusal to end in the acquisition of property or the formal achievement of couplehood is remarkable for the ways in which it draws out possibilities of queer intimacy that exceed or reject those forms. Rather than end in failures of romance, *Let's Love* presents a detailed catalog of how queer women utilize public or semi-public space as sites for intimacy.

At the point in time when Chan visits these apartments to look for an inhabitable space and life, we already look upon these spaces with the gaze of hindsight – with nostalgia and perhaps recognition: it is only with the predominance of finance capital and its shaping of the city that we begin to see these spaces as desirable and enabling. The banter of the real estate agent supports this reading: his sales pitch is all about boutique living and potential profit – highlighting the current propensity to replace housing with lifestyle, the fulfillment of needs with boutique marketing, and rights with privilege. However, the affective relation that unfolds between the two queer women in this space exceeds these reductive occupations of the contemporary city.

Semi-public intimacy is intensified in the film's climax in which Zero approaches Chan on the train and massages her foot. Rather than inhibit lesbian intimacy per se, city spaces in *Let's Love* appear as sites that stimulate the desire for female same-sex intimacy. It is especially the interstitial spaces – those that are public or semi-public, or those that have not fully transitioned to the logics of finance capital – that stimulate such desire. Cinematographically this is underwritten by the film's slow pacing and, according to Bérénice Reynaud, by the realist-expert *and* intimate gaze that "director Yau Ching casts over the city of her birth – . . . the[se] working-class buildings, cramped apartments, crowded streets, endless stretches of small shops . . . the urban decay/permanent renewal that keeps hovering between nostalgia and a desperate quest for modernity" (Reynaud 2002).

Intimacy

In this film everyone is matter of fact about sex, but critics have questioned the characters' capacity for intimacy. Several characters' desires are virtual; they don't always want real persons. Others have been understood as having evacuated desire from their everyday, physical lives. The closest that Chan seems to come to intimacy is sleeping in her mother's bed in one scene and secretly watching Zero cry in another.[7]

However, the film's reticence in this regard prompts us to develop a wider sensorium for what intimacy can include. Thus, a scene of turnip cake making, in which Chan sits in front of her mother, between her legs, appears as a scene of intimacy. Chan's mother envelops her in a close embrace as they stir the cake mass together. The scene can further be understood to approximate an intimate sex scene, especially when viewed in conjunction with slang for lesbian sex that uses food metaphors. Thus, the Cantonese title of Ann Hui's film *All About Love* is *Tak Haan Chao Faan*, roughly, "when you're free, why don't you fry some rice" – slang for lesbian sex adopted from mainland usage.

The simultaneity of Nicole's cybersex with the scene in which Zero massages Chan's foot on the train and with scenes of Chan's mother cooking further underlines this. Parallel editing presents these scenes not only as a collective climaxing but also does not differentiate between the cyber domain, physical touch, and a broader sensorium of smell, intimacy, and the haptic. The simultaneity of these scenes further draws the mother-daughter relationship into close proximity to lesbian desires.

Finally, Chan's regular meetings with a sex worker, also do not foreclose intimacy but rather broaden its repertoires. Rather than classify these scenes merely as a refusal of intimacy, we can understand them as ones in which the inevitable transactions that accompany and shape intimacy are thematized. As Tang (2011) writes, "I want to know, how are the grey areas defined between Kwok Chan and her lover? Are there moments where she would rather know her as a lover, or am I asking the wrong question and making a forbidden assumption? A lover to me does not preclude monetary exchange" (132). Rather than assume conventions of ownership or of monetary exchange, such conventions are played out and *worked through* by the women in these scenes. Noticeably, they are stimulated by transactionality itself. The first scene of Chan's meeting with the sex worker begins with the shot of HKD 100 bills and returns to them several times. That the women engage with these thematics playfully however underlines their questioning of the parameters of transactionality and the assumed conventions of reciprocity in general – and that they in fact ultimately do not adhere to a notion of "ownership" of the other.

During a further meeting (at around the 45th minute of the film), Chan and the sex worker tease each other over which one of them won't have any customers anymore in how many years and start a pillow fight. In the continuation of the scene, the sex worker rejects payment from Chan, asking, "How will you know you paid for these various body parts?" while pointing to each one. Chan counters, "I paid for this and this and this." The sex worker retorts, "So who do you belong to?" They start to wrangle again.

Tani Barlow (1998) identified in the Sinophone cinema of the 1990s the close association of women, rather than men, with the production of surplus value: "The laboring subjects who produce the wealth are all female" (148). An iconic image that underlines this point in a film that Barlow analyzes is a "crotch shot of [of a character] "Ermo" sitting on her kang [platform] with a mound of small-denomination banknotes flowing as though out of her vagina" (146). Barlow argues however that, while women are incredibly productive in economic terms, such plenitude does not extend to their social and sexual satisfaction. Like in the 1990s films that Barlow describes, labor is all female in *Let's Love*. However, in this film, labor and precarity provide the setting for and enable lesbian desire. *Let's Love* points both to the destructive aspects of the feminization of the constantly updating modes of labor in East Asia as well as searching for enabling features of the same.

The film introduces an updated version of a world in which "women rather than men are the producers of surplus value."[8] Women are intimately aligned with an economy both sexual and electronic, the latter of which augments surplus value to a never known extent in an economy in which "the perpetual need to find profitable terrains for capital surplus production and absorption shapes the politics of capitalism." David Harvey (2008) describes the ways in which the city takes on certain configurations under these conditions: "The result of continued reinvestment [in the city] is the expansion of surplus production at a compound rate – hence the logistic curves (money, output and population) attached to the history of capital accumulation, paralleled by the growth path of urbanization under capitalism" (24). In *Let's Love* it is both the city, the female protagonists of the film, and the coordinates of desire and sexuality that operate under the augmented logics of value in electronic capitalism.

In fact, the real estate agent who becomes Zero's drinking partner states that his biggest regret is that he is not a woman. He is obsessed with both sex workers and with the digital economy – "Let's start a dot com," he urges Zero. The world of *Let's Love* is thus one that associates women not only with industrial production and trade, but even more closely with the multiplicatory characteristics of electronic capitalism. The film thereby investigates erotic and relational possibility under a new regime of value. Scoping out these possibilities from inside this world, so to speak, *Let's Love* thus shows that Chan and the sex worker eroticize transactionality on the one hand, but on the other hand do not entirely subordinate their desires to it.

One way in which *Let's Love* intervenes in a contemporary world, in which all areas of social and emotional life are subordinated to and suffused with market logics is that, ultimately, it is nonproductivity that turns the women on and becomes "sex talk" in the scene between Chan and the sex worker described. In the film as a whole, it is the spaces, aesthetics, and discourses of precarity that inform the attractiveness of the characters *and* provide the grounds for the women's attractions to each other. Zero, is the character in the film who, true to her name, is most precariously positioned and makes the least money. She constantly appears in new functions (and thereby as incredibly versatile in the contemporary economy), selling everything from sex potions to cell phones. While she exemplifies precarious labor, Zero is also shown as the character who seems happiest, takes time to go enjoy herself, and possesses the greatest mobility in the city.

A final remark pertains to reception or to the labor that audiences and critics of *Let's Love* invest in their apperception of the film. Thus, a passage in Tang's analysis concludes, "I feel the urge to tear down what I have imposed on myself and what others have expected of me" (Tang 2011, 133). What is striking is the degree to which *Let's Love* elicits in its viewer-critics the desire to realize the possibilities that at times remain foreclosed in the film. Olivia Khoo (2008) asks, "How do we learn to feel movement and in doing so hold, if not enact, possibilities for change?" (114). The reviews of the film tend to be passionate and highly invested in producing queer possibilities: "Chan Kwok Chan dreams of the grandiosity of lesbian desires. Curiously, we know, it could be difficult to arrive at, but not impossible. We just need to carve our own space in hyper-density. Queer desires are to be reckoned with" (Tang 2011, 140). In addition, the precision with which *Let's Love Hong Kong* allows critics to describe privacy and intimacy also stands out (Leung 2007, 34–35). We might thus direct attention also to the perceptual and affective avenues that the film opens up: it is not only the diegetic possibilities, or lack thereof, for queer lives that we should evaluate but also the utopian-activist impulses that *Let's Love* stimulates.

Let's Love skillfully navigates the digital domains of cybersex, urban spaces built and redefined by finance capital, and the negotiations of commercial sex. The film is perceptive in marking these as parallel spaces of an at least partial virtuality that all our lives are suffused with. In a 2008 analysis Khoo casts the film's promise for lesbian possibility into the future (as well as into the temporality of a "natural, always already"): "The real space of Hong Kong, which continues to deny visibility or full presence to lesbian bodies, is articulated with two other metaphoric or imagined spaces shown on-screen. These alternative imaginings seem to suggest that one of the few places that Hong Kong lesbian bodies *can* exist at present is in utopia – either a virtual reality utopia (set in the future as a hopeful possibility) or a utopia of giraffes running in the field (seen as natural, always already there, and therefore unquestionable)" (Khoo 2008, 108). But I think that we should extend Khoo's "always already" of lesbian possibility also to the concrete world of the city delineated by *Let's Love*. Although the film casts skepticism on the contemporary city and on lesbian relationality, it is equally concerned with drawing out the possibilities that we do have within contested worlds overdetermined by coding, finance, and transactionality. A further, chilling note on the temporalities of queer desire is, however, presented by the fact that the filmmaker herself at present resides outside of Hong Kong as her political stances exceed the limits of what can currently be expressed in the SAR. In hindsight *Let's Love*'s *ho yuk* (which "connotes a sense of rapid, disorienting, jarring motion") quality might then also be taken as an injunction not to rest content in our interpretive conclusions but to continue to shake up all notions of queer presents, futures, and political possibility (Martin 2002, 43).

Notes

1 Examples include *Blade Runner* (1982), *SPL II: A Time for Consequences* (2015), *Ab-normal Beauty* (2004), *Contagion* (2011), and the films of Johnny To or Wong Kar-wai. Denise Tang introduces the terms "hyper-dense" and "hyper-density" in *Conditional Spaces* (2011), 139–40.
2 See also Denise Tse-Shang Tang, "Of Longing and Waiting: An Inter-Asia Approach to Love and Intimacy Among Older Lesbians and Bisexual Women." *Sexualities* 25, no. 4 (2020): 1–16.
3 Olivia Khoo (2008) and others have also incorporated time into their analyses as they, for instance, investigate elements such as speed with regard to lesbian desire in the film.
4 "Thus the 'culture' or 'subject' of the virtual megacity is not only diversified in the usual race-class-gender way alone, but is also capital-fractured in agency – between active and passive, or, if you like, 'control' and its antonym, although that is already too crude when the movement is electronic. Yet, the nation-state is the name of that crude episteme that will not go away. . . . The culture-subject-agent trinity remains as necessary as it is impossible. If the subject does not dream of controlling the agency of capital, capital does not move." Spivak (2000), 12–13.
5 Ackbar Abbas (1997) writes: "It is possible to think of this period as a period when an 'older' but still operative politics of national legitimacy and geophysical boundaries comes into conflict with a 'newer' politics of global flows, information, and the devalorization of physical boundaries" (4). However, we may instead understand antiquated narratives of self and location/nation as precisely animating the unbounded operations of global capital.
6 See also Leung (2007, 34) and Martin (2002, 46).
7 See also Khoo (2008, 104–5).
8 This is what Barlow argues in "Green Blade."

References

Abbas, Ackbar. 1997. *Hong Kong: Culture and the Politics of Disappearance*. Minneapolis: University of Minnesota Press.
Barlow, Tani E. 1998. " 'Green Blade in the Act of Being Grazed': Late Capital, Flexible Bodies, Critical Intelligibility." *Differences: A Journal of Feminist Cultural Studies* 10 (3): 119–58.
Berlant, Lauren. 2000. *Intimacy*. Chicago: University of Chicago Press.
Cheung, Esther M. K. 2010. "On Spectral Mutations: The Ghostly City in *The Secret*, *Rouge* and *Little Cheung*." In *Hong Kong Culture: Word and Image*, edited by Louie Kam, 169–91. Hong Kong: Hong Kong University Press.
Harvey, David. 2008. "The Right to the City." *New Left Review* 53 (September–October): 23–40.
Khoo, Olivia. 2008. "The Ground Beneath Her Feet: Faultlines of Nation and Sensation in Yau Ching's *Ho Yuk: Let's Love Hong Kong*." *GLQ: A Journal of Lesbian and Gay Studies* 14 (1): 99–119.
Leung, Helen Hok-Sze. 2007. "Let's Love Hong Kong: A Queer Look at Cosmopatriotism." In *Cosmopatriots: On Distant Belongings and Close Encounters*, edited by Edwin Jurriens and Jeroen de Kloet, 19–39. Leiden: Brill.

Marchetti, Gina. 2017. "Handover Bodies in a Feminist Frame: Two Hong Kong Women Filmmakers' Perspectives on Sex After 1997." *Screen Bodies* 2 (2): 1–24.

Martin, Fran. 2002. "Floating City, Floating Selves: Let's Love Hong Kong." In *Ho Yuk – Let's Love Hong Kong: Script and Critical Essays*, edited by Yau Ching, 43–49. Hong Kong: Youth Literary Press.

Reynaud, Bérénice. 2002. "Let's Love Hong Kong." *Senses of Cinema* 22 (October). https://www.sensesofcinema.com/2002/feature-articles/love_hk/.

Sassen, Saskia. 1996. "Whose City Is It? Globalization and the Formation of New Claims." *Public Culture* 8: 205–23.

Spivak, Gayatri Chakravorty. 2000. "Megacity." *Grey Room* 1 (Fall): 8–25.

Tang, Denise Tse-Shang. 2006. "A Dialogue on Intimacy with Chan Kwok Chan in Yau Ching's *Ho Yuk: Let's Love Hong Kong*." *Intersections: Gender, History and Culture in the Asian Context* 14 (November). http://intersections.anu.edu.au/issue14/tang.html.

———. 2011. *Conditional Spaces*. Hong Kong: Hong Kong University Press.

———. 2020. "Of Longing and Waiting: An Inter-Asia Approach to Love and Intimacy Among Older Lesbians and Bisexual Women." *Sexualities* 25 (4): 1–16.

Yau, Ching. 2010. *As Normal as Possible: Negotiating Sexuality and Gender in Mainland China and Hong Kong*. Hong Kong: Hong Kong University Press.

36
CARE IN FILMING, CHANGE BY LOVE

Shuting Li

Care in Filming, Change by Love

As affordable DV technology developed in the 1990s, independent women filmmakers in China and Taiwan spontaneously embraced this technology and started making independent documentaries about the family. Yang Lina decided to start her first documentary *Lao Tou* (Old Men, 1999) after encountering a group of elderly men sitting on the sidewalk, although she did not have any professional training or previous experience in documentary filmmaking (Zhang 2018). She walked into these elderly neighbors' personal lives along with a DV camera to document their everyday lives in Beijing, which were transformed by the waves of reform and opening-up, modernization, and urbanization rippling across mainland China. Transformations in the Chinese family during the late 1990s, such as changes in marriage, intergenerational relations, and practices of intergenerational care, unfold through a glimpse into the everyday lives of a group of old men. Across the strait, Jasmine Ching-hui Lee became an independent filmmaker after graduating from the Graduate Institute of Sound and Image Studies in Documentary, Tainan National University of the Arts (Zhang 2023). Compared with Yang's serendipitous entry into the documentary world, Lee's filmmaking trajectory mingles with her personal life in the family domain. Her first documentary *Jia Zai He Fang* (Where Is My Home, 1999) narrates the story of how her family cared for her *waipo* (maternal grandmother) after sending her to a nursing home far away from home. She sheds light on tensions and challenges faced by the old generation and different generations of women, including wives, daughters, daughters-in-law, and granddaughters, in care practices (Lee 2011).

Yang and Lee started their filmmaking journey on different occasions. However, both women filmmakers coincidentally end up using their cameras to tell the stories of women, particularly of their roles as caregivers, and interrogate the ideas of care and love they encounter in intimate family relationships. Care is a moral practice of taking responsibility for those in need (Kleinman 2009; Buch 2015). It demands "all the supporting activities that take place to make, remake, maintain, contain and repair the world we live in and the physical, emotional and intellectual capacities required to do so" (Dowling 2021, 25). Care not only involves people's recognition and reaching out to care about something but

DOI: 10.4324/9781003266952-47

also leads to certain actions of taking some responsibility and giving care (Tronto 1993). In addition to its moral and ethical aspects, care can be understood as the practice of social reproduction that makes the world and holds society together (Dowling 2021). However, care practices depend on the chemistry between caregivers and receivers, often form intertwined but conflicting relationships, cause indescribable affect like bittersweet feelings, and raise concerns and questions about love and intimacy. As Annemarie Mol (2008) argues, the logic of care entails a complex of negotiations over "competing notions of the good" for people in need (46). The documentary as a medium records stories about the daily care practice; at the same time, it conducts practices of care that filmmakers, film subjects, and audience involved. I argue that care in the documentary is more than a theme; it is embedded in practices of production, circulation, and consumption.

In this chapter, I will compare the bodies of work of Yang Lina and Jasmine Ching-hui Lee to show how care practices in the Chinese family are depicted in the documentary and how care can become a driving force in documentary filmmaking and circulation practices. By examining how Yang and Lee direct their cameras to the family, I will discuss why the family is a critically important topic in Chinese-language documentaries,[1] particularly among women filmmakers. Following the flow of care in the documentary, I bring Maria Puig de la Bellacasa's "matter of care" (MoC) approach into the discussion about how care practices shape the relationships between filmmakers and subjects, how filming and aesthetics can do care work, and how to understand the concept of *xianchang* (on the scene). *Xianchang* is a seminal concept for Chinese-language documentaries during the 1990s. It indicates the changing aesthetics from *xianshi zhuyi* (social realism) to *jishi zhuyi* (documentary realism), directs attention to ordinary people and marginalized voices, highlights spontaneity and contingency in space, place, and time, and distinguishes itself from political propaganda officially produced by the state (Zhang 2007; Robison 2010; Chiu and Zhang 2015). Puig de la Bellacasa's MoC approach provides us with an inspiring way to expand the understanding of *xianchang* into a web of interactions among multiple participants. Through looking into care practices, both filmmakers encounter multiple faces of love ranging from romantic, altruistic, to exploitive. The last part will discuss how Yang and Lee question love in their films and raise the question: how can love be used as a powerful tool for social change and advocacy in the care practices of the documentary?

Why the Family Is Important in Chinese-Language Documentaries?

Intrigued by a group of old men sitting on the curbside, Yang started her filmmaking journey with *Lao Tou*. Concerned with great changes in the Chinese family, she directed her camera to explore the complexity, paradoxes, and struggles of intimate and loving relationships in the family. Driven by her questions about her family of origin, Yang took the roles of a director as well as a daughter in her second documentary *Jiating Luxiangdai* (Home Video, 2000) to investigate her parents' divorce that she was absent from and record different family members' memories about that divorce. In *Lao'an* (The Loves of Lao'an, 2008), the *huanghun lian* (twilight love story)[2] between Lao'an and Xiaowei unfolds in front of her camera. Although Lao'an and Xiaowei have their own families, they fall in love and care for each other without changing their current status of marriage. Motivated by her previous experiences in making documentaries about the family and her personal struggles in the family, Yang started conceiving a "Women's Trilogy" of narrative features about three generations of women since the Cultural Revolution (Zhang 2018). While Yang's focuses, styles, and genres vary from film to film, her body of works is always inspired and moti-vated by her care for aging neighbors, elders in the park, and her elderly parents.

In comparison, Lee's *Jiaguo Nüxing Xilie* (Women and Homeland Series)[3] is a series of documentaries that revolves around a major theme: the care for the elderly and women's roles in the family (Taiwan Docs 2023). Lee started her first documentary *Jia Zai He Fang*, when her *waipo* was transferred to a nursing home in 1996, and finished the series with *Mianbao Qingren* (Money and Honey, 2012), which is about stories of women migrant workers from the Philippines who look after the elderly in nursing homes in Taiwan. Com-pared with Yang's various approaches to the elderly and the family, Lee's filmmaking trajec-tory centers around the nursing home – the place that offers her inspiration and the ground that nurtures her creation. Immersing herself in the nursing home where her *waipo* stays, Lee examines her family's struggles in sending her *waipo* to the nursing home, records love stories of different generations of women in the family, presents the everyday life of Grandma Zhang[4] living in the nursing home, and narrates bittersweet stories of migrant care workers there (Lee 2011). If Yang's filmmaking path is described as searching for answers to questions about the family in relation to socio-economic changes in post-reform China, Lee's path is more like collecting stories in the nursing home from her family, elderly residents, and migrant care workers to create a picture of elder care in the post-bubble economy of Taiwan.

Although Yang's and Lee's paths to filmmaking emerge in different contexts, both of their works center on women, care, and the family. As women filmmakers, Yang's and Lee's gender and social roles make them more open and interested in personal stories, gender politics, the family, and the private sphere, which have been neglected by most dominant male filmmakers in China and Taiwan during the late 1990s. At that time, many Chinese independent filmmakers, such as Wu Wenguang, Jiang Yue, and Zhang Yuan, struggled to form alternative voices, aesthetics, and styles to differentiate themselves from films or *zhuantipian* (special topic program) produced within the state system. The lives of ordinary people after the Tiananmen Square demonstrations in 1989 became a central theme of Chinese independent documentary during that period. However, Paul Pickowicz (2006) underscores the fact that many independent documentaries are neither politically illicit nor are they against the state, and argues that these Chinese filmmakers created a phenomenon of "dancing" or "negotiating with the state" on the content rather than form in the 1990s (6). Focusing on marginalized subjects who are neglected by the state, such as amateur actors, drifters in Beijing, and migrant workers, allowed these filmmakers to circumvent sensitive topics and political censorship in order to survive in that period. At the same time, the emphasis on spontaneity, inspired by cinema verité, equipped these independent filmmakers with the tactic of avoiding institutional and self-censorship (Berry 2007). There are no scripts for filmmakers to submit because they do not know what will unfold during the process of filmmaking. The absence of a collective discussion on the Tiananmen Square demonstrations in 1989 and the circumvented conversations with the authoritative state are the backdrop of the development of independent documentaries concerned with the public and social issues in China during the 1990s. Among the generation of independent filmmakers in the 1990s, only the female documentary director Li Hong features women migrant workers in her first documentary, *Out of Phoenix Bridge* (1997).

At the same time, new Taiwan documentary (NTD) thrived in the mid-1980s and aimed to "give voices to the voiceless" and intervene in "the state apparatus's manipulation of media representation" of social injustices (Chi 2003; Chiu and Zhang 2015, 42). In contrast with "objective reports" of the mainstream media in Taiwan, documentary filmmakers in "*Lüse Xiaozu* (the Green Group)" emphasize the power of witness and grassroots vision and use their films as ethical action to advocate for social justice and rights (Chiu and Zhang, 42). Continuing this tradition, Wu Yi-feng's groundbreaking participatory mode that emphasizes close interactions and emotional involvement between filmmakers and film subjects in both the production and screenings became prevalent in the 1990s (Chiu and Zhang, 55). Lee also shares the zeitgeist of the NTD and advocates for social justice and political transformations through her documentary-making practices (Zhang 2023). Lee's *Jia Guo Nüxing Xilie* aims to raise people's awareness of the elder care issue and facilitate changes in public perception and government policies about migrant care workers. In order to give an alternative voice that differed from the state, the independent documentary filmmakers in China and Taiwan at that time sought inspiration from everyday life and trained their cameras on ordinary people. In contrast with the emphasis on the public space of civil society in the male-dominant documentary world, Yang's and Lee's films shed light on the private space in the family and add female voices to the landscape of Chinese-language documentaries.

In the Chinese Confucian tradition, women's social roles are constructed in the family, from daughter, to wife, to mother. Being female filmmakers in societies shaped by Chinese culture and Confucian values drives both Yang and Lee to look for personal stories happening in the family. However, the focus on the family does not limit the broad social and political impact of their works. The family, as a microsite of society, not only reflects but also embodies the ongoing transformation of society that keeps reconstructing people's everyday lives. In Confucianism, filial piety is the root of Confucian ideas of *li*, *tao*, and *ren*, and the family is the ground where Confucian persons develop their relational selves and realize role ethics (Rosemont and Ames 2009). Nevertheless, the parental authority and practices of filial piety have been challenged by a series of social and economic reforms in China since 1978 and neoliberal marketization in Taiwan since the 1990s. As the declining parental authority and children's increasing pursuit for freedom compromised in practices of caring for the grandchildren, a new notion of filial piety – "caring and supportive but not obedient" – has emerged and gradually gained acceptance by both generations in China (Yan 2016, 250). In Taiwan, transferring care work in the domestic sphere to hired care workers has become a common solution to the unfeasible overload of carrying out traditions of filial piety (Lan 2001, 2004). Due to the shortage of labor and offshore manufacturing, a large population of migrant workers is drawn to Taiwan to fulfill labor shortages in manufacturing as well as care institutions.

Simultaneously, the family in Confucianism works as a governing metaphor for the state with the self as its core (Xu 2015). Deeply influenced by Confucianism, the family in China and Taiwan becomes the site where individuals and the state entangle, as the juxtaposition of *jia* (family) and *guo* (the state), as the name of Lee's series indicates. Growing up in a multi-generation Christian family and being a pious Christian, Lee is also deeply influenced by Chinese Confucian values, particularly filial piety (Zhang 2012; IFENG Entertainment News 2013). Although God as the Christian authority conflicts with the Confucian emphasis on ancestors and father, Confucian values *ren*, *li*, and *xiao*, and some care practices, such as respecting and nurturing parents and the elderly, conflate with Christian teachings and discipleship in Taiwan (Hong 2017; Wu 2022). As Catherine Russell argues, "autobiography becomes ethnographic at the point where the film or video maker understands his or her personal history to be implicated in a larger social formation and historical process"

(Yu 2014, 26). The filmmaking process in the family context becomes the field site for Yang and Lee to conduct their ethnographic observation and the node for them to connect their personal life stories in a larger historical and social context. The radio broadcasting news in old men's homes and the demolition sweeping their leisure space on the sidewalk in *Lao Tou* are epitomes of urbanization that have undergone in Beijing. In *Money and Honey*, community events and legal workshops organized by KASAPI (Kapulungan ng Samahang Pilipino) as well as the multiple languages spoken in the nursing home are indicators of a phenomenon that migrant workers becoming a part of family care practices and labor source in Taiwan. The family becomes an epitome of broad social and cultural contexts, where individuals look for their relational selves within and beyond the family. Yang and Lee bring a feminist perspective to interrogate social issues from their relational and gender roles in the family, which is always neglected in the patriarchal and Chinese Confucian world.

"Matter of Care" in Documentary Practice

In the early 1990s, *xianchang*, which is considered an alternative to socialist realism, became a term for filmmaking practices and aesthetics in the Chinese context. *Xianchang* not only emphasizes spontaneity and contingency in the representation of reality but also raises ethical questions about the relationship between the directors and subjects and the directors' social responsibility in the process of film production (Robison 2010). Yiman Wang (2005) uses "searing" to describe the intimate but distanced, objective while emotional relationships between filmmakers and film subjects. The "searing" relationship emphasizes "cruelty" and "violence" imprinted in both the production of documentary and the reality where film subjects live. Through examining the body of Yang's works, Zhen Zhang (2018) proposes a different way of understanding Yang's relationship with her film subjects: Yang as a filmmaker is *zhaogu* (looking after) those elders in her film through the act of *zhaoxiang* (photographing). *Zhaogu* and *zhaoxiang* have a common Chinese character *zhao*, whose literal meanings relate to the direction of photographing, attention, and care. Zhang (2018) argues:

> They felt they were being "taken care [or picture] of" in a special way and taken seriously, even well after their deaths, as their images and voices had been preserved by someone they trusted – a young member of the residential community who gave them extra attention and patiently saw them into the dark of the night.
>
> *(43)*

Yang's intentionality of caring for film subjects is centered in her practices of filming. Yang's camera observes elders either from a low angle or at eye level. Although Yang does not appear in the film, we can always hear elders in *Old Men* and *The Loves of Lao'an* call her "Yangzi" amicably. In both films, Yang always accompanies or takes elderly protagonists to their destinations. When Lao'an is sick and stays in hospital, Yang drives Xiaowei or Lao'an's wife to visit him. She knows nurses or roommates living with Lao'an in the hospital too. Yang's care for the elderly is practiced through following, accompanying, and filming them to do their daily activities, such as hanging out with friends, dancing in the park, staying at home, and going to the hospital. The practices of "looking after" and "photographing" are inseparable in Yang's process of making films. The relationships between filmmakers and film subjects can be "searing" while "caring," "cruel" but "intimate."

Puig de la Bellacasa's "matter of care" (MoC) approach originates in the field of Science and Technology Studies (STS) but brings the feminist thinking of care into complicated relationships between humans and nonhumans. The MoC approach provides us with another way of understanding *xianchang* and how documentaries can become practices of care. Drawing from Latour's (2004) foreground of politics and concerns in actor network theory, the MoC approach underscores care with an intention in the reality complex and motivates people to attend to marginalized voices, make inquiries about "who will do the work of care, as well as how to do it and for whom," and reflect on "what are we encouraging caring for" (Puig de la Bellacasa 2011, 91–92). At the same time, the MoC approach highlights how affect can shape interactions between things and humans without being assimilated into rigid categories. Pre-established categories are not applicable in the MoC approach, because learning to care is a process of constantly interacting, contesting, and adapting (Puig de la Bellacasa 2011). Without the shackles of categories and identities, the MoC approach allows people to explore the possibilities of who they are, embrace the partiality of identity, and create an affinity for a particular political goal across gender, race, class, nationality, and other bounded labels. In *What's the Use?* (2019), Sara Ahmed follows bell hooks' critique on how theory can be used to reinforce domination and argues that if the past use of theories is not exhaustive, we need to enable these tools to be used for other useful purposes. Inspired by Ahmed, I apply the MoC approach to analyze the Chinese-language documentary as a "queer use," which offers us an entry point to challenge the binary understanding of filmmakers and film subjects and foreground the intentionality of care in complicated interactions among humans and nonhumans in the practices of filmmaking.

The intentionality of care is centered on the practice of making documentaries. Care embedded through the act of "photographing" appears in the documentaries of Yang and Lee. Their cameras always accompany and interact with film subjects like their close friends. Similar to Yang's low or eye-level angles, Lee and her camera become the medium that connects migrant workers in Taiwan with their families in the Philippines. When filming *Money and Honey*, Lee joined the family union of Lolita, delivered video messages between migrant workers and their families across the country, and traveled with Baby to find her coworker Arlene in the Philippines (Figure 36.1). Filmmakers care for subjects by means of filming. In an interview by *Tai Feng*,[5] Lee (IFENG Entertainment News 2013) said, "Although I have been working in the documentary field for many years, I am deeply aware of the fact that the trust between film subjects and film director cannot be achieved by any technologies or theories. It needs to be exchanged by time and sincerity."

At the same time, care flows from film subjects to filmmakers by revealing their personal stories, emotions, and cooperating with directors to make the film together. Near the end of *Money and Honey*, Lolita says, "Before Jasmine,[6] I'm not a woman that's very interested in what happened to the world. Only when I go to Taiwan, I said, 'Why? I'm Filipina. Why I go here to earn money?'" These optimistic and brave migrant workers contribute not only to the physical care for elders in nursing homes in Taiwan but also through their affective labor for elders, directors, and audiences who watch this film. In *The Loves of Lao'an*, Yang drives Xiaowei to the hospital and helps her with the errands of caring for sick Lao'an. Yang also conceals the sad news of Xiaowei passing away with the help of Lao'an's roommates and nurses in the hospital for the goodness of Lao'an. Filmmakers, film subjects, and the camera form a network of humans and nonhumans that connect by

Figure 36.1   A photo of Baby, Arlene, and Jasmine (from left to right).

social relationships in filmmaking practices. The center in the network of filming will be where the care flows.

Things or nonhumans matter in the practice of making documentaries. One of the powerful objects we can consider in the production of documentaries is the camera, which plays a vital role in transforming relationships between filmmakers and film subjects. In addition to the camera, things in filming sites can become another protagonist in the documentary. In *The Loves of Lao'an*, the dead golden fish becomes a protagonist to tell the story of unpredictable death and loss in life. It resonates with the unanticipated death of Xiaowei, and implies thoughts about death and dying that haunt these elders in the film but are not openly discussed. When Yang takes a video of Lao'an and his wife, his wife's sudden act of caressing the plastic dog attracts our attention and challenges us to think about what companionship means in people's intimate relationships, which may form between humans and things as well (see Figure 36.2). Expanding from things shot on the spot, Lee in *Money and Honey* experiments with fictional elements, such as hand-painted animation, poems, and songs to express these migrant workers' feelings, sentiments, and emotions. The blend of humans and nonhumans or of fictional and non-fictional elements is driven by the flux or diffusive flow of care in the practices of making documentaries rather than the voice of directors.

Focusing on the "matter of care" in the documentary decenters the dominant voice of filmmakers and foregrounds various participants in the documentary, including humans and nonhumans. At the same time, the MoC approach provides us with a different angle to understand *xianchang*. In previous debates on *xianchang* in the Chinese-language documentary, the understanding of *xianchang* is developed from "on the scene" into ongoing

Figure 36.2 Lao'an asks Yang to take a photo of him and his wife, while Yang uses her DV to capture the moment that his wife is caressing the plastic dog.

interactions between filmmakers and subjects (Zhang 2007; Robison 2010). Following care from production to circulation of the Chinese-language documentary, I further expand *xianchang* from "on the spot" to every encounter between filmmakers and film subjects beyond the production, between films and audiences, and between films and various forums. The scope of *xianchang* becomes a complicated and overlapping network connected by the flow of care from multiple parties in the documentary practices. Every time a documentary is screened, a different *xianchang* is formed between the film, the audience, and the forum. Although Yang's *Old Men* has not circulated in public recently, this film was on Bilibili, a video-sharing website in China, for a period and is now distributed on a streaming platform CathayPlay, which aims to promote Chinese independent films to a global audience (Cathayplay n.d.). A short version of Lee's *Money and Honey* can be found on Bilibili as well. Through these informal ways of circulation, many audiences can watch this film outside the forum of film festivals, classrooms, and particular screening events. Connections between the documentary and audiences are continually built and reformed through re-circulation and re-mediation in different forums. *Money and Honey* was also promoted and screened in Christian communities on a transnational scale. Through her network in the Christian community, Lee associates the distribution of *Money and Honey* and her other films with "mission trip," which calls on people to become "angels" to donate or promote this film to more communities under God's love (Money and Honey Films Org 2018). The screening information of *Money and Honey* was promoted on websites of Christian communities, such as *Jidujiao Jinri Bao* (Christian Daily) and *Fuyin Zhan* (J Gospel Net) (JGospel 2012; Zhang 2012). Multiple *xianchangs* happen and become laminated in every screening of these films.

Rethinking "Love"

Along with care, love is another important theme in *The Loves of Lao'an* and *Money and Honey*. In the former, Lao'an falls in love with Xiaowei, while their spouses are aware of their relationship. The love between Lao'an and Xiaowei in their old age seems to be romantic but deviant according to social norms. The film could have ended with Lao'an's lonely and sorrowful life after the death of Xiaowei, but Yang decides to end it with Lao'an spending time with his new "girlfriend," Zhang Li, in the park six months after the death of Xiaowei. Sitting on the bench in the park, Lao'an intimately interacts with Zhang Li and puts 50 yuan in her handbag. Lao'an's explanation of hiring someone to look after him when he gets sick, his wife's accusation of Xiaowei taking away the money of Lao'an, and the money exchange between Lao'an and his lovers cast gloom over the romantic love between Lao'an and Xiaowei. The ending of Lao'an is Yang's question about romantic love constructed by masculine fantasy and desire and the commodification of care in post-reform China. Romantic love in the patriarchal world is also interrogated in *Money and Honey*. Driven by love for the family, these women migrant workers came to Taiwan to make money for their families. Nevertheless, either the romantic love between husband and wife or the parental love between mother and children may collapse into quarrels, strangeness, and even abuse in intimate relationships over the distance. When beautiful fireworks shoot off the landmark building Taipei 101 on New Year's Eve, Lolita's younger sister said, "I'd rather eat dried fish, as long as I can be with my family." Love is beautiful fireworks that captivate people but can never be reached in both films.

Yang and Lee direct their cameras to care and love in the family and reflect on different faces of love. Love is a sensible bonding between humans as well as a mesmerizing fantasy rooted in masculinity, patriarchy, and Confucianism under the examination of Yang's and Lee's cameras. In *All About Love* (2001), bell hooks criticizes the understanding of love rooted in the popular culture built on male fantasy and the strong association between love and sexual attraction. From "dysfunctional" love in the family, bell hooks encourages us to imagine a different love and think of love as an action that assumes care, accountability, and responsibility. Yang and Lee engage and raise sensory resonances with the audiences through love stories, while motivating audiences to reflect on, question, and rethink love.

In the marketing campaign of *Money and Honey*, Lee turns love into the driving force of social advocacy. But what kind of love does Lee refer to? Is it the love of the Christian God, the love in the Confucian family, or the love emerging from sisterhood? It is ambiguous. When examining the feminist view of "personal is political," Kuo Li-Hsin (2012) argues that sentimentalism raises sympathy without motivating audiences to engage in social issues and political affairs. As Zhang (2023) argues, his concerns about apolitical sentimentalism in mainstream Taiwanese documentaries are shaped by the geopolitics of post-martial law Taiwan, which is engulfed by the U.S. military-capitalist presence in Asia and the rising power of mainland China (Heberer 2019). Simultaneously, Kuo's critique is based on the patriarchal understanding of love that reinforces gender bias and represses women through the narrative of romance, egalitarian marriage, and motherhood (Rapp 1978). However, in *Living a Feminist Life* (2017), Sara Ahmed writes, "I want to explore how feminism is sensible because of the world we are in; feminism is a sensible reaction to the injustices of the world, which we might register at first through our own experiences" (21). We need to be wary of fantasy traps created by patriarchy, capitalism, and Confucianism, but we should also be aware of the power of our sensations, feelings, and affect when facing social injustices and gender inequality. Registering through personal experiences is the initial motivation for Yang's and Lee's filmmaking practices. Directly or indirectly, Yang and Lee use their cameras to express their care for social injustices in a feminist way.

In contrast with Kuo's concerns about depoliticized sentimentalism and humanitarianism, Feng-mei Heberer (2019) proposes the concept of "sentimental activism" that highlights the use of a sentimental narrative of love and pain to raise sympathy and realize social justice mobilization. By closely examining the documentary *T Po Gongchang* (*Lesbian Factory*, 2010), Heberer (2019) elaborates on how the radical discourse of liberal rights and its sentimental legibility makes sentimental activism work in Taiwan and how the director Susan Chen creatively draws from transnational feminist and queer practices to make radical progress in laws, policies, and public awareness about Filipino migrant workers' rights in Taiwan. Puig de la Bellacasa (2011) also argues, "From this affective perspective, transforming things into matters of care is a way of relating to them, of inevitably becoming affected by them, and of modifying their potential to affect others" (99). Love, sentiments, emotions, and affect are sensible ways of making connections with others in care practices of the documentary. In the MoC approach, feminist love can channel through the threads in the network without leaving its reflection on social issues and political agendas behind. Simultaneously, it also acknowledges the fluid and shifting possibilities of caring and being cared for in various local contexts. Care is not a panacea to social injustices, the same with love. When rethinking love and care in the documentary, we should constantly question, reflect, and resist the dominant power, ranging from patriarchy, the state, capitalism, to modernity. Looking to MoC is a feminist way of building local, sensible, and alliance relationships with the cared and creating an alliance to fight for what we care about together.

Conclusion

When I first encountered the works of Yang and Lee, I was interested in the everyday practices of caring for the elderly. I treated their works as ethnographic archives that allowed me to glimpse into the everyday life of the elderly and the persons who look after them in the Chinese Confucian family. Following characters and tracing the life paths of both directors, I find that care flows through every active or passive and every human or nonhuman participant in the documentary practice, which is beyond the theme and the story of the documentary. In *Culture/Media: A (Mild) Polemic*, Ginsburg (1994) writes, "It is crucial that we understand media not only intertextually but also in the context of broader social relations that are constituted and reimagined in film and video works explicitly engaged in presenting culture" (4). She suggests that people look at media in relation to other cultural forms, such as production, distribution, and reception in different local contexts. As practices of social production, care practices in the documentary provide us with a map to follow and examine social relationships constructed and reconstructed in film. Introducing the MoC approach to the media world aims to reuse the understanding of media as social practices and interactions between humans and nonhumans, and provide an alternative way of examining the power of emotion, sentiment, and affect in the Chinese-language documentary practice.

Notes

1 By following Chiu and Zhang's (2015) choice and argument, I use "Chinese-language" to refer to the common ground of Chinese-language cultural productions while recognizing the heterogeneity and locality of Chinese-speaking societies other than mainland China.
2 *Huanghun lian* (twilight love story) refers to the romance of the elderly.
3 According to Taiwan Docs (2023), Jasmine Ching-hui Lee's *Jiaguo Nüxing Xilie* (Women and Homeland Series) includes *Jia Zai He Fang* (Where Is My Home? 1999), *Ama De Liange* (The Blades of Grandmothers, 2003), *Sinian Zhi Cheng* (City of Memories, 2007), *Qinqin Wo De Ai* (My Dear Love, 2008), *Anye Feixing* (Flying in the Darkness, 2010), and *Mianbao Qingren* (Money and Honey, 2012).
4 Grandma and Grandpa followed by the last name can be used as the honorific, by which young people use to address the elderly respectfully.
5 *Tai Feng* is a channel under the *Feng Huang Yu Le* (IFENG Entertainment) that focuses on news about films in Taiwan. Jasmine Ching-hui Lee was invited to talk about *Money and Honey*.
6 Featured care workers in *Money and Honey* called the director as Jasmine.

References

Ahmed, Sara. 2017. *Living a Feminist Life*. Durham, NC: Duke University Press.
———. 2019. *What's the Use? On the Uses of Use*. Durham, NC: Duke University Press.
Berry, Chris. 2007. "Getting Real: Chinese Documentary, Chinese Postsocialism." In *The Urban Generation: Chinese Cinema and Society at the Turn of the Twenty-First Century*, edited by Sheldon H. Lu, Chris Berry, Jason McGrath, and Zhen Zhang, 115–36. Durham, NC: Duke University Press.
Buch, Elena D. 2015. "Anthropology of Aging and Care." *The Annual Review of Anthropology* 44: 277–93. https://doi.org/10.1146/annurev-anthro-102214-014254.
Cathayplay. n.d. "About Us." *Cathyplay.com*. Accessed January 5, 2023. https://www.cathayplay.com/en/about-us.
Chi, Robert. 2003. "The New Taiwanese Documentary." Modern Chinese Literature and Culture. 15, no. 1: 146–96. http://www.jstor.org/stable/41490897.
Chiu, Kuei-Fen, and Yingjin Zhang. 2015. *New Chinese-Language Documentaries: Ethics Subject and Place*. London: Routledge.
Puig de la Bellacasa, Maria. 2011. "Matters of Care in Technoscience: Assembling Neglected Bethings." *Social Studies of Science* 41 (1): 85–106. https://doi.org/10.1177/0306312710380301.
Dowling, Emma. 2021. *The Care Crisis: What Caused It and How Can We End It?* New York: Verso.
Ginsburg, Faye. 1994. "Culture/Media: A (Mild) Polemic." *Anthropology Today* 10 (2): 5–15. https://doi.org/10.2307/2783305.
Heberer, Feng-Mei. 2019. "Sentimental Activism as Queer-Feminist Documentary Practice; or, How to Make Love in a Room Full of People." *Camera Obscura: A Journal of Feminism, Culture, and Media Studies* 101 (2): 41–69. https://doi.org/10.1215/02705346-7584904.
Hong, Jingyi. 2017. "盡孝是從祭祖開始嗎？認清至大的孝道" [Does Filiality Start from Honoring Ancestors? Recognizing the Ultimate Filiality]. 基督教日報/*Christian Daily*, July 27, 2–217. https://cdn-news.org/News.aspx?EntityID=News&PK=0000000000652e5959c1dc7f67e33f42800677ccd9909f70.
hooks, bell. 2001. *All About Love: New Visions*. New York: Perennial.
IFENG Entertainment News. 2013. "专访《面包情人》导演李靖慧：东南亚移工的现代史诗" [Interview with the Director of Money and Honey Jasmine Ching-Hui Lee: The Modern Poem of East Asian Migrant Workers]. 台风：凤凰娱乐/*Taifeng: IFENG Entertainment News*. https://ent.ifeng.com/movie/taifeng/lijinghui/#pageTop.
JGospel. 2012. "《麵包情人》money與honey的兩難抉擇" [Money and Honey, the Dilemma Between Money and Honey]. 福音站/*J Gospelnet*, July 24. https://www.jgospel.net/ContentDetail.aspx?contentID=78223&contentTypeID=346&urlRewrite=true&languageID=2.
Kleinman, Arthur. 2009. "Caregiving: The Odyssey of Becoming More Human." *Lancet* 373 (9660): 292–93.

Kuo, Li-Hsin. 2012. "Sentimentalism and the Phenomenon of Collective 'Looking Inward': A Critical Analysis of Mainstream Taiwanese Documentary." In *Documenting Taiwan on Film: Issues and Methods in New Documentaries*, edited by Sylvia Li-Chun Lin and Tze-Lan Deborah Sang, 183–203. New York: Routledge.

Lan, Pei-Chia. 2001. *Subcontracting Filial Piety*. Working Paper No. 21. Berkeley: Center for Working Families, University of California.

———. 2004. "女人何苦为難女人？僱用家務移工的三角關係" [Jealous Madams, Anxious Mothers: Triangular Relationships in the Employment of Migrant Domestic Workers]. 台灣社會學 [*Taiwanese Sociology*] 8: 43–97.

Latour, Bruno. 2004. "Why Has Critique Run Out of Steam? From Matters of Fact to Matters of Concern." *Critical Inquiry* 30 (2): 225–48. https://doi.org/10.1086/421123.

Lee, Ching-Hui. 2011. "Director's Profile: Jasmine Lee Ching-Hui." *Money and Honey Official Blog*. https://moneyandhoney.pixnet.net/blog/post/2862856-director's-profile:jasmine-lee-ching-hui.

Mol, Annemarie. 2008. *The Logic of Care: Health and the Problem of Patient Choice*. London: Routledge.

Money and Honey Films Org. 2018. "Money and Honey Mission Trip." Online. https://www.youtube.com/watch?v=YXT8U6D7BZI&list=PLYwCE5OCevVrbK3bVY1PXbnFhmgK-wP9P.

Pickowicz, Paul G. 2006. "Social and Political Dynamics of Underground Filmmaking in China." In *From Underground to Independent: Alternative Film Culture in Contemporary China*, edited by Paul Pickwicz and Yingjing Zhang, 1–22. Lanham: Rowman & Littlefield Publishers, Inc.

Rapp, Rayna. 1978. Family and Class in Contemporary America: Notes Toward an Understanding of Ideology. *Science & Society* 42:278–300.

Robison, Luke. 2010. "From 'Public' to 'Private': Chinese Documentary and the Logic of Xianchang." In *The New Chinese Documentary Film Movement: For the Public Record*, edited by Chris Berry, Lu Xinyu, and Lisa Rofel, 177–94. Hong Kong: Hong Kong University Press.

Rosemont, Henry, and Roger T. Ames. 2009. *The Chinese Classic of Family Reverence: A Philosophical Translation of the Xiaojing*. Honolulu: University of Hawai'i Press.

Taiwan Docs. 2023. "Jasmine Ching-Hui LEE." https://docs.tfai.org.tw/en/filmmakers/5882.

Tronto, Joan C. 1993. *Moral Boundaries: A Political Argument for an Ethic of Care*. New York: Routledge.

Wang, Yiman. 2005. "The Amateur's Lightning Rod: DV Documentary in Postsocialist China." *Film Quarterly* 58 (4): 16–38.

Wu, Kijin James. 2022. "Chapter 23, a Contextual Comparison of Conceptual Categories: A Christian-Confucian Test Case in Taiwan from a Ritual Perspective." In *A Companion to Comparative Theology*, edited by Pim Valkenberg, 446–66. Leiden: Brill. https://doi.org/10.1163/9789004388390_025.

Xu, Jilin. 2015. "'大脱嵌'之后: 家国天下与自我认同" [After the 'Great Disembedding': Family-State, Tianxia and Self]. China: *Fudan Xuebao*/复旦学报.

Yan, Yunxiang. 2016. "Intergenerational Intimacy and Descending Familism in Rural North China." *American Anthropologist* 118 (2): 244–57. https://doi.org/10.1111/aman.12527.

Yu, Tianqi. 2014. "Toward a Communicative Practice: Female First-Person Documentary in Twenty-First Century China." In *China's iGeneration: Cinema and Moving Image Culture for the Twenty-First Century*, edited by Matthew D. Johnson, Keith B. Wagner, Tianqi Yu, and Luke Vulpiani, 23–44. London: Bloomsbury.

Zhang, Jiahui. 2012. "《麵包情人》歷13年拍攝 記錄移工兩難抉擇" [Thirteen Years of Filming the Recording of Dilemmas of Migrant Workers]. July 17. https://cn.cdn-news.org/News.aspx?EntityID=News&PK=0000000000652e59eb3d91179950d942882f8d6364ec5048.

Zhang, Zhen. 2007. "Introduction: Bearing Witness, Chinese Urban Cinema in the Era of 'Transformation' (*Zhuanxing*)." In *The Urban Generation: Chinese Cinema and Society at the Turn of the Twenty-First Century*, edited by Sheldon H. Lu, Chris Berry, Jason McGrath, and Zhen Zhang, 1–48. Durham: Duke University Press.

———. 2018. "From Sidewalk Realism to Spectral Romance: Yang Lina's Beijing and Beyond." In *Visual Arts, Representations and Interventions in Contemporary China: Urbanized Interface*, edited by Minna Valjakka and Meiqin Wang, 35–59. Amsterdam: Amsterdam University Press.

———. 2023. *Women Filmmakers in Sinophone World Cinema*. Amsterdam: Amsterdam University Press.

37
DOMESTIC TEMPORALITIES AND FILM PRACTICE

Los Otros, Quezon City, and Forum
Lenteng, Jakarta

Jasmine Nadua Trice

It is possible to trace a map of recent Southeast Asian filmmaking that would lead in and out of film practitioners' homes. Rather than the movie theater, the studio, or the street – common locations found in scholarship situated at the intersection of film and spatial history – this map would reveal the home as a site of both formal and informal labor among film practitioners. It would also chart the home's emergence as a framework for experimenting with space, memory, and historical narration.

Like the moviehouse, the home is a technology for organizing space and time and "a technique for expressing lifeworlds" (Lee 2016, 151). While there has been a great deal of scholarship on the home in the humanities and social sciences, its definition is unwieldy. In its classical iteration, it demarcates boundaries between public and private, providing sanctuary from that deemed unfamiliar, strange, or threatening.[1] In this model, its material, architectural form demarcates socio-economic status and evokes an ideology – if not an economic reality – of property and ownership (Rhodes 2017). As feminist historians have demonstrated, the home is not separate from capitalism, colonialism, and industrial labor, but it is a crucial part of their infrastructure (Blunt and Dowling 2006; Blunt 2008; Legg 2018). At the same time, in much of the world it has long been a space of informal enterprise and outsourced domestic labor (Tipple 2005; Mezzadri 2020; Yeoh et al. 2020). In more utopian imaginings, the home activates a different kind of lifeworld, defined through the porousness of its boundaries. This has been particularly the case for grassroots arts and activist movements, where the home trades regimes of privacy for more public forms of collective habitation.

Through examining the work of two experimental film groups – Forum Lenteng, in Jakarta, Indonesia, and Los Otros in Quezon City, Philippines – this chapter will consider the role of the home in Southeast Asian film practice. I seek to trace the home's various meanings as a space of creative labor and care work, as well as a space of cinematic representation on screen. I would suggest that this turn to the home as a site of possibility for shooting locations, screenings, and organizing can be read as a response to the transformation of urban space within sprawling mega cities like Manila and Jakarta, where radical

DOI: 10.4324/9781003266952-48

forms of hospitality take shape amid ecological crisis, infrastructural unevenness, and the encroaching authoritarianism that the COVID-19 pandemic heightened (Docot 2021; Walton 2021; Crace 2021). While alternative and experimental film production has taken place within practitioners' homes in many settings (Raven 2010), the material conditions of the spaces that urbanists have referred to as "cities of the global south" (Dawson and Edwards 2004; Simone 2020) offer a different vantage point. Here, the home becomes a medium for intervention into the developmental temporalities that constitute Manila and Jakarta's contradictory, uneven 21st-century urbanisms. Such cities are constituted by a range of urban temporalities. State discourses emphasize futurity (Roy 2016) and "fast urbanism" (Shin et al. 2020) while also promoting historical amnesia (Lim 2023) and selective forms of architectural remembrance (Kusno 2010). Meanwhile, ecological collapse has created a sense of urban futures as both uncertain and ominously finite. In January 2022, Indonesia's Parliament passed a bill to leave the sinking capital city, relocating the capital to a new site (Lim 2023). The same plans have been discussed in relation to Manila, with speculative renderings of "New Clark City" envisioning a new capital on the site of the former US military base, sanitized and free from the traffic, congestion, and pollution of the city (Garfield 2018). How do home, dwelling, and domesticity become meaningful amid these urban temporalities, in spaces where colonial, authoritarian, neoliberal, and ecological times interweave and collide? What can we gain from understanding how home-based film texts and practices of production and exhibition rework domestic temporalities?

Living and working in rapidly and unevenly transforming urban spaces, Forum Lenteng and Los Otros have turned to the home as a site of temporal reinvention. The home has been a space to make films and to evolve new modes of working, from Los Otros members' negotiation of filmmaking and childcare, to Form Lenteng's pedagogical experiments with duration. In both cases, the home becomes a space to cultivate temporalities that exist in friction with the tempos of the cityscape. These modes of film practice find textual counterparts in films like *Dolo* (Hafiz Rancajale 2021), *Nervous Translation* (Shireen Seno 2017), and *Years When I Was a Child* (John Torres 2008). In these films, homes filled with collected objects become sites for gathering, rest, care, education, and anticipation, on-screen counterparts for the spaces their makers inhabit.

In drawing attention to the spatiotemporal organization of the home, this chapter ventures a methodological rescaling of scholarly engagements with the spaces of film practice, moving from locations like the city and the studio to domestic interiors. In emphasizing the home's spatiotemporal dimensions, it joins other projects that expand and contract the geographic boundaries of analysis to conceive of film production spaces as comprising myriad economic, technological, environmental, institutional, and social relations; such work traces the dynamic entanglement of environments (built and "natural") and film practice (Jaikumar 2019; Jacobson 2020; Mukherjee 2020). My own approach to this imbrication of media and environment uses the home to consider the temporal dimensions of film practice (i.e., the social, embodied experience of time), tracing how such spatialized, small-scale temporalities correspond to other temporal registers, such as historical narrative and urban transformation. Independent film movements in Southeast Asia emerged in the early 2000s alongside the rise of low-cost digital video for production and dissemination, socio-political transformation in sites like the Philippines and Indonesia (e.g., the overthrow of Estrada and Suharto), as well as the rapid urbanization that accompanied a decade of liberalization, culminating in the 1998 financial crisis spurred by the speculative housing market (Campos 2016; Ainslie et al. 2020). As housing markets collapsed under regimes of property, varied definitions of home circulated on screen and in film practice. In this chapter, shifting critical focus to the home is a gesture toward this originary moment, a common touchstone in 21st-century Southeast Asian film historiography.

I use "home" as a broad term for describing spatial and temporal arrangements that include the architectural materiality of a house or other living space, as well as connotations of refuge – though not retreat – from public life. This idea of home overlaps with but is not synonymous with "domesticity," which evokes more politicized implications around gender, race, class, sexuality, and labor (Chee 2012; Burton 2019). This chapter is situated in that overlapping space, using the terms interchangeably. In the cases I discuss here, "home" is the term filmmakers and on-screen speakers employ (sometimes through translation); domesticity is useful for considering urban temporalities' impact on home-based film practice because the concept is often conceived as temporal, tied to the routines of daily living, to seasonal life cycles, and to the temporalities of domestic labor. The domestic has been a site of contestation, at once a globally hegemonic set of ideas and practices enforced through colonial and capitalist expansion, as well as a site of resistance to those vectors of power (George 2020). The home is always information, and for process-based film work taking place within contexts of fast urbanism and relentlessly paced futurities, it offers different kinds of temporal orientation, discernible in moving-image practices and texts.

Forum Lenteng: Thresholds and Anticipatory Time

Forum Lenteng locates its origins in the May 1998 student protests and violent riots that ended the US-backed New Order regime, which had been in power since 1966. In the *reformasi* (reformation) period that followed, the country saw a wave of audiovisual media production, both independent and industrial, after decades of censorship and propaganda. Noticing a gap in arts and media criticism, members founded Forum Lenteng in July 2003 as a group devoted to studying the history of audiovisual film and media. The organization was established in Lenteng Agung, South Jakarta, at the same time as several media arts collectives that thrived in the years of the post–New Order era.[2] Established in the wake of revolution, over the past two decades Forum Lenteng has become one of the most enduring, active arts organizations in Southeast Asia. Their focus is what members describe as "cultural activism," and in addition to producing work, this involves creating spaces for discussion: producing and posting films, publishing research, hosting screenings, art exhibitions, workshops, and trainings, and collaborating with other collectives around the archipelago.

In August 2019, my research partner and I visited Jakarta to participate in the annual Arkipel: Jakarta International Documentary and Experimental Film Festival.[3] During the event, Forum Lenteng cofounders Otty Widasari and Hafiz Rancajale invited us to the space Forum Lenteng rented at the time, a modest two-story house on a narrow residential street in Pasar Minggu, an area of South Jakarta. The small architectural flourishes on the structure's roofline evoked the *rumah adat* style of traditional Indonesian houses. The airy downstairs workspace was simple, with a whiteboard, chairs, and tables that could be easily moved to accommodate screenings, workshops, and performances. Forum Lenteng's publications and artworks were displayed around the space. Upstairs, rooms served as storage for archival materials and artworks, video-editing space, and sleeping quarters for the five to six members who might live in the house at a given time. There was also space for artists passing through town, who would occasionally stay on a short-term basis. In an interview, one younger member had noted her surprise upon finding that the group used a residential house as its base when she had joined two years earlier, commenting that other film festivals she had worked with used more formal offices. The Forum Lenteng space was more informal, in keeping, perhaps, with the grassroots ethos that it managed to maintain, even as it became more established. Otty and Hafiz lived across the street from Forum Lenteng, and there was a fluid sense of space between the two houses.[4] Other active members rented apartments nearby. As members described, there was always someone in the Forum Lenteng space, awake and working, at all hours.

Because the house was situated within a residential area, the group was careful to avoid arousing suspicion from neighbors; watchful eyes could view their work as politically subversive or disapprove of young men and women living together. To mitigate potential distrust, the group loaned their projector for a neighborhood event and painted a mural near a local sports field. While the house was unusual for the area in its use as an arts organization headquarters, it was also embedded in the cycles of the street's daily life and annual rituals. At times, events like Arkipel director Yuki Aditya's film history course would have to be put on hold due to the call to prayer from the nearby mosque, a reminder of more traditional sectors' proximity. Forum Lenteng researcher Anggraeni Widhiasih noted that the house was a vantage point for observing what she described as the city's spatial "fluidity." The street would fill with passing cows during the Hajj, and the neighborhood hosted "spontaneous" markets. The group would capture this spatial fluidity in the videos it produced for its 2019 *Capital* project.[5]

Activist histories of the home also appear in moving-image work. *Dolo*, a 2021 documentary about activist and artist Dolores Sinaga, considers the relationship between art and politics. In the film, shots move from intimate proximity to the scale of history. The film opens with a quote from Sinaga's spouse, musician Ardjuna Hutagalung: "Boleh kau punya rumah kecil tapi seluruh dunia harus bisa masuk ke dalamnya" ("You can have a small house, but the whole world must be able to enter it"). It then cuts to two slow tracking shots totaling eight minutes, depicting a domestic interior. As the sound of off-screen, diegetic piano plays, the camera moves down a corridor toward closed doors, and the film cuts to Ardjuna in the process of composing. As he taps out atonal notes, the film cuts to documentary footage of the street, the on-screen text locating the image in 1998 Jakarta, during riots that ended with a death toll of over 1,100 people. The sound of the piano carries over, intertwining domestic and public spheres, refiguring hierarchical scalar relations between home and nation. In interviews later in the film, activists remember leaving their dorms to visit Sinaga's house, in order to gather and talk with like-minded people. As one interviewee recounts, the veranda, in particular, was an important space – the threshold between indoors and outside. Several interviewees echoed this comparison with home, describing Garuda as a site for political debates and disagreements that could be worked out in the spirit of kinship; for some who were in hiding at the time, it became a literal safehouse from authorities. *Dolo* visualizes the home as a spatial threshold between reflection and action, an architectural and conceptual form that Forum Lenteng continues.

Los Otros: Scale and the Temporalities of Care

Based in Quezon City, Metro Manila, Philippines, Los Otros uses the space of the home in ways that both parallel and depart from Forum Lenteng's work. I seek to trace the ways that Los Otros engages with the politics and poetics of scale through the urban home, in their films and in their studio space, which becomes a site of both creative and caregiving labor. Scale is a complex category of analysis. For Marxist geographers, scale describes the relations from the home, to body, neighborhood, city, nation, and beyond (Brenner 2019). In film studies, scale has been largely a question of film form; as Mary Ann Doane has recently written, film theorists have long argued that cinematic scale is inherently disorienting due to formal techniques that show objects at unsettlingly close range, leaving the spectator unable to locate their relation to the image (2021).

Los Otros refigures scale through foregrounding domestic temporalities in their films and through public narratives of their practice. These questions around domestic time and care work have been an area of concern in film production studies since the COVID-19 pandemic (Mayer and Columpar 2022). Unlike Forum Lenteng, the house where Los Otros is based is not a regular living space/workspace for artists beyond Seno and Torres themselves, though it doubles as a studio and lab and has become a site for teaching, making, and gathering. Rather than focusing on the home as a site for cultivating alternative or communal formations, in this section, I am interested in the ways that Los Otros upends conventional scalar models, in part through making visible the kind of feminized care labor typically dismissed as social reproduction (Bhattacharya 2017). Domestic timespace becomes a platform and a medium for this interweaving of care and creative labor. If the time of the city is based on futurism and teleology, domestic care is predicated on a temporality of interruption, a fragmented, non-teleological temporality that foregrounds the potential of gaps and interludes (Baraitser 2009). These patched-together fragments of time, taking place in domestic spaces, offer alternatives to the grander scale of larger historical narratives.

Ideas of scalar relations as produced through dispossession and disorientation resonate with several of Los Otros's projects.[6] The group's exhibition for the Trans-Southeast Asia Triennial (March 2021) paid homage its living space/workspace. Titled *My Home Is the Other*, the installation included artifacts from workshops, as well as screenings of works such as Seno's *A child dies, a child plays, a woman is born, a woman dies, a bird arrives, a bird flies off*. Images of their daughter are projected over a human-size bird's nest, where visitors could sit and peruse a photo album of artists' talks. The giant nest reduces humans to avian size and evokes a resting place amid winged migrations. The exhibit positions home as a hub among ongoing routes, a space both disorienting and familiar. In Seno's *Nervous Translation* and Torres's *Years When I Was a Child Outside*, manipulations of scale portray the home as an unstable measure of economic prosperity and precarity. While the scales of the body and the home sit at the bottom of the ladder in conventional geographic orders, Los Otros's production practices elevate these spatial registers through foregrounding the typically invisibilized work of care labor.

Like Forum Lenteng, the home is also the site of Los Otros's studio and film lab, though they operate at a much smaller scale. The group includes Seno and Torres, alongside a small, rotating roster of fellow artists and filmmakers. It began in 2003 as an informal gathering of musicians and friends led by Torres, then a recent college graduate who was exploring the possibilities of new digital video tools and music. After a few years, Shireen Seno joined the group when she moved to Manila after graduating from college in Toronto, and it became more formalized. It also moved from a condominium to its current space, a house that Torres's father had long rented for his work. The Los Otros house is located in the Teachers Village area of Quezon City. The area has undergone tremendous changes over the past two decades, transitioning from a primarily residential space to a "hip" neighborhood that offers eateries and bars for students attending the nearby universities. Like Jakarta, the 16 cities comprising Metro Manila have undergone significant transformation over the past three decades. Neoliberal restructuring has taken the form of market-oriented urban renewal projects, the privatization of public lands, and the displacement of the urban poor, in efforts to attract global investments (Ortega 2015). For much of the city, such trends take the form of high-rise condominiums and sprawling malls, material manifestations of the city's futurist imaginings, which have displaced informal settlements or kept them out of view. The area around Maginhawa, a Teachers Village street, offers a more complex form of temporal imagining. The area is lined with cafes, restaurants, and more recently, street art. The neighborhood stands out as one of a few "bohemian" centers in the city, evoking an aestheticized past of low-rise buildings, independent businesses, and pedestrian traffic, largely catering to a middle-class clientele of students and young professionals. Some commenters online have described it as "gentrified," a term Seno herself used to describe the ways the neighborhood has changed over the years. Due to the location of the house passed on to them, this is where Los Otros is based – an enclave in the city that has become a sort of spatial experimentation, reflecting a search for authenticity that urbanists in different contexts have pointed to as a localized response to globalization (Zukin 2009). For good or ill, like many gentrifying neighborhoods, it is a space of spatiotemporal invention.

As Seno describes, they host workshops for visiting filmmakers and artists, posting announcements on their social media. They have food and drink, which encourages people to linger. The events draw familiar faces, but friends sometimes bring someone new. She recalled that one attendant, nervous to participate in the workshop because he hadn't worked with film previously, offered to cook a meal and sit in as an observer. Visitors come and share their skills; sometimes these skills are arts-related, but sometimes they are not, and the goal is not always to produce work but to cultivate a community of different kinds of makers. Care work and creative work are intertwined.

Creative practice became a process of tactically managing time when Seno and Torres had two children, and this temporal negotiation, usually confined to the private household, became a part of their public discussion of their arts practice. Through a 2019 residency with Nanyang Technological University's Centre for Contemporary Art in Singapore, Torres began to experiment with what he described as "parasitical filmmaking strategies." Because he had little time outside his childcare responsibilities, he would leave the house for three-hour sessions, visiting other filmmakers' sets to shoot footage, which he would then repurpose into his own short film, *We Still Have to Close Our Eyes*. He describes this process as "a way of structuring the artist's work schedule around his daughter's sleep and feeding schedule so as to strike a balance between making art and raising a family."[7] Seno has used similar tactics. In describing her ongoing multimedia project, *A child dies, a child plays, a woman is born, a woman dies, a bird arrives, a bird flies off*, Seno recounts her efforts to create small segments of time, a need heightened during the COVID-19 pandemic: "The work thus far has been in parallel to the birth of my daughter, so I was limited to footage I was able to shoot in two locations a few hours by car from Manila."[8] The project is itself about more conceptual, affective registers of home, recounting her own father's migration to the US. In their current state, the work of care becomes an active part of their everyday creative lives. Privileging the scale of the domestic and the home, their intertwined creative and care work exchanges hierarchical notions of scale for a different model, one that centers the body and the home.

This is not to suggest that home is solely where norms of family life play out. Instead, it becomes a site to consider questions of domesticity and dwelling. As Lilian Chee and Eunice Seng have argued, questions of dwelling have become vital in Asia, a

networked region . . . collectively bound to particular socio-cultural and political tendencies: filial piety, the suppression of the individual in favour of the importance of family and affinity to tradition, as well as being, conversely, also complicated by a neo-liberal capacity for uninhibited development.

(2017, 993)

Within this context, questions of dwelling have become vital:

If the question of dwelling must ultimately be interrogated through an architectural setting – a home, a house, a homeland, a nest, somewhere to lodge, belong, return to, depart from – then the circumstances of this context become more complex with the onset of globalisation, gentrification, privatisation, immigration, migration, forced and elective dislocation, and self-exile . . . "What does it mean to dwell?" takes on completely different implications.

(993)

Dwelling shifts from being a "thing," as it has existed in architectural theory, and becomes "architecture-in-the-making, continuously produced, co-produced and re-produced through everyday domestic practices and rituals" (Chee and Seng 2017, 996). For Seno and Torres, filmmaking has become one of those domestic practices and rituals, as they stitch together fragments of time for creative labor amid the demands of care work.

The home is a generative spatiotemporal form in Los Otros's films and in their work as arts organizers; their filmic experimentations with the home become a means of manipulating scalar relations, creating a micro-cartography of interiors that rescales Philippine history to the terrain of the embodied and the personal, but does so in a way that renders that history disorienting, its proximity illegible and unclear. This scalar intervention configures the personal not as individualism, but as a way of reanimating domesticity; here, the home becomes a site for an intertwined project of collaborative making and care work, an enterprise that values process over product.

Domestic Temporalities and Film Practice

Forum Lenteng and Los Otros signal the kinds of spatiotemporal experimentations that filmmakers in Southeast Asia have undertaken over the past two decades, in efforts to create models of collaboration and creative making. Situated within sprawling megalopolises reeling from the effects of failed futurism, the home becomes one mechanism for facilitating other forms of temporal intervention: combining care work with film practice, developing pedagogical models, and documenting a transforming cityscape. The home becomes a space of respite from neoliberal urbanism and environmental crisis but also a space to recoup spent energies and fashion them into something new. Activating the home's capacities to reframe historical narratives and rescale hierarchical geographic imaginings, Forum Lenteng and Los Otros have reframed the home as a place of intertwined creative and care work, as well as a generative threshold between public narratives and collective memory. The home has become a platform for different forms of worldmaking.

Notes

1 See, for example, Annette Burton's caution that discussions of domesticity often take for granted the categories established in Western 1970s feminist theory (Burton 2019).
2 There has been some research on Forum Lenteng from a range of disciplines. See Ratna 2007; Jurriëns 2014; Engchuan 2021.
3 This chapter is part of a larger project undertaken with Philippa Lovatt as a part of our work with the Association for Southeast Asian Cinemas. We collaboratively conducted interviews with film practitioners, many of which are available at aseac-interviews.org.
4 I refer to Otty and Hafiz by their given names as is customary in Indonesia.
5 Led by Seoul-based collective Space Cell and sponsored by the 2019 Asian Film and Video Art Forum (AFVAF) in Seoul, Korea, the Capital project was a collaboration across several small film groups, including Forum Lenteng and Los Otros.
6 Dispossession has become a touchstone in critical theory, often in relation to territorial expansion of settler colonial states (see Nichols 2020). I am using the term more broadly here, to point to the economic precarity within a middle-class, postcolonial context.
7 "John Torres," NTU Centre for Contemporary Art, 2019, https://ntu.ccasingapore.org/residency/john-torres/.
8 "A child dies, a child plays, a woman is born, a woman dies, a bird arrives, a bird flies off (Arcade 4walls edition)," Shireen Seno, https://shireenseno.tumblr.com/post/639907598434484224/a-child-dies-arcade-4walls.

References

Ainslie, Mary, Thomas Barker, and Gaik Cheng Khoo, eds. 2020. *Southeast Asia on Screen: From Independence to Financial Crisis (1945–1998)*. Amsterdam: Amsterdam University Press.
Baraitser, Lisa. 2009. *Maternal Encounters: The Ethics of Interruption*. Milton Park: Routledge.
Bhattacharya, Tithi, ed. 2017. *Social Reproduction Theory: Remapping Class, Recentering Oppression*. London: Pluto Press.
Blunt, Alison. 2008. *Domicile and Diaspora: Anglo-Indian Women and the Spatial Politics of Home*. Hoboken: John Wiley & Sons.
Blunt, Alison, and Robyn Dowling, eds. 2006. *Home*. Milton Park: Routledge.
Brenner, Neil. 2019. *New Urban Spaces: Urban Theory and the Scale Question*. Oxford: Oxford University Press.
Burton, Antoinette. 2019. "Toward Unsettling Histories of Domesticity." *The American Historical Review* 124 (4): 1332–36.
Campos, Patrick F. 2016. *The End of National Cinema: Filipino Film at the Turn of the Century*. Quezon City: University of the Philippines Press.
Chee, Lilian. 2012. "The Domestic Residue: Feminist Mobility and Space in Simryn Gill's Art." *Gender, Place & Culture* 19 (6): 750–70.
Chee, Lilian, and Eunice Seng. 2017. "Dwelling in Asia: Translations Between Dwelling, Housing and Domesticity." *The Journal of Architecture* 22 (6): 993–1000.
Crace, John. 2021. "Philippines President Duterte: You Choose, Covid Vaccine or I Will Have You Jailed." *The Guardian*, June 21. https://www.theguardian.com/world/2021/jun/22/philippines-president-duterte-you-choose-covid-vaccine-or-i-will-have-you-jailed.
Dawson, Ashley, and Brent Hayes Edwards. 2004. "Introduction: Global Cities of the South." *Social Text* 22 (4): 1–7.
Doane, Mary Ann. 2021. *Bigger Than Life: The Close-Up and Scale in the Cinema*. Durham and London: Duke University Press.
Docot, Dada. 2021. "Carceral and Colonial Memory During Pandemic Times in the Philippines." *Commoning Ethnography* 4 (1). https://ojs.victoria.ac.nz/ce/article/view/7089
Engchuan, Rosalia Namsai. 2021. "Situated Assemblages of Un-Situated Things." *Afterall: A Journal of Art, Context and Enquiry* 51: 34–47.

Garfield, Leanna. 2018. "The Philippines Is Planning a $14 Billion 'Pollution-Free' City That Will Be Larger Than Manhattan." *Business Insider*, May 26.

George, Rosemary Marangoly, ed. 2020. *Burning Down the House: Recycling Domesticity*. Milton Park: Routledge.

Jacobson, Brian. 2020. "Studio Perspectives." In *In the Studio: Visual Creation and Its Material Environments*. Berkeley: University of California Press.

Jaikumar, Priya. 2019. *Where Histories Reside: India as Filmed Space*. Durham: Duke University Press.

Jurriëns, Edwin. 2014. "Mediating the Metropolis: New Media Art as a Laboratory for Urban Ecology in Indonesia." In *Art in the Asia-Pacific: Intimate Publics*, edited by Larissa Hjorth, Natalie King, and Mami Kataoka. Milton Park: Routledge.

Kusno, Abidin. 2010. *The Appearances of Memory: Mnemonic Practices of Architecture and Urban Form in Indonesia*. Durham: Duke University Press.

Lee, Doreen. 2016. *Activist Archives: Youth Culture and the Political Past in Indonesia*. Durham: Duke University Press.

Legg, Stephen. 2018. "Gendered Politics and Nationalised Homes: Women and the Anti-Colonial Struggle in Delhi, 1930–47." In *Culture and Society*, 229–49. Milton Park: Routledge.

Lim, Bliss Cua. 2023. "A Tale of Three Buildings: The National Film Archive, Marcos Cultural Policy, and Anarchival Temporality." In *Beauty and Brutality: Manila and Its Global Discontents*, edited by Martin F. Manalansan IV, Robert Diaz, and Roland B. Tolentino, 56–77. Philadelphia: Temple University Press.

Lim, How Pim. 2023. "Indonesia's New Capital Nusantara Seeks to Achieve Net Zero Carbon Emissions, Lead in Competitiveness." *Borneo Post Online*, February 10. https://www.theborneopost.com/2023/02/10/indonesias-new-capital-nusantara-seeks-to-achieve-net-zero-carbon-emissions-lead-in-competitiveness/.

Mayer, So, and Corinn Columpar, eds. 2022. *Mothers of Invention: Film, Media, and Caregiving Labor*. Detroit: Wayne State University Press.

Mezzadri, Alessandra. 2020. "The Informal Labours of Social Reproduction." *Global Labour Journal* 11 (2): 156–63.

Mukherjee, Debashree. 2020. *Bombay Hustle: Making Movies in a Colonial City*. New York: Columbia University Press.

Nichols, Robert. 2020. *Theft Is Property! Dispossession and Critical Theory*. Durham: Duke University Press.

Ortega, Arnisson Andre C. 2015. "Manila's Metropolitan Landscape of Gentrification: Global Urban Development, Accumulation by Dispossession & Neoliberal Warfare Against Informality." *Geoforum* 70: 35–50.

Ratna, Lulu. 2007. "Indonesian Short Films After Reformasi 1998." *Inter-Asia Cultural Studies* 8 (2): 304–7.

Raven, Lucy, ed. 2010. *Radical Light: Alternative Film and Video in the San Francisco Bay Area, 1945–2000*. Berkeley: University of California Press.

Rhodes, John David. 2017. *Spectacle of Property: The House in American Film*. Minneapolis, MN: University of Minnesota Press.

Roy, Ananya. 2016. "When Is Asia?" *The Professional Geographer* 68 (2): 313–21.

Shin, Hyun Bang, Yimin Zhao, and Sin Yee Koh. 2020. "Whither Progressive Urban Futures? Critical Reflections on the Politics of Temporality in Asia." *City: Analysis of Urban Change, Theory, Action* 24 (1–2): 244–54.

Simone, AbdouMaliq. 2020. "Cities of the Global South." *Annual Review of Sociology* 46: 603–22.

Tipple, Graham. 2005. "The Place of Home-Based Enterprises in the Informal Sector: Evidence from Cochabamba, New Delhi, Surabaya and Pretoria." *Urban Studies* 42 (4): 611–32.

Walton, Kate. 2021. "Post-Pandemic Authoritarianism Looms in Indonesia." *Foreign Policy*, October 13. https://foreignpolicy.com/2021/10/13/indonesia-pandemic-authoritarianism-jokowi-cyberlaw/

Yeoh, Brenda S. A., Charmian Goh, and Kellynn Wee. 2020. "Social Protection for Migrant Domestic Workers in Singapore: International Conventions, the Law, and Civil Society Action." *American Behavioral Scientist* 64 (6): 841–58.

Zukin, Sharon. 2009. "Changing Landscapes of Power: Opulence and the Urge for Authenticity." *International Journal of Urban and Regional Research* 33 (2): 543–53.

38

UNSTABLE PIXELS, MODULAR SELVES

Digital Subjectivity in Chinese Independent Animation

Jinying Li

Animation has become a major part of the Chinese film industry. But long before the market success of animated blockbusters, independent artists and animators outside the mainstream system had been gaining momentum on the Internet since the early 21st century. In 2001, an animated short video featuring a stick figure named Xiao Xiao generated an international sensation. Created by a young Chinese animator using Adobe Flash, the short video drew millions of viewers almost immediately after its release on video-sharing websites. Xiao Xiao's creator, Zhu Zhiqiang, had neither college education nor formal art training, but his self-taught proficiency in Flash paved the way for his artistic ambition. He created a series of animation videos on the character of Xiao Xiao. The success of the series not only launched a global fad of animated stick figures populating YouTube, but also pointed to a new direction for a young generation of Chinese artists to take advantage of accessible digital tools.

There soon emerged a wave of Flash animators in China, celebrated as *shanke* (Flash-er). One of them was Pi San, an emerging artist who recognized Flash as a powerful tool that gave him "the right to speak" (*hua yu quan*).[1] Pi San launched his own independent animation studio in 2004, which gained international fame by creating the Flash animation sequences in Jia Zhangke's film *Shijie* (World, 2004). The rise of video-sharing platforms expanded online viewership, which made Pi San's animation series, *Kuang Kuang Kuang*, an Internet hit. Combining youthful cuteness with rebellious violence, nostalgic romance with sarcastic humor, the *Kuang Kuang Kuang* series was both appealing and provocative, a stance that reflects the popular ethos of the *shanke* movement. Although Flash as a web-based technical format is no longer supported by Adobe since 2017, Flash video as a digital form of vector-based moving images continues to flourish, especially in the Global South, thanks to its low-cost accessibility.[2] The cultural life of Flash as digital aesthetics is far beyond its technological life. If the Flash aesthetics, as Lev Manovich (2006) argued, exemplifies the cultural sensibility of digital making, the Chinese *shanke* movement embraced that sensibility as a powerful cultural statement to make sense of the new technological and socio-political realities

That cultural statement had been so deeply anchored on digital networks that a younger generation of artists – after and beyond the "generation Flash" (*shanke*) – began to take

DOI: 10.4324/9781003266952-49

advantage of networked connectivity to create a new mode of animation production. The result is Bingtanghuluer, an online crowdsourcing platform developed in 2010 at the video-sharing website AnimeTaste.net for animators to collectively participate in animation production in a distributive manner. The collaborative animation productions organized by Bingtanghuluer resemble the crowdsourcing process in the open-source software movement, transforming Chinese independent animation from individual pursuits to collective efforts.

From *Xiao Xiao* to Bingtanghuluer, the brief history of Chinese independent animations points to a broader socio-cultural shift in postmillennial China that was moving toward information society and digital economy (Wu 2005; Wu and Fore 2015). As digital production and distribution profoundly changed Chinese screen cultures, what can we learn from this not-too-distant history of independent digital animations that once saturated Chinese cyberspace? Marked by their DIY flexibility, networked distributiveness, and collaborative creativity, these independent animations formed the aesthetical and technical foundation of China's burgeoning digital culture at its defining moment. Therefore, understanding their historical and cultural significance, I believe, is the key to understanding the changing ethos of the digital-age China.

Of particular significance is the ways in which these independent digital animations formed a networked producer culture that provides us with a powerful model to rethink digital subjectivity and epistemology in relation to digital production. It is a model of subject formation that shifts from the ontological relation between image and reality to the production relation between image and image-making. Zhen Zhang and Angela Zito (2015) once called our attention to an emerging yet often-ignored dimension in digital subjects – "the creative agents-as-subjects." This notion suggests a radical departure from the existing theoretical frameworks in film studies that are often exclusively focused on spectators-as-subjects. The shift is not simply to address the post-Fordist condition of blurred boundaries between consumers and producers, but is to underline the *changing modes of production* as the material foundation for constituting a digital subject.

This essay, therefore, focuses on the subject effects in the digital production of independent animations, and re-examines the historical formation of digital subjects at the pivotal moment in China when the tools for producing animated images, which used to be contained within art institutions and film industry, began to be available to the grassroots. I first call for a theoretical rethinking of digital subjectivity by shifting the focus from indexicality to modular production, which involves imagemakers-as-subjects more than spectators-as-subjects. My study demonstrates the subject effects of modular production and their socio-cultural ramifications through three cases – *Xiao Xiao, Kuang Kuang Kuang*, and AT Bingtanghuluer. I underline three key elements that characterize the digital subject effects: *plasmaticness* in aesthetic forms, *pluralism* in knowledge production, and *precarity* in labor conditions. These three elements formulate the material-symbolic foundation for the formation of "creative agents-as-subjects," whose subjectivity constitutes a new folk identity in digital cultures.

Rethinking the Digital Subject: From Indexicality to Modularity

Studies of Chinese digital moving images are often tied to the digital video (DV) movement, a digital form that is celebrated for its on-the-spot immediacy and documentary-style engagement with everyday realities. Realism is thus taken as the theoretical anchor. The fixation on realism is so strong that Paola Voci labeled Chinese digital videos – including animations – as "small-screen realities" (Voci 2010). Overshadowed by such obsession with realism, animations occupy an uneasy position because they deny photographic realism, which not only problematizes the dominant approach to Chinese digital cinema but also calls for a rethinking of digital subjectivity and epistemology. Since the beginning, theoretical engagements with digital images have been wrestling with the notion of indexicality that anchors the realistic claim of photographic media through physical connections with real objects. The digital is thus conceptualized as the defining "other" of the indexical, as digitalization is believed to weaken the physical relation between the image and the reality (Rodowick 2007; Doane 2007). As Philip Rosen (2006) noted, it is "not the analogue in general but the indexical becomes the opposing term, against which the digital may be defined and which it surpasses" (302). However, the fact that digital images include both indexical elements (e.g., documentary) and non-indexical ones (e.g., animation) indicates that the theoretical fixation on indexicality has less to do with the technological conditions than with the ideological conventions focused on visual representation and verisimilitude.

The actual technological distinction between the digital and the analog, in fact, is less about the ontology in representing reality than the modality of representing media – in discrete, numerical forms (digital) or in continuous, non-numerical forms (analog). Such a distinction defines digital media as *modular*, because the material difference between the digital and the analog lies in their operational procedures: while analog machines perform in "live" continuous processes, digital ones rather solve problems in a modular fashion with discrete, reiterative steps. Therefore, instead of indexicality, the parameter with which digital media should be measured is *modularity*. According to Lev Manovich (2002), one of the defining principles of digital media is modularity, which is the result of the structural discreteness of numerical representation. Digital modularity characterizes a media entity as an assemblage of discrete units (pixels, characters, scripts) that can be individually changed, manipulated, and replaced without breaking the whole. Modularity inevitably leads to *variability*, which defines digital media as "not something fixed once and for all, but something that can exist in different, potentially infinite versions" (Manovich 2002, 36). Therefore, instead of an indexical connection between image and reality, the actual impact of digitalization is on the relation *between image and image-making* (and image-makers), because digital modularity and variability allow images to be changed, reshaped, and manipulated with a greater level of convenience and easiness. In other words, what digital technologies really changed *is not ontology but the mode of production*.

The changing mode of production aligns digital media with animation, which is also marked by modularity and variability. The digital mode of production returns cinema to its roots in animation. Manovich (2002) famously claimed: "Digital cinema is a particular case of animation" (302). Like digital media, animation is notably malleable thanks to its modular mode of production. Its defining feature is metamorphosis, the ability of animated images to fluidly change shapes because they are created frame by frame in a modular fashion. This aesthetic is celebrated by Sergei Eisenstein as *plasmaticness*: "a rejection of once-and-forever allotted form, freedom from ossification, the ability to dynamically assume any form" (Eisenstein 1988, 21). Eisenstein's notion of plasmaticness echoes Manovich's characterization of digital variability. We may describe it as *digital plasmaticness*, for the modular structure of a discrete, numerable representation allows a media object the "freedom from ossification" and "the ability to dynamically assume any form." This sense of digital plasmaticness, which characterizes the tendency to constantly oscillate, mutate, and proliferate, is arguably the defining characteristic of digital cultures. Such modular plasmaticness also entails a shift in the labor organization toward individuals. As Thomas Elsaeser (1998) noted, the digital mode of production "requires a new kind of individual input, indeed manual application of craft and skill, which is to say, it marks the return of the 'artist' as source and origin of the image" (205).

It is from this perspective of the digital turn that a new model of digital subjectivity emerged, a model that centers on the effect of digital production (rather than consumption) on individual subjects. Embracing digital modularity and plasmaticness, Chinese independent animations put such digital subjects in motion, advocating a mode of cultural expression and knowledge production that resonated with broader socio-economic transformations: the economic transition from the industrial to the post-industrial capitalism, and the emergence of an urban knowledge class that was simultaneously cultivated and exploited. To understand Chinese independent animations, therefore, is to understand how digital subjects interact with these realities – not through indexical representation but through modular interplay. I characterize the socio-cultural ramifications of such digital subjects of modular production through three key elements: aesthetic plasmaticness, semiotic pluralism, and labor precarity.

Xiao Xiao: The Cartoon Logic of Digital Plasmaticness

At first glance, it may seem strange to describe a Flash animation as "plasmatic" because Adobe Flash, a technique originally developed for Web design, creates motion graphics through vector-based movement and is not good at generating fluid metamorphosis or even smooth motion, which is why Flash animations often appear distinctively jittery, disjunctive, and graphically simple. The animations in the *Xiao Xiao* series, however, create a peculiar sense of plasmatic energy despite the limited animating ability. Without fluid bodily transformations, the sense of plasmaticness in *Xiao Xiao* comes from the ways in which the dynamic, spectacular figural movements destabilize visual coherence, freeing the minimally composed Flash imagery (with mostly lines and circles) from geometrical ossification. When animated Xiao Xiao bounces and kicks, the entire image is (literally) shaking (in *Xiao Xiao No. 5*) or punctuated (in *Xiao Xiao No. 3*), as if the rectangular onscreen space is too constraining for the dynamic motion of this simple stick figure. Xiao Xiao reminds me of Felix the Cat, a cartoon figure from the early animation history of the 1910s, whose unruly exploitation of the graphic surroundings puts the entire visual environment and diegetic universe in flux.

Both Xiao Xiao and Felix seem to magically possess an alternative logic that is not restrained by physical rules, a logic that transcends the boundaries and constraints of mundane reality. That is the cartoon logic, or what Scott Bukatman (2014) calls "cartoon physics," a set of unnatural laws of an alternative universe where "momentum trumps inertia, gravity is a sometime thing, solid matter often isn't. And cartoon bodies are possessed of a nearly infinite pliability" (303). Such a crooked logic not only governs cartoons but is also widespread in video games and superhero movies. What is fundamentally challenged by the cartoon logic is "the logic of the cosmos itself." Therefore, underlying the cartoon logic is the essence of Eisenstein's notion of plasmaticness, for "[t]he freedom claimed for the cartoon by Eisenstein here becomes a freedom from traditional causality, freedom from natural laws, and freedom from consequence (punishment, death, skinned knees)" (Bukatman 2014, 311).

For Xiao Xiao, the logic of cartoons – freedom from death, causality, and physical laws – is also the logic of kung fu. The flying, jumping, and bouncing body of Xiao Xiao, for the most part, is playing kung fu. Kung fu provides the aesthetic and diegetic condition for the cartoon logic to prevail and for the cartoon body – the stick figure – to dynamically destabilize and invigorate the otherwise plain, geometrical graphics. If the cartoon logic is essentially "a reimagining of the body and its relation to the world" (Bukatman 2014, 304), so is kung fu. Who can forget the spectacular body of Jackie Chan trespassing the global geo-boundaries from Hong Kong to New York? In fact, Xiao Xiao's creator, Zhu Zhiqiang, had been drawing stick figures to imitate his favorite kung fu hero, Jackie Chan, since childhood.[3] Compared with Jackie Chan's concrete, physical body, however, Xiao Xiao's sketchy, caricature body may possess even more potential to be liberating, because the stick figure, a highly abstracted representation of a human body, is more iconic and thus more identifiable. While the flesh-and-blood masculine body of Jackie Chan is deeply associated with Chinese nationalism (Li 2001), the stick figure of Xiao Xiao seems to be freed from identity markers of various kinds. That's why Scott McCloud (1993) argues for the universal identifiability of cartoon:

> The more cartoony a face is, for instance, the more people it could be said to describe . . . Thus, when you look at a photo or a realistic drawing of a face, you see it as the face of another. But when you enter the world of cartoon, you see *yourself*. . . . We don't just *observe* the cartoon. We *become* it!
>
> *(36)*

Indeed, we don't just enjoy watching Xiao Xiao. We become it! We become this almighty stick figure, whose cartoony kung fu logic leads us to break physical laws, to destabilize cultural norms, to transgress identity boundaries, and above all, to reject "once-and-forever allotted form."

The abstract yet powerful body of Xiao Xiao mirrors the ambition of Chinese independent animators who embrace Flash and other digital tools as potential means of empowerment. Although computer technologies have increasingly been colonized by the global empire of information capitalism, the critical potential of affordable digital tools may not be completely lost. The personal experience of Xiao Xiao's creator, Zhu Zhiqiang, who rose from a humble background with little formal education to become an internationally acclaimed animation artist, testifies to the possibility of grassroots empowerment. In fact, when Manovich (2006) mourned the loss of digital empowerment, his main evidence was the lack of digital artists from the non-Western world. But he spotlighted one exception:

> Tirana Biennale 01 did include one artist from China who contributed a beautiful animation of martial arts fighters. But we never found out who he was. . . . Maybe he did not even live in China.
>
> *(215)*

The artist Manovich was referring to is no other than Zhu Zhiqiang, and he did live in China, as a poorly paid programmer in a software company. Many Chinese independent artists and filmmakers were just like him, who had no formal training in arts or cinema, and who worked as underpaid laborers struggling with China's technological booms. These were the so-called IT *mingong* (IT peasant-workers) who flooded to Beijing and Shenzhen, programming software or selling computer parts. For these IT *mingong*, using Flash vectors and stick figures is less an aesthetic choice than practical necessity because it is probably the easiest way to make an animation. The ways in which a stick figure created by a crude technique can transcend physical boundaries and logical rules, to some degree, reflect the animators' own aspiration to break free from socio-economic constraints.

Such a grassroots aspiration echoes Eisenstein's (1988) political interpretation of the utopian appeal of animated plasmaticness, which is its revolt against the mechanical enslavement of industrial labor on Fordist assembly lines:

> In a country and social order with such a mercilessly standardized and mechanically measured existence, which is difficult to call life, the sight of such "omnipotence" (that is, the ability to become "whatever you wish"), cannot but hold a sharp degree of attractiveness.
>
> *(21)*

What Eisenstein considered liberating in the 1930s Ford is equally so in today's Lenovo. For Chinese IT *mingong* prisoned in cubicles, the ability to create and enjoy Xiao Xiao's plasmatic freedom must feel exhilarating. In fact, the space where Xiao Xiao fights (and frequently destroys) is often a generic office space, with elevators and glass walls being kicked and mashed by Xiao Xiao (in *Xiao Xiao No. 3* and *No. 7*). The animated spectacle of Xiao Xiao destroying a modern, sleek office space with his kung fu body feels strangely empowering because it reorganizes the residual elements of digital media (Adobe Flash) into a plasmatic revolt (the cartoon logic of a stick figure) against the informationally measured existence in post-industrial cubicles.

Kuang Kuang Kuang: Compositing Layers of Semiotic Pluralism

If Xiao Xiao somehow manages to be freed from the "once-and-forever allotted form," Kung Kuang, unfortunately, does not. In fact, the whole animation series of *Kuang Kuang Kuang* is about identity construction by socio-cultural institutions. Taking advantage of the "notorious" graphic limitation and inflexibility of Flash vectors, *Kuang Kuang Kuang* creates a dark, uncanny metaphor of social suppression in China by featuring strikingly uniformed character designs in fixed geometrical shapes – they are all identical squares! But Kuang Kuang, the central character, is different. He is not a square but a circle, thus a disrupter, a provocateur. What is more destabilizing, however, is not the shape but the line. The outline of the character design is deliberately hard so that these figures stand out from the background they inhabit, as if they are detached elements thrown into an alien space that they don't belong to. In fact, the hard-edge figures – the walls, the trees, and the buildings – are all drawn as assemblages of paper cutouts pasted on the background.

The pronounced distance and division between these layers of cutouts expose the composited nature of the animated images in *Kuang Kuang Kuang*. They are discrete and fractured, forming a sharp contrast with photorealistic images that are continuous and unified. Compositing has been an inherent element of animation production since its pre-digital age. A single frame is divided to layers of cells to speed up production and to facilitate division of labor. Digital compositing turns this industrial standard into a cultural norm. But compared with the conventional use of digital compositing, *Kuang Kuang Kuang* distinguishes itself by emphasizing the internal boundaries and divisions *within* the composited images.

Compositing in digital cinema (e.g., CGI movies) is often operated to imitate the appearance of continuity in photographic images: composited elements are to be blended seamlessly and internal gaps are to be erased or concealed. The compositing in *Kuang Kuang Kuang*, however, does the opposite by opening (and sometimes exaggerating) the gaps and distances among different visual elements. It pronounces disparities in a disjunctive fictional space rather than smoothing them to create the illusion of a seamless virtual world. It is what Thomas LaMarre (2009) calls "open compositing," as opposed to the "close compositing" favored by Hollywood cinema.

In *Kuang Kuang Kuang*, the aesthetic effect of open compositing is so loudly pronounced that it amounts to a political metaphor: what kind of a society generates so many identical cutouts and assemble them into a fundamentally divided universe? The hard-edged open compositing in *Kuang Kuang Kuang* creates a graphic cacophony that is on the verge of collapse. The images look too unstable, and the visual elements are under constant threat of erasure and disappearance. In one episode titled "Bombing the School" (2008), Kuang Kuang is kicked out of school in a graphic manner that resembles crossing out a word on paper, and the school's name is written on cutout papers that are falling apart. Every visual element is in crisis. The animation thus appears to be a messy assembly of interfering signals instead of a coherent diegesis. Such composited visual incoherence and instability are certainly provocative. But what is more provocative is the semiotic chaos. Since the compositing effect is too divided to hold the image as a unified whole, these discrete visual elements are distributed evenly and all call attention to themselves, begging to be read symbolically. In "Bombing the School," the visual chaos is particularly evocative (Figure 38.1): What are the meanings of the burning stove, the crumbling walls, the chicken, the bomb, or the automatic toothbrush that is transformed from a machine gun? Facing such disjunctive and diverse

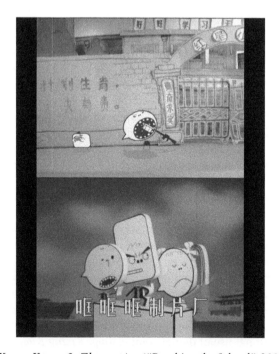

Figure 38.1 Kuang Kuang Kuang 2: Zhaxuexiao ("Bombing the School" 2008, Dir. Pi San).

visual elements that are busily composited together, even the most naïve viewer is compelled to read them as a collection of discrete signs awaiting to be assembled into eligible meanings.

But compositing is not all to be blamed. Modern semiotics, after all, is fundamentally about discreteness. Roland Barthes (1977, 64) said: "Language is, as it were, that which divides reality." So is cinema, according to Christian Metz, who argued that cinema can be considered a language because it is composed of discrete elements (e.g., shots, frames) that can be arranged and assembled into a discourse. However, Metz also recognized that cinema is derived from analog and continuous media (e.g., photography), and it does not have purely distinctive units. Therefore, "[t]he analysis of a shot consists in processing from a non-discrete whole to smaller nondiscrete wholes: One can decompose a shot, but one cannot reduce it" (Metz 1974, 116). It seems that Metz was struggling between cinema's structural discreteness (editing, montage) and ontological wholeness (indexical representation of reality). Things may be much easier if Metz was dealing with digital animation, because digital images do have a smallest discrete unit (at least in theory) and that is a pixel. Digital modularity and variability offer greater levels of operational possibilities for visual elements to be manipulated and composited into semiotic discourses.

The *Kuang Kuang Kuang* animation series, with its open compositing and graphic diversity, experiments with a kind of semiotic plurality. It generates a plasmatic signification field that refuses to be locked down to a singular meaning, and thus destabilizes, transforms, and even subverts the existing visual signs that tend to be heavily coded and over-determined by various socio-political forces in China. For example, the square-shaped character design is modeled after a dialogue box in the computer user interface, and it is an allegorical sign – what is constrained is not just identity but is *hua yu quan* (the right to speak). The logo of the animation is referencing old propaganda movies from the socialist era (Figure 38.1). What Kuang Kuang is challenging is the discursive fixation that has been tightly controlled by state institutions in China.

For the filmmaker/artist Pi San, the gesture of semiotic pluralism expresses a somewhat oppositional stance of an individual against the state. The fact that several videos from the *Kuang Kuang Kuang* series were banned by state censorship further reinforces this sensibility. However, the casual, playful manner of the animation also suggests something less oppositional than habitual and intuitive. The animation's composited visual disjunction points to a broader and more pervasive cultural sensibility on digital media. It is the cultural logic of remix, an aesthetic condition that is especially highlighted by the operational principle of Flash. It takes artwork as a set of samples instead of a coherent whole. As Manovich (2006, 210) argued, "[i]t invites us to play with the dialectic of the sample and the composite, of our own works and the works of others." It is the logic of cut, copy, and paste, or that of sampling, selecting, and morphing.

Therefore, semiotic pluralism is less a political stance than a cultural condition of digital subjectivity, a condition of modular media structures that cannot be fixed to a singular form but are always composited from diverse samples. But there are political implications in such digital subjects. The proliferation of various kinds of digital sampling, remix, and redux has created a mounting challenge for the Chinese government that is struggling to simultaneously promote the digital economy and to maintain cultural control. Semiotic pluralism in digital subjects, therefore, is an inherent cultural contradiction of the modular mode of digital production that oscillates between protocological control and distributive chaos (Galloway 2004). The playful and provocative tone of the *Kuang Kuang Kuang* series testifies to such a cultural contradiction.

AT Bingtanghuluer: Precarious Free Labor in Modular Production

Unlike the individualist stance taken by *Xiao Xiao* and *Kuang Kuang Kuang*, AT Bingtanghuluer is rather a collective initiative. Founded in 2008 as a video-sharing website for Chinese independent artists, AnimeTaste.net (AT) soon evolved into an organizational platform for animation enthusiasts to gather and socialize both online and offline: they started their own circles on social media and organized meetings, forums, and screenings at cafes, clubs, and college campuses. In 2010, AT organized its first "one-minute party," and each participant produced a one-minute animation video within hours. Such activities quickly developed into collaborative production projects, in which animators each created a short segment and these segments were compiled and edited together into a complete animation video. It thus became an effective online platform for organizing collective animation production, and it was aptly named "Bingtanghuluer," a reference to a popular snack that consists of candied fruits on skewers.

Since the release of its first project *GoGoGo* in 2012, AT Bingtanghuluer has produced over 20 animated short films with hundreds of participants. One of the most successful projects is *Da Yezi* (*Coconut*, 2012), a music video for the Chinese rock band Hey!, whose lead singer, Lei Lei, is also a renowned animation artist. The film was collectively created by 18 teams of animators, each producing a short segment with distinctive styles. These 18 segments were then edited together by the director/producer Wang Tianfang, who skillfully combined these diverse units in a playful manner that is full of lyrical disjunctions: a 2D sketch is juxtaposed with 3D rendering, the screen capture of a webpage full of texts is cut to the motion graphics that are imitating a cellphone game. As an assembly of so many diverse styles, the animated film is a dazzling bricolage.

The ways in which AT Bingtanghuluer organized collective production exemplify the trendy practice of online crowdsourcing, which was first popularized by the open-source software movement and was quickly adopted by digital businesses of various kinds. A method for distributed problem solving, crowdsourcing has been fashioned as a crucial mode of organizing labor and production in digital economies. The fact that both animation production and software programming can be organized in a similarly distributed manner suggests that the foundation of crowdsourcing is not computational technology but structural modularity. Both animation and software require a modular mode of production: frame by frame (animation) or function by function (programing). The inherent modularity of digital production brings animation and software together as they operate with the same structure of modularized design.

In fact, modularity has become the organizational principle of not only digital media but the entire digital economy for managing production and labor (Langlois 2002). In the so-called Web 2.0 era, user participation such as crowdsourcing is largely enabled by the modular architecture of media platforms, whose standardized and accessible structure is fashioned as an open egalitarian facilitation of collective endeavors (Gawer 2014). From computer programming to media production, modularity is the key to the techno-culture of post-industrialism that is branded as flexible, participatory, and "user-friendly" (Baldwin and Clark 2000). But we must remember that the principle of modularity is nothing new. It originated from the Fordist mode of production in the industrial era, when animation, as a cultural forms of mechanical modularity, established its currency. There is a deeply rooted archaeological connection between the division of labor in Disney studio's cel-animation production and the collective crowdsourcing in Bingtanghuluer's digital creation. The continuous reliance on modularity from Fordist assembly lines to post-Fordist crowdsourcing suggests a conjunctural history, whereby the relations between labor, technology, and cultural production were repeatedly entangled, restructured, and resolved in the changing systems of capitalism.

As a distributed mode of production, crowdsourcing is frequently celebrated as what Pierre Lévy (1997) called "collective intelligence." The animation community at AnimeTaste certainly embraced such utopian ideals, and they explicitly branded Bingtanhuluer as an open, collaborative platform to generate collective passion, creativity, and knowledge for communal aspiration and fulfillment, a stance in opposition to the profit logic of media industries. Underneath such a utopian statement, however, the actual works that were collectively created by these animators rather paint a much darker picture. For instance, the film *Coconut* tells a gloomy story of a young, unemployed college graduate who is desperately looking for a job while searching for his lost "coconut" (a metaphor for the future, soul, or identity). As a music video, the animation pairs the black humor in the colloquial lyric ("Did you get a job yet?" "Not a single interview") with uncanny images (a tiger weeping behind fleeing mice, a coconut turning to an exploding bomb) that resemble both surrealism and pop art (Figure 38.2). Identified as an "artist," the main character is a self-reference to the thousands of animators who gather at AT. For them, creating animation as collective, "free" (unpaid) artists – as opposed to joining the industry as paid workers –

Figure 38.2 Da Yizi (Coconut, 2012), AT Bingtanghuluer.

may not be an intentional choice but a degrading reality, a reality of precarious labor over-shadowed by China's much-hyped economic miracle.

Despite the rapid boom in Chinese digital media, the precarity of creative labor has increasingly become a serious social problem. The situation is especially pronounced in animation production, which has one of the highest unemployment rates among college graduates. For those unemployed or underpaid college graduates, who constitute the so-called *yizu* (ant tribe) in China, "collective intelligence" comes as a compromise rather than a utopia. It is a mode of collective free labor, which is a defining feature of the post-Fordist mode of digital production where collective creativity is "translated into excess productive activities that are pleasurably embraced and at the same time often shamelessly exploited" (Terranova 2004, 78). This crucial yet unrecognizable labor force is the outcome of the modular mode of production that is reshaping the relationship between labor, capital, and culture.

In China, where the economy is still transitioning toward post-industrialism, free labor is both a feature and a symptom. It represents a structural failure for society to valorize a surplus labor force, a new generation of college-educated knowledge labor that is over-produced and impossible to be fully incorporated. For Chinese knowledge workers who are facing an alluring promise ("China Dream") and a depressing reality (unemployment), joining collective free labor on the Internet is an investment of both desire and frustration, a process of self-valorization of excess productivity that is longing yet fails to be actualized by the socio-economic system. Such ambiguity and uncertainty entailed in the digital subjects-as-free-labor are underlined by the creative force at AT Bingtanghuluer. The community's celebratory note on the website ("we are self-organized enthusiasts") vis-à-vis the gloomy message in their films ("you will never find a job") opens a peculiar space for negotiating the unevenness and contradiction in China's transition toward informational capitalism.

Conclusion: Digital Subjects in a Producer Culture

As digital technologies transformed the relationship between image and image-making, the changing subject effects are located in the shifting dynamics between media objects and their creators in a networked culture that is tilted toward production. The Chinese independent animations demonstrate the profound subject effects of digital plasmaticness, pluralism, and precarity in an emergent producer culture at the pivotal moment of China's post-industrial transition: *Xiao Xiao*'s rebellious energy against the post-Fordist entrapment with its plasmatic logic; *Kuang Kuang Kuang*'s satirical critique of the homogenous discursive formation with semiotic pluralism; and Bingtanghuluer's playful exposure of labor precarity in digital economies. They raise social, cultural, and political questions regarding the problematic identity of the so-called creative class and its ambivalent existence in China. Taking advantage of the modular logic of sampling, selection, and remix, these animations demonstrate how digital subjectivity, as unstable and contradictory as it is, may challenge the constructed uniformity of an "ideal" subject of knowledge work that is demanded and exploited by both Chinese authoritarianism and post-industrial corporatism. These animations also call for a theoretical shift in our political evaluation of digital media from indexicality of images to plurality of knowledge, for such plurality may become the critical source where the residual subcultural and countercultural elements in digital media can be reorganized to form what Allan Liu calls "an ethos of the unknown." It is "a counter-ethos within the dominant ethos of informationalism that spends its days and nights locked within the cubicles of post-industrialism but also 'gesture' all the while that it is something else," something that can constitute "the *basis* for a renewed folk identity" (Liu 2004, 71). It is this counter-ethos for "a renewed folk identity" *within* the digital producer culture that identifies the political spirit of Chinese independent animations and their creative energy.

Notes

1 Interview with Pi San.
2 China is one of the few places still supporting Flash Player (as of 2022).
3 Interview with Zhu Zhiqiang.

References

Baldwin, Carliss Young, and Kim B. Clark. 2000. *Design Rules: The Power of Modularity*. Cambridge: MIT Press.

Barthes, Roland. 1977. *Elements of Semiology*. Translated by Annette Lavers and Colin Smith. New York: Hill and Wang.

Bukatman, Scott. 2014. "Pertaining to Cartoon Physics: Or, the Cartoon Cat in the Machine." In *Animating Film Theory*, edited by Karen Beckman, 301–16. Duke University Press.

Doane, Mary Ann. 2007. "The Indexical and the Concept of Medium Specificity." *Differences* 18 (1): 128–52.

Eisenstein, Sergei. 1988. *Eisenstein on Disney*. London: Methuen.

Galloway, Alexander R. 2004. *Protocol: How Control Exists After Decentralization*. Cambridge: MIT Press.

Gawer, Annabelle. 2014. "Bridging Differing Perspectives on Technological Platforms: Toward an Integrative Framework." *Research Policy* 43 (7): 1239–49.

LaMarre, Thomas. 2009. *The Anime Machine: A Media Theory of Animation*. Minneapolis: University of Minnesota Press.

Langlois, Richard N. 2002. "Modularity in Technology and Organization." *Journal of Economic Behavior & Organization* 49 (1): 19–37.

Lévy, Pierre. 1997. *Collective Intelligence: Mankind's Emerging World in Cyberspace*. Cambridge, MA: Perseus Books.

Li, Siu Leung. 2001. "Kung Fu: Negotiating Nationalism and Modernity." *Cultural Studies* 15 (3–4): 515–42.

Liu, Alan. 2004. *The Laws of Cool: Knowledge Work and the Culture of Information*. Chicago: University of Chicago Press.

Manovich, Lev. 2002. *The Language of New Media*. Cambridge, MA: MIT Press.

———. 2006. "Generation Flash." In *New Media, Old Media: A History and Theory Reader*, edited by Wendy Hui Kyong Chun and Thomas Keenan, 209–19. New York: Routledge.

McCloud, Scott. 1993. *Understanding Comics: The Invisible Art*. New York: HarperCollins.

Metz, Christian. 1974. *Film Language: A Semiotics of the Cinema*. Chicago: University of Chicago Press.

Rodowick, David Norman. 2007. *The Virtual Life of Film*. Cambridge: Harvard University Press.

Rosen, Philip. 2006. *Change Mummified: Cinema, Historicity, Theory*. Minneapolis: University of Minnesota Press.

Terranova, Tiziana. 2004. *Network Culture: Politics for The Information Age*. London: Pluto Press.

Thomas, Elsaesser. 1998. "Digital Cinema: Delivery, Event, Time." In *Cinema Futures: Cain, Abel or Cable? The Screen Arts in the Digital Age*, edited by Thomas Elsaesser and Kay Hoffmann, 201–22. Amsterdam: Amsterdam University Press.

Voci, Paola. 2010. *China on Video: Smaller-Screen Realities*. London: Routledge.

Wu, Weihua. 2005. "Independent Animation in Contemporary China." *Cartoons* 1: 21–25.

Wu, Weihua, and Steve Fore. 2015. "Flash Empire and Chinese Shanke: The Emergence of Chinese Digital Culture." *Animation Journal* 13: 28–51.

Zhang, Zhen, and Angela Zito, eds. 2015. *DV-Made China: Digital Subjects and Social Transformations After Independent Film*. Honolulu: University of Hawaii Press.

39

EXPERIMENTATION AND TRANSNATIONAL INFLUENCES

Documentary Film in Post-Authoritarian Indonesia

Eric Sasono

Introduction

Amid the lack of academic writing on documentary film in Indonesia, discussion about the subject revolves around the success of the authoritarian New Order regime in controlling media production and circulation and, as a result, dictating the aesthetics of documentaries produced in the country. The New Order (1966–98) was a term used by the late Indonesian President Soeharto to characterize his anti-Communist, militaristic regime established after the 1965–66 massacre of political leftists and members and sympathizers of the Indonesian Communist Party. The regime exerted extensive control over the Indonesian media landscape, including complete control over media production and distribution, as well as the institutions involved in media and film culture.

Discussion in documentary aesthetics has been dominated by the idea of the pervasiveness of the New Order control that left almost and lack of artistic space for documentary filmmakers. Filmmaking is seen to be fully controlled by the New Order regime and this has created a situation to the extent that the regime had their distinctive New Order style of which filmmakers were somehow observed in their creative decisions. In commenting to ethnographic style documentary that occupied the state broadcaster in the 1980s, many dismiss the artistic potential and call it part of that New Order visual style and a self-exoticization attempt from the filmmakers, which in the end strengthened the dominance of national culture over the local and regional expressions.

In this perspective, documentary film is marginalized by being equated with an instructional medium for the general public or a propaganda machine to promote national development, the quasi-ideology of the New Order regime. Consequently, documentary public screenings were regarded as instruction to the audience to be obedient subject to the state ideology that is necessary for economic development. Documentary film screenings were dominated by documentaries and newsreels produced by the state-owned film company PFN (Perusahaan Film Nasional), under the title of Gelora Indonesia (Zeal of Indonesia) containing government official's activities, state ceremonies, the arrival of international

DOI: 10.4324/9781003266952-50

guests and other public information services.[1] This is elaborated by a Dutch researcher, Van Heeren:

> The object of the documentary was to depict the success of some development projects or the exoticism of the preferably remote area, or a combination of both. All was accompanied by a voice over, using a particular documentary pitch, with some cheery music typically associated with this type of film.[2]

This narrative model was viewed as the norm for Indonesian documentaries at that time, and documentary role as public instruction tools and propaganda dominated public perception for decades. Many believe that in the post–New Order era, this view still dominates the perception of documentary filmmakers and broadcast executives.[3] Documentary is equated with its instructional format, to influence public behavior to be good citizens under the New Order.

Documentary film in Indonesia has also been viewed in isolation from transnational influences with a focus on the omnipotent power of the New Order in controlling the production and the aesthetics. Documentary films and their institutions were seen as the by-product of the New Order regime in controlling the public space and promoting order, national unity, and the success of development. The roles of external influences in documentary institutions and artistic decisions have been limited.

Since the political change in 1998, the influence of international factors on documentary filmmaking and distribution has been a topic of discussion. However, many perceive these international factors as simply replacing the controls that were previously imposed by the New Order regime after it collapsed. Rather than viewing transnational influences as a necessary part of driving creativity and production through strategy and tension, some see it as a form of political and creative control over a medium that is traditionally used to convey instructional messages to the audience. The perception of documentaries as solely instructional format remains.

These views have limited the discussions on documentary films in Indonesia by focusing mainly on their role as instructional films, ignoring their critical and artistic potential. On the other hand, when documentary institutions are discussed, they are often seen as being confined to the New Order regime or viewed only as producers of instructional media. There have been few studies putting documentary as an integral part of society and politics, or to put it in Krishna Sen's phrase "has been the site of every momentous transition in living history."[4] Discussion on documentary aesthetics is often overshadowed by the focus on documentary institutions being the extension of foreign agency interests.[5]

This chapter aims to shed light on documentary film in Indonesia from two perspectives to broaden our understanding of the medium in Indonesia. First, by focusing on Sinema 8, a short-lived movement initiated by students at the Jakarta Art Institute during the New Order, this chapter aims to highlight the function of documentary as a platform for filmic experimentation and storytelling, rather than an instructional tool. Second, the chapter will explore the role of transnational influences in the production and circulation of documentary film, as an integral part of the historical development of the medium in Indonesia, and not separate from its institutional and political context. By viewing documentary film in this manner, the chapter intends to provide insights into how documentary film has been a part of the political transitions in Indonesia.

Documentary film is seen not in the confinement of its textual interpretation nor insularity of its institution but seen as institutional practices involving the tension between national relevance and transnational drive. This chapter will see how documentary film development has been interlinked with international elements such as international donor agencies and charity organizations that played important roles in Indonesia's political transition. Under the pretext of democratization in a post-authoritarian setting, these agencies' funds enabled documentary filmmakers to produce and circulate documentary film to meet its public amid the lack of infrastructural supports, such as funding opportunities and dedicated screening venues and platforms. The discussion will be limited shortly before and after the political transition of 1998, where the authoritarian New Order regime was toppled from its position by a democratic movement in Indonesia.

Sinema 8

The equating of documentaries with their instructional purpose during the authoritarian New Order Regime (1968–98) cannot be dissociated from the substantial control over the production and distribution of media, including documentary film. During this time, most of the documentaries were produced by the state-owned film company and only broadcast on the state-owned station, Televisi Republik Indonesia, or TVRI, established in 1962. The dominant genre was newsreels and documentaries about national development were dominant, with occasional documentaries about ethnic tribes in Indonesia also shown. This type of ethnographic documentary is believed to have been part of the New Order's efforts to dominate and incorporate local cultures into the national identity. The depiction of local cultures and remote ethnic groups was framed within the narrative of national culture development that was deemed crucial to support the New Order's primary objective of national progress.

Despite the various evaluations, the presence of documentary film on TVRI, the sole TV station in the country until late 1989, was pivotal in supporting the development of artistic documentary in Indonesia. The ethnographic films on TVRI started around the same time that the station ceased airing commercials. The ban on commercials caused TVRI to seek alternative sources of revenue, which led them to partner with government agencies. These agencies paid filmmakers to produce content that highlighted their achievements in national development, providing a business opportunity for film lecturers and students at the Jakarta Institute of Art, or IKJ,[6] the only film school in Indonesia at that time. IKJ responded to these demands and used the profits to purchase equipment for the school.[7] As a result, 14 documentary films were produced in the early 1980s, mostly directed by David Albert Peransi.[8] Peransi and his peers were instrumental in advocating documentary as an art form, equal to fiction film, and emphasizing its artistic quality as a contribution to the concept of national cinema. Peransi's documentaries primarily focus on environmental issues, transmigration, and socio-cultural problems. Although the titles[9] may suggest otherwise, these documentaries are not intended as promotional materials about economic development. Instead, Peransi believed in the power of documentary aesthetics and sought to advocate this medium. He understood its potential to serve as a tool for "cultural education," a directive from the New Order government to the filmmakers in the 1980s to produce films with educational values.[10] While this directive was mainly aimed at fiction filmmakers,[11] Peransi argued that documentary films have the capability of "opening new perspectives (cultural function) while at the same time exposing new facts for learning and observation."[12] He advocated for the recognition of documentary film in the national film scene, as they were often considered as *anak tiri* (stepchildren) compared to fiction film,[13] indicating their marginal position and unfavorable treatment. Peransi explains this:

> The attention of the public and film institutions has been directed to feature films, maybe because these films are more glamorous. Meanwhile they forget about documentary film, which is essentially the cultural-educational film.[14]

Peransi was appealing for the documentary film used a lexicon that was popular in the context of *film nasional*, or "national film," in the 1980s. *Film nasional* is more than just an Indonesian term for national cinema; it is a concept that has been used by the government, filmmakers, critics, and officials at film institutions as "a nationalist project with both material and cultural aspirations" to define what Indonesian film is.[15] The concept was formalized by a presidential decree in 1999 following inputs from people in the film industry.[16]

Building upon this idea, Peransi proposed the government establish an independent body to support documentary filmmaking. He also encouraged filmmakers to adopt an anthropological approach in their documentaries, focusing on documenting the lives of different ethnicities and tribes,[17] as he believed this format had the potential to instigate sociocultural dialogues.[18] He urged the government, and also documentary filmmakers whom he referred to as "intellectuals," to move beyond the use of documentaries as propaganda[19] and instead embrace their distinct artistic value. Peransi's call was one of the earliest efforts to position documentary films as having intrinsic artistic merit and not simply serving as a means of delivering information to the public.

Peransi was part of a group at IKJ founded by students and graduates, which aimed to experiment with film and audiovisual media. The group started an experimental film festival called Festival Film Mini (Short Film Festival) to showcase 8 mm film.[20] They experimented with 8 mm film and screened short, experimental, animation, and short documentary films and unfinished works under the group name Kelompok Sinema Delapan (Eight Cinema Group).[21] This group viewed documentary film in the same light as experimental film to provide an avenue for experimenting with film storytelling and aesthetics. As film students, they are influenced by foreign filmmakers, especially from France and Russia. Peransi was also influenced by Dutch filmmaker, Joris Ivens, whom he met during a trip to Paris. Members of this group, including experimental filmmaker Gotot Prakoso and dancer/filmmaker Sardono Kusumo, blended animation or dance with documentaries, a novel concept at the time. For instance, *Meta Ekologi* (dir. Gotot Prakosa), 1979, documented a dance performance staged by Kusumo and his company in a mud pool, exploring the fusion of dance and cinema as a form of poetry. In Prakoso's words:

> This film is a response to the dialogue with the ecology of soil and water. Humanity expresses their feelings through their bodies, squirming to become one with the universe, much like farmers who work on their land and struggle with mud. [This is] a process of poetization.[22]

In principle, this non-fiction film has opened up the possibility of approaching documentaries beyond their instructional format, demonstrating the artistic potential of documentaries in Indonesia that many scholars overlook in their examination of documentary film aesthetics during the New Order.

Another noteworthy filmmaker is Garin Nugroho, who later became the most decorated filmmaker in the country. Although not a member, he was an IKJ student who was exposed to Sinema 8 experimentation and became part of a wider conversation about exploration in cinematic storytelling. Nugroho made an important breakthrough with his film, *Air dan Romi* (Water and Romi) (dir. Garin Nugroho) 1991, which impressed the international community, including an academic from Monash University, Australia, David Hanan.[23] *Air dan Romi* is a short documentary that portrays the dire conditions of water pollution in Jakarta through the eyes of three poor people living in the city's slum area. The subject matter – the depiction of poverty and environmental problems in Jakarta – was unusual for documentary films in the New Order era, and Hanan also noted that the aesthetics were particularly intriguing compared to its contemporaries. Hanan referred to this documentary work as a "poetic" documentary, where movement and flow are at the center of the aesthetics.[24] The day-to-day activities of the three subjects are depicted without any narrative interventions, and they do not speak to the people behind the camera throughout the film. This approach was completely different from documentaries aired on TVRI, which were dominated by voice-overs and excessive explanations about what was happening on the screen. Hanan considered the voices of the subjects in Nugroho's *Air dan Romi* to be "dignified commentary over shots of their own daily activities."[25] This artistic style also attracted the attention of a Japanese critic and film programmer at the Yamagata Film Festival, Kenji Ishizaka. During a conversation with Nugroho, Ishizaka made a very strong remark about *Air dan Romi*, especially in comparison to documentary films during the New Order era:

> [T]here's hardly any difference in eye level between you as filmmaker and the filmed subject of your gaze. As you said, if you make a documentary badly, then be it propaganda or enlightening, it will still be about those on top teaching the weak at the bottom. Your work has an exceedingly level gaze, and features society's weak and oppressed. I have never seen anything like this in other Indonesian films from the Suharto era.[26]

The documentary was regarded to have a political impact, and as noted by film scholar David Hanan, it faced an attempted ban and destruction of the Betacam master by the Indonesian Intelligence Service.[27] Despite this, the film was never banned and has been shown on various occasions, including in a special event in 2009,[28] showing that the master still exists. However, Nugroho's contribution to the development of documentary industry is likely to be more significant than its artistic development, as will be discussed later.

These documentaries and other experimentations receded into obscurity as they were only shown at the IKJ festival and limited events and were not widely circulated beyond film and art students at IKJ. They failed to make an impact on the general public due to limited distribution and reinforced the view that equated documentary films with propaganda.[29] Even when commercial TV stations started broadcasting in the early, they were reluctant to produce documentary programming based on this perception.[30]

In this period, documentary films played a role in defining the national image of Indonesia for two reasons. First, the themes explored in these films aimed to satisfy the demand of broadcasters while also conforming to the concept of national unity in Indonesia, which was heavily promoted by the state to showcase the success of the regime in uniting the nation to support the economic and cultural development of the country. Second, documentary film was trying to assert their position in the "national film" discourse because documentary film was made by the country's intellectuals and are capable of instigating socio-cultural dialogues among different cultural groups that share the country. Peransi sought to place documentary film at the center of the national cinema discourse by emphasizing its artistic quality and educational function that align with the idea of "cultural education" promoted by the New Order. Despite being subsumed into the national cinema narrative, Peransi believed that documentaries should be seen beyond instructional medium and should be recognized for their artistic merit. Documentary aesthetics were explored within the restriction of the New Order regime, and a more extensive examination of Sinema 8's work is needed.

Beyond National Discourse

After the collapse of the New Order regime in 1998, documentaries were freed from institutional constraints. New production and circulation arrangements were necessary. In the 1990s, audiovisual companies existed to meet the market demands, but a significant change occurred when filmmakers established non-profit organizations alongside their private companies to produce documentaries. Garin Nugroho played a crucial role in this development.

Audiovisual production companies were prevalent in the late 1980s when the Indonesian government allowed private commercial television stations to broadcast in 1987.[31] During the early years of the television industry boom, many filmmakers left film studios to work for TV stations, while some established their own production companies, such as former member of Kelompok Sinema Delapan Johan Teranggi, who founded PT Cinevisi Inc. to produce documentaries for private companies and foreign broadcast.[32] Garin Nugroho, however, chose a different path by creating a non-profit branch of his company, SET Foundation, to address the increasing needs of civil society after the political change in 1998. While Nugroho produced films through his commercial production company, SET Workshop, his non-profit wing, SET Foundation, joined forces with non-government organizations (NGOs) to campaign for citizen participation in politics and welcome the opening up of civic space at large in Indonesia.

After the fall of the New Order in 1998, a general election was held in 1999 and Nugroho was, in his own words, "actively participating in guarding the 1999 election from any frauds to happen again like what happened during the Suharto era."[33] For this purpose, Nugroho claims that "SET Workshop that I led has transformed into an NGO (non-government organization), to collaborate with 15 other non-profit organizations working in the field of democracy."[34] SET Foundation received funding from international donors and NGOs such as USAID (United States), HIVOS (the Netherlands), and TIFA Foundation (part of Soros Foundation in Indonesia),[35] and Nugroho considers these activities as their "public role." After the election, SET continued to work on issues such as civic education, promoting multiculturalism, democratization in broadcasting, and producing audiovisual materials for those purposes.[36] Nugroho claims that many filmmakers, especially in the 2000s, followed his footsteps by creating non-profit wings or NGOs to secure funding for film and documentary production through non-profit funding mechanisms.[37]

Garin Nugroho and SET's dual identity enables them to seek funding from the "non-profit sector," rather than relying solely on commercial sources. This is possible because many aid agencies, international NGOs, and philanthropic organizations that fund documentary film activities require their partners to be non-profit institutions rather than commercial entities. These foreign organizations provide grants based on the belief that such partnerships with civil society organizations are important to work on themes, such as community development, democratization, capacity building, and other non-commercial causes.[38] Meanwhile, this gives an advantage to SET, and with their non-profit arm, they are able to offer internships to novice and aspiring filmmakers, giving them a taste of real filmmaking experience. SET has been offering these opportunities since its establishment, and this also applies to its fiction film projects, workshops, and film festivals.[39] This division between the profit and non-profit arms has become a model followed by other filmmakers, such as Shanty Harmayn with YMMFI (JIFFest and In-Docs) and Nia Dinata with the Kalyana Shira Foundation.[40]

The non-profit face of these organizations became a starting point for the growth of documentary film in Indonesia after 1998, as they formed partnerships with local and international NGOs (such as Ford Foundation or the Asia Foundation), foreign funding agencies (such as USAID), and international philanthropic organizations that were looking for partners to work in audiovisual media as part of institutionalizing democracy in Indonesia in the post-authoritarian setting. These international organizations were required to work with local non-profit entities, leading them to collaborate with NGOs such as SET Foundation, In-Docs, and Kalyana Shira. The non-profit form was crucial, as during the New Order era, NGOs were seen as the embodiment of civil society in a country where political institutions, such as opposition parties, were tightly controlled.[41] This perception continued into post-authoritarian Indonesia, where the sudden openness happened, alongside with the idea that citizen participation and civic engagement should be developed in the public sphere; these NGOs were considered to be the ideal partners for advancing these efforts.[42]

Since then, this model has been a strong alternative for documentary film production and training in Indonesia. With funding from the non-profit sector, it has helped to cultivate documentary film culture in Indonesia. The development of documentary film culture in Indonesia is directly linked to the narrative of building civil society and advancing political reform in Indonesia. Some of the prominent younger generations of filmmakers who have emerged from this funding model include Aryo Danusiri, Lexy Rambadetta, Shalahuddin Siregar, Ucu Agustin, Daniel Rudi Haryanto, Fanny Chotimah, and Chairun Nisa.

Documentary Film Audience

The role of international funding agencies was also significant in fostering the audience for documentary films at the Jakarta International Film Festival or JIFFest, the first international film festival held by civil society in Indonesia. JIFFest, co-established in 1999 by documentary filmmaker Shanty Harmayn and French film enthusiast Natascha Deviller, screened documentaries in theatrical settings, providing Indonesian film audiences and filmmakers to watch such films.[43] For many years, JIFFest relied on foreign funding as government funding (local and national) and domestic commercial sponsors were barely available, except for a few years in the 2000s.

JIFFest screened international documentary films, obtained from embassies and foreign cultural centers, and less-distributed Indonesian titles, which captivated and intrigued Indonesian audiences with their storytelling and subject matters. The response toward documentary films at JIFFest was overwhelmingly positive, and they even became most most-watched films in 1999 and 2002 outperforming fiction films. In 1999 *Jalan Raya Pos – De Groote Postweg* (Post Boulevard) (dir. Bernie Ijdis) 1996), a Dutch documentary about the famous Indonesian author, Pramoedya Ananta Toer, became the most watched film; in 2002 *War Photographer* (dir. Christian Frei), 2001, outperformed the opening film, the Golden Lion winner at 2001 Venice Film Festival, *Monsoon Wedding* (dir. Mira Nair), 2001).[44] JIFFest 2002 edition also set a new record by screening a total of 38 documentary films.[45] Abduh Aziz, an activist, filmmaker, and program manager at Garin's SET Foundation, said the success of *War Photographer* was a turning point for Indonesian filmmakers, such as himself, to believe that there was already an audience for documentary films in Indonesia.[46] In Aziz's words,

> [t]here had been the passion, there had been growth, but we didn't have any structure. Therefore, we created In-Docs. We started training, by inviting some renowned filmmakers such as Harun Farocki.[47]

The documentaries shown at JIFFest also played a key role in expanding the understanding of documentary aesthetics. According to Aziz, they provide "a space for contemplation beyond voice-over explication, contributing to a collective experience for its public."[48] Since JIFFest introduced these documentaries, artistic quality has become the primary consideration both for audiences and for filmmakers in documentary film production and exhibition. This has complemented and even surpassed the prior perception of documentary film as a mere information tool or propaganda for the general public, which was prevalent during the New Order era.

Conclusion

The experimentation by the Sinema 8 group may not have made a significant impact during the New Order and their films quickly receded into obscurity, but it was crucial in providing a defense of the documentary's artistic value and potential in an authoritarian political context that suppressed exploration of content and form. The role of documentary was also important in opening up space after the fall of the authoritarian regime. With transnational support, documentaries were able to be part of a momentous transition in opening up space from authoritarian politics, taking documentaries beyond the search for national relevance that was advocated for by some filmmakers during the New Order.

The growth of documentary film culture in Indonesia is further supported by foreign funding, and it gets traction from festival screenings. This growth is then pushed by those who know how to use their leverage to secure foreign funding for advancing the role of documentary film in the political transition. Today, more documentary films are seen as more than just a means of instruction for citizen, as they have established their place in the hearts and minds of Indonesian audiences, becoming part of the transition from authoritarian politics.

Notes

1 Srie Atmano, *Katalog Film-film Produksi PFN 1962–1968*. (*PFN Film Catalogue 1962–1968*). (Jakarta: Pusat Film Negara, 1969), 6–30. (My translation).
2 Katinka van Heeren, *Contemporary Indonesian Film: Spirits of Reform and Ghosts from the Past*. (Leiden: KITLV Press), 89.
3 Gotot Prakoso, *Film Pinggiran: Antologi Film Pendek, Film Eksperimental & Film Dokumenter* (Jakarta: Yayasan FFTV IKJ, 1997), 185.

4 Krishna Sen, "Introduction: Re-Forming Media in Indonesia's Transition into Democracy," in *Politics and The Media in Twenty-First Century Indonesia*, ed. Krishna Sen and David Hill (New York: Routledge, 2011), 1.

5 See, for example, Kukuh Yudha Karnanta in an article about influence of Ford Foundation to Indonesian institution work on documentary film: https://www.e-journal.unair.ac.id/LAKON/article/download/1908/10697.

6 Jakarta Art Institute (IKJ) is an art education institution established in 1976 during the presidency of Soeharto, the leader of New Order regime. The institution hosts the first film studies department in the country that trained Indonesian in fiction and documentary filmmaking, besides other art-related subjects, such as fine art, theater, and music. Many of the teachers at this institute were graduated from foreign institutions, including graduates from the Russian State University of Cinematography (VGIK).

7 Prakoso, *Film Pinggiran,* 188.

8 Garin Nugroho and Dyna Herlyna, *Krisis dan Paradoks Film Indonesia (Crisis and Paradox of Indonesian Film)* (Jakarta: Kompas, 2015), 174 (my translation). See also Prakoso, *Film Pinggiran*, 188. David Albert Peransi was once a student at IKJ and he was one of the few film students who wrote about film in its formative years as an art form in Indonesia. Besides at IKJ, Peransi also obtained his film education at New York University, majoring in film studies. Peransi's name nowadays is used by a Jakarta-based documentary and experimental film festival, Arkipel, as their award's name.

9 Prakoso mentions such titles as *Cinta Kasih dan Harapan* (Love and Hope), *Wayang Golek* (Shadow Play), *Wayang Kulit Purwa* (Ancient Shadow Puppet), *Jakarta Kota Pariwisata* (Jakarta the City of Tourism), *Perkembangan dan Pengembangan Seni Budaya di Jakarta* (Progress and Development of Art and Culture in Jakarta), *Paru-paru Hijau* (Green Belts), *Problem Sosial di DKI* (Jakarta's Social Problems), *Tanjung Priok Membenah Diri* (Tanjung Priok Self-Refurbishment), *STM Pembangunan* (Vocational College of Development) and *Transmigration* (Inter-Islands Migration). See Prakoso, *Film Pinggiran*, 188.

10 van Heeren, *Contemporary Indonesian Film*, 43.

11 Ibid.

12 "*Membuka perspektif-perspektif baru (kultural) dan sekaligus memaparkan kenyataan-kenyataan untuk dipelajari dan ditelaah*" (my translation). See D. A. Peransi, "Film Dokumenter di Indonesia (beberapa pokok pikiran) (Documentary Film in Indonesia, Some Initial Thoughts)," in *DA Peransi dan Film (DA Peransi and Film)*, ed. Marseli Sumarno (Jakarta: Lembaga Studi Film, n.t), 43.

13 Ibid.

14 Original text from Peransi: Perhatian masyarakat dan lembaga-lembaga yang mengurusi film lebih tertuju pada film cerita, mungkin karena film cerita lebih glamur [sic], sementara dilupakan bahwa film dokumenter pada hakekatnya adalah apa yang disebut film kultural edukatif. Ibid., 41.

15 Thomas Barker, "Historical Inheritance and Film Nasional in Post-Reformasi Indonesian Cinema," *Asian Cinema* 21, no. 2 (September 2010): 12.

16 See Presidential Decree No. 25, year 1999, about Film Nasional Day (Keputusan Presiden No. 25 tahun 1999). The National Film Day is actually decided based on the first day of the shooting of *Long March*, a 1950s film directed by Usmar Ismail, with Asrul Sani as screenwriter. Both names became famous as the "founding fathers" of Indonesian cinema. Film has been made in Indonesia since 1926 and screened since 1900, but this date was chosen for its connotation with its ethno-nationalistic spirit and resistance against colonialism. See Barker, Ibid, 7–24.

17 Peransi, "Film Dokumenter," 45.

18 Ibid.

19 Ibid.

20 Prakoso, *Film Pinggiran*, 2.

21 Ibid.

22 In Prakoso words: "Film ini adalah sebuah tanggapan terhadap usaha berdialog dengan ekologi bumi dan air. Kemanusiaan mengekspresikan perasaan melalui badannya, bergeliat untuk menjadi satu dengan jagat raya. Seperti petani yang menggarap tanah dan bergumul dengan lumpur. Sebuah proses mem-puisi-kan." See here: Accessed February 13, 2022, http://filmindonesia.or.id/movie/title/sd-m011-79-942771_meta-ekologi.

23 David Hanan, "The Films of Garin Nugroho, Political Documentaries and Essay Films by Garin Nugroho in Late New Order and Post Reformasi Indonesia," *Screening Southeast Asia, Spectator* 24, no. 2 (Fall 2004): 43.

24 Ibid.

25 Ibid.

26 Ishizaka Kenji, "An Interview with Garin Nugroho," *Docbox Yamagata International Film Festival*, accessed December 6, 2018, https://www.yidff.jp/docbox/14/box14-2-1-e.html.

27 Hanan, "The Films of Garin Nugroho," 43.

28 Anonymous, "Perayaan Hari Bumi dan World Cinema Features @kineforum (Celebration of the Earth Day and World Cinema Features @kineforum)," *Kineforum*, April 20, 2009, accessed October 12, 2017, https://kineforum.wordpress.com/2009/04/20/pemutaran-film-dalam-rangka-hari-bumi/.

29 van Hereen, *Contemporary Indonesian Film*, 89.

30 Prakoso, *Film Pinggiran*, 190.

31 Ade Armando, *Televisi Indonesia di Bawah Kapitalisme Global (Indonesian Television Under Global Capitalism)* (Jakarta: Kompas, 2016), 149. (My translation).

32 Thomas Barker, "A Cultural Economy of The Contemporary Indonesian Film Industry," PhD thesis (Singapore: National University of Singapore, 2011), 72.

33 "Saya secara aktif turut menjaga Pemilu 1999 agar tidak mengulangi berbagai kecurangan pemilu saat Soeharto masih berkuasa." Nugroho and Herlyna. *Krisis dan Paradoks*, 250.

34 Ibid.

35 "Sains Estetika dan Teknologi (SET)," ANSA-EAP, accessed October 16, 2017, http://www.ansa-eap.net/networking/geographic-focus/java-conveners-group-indonesia/country-partners/sains-estetika-dan-teknologi-set/. (My translation)

36 Ibid.

37 Nugroho and Herlyna, *Krisis dan Paradoks*, 250.

38 For example, see Hans Antlöv, Derick W. Birkehoff, and Elke Rapp, "Civil Society Capacity Building for Democratic Reform: Experience and Lessons from Indonesia," *Voluntas* 21 (May 2010): 417–39.

39 "About LA Lights Indimovie," LA Lights Indiemovie, accessed October 16, 2017, http://enjoy-indiemovie.blogspot.com/p/about-la-lights-indiemovie.html. (My translation)

40 "*Tentang Kami*" (About Us), Kalyana Shira Foundation, accessed October 18, 2017, http://www.kalyanashirafound.org/index.php?option=com_content&view=section&layout=blog&id=7&Itemid=88&lang=en. (My translation.)

41 Hans Antlöv, Rustam Ibrahim, and Peter van Tuijl, "NGO Governance and Accountability in Indonesia: Challenges in a Newly Democratizing Country," in *NGO Accountability: Politics, Principles and Innovation*, ed. Lisa Jordan and Peter van Tuijl (London: Earthscan, 2006), 150.

42 Antlöv, Birkehoff, and Rapp, "Civil Society Capacity Building," 417–39.

43 Abduh Aziz, Interview, 2016.

44 JIFFest, "Statistics on the 1st to 9th JIFFest," in *An Annex to 9th Jakarta International Film Festival 2007, Official Report, December 7–16, 2007* (Jakarta: JIFFest, 2007).

45 YMMFI, *Narrative Report to Ford Foundation. Grant No.1025-0225* (Jakarta: YMMFI, n.d.).

46 Ibid.

47 Aziz words:"Kita lihat passion-nya ada, pertumbuhannya ada, tapi kita ngga punya struktur. Makanya kita bikin In-Docs. Kita mulai training, ngundang beberapa filmmaker terkenal seperti Harun Farocki." Source: Aziz, Interview.

48 Ibid.

40

FILMING RESISTANCE

A Conversation with Deepa Dhanraj

Fathima Nizaruddin

India has a vibrant tradition of independent documentary film practice that stands apart from market-oriented as well as state-sponsored documentary work. While the Films Division, the state body that has produced over 8,000 films, used to have a firm hold over the documentary landscape in the country, a range of political, social, and technological changes radically transformed this configuration and ushered in the age of a new kind of independent practice in the field of documentary production and circulation (Battaglia 2014). Since at least the 1980s, independent documentary film practice in India has been a site where diverse narratives from various marginalized groups and peoples' movements were articulated. The close links that this practice maintained with a range of people's struggles and movements across the country, including the women's movement, led to a way of working that did not rely on a fee-paying cinema audience or television networks for its survival. An artisanal way of working, as well as the itinerant practices of filmmakers who traveled across the country to show their films in diverse makeshift spaces in a range of communities, is closely tied to the emergence of involved publics around independent documentary practice in India (Kishore 2018).

Within the lineage of these practices, the work of feminist documentary filmmaker Deepa Dhanraj is firmly located in the category of films that work outside the parameters of commercial documentary production that adheres to the demands of specific markets. Born in 1953, Deepa's entry into documentary filmmaking was a result of her involvement with activist movements. Her work of over four decades contains filmic responses to a range of issues such as the violence that a repressive state apparatus waged on the bodies of marginalized groups in the country – especially women – in the name of population control as well as the casteist university structures in India that push Dalit scholars, who are termed lower caste in the hierarchy of the system, to the brink of suicide.

Collaborative practices have always been at the heart of Deepa's work and in 1980 she formed the collective Yugantar along with three colleagues. The films made by the collective were a result of a deep engagement with workers' movements and feminist politics. Several decades after these initial films, Deepa's work, which has been an important part of documentary history in India, continues to display a strong sense of political commitment. Some of the landmark films from Deepa's rich repertoire include *Kya Hua Is Shahar Ko* (What

DOI: 10.4324/9781003266952-51

Has Happened to This City 1986), *Something Like a War* (1991), and *We Have Not Come Here to Die* (2018). In this conversation, Deepa talks about how societal transformations and the women's movement in India contributed to the rise of a group of women documentary filmmakers like herself who brought distinct shifts in existing modes of documentary practice in India.

Fathima: **You have a deep involvement with people's movements and feminist activism; many of your films emerge from this involvement. Can you please speak about the socio-political climate around you in the 1970s and '80s?**

Deepa: In the early '70s I had left college after completing a degree in English literature and journalism.[1] University campuses then were vibrant spaces with students taking part in various political campaigns, both on and off campus. For the most part, left politics dominated – though there were student unions like the ABVP as well that belonged to the right-wing Hindu supremacist organizations[2] and the National Students Union of India that was associated with the Congress party.

To give you a brief history of the context in which the third women's movement arose in the late '70s, we would have to look at the economic and political crisis India was going through in the late '60s. The promises of the freedom movement (about a new and equal society following the struggle against colonialism) had collapsed. Prices were rising, urban unemployment was at a high, food shortages and large-scale rural unrest led to a questioning of the Nehruvian[3] model of planned development, which favored landed interests. In

Figure 40.1   Deepa Dhanraj.

urban India, industrial workers were on strike for higher wages. Peasant and tribal revolts against debt bondage, low wages, unequal land distribution, and caste atrocities broke out in many states, including Bengal, Andhra Pradesh, Kerala, Bihar, and Tamil Nadu.

From the 1960s to the 1970s, there were stirrings within the broad left, including the CPI[4] (which in 1964 had split into two parties, the CPI [M][5] and the CPI), the Socialists (who were themselves divided into different groups), new left formations, those that believed in organized mass action and building mass movements, and those that took to armed struggle within the left movements. These parties had student wings with impressive memberships.

Other political groups, the Gandhians and those who advocated anti-caste politics, also took to public action; these actions were centered around many issues including ensuring and protecting access to forests and the commons. Some groups focused on mobilization against the discriminatory caste system. Intellectuals, writers, and students (many of them women) left formal education to join these movements in large numbers.

Protests against the state were widespread. Thousands of poor and middle-class women in Gujarat – including teachers, doctors, [and] civil servants – stepped into political activity for the first time, agitating against rising food prices, corruption, and profiteering. They succeeded in forcing the government to resign. It seemed as if women were everywhere!

Women who emerged in such large numbers into public life, adivasis (as indigenous peoples are referred to in India), peasants, industrial workers, municipal workers, students, and women from different class and caste backgrounds were speaking up. Very organically, women in all movements began to interrogate their gender roles in family, society, and public life. Reacting to the widespread political unrest in the country, then Prime Minister Indira Gandhi declared a state of emergency on 25 June 1975 that lasted until March 1977.[6] Apart from the political opposition, leaders of mass organizations, trade unions, and student organizations were imprisoned. Press censorship was imposed, elections were postponed, and civil liberties were violated with impunity through the suspension of fundamental rights under the Constitution. Large-scale demolitions took place in Delhi, and thousands of people were evicted. Coercive sterilizations took place. All protests were crushed, hundreds of activists – men and women – were driven to work underground, many got arrested, and many activists were killed; women were assaulted.

Living through the emergency was for many young women of my generation an experience that radicalized us permanently. For the first time, the experience of absolute state power and impunity was crushing. We observed impunity in its everyday manifestations. Encounters in court with political prisoners who were brought in chains for bail hearings was a way to list and verify the names of prisoners for families (once they were picked up no one knew which jail they were in or even if they were alive). There were visits to friends in prison, where one had no influence [over] the medical treatment that was being administered, despite knowing that appropriate treatment was critical. News of encounter killings and disappearances of students had started trickling in, and these could not be dismissed as rumors. The continuous work of making lists of prisoners' names and missing persons and altering them according to information led to the making of a complex underground network.

Many small pamphlets and articles written by people underground had to be typed up from handwritten notes for cyclostyling and distributing. The language and ideas in those pieces made a deep impact as they ranged from pleas by people to locate family members to polemical writings across the political spectrum; this spectrum included Gandhians, Lohiaites, socialists, Trotskyites, and other left groups. With no discrimination against any group, we distributed them all! Through these processes, one was getting a powerful political education.

This experience has marked my work indelibly. As a result, most of my films are framed as an interrogation of state power and impunity, sometimes overtly and sometimes in the overall perspective of the film. Once the emergency was lifted, the experience of the violence and curtailment of human rights sparked newly politicized groups. Some women activists, foregrounding the gender question, formed women's groups within movements, and others left to form independent feminist organizations. Many groups were formed after the vigorous campaigns against rape. Declaring themselves autonomous from political parties and institutional funding, these groups were non-hierarchical in structure and practice. I joined this movement immediately.

Fathima: **How did your involvement with these groups influence your work with Yugantar?**
Deepa: The women's groups began to work on violence against women, both in private and public realms: expanding the notion of violence to include gender discrimination at different stages of women's life cycle, including marital violence and dowry murders. In questioning patriarchy and asymmetries of power within the family as well as challenging how these are played out in the public realm, feminists began to play a major role in making violence against women visible and important to be acted upon. The radical upsurge in political actions by feminists across caste, class, and regional locations included an explosion of street protests shaped and attended by many. A burst of myriad cultural and political activities followed, such as feminist research, publishing, street theater in many cities, poster productions, writing songs, and more.

It was an exciting and energizing time; this was the vibrant and innovative ground from which the Yugantar film collective emerged in 1980. We hoped that the collective's name (Yugantar/Change to a New Era) would point to a radical historical transformation. There were four of us, Abha Bhaiya, Navroze Contractor, Meera Rao, and myself. I had never been to film school. I had previously worked as an assistant to feature film directors. Abha had been a full-time activist, Navroze Contractor was the only one who had a film education; he was trained at the Film (and Television) Institute of India. Our audacity in undertaking this experiment was fueled largely by the euphoria of being part of feminist politics at the time! We were conscious that many working-class women's participation and leadership in political struggles were often invisible and not being documented. Academic texts and articles written by feminists were available, but at the time it was impossible to see or hear rural or urban working-class women speak on film. Participating in meetings where vibrant combative discussions took place was exhilarating. The physical presence of women, the vitality of their voices and richness of their expressions we felt was crucial to animate the record of their movements.

Fathima: **Can you please expand [on] the collaborative dimension of the work that was produced through Yugantar?**

Deepa: For example, the film on the Nipani Tobacco Workers Union[7] and the spontaneous manner in which the women took to the streets; this was taken ahead by the socialists, who had a presence in parts of Maharashtra. The women – many of whom were *devadasis*[8] – were not entirely unaware of their social situation. There had been a measure of organizing around the issue of sexual servitude and to that extent there was unrest among this class of women. The conditions of labor and the labor militancy that happened in its wake have to be viewed in this context. They addressed not only labor concerns, but also social issues to do with caste and culture.

Molkarin (Maid Servant 1981), the film on the Pune domestic workers union was one of the first of its kind. It was organized by one of the new left formations of this time – Lal Nishan – which was active in Maharashtra. They had an openness to gender and attracted women organizers. This was unusual, organizing domestic workers was difficult and fraught since one had to address the precarity of their lives as well as the injustice that shaped it.

As with the film around Nipani tobacco workers, at Pune also women took matters into their own hands. They came to address not just labor concerns, but also the broader concerns around [the] gendered realities of their lives. The other two Yungantar films were on domestic violence and on the ecological Chipko movement, led by rural women to protect trees and the environment in the foothills of the Himalayas.

Each film produced by the Yugantar collective was developed through collaborative processes with the groups we were filming: of domestic workers in Pune for *Molkarin*

Figure 40.2   An image from the film *Molkarin* (1981)

(Maid Servant 1981),[9] female factory workers in Nipani for *Tambakoo Chaakila Oob Ali* (Tobacco Embers 1982), with members of Stree Shakhti Sanghatana (SSS) in Hyderabad for *Idhi Katha Matramena* (Is This Just a Story? 1983)[10] on marital violence, and lastly with members of the Chipko Andolan for *Sudesha* (1983).[11]

Fathima: **You have worked with the fiction form and reconstruction in the Yugantar films. Will you use these forms to look at any contemporary issue in the future?**

Deepa: We had to craft a practice each time, to enable the women we filmed with to indicate how they wanted to be represented, and how they wanted their stories to be told. These discussions were long and they would identify the most crucial milestones in the history of their movements. Recreating a strike or an incident that they felt was pivotal led us to do fictional reconstructions! And then we tried to shoot it in *vérité* style! On the whole we were trying to create a consciously feminist practice of collective research, filmmaking, and distribution in an organic loop. It was an exciting experiment.

I don't have a formal "style" that identifies my films. Each film is crafted based on the strength, possibilities, and limitations of the material. Often, since I am filming "live" situations, one cannot control the aesthetics of what one is covering, either. The form emerges from there. I work intuitively and analytically in a weird dance. My main motivation is to move the viewers cerebrally and emotionally to go against the grain of existing orthodoxies. And each film, of course, rises out of a critical understanding of the social and political historical moment; it is a response to that.

I am not particularly attached [to] or invested in any particular form and am quite reckless in the risks that I take. I am not averse to mixing up different formal styles if the material demands it. Formally my work has been in the *vérité*, observational mode – following events as they unfold, this informs the final narrative structure. I have experimented with dramatic reconstruction, no narration as well as narration, testimonies, and fly on the wall *vérité* techniques. I have made observational films, essay films, investigative films, and hybrids, too! Apart from documentaries, I have also worked using the documentary method in creating video training materials for government primary school teachers, first-generation learners who are mainly dalit, adivasi, and Muslim, as well as elected Panchayat Raj[12] representatives. This work has been more pedagogic in intention.

Fathima: **What kind of links have you had with other Asian filmmakers? Do you think that independent Indian documentary filmmaking community needs to have closer ties with the broader Asian filmmaking community? What will be some of the ways to form such ties?**

Deepa: I haven't had opportunities to interact with filmmakers from many parts of Asia. I would be very keen to. Having said that, however, through HIMAL South Asia,[13] one has a chance to see work from the Indian subcontinent. I am always eager to meet filmmakers from the region and to watch their work. Often, I feel we haven't recovered from the brutal experience of partition and its aftermath and postcolonial traumas. The Tamil-Sinhala story in Sri Lanka is another case in point. I look forward to the day when we can work together in some ways.

Fathima: **How would you look at your film practice in relation to the social issues which have, in a way, shaped the very course of this practice?**

Deepa: I have been making short and feature-length documentaries since 1980. Over the years I have returned, in a continuous engagement, to questions of caste, sectarian violence, women's status, political participation, health, and law – both formal and customary. Law as a site of inquiry has been an enduring theme, whether it is films that interrogate customary law and the strategies that tribal and Muslim women use to counter patriarchal verdicts, or formal law, examining how a human rights legal practice began invoking the protections of the Constitution against the suppression of dissent, custodial violence, and state impunity. Most crucially, the focus was on how one could insist on governments taking responsibility for safeguarding the constitutional right to life and liberty of all its citizens. The caste question and the myriad forms of discriminations that Dalits experience and the rise of Dalit assertion is another theme that I try to explore in many films.

Fathima: Among your work, the film *We Have Not Come Here to Die* (2018) is an extremely powerful film on the question of caste. Can you please describe the process behind the making of this film? It is a film that has the capacity to leave a deep emotional impact on the viewer. This film, which was made in 2018, was filmed at a time when a large number of people have access to mobile cameras. But the viewpoint of your film stands apart, it often comments on the other cameras that are present at the scene. Amid so many cameras, how difficult was it to forge a different filmic space?[14]

Deepa: On 18 January 2016 one day after Rohith Vemula hanged himself in a friend's hostel room in Hyderabad Central University, Hyderabad, I read the handwritten letter he had left behind. A close friend of his who entered the room with the police photographed the letter at once with the apprehension that the police could destroy it later to create a counter-narrative of [his] death. He described to me how neatly Rohith had left those pages on the desk. He proceeded to upload the letter online and, almost instantaneously, it was everywhere. The student movement against his institutional murder, which [was] comprised of students from all castes, was as much a response to the letter as it was to the circumstances leading up to his death. The outpouring of online support across castes and generations seemed to acknowledge that it was a unique historic moment. His words managed to puncture and make visible the societal discrimination that marks caste relations as well as the continual violence that Dalits face.

For me, reading those three pages had a visceral impact. Not just for the lines "My birth is my fatal accident" which is the brutal burden that Dalits must bear, but for the clarity of suggesting a way to reimagine a life that could move beyond being marked by that identity into a life of infinite possibility, "to be treated as a mind. As a glorious thing made up of stardust. In every field, in studies, in streets, in politics, and in dying and living." Rohith physically was no more, but I felt his letter carried his pain, his indomitable courage, and his dream of a future not just for himself but for all of us. I felt compelled to go to the Hyderabad University Campus, we began filming and covered the student movement that began both in Hyderabad and nationally for 18 months.

It was a very difficult shoot as public events attracted many news cameras. Students were shooting on their phones, citizen journalists and members of other political groups were shooting, and hours later the footage was uploaded onto social media and TV news channels. It was a movement that was covered extensively for months. Often, I would wonder if viewers wouldn't feel a sense of *déjà vu* when watching our film some months down the line as [many people] were very often filming physically from the same spaces. But those were not the real challenges. I think structuring the film was very difficult. As we were filming as well as participating as much as we could in the protests, I felt the film should somehow represent the multitude of images, to convey the role of images in creating alternative narratives of the movement to (counter) the mainstream casteist reportage. This is the first film of ours which has almost 40% of material filmed by others [including platforms such as] Dalit Camera, students, and other documentary filmmakers; we have credited [these contributions].

The other challenge was the representation of Dalit subjects; for me it was not about speaking for or speaking about but of speaking with. Is it possible to do so by the filmmaker and the subjects and situations one is filming being "present" in a cinematic conversation (can be visual and metaphorical not only verbal!).

Fathima: **How has your understanding of caste informed your work?**
Deepa: My first opportunity to understand the caste question and to then deal with its cinematic representation was in Karnataka in 1993 when legislation was enacted to ensure 33% reservation for women in all three tiers of self-governance. For the first time, 36,000 women entered the public domain at the Gram Panchayat (village) level alone. Thirty-three percent of these women were from Dalit (Scheduled Caste) and adivasi/indigenous (Scheduled Tribe) communities. We were given the task of creating materials that could give rise to discussions in training programs for women Panchayati Raj members. Apart from the formal "curriculum" of learning the ropes of Panchayati Raj functioning, we were keen to enable conversations on the shift in power relations that had resulted from reservation.

We traveled to 22 districts filming intense meetings of women – both Dalit and dominant castes – on their new role as well as the challenges of being permitted to function. They spoke of the hostile attitudes and discrimination that they faced from dominant caste men, panchayat members, and officials. The government trainers, after watching the videos and listening to the testimonies of discrimination and resistance, flatly refused to touch the caste question, as they felt it would be too hot to handle in a mixed caste session. This led to displacing this material onto small plays which were then filmed and inserted into the documentary footage. I was fortunate enough to work with Dalit poet-writer Kotiganahalli Ramaiah as the writer and C. Basavalingaiah as the director, and theater artists from *Rangayana*. Though this video training material had a pedagogic intention, the process of crafting the documentary sections and observing the writing and direction of the plays was, for me personally, a very rich experience of understanding the complexities of the caste and gender question.

A similar exercise followed with government primary school teachers in 1998 when we had to interrogate dropout rates of Dalit and tribal children. What were the factors – both structural as well as attitudinal – that led these children to feel excluded and fearful in the classroom? Physical access did not mean substantive access. Teachers often used practices in the classroom that were blatantly discriminatory against Dalit, tribal, and Muslim children. In 2004/2005, while creating video lessons for government primary school children on historiography and science, working continuously over a period of two months with children from [a] government school in Belvanakki, a village near Gadag, we had to find a way to start a conversation with children about caste in a mixed-caste classroom. It was challenging to devise a pedagogy that could create a fearless classroom where children could speak freely. In every instance, what grew and stayed for me was a very strong commitment to an anti-caste political position.

Fathima: India is currently witnessing an unprecedented surge in Hindu majoritarianism. As a documentary filmmaker, how has this affected your work? How would you compare the times when you made *What Has Happened to This City?* (1986),[15] with the present socio-political climate? What similarities and differences do you see?

Deepa: Interrogating Hindu majoritarianism is a subject I have returned to in different films over 30 years. It appears in different aspects either directly or in the context in which the narratives play out. The film *Kya Hua Is Shahar Ko* (What Has Happened to This City? 1986) in the '80s was an autopsy of an engineered sectarian riot between Hindus and Muslims for political gain. At the time it was still early days, in terms of mobilizing Hindus around the majoritarian agenda. Religious processions around the Hindu god Ganesh were taking on a public militant tone, a slogan of the day was "Hindu Hindu Bhai Bhai" (Hindus are brothers); the slogan was tellingly direct in acknowledging that the caste divide had to be overcome to create a Hindu brotherhood. Another film of mine, *The Advocate* (2007), a political biography of one of the founders of the civil liberties movement in India, K.G. Kannabiran, also looks at raising concerns about majoritarianism. He took up a case of the custodial gang rape of a Muslim woman, Rameeza Bee. When her husband protested, he was beaten to death by the police. Riots against the police broke out in the city. However, both her poverty and her Muslim identity made it easy in court for the police to bring in fake witnesses to declare that she was a prostitute, and so sexual assault could have been her soliciting for custom. In a communal atmosphere, her identity was deemed fit for such treatment.

In *Invoking Justice* (2011), a film about the Tamil Nadu Muslim Women's Jamaat and their successful women's court that delivers verdicts on family law cases, my intention was to showcase their brilliant agency in negotiating between customary and formal law and the criminal justice system. In discussions with members of the Jamaat prior to filming, they were adamant that two issues, triple *talaq*[16] and the hijab, that were led nationally by Hindutva forces to "rescue" Muslim women, were *not* to be included in the film.

In an atmosphere where Muslim women are stigmatized as backward and in the grip of Islamic fundamentalist beliefs and practices, lacking all agency and critical thinking, during post-screenings within mixed community audiences, there is always shock and an incredulous appreciation at having their assumptions overturned.

In *We Have Not Come Here to Die* (2018), the accusations about Rohith Vemula and his friends being anti-national by the president of the ABVP (the right-wing students organization), in Hyderabad Central University are directly linked to his suspension and institutional murder. This was because [the] Ambedkar Students Association, the student group Rohith Vemula belonged to, was vehemently opposed to majoritarian Hindutva politics. Rohith wrote regularly on Facebook attacking the ABVP and the RSS. After his death, cases were filed against the vice chancellor as well as a central minister who had brought pressure on the university administration to take action against Rohith and his friends for their "anti-national" activities on campus. The cases were filed under the SC/ST Atrocities Act, which is a special law that deals with offenses committed against Scheduled castes and Tribes.

By 2018 the BJP (Bharatiya Janata Party), which is closely linked to the RSS both ideologically and organizationally, had been in power for four years. The efforts by Union ministers of the BJP to protect one minister to enable him to escape the provisions of the SC/ST Atrocities Act were incredible. All state and central government agencies were involved at the highest levels to suppress the case by declaring that Rohith was not a Dalit and that no one was responsible for his death.

Fathima: **Before we end, can you please talk about what you are working on currently?**
Deepa: During the period from 2016 to 2018, when I was filming the student movement after Rohith Vemula's death, I found many responses to his suicide note. For Dalit students in campus after campus across the country, Rohith was the critical organic intellectual and his letter had turned into a primal text, both as a *cri de coeur* and as a liberatory manifesto to unlock tongues, to enter into an exciting new world of Dalit assertion. Social media posts by Dalit students were exploding, they wrote moving personal letters to Rohith: some, grateful for their "release from the dark," wrote confessional testimonies, and others deeply grieving texts.

Many artistic responses from established artists, writers, poets, music groups, and playwrights followed, either they would respond conceptually to the questions raised by the letter or inscribe his words into their artwork, songs, and poetry. Both responses, artistic as well as the student's letters, felt like deferred personal conversations that they were having with Rohith.

Six years later I would like to start a conversation on caste with selected writers, poets, and musicians who engaged seriously with his letter. What drew them to it? Why was the engagement so personal? Did anything shift in their understanding of caste?

It will be a challenging film to make, but I am looking forward with nervous excitement as to what we will encounter on this journey.

Conclusion

Deepa Dhanraj's trajectory of documentary practice provides an extremely important vantage point from which to make sense of some of the major socio-political transformations that have occurred in India since the 1980s. Her work is informed by a collaborative logic, and it is possible to make an argument that this logic guides her choice of filmic form in different films. The deep embeddedness of her work in feminist politics has been extremely influential, and it has markedly influenced the course of feminist documentary practice in India. As Deepa mentions in this interview, she began her work as a filmmaker in the atmosphere of charged political activism that followed the Emergency period in India when democratic rights were suspended. Today, when India is witnessing the emergence of a majoritarian state (Chatterji, Hansen, and Jaffrelot 2019), with the consolidation of Hindu majoritarianism, Deepa's work continues to stand with the marginalized by being part of a language of resistance that refuses to accept the prevailing hegemonies.

Notes

1 Deepa did her education in Madras University (English literature) and Osmania University (journalism).
2 ABVP (Akhil Bharatiya Vidyarthi Parishad) is part of the group of Hindu majoritarian right-wing organizations in India that are commonly referred to as the Sangh Parivar or Sangh family; the central organization within this family is the RSS (Rashtriya Swayamsevak Sangh).
3 Nehru was the first prime minister of independent India. For a detailed account of the policies in the Nehruvian period, see (Menon 2021).
4 CPI: Communist Party of India.
5 CPI (M): Communist Party of India (Marxist).
6 During this period, civil liberties were suspended.
7 The film *Tambaku Chaakila Oob Ali* (Tobacco Embers, 1982) centers on the struggles of women tobacco factory workers at Nipani in the state of Karnataka, India.
8 For a detailed account of the devadasi system which resulted in sexual exploitation of women, see (Torri 2013).
9 *Molkarin* (Maid Servant, 1981) focuses on the life and struggles of domestic workers in Pune.
10 *Idhi Katha Matramena* (Is This Just a Story? 1983) is a fiction film that depicts the plight of women within oppressive family structures.
11 *Sudesha* (1983) looks at Sudesha, a villager who was part of the ecological conservation movement called Chipko movement in the Himalayan region which aimed to conserve forests and trees.
12 Elected representatives at the village level.
13 Here the reference is to Film South Asia (Rana 2022).
14 The death of Rohit Vemula, a promising young student leader from the Dalit community, can be located as an institutional murder in the context of casteist academic and university structures in India that privilege upper caste hegemony, comparable to the whiteness of academia in other parts of the world. It led to a massive student led movement.
15 *Kya Hua Is Shahar Ko* (What Has Happened to This City? 1986) is a landmark film that examines the violent configurations of politics around Hindu-Muslim conflict by focusing on the Hindu-Muslim riots that took place in 1984 in the city of Hyderabad in India.
16 Triple talaq refers to the practice of instantly divorcing a woman within the Muslim community. For details see (Chakrabarti et al. 2022).

References

Battaglia, G. 2014. "The Video Turn: Documentary Film Practices in 1980s India." *Visual Anthropology* 27 (1–2): 72–90. https://doi.org/10.1080/08949468.2014.852461.
Chakrabarti, A., K. C. M. Rahman, and S. Ghosh. 2022. "Of Marriage, Divorce and Criminalisation: Reflections on the Triple Talaq Judgement in India." *Journal of Legal Anthropology* 6 (1): 24–48. https://doi.org/10.3167/jla.2022.060103.
Chatterji, A. P., T. B. Hansen, and C. Jaffrelot. 2019. "Introduction." In *Majoritarian State: How Hindu Nationalism is Changing India*, edited by A. P. Chatterji, T. B. Hansen, and C. Jaffrelot. Oxford: Oxford University Press.
Kishore, S. 2018. *Indian Documentary Film and Filmmakers: Independence in Practice.* Edinburgh: Edinburgh University Press.
Menon, N. 2021. "Developing Histories of Indian Development." *History Compass* 19 (10): e12689. https://doi.org/10.1111/hic3.12689.
Rana, P. S. 2022. "Twenty-Five Years of Popularising the Documentary Filmmaking Genre." https://kathmandupost.com/art-culture/2022/04/21/twenty-five-years-of-popularising-the-documentary-filmmaking-genre.
Torri, M. 2013. "Abuse of Lower Castes in South India: The Institution of Devadasi." *Journal of International Women's Studies* 11 (2): 31–48.

Films Cited

Dhanraj, D. (Director). 1981. *Molkarin* (Maid Servant*)*.

———. 1982. *Tambaku Chaakila Oob Ali* (Tobacco Embers).

———. 1983. *Idhi Katha Matramena* (Is This Just a Story?*)*.

———. 1983. *Sudesha*.

———. 1986. *Kya Hua Is Shaher Ko* (What Happened to This City).

———. 1991. *Something Like a War*.

———. 2007. *The Advocate*.

———. 2011. *Invoking Justice*.

———. 2018. *We Have Not Come Here to Die*.

SECTION VI

Archives, Festivals, and Film Pedagogy

INTRODUCTION

Sangjoon Lee

Routledge Companion to Asian Cinemas' final section, "Archives, Festivals, and Film Pedagogy," introduces new perspectives on film festivals and film archives studies in Asia. This section is designed both to respond to the popular interest in film festivals and film archives and to meet the new demand for high-quality academic publications on the subject. By bringing a wide range of academic specialists together in a section with six chapters, this section aims to situate current scholarship on the subjects within the ongoing theoretical debates in contemporary global film studies.

Much has been written about film festivals and film archives over the past two decades. Regarding film festivals, Marijke de Valck's *Film Festivals: From European Geopolitics to Global Cinephilia* was published in 2007. It was one of the first book-length studies of its kind, excluding festival program booklets and collections of short essays by journalists, festival programmers, and film critics. And, following the publication of de Valck's seminal work, the first edition of the *Film Festival Yearbook*, initiated by Dina Iordanova, was released in 2009. Cindy Wong's *Film Festivals: Culture, People, and Power on the Global Screen* appeared in 2011. Since then, film festival studies have flourished in the form of monographs, edited volumes, and special issues on a range of topics, including histories, cities, politics, industries, themes, programming, and reception. Dozens of monographs, anthologies, and special issues and hundreds of articles address a wide range of topics in film festival studies from various methodological perspectives.

Although the extensive body of literature in the field of film festival studies has provided significant insights into the subject, it is important to recognize its limitations. First, most of the publications have stated that the annual international film festival is a European phenomenon, and that the history of the international film festival prior to the 1970s can be condensed into the story of several prestigious European film festivals, including Venice, Cannes, Edinburgh, Rotterdam, and Berlin. De Valck (2007) and Elsaesser (2005) both emphasize the European specificities of the film festival by defining it as a European institution, and they often claim that the phenomenon later spread throughout the world, as we are now witnessing the burgeoning of new film festivals in formerly peripheral nations. In other words, the West set the standard, or form, and then disseminated it to other parts of the world. Elsaesser brings up Busan International Film Festival, one of the most important film festivals in Asia,

DOI: 10.4324/9781003266952-53

as a clear example of how the "phenomenon" was disseminated to Asia during the 1990s. Scholars of film festivals generally have little knowledge that Asia had its own film festivals – not one but many – long before the 1990s film festival boom. And, contrary to common belief, these festivals thrived until the late 1980s. Among those bringing back forgotten histories are Lee (2012, 2020), Baskett (2014), Poon (2019), Djagalov (2020), Razlogova (2021), Govil (2022), and Salazkina (2023), who have written about the film festivals in East, South, Southeast, and Central Asia that flourished during the height of the cultural Cold War.

Second, because the scholarship generally focuses on European festivals, until recently less emphasis was placed on the roles of non-Western festivals, and Asian narratives and perspectives consequently remain under-studied and marginalized in film festival scholarship. In recent years, Iordanova and Cheung (2011), Wong (2011), Ahn (2012), and Berry and Robinson (2017) have opened the door to the study of film festivals in contemporary Asia from Asian perspectives. Since these foundational studies were published, the field of Asian film festival studies has grown rapidly. Today it continues to shed light on the lesser-known histories of festivals in Asia.

As a contribution to this field, the first four chapters, written by Anne Ciecko, Subasri Krishnan, Beth Tsai, and Roger Garcia and Thong Kay Wee, explore the histories, politics, and institutional networks of film festivals in Asia and beyond. The chapters suggest new avenues for researchers of film festivals outside the West by discussing the histories of film festivals in Asia, a lesser-known documentary film festival in India, a women's film festival in Taiwan, and the early history of Hong Kong International Film Festival and the future of film festivals in Asia. In her illuminating first chapter, Ciecko offers a descriptive and dialogic overview of conceptualizations of festivals in relation to culture and discourses on the emergence of international film festivals. The chapter addresses the ways festivals and related awards have reflected legacies of colonialism and geopolitical negotiations and reifications of film art, auteurism, and canon formation – underscoring the problematics of "discovery." Informed by reflective observations gleaned from Asian cinema scholarship and festival experiences, the chapter concludes with examples from the contemporary global film landscape: breakthroughs, transformations, diversifications, mediations, branding and commodification, acts of resistance, interventions, and ongoing globalization.

This first chapter is followed by two chapters on distinctive and rarely studied film festivals. First, Subasri Krishnan delves into the Urban Lens Documentary Film Festival in Bengaluru. The Urban Lens festival was established in 2013 so that film academics, practitioners and audiences could co-create a new language to discuss viewing practices for films, especially from countries in South Asia and the Global South. The festival showcases primarily non-fiction films that engage with the real and imagined idea of the city. These films come from different storytelling traditions and formal practices, including ethnographic accounts of the city, personal essay films, and animated films. All of the films that are part of the Urban Lens interrogate facets of what the urban produces – from the granularity of everyday life to a macro-level picture of what it means to inhabit a city. Next, Beth Tsai discusses Taiwan's Women Make Waves International Film Festival, a gender-specific initiative that has been showcasing independent world cinema since its inception in 1993. Although the festival is Taiwan's only festival dedicated to moving images created by women filmmakers – and the largest such festival in Asia – academic scholarship and film festival reports covering this event in the Anglophone world remain limited and sparse. By delineating the history of Women Make Waves and its relationship to feminist movements in Taiwan, Tsai demonstrates that this film festival is more than an identity-based practice;

it also functions as a "subaltern festival" to disrupt patriarchy, while using feminist tactics and controversy as market branding to challenge the patriarchal beliefs and structures that are so deeply ingrained in Taiwanese society.

The fourth chapter in the section is a dialogue between Roger Garcia, a veteran film festival curator and executive, and Thong Kay Wee, the programming director of the Singapore International Film Festival. Most renowned for his status as co-founder and former executive director of the Hong Kong International Film Festival (HKIFF), Garcia has established himself as a well-respected veteran of the film industry across the world and continues to enjoy a multifaceted career that has spanned more than four decades. Many credit him as being one of the pioneers in drawing attention to the framing of Asian cinema, and his time at HKIFF inspired many newer festivals and film organizations in Asia to develop a similar regional focus. Throughout the dialogue with Thong, Garcia recalls the early days of HKIFF in the 1970s and 1980s and reflects on how the festival in Asia has evolved in the face of the pandemic, streaming services, and other challenges of today's world.

The last two chapters in this section reflect recent trends in film archive studies in Asia – their histories, strategies, agendas, and contributions to the field of Asian cinema studies. In recent years, many Asian governments have turned their attention to cultural heritage, including cinema, and consequently academic research has proliferated, particularly in film archives, university libraries, and national archives. Writing histories of national cinemas, especially Asian cinemas, was until recently almost impossible for non-native speakers, since few films had circulated in the West and most of the sources were almost entirely written in local languages. Even if a researcher was lucky enough to acquire the relevant statistics, they were not always reliable. However, things have changed. Film archives in Hong Kong and South Korea have published an impressive number of English-language books, anthologies, and catalogues that give non-Cantonese and Korean-speaking film historians access to their film history. The Korean Film Archive has also been putting energy into making the materials accessible by releasing DVDs of restored old films and running a YouTube channel for classic films with English subtitles. As Lisabona Rahman and Sanchai Chotirosseranee and Atit Pongpanit discuss in their chapters, film archives in Thai, Indonesia, and Singapore have been actively restoring classics and rediscovering overlooked or forgotten histories of Southeast Asian cinemas. Thanks to the accessibility of the archives, new historical studies have emerged.

Lisabona Rahman tells the story of the restoration of two Indonesian classics of the 1950s, Usmar Ismail's *Lewat Djam Malam* (After the Curfew, 1954) and Tan Sing Hwat's *Aladin* (1953). This chapter shows that restoration technology can facilitate listening to multiple voices from the past. The different circumstances and conditions of each project also show that technology should be used with strategies that ensure the diversity of perspectives. *Lewat Djam Malam* restoration is a complex transnational organization involving support from Singapore and the US, with a technical process that took place in a specialized laboratory in Bologna, Italy. Meanwhile, *Aladin*'s restoration took place on a much smaller scale, involving Indonesian institutions and using locally available means. In their last chapter in the section, Sanchai Chotirosseranee of the Thai Film Archive, together with the film scholar Atit Pongpanit, reexamines Thai queer cinematic history by exploring every Thai film possible either with or without a non-heteronormative focus, together with the accompanying filmic materials (such as film posters, screenplays, film magazines, or booklets) preserved in the Thai Film Archive (a public organization), especially those before 1985. This last chapter in the section offers the first synthesized archival database of the history of early Thai queer cinema.

Bibliography

Ahn, SooJeong. 2012. *The Pusan International Film Festival, South Korean Cinema and Globalization*. Hong Kong: Hong Kong University Press.

Baskett, Michael. 2014. "Japan's Film Festival Diplomacy in Cold War Asia." *The Velvet Light Trap* 73 (1): 4–18.

Berry, Chris, and Luke Robinson, eds. 2017. *Chinese Film Festivals: Sites of Translation*. London: Palgrave Macmillan.

De Valck, Marijke. 2007. *Film Festivals: From European Geopolitics to Global Cinephilia*. Amsterdam: Amsterdam University Press.

Djagalov, Rossen. 2020. *From Internationalism to Postcolonialism: Literature and Cinema between the Second and Third Worlds*. Montreal, Quebec/Kingston, Ontario: McGill-Queen's University Press.

Elsaesser, Thomas. 2005. "Film Festival Networks: The New Topographies of Cinema in Europe." In *European Cinema: Face to Face with Hollywood*. Amsterdam: Amsterdam University Press.

Govil, Nitin. 2022. "In and Out of Alignment: Cold War Sentiment and Hollywood–Bombay Film Diplomacy in the 1950s." In *A Companion to Indian Cinema*, edited by Neepa Majumdar and Ranjani Mazumdar. Hoboken, NJ: Wiley Blackwell.

Iordanova, Dina, and Ruby Cheung, eds. 2011. *Film Festival Yearbook 3: Film Festivals and East Asia*. St. Andrews: St Andrews Film Studies.

Lee, Sangjoon. 2012. "The Emergence of the Asian Film Festival: Cold War Asia and Japan's Reentrance to the Regional Film Industry in the 1950s." In *The Oxford Handbook of Japanese Cinema*, edited by Daisuke Miyao. Oxford: Oxford University Press.

———. 2020. *Cinema and the Cultural Cold War: US Diplomacy and the Origins of the Asian Cinema Network*. Ithaca, NY: Cornell University Press.

Poon, Ka-yan Erica. 2019. "Southeast Asian Film Festival: The Site of the Cold War Cultural Struggle." *Journal of Chinese Cinemas* 13 (1): 76–92.

Razlogova, Elena. 2021. "Cinema in the Spirit of Bandung: The Afro-Asian Film Festival Circuit, 1957–1964." In *The Cultural Cold War and the Global South*, edited by Kerry Bystrom, Monica Popescu, and Katherine Zien. New York: Routledge.

Salazkina, Masha. 2023. *World Socialist Cinema: Alliances, Affinities, and Solidarities in the Global Cold War*. Berkeley: University of California Press.

Wong, Hing-Yuk Cindy. 2011. *Film Festivals: Culture, People, and Power on the Global Screen*. New Brunswick, NJ: Rutgers University Press.

41

FESTIVALIZATIONS AND CULTURAL CONSTRUCTIONS OF "ASIAN CINEMA"

Anne Ciecko

I begin with a brief tribute to the film critic, scholar, and festival programmer, Sato Tadao (1930–2022), who recently passed away. Among his many accomplishments, he trained generations of filmmakers at the Japanese Institute of the Moving Image and served as director (1991–2006) at the "Focus on Asia" Fukuoka International Film Festival. In the latter context, I met him in 2005 during the penultimate (15th) installment of the festival under his direction and was deeply impressed by the sensitive and inclusive curation of the festival, embracing, for example, the first Syrian feature film made by a woman, Waha Al-Raheb – *Ruaa Halima* (also known as *Dreamy Visions* 2003). The programming included 24 other noteworthy films that mainly flew under the A-festival radar. During the festival in Fukuoka, I saw ample evidence of Tadao Sato's efforts in introducing Japanese and international audiences to cinema from throughout the Asian continent (including West and Central Asia), as well as helping to develop the city of Fukuoka into a major Asian gateway and cinema hub (Corkill 2011). He is not as well known in the West as he deserves to be, as only two of his many books have been translated into English, most notably *Currents in Japanese Cinema* (Sato 1987). His work, as noted in a heartfelt homage by film scholar Aaron Gerow (2022), has profoundly enriched Japanese cinema studies. For me, his critical efforts and festival programming increased my own exposure to diverse Asian cinema, and his expansive curatorial vision continues to inspire.

In this chapter, I explore the concept and category of Asian cinema in film festival contexts. I dialogically address and problematize some of the ways hegemonic models of film festivals have selectively launched Asian cinema into the global auteurist pantheon and the international image market. I discuss the development of some festivals and initiatives focus on Asian cinema and recognize diverse Asian films and makers worldwide.

Cultural Encounters and Other Festival Negotiations

Festivals can be variously viewed as sites of cultural encounter (Duffy and Mair 2018), cultural legitimization (de Valck 2016), cultural translation (Berry and Robinson 2017), and cultural consolidation and synergistic identity-building (Ahn 2009, 2012). In showcasing filmmaking from less visible Asian countries in the international film culture

DOI: 10.4324/9781003266952-54

landscape. "Focus on Asia" Fukuoka International Film Festival was a pioneer in making, for example, Mongolian cinema more globally visible. While I have viewed Asian films at many festivals worldwide, my first encounter with a Mongolian film at a festival was at Fukuoka in 2005, with a premiere screening of a striking video-film epic, *Uuliin Tumur* (Tumur of Mountain, 2005), directed by Osor Bat-Ulzii, whose previous work, *Words from the Heart*, had also premiered in Fukuoka two years before. In the preceding decade, the Mongolian films curated for the Third "Focus on Asia" Fukuoka International Film Festival in 1993 in a landmark program would be subsequently shown at other festivals, including a Mongolia-focused Forum program at Berlinale the following year.[1] Mongolia's oldest and largest film festival, Ulaanbaatar International Film Festival, was later established (in 2013) to build an infrastructure for sustainable film culture by exposing local filmmakers and audiences to films that won recognition at high-profile European and North American film festivals, supporting film education, and developing co-production opportunities.[2]

As I have asserted elsewhere, the largest continent in the world and its cinematic productions are extraordinarily heterogeneous, although they have been narrowly and relationally defined through geopolitics, especially the perspective of and proximity to Europe (Ciecko 2006, 4). In my most recent work on this topic, I have adopted the concept of "other Asias" to consider the role for example of interstitial and exilic cinema, such as that of Armenia and its film cultural institutions, such as the Golden Apricot Film Festival in Yerevan (Ciecko 2018), an often-overlooked and peripheral film festival positioned between Europe and Asia, that emerged in 2004 in the decade after Armenian independence and the disaggregation of the Soviet Socialist Republics.

As Lindiwe Dovey (2015) states in her book, *Curating Africa in the Age of Film Festivals*, the origins of film festivals can be found "within a two-millennia history of practices of collecting, curating, and displaying objects in Europe" (29); proto film festivals are entwined with colonialism. A critical historiographic contention among film festival scholars is that the concept and institutionalization of film festivals can be viewed as a European phenomenon first that, while retaining hegemonic centrality in the European festival nexus, has expanded and somewhat shifted with the proliferation of film events and cinephilia worldwide (De Valck 2007; Wong 2011, 7; Iordanova 2011, 1, as cited in Stringer 2016, 35–36). Established in 1932, the Venice International Film Festival as the reputed oldest film festival in the world is connected with fascism and the assertion of national power through the festivalization of culture. Film festival operations have overtly or implicitly demonstrated the workings of geopolitics and ideology. As film festival scholar Cindy Hing-Yuk Wong notes, "All film festivals are shaped by and comment upon their local environment, cultural, political, financial, and bureaucratic" (221). Historically, international film festivals in Europe expanded and consolidated their power and influence after World War II (Wong, 11) and, influenced by auteur theory and related critical trends, celebrated film directors and unveiled new film movements and related discoveries (Ostrowska 2016, 20). Festivals, such as Cannes, Locarno, and Berlin, with first official installments soon after World War II, were linked also with cultural revitalization and urban renewal (Ahn 2012, 6–7; Dovey 2015, 33). The Berlin International Film Festival in particular, inaugurated in the divided city and nation in 1951, was entrenched in Cold War conceptualizations of "East" and "West" and is especially integral in the evolution of the spatial imagination of the "international festival circuit" (de Valck 2007, 45–83).

Festival Prestige and the Rise of Cinematic Authorship and Canonization

International film festivals, particularly those in Europe, have historically promulgated reifications of cinematic art and film authorship and auteurism. In 1951, Kurosawa Akira *Rashomon* became the first Asian film to win the top award, the Golden Lion, at the 12th installment of the Venice film festival, attracting worldwide attention. Across the top three European fests recognized as "competitive" by the International Federation of Film Producers Association (FIAPF) – Venice, Cannes, and Berlin – Japan is the Asian nation most recognized for highest accolades, with ten Golden Lions, Palms, and Bears combined, as of May 2023. Daiei Studio was reportedly reluctant to send *Rashomon* (recommended by Giuliana Stramigioli, an Italian journalist and professor who saw the film in Japan) to overseas festivals such as the Venice International Film Festival, fearing it was too Japanese and complex and thus unintelligible to be intelligible and appreciated by Western audiences (Prince 2012). The press, critics, and scholars have played critical roles in canon formation and exaltation of auteurs in their roles as interlocutors and disseminators of information on films, directors, and festivals (Wong, 112). Marking the beginning of a wide-scale global interest in Japanese film (especially period dramas, or *jidaigeki*), *Rashomon* became the first Japanese film to get a North American release from a major studio, RKO, in a kind of release that prefigured art-house distribution that would later develop fully (Sharp 2020).[3] The film about a crime that is recalled differently by all witnesses also inspired the judicial and epistemological concept of the so-called "Rashomon Effect," used to describe conflicting accounts and descriptions of certain events by unreliable eyewitnesses (Anderson 2016). *Rashomon* became in 1952 the first Asian film to win a Special/Honorary Academy Award in the United States (the category later known as Best Foreign Language Film, and after that, Best International Feature). While David Bordwell (2009) notes that the French critics of *Cahiers du Cinema* in the 1950s favored Japanese auteur Kenji Mizoguchi over Akira Kurosawa, he contends that elsewhere Akira Kurosawa, a "problematic auteur," was embraced and "[s]old, like [Indian filmmaker] Satyajit Ray, as a humanist from an exotic culture, he played into critics' eternal admiration for significance." Kurosawa was a key figure in the acceptance of "foreign" cinema in the West, and recognition of what Tino Balio (2010) has called "auteurs from outside the epicenter" and the postwar "foreign film renaissance" on American screens. As Meghan Warner Mettler (2018) asserts, the critically lauded *Rashomon*, in contrast to Toho Studio's *Gojira/Godzilla* from 1954 was received as an art-house film and also posed no challenge to US foreign policy images of Japan as ally.

While some Japanese films had played at Venice earlier and had theatrical release in the West, the recognition of *Rashomon* (and the talent of Kurosawa) was a breakthrough. Later in the same decade, another Japanese film, *Muhōmatsu no isshō* (Rickshaw Man, 1958), directed by Hiroshi Inagati would win the top prize at Venice in 1958. Unlike *Rashomon*, this film has not had an enduring impact in the world cinema canon, although the Tokyo International Film Festival recently (in 2020) screened a restored and digitally remastered version of the film. The Cannes Film Festival's first Asian Palme d'Or winner was Kinugasa Teinosuke's *Jigokumon* (Gate of Hell) in 1954, and the Berlin International Film Festival's inaugural top award to an Asian film was Imai Tadashi's *Bushido Samurai Saga* in 1963 (a shared prize with the Italian film, *Il Diavalo*, directed by Gian Luigi Polodoro). Japanese films have won five jury prizes throughout Cannes' history (as of 2023) – four of them between 1960 and 1965. As scholars such as Sharon Hayashi (2010) have noted, Japanese historical dramas had particular exotic appeal for European festival audiences in the post–World War II era, and their successes, from Kurosawa's *Rashomon* in 1951 onward, influenced subsequent festival submissions by the Japanese Film Producers Association (52–53).

In 1956, India's most celebrated auteur Satyajit Ray, won the Best Human Document award at Cannes for the first film in his Apu Trilogy, *Pather Panchali*, that can be regarded as a milestone for "world cinema in the cultural imaginary" (Nagib, Perriam, and Dudhah 2012, xvii).[4] The second film in the series, *Aparajito,* would win the Golden Lion at Venice in 1957 (as well as the FIPRESCI prize and New Cinema award for best film), and other awards elsewhere including the Selznick Golden Laurel at the Berlin International Film Festival and Golden Gate awards for Best Picture and Director at the San Francisco International Film Festival in 1958. The filmmaker himself deconstructed his experiences in festival materials for the Fifth International Film Festival of India, established in 1952 and currently held in Goa, a festival that from its inception became entwined with geopolitics, diplomacy, and Cold War era cultural exchange (Govil 2022). Satyajit Ray asserts,

> My first film *Pather Panchali*, found its way to the Cannes Film Festival through the efforts of some sympathetic friends. I had no means of going, so I stayed back and held my breath. As I learnt later, the official screening of the film took place around midnight. The jury had already on the same day, sat through four long features and decided to skip the Indian entry. Among the handful who attended were some critics, apparently with insatiable appetites, who sat through the film and liked it enough to insist on a second screening for the jurors. This was arranged, and the film went on win a special prize as the "best human document." The next year, my second film, *Aparajito* went to the Venice festival and won the Golden Lion. This time I was present and experienced the rising tension that marks the occasion for a competing director . . .[5]

Ray would twice go on to win Best Director awards (Silver Bears) at Berlin in 1964 and 1965. Festival recognition contributed enormously to the world cinema canonization of the Apu Trilogy and Bengali art cinema, as did the enthusiastic endorsement of peer auteurs such as Kurosawa.

We can also see in the recognition of Chinese films (Zhang Yimou's *Hóng Gāoliáng* [Red Sorghum, 1987] at Berlin in 1988 and *Qiū jú dǎ guānsī* [The Story of Qui Ju] at Venice in 1992 and Chen Kaige's *Farewell My Concubine* at Cannes in 1993) and Zhang Yimou's *Yīgè dōu bùnéng shǎo* (Not One Less) at Venice in 1999, the cultural ascendance and prominence of so-called fifth-generation Chinese cinema. Their successes also reveals disconnects within the production and reception nexus, and signs of "cross-cultural commodity fetishism" (Chow 1995, 59). Made by graduates of the Beijing Film Academy after the Cultural Revolution, these films were variously impacted by censorship and governmental intervention in the People's Republic of China. In the mid-2000s, the post-socialist neorealism of the Sixth Generation, or "Urban Generation" (Zhang 2007), Chinese filmmakers Jia Zhangke and Wang Quan'an would be celebrated with wins for, respectively, *Sānxiá Hǎorén* (Still Life) at Venice in 2006 and *Túyǎ de hūnshì* (Tuya's Marriage, 2006) at Berlin in 2007. Fellow Sixth Generation/Urban Generation Chinese filmmaker Zhang Yuan won Venice's Silver Lion for Best Director in 1999 with for *Guò nián huí jiā* (Seventeen Years), his first film that could be shown in Chinese theaters (Berry 2002, 153).

Expanding the frame of Chinese-language cinema, Wong Kar-wai, the Hong Kong filmmaker whose work is "[c]entral to the contemporary Chinese renaissance" (Stringer 2002, 417) won Best Director at Cannes in 1997 for *Happy Together*, the film that "thoroughly consolidated Wong's international reputation" (Stringer, 422). Taiwanese filmmakers Edward Yang and Hou Hsiao-hsien came into global prominence as "world class auteurs" (Ma 2010, 341). Along with Malaysian-born, Taiwan-based Tsai Ming-liang, the acclaimed filmmakers' wins at international festivals including Venice (Golden Lions for Hou's *Bēiqíng chéngshì* (A City of Sadness) in 1989 and Tsai's *Àiqíng wànsuì* (Vive l'Amour) in 1994, Grand Jury Prize for Tsai's *Stray Dogs* in 2013 and Cannes (Jury Prize for Hou's *Xìmèng rénshēng* (The Puppetmaster) in 1993, Best Film for Hou's *Hǎishàng Huā* (Flowers of Shanghai) in 1998, Best Director for Yang's *Yi Yi* in 2000, Best Director for Hou's *Cìkè Niè Yǐnniáng* (The Assassin) in 2015. The Nantes Three Continents Festival (a festival established in 1979, focusing on films from Asia, Africa, and Latin America, with a funding project for independent filmmaking), was the first international high-profile film festival to "discover" Taiwanese cinema and auteur Hou Hsiao-hsien back in the 1980s. According to As Beth Tsai (2018), Hou's films were placed into competition as entries from "Taiwan, China" for several years until 1986 when the Nantes festival recognized Taiwan, and Taiwanese filmmakers were subsequently misidentified at multiple A-list film festivals. *The Assassin*, was listed in the 2015 Cannes program as Chinese from the Republic of China, and Tsai Ming-Liang's *Stray Dogs* was mislabeled at the 70th Venice Film Festival in 2013 as from "Chinese Taipei" because the Italian government did not recognize Taiwan as a country (Tsai 2018, 179–180). Film festivals shape and create perceptions of the sudden emergence of new cinematic waves with their "cultural and political interventions, mediated by both domestic contexts and international forces" (Tsai 2018, 193). Song Hwee Lim (2014), a progenitor of the concept of "slow cinema," contends that "Tsai Ming-liang's films are uniquely placed to illuminate the relationship between slowness and cinephilia and that this relationship is cast within the notion of film authorship and shot through with a dose of nostalgia" (43). Given the exceptional successes of Taiwanese cinema at international festivals of filmmakers like Hou, Yang, Tsai, and Ang Lee), Lim's most recent book demonstrates that Taiwanese cinema can be viewed as "small nation" cinema with enormous "soft power," and with authorship as the secret weapon (Lim 2022, 2). Such authorship can be evidenced by generic transformation. Daniela Berghahn (2021) asserts that with a film such as *The Assassin*, the *wuxia pian* swordplay film genre is adapted into slower and more aesthetically lavish art cinema (223, 233–35).

The Cannes Film Festival would be the first of the big three to recognize an auteur of the so-called New Iranian cinema of the post-revolutionary period with Abbas Kiarostami's *Ta'm-e Gīlās* (The Taste of Cherry) in 1997, sharing a prize with *Unagi* (The Eel), by Imamura Shohei, who had been previously recognized for his 1983 film, *The Ballad of Narayama*. This programming pattern of revisiting an auteur at late career was also demonstrated by Kurosawa Akira's *Kagemusha* sharing a Palme d'Or in 1980. Following wins in the 1980s by Iranian films at the Nantes Festival of Three Continents, and the emergence of Locarno as "an important festival gateway through which Iranian cinema moved onto the world stage" (Wong, 110), Iranian films premiered and took major prizes at Cannes, Venice, and Berlin.

Jafar Panahi's controversial *Dâyere* (The Circle, 2000) (an Iranian, Italian, and Swiss co-production), banned in Iran, won the Golden Lion in Venice 2000 and was described by film critic Deborah Young (2000) in *Variety* as the second Iranian film screened at Venice about female oppression that year, after Marzieh Meshkini's allegorical *Roozi ke zan shodam* (The Day I Became a Woman, 2000). Berlinale in particular has embraced and endorsed Iranian films and filmmakers, acknowledging Panahi during his house arrest and with him winning the Golden Bear in absentia in 2015 with *Taxi*, made despite a filmmaking ban imposed by the Iranian government. Other Iranian winners at Berlinale include Asghar Farhadi's 2011 film, *A Separation* (which would also become the first Iranian Academy Award winner for the category then known as Best Foreign Language Film) and Mohammad Rasoulof's 2020 film, *Sheytân vojûd nadârad* (There is No Evil), focusing on capital punishment and banned in Iran.

The familiar narrative of international embrace of films banned or censored at home is also part of the festival trajectory of films of the much-lauded independent Thai auteur Apichatpong Weerasethukul, whose films engage with queer sexuality and employ political allegory. *Sud saneha* (Blissfully Yours) was a 2002 Cannes *Un Certain Regard* award winner, and *Satpralat* (Tropical Malady), a 2004 Palme d'Or nominee was a Cannes Jury Prize winner. Apichatpong's *Lung Bunmi Raluek Chat* (Uncle Boonmee Who Can Recall His Past Lives, 2010) is a Cannes Palme d'Or winner, the first Asian film to win the award since 1997, when the Palme d'Or was jointly awarded to Kiarostami's *A Taste of Cherry* and Imamura's *The Eel*. *Uncle Boonmee* can be viewed as a quintessential "festival film" (Falicov 2016, 209), with funding endorsements from the International Film Festival Rotterdam's Hubert Bals Fund and Berlinale's World Cinema Fund.

Across the European big three festivals, there have (as of summer 2023) been 20 Best Director awards (Prix de la Mise en scène, Silver Bear, Silver Lion) awarded to Asian filmmakers. For example, Cannes awards have gone to Oshima Nagisa (Japan, 1978), Wong Kar-wai (Hong Kong, 1997), Im Kwon-taek (South Korea, 2002), Nuri Bilge Ceylan (Turkey, 2008), Brillante Mendoza (Philippines, 2009), Hou Hsiao-hsien (Taiwan, 2015), and Vietnamese-born French filmmaker Tranh Anh Hung (2023). Asian filmmakers were invited to contribute to multi-director omnibus film projects connected to festivals such as *Chacun son cinema* (To Each His Own Cinema, 2007), a cinephilic commemoration of the 60th anniversary of Cannes, with a total of 34 short films, including ones by Kitano Takeshi from Japan, Hou Hsiao-hsien, and Tsai Ming-liang from Taiwan, Zhang Yimou and Chen Kaige from China, Amos Gitai from Israel, Elia Suleiman from Palestine, and Abbas Kiarostami from Iran. Kiarostami would subsequently would grow his short film, *Where is My Romeo* (entirely comprising close-up shots of Iranian actresses presumably watching an adaptation of Shakespeare's *Romeo and Juliet*), into an extraordinary 2008 feature film *Shirin*, featuring more than 100 Iranian actresses (and also French actress Juliette Binoche, who was visiting Iran at the time), watching and reacting to a filmic adaptation of the Persian tragic romance "The Tale of Khosrow and Shirin." (The feature film *Shirin* was included in the 65th Venice Film Festival.) More recently, the 2021 pandemic-themed seven-segmented global anthology film titled *The Year of Everlasting Storm*, produced and distributed by Neon (known for bringing films like *Parasite* to international triumph), included contributions from Jafar Panahi (Iran), Anthony Chen (Singapore), and Apichatpong Weerasethakul (Thailand). Turning the transauthorial omnibus (Diffrient 2014) into a festival event, *The Year of Everlasting Storm* premiered at Cannes in 2021.

Exposure at these high-profile European film festivals and industry market initiatives also contributed to the proliferation of more international co-productions and collaborations such as Juliette Binoche (the first actress to win top acting honors at Berlin, Cannes, and Venice) working with Asian auteurs. These examples of film star and director clout convergence include Kiarostami's Tuscany-set Iranian/French/Italian/Belgian co-production, *Certified Copy* (2010); Naomi Kawase's Japanese/French co-production *Vision* (2018); Hou Hsiao-hsien's French and Taiwanese co-production, *Flight of the Red Balloon* (2007), Hou's first project filmed outside Asia; and Kore-eda Hirokazu's *The Truth*, a Japanese and French co-production and the opening film at the 2019 Venice Film Festival.

Asian Film Festival Historiography

One central problematic paradox of "discovering" Asia in the international film festival circuit is a replication, in the narrative of European invention, of the colonialist or imperialistic narrative of film history that we read again and again in historical accounts of the emergence of Asian cinemas and film cultures. It often looks something like this: The brothers Lumière and company or the Edison team come to Asian countries bringing "the world to the world" as they shoot and screen cinematograph actualities and peepshow novelty entertainment (Deocampo 2017a, 299–312). Western industrialization and commerce introduce the mechanical cinematic apparatus and motion pictures (Deocampo 2017b, 2). However, pre- or proto-cinematic cultural forms, the "seeds of cinema" in traditional performing arts, such as Malay *wayang kulit* (Multhalib 2017, 240), offer us a much longer narrative, locating a shadow play public spectacle centuries before the Lumière Cinematograph, the Edison Projectoscope, or Cannes, Venice, or Berlinale.

The Southeast Asian Film Festival established in the mid-1950s (and later renamed the Asian Film Festival and the Asia-Pacific Film Festival) can be viewed as a pioneering pan-Asian film event and the "oldest continuous film festival in Asia" (Stringer 2016, 36; n. 9, 44, citing Yau 2003), that was also a site of Cold War era cultural struggle (Poon 2019; Lee 2020). The Afro-Asian Film Festival, a transnational cooperative effort to contest colonialism, was inaugurated as the Asian Film Week in Beijing in 1957, Tashkent in 1958, Cairo in 1960, and Jakarta in 1964 (Djagalov 2020; Razlogova 2021; Salazkina 2023). As articulated by Stephen Teo, while there were also precursors in Asia back in the 1950s, such as the aforementioned International Film Festival of India, the founding of film festivals in Asia "as a form of cultural practice and recognition of cinema as an artistic medium" was galvanized by Hong Kong International Film Festival in 1977, a festival that soon gained a reputation as a platform for Asian films (Teo 2009, 109) and helped cultivate local film criticism (Bordwell 2000, 45). The origins and ongoing development of the Hong Kong International Film Festival, with increasing emphasis on popular entertainment, are linked with colonial history and its current postcolonial identity (Cheung 2016). Hong Kong still remains a major Asian international film festival, with others in the calendar including Metro Manila Film Festival (formerly Manila Film Festival between 1966 and 1975), Singapore International Film Festival (founded in 1987 offering a platform for international films, but especially from Singapore and the Southeast Asia region), the Shanghai International Film Festival (established in 1993), the Fajr International Film Festival (inaugurated in Iran in 1982), Busan International Film Festival (arguably Asia's most influential film festival, established in 1996), Tokyo International Film Festival (launched in 1985, with an international competition, the Tokyo Grand Prix, which has had winners over the years from Japan, China, South Korea, China, Hong Kong, Israel, and Kazakhstan and, over the past decade, a number of European co-production winners, including a Turkish/German/French/Swedish co-production in 2017), the Golden Horse Film Festival and Awards founded in Taipei in 1962, and Jakarta International Film Festival (raising the film cultural profile of Indonesia since 1999 – Indonesian film director and producer Christine Hakin served on the Cannes film festival jury in 2002), among others.

The Busan International Film Festival (formerly the Pusan International Film Festival) is incredibly Asia-forward, creating spaces for new and retrospective programming, "New Currents" section award recognition for first and second feature Asian films, an Asian Project Market and Asian Film Market, script development, and post-production support. With Busan's exemplary Asian cinema "Panorama" programming, for example, I have had the opportunity to view films in a festival context that stretched the familiar representations of East, South, and Southeast Asian cinema to early cinema from Central Asia. As demonstrated by scholars such as SooJeong Ahn (2012), a former employee of the Pusan International Film Festival between 1998 and 2002, the festival's growth and emergence as a preeminent Asian festival, in tandem with transformations of the South Korean film industry, reflect engagement with national identity, Asian regionalism, and globalization.

North America's first and longest-running Asian-focused festival, the New York Asian American Film Festival, was founded in 1978 in conjunction with the grassroots media arts collective Asian CineVision, with a remit extending to the Asian diaspora and embracing artistic experimentation and video expansion (Okada 2009, 22–23). The New York Asian Film Festival, inaugurated in 2002, has grown significantly over the years in scale, and now includes multiple awards (audience, feature film, Screen International Rising Star Award Asia). The San Francisco–based CAAMFest, established in 1982 (formerly the San Francisco International Asian American Film Festival), coordinated by the Center for Asian American Media, is a large showcase for Asian American and Asian films. Films by Kurosawa Akira and Satyajit Ray were among the first ones screened at the San Francisco International Film Festival, America's longest running film festival, in 1957. The festival's annual directing award was initially named for Kurosawa, its first recipient in 1986. Satyajit Ray also won this award (in 1992), as well as awards for Best Director and Best Film for *Pather Panchali* (1957) and *Aparajito* (1958) in the early years of the festival. The Hawaii International Film Festival, established in 1981, has a very strong Asia-Pacific focus, and its premieres include Ang Lee's *Crouching Tiger, Hidden Dragon* (2000).

In Canada, the Vancouver Asian Film Festival (that debuted in 1997) claims to be the nation's longest running Asian film festival, and the Vancouver International Film Festival (founded in 1958), includes an East Asian film strand, Dragons & Tigers, originated by programmer and critic Tony Rayns. The festival also formerly hosted an award for emerging Asian-Pacific filmmakers (1994–2013), subsequently opened to international filmmakers more generally. The Toronto International Film Festival, founded initially in 1976 as the "Festival of Festivals" showing films from festivals around the world, has become one of the largest and most influential film festivals in the world, and has included extensive programming of Asian and Asian diasporic features and short films. The Taiwan/PRC/Hong Kong co-production, *Crouching Tiger Hidden Dragon*'s People Choice Award win at TIFF in 2000, helped predict its amazing run at the Oscars in 2021 with ten nominations and four wins. The remarkable success of the film also inspired a namesake film festival, Pingyao Crouching Tiger Hidden Dragon Film Festival (also known as the Pingyao International Film Festival), founded by Chinese filmmaker Jia Zhangke in 2017. Established in 1997, Toronto Reel Asian International Film Festival is Canada's largest pan-Asian film festival, and also claims to be its longest-running.

Other entities committed to raising global exposure of pan-Asian cinema include the Network for the Promotion of Asian Cinema (NETPAC), the resource organization Asian Film

Festivals, and the pan-Asian talent incubator/educational initiative Asian Film Academy.[6] Founded in 1990 by New Delhi–based film critic-scholar Aruna Vasudev, the Network for the Promotion of Asian Cinema (NETPAC) is a film organization for the promotion of Asian cinema worldwide, associated with the film journal *Cinemaya: The Asian Film Quarterly* (established by Vasudev in 1988). NETPAC has collaborated with numerous film festivals worldwide with special juried awards to recognize Asian cinema. Established in 2016 by Buenos Aires–based Sebastian Nadilo, Asian Film Festivals' resource website lists current film festivals in the Asian continent, as well as Asian cinema-focused festivals in 13 countries outside Asia. Asian Film Festivals (as of 2022) recognizes festivals across 14 Asian countries and 2 special administrative regions, including 43 film festivals in South Korea, 36 in the Philippines, and 27 in Japan. Built into the infrastructure of the Busan International Film Festival (BIFF), the Asian Film Academy enables emerging Asian filmmakers (with eligibility as determined by the United Nations Asian nationality geoscheme or "overseas" Korean heritage, as well as some short film production experience) to take workshops and attend lectures and masterclasses with acclaimed directors and create short productions, several of which are selected for presentation at BIFF. Arguably, such initiatives and programs point to national, regional, and global iterations of the desire and possibilities for what Aaron Han Joon Mangan-Park has called a "Poly-Asian Continental Film Movement" (Mangan-Park 2018).

Conclusion: New Accolades, Challenges, Milestones?

In the international image market, the concept and products of festivalized "Asian cinema" continue to be diversified, disaggregated, and globalized due to countless factors. Among them, the impacts of the recent global COVID-19 pandemic and the rise and expansion of streaming platforms have catalyzed further hybridization of filmic objects and screening experiences. The global spread of pan-Indian and regional film is heralded with amazing ascendance of Tollywood, with the commercial and critical success of a Telugu film like *RRR* (2022). Feted as the first Indian and first Asian winner of Best Song, for "Naatu Naatu," at the 2023 Academy Awards, it is also the first Indian-produced film to win any Academy Award. *RRR* enjoyed huge success at the worldwide box office (becoming the highest grossing Indian film of 2022) and also on the Netflix streaming platform.

At this cultural moment of global embrace of Korean popular culture and the expansion of its discursive extensions, what I call transnational cinemediations (Ciecko 2022), *Parasite* became the first Korean winner of the Palme d'Or at the Cannes Film Festival in 2019, and its director, Bong Joon-ho, the first Korean to serve as president of the Venice Film Festival's jury in 2021. After its international festival debut, *Parasite* (2019) would proceed to a groundbreaking performance at the US Academy Awards in 2020, receiving Oscars for Best Picture, Best Director, Best Original Screenplay, and Best International Feature. The first South Korean and Asian movie to win in all four categories, it was also the first non-Anglophone film to win Best Picture (Sharf 2021).

Beyond the most visible and dominant festival players from India and South Korea and elsewhere, auteurs from Southeast Asia, including Apichatpong Weerasethakul from Thailand, Brillante Mendoza and Lav Diaz from the Philippines, and Cambodian filmmaker Rithy Panh, have been prominent at Cannes, although the latter resigned as president of the jury of the inaugural TikTok-branded short film competition in 2022, "citing pressure on the jury choices from the European team of the China-owned social network" (Wiseman 2022). Spanning decades of acclaimed filmmaking, Vietnamese-born Tranh Anh Hung won the Camera d'Or for best first feature for *The Scent of Green Papaya* in 1993 and, 30 years later, Best Director for *The Pot-au-Feu* (The Taste of Things) in 2023. Film critic Liza Shackleton, reporting from Cannes 2023, described a "new wave" of Southeast Asian talent, including Malaysian filmmaker Amanda Nell Eu premiering her horror film *Tiger Stripes* in Critics Week, the selection of Vietnamese filmmaker Pham Thien An's *Bên trong vỏ kén vàng* (Inside the Yellow Cocoon Shell, 2023) for Director's Fortnight, and returning Singaporean director Anthony Chen (winner of the Camera d'Or in 2013 for his debut feature, *Ilo, Ilo*) with a mainland Chinese project in in the Un Certain Regard strand. Shackleton correlates this boom with the increase in film labs, workshops, budgets, and co-production initiatives due to government-supported production schemes, regional and international film/media development partnerships and funds, new business models and networks and European festival markets, such as Torino Film Lab, International Film Festival Rotterdam's Cinemart, and Locarno's Open Doors. In order to generate co-production activity within and beyond Asia, Locarno's Open Doors, for example, has, since 2003, coordinated cycles of film projects and makers/producers from an array of georegional and geocultural configurations: Southeast Asia, South Asia, the South Caucasus, Greater China, Central Asia, the Near and Middle East, and the Mekong (Cambodia, Laos, and Vietnam).

In 2023, Singaporean filmmaker Nelson Yeo's feature debut, *Dreaming and Dying,* won both the Filmmakers of the Present – Golden Leopard award and the Swatch First Feature Award, at the Locarno Film Festival, the first win for a Southeast Asian filmmaker in either category (Lim 2023). Previously, the Singapore/France/Netherlands co-production *A Land Imagined* (a thriller about the disappearance of Chinese and Bangladeshi migrant workers), won the top Golden Leopard award for best film at Locarno in 2018. This was the second feature directed by Yeo Siew Hua, a first-time win in this prestigious category by a Singaporean filmmaker. Recognizing contributions to global art cinema but also expanded screen experiences in installations and with virtual reality, a career achievement award, Pardo alla carriera (bearing the sponsor's name, Ascona-Locarno Tourism award, demonstrating the Swiss festival's ongoing embeddedness with tourism) was bestowed on Taiwanese auteur Tsai Ming-liang in 2023. (Tsai was the second Asian filmmaker to receive this award recognition, following Hong Kong director/producer Johnny To, back in 2012.)

With 2023's Golden Leopard top prize for the Iranian film *Mantagheye bohrani* (Critical Zone), directed by Ali Ahmadzadeh, Locarno offered a public stance of support to an endangered film and filmmaker. The festival was pressured by Iranian authorities to pull the gritty film, described by *The Hollywood Reporter* as " 'Taxi Driver' Meets 'Taste of Cherry' " (Mintzer 2023), on the grounds that it was not made without official permission; further, the director was banned from leaving Iran (Balaga 2023). Given the jail sentencing of Iranian filmmaker Saeed Roustayi for "anti-regime propaganda activity" for unauthorized festival submission, one year after the 2022 Cannes screening of his film, *Barādarān-e Leilā* (Leila's Brothers), it remains to be seen whether festival award recognition and global interventions will open up possibilities for further filmic authorship, freedom of expression, career development, and exposure in global film culture for filmmakers, such as Ali Ahmadzadeh.

Notes

1 See the archival documents for the "Focus on Asia" Fukuoka International Film Festival in 1993 and the 1994 Berlin International Film Festival at https://www.focus-on-asia.com/archives/1993-3rd/ and https://www.berlinale.de/en/archive/jahresarchive/1994/01_jahresblatt_1994/01_jahresblatt_ 1994.html.
2 See the Ulaanbaater International Film Festival's website: http://www.ubiff.mn/about/.
3 David Desser explains that Japanese cinema of the prewar period (1927–44) was dominated by the jidai-geki (Desser 1992), "particularly stories concerning samurai, or feudal swordsmen" (145). The samurai film genre was essentially banned by the American occupation army but experienced a renaissance and renewed interest when *Rashomon* won favor in the West.
4 Cannes did a major retrospective of the Bengali auteur's films in 2022. See the *Times of India* coverage, "Cannes to honour Satyajit Ray with a 10-film retrospective," March 23, 2022, https:// timesofindia.indiatimes.com/entertainment/bengali/movies/news/cannes-to-honnour-satyajit-ray- with-a-10-film-retrospective/articleshow/90389508.cms?frmapp=yes&from=mdr#:~:text=For%20 the%20unversed%2C%20in%201956,a%20fitting%20tribute%20to%20him.
5 See the post at the India Film Institute's online archive: https://www.indianfilminstitute.org/ post/1975/01/03/satyajit-ray-the-feel-of-festivals-iffi-1975.
6 The website for the Network for the Promotion of Asian Pacific Cinema (NETPAC) is https://netpacasia. org/homepage. AsianFilmFestivals.com has the declared mission of helping film festivals reach a wider audience, developing interest for Asian audiovisual content, and keeping Asian filmmakers updated on open calls, financial grants, and opportunities to grow their skills and connections (https://asianfilmfesti- vals.com/about-us/). The details of the Asian Film Academy, currently hosted by the Busan International Film Festival along with the Busan Film Commission, and the Grand Korea Leisure Foundation are available here: https://afa.biff.kr/eng/. After a short hiatus because of the COVID-19 pandemic, the pro- gram reemerged, rebranded as a collaborative partnership with the luxury fashion brand CHANEL X BIFF Asian Film Academy. The Asian Film Festivals website posted the call for applications here: https:// asianfilmfestivals.com/2022/04/13/asian-film-academy-call-for-entry-2022/#:~:text=Eligibility%20 %3A,%E2%80%93%20Can%20communicate%20in%20English.

References

Ahn, S. 2009. "Building up Asian Identity: The Pusan International Film Festival in South Korea." In *Cinemas, Identities and Beyond*, edited by R. Cheung with D. H. Fleming, 115–31. Newcastle upon Tyne: Cambridge Scholars Publishing.

———. 2012. *The Pusan International Film Festival, South Korean Cinema and Globalization*. Hong Kong: Hong Kong University Press.

Anderson, R. 2016. The Rashomon Effect and Communication. *Canadian Journal of Communication* 41: 249–69.

"Asian Film Academy" Website. Accessed May 2022. https://afa.biff.kr/eng/.

"Asian Film Festivals" Resource Website. Accessed May 2022. https://asianfilmfestivals.com/.

Balaga, M. 2023. "Locarno Film Festival Awards: 'Critical Zone', the Film the Iranian Government Doesn't Want to Be Seen, Wins Big at Swiss Fest." *Variety*, August 12. Accessed August 2023. https://malaysia.news.yahoo.com/critical-zone-film-iranian-government-133759809.html?soc_ src=social-sh&soc_trk=ma

Balio, T. 2010. *The Foreign Film Renaissance on American Screens, 1946–1973*. Madison: University of Wisconsin Press.

Berghahn, D. 2021. "Performing Exoticism and the Transnational Reception of World Cinema." *Studies in World Cinema* 1 (2): 221–38.

Berlin International Film Festival. 1994. Accessed May 2022. https://www.berlinale.de/en/archive/ jahresarchive/1994/01_jahresblatt_1994/01_j ahresblatt_1994.html.

Berry, C., and L. Robinson. 2017. "Introduction." In *Chinese Film Festivals: Sites of Translation*, edited by C. Berry and Robinson, 1–11. New York: Palgrave Macmillan.

Berry, M. 2002. *Speaking in Images: Interviews with Contemporary Chinese Filmmakers*. New York: Columbia University Press.

Bordwell, D. 2000. *Planet Hong Kong: Popular Cinema and the Art of Entertainment*. Cambridge: Harvard University Press.

———. 2009. "Kurosawa's Early Spring." *Observations on Film Art*, December 8. Accessed August 2023. http://www.davidbordwell.net/blog/2009/12/08/kurosawas-early-spring/.

"Cannes to Honour Satyajit Ray with a 10-Film Retrospective." 2022. *The Times of India*, March 23. Accessed May 2022. https://timesofindia.indiatimes.com/entertainment/bengali/movies/news/cannes-to-honnour-satyajit-ray-with-a-10-film-retrospective/articleshow/90389508.cms?frmapp=yes&from=mdr#:~:text=F or%20the%20unversed%2C%20in%201956,a%20fitting%20tribute%20to%20him.

Cheung, R. 2016. "Ever-Changing Readjustments: The Political Economy of the Hong Kong International Film Festival (HKIFF)." *New Review of Film and Television Studies* 14 (1): 59–75. Film Festivals: Origins and Trajectories.

Chow, R. 1995. *Primitive Passions: Visuality, Sexuality, Ethnography, and Contemporary Chinese Cinema*. New York: Columbia University Press.

Ciecko, A. 2006. "Chapter 1: Theorizing Asian Cinema(s)." In *Contemporary Asian Cinema: Popular Culture in a Global Frame*, edited by A. Ciecko, 13–31. Oxford: Berg/Bloomsbury.

———. 2018. "Theorizing Other Asian Cinema: The Sensorium of Transcaucasia." In *The Palgrave Handbook of Asian Cinema*, edited by A. H. J. Mangun-Park, G. Marchetti, and S. K. Tam, 71–88. London: Palgrave Macmillan.

———. 2022. "Contemporary Film Culture and Convergence: Cinemediated Solidarity." In *Routledge Handbook of Asian Transnationalism*, edited by A. K. Sahoo, 380–93. London: Routledge.

Corkill, E. 2011. "Fukuoka Fast becoming Asia Film Hub." *The Japan Times*, September 9. Accessed May 2022. https://www.japantimes.co.jp/culture/2011/09/09/events/events-outside-tokyo/fukuoka-fast-becoming-asia-film-hub/.

De Valck, M. 2007. *Film Festivals: From European Geopolitics to Global Cinephilia*. Amsterdam: Amsterdam University Press.

———. 2016. "Fostering Art, Adding Value, Cultivating Taste: Film Festivals as Sites of Cultural Legitimization." In *Film Festivals: History, Theory, Method, Practice*, edited by M. De Valck, B. Krendell, and S. Loist, 100–16. London and New York: Routledge.

Deocampo, N. 2017a. "Appendix: Chronology of Film Beginnings in Asia." In *Early Cinema in Asia*, edited by N. Deocampo, 299–312. Bloomington: Indiana University Press.

———. 2017b. "Introduction: The Beginnings of Cinema in Asia." In *Early Cinema in Asia*, edited by N. Deocampo, 1–31. Bloomington: Indiana University Press.

Desser, D. 1992. "Toward a Structural Analysis of the Postwar Samurai Film." In *Framing Japanese Cinema: Authorship, Genre, History*, edited by A. Nolletti, Jr. and D. Desser, 145–64. Bloomington: Indiana University Press.

Diffrient, J. S. 2014. *Omnibus Films: Theorizing Transauthorial Cinema*. Edinburgh: Edinburgh University Press.

Djagalov, R. 2020. "The Tashkent Film Festival (1968–1988) as Contact Zone." In *From Internationalism to Postcolonialism: Literature and Cinema between the Second and Third Worlds*, 65–110. Montreal, Quebec/Kingston, Ontario: McGill-Queen's University Press.

Dovey, L. 2015. *Curating Africa in the Age of Film Festivals*. New York: Palgrave Macmillan.

Duffy, J., and M. Mair. 2018. *Festival Encounters: Theoretical Perspectives on Festival Events*. London: Routledge.

Falicov, T. 2016. "The 'Festival Film': Film Festival Funds as Cultural Intermediaries." In *Film Festivals: History, Theory, Method, Practice*, edited by M. De Valck, B. Krendell, and S. Loist, 209–29. London: Routledge.

"Focus on Asia" Fukuoka International Film Festival, 3rd Annual. 1993. Accessed May 2022. https://www.focus-on-asia.com/archives/1993-3rd/.

Gerow, A. 2022. "Sato Tadao sensei (1930–2022)." Tangemania: Aaron Gerow's Japanese Film Page. Accessed August 2023. http://www.aarongerow.com/news/sato-tadao-sensei-19302022.html.

Govil, N. 2022. "In and Out of Alignment: Cold War Sentiment and Hollywood-Bombay Film Diplomacy in the 1950s." In *A Companion to Indian Cinema: Transnational and Transregional Circuits*, edited by N. Majumdar and R. Mazumdar, 398–411. Hoboken: Wiley-Blackwell.

Hayashi, S. 2010. "The Fantastic Trajectory of Pink Art from Stalin to Bush." In *Global Art Cinema: New Theories and Histories*, edited by R. Galt and K. Schoonover, 48–61. Oxford: Oxford University Press.

Iordanova, D. 2011. "East Asia and Film Festivals: Transnational Clusters for Creativity and Commerce." In *Film Festival Yearbook 3: Film Festivals and East Asia*, edited by D. Iordanova and R. Cheung, 1–33. St. Andrews: St. Andrews Film Studies.

Lee, S. J. 2020. *Cinema and the Cultural Cold War: US Diplomacy and the Origins of the Asian Cinema Network*. Ithaca: Cornell University Press.

Lim, R. Y. 2023. "Singapore Filmmaker Nelson Yeo's Dreaming and Dying Wins 2 Awards for First Feature Film at Locarno Film Festival." August 14. Accessed August 2023. https://www.straitstimes.com/life/entertainment/singapore-film-maker-nelson-yeo-s-dreaming-dying-wins-two-awards-for-first-feature-films-at-locarno-film-festival.

Lim, S. H. 2014. *Tsai Ming-Liang and a Cinema of Slowness*. Honolulu: University of Hawaii Press.

———. 2022. *Taiwan Cinema as Soft Power*. Oxford: Oxford University Press.

Ma, J. 2010. "Tsai Ming-Liang's Haunted Movie Theater." In *Global Art Cinema: New Theories and Histories*, edited by R. Galt and K. Schoonover, 334–50. Oxford: Oxford University Press.

Mangan-Park, A. H. J. 2018. "The Desire for a Poly-Asian Continental Film Movement." In *The Palgrave Handbook of Asian Cinema*, edited by A. H. J. Mangun-Park, G. Marchetti, and S. K. Tam, 15–52. London: Palgrave Macmillan.

Mintzer, J. 2023. "Critical Zone Review: 'Taxi Driver' Meets 'Taste of Cherry' in Provocative Iranian Road Movie." *The Hollywood Reporter*, August 16. Accessed August 2023. https://www.hollywoodreporter.com/movies/movie-reviews/critical-zone-review-iran-1235567852/.

Multhalib, H. A. 2017. "From Shadow Play to the Silver Screen: Early Malay(sian) Cinema." In *Early Cinema in Asia*, edited by N. Deocampo, 240–54. Bloomington: Indiana University Press.

Nagib, L., C. Perriam, and R. Dudrah. 2012. "Introduction." In *Theorizing World Cinema*, edited by Lucia Nagib, C. Perriam, and R. Dudrah, xvii–xxxii. London/New York: I.B. Tauris.

"Network for the Promotion of Asian Pacific Cinema (NETPAC)" Website. Accessed May 2022. https://netpacasia.org/.

Okada, J. 2009. " 'Noble and Uplifting and Boring as Hell': Asian American Film and Video, 1971–1982." *Screen* 49, no. 1 (Fall): 20–40.

Ostrowska, D. 2016. "Making Film History at the Cannes Film Festival." In *Film Festivals: History, Theory, Method, Practice*, edited by M. De Valck, B. Krendell, and S. Loist, 18–33. London: Routledge.

Poon, E. K.-Y. 2019. "Southeast Asian Film Festival: The Site of the Cold War Cultural Struggle." *Journal of Chinese Cinemas* 13 (1): 1–15.

Prince, S. 2012. "The Rashomon Effect." *Criterion Collection Blog*, November 6. Accessed May 2022. https://www.criterion.com/current/posts/195-the-rashomon-effect.

Ray, S. 1975. "Satyajit Ray: The Feel of Festivals (IFFI – 1975)." Festival News: 5th International Film Festival of India, via Indian Film Institute Archives (April 14, 2018 Post). Accessed May 2022. https://www.indianfilminstitute.org/post/1975/01/03/satyajit-ray-the-feel-of-festivals-iffi-1975.

Razlogova, E. 2021. "Cinema in the Spirit of Bandung: The Afro-Asian Film Festival Circuit, 1957–1964." In *The Cultural Cold War and the Global South*, edited by K. Bystrom, M. Popescu, and K. Zien, 111–28. New York: Routledge.

Salazkina, M. 2023. *World Socialist Cinema: Alliances, Affinities, and Solidarities in the Global Cold War*. Berkeley: University of California Press.

Sato, T. 1987. *Currents in Japanese Cinema*. Translated by G. Barrett. New York: Kodansha USA.

Sharf, Z. 2021. "Bong Joon Ho Makes History Again as 2021 Venice Jury President, the First from South Korea." *IndieWire*, January 15. Accessed May 2022. https://www.indiewire.com/2021/01/bong-joon-ho-venice-jury-president-1234609687/.

Sharp, J. 2020. "70 Years of Rashomon – A New Look at Akira Kurosawa's Cinematic Milestone of Post-Truth." *British Film Institute*, August 25. Accessed May 2022. https://www.bfi.org.uk/features/rashomon-akira-kurosawa.

Stringer, J. 2002. "Wong Kar-wai." In *Fifty Contemporary Directors*, edited by Y. Tasker, 417–25. London: Routledge.

———. 2016. "Film Festivals in Asia: Notes on History, Geography, and Power from a Distance." In *Film Festivals: History, Theory, Method, Practice*, edited by M. De Valck, B. Krendall, and S. Loist, 34–48. London: Routledge.

Teo, S. 2009. "Asian Film Festivals and Their Diminishing Glitter Domes: An Appraisal of PIFF, SIFF and HKIFF." In *dekalog 3: On Film Festivals*, edited by R. Porton, 109–21. New York: Wallflower.

Tsai, B. 2018. "Visible Art, Invisible Nations? On the Politics of Film Festivals, Hou Hsiao-hsien, and Taiwan New Cinema." In *International Film Festivals: Contemporary Cultures and History Beyond Venice and Cannes*, edited by T. Jenkins, 179–96. London: I.B. Tauris.

Ulaanbaater International Film Festival Website. Accessed May 2022. http://www.ubiff.mn/about/.

Warner Mettler, M. 2018. "Godzilla versus Kurosawa: Presentation and Interpretation of Japanese Cinema in the Post World War II United States." *Journal of American-East Asian Relations* 25 (4): 413–37.

Wiseman, A. 2022. "Rithy Panh Further Explains His Resignation as Jury President of Cannes' Tik-Tok Competition." *Deadline*, May 19. Accessed August 2023. https://deadline.com/2022/05/cannes-tiktok-jury-rithy-panh-resigns-competition-1235028792/.

Wong, C. H.-Y. 2011. *Film Festivals: Culture, People, and Power on the Global Screen*. New Brunswick: Rutgers University Press.

Yau, K. S.-T. 2003. "Shaws' Japanese Collaboration and Competition as Seen Through the Asian Film Festival Evolution." In *The Shaw Screen: A Preliminary Study*, edited by A.-L. Wong, 279–94. Hong Kong: Hong Kong Film Archive.

Young, D. 2000. "The Circle [Review]." *Variety*, September 11. Accessed May 2022. https://variety.com/2000/film/reviews/the-circle-1200464326/.

Zhang, Z. 2007. *The Urban Generation: Chinese Cinema and Society at the Turn of the Twenty-First Century*. Durham, NC: Duke University Press.

42

CURATING THE CITY

The Urban Lens Film Festival

Subasri Krishnan

Introduction

The Urban Lens film festival, curated by the Media Lab at the Indian Institute for Human Settlement (IIHS) Bengaluru, an educational institution that works on urban practices, was set up in 2013 to bring into the public domain a complex set of questions: How does one understand cinematic representations of a city, over a long period of history? How does the construction of time and space in cinema provide insight into the complex nature of what cities can be? How do we understand films about and set in cities of past times in the present? How does film practice create new forms of knowledge and ways of seeing? The film festival was established so that film academics, practitioners, and audiences could co-create a new language of conversation and viewing practice of films, especially from countries in South Asia and the Global South.

Typically, conversations about film forms and practices have been siloed between academics and practitioners – while film academics have theorized about films in books, journals, and conferences, their works, alongside the films/filmmakers they write about, have largely been unexplored in a film festival space. The festival has tried to create a platform where the gap between those who theorize and those create can be lessened – through a dialogue about films between film academics and practitioners, that is not only available to the public who attend the festival but in an online space as well.

The industrialized First World, or Global North, has so far been the benchmark for the discipline of urban studies. This has shaped the public imagination of cities in various cultural expressions, including cinema. Countries in Latin America, Africa, and South Asia have always had strong cinematic traditions coming from different storytelling heritages and formal practices. They confound/challenge stereotypes of what Third World cities are supposed to be, excavating distinctive features of urban life and imagination. The Urban Lens film festival is an attempt at providing a platform for filmmakers from the global south to be able to screen and talk about their films on their own terms, outside the logic of the commercial or state-sponsored film festivals nationally and internationally.

The Urban Lens film festival primarily showcases non-fiction films that engage with the real and imagined idea of the city. These films come from different storytelling traditions

DOI: 10.4324/9781003266952-55

and formal practices: from ethnographic accounts of the city, to personal essay films and animation films – all the films that are part of the Urban Lens seek to interrogate different facets of what the urban produces – from the granularity of everyday life to a macro picture of what it means to inhabit a city.

This chapter will be divided into three sections. The first section will focus on the eco-system of non-fiction screening and festival spaces in India, both within and outside formal institutions. The second section will delve into what has shaped the curatorial choices of the Urban Lens film festival for the past nine editions. The concluding section will examine what it means to reintroduce older films to a newer generation of audience and the possibilities it holds for viewing practices.

Non-Fiction Film Screening Cultures/Festivals in India

India has a rich history of non-fiction film practice, in institutional and independent spaces. The Films Division, established after the Indian independence in 1948 under the Ministry of Information and Broadcasting was the primary producer of non-fiction films until independent non-fiction films began to emerge in the mid-1970s. They were mostly government propaganda films that were made on government campaigns and issues important to the state in post-independent India. It was seen as a mass medium through which the "uneducated" population could be refashioned into an upright citizen, who would contribute to the making of the post-colonial republic. Some of the films made under Films Division were on large dams, steel plants, population planning, and the state's contribution to various facets of the Indian citizen's life. These films were issue based, had a social message, and were made with an eye on the nation-building project.

As journalist Abhay Vaidya writes in his article on the legacy of Films Division that "the use of documentary films for communicating development initiatives by the government" was in many ways echoing British filmmaker John Grierson who believed that "training natives in the colonies in documentary filmmaking" would enable citizens to spread the word of the government in the newly formed nation-states (Vaidya 2022). Most of the films produced by Films Division were exhibited in commercial movie theaters before the screening of a feature film. Though, to produce a history of films made Films Division as only government propaganda would be inaccurate. There were filmmakers within the institution who directed films that not only critiqued the project of the nation-state (S. Sukhdev's *India 69*) but were also experimental (Pramod Pati's *Explorer*) and were reflecting on the film form (S.N.S. Sastry's *And I Make Short Films*). These films were exceptional because not only were they working within a state institution and its infrastructure, but they managed to create a body of work that is still screened and written about when one thinks of the history of Indian non-fiction films.

From the mid-1970s onward, independent non-fiction films emerged through the works of Anand Patwardhan, Deepa Dhanraj, Manjira Dutta, Tapan Bose, Suhasini Mulay, and others. They were activist films that questioned the state and its excesses and, in many ways, were the harbinger of independent non-fiction practice in India. The rise of the independent non-fiction films outside the structure of state institutions is closely tied to what India was going through at that moment. The events leading to it was because on 12 June 1975 the Allahabad High Court (a state high court in India) declared Indira Gandhi's election in her constituency null and void and barred her from contesting elections for six years. The court also asked the Congress party (to with the prime minister belonged), to find a replacement in 20 days. This led to nationwide protests for her to be removed.

On 26 June 1975, a national emergency was declared by Prime Minister Indira Gandhi, where many of basic fundamental rights were suspended with curbs on the press and freedom of speech and expression. In many ways, the rise of the independent non-fiction films is tied to this history. For many years, these films were a counter to the production of state narratives through the trope of the audiovisual oral testimony of people affected by policies of the state. From Anand Patwardhan's *Zameer Ke Bandi* (Prisoners of Conscience, 1987), Deepa Dhanraj's *Kya Hua Is Shahar Ko* (What Happened to This City? 1986) to Ranjan Palit and Vasudha Joshi's *Voices from Baliapal* (1988) – these documentary films employed the first-person interview to the camera alongside the commentary of the filmmaker to challenge hegemonic narratives produced by the state. From the late 1980's onward, there was a rupture to this form in the Indian documentary film practice. From Manjira Dutta's *Babulal Bhuiya ki qurbani* (Sacrifice of Babulal Bhuiya, 1988), Ruchir Joshi's *Tales from Planet Kolkata* (1993), Amar Kanwar's *A Season Outside* (1997), a different kind of film aesthetic emerged. Loosely termed as essay films – these documentaries did not rely on oral testimonies to produce a landscape of ideas and counter narratives of the state. These films relied on the filmmaker stitching together a diverse set of moving images from different places. The filmmaker's aesthetic choices and commentary produced meaning for the viewer.

Alongside this, new avenues for screening films outside the theatrical space opened up as well. These were film collectives and film clubs that emerged. They were taken to people in their cities and communities by different activist groups, community organizers, and film collectives burgeoning in the country, especially in the states of Kerala and West Bengal. Perhaps one of the reasons that these two states in the country saw the rise of a film screening culture (along with other forms of cultural expression) is because they had elected state governments that were left parties. Many artists, that included filmmakers/members of film collectives, were either members of the left party or were sympathizers. They were committed taking films to a non-metropolitan audience who could access films made in India and different parts of the world. From the 1960s onward, there were various film societies that emerged in different cities in India like Madras (Chennai), Bombay (Mumbai), Delhi, Patna, and Calcutta (Kolkatta), but they screened mostly fiction films.

The Mumbai International Film Festival (MIFF) began in 1990, supported by the Ministry of Information and Broadcasting. The festival was conducted once in two years and continues to be one of the largest spaces to showcase independent documentary films. A parallel history to MIFF emerged in 2004 when many independent filmmakers boycotted the festival as a result of a new censorship regime to screen films emerged. They organized a film festival called Vikalp: Films for Freedom, which ran for six days. Vikalp continues to screen non-fiction films in the Mumbai and Bengaluru and is run by filmmakers in the city. Apart from MIFF, some of the other film festivals that are in India today are Madurai International Documentary and Short Film Festival (1998); Experimenta India (2003), which screens experimental films and is held in the city of Bengaluru; Bring Your Own Film festival, BYOFF (2004), in Puri, Orissa, where filmmakers and artistes bring their films and screen it in makeshift tents; Asian Women's Film Festival (2005), run by IAWRT India, which showcases films by Asian women filmmakers in the city of New Delhi; VIBGYOR film festival (2006); Thrissur (Kerala), which screens non-fiction films and includes activist films as well; International Documentary and Short Film Festival of Kerala, IDSFFK

(2009); SIGNS Film Festival (2008), which takes place in the city of Thiruvananthapuram, Kerala; Bangalore Queer Film Festival, BQFF (2009), which is held in the city of Bengaluru and screens national and international films (fiction and non-fiction) on queer issues; and Kashish Mumbai International Queer Film Festival (2010), which takes place in the city of Mumbai. This list is in no way exhaustive as in the past decade many non-fiction film festivals have mushroomed in different cities of India. There are a variety of reasons for this – the turn from analog to digital that made the infrastructure for screenings easier, a larger production of non-fiction films with diverse aesthetic and storytelling methods that has increased audience, and corporate sponsorship and government support in some states in India. But what the list illustrates is that it was in this fecund screening culture that Urban Lens film festival emerged within an institutional framework in the year 2013.

Urban Lens Film Festival

The Indian Institute for Human Settlement (IIHS) is a private interdisciplinary institution that was set up to understand different forms of urban practice and the Urban Lens film festival, is in many ways, an extension of IIHS' interdisciplinary core. Historically, in academia and in the world of knowledge production certain canons and methods have always been privileged over tacit modes of understanding and making visible the world. The festival began in 2013 as a way to understand how filmmakers and artists engaged with the urban questions and what new forms of knowledge (outside the domain of academia) this encounter has produced. Urban Lens film festival is non-competitive and curated by the programming team at the IIHS, Media Lab. The programming is curated by the IIHS Media Lab (and in some years working with external film curators) and supported by the institution. There are no corporate sponsors for the festival, but in some editions of the festivals, there have been collaborations with cultural institutions like the Goethe Institut Max Muller Bhawan, Alliance Francaise, the Danish Cultural Centre, and the India Foundation for the Arts.

The management of the festival is led by the Media Lab but supported by various programs in IIHS that help execute the festival. The festival has no sponsorship and is entirely by the labor and resources of those working at IIHS. While the film festival takes place in the city of Bengaluru, some years have also seen the festival travel to Delhi and Mumbai. While in the initial editions of the festival from 2013 to 2016, mostly non-fiction films were screened, subsequently fiction films also began to be screened. The festival currently screens films from all genres where films from Latin America, Africa, North America, and Asia have been screened.

The festival, over the years, has attempted to not just bring film practitioners and academics in dialogue with each other but to also have filmmakers screen their film and speak about their work to a larger public, on their own terms. The festival programming is not restricted to the screening of films made in the not-too-distant past, as is common with most film festivals. While the exhibition of recent and innovative work provides audiences with the excitement of encountering the new, it leaves the task of creating a deeper discourse around films to film academics/historians and disseminating in the limited domain of academic conferences. This has tended to separate out from the possibilities films have to offer through broader public viewing and conversations. This is the reason that the Urban Lens film festival has always remained non-competitive.

The Urban Lens festival addresses the question of how one reconciles the worlds of film practice and theory while recognizing that each has its own place. This is why conversations around films are a very important feature of the festival, which has, over the years, tried to create a space for film practitioners and artists to have a dialogue among themselves and with a larger public about the relationship between aesthetics, ideas and urban life. While the first few editions of the festival mostly featured non-fiction films, in 2017 fiction films were introduced into the programming. This is because while "fiction" and "non-fiction" are categories that offer a starting point for understanding certain cinematic histories and formal impulses, filmmakers have always complicated the distinction. Non-fiction filmmakers have always used tropes of fiction, and vice versa. And yet there is limited conversation among practitioners, scholars, and a film-going public to explore how fiction and non-fiction practices are two sides of the same coin and emerge from shared histories. Over the years, no matter which genre of film is being screened, the programming has asked certain fundamental questions time and again – what are the minutiae of urban life in different cities, and what new forms of narrative emerge that make us reflect on the idea of cinema itself?

The festival runs for three to four days in the city of Bengaluru. The curation is a mix of screenings followed by conversations with the director, and sometimes the crew, of the film. Conversations with filmmakers unpacking the narrative and form of the film are an important element of the festival – as crucial as the screening itself. Apart from this, Urban Lens has a curated section every year that are conversations with film practitioners – cinematographers, editors, and sound-recordists (often described as "technicians") – around their body of work and how their practice feeds into the vision of the film. This is because a film is often seen as an extension of a director's vision and what she brings to the table. While that may be true to some extent, film is a collaborative form, and each person in the crew brings in not just their skills but also their aesthetics and thoughts. How one then begins to understand the nature of collaboration and its generative possibilities is something the festival has tried to pay close attention to. Another feature of Urban Lens film festival is that it screens films around the urban in the broadest possible manner. The term urban produces a certain imagery of the city with its built environment. The films screened at the festival interrogate this idea of the urban and produce broader ideas of what we mean by the city and the urban condition. This is also a part of the reason that the festival has never had a thematic curation under the urban. A thematic curation has the danger of fixing the meaning of the text of the film, and drawing the attention of the audience to only a particular set of things. Leaving the audience to create their own meanings and subtexts opens out the possibility of a diverse reading of films in the post-screening discussion. The audience who attend the festival is quite diverse – cinephiles, urban researchers/students, people living in the neighborhood – different forms of public constitute the Urban Lens audience.

Looking Back

In the past, while two editions of the festival have had an open call entry for submission of films, the curation is largely driven by cinephiles' gaze. This has meant that the festival does have a fidelity to some of the norms that govern most film festivals in India or internationally, namely, the year of production. In most competitive festivals, screenings are determined by the "newness" of the film or how successful or "big" the film is. The logic of the film festival circuit and screenings follow a predictable pattern, which in many ways determines the life of an independent film. While these spaces are extremely crucial for independent films outside the studio system, they create their own hierarchies and networks of privilege which determines which films get watched, where and for how long. At Urban

Lens, the year of production of the film is irrelevant. This is because film as a text is open to different readings, over time. How one responds to a film can and does change with the passage of time. So a film made in the 1970s or 1980s would have had a different relationship with the audience viewing it at that time, as opposed to the audience viewing it today, who will imbue it with meanings from their present contexts. I would like to illustrate this by sharing examples of three films that have been screened at the Urban Lens film festival, followed by conversation with the directors of the film.

The first one is *Kya Hua Is Shahar Ko*, made in 1986 by filmmaker Deepa Dhanraj. The film chronicles the communal violence that took place between the Hindu-Muslim community in 1984 in the city of Hyderabad, India. Perhaps the first film to document a riot as it was happening in a pre-mediatized time, the film was denied a censor certificate and was eventually granted it nine months after the completion of the film. For three years after it was granted the censor certificate, the film was screened in various cities across India. The filmmaker's own VHS copy was damaged as a result and the film disappeared from public circulation. Twenty-three years later, a subtitled print of the film that remained in the Arsenal film archive was restored into a digital copy, and screenings of the film began to take place once again from 2013. Film academic Nicole Wolf (2013), responsible for the digitization of the film and its circulation in the public domain in the present, writes about its reappearance:

> How do we project and view this film today? What might the film evoke in those who lived through the period it reflects on and what does it propose for a younger generation? To which time, to which context, to which politics does it belong or how does it transcend those parameters and pose questions towards the making of politics, and of political film, on a wider geopolitical platform? How to meet the concerns that inspired the film then and extend those to the urgencies of now?

The film was screened in 2014 at the Urban Lens film festival to a new generation of audience and for many who have no memory of that time (Dhanraj 2019) They were encountering an image and a form that belonged to its time. And yet in reencountering it materially (film stock that had been converted to digital) and the formal choices the filmmaker made at the time, *Kya Hua Is Shahar Ko* transforms itself from an artifact in an archive to a piece of work that has resonance with an audience living with the memory of 2002 Gujarat pogrom and many things that followed in its wake.

The second film that I would like to take the example of to illustrate my point is *Kamlabai* by editor and director, Reena Mohan. Made in 1992, the film shot on celluloid is a portrait of Kamlabai Gokhale, one of first actresses of Indian silent cinema. The film is a series of conversations with her, aged 88, and the filmmaker. It took Mohan three years to complete the film using her own resources and borrowing equipment and time from friends and fellow journeypersons. In the post-screening discussion of the film (available on the IIHS YT channel) at the festival in 2019, Mohan speaks of the difficult task of arriving at the final cut of the film (Mohan 2019). She was severely constrained not only with money and film stock but also the challenges of shooting an interview with a person who was elderly and could not move around. *Kamlabai* was perhaps the first non-fiction film in independent non-fiction filmmaking, that pushed the interview format beyond what one was used to seeing. The outtakes of the film, where Kamlabai turns the gaze and asks the filmmaker questions, finds its way in the final film, thereby turning the gaze back at the person asking the question. Many non-fiction filmmakers thereafter have used this method as a way to acknowledge their positionality and gaze. For the audience, watching the film 28 years later gives an insight into documentary film practice history and ways in which independent filmmakers were pushing the envelope in pre-digital times. The film, in many ways, also expanded the meaning of political filmmaking, which until that point had only meant films that had challenged state power.

The third film I would like to illustrate my point with is *Unlimited Girls* by Paromita Vohra (2019). Made in 2002 with the ushering of the digital age and lighter/smaller film equipment and non-linear editing, the film is an exploration of the many meanings of feminism. The film is a pastiche of different forms – interviews, songs, fictionalized sequences, chat room conversations – to unpack what feminism could mean for the fictional character in the film. It was perhaps the first non-fiction Indian film that was used humor as a way to explore an issue. Vohra creates a kaleidoscope of formal choices, unseen up until that point, to ask the question "What is feminism?" Her film also illustrates the deep relationship between technology and aesthetics. In her post-screening discussion at the Urban Lens film festival, she says that the film would not have been possible if it weren't for smaller camera equipment and non-linear editing. Much of the formal choices were enabled because of leaps in technology.

Kya Hua Is Shahar Ko?, *Kamlabai*, and *Unlimited Girls* were made by women non-fiction filmmakers who were responding to the world around them and the curiosities that they felt. They expanded the meaning of "political documentaries" through different methods. To encounter their works in a film festival space followed by a conversation exposes a new generation of audience not only to read their work carefully but also to be able to connect the dots between different generations of filmmakers and their practices.

The pulsating heart of cinema has always been about sitting in a dark room and encountering films collectively, each in their private universe, creating their own fantasies and meanings. A film festival is a shared space where ideas, feelings, and ways of seeing the world find a home. For it is in the viewing and conversations that the future of cinema lies, in a world rapidly moving toward an atomized viewing culture in the privacy of one's home or private space. The Urban Lens film festival will have its tenth edition in 2024. The first edition of the festival in 2013 began modestly with the screening of ten non-fiction films followed by conversation with filmmakers. While over the past ten years, the festival has expanded in its scope and reach, it hopes to continue remaining a space for many kinds of cinemas on the city, especially of the global South, and conversations.

References

Dhanraj, Deepa. 2019. "Deepa Dhanraj: In Conversation with Avijit Mukul Kishore." *Urban Lens Film Festival*, September 26. https://www.youtube.com/watch?v=WTXj5waVLGM

Mohan, Reena. 2019. "Reena Mohan in conversation with Shabani Hassanwalia." *Urban Lens Film Festival*, September 21. https://www.youtube.com/watch?v=Ff94DvcxsBY

Vaidya, Abhay. 2022. "With Its Impressive Legacy, Films Division Should be Allowed to Remain Autonomous." *Wire.in*, January 13. https://thewire.in/film/films-division-india

Vohra, Paromita. 2019. "Paromita Vohra in conversation with Swati Bandi." *Urban Lens Film Festival*, September 22. https://www.youtube.com/watch?v=jCUJkJ4yInc

Wolf, Nicole. 2013. "Kya Hua is Shahar ko?/What Happened to this City? History, Context and Reflections on Re-Screening a Political Film Booklet." Essay and Video Interviews for DVD Edition of *Kya Hua is Shahar Ko?* (1986). Released by Filmgalerie 451, Berlin.

43

TO BE CONTINUED

Women Make Waves International Film Festival

Beth Tsai

Taiwan's film industry, like other national film industries since the colonial era, struggles with gender disparity after inheriting Japan's film business structure and rigid filmmaking practices (Lee 2021).[1] This resulted in, not surprisingly, a working environment and a field of film professionals dominated by men, not to mention that the production resources created and shared have reflected an implicit gender bias. The names of a few Taiwanese women directors, screenwriters, and film festival curators did not go unnoticed. However, the fact remains that these women still occupy a secondary role in the industry and their voices remain stifled. To this day, women directors are still largely absent in feature-length film production in this island nation. Although many of them were able to pivot and flourish in the documentary field (Sang 2022), women's under-representation in Taiwan's film industry remains endemic.

It was in this context that Taiwan's Women Make Waves International Film Festival, commonly referred to Women Make Waves, was inaugurated in 1993. Despite it being Taiwan's only and Asia's largest film festival dedicated to moving images created by women filmmakers, academic scholarship and film festival reports covering this event in the Anglophone world remains limited and sparse, outdated even (cf. Huang 2003; Aufderheide and Zimmerman 2004). By delineating the history of the Women Make Waves and its intertwined relationship with feminist movements in Taiwan, this chapter can demonstrate that this film festival is more than an identity-based practice; rather, it functions as a "subaltern festival" (Wong 2011) to disrupt patriarchy, while employing feminist tactics and controversy as market branding – juxtaposed with the example of Cannes – to necessarily challenge the patriarchal beliefs and power that are so deeply ingrained in Taiwanese society. Also, by looking at spectator genre preferences in feminist cinema, I draw attention to how these preferences mirror the conservative Confucian ethics that have had a long history in this country, reflecting values that support heterosexual normativity and male superiority. Confucianism-influenced dominant ideology also perpetuates the general public's reluctance, inability, mortification, and even unwillingness to explore topics that are incompatible with conservatism (e.g., female sexual pleasure). Lastly, a film festival is not just an alternative exhibition and deterritorialized network for women filmmakers but also constructs women's history, writing herstory.

DOI: 10.4324/9781003266952-56

The Entangled Histories of Taiwan's Women's Movements

The history of Women Make Waves is intimately intertwined and codependent with the domestic women's rights movement. The 1980s can be considered an "awakening" period for Taiwan, involving the political transition after the ending of 38 years of martial law in 1987; changes in macroeconomic conditions, including the shift from an unskilled labor workforce to capital-intensive and knowledge industries; and, most importantly, political movements and ideological progression. The women's rights movement in the post-martial-law era in Taiwan helped raise and shape women's consciousness, drawing attention not only to the recognition of women's issues in women's cinema, but simultaneously identifying the gender inequality that has existed in the screen industries. Treating cinema as radical and reactionary, the joint effort between feminist organizations and the festival platform solidified itself with independent filmmaking worldwide by highlighting the underrepresented and unacknowledged work of women directors and presenting worthy issues often ignored in Taiwan's mainstream cinema. These issues include the perpetuation of gender-biased and stereotypical representation of women on screen, the under-representation of women film professionals in the workforce, unequal access to an uneven distribution of production funds and governmental subsidies, and the lack of advocacy and opportunities for women to advance their careers.

The festival was launched by two feminist NGOs – the Women Awakening Association and the Black and White Film Studio – which aimed to inform women in Taiwanese society about women's issues and raise their consciousness and foster their empowerment. First-named Taiwan Women's Visual Arts Festival, the event was founded by activist and writer Lee Yuan-chen, academic scholars Chang Hsiao-hung and Fifi Ding, and film directors Wang Ping and Huang Yu-shan (the latter a founder of the Black and White Film Studio), initially set out to screen more narrowly defined moving images, media art, and experimental cinema in gallery spaces. The lineup included, for example, Trinh T. Minh-ha's experimental documentary *Surname Viet Given Name Nam* (1989), Kathy High's short video *I Need Your Full Cooperation* (1989, now part of the permanent collection of the Museum of Modern Art), and a black and white experimental short *Prayjob* (1995) by Danish director Bynke Maibøll, featuring explicit sex scenes.

Women Make Waves did not expand outside of the museum gallery until its third year when it began to curate around a dedicated theme. The screenings of these films were accompanied by program information that provided the context of the film (explaining the curatorial decisions and why films of specific directors were chosen). There would be special focus offered (such as, in one case, a retrospective on Chantal Akerman or a theme on self-portrait film), and essays that provided insights and reflections on their selection process and op-ed writings – insisting that only women directors could render these topics and sentiments. The range of the topics reflected in their film curation included women in the workplace, gender and bodies, the cultivation of women's consciousness, racial and ethnic representations in the media, and feminist movements, to name a few. Women Make Waves considered its duty to be a platform spotlighting intimate and sometimes taboo or controversial subjects and assumed an institutional role to dialogue with the public. The festival presumed the function of cinema to generate discussions and debates, building on the belief that cinema is an art form that can potentially create social change. The contention was, that if the festival could screen women's cinema from different parts of the world, it would allow the audience to recognize that some of the narratives presented shared the same stories that Taiwanese women face today. In other words, the festival hoped to show that these struggles and the social injustice they experienced were universal.

The early days of Women Make Waves coincided with the burgeoning of new teaching institutions, media platforms and broadcasting channels, and art practices, such as the establishment of the Tainan National University of the Arts in 1996 (formally the Tainan National College of the Arts), known for their training in sound and image arts. Around the same time, one of the organizations that co-founded Women Make Waves – Black and White Film Studio – branched out and partnered with the Democratic Progressive Party and organized a Tsa-bóo Film Festival in 1995 (Tsa-bóo means woman or female in the Hokkien/Taiwanese dialect). Taiwan's Public Television Service (*Gonggong dianshi*), the country's first independent public broadcasting institution, created the Viewpoints program, dedicated specifically to programming and curating documentary films. A decade later, Women Make Waves continued its expansion and formed a global alliance with city-based women's film festivals in the neighboring countries (South Korea and Japan) called the Network of Asian Women's Film Festival. India and Israel later joined the alliance in 2009. These efforts and institutional expansions created new cosmopolitan spaces in which independent and women filmmakers could showcase their work, specifically encouraging women to explore gender issues with documentary filmmaking, and thereby subvert the reality of the Taiwan film industry's "woman problem," a system that was and is headed by men for the benefit of men.

Herstory, Her Mission, and Feminist Tactics

As stated on their official website in its historical overview and mission statement, at its inception the programming strategy of Women Make Waves was to create an alternative exhibition platform "outside the mainstream male-centric perspective." The 1993 first run highlighted the theme of women's bodily autonomy as a way in which to position the film festival within the discourse of feminism and local women's rights movements (Y. Wang 2003). By the third rendition of the event, the festival began to adopt an even more empathetic approach to the selection of feature-length films, by choosing films that explicitly dealt with women's erotic desires, sexual potential, arousal, temptation, affection, and love. Sometimes women's lust is not inextricably bound up with emotional connection but instead with a craving for sexual variety. The dedicated theme and the focus on women's erotic desire were not only daring for its time, but these film screenings extended a sanctuary for women to extricate themselves from traditional gender roles that require women to be passive and submissive, focusing more on pleasing others than on their own pleasure. The curatorial tactic to focus on women's sexual desire is audacious as gender politics in Taiwan in that period was still much constrained by the traditional values and principles of Chinese culture – a patriarchal system promoted by the Confucian-oriented ideology in which women should be subjugated to men and dominated by them.

Of note is a proverb familiar to the many Taiwanese: *wen liang gong jian rang*. Its literal translation means to be warm, kind, and respectful to others, while living on very little money (*jian*, or frugal) and to always compromise and be amicable when facing a disagreement (*rang*, or compromise). This conveys the basic belief and value governing women's etiquette, indirectly, without explicitly saying so. Because the proverb is ingrained in thoughts and every facet of life, Taiwanese society expects women not to deviate from this model. Women Make Waves' selection of films focusing on women's liberated sexual desire thus allows the audience the opportunity of exposure to these vanguards, these contrasting views, during a time before the HBO series *Sex and the City* (1998–2004) aired in syndication worldwide – a series that was recognized as a trailblazer for its sex-positive commentary that allowed women to engage in these conversations more openly. Women Make Waves broadened private discussions on eroticism by creating a public space (and a public discourse) for dialogue on sexuality and women's rights in Taiwanese society (Y. Wang 2003, 19).

To combat mainstream "male-centric" domination, as the Women Make Waves declared in their mission statement, the film festival set out with exclusionary practices to ensure work by women. At that time, those who fit the narrow definition of "biologically female" were guaranteed a spot in the program. At its outset, to be qualified for program consideration, applicants had to adhere to the festival's three ground roles: One, the film work must be directed or created by a female director. Two, the content of the work must be women-centric, whether by positioning women at the forefront or by telling an empowering story through its on-screen female characters. Three, the film should feature themes and issues related to women and girls (P. Wang 2003, 141). The festival's founders saw the qualification rules as necessary to subvert the under-representation of women directors in the industry. By extension, these rules represent a continuation of the feminist ideologies of the co-founder of the Women Awakening Association, the feminist pioneer-turned-vice-president Lu Hsiu-lien (also known as Annette Lu). Without a doubt, in today's crowded market of international film festivals worldwide, Women Make Waves would be pigeonholed as a niche LGBTQ film festival that emerged out of identity politics, practiced identity-based (or gender-based) programming, and assimilated identity politics into a wider public community discussion through the festival site.

Why mention Lu Hsiu-lien? Taiwan's first-wave feminist movement in the 1970s is indebted to Lu Hsiu-lien, a student turned government worker and an undeniably critical figure in women's liberation, who, by setting up various activities had helped organize the women's movement in Taiwan. Influenced by the 1960s second-wave feminism in the US that heightened consciousness of legal inequalities to a wider range of issues (voting and property rights), Lu introduced these radical concepts to Taiwan and focused on critiquing the patriarchal institutions and cultural practices, in particular, those affecting women in the workplace and reproductive rights (and the right to make autonomous decisions about her own body). The women's contraception conundrum, especially the right to choose when and if a woman wants to start to grow a family, has been a hot public debate. From the festival founder and programmer Huang's (2003) perspective, Lu's legacy and her involvement in women's liberation greatly shaped how she envisioned the direction of the festival and the films selected.

Abortion may have been legalized in Taiwan when Women Made Waves was inaugurated in 1993, but the right to safe and legal abortion laws had just been passed in 1984, less than a decade before. Abortion access may have been technically legal and available since the Japanese colonial era (1895–1945) – but in actuality, access was only permitted (or without the fear of repercussion) to those when pregnancy led to life-threatening health complications. Physicians and healthcare professionals in Taiwan began publicly supporting woman's rights and autonomy to abortion in the 1970s, but it was until 1984 that the legal right to abortion was enacted under the Eugenic Health Law. The feminist tactics are about putting women and women's issues on center stage, creating a platform, and amplifying these dissenting voices. However, through curation and programming, it became apparent that the film festival selection was not only intended to broaden the scope of feminism and to encourage a public discussion about a controversial subject, but that the fight for feminism was also the fight for democracy, to go against the authoritarian Nationalist Party that has been governing Taiwan since 1949.

The feminist movements in Taiwan have led Women Make Waves to continuously foster kinship and build bridges with other supporting organizations, such as Foundation for Women's Rights, the Public Television Service, and the Taipei Women's Rescue Foundation. The collaboration arrived at a consciousness of treating an identity-based film festival as a site of the production of knowledge serving the public sphere. Some of the films the festival featured were meant to spotlight how far women's liberation has come to challenge the dominant views of Taiwanese society in the 1980s and 1990s. These films exhibited women's involvement as democracy advocates, demonstrated how women's groups sought to intervene in domestic violence and abuse, and documented how women who have been involved in politics or participated in protests or political movements have faced retaliation from their friends and co-workers, and those of their supervisors or administrators.

One quintessential example is Chien Wei-Su's one-hour documentary, *Echo with Women's Voices – Their Involvement in Political Movements* (2005). This work documented women's political participation in Taiwan over the past 30 years. It includes valuable historical and rare photographs, starting from First Wave Feminism in 1971 and bookended with the scandalous, cold-blooded murder of Peng Wan-ru in 1996. The film includes interviews with many high-profile, influential feminist pioneers, including Lu Hsiu-lien, Peng Wan-ru, Chen Chu (part of the Kaohsiung Eight, who were arrested and put behind bars after the Kaohsiung Incident in 1979), Yeh Chu-lan (former secretary to the president of Taiwan), and many other influential figures. Among these interview clips, Peng Wan-ru (recorded before she was raped and killed) commented that the Confucian ethics in Taiwanese education fuels the patriarchal belief that women are weak and that a Taiwanese woman is expected to perform a subservient role to men. Peng's statement and her cruel death also explain why authoritarianism is fearful of empowered women – because their robust participation in the workforce, in politics, and in civic life not only challenge the traditional binary patriarchal model but also transform society and build a global ascendant pro-democracy coalition.

Controversies and Contradictions

In thinking about how film festivals interconnect with the public sphere and cinema culture, we can consider festivals as the material practices of a cultural industry driven by cultural policy (Rhyne 2016). The web and reach of this industry are complex as well. The worldwide proliferation of film festivals has been regarded as an alternative exhibition to movie theaters and multiplexes. But festivals are also a site of distribution networks and cultural designations of knowledge and taste (de Valck 2007). Film festivals have been easily misconstrued as "concrete events, encompassing both time and physical spaces that allow people to congregate" (Wong 2016, 85), when even with archives[2] a festival is still ephemeral in essence (Damiens 2020).

Curiously, film festivals strive to live on the reputation of "things that went wrong" or dealing with "unplanned" incidents and make their way to newspapers' headlines. It signals an almost perhaps intentional distraction of going against a festival's presumed ability to "perform reliably," which creates a paradox of the festival interlaced with media coverage of the event's predictable "unreliability" (Harbord 2016, 77). Cannes, for example, has a reputation for its consistent scandals and controversies on all fronts, from the mildest instances of choosing controversial movies that earned walkouts (e.g., films by Lars von Trier, Gaspar Noé, and even Tsai Ming-liang's *Visage*) to the festival's general complacency and the director Thierry Frémaux's unabashed defense of supporting sexual predators (e.g., defending director Roman Polanski, who is a convicted rapist and has a long history of sexual abuse). From the festival's interruption in May 1968 to the many and recent controversial statements ushered by film directors and movie stars, it ostensibly points to "controversy" as a label and its almost deliberate self-branding strategy. The strategy to invoke controversy and provoke public debates isn't unique to Cannes: it almost seems that festivals need controversies, that they can't survive without them. Controversies, as an added force, would only extend and expand the public exposure of an event that relies on them.

   This insistence on garnering media attention also reemphasizes the particularities of the "happening," that events are unfolding in real time and on locations instead of diverting to a pre-recorded, (re)mediated situation in which film screening and the experience of viewing them are not only separate in time and space but also only relevant to what could have happened during the spontaneous discussion on site. A festival event wants the "immediacy" that screening a pre-recorded film reel couldn't have achieved at a Cineplex. As Janet Harbord describes it, the festival, like the early cinema of attractions, "harnesses the time of contingency through live events that bookend screenings, introducing into the offering the singularity of an experience that *cannot be reproduced* at a later date or location" (my emphasis, Harbord 2016, 76).

   With its aspiration and the French discourse to position itself as an alternative global cultural powerhouse to Hollywood, Cannes presents another paradox of the film festival construct, concocting a contradictory image as both a champion of art-house cinema along with courtship of Hollywood stars on the red carpet.[3] Cannes' competition sections and its crown jewels prize Palme d'Or favor art films over blockbuster movies, but Cannes persists in pursuing Hollywood stars for "ambiance and attraction" (Wong 2016, 86). Because of the paradoxical nature of these A-list festivals (Cannes' situation very much applies to Venice and Berlin), Cindy Wong's (2016) postulation of attuning to "subaltern festivals," by which she means "women's festivals, ethnic festivals, or any festivals that promote the voices of subordinated classes or issues" should be further examined when exploring the discursive and counter-formations of the public sphere (90).

Dialogue and Positionality: An Urban-Rural Divide

If Cannes has never been afraid to embrace – or leverage – controversial moments, Women Make Waves had to lean into the unrecognized contradiction, biases, and blind spots within a position to advocate marginalized voices. Indeed, Cindy Wong (2016) noted that "the very contradictory tendencies within film festivals can give rise to a better understanding of how different public spheres – bourgeois, counter, and subaltern – either complement each other or demand their own 'spaces' within negotiated contestations" (90). Film festivals throughout the world usually take place in major cosmopolitan cities as a form of state-sponsored or state-sanctioned cultural diplomacy to promote tourism and city economics. With the type of vanguard feminist films selected, Women Make Waves inevitably created a space that circumscribes dissension among city versus rural viewers. Namely, the festival faces the critique of orchestrating a chasm between the rural and urban divide on spectatorship and feminist ideology.

One of the criticisms had to do with the festival's heavy-handed Euro-American film programming. When radical women's cinema was introduced and screened in Taiwan, most of these films were from Euro-American countries. In 2001, at the eighth Women Make Waves event, the film festival featured a retrospective of Agnès Varda (see Figure 43.1), screening eight of her films. Of all the 42 films shown in conjunction, only 19 were domestic productions. In collaboration with Cinematek (Cinémathèque royale de Belgique), a retrospective of Chantal Akerman was featured in 2016, dedicated to celebrating newly preserved and digitally restored films. In the program guide, Akerman's films were introduced as more than a lesbian tribute but about validating the perspective of queer women. The radical lesbian gaze manifested in films, for example, *Je Tu Il Elle* (I, You, He, She, 1974), deconstructs the heteronormativity binary and "rewrites film history" (Chang 2016). It was

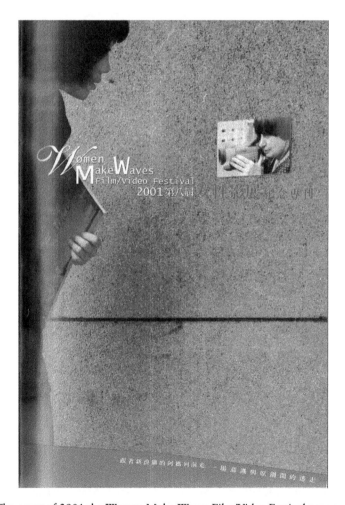

Figure 43.1 The cover of 2001 the Women Make Waves Film/Video Festival program guide.

502

in 2008 that the festival featured a more substantive, curated program spotlighting films entirely from East Asia (named "Korean Passion"); only recently in 2021 did the festival feature a retrospective on a singular women auteur, Mi-Mi Lee, from Taiwan.

Yet to some this repeated spotlight on art-house cinema seems to be a slippery path to indoctrinate the feminist movement for all its intents and purposes with an elitist perspective, which would further marginalize the situation of the working class, the underserved communities, and racialized women (typically women from Southeast Asian nations who married citizens of Taiwan, also referred to as "new immigrant women"). As an attempt to redress some of the criticisms that Women Make Waves is anchored in exclusive practices, the festival began to increase the scale of the event by diversifying its screening locations to cities and towns outside the capital, Taipei. The festival wanted to avoid being invoked as perpetrating the postcolonial notion of the "center" (projecting a hegemonic view of a progressive society) to thereby fall into the pattern of neglecting geographical, economic, ethnic, and cultural peripheries (Lo 2016).

One of the early challenges Women Make Waves encountered was how to educate the public about social issues through these films beyond public screenings. Women Make Waves primarily partnered with schools, community colleges and public agencies in its initial community outreach. The festival also recognized the importance of broadening its audience, from college students to local women's support groups, hoping that the curated films could reach a wider general audience outside the intellectual presupposition. According to Ting Ching You's (2003) field research, city moviegoers value the ritual aspect of a film festival and would be willing to block out an entire day to spend in the theaters, going from one screening to the next. This was not the case for viewers based in the countryside and rural towns; for them, time is limited, and they may be preoccupied with labor-intensive work, so they would tend to be selective with movie times and their genre preferences. For example, rural viewers much prefer documentaries, such as *Xiao Wei* (dir. The Su-jun, Yang Ke-fan, Wu Yi-fang 2000) and *Going Solo* (dir. Huang Chun-man 2001; You 2003, 50–51). The former film portrays the conflict matrimony between indigenous people and the Han community; the latter documented two widows coping with the grief of losing a partner while trying to raise children. Both documentaries foregrounded the emotional core of their human subjects and intimately examined all aspects of women's lives, especially their hardships. These genre types proved to be more popular among rural viewers than urban attendees.

On the other hand, college students preferred documentaries that offered an alternative view of women's solidarity: films that narrate the possibility of creating a parallel subculture as a resistance to Confucian piety and male dominance. For instance, *Nu Shu: A Hidden Language of Women in China* (dir. Yue-Qing Yang 1999) is a cross-cultural production between Canada and China that explores the undiscovered history of "écriture feminine" in feudal China. Urban audiences have also favored Vietnamese-born acclaimed filmmaker Trinh T. Minh-ha's work – who is also a scholar herself (You 2003, 51). *The Fourth Dimension* (2001) is Trinh's venture into digital filmmaking, and this work, as is the case with her previous lyrical films, sutures visual compositions and poetic narration that examine Japanese art meditating on time, travel, ceremony, and rituals. Urban viewers who were college students or who had received higher education have been more attuned to filmic themes that explore women's lust, attraction, and body autonomy. In contrast, community audiences and members who assumed the role of a mother were more drawn to films that grapple with day-to-day gendered hassle and emotional core issues (You 2003).

Considering the changing experience of women throughout history, Taiwanese society has not evolved from traditional gender values and expects a woman to take care of the home while a man provides financially for his family. Women most often are the ones who make compromises when the needs of children and other family members collide with their work. In her work, Yu Pin (1999) observes how the rural landscape shapes women's identities and their experience of leisure living in rural areas. If leisure is defined by an individual's ability to choose the activity or experience free from family or financial obligations, the agrarian culture restricts a woman's time and mobility; women possess little substantial freedom and choice of leisure activities in rural areas because their work patterns and where they are located determines their use of time. For many of them, the dilemma is not about choosing between work and free time; it is about the "meaning" of leisure as women's lives have been taken over by routine and compulsory housework. This framework thus provides a vital understanding of how the urban and rural settings impact community members' film viewing preferences. On the flip side, going to these feminist film screenings was not only a social visit for women living in the suburbs or the country-side; the experiences of being at the festival allowed patrons to consider that gender is a social-cultural construction, and to wrestle with how that construction shapes women's everyday life and leisure.

Call for Intersectionality

Women Make Waves is very aware of the spectatorial split and has since revised its mission statement to reflect that the festival has been committed to working with local communities, educational institutions, performing arts centers, and exhibition venues "to decrease the gap in Taiwan's urban-rural divide." While the festival continued to label itself as the largest festival in Taiwan "dedicated to supporting female talents," the language they use to lay out film eligibility has changed from "by a female director" to "directed at least by one FEMALE (including a self-identifying female) director" (original emphasis). In their most current film submission requirements, Women Make Waves have also broadened the content requirements using more inclusive language as, for example, their opening line writes: "WMWIFF is open to all forms, styles, lengths, and formats. Anything related to LGBTQI communities, women issues [*sic*] and ideologies such as feminism and post-feminism, and current events around the world that reflects the status quo of women." The festival also makes clear about submission it prohibits: they do not tolerate films that indicate "appearance anxiety" and "digital sexual violence." The latter category points to two major ethical concerns: obtaining consent is a must in creating any audiovisual work in the digital era. Second, when intimate and sexualized images of a person are distributed online without their consent, this is considered an image-based sexual abuse and assault facilitated by technology (such as via photos, videos, and social media).

As one of the core founders of the festival, Director Wang Ping has long meditated on definitions of "woman." She asks the following: Are trans women not considered "real women"? Shouldn't Women Make Waves allow trans women to be qualified for film submissions? Should films focusing on women and women topics but directed by men be included in the festival lineup? And to continue to reflect on transgender identities, Wang (2003) advocates that even though Women Make Waves is a film festival that foregrounds "woman," the festival programming should encompass all gender-related issues and should consider the practice of non-binary inclusion.

Over 30 years, the Women Make Waves Film Festival has undergone changes and transformation. While the festival program has continued to be dominated by world cinema, the festival carved out a Taiwan Competition category to offer a center stage for domestic production since 2013. Wang Ping (2003) lamented that compared to domestic production, international cinema continues to be more powerfully dialogue-provoking and offends and inspires curiosity and conversation in equal measure. It may seem Wang's criticism of Taiwan is rather harsh; she is right that there is still much room for growth in gender equality awareness in Taiwan (and in most parts of the world).

A recent scandal involving two students from the National Taiwan University reveals underlying gender biases in Taiwan's education system and social environment. Two economics students running for student council president caused public outrage by circulating an offensive set of proposals. The students' entire proposal was bigoted, sexist, full of body-shaming remarks, and completely discriminatory masked under "locker room jokes." Their ill-phrased remarks included mandating girls with "boobs smaller than an A cup" to enroll in elective classes, barring LGBTQ students from student council meetings, and opposing admission quotas for indigenous people (Taipei Times 2023). Other similar incidents in the past include an uproar among communities when a legislative politician publicly victim-shamed a firefighter who experienced sexual harassment in Taiwan's Yilan county, telling her she should have locked her bathroom door if she didn't want Peeping Toms. Neither incident should be seen as an isolated event or as examples of trivial speech. These impulsive acts and poorly phrased remarks are truth-telling: the politician's insensitive mansplaining reveals a harsh victim-blaming culture in the country's workplaces, schools, and society at large, and both examples mean that the concept of gender equality is completely lost on them.

This is why this chapter opens with the title "To Be Continued" so as to underscore that the gender equality issues under discussion have not resolved. Even though women filmmakers do not necessarily take to the streets or engage in demonstrations to demand immediate social changes, Women Make Waves has been able to construct a meaningful film culture and spectatorship *about* women and *for* women. The fight for women's equality is a fight against authoritarianism, and it isn't over yet.

Notes

1 Unlike the Taiwanese film industry where a film professional may wear multiple hats at work, the studio system, first introduced during the Japanese colonialization, emphasized clear divisions of positions and separate responsibilities and contributed to a film crew hierarchy. In an interview, director Mi-Mi Lee recalls that when she was working as a script supervisor for Tetsuya Yamanouchi in 1969, the Japanese film crew valued punctuality on the set more than everything else. Being one of the few women film crew on set gave her the privilege of learning from her male counterparts, and she reached the director position fairly quickly. At the same time, to maintain creative freedom and produce films that focus on the everyday experiences of women without having to resort to the themes of sexploitation or sacrificial woman surrender to piety and patriarchal values, Lee had to remove herself from Taiwan and start her own production company called Qian Kee Film Company in Hong Kong.
2 The concreteness of the festival platform can come from its archival practices, given the multitude of materials a festival produced, including festival reviews, press releases, program notes,

newspaper articles, and other documents (Burgess and Kredell 2016). But Antoine Damiens in his book *LGBTQ Film Festivals: Curating Queerness* (Amsterdam: Amsterdam University Press, 2020) details that identity-based film festivals are ephemeral in essence, they often only exist as traces within archival collections, and not all film festivals are archived or accessible to organizers, scholars, and historians.

3 For example, outsiders and non-regular festival attendees wondered why Harrison Ford walked the red carpet at the 76th Cannes Festival in 2023 or why the latest Indiana Jones movie premiered at Cannes, a site that seemingly only advocate art house and independent films.

Bibliography

Aufderheide, Pat, and Debra Zimmerman. 2004. "From A to Z: A Conversation on Women's Film-making." *Signs* 30 (1): 1455–72.

Burgess, Diane, and Brendan Kredell. 2016. "Positionality and Film Festival Research: A Conversation." In *Film Festivals: History, Theory, Method, Practice*, edited by Marijke de Valck, Brendan Kredell, and Skadi Loist, 159–76. London/New York: Routledge.

Chang, Yi-Seun. 2016. "Films that Worth Destroyed Destruction that Deserves Films a Gift from Chantal Akerman." In *23rd Women Make Waves Film Festival 2016*, 38–40. Taipei: Taiwan Women's Film Association.

Damiens, Antoine. 2020. *LGBTQ Film Festivals: Curating Queerness*. Amsterdam: Amsterdam University Press.

de Valck, Marijke. 2007. *Film Festivals: From European Geopolitics to Global Cinephilia*. Amsterdam: Amsterdam University Press.

Harbord, Janet. 2016. "Contingency, Time, and Event: An Archaeological Approach to the Film Festival." In *Film Festivals: History, Theory, Method, Practice*, edited by Marijke de Valck, Brendan Kredell, and Skadi Loist, 69–82. London/New York: Routledge.

Huang, Yu Shan. 2003. "Creating and Distributing Films Openly: On the Relationship between Women's Film Festivals and the Women's Rights Movement in Taiwan." *Inter-Asia Cultural Studies* 4 (1): 157–58.

Lee, Mi-Mi. 2021. Interview by Chih Heng Su. Taiwan Film and Audiovisual Institute, October 14, 2021, 15:05. https://youtu.be/KHd_A7N2tpA

Lo, Pecha. 2016. "Dual-direction Exposition (Dual Narratives): The Mingling of Sense and Sensibility." In *23rd Women Make Waves Film Festival 2016*, 4–5. Taipei: Taiwan Women's Film Association.

Rhyne, Ragan. 2016. "Film Festival Circuits and Stakeholders." In *Film Festival Yearbook 1: The Festival Circuit*, edited by Dina Iordanova and Ragan Rhyne, 9–39. St Andrews: St Andrews Film Studies.

Sang, Tze-lan Deborah. 2022. "Small Talk (2017): Critiquing Heteronormativity, Resisting Homonormativity." In *32 New Takes on Taiwan Cinema*, edited by Emilie Yueh-yu Yeh, Darrell William Davis, and Wenchi Lin, 439–50. Ann Arbor: University of Michigan Press.

Taipei Times. 2023. "No Place for Bigots." May 26, 2023. https://www.taipeitimes.com/News/editorials/archives/2023/05/26/2003800444.

Wang, Ping. 2003. "Nuxing yingzhan shi nian: pochu xingbie eryuan de 'nu' xing xingmao [Tenth Anniversary of Women Make Waves Film Festival: Breaking the Gender Binary and 'Feminine' Traits]." In *Retrospect and Perspectives–Aesthetics, Social & Cultural Perspectives of Women's Film/Video Works: Women Make Waves International Forum, Taipei and Kaohsiung, September 25–28*, 139–41. Taipei: Taipei Women Film and Video Association.

Wang, Ya-ko. 2003. "Taiwan Women Film Festival: History and Prospect [Tenth Anniversary of Women Make Waves Film Festival: Breaking the Gender Binary and 'Feminine' Traits]." In *Retrospect and Perspectives–Aesthetics, Social & Cultural Perspectives of Women's Film/Video Works: Women Make Waves International Forum, Taipei and Kaohsiung, September 25–28*, 15–22. Taipei: Taipei Women Film and Video Association.

Wong, Cindy Hing-Yuk. 2011. *Film Festivals: Culture, People, and Power on the Global Screen*. New Brunswick, NJ: Rutgers University Press.

Wong, Cindy Hing-Yuk. 2016. "Publics and Counterpublics: Rethinking Film Festivals as Public Spheres." In *Film Festivals: History, Theory, Method, Practice*, edited by Marijke de Valck, Brendan Kredell, and Skadi Loist, 83–99. London/New York: Routledge.

You, Ting Ching. 2003. "Zouchu Taipei: nuxing yingzhan zaidi xunhui de guanzhong xinli yu yingyan zhi jian de guanxi [Leaving Taipei: The Relationship between Audience Psychology and Screenings at Women Make Waves Film Festival]." In *Retrospect and Perspectives–Aesthetics, Social & Cultural Perspectives of Women's Film/Video Works: Women Make Waves International Forum, Taipei and Kaohsiung, September 25–28*, 46–59. Taipei: Taipei Women Film and Video Association.

Yu, Pin. 1999. "Funu yu xiuxian wenhua [Women's Leisure Lifestyles]." In *Xing shu guan xi (shang): xing bie yu she hui, jian gou* [Sexuality (I): Gender and Society, Construction], edited by Ya-ko Wang, 305–33. Taipei: Xinli Press.

44

FILM FESTIVAL JOURNEYS – PAST, PRESENT, FUTURE

A Conversation with Roger Garcia

Thong Kay Wee and Sangjoon Lee

Most renowned for his work in establishing the Hong Kong International Film Festival (HKIFF), Roger Garcia is a well-respected veteran of the film industry across the world and continues to enjoy a multi-hyphenate career that has spanned across more than four decades so far. Many would credit him as one of the pioneers for bringing consciousness to the framing of Asian cinema, and for his time at HKIFF (in the late 1970s and, later, in the 2000s) which inspired many newer festivals and film organizations in Asia to develop a similar regional focus. Roger has also advised and programmed many film festivals around the world including Berlin, Hainan, Locarno, London, San Francisco, Torino, and Udine. He has served on festival juries in Manila, Mumbai, Rotterdam, and Venice, among others.

As a film producer, he has worked on studio pictures in Hollywood and independent films in Asia and created the first US program on Asian and Asian American cinema for Comcast cable television. His writings on film have been published extensively by *Asiaweek*, *Cahiers du Cinema*, and the British Film Institute, among others. He was made Chevalier de l'Ordre des Arts et des Lettres by the French government in 2018. He is currently an adviser to the Asian Film Awards (AFA) Academy and continues to advise several film festivals around the world. This profile interview offers an insight into his professional history, his current thoughts about cultural work through film festivals, and his ideas for the film sector moving forward.

Thong Kay Wee (TKW): **You have been many things in your career: producer, critic, consultant, even policymaker in the government sector to name a few. But your name will always be synonymous with the work you do with film festivals in Asia. How did this relationship with film festival work begin, especially at a time when not many in Asia were doing it?**

Roger Garcia (RG): I was very lucky. I was in the right place at the right time when I went back to Hong Kong after studying art in England. I started working in the government in

DOI: 10.4324/9781003266952-57

1977 and because of my educational background, I was sent to work in the then nascent cultural services department. My first boss was Darwin Chen, who had the vision to improve and modernize the cultural life of Hong Kong – it was a response to the oft-heard description of Hong Kong as a "cultural desert" in the 1970s. So, we were involved in setting up local cultural institutions including building cultural centers, museums, and libraries. Looking back on that era (the late 1970s) I place the cultural initiative as one of the colonial government's efforts in localization in various fields such as district level representation, and the higher echelons of the administration.

One of the managers in the department was Paul Yeung. He had just come back from a professional visit to the UK with many ideas, and in quick succession, the department set up a Cantonese theater group, a dance company, a Chinese music orchestra, and the film festival. At the time the cultural film programs put on by institutions like the Goethe Institute and the Alliance Françoise were popular so the setting up of the film festival, as a showcase for international cinema, was partly a response to this audience demand.

Paul launched the Hong Kong International Film Festival (HKIFF) in the summer of 1977. I worked with him on festival programming and strategy such as introducing a contemporary Hong Kong film section, and the Hong Kong film retrospective, but he left shortly after to emigrate to Canada. Although I was in my mid-20s at the time, Darwin asked me to take his place. I had never run a film festival, of course, but I was up for it! I should add that there had been no other international film festivals in Asia at the time, we were the very first.

TKW: **That must have been a lot on your young shoulders. Did you set out any objectives with the Hong Kong International Film Festival at the beginning, and were there any reference points you could rely on?**

RG: set about trying to structure the film festival into something that would be sustainable and would last. Two things were very important to me: one was to bring international cinema to Hong Kong in a more curated form, not just showing anything and everything, and the other was to deep dive into Hong Kong's film history. In the latter I was influenced by the late Mr. Lin Nien-tung who had a great knowledge of Chinese aesthetics, and Hong Kong Cantonese and Mandarin language cinema. He curated the first HKIFF retrospective, a program on Hong Kong Cantonese cinema of the 1950s. It really was my first introduction to the rich history of Hong Kong cinema, especially coming back from England where I had been studying filmmakers like Douglas Sirk and Frank Borzage and had developed an interest in melodrama. I could see in the works of Zhu Shi-Lin, Lee Tit and Lee Sun-fung the kind of mise-en-scene that existed around the world at that time in the '50 s. As both a festival director and a cinephile this was a wonderful starting point and persuaded me that there was a cinema without borders and its common language was mise-en-scene and auteurship. For me, the (family) melodrama is as much of a cornerstone of Asian cinema as martial arts action. At the time most people thought of Hong Kong cinema as action cinema so the melodrama angle gave it a different, if not new, perspective.

And once again, I was in the right place at the right time because the Hong Kong New Wave was just emerging in the late '70s – people like Tsui Hark, Ann Hui, Allen Fong, Yim Ho, Ronnie Yu, and everybody else you care to name from New Hong Kong cinema. And I met some of them, including Allen Fong whose work I truly admire. *Ah Ying* (1983) is one of the masterpieces of Hong Kong cinema. I also met Po-chih, Leong who had just made *Foxbat* (1977), one of the first Hong Kong international co-productions. He's regarded as one of the precursors to the Hong Kong New Wave (through his first feature *Jumping Ash*) and Edward Yang thought of him as his mentor even though they make completely different types of films. He's still as energetic as ever. [*Post-interview note: Garcia prepared a small tribute program to Leong at the Far East Film Festival Udine, Italy in 2023.*] I truly enjoyed my interactions with filmmakers – three years before I had been studying the work of Satyajit Ray and Nagisa Oshima, reading Cahiers du Cinema in university. I had heard of Lino Brocka but hadn't had a chance to watch his films. Now I was having dinner with them and talking cinema with Serge Daney. I had been thrown in at the deep end of a pool I loved to swim in!

I think it's very easy nowadays, in film festival culture, to just say "Oh, I want to be a programmer at a film festival" or "I love to watch movies, and I'd like to choose them and show them to people." But it's very important to have a vision of what it is you're trying to do at the film festival. As an undergraduate, I attended the Edinburgh International Film Festival under the Screen group in the early 1970s, and it showed me that a film festival could really mix it up, not only in the range of films but also in mixing theory and practice. Peter Wollen and Paul Willemen (both of whom I got to know later) were really crucial

Figure 44.1   Roger Garcia with Ulrich Gregor and Hong Kong experimental filmmaker Jim Shum at Berlinale Forum press conference, 1987 (photo credit: Roger Garcia Collection).

in demonstrating how this could be done through festival activity. There are also three people whom I think had a vision: Richard Roud at the New York Film Festival in the '60s; Hubert Bals at the Rotterdam International Film Festival in the 1970s; and the most important – Ulrich Gregor, who created the Berlinale Forum in 1971. He is truly one of the most visionary programmers I've ever met. The Berlinale Forum in the '80s was very important to me because not only did Ulrich show some of my first productions there, but his program helped me understand more about the international perspective of what avant-garde and independent cinema could be. He was really one of the first to be very open to Asian cinema, understanding its growing importance – a real pioneer. I first met him in Hong Kong in the early '80s, and in that decade, I often suggested Hong Kong and other Asian films to him for the Forum. I think he's often not given the due that he deserves for the work not only for Hong Kong cinema but also for Korean, Japanese, and Chinese films.

These three people and Edinburgh of the '70s certainly showed me how a film festival could be programmed for a larger purpose rather than a personal agenda. Like everyone, I had ideas about films and film theory, but at that time in the early 1980s, the larger purpose for me was to help create a film culture centered around Asian cinema with Hong Kong as its hub, and for Hong Kong cinema to be taken seriously, because it wasn't really at that time. HKIFF, at the time, became a leader of this vision in our region.

TKW: **In retrospect, Hong Kong International Film Festival (HKIFF) did play a pioneering role in platforming Asian cinema. Can you share with us the process of creating this shift and the challenges you may have faced along the way?**
RG: In 1979, I was running the film festival and was driven by a desire to be different. I had to give HKIFF a distinctive "brand" as we say nowadays. We were the only film festival in Asia, but I could see that there would be others (indeed I met and gave ideas to some of the folks who wanted to start their film festivals in Asia and also the US) and just being an international film festival was not enough. So how do we lead, you know, at this point? During my staff meeting, it was Lin Nien-tung, the retrospective curator who said, "Well, you know, you should do Asian cinema," and suddenly light bulbs went off in my head because the only Asian cinema that had been shown in festivals – and these were Western festivals, of course – were basically films by the so-called masters: Kurosawa Akira and Satyajit Ray. And Oshima Nagisa because of *Ai no Korīda* (In the Realm of the Senses 1976). There were of course others, but these were the main representatives at the time. So this set me on a course that has occupied a lot of my life.

Pierre Rissient, who was scouting for the Cannes Film Festival, among many other things, had introduced me to Lino Brocka, and so I knew that there were interesting things going on in the Philippines. I went there myself and met various filmmakers: Ishmael Bernal, Mike De Leon, Raymond Red, et cetera. And I thought that this was the way to go – I mean, we're in Asia, in Hong Kong, we're supposed to be the crossroads of Asia where East meets West. So, I set up a section on Asian films separate from our international selection, and consolidated the Hong Kong film retrospective and contemporary Hong Kong cinema sections. A number of programming and festival people came to the festival to discover more about Asian cinema both historical – we did a great program on Indonesian cinema in the early 1980s including the master, Teguh Karya – and contemporary works by filmmakers such as Kidlat Tahimik in the late 1970s. I also believe that our contemporary Hong Kong Cinema section, an annual look back at the year's output, helped introduce a lot of people to the Hong Kong new wave and drew their attention to the developments in Hong Kong movies that eventually blossomed in the 1980s. Jeanette Paulson and the folks from Hawaii showed up in the early 1980s and then created their own international film festival (Hawaii International Film Festival) in 1981 with an emphasis on Asia programming. I met Philip Cheah in the mid-1980s when he was working on what would become the Singapore International Film Festival. There were quite a few others but one of the most important for me was Serge Daney, who was finishing up at editor of *Cahiers du Cinema*. The *Cahiers* analysis of John Ford's *Young Mr Lincoln* (1939) had been seminal for me so discussions with Serge were always an education. Later he sent critics Olivier Assayas and Charles Tesson to Hong Kong to edit the "Made in Hong Kong" special edition of *Cahiers* – it's still something of a classic.

I'd like to add that I also helped establish the HKIFF publications program and its bilingual policy, especially with writing by Hong Kong critics. I thought that the way to promote HKIFF and Hong Kong cinema (contemporary and retrospective) in particular was through the publications and some "serious writing," especially on the retrospective side. And as a putative film theorist, I made it a personal project to write quite theoretically about Hong Kong films! Not sure if it worked but my general embrace of strange bedfellows led me to mix Lacan and Liu Jialiang. When I began, we had precisely two and a half books in English on Hong Kong cinema. Over the years the HKIFF publications expanded the number of books exponentially and also influenced studies and other publications about Hong Kong movies. The impact has been profound and is rarely acknowledged.

Nevertheless, I'm very proud of these initiatives and I think this is how I helped bring Hong Kong and Asian cinema to the international scene.

TKW: **Yes, and I also believe you have created a blueprint for other film festivals in Asia to follow and adapt, including the Singapore International Film Festival that started in the late '80s. How about the types of challenges your team faced, if any?**
RG: Many of the challenges were practical. Video was just coming in but we were not yet able to watch screeners that way. If we really wanted to watch a movie, it had to be shipped to us on 35 mm, which is ten cans' worth. Quite expensive freight, actually.

So, that was the first challenge. Being a film critic myself, I know that reading about a film doesn't necessarily present an accurate portrayal of what that film really is. But as we were not traveling around a lot at the time, we had to base our programming on hearsay, reports that we trusted, and friends of ours who traveled overseas and watched some of the films.

On the Asian side, we didn't know many people around the region. We knew some guys in Japan. None of us had really been exposed to Korean cinema and I certainly hadn't. So, actually finding out what was going on in the cinema around Asia was something of a challenge.

I remember we were interested in some Thai films and we called up this guy in Thailand. And of course, we didn't speak Thai, and he didn't speak English or Chinese or anything. So, the communication was quite surreal, to put it mildly, and eventually, we had a friend – I think it was an American guy who lived in Thailand – who helped us there. We knew quite a lot about Taiwan, but it was a little problematic at the time because we were a British colony and had to avoid China provocations. Hence, showing Taiwanese films was something of a challenge but we managed mainly through the cultural avenue.

The Philippines was a little easier for me because I already knew a few people there. China was emerging from the Cultural Revolution. I visited China for the first time in 1981 on a UN mission and understood pretty quickly that things were really happening. Later, after my time, HKIFF grew in importance because it was the nexus of the Hong Kong new wave, Taiwan new cinema, and China's fifth generation – exciting times for Chinese-language cinema!

TKW: **It does sound to me like some of these challenges have evolved and some have stayed the same. Coming back to the present day, what are your thoughts about the evolution of cinemas in Asia and what are some of the aspects in contemporary Asian cinema that you find exciting today?**

RG: I think very few people knew about the region's cinema back in the 1970s. The industries were generally parochial, absorbed only in their own markets. Japan was the exception because they had the international attention and exposure – in contemporary terms at the time, this was mostly led by Oshima Nagisa. We have to give a lot of credit to the Japanese for developing the cinema in a more international way. It had its ups and downs but the co-productions that Oshima's work initiated laid the groundwork for the future. In Hong Kong, films were basically being shown around Southeast Asia for the Chinese diaspora, thanks to Shaw Brothers, Cathay, and others, but they weren't really that well known to non-Chinese audiences. Golden Harvest was more adventurous, especially after international hits with Bruce Lee. But the "Bruce Lee effect," if I can put it that way, was to typecast Asia into kung fu mode. I mean, Hong Kong does action movies really well, but there was also Allen Fong, Ann Hui, and Patrick Tam . . . eventually, it took Wong Kar-wai to show international audiences in a big way that our cinema was not only kung fu.

Since the late 20th century, the evolution toward more international aspirations has largely come about from Asian films being increasingly shown in prestigious film festivals. As I mentioned earlier, the Berlinale Forum of Ulrich Gregor and Rotterdam of Hubert Bals were pioneering – to some extent they showed me that commercial films from Asia could break through internationally as art-house cinema.

Nowadays the regional industries have become more used to overseas festival screenings where they hope to get a distribution pickup. Many Asian filmmakers hope to show their films in an international film festival and quite a number of films reflect this aspiration. However, the idea of making films for film festivals can also become self-indulgent. Film festivals are like a hothouse – the audience has paid quite a lot to be there which influences their response to films which naturally is generally positive. When a film is only shown on the festival circuit, it may never get the critical feedback that can enrich the cinema more. Filmmakers may just end up making the same film over and over again because they try to second-guess that the festival likes that film, and it becomes an unending spiral.

Regardless, I think one of the things that I like about Asian cinema – on the tail of some of these developments – is that nowadays you can have the coexistence of extremes. Two examples, for instance, are Thailand and the Philippines. You have a Filipino filmmaker like Lav Diaz who makes ten-hour movies with long takes about Filipino histories, but screenings at home are limited. On the other end of the spectrum, there's a Sharon Cuneta melodrama or a Joyce Bernal comedy made for the mass audience, which do really well at home but not so well overseas. A similar situation exists in Thailand where you have an artist/filmmaker like Apichatpong Weerasethakul working with a big star like Tilda Swinton on art films, while there are also popular commercial movies with stars such as Tony Jaa. In the end, it's important that there is some kind of dynamic between these two types of film practice, but it's rare that the two poles are combined in one auteur.

Wong Kar-wai in Hong Kong is one of the rare filmmakers who has managed this balancing act, and he's perhaps the best at it. He makes international art-house films, but they are constructed as commercially ambitious works with big stars, high budgets, and great production value. *The Grandmaster* (2013) was commercially successful in China. *Chungking Express* (1994) and *In the Mood for Love* (2000) have been international hits. He has successfully realized the potential of international distribution possibilities while maintaining his auteur ambitions. Jia Zhangke is perhaps another example. He began making indie art-house films like *Xiao Wu* (1997), but he has now become a powerhouse in his own right through a judicious choice of films and international distributor. Wong and Jia are among the very few Asian filmmakers who have achieved this very difficult balancing act between art and commerce, between local and international audiences. In the Asian region, they are the ones who can and have made a difference.

Historically it's been tragic for me to see that friends who are no longer with us could have made a huge difference if they had lived to experience the growing recognition today of their genius – King Hu and Lino Brocka are the best examples, but Edward Yang was another who left too early.

TKW: **Bringing the conversation back to film festivals, I think we all know that the so-called top film festivals are still widely regarded as the ones from Europe, maybe from North America as well. This naturally means that they heavily influence and even define an "international" film culture. So, what are your thoughts about this status quo in today's context?**

RG: That's a really good question to which I don't have a simple or definitive answer! I do recognize that a lot of film festival culture is determined by Europe and the European sensibility. And when I say European sensibility, I also mean a European view of Asian cinema, which is not exactly the same as Asian cinema viewed by Asian film critics or Asian film festivals.

One of the measures that Asian festivals need to undertake is to develop and create their own aesthetic on what Asian cinema means and not necessarily follow, for example, the trends set by Europe. It's not a neocolonialist thing. The European festivals are generally very sympathetic and open, but at the same time, they are balancing their film festival concerns between Asia, Africa, Europe, and North America. They are also trying to appeal to audiences who want to see everything: Hollywood movies, art-house movies, Asian film discovery, something from Africa, women's films, et cetera. Can Asian film festivals develop their own aesthetic, and do they have to play this game as well?

If I were to start an Asian film festival today, I would have it express an Asian view of European cinema or an Asian view of Hollywood cinema, which is different from the mainstream European or American film festival view. It's always good to see yourself from an outside position – you develop a much better perspective and the cinema – well, it's all about angles and points of view. It's complicated and convoluted but consider this fact: all Asian box office earnings except South Korea are dominated by Hollywood films. The US box office is dominated by Hollywood films. So, the view of Asian films from a theatrical distribution and box office point of view is very narrow.

On the other hand, the non-theatrical window has been blown open completely by streaming platforms. Viki.com, Amazon, Netflix, all carry a load of Asian series and films, and co-produce their own material such as *Ojingŏgeim* (Squid Game 2021). So, a person outside Asia can watch a lot of different material from the region. But how do they distinguish between what is worth watching or what is not? A lot of soap operas online is historical stuff particularly from South Korea or China, and fundamentally these are not too different from soap operas that you see in the West. And does it really matter?

So, if we are looking at film festivals in Asia, what do we really want to see? For example, you have an audience in Singapore that is really in tune with a lot of what's going on around the world. Most of your audience speaks good English and so they can have access to a lot of different materials. In terms of an Asian film festival, I'm sure you're asking yourself questions like: What can I bring to the audience that they don't know? A film festival is always about showing something that people want to see and what they don't know about.

With film festivals in the other parts of Asia – particularly in Southeast Asia – you have developing economies, you have a very young demographic, a lot of young people who are essentially growing up on TikTok videos and online platforms. So, the challenge for a film festival is how to develop an audience and bring them into the theater. Mature festivals, like Berlin, Venice, Sundance, and Cannes, already have built-in audiences that we don't necessarily have in some parts of Asia. By comparison, I think our idea of film history in Asia may not have been so strong before because we were not cognizant of our own film histories. A lot of it has been lost. However, I know from my own experience of the Hong Kong film retrospectives at HKIFF that bringing this history to light to local audiences really increases their curiosity and their appreciation of their own cinema. I think the Busan International Film Festival (BIFF) in South Korea has accomplished some of this too – their Korean film retrospectives have been revelatory and well-programmed. They have a good domestic audience and local and overseas industry attendees for the market.

There are very, very few film festivals in the world today that do complete retrospectives. I believe the Locarno Film Festival is the only festival in Europe now that does really big retrospectives. BIFF is one of the few in Asia. I think there is more space in Asia for a film festival to do a really good retrospective section. It would be great to organize a film festival where it can help piece together the knowledge of film history around the Asian region and maybe fill in some of the gaps. The Memory Film Festival in Cambodia has been doing some of this. There is value in making this kind of retrospective film festival that recognizes, dignifies, and positions that country's film history within the larger context of cinema practice.

TKW: **I also want to address some of these recent anxieties about the future of film festivals. Especially in recent years, there have been these almost seismic changes with the rise of streaming services and the consequences of the pandemic. So, with current conditions in mind, do you think anything needs to evolve with film festivals, whether for it to stay relevant with the public or to remain financially sustainable?**

RG: I believe that the shift caused by COVID would have happened anyway – the pandemic just accelerated an inevitability of watching films mostly online at home. This acceleration has forced large companies to make their films accessible online with shortened windows.

A few years ago, I was quite taken with the remarks by Steven Spielberg and George Lucas, who said that in the future, going to the movie theater instead of watching in-home would be a premium event and you'd pay 50 dollars or something. It would be like an opera ticket.

We are not there yet but I think that premium could be applied to a film festival. For example, in some time zones, an audience could go to a movie house near their home and watch the red carpet, and the opening film in Cannes streaming live, all on a big screen. This live theater streaming already happens for sports events, and for events like the New York Metropolitan Opera. And they charge premium amounts. Maybe demand is already there – movie fans stay up to watch the live Oscars show, for example. The better-known film festivals already have a kind of built-in audience internationally and I see streaming live in a public theater as a natural place for such events. There are people who would love to see the opening film in Cannes, and they don't want to wait. So, they are prepared to pay, say, 50 to 100 dollars to watch that movie. Of course, time zones are a challenge, but for something like Cannes, there could be an audience across Europe and the UK and for late mornings in America.

I know this is difficult to execute at the moment largely due to territorial rights and piracy, but I don't see why we would not be moving in that direction in future. Film festivals need money and premium screenings could help, and distributors may be open to the idea if they get a cut of the box office.

Figure 44.2 On the yellow carpet: Filipino filmmaker Raymond Red and Roger Garcia, then artistic director of Hainan Island International Film Festival, China, 2019 (photo credit: Roger Garcia Collection).

Following that thought, the audience would expand worldwide if they were able to watch all of this at home on a big-screen TV in real time at a premium price. With this model you get to see more of a film festival – the premieres, red carpets, press conferences, interviews, et cetera, in real time and with an international reach. That would be great for sponsors! Once again there are rights and piracy issues, but the current models are difficult too, and new generations of cinephiles are being brought up to watch films online, whether they like it or not! You need to meet your audience on their own ground if the festival is going to succeed in the long term.

I think film festivals have moved from being a purely cultural phenomenon to an economic one with tourism benefits. There is an economic benefit to a film festival that I know a lot of governments don't necessarily understand because it's not specifically cause and effect. It's not as if you have a film festival and then suddenly your tourism numbers go up, you know? The way it works is that you have a film festival and it puts your city on the map and grows its reputation and appeal internationally over the long term. The only reason that, for example, a lot of people have heard of Udine in Italy is because of its Far East Film Festival which over 25 years of operation is now one of the best festivals showcases in Europe for Asian cinema. The reputation of the festival, especially in Asia, is very good. Asian filmmakers like to go there because it's Italy, it's food, and it's in the wine-growing Friuli region! The festival hospitality is well known. All of these ancillary points are positives and add to the film festival and its growing numbers. So, there is an economic, cultural, and geopolitical benefit to having a film festival, and I think that is the way in which financial sustainability could work.

On the question of relevance, I think film festivals still serve to point us to the latest and/ or most interesting movies out there and still act as a good publicity vehicle to spotlight them. When you go on Netflix, for example, there are millions of films there and where do you even begin? So, a film festival can help to publicize a movie that could really get lost in the shuffle. Maybe film festivals will need to develop a greater understanding that the end point is not only to show films to people who are coming to the theater but also to highlight films that people will be able to watch online.

Although I have grown up in the film festival world, I think there are too many film festivals nowadays. Every village has a film festival which lasts say two days, and it's really not a film festival at all. If the point of a film festival is to present a point of view, or a report on the state of contemporary cinema, then I would say there are probably about 50 film festivals in the world that are worth attending. Everything else is there to basically promote something other than cinema, in their own communities. Less is definitely more in this case.

TKW: **If you can sum it up for us as a conclusion to this interview, what then do you think are some of the defining characteristics that an ideal film festival should have, and why so?**
RG: I think one of the major things that a film festival has to do is to build trust with its audience. I did this in Hong Kong in my first year – but that's because Hong Kong was a new film festival at the time and something of a novelty. But I believe when there is trust, your audience will then become more open to the different stuff, the weirder films that you will want to show. This is very important because when we talk about culture, we are talking about stretching the boundaries of people's appreciation, their understanding of the world, and their understanding of how to view the world, because cinema is all about how you view the world and how you project

yourself into it. In a good and bad way, the cinema is a culture of aspiration, and film festivals reflect that. As a curator, I think it's important to develop an audience that is receptive to having something different brought into their consciousness. I have always believed – because it happened to me – that cinema can expand your horizons of life. I also believe that festivals should show films that broaden the horizons of the cinema itself whether in film history, or some latest reinvention of the cinematic vocabulary.

I think this characteristic is very rare today. In a world numbed by media, I think sometimes film festivals show too many movies. Quantity seems to be more important, sometimes, than quality. This is why I admired Richard Roud when the New York Film Festival would show say around 20 films. Today you are run around watching five, or six films a day in a festival, and it becomes more difficult to appreciate what you saw and the reasons for seeing them quite apart from the reason why the film seeks to exist!

So that takes me to the second important characteristic of a film festival, which is that less is actually more. I've had this experience where there are so many sections in a film festival that your audience actually falls away from confusion. So, it's good to create some clear-cut roadmaps in a film festival. I'm a big advocate of different theaters in a film festival where each venue specializes in one strand of the program so that the audience can work out better where to go and design their film-watching experience accordingly. The location also matters. What I like about the Berlinale, for example, is that it takes place mainly in the Potsdamer Platz where there are a few cinema complexes that you can just go from one to another in five minutes. Unfortunately, I didn't have that proximity and infrastructure in Hong Kong, and it was difficult to program where you could go from one film to another in a matter of minutes. In the early years, HKIFF was based around one venue, and I structured the program into only four sections. I think that compactness contributed to the festival's success, but today that kind of capacity would limit ticket sales.

But having said all that, and by way of conclusion, I still think that a good film festival is one where you show the films that you yourself would really want to see. And then you hope that people will get your vision too!

45

REFLECTION ON FILM RESTORATION, *ACCULTURATIE* AND DEMOCRACY

The Case Studies of *Lewat Djam Malam* and *Aladin*

Lisabona Rahman

Film restoration is a tool which enables film archives to reach a wider contemporary audience without putting a high risk on the safety of the vintage materials in its collection. The workflow of a restoration involves complex technical knowledge that is not very widely or evenly spread around the globe. The acknowledgment for the need for film restoration stems from realizing that film is an important art form of the 20th century, that films can be lost due to their chemical instability, as well as market demand for video content (Read and Meyer 2000).

In a country like Indonesia, where film preservation is hardly a priority in the cultural agenda, archive institution is precarious and under-resourced. Maintaining a film collection is already a big task and therefore film restoration projects are an extra challenge (Wardany 2013). It is worth noting that the distribution of knowledge of film restoration worldwide remains dominated by the knowledge based on Euro- or US-centric institutional experiences.

The development of the infrastructure for film restoration in Asia and the Pacific is not very well documented yet. Following the digital turn in film production and distribution technology, commercial laboratory facilities started offering restoration services, such as Imagica in Japan (since 2003), Technicolor Bangkok (since 2009), Render Digital in Indonesia (since 2013), and L'immagine ritrovata Asia in Hong Kong (since 2015). Film archives in the region also equip themselves with scanning facilities, such as the China Film Archive (Iordanova 2020) and a combination of a digital and analog facility in the National Film and Sound Archive in Australia, the Thai Film Archive, and the Korean Film Archive. The history of film restoration infrastructure and the development of its knowledge in Southeast Asia and the Pacific, to my knowledge, has not been extensively researched, except for its practice in Japan's Imagica West Corporations (Shibata 2020) and Technicolor Bangkok (Cipriani 2021); therefore, it remains an area that is interesting to develop in the future. A study or an account about the practices of restoration in Asia should not only be based

DOI: 10.4324/9781003266952-58

on institutional practices but also take into account community participation such as illustrated by the two following case studies.

Listening to Multiple Voices from the Past

This chapter looks at the circulation of knowledge about film restoration, from two case studies: Usmar Ismail's *Lewat Djam Malam* (After the Curfew, [1954] 2012) and Tan Sing Hwat's *Aladin* ([1953] 2019). Both films come from the Sinematek Indonesia film archive, which mainly collects fiction films produced in the country. The institution was founded by filmmaker/archivist Misbach Yusa Biran (1933–2012). Biran started his career in filmmaking in 1954 under the mentorship of Usmar Ismail. Throughout the 1960s he gradually gained recognition as a scriptwriter and director, working until the late 1970s. When his mentor passed away suddenly in early 1970, an idea about preserving his legacy grew in Biran's mind. He shifted away from filmmaking to focus on film preservation and teaching film history (Ardan 1979). Biran eventually launched the Sinematek Indonesia film archive in October 1975.

He started the collection in 1971 with one short and two long feature films among hundreds of still photos and magazine copies (Biran 1973, 3), which continued to grow until 1998. By then, the collection included 455 titles of feature films with thousands of others in video formats along with photos, film publicity items, and scripts (Biran and Andoko 1999).

Both *Lewat Djam Malam* and *Aladin* were made in the early 1950s, during the postcolonial period. They are proof of the diverse film culture of the period, in which the circulation of at least two kinds of film genres was acknowledged by historians, such as Biran (2009) and Tanete Pong Masak (2016). The first genre was nationalist realist drama identified as *film idealis* (idealistic film) and the second was fantastic genre films. Director Usmar Ismail was the most famous proponent of *film idealis*. The fantastic genre films have always been stigmatized as the antithesis of idealist films since they are produced as profit-seeking entertainment. Restoring the two titles opened up more possibilities to complicate our understanding of this period.

This essay shows that restoration technology can facilitate listening to multiple voices from the past. The different circumstances and conditions of each project also show that technology should be used with strategies ensuring the diversity of perspectives. The *Lewat Djam Malam* restoration is a complex organization of transnational work involving support from Singapore and the US, with the technical process taking place in a specialized laboratory in Bologna, Italy. Meanwhile, the *Aladin* restoration was a much smaller scale of organization, involving Indonesian institutions and using locally available means. The collaborative efforts to restore both films and to bring them back to the public reflects the character of film technology itself, which post-colonial Indonesian writer/poet Armijn Pane calls *acculturatie*: "a Western seed of knowledge planted in this country, becoming a sign of acculturation in today's Indonesia, just like in the field of politics, 'democracy' can be seen in a similar way" (Pane 1953, 5).

In using *acculturatie*, or the hybrid interaction of cultures and "democracy," as a parallel to film, Pane sees film as a social technology which is adopted and adapted, enabling more voices to contribute. Film restoration, when carefully adopted and adapted, could also result in opening up the vocabulary of world cinema, offering a more diverse point of view and interrogating existing hegemonic assumptions. Both restorations were done in the context of heritage activism (Gilliland and McKemmish 2014, 78) by the community to engage in a participative history-making practice, creating equal possibilities to encounter people or film works made by minorities or less privileged political groups instead of only perpetuating the knowledge coming from the privileged majority.

This chapter is also especially addressing film restoration practices which are done as communal and collaborative endeavors, external to institutional film archives. The process included a lot of learning by doing, getting help, absorbing and adopting knowledge – a messy entanglement. The curatorial strategies organization of technical works in the two case studies are very different, yet they complement one another. *Lewat Djam Malam* enabled a more complex and critical look on film history through the body of work of Usmar Ismail. The scale of resources mobilized for this project required justification in order to get enough attention from the international partners. The known reputation of Usmar Ismail in Indonesia as the father of national cinema, the mainstream hero whose visibility was already acknowledged in international festivals such as in Asia Pacific with *Harimau Tjampa* (Tiger from Tjampa; released in 1953) and in Europe with his film *Pedjuang* (Warriors for Freedom; released in 1960) certainly helped in fulfilling the requirements. The *Aladin* project, on the other hand, focused on questioning dominant historical narratives by working with a marginalized "unidentified" film. The project was designed to combine basic training in film restoration, as well as to explore collaboration with commercial postproduction facilities in Jakarta, which are not especially designed for film restoration. This restoration made way for the rediscovery of Tan Sing Hwat, and his work as a filmmaker. Tan (1918–86) was a writer, journalist, filmmaker, and a leader of the film and theater labor union of Indonesia's political left. Following the political conflict which resulted in persecution against leftist artists and activists in 1965, Tan stopped making films (Setiawan 2019). His name and filmography was not very often cited, a proof of the perpetual erasure of Chinese migrant filmmakers' contribution to Indonesian film history (Sen 2006).

Benefit and Problem: "Monumental" Approaches to Film Heritage Practice

The *Lewat Djam Malam* project started in early 2010, when Singaporean film critic Philip Cheah asked his Indonesian colleague JB Kristanto to recommend a title of an important local classical film. Both Philip Cheah and JB Kristanto have shown deep concerns about the limited accessible materials on Southeast Asian film histories (Rahman 2013). JB Kristanto proposed *Lewat Djam Malam*, by Usmar Ismail, with this reason: "Spontaneously, *Lewat Djam Malam* by Usmar Ismail popped in my mind, as I consider it as the best Indonesian film of all time. The film is significant not only for its [aesthetic] achievements, but also its historical values" (Pasaribu and Kristanto 2012, viii). Kristanto's choice clearly showed his intention of identifying a monument of prominence within Indonesia's film history. In her revised edition of *From Grain to Pixel* (2018), film heritage scholar and curator of EYE Filmmuseum, Giovanna Fossati, addressed the need to move away from seeing film heritage as merely identifying monuments (332) as that merely reinforces the dominant perspective on art, culture, and heritage (333). She instead proposed to enlarge the field of vision, acknowledging the "complementary dimensions of Documents and Events as equally informing the *life of archival life of film.*" The consequence of this proposition is to engage in archival films as part of a body of collection and discover them rather than treating the collection as a mere site to locate familiar items. Fossati further argued for decolonization and transcending traditional conceptions revolving around national cinema, auteurist approaches, and film-as-art discourse (Fossati 2021).

Figure 45.1 Still from *Lewat Djam Malam*. Courtesy of Usmar Ismail Cinema Society (UICS).

Kristanto's choice applies the monumental approach with a twist. Usmar Ismail got his status as the father of Indonesian national cinema from *Darah dan Doa* (The Long March, 1950), a film that reconstructs the independence guerilla war. He proclaimed it as the first nationalist film (Ismail 1963, 127), being a story about national struggle. Kristanto knowingly did not pick *The Long March*, subverting its existing monumental status, although he still wished to acknowledge the prominence of Usmar Ismail as an auteur. Choosing a work of Usmar Ismail had the benefit of his prominent status in the national film industry, as well as his collaboration with film companies in Malaysia and the Philippines. *Lewat Djam Malam*, however, is his lesser-known work. The film depicts a fallen hero who is traumatized by the war and has trouble reconnecting with society. Since its completion, *Lewat Djam Malam* was not among the most popular Perfini productions even though it was critically well received at the national film award in 1955 (Sen 1994, 40). The film was actually created for the international market, with the intention of participating at the Southeast Asian Film Festival in Tokyo in 1954, although a diplomatic row between Indonesia and Japan stopped it from being screened (Lee 2020, 70).

Transnational Collaboration: Adoption of Knowledge and Asymmetry of Power

The initial fund for the *Lewat Djam Malam* restoration project came from the National Museum of Singapore. Zhang Wenjie, the director of the Cinemathéque at the National Museum of Singapore at the time, proposed a collaboration with L'immagine ritrovata laboratory (Pasaribu and Kristanto 2012, 16). At that time, Zhang had just attended the FIAF Film Restoration Summer School at the lab in summer 2010 (FIAF n.d.). Through this collaboration, the knowledge to do research on source materials for film restoration was passed on from laboratory director Davide Pozzi to Indonesian film activists Lisabona Rahman and Lintang Gitomartoyo. After the restoration, the learning process for Rahman and Gitomartoyo was extended to participation at the next Film Restoration Summer School in 2012.

Zhang's initiative of restoring a work of Usmar Ismail shows a commitment to acknowledging a generation of Southeast Asian filmmakers who had co-production projects with the Singapore-based Cathay-Keris (Mydin 2012, 19). The involvement of the World Cinema Foundation (WCF) added more resources to the project, although it also completely altered the launching plan. The project that ironically started with the intention of introducing a Southeast Asian classic in the region had to wait until after its world premiere in Cannes. The WCF proposed to launch the restoration result at the 2012 Cannes Film Festival, which required exclusivity, so it had to come first before any screenings in Asia or other parts of the world. Cheah has critically argued for balancing the curatorial powers of international film festivals with reserving curatorial privilege to channel the "voice" of Southeast Asian filmmakers, critics, collectors, and festivals. He reflected the asymmetry of power from his experience as programmer and promoter of Asian cinema in concurrence with non-Asian fellow programmers (Cheah 2012, 75) and the priority of a premiere at Cannes certainly was another bitter example.

Inside of Indonesia, a nationalist sentiment arose. In late April 2012, *Lewat Djam Malam*'s premiere at the Cannes Film Festival was officially announced. The reactions in Indonesia regarding the premiere were ambiguous, as they were laden with a mix of xenophobic suspicion and admiration for Martin Scorsese's involvement in the project. News articles came up with titles ranging from "Martin Scorsese Brings *Lewat Djam Malam* Back to Life" (Suara Pembaruan 2012) to "National Film with 'Foreign' Taste" (Ismayanto 2012). Mass media and social media alike questioned the Indonesian government's neglect over archival films' stewardship. At the same time, the digital restoration techniques, which allow simulation of pristine images and sound, were being celebrated (Ismayanto 2012; Ginanjar 2012).

The amount of publicity generated inside the country pushed the project further into public attention. Following the Cannes premiere, a plan to screen the film in commercial Indonesian theaters was announced in early June 2012 (Kamil 2012). The film was playing in ten different Indonesian cities, attended by nearly 6,000 viewers. It is certainly not comparable to a contemporary blockbuster. However, as the first local old film to be re-released, this result was encouraging. It also showed that Asian forums for art cinema as well as archival films were growing. The *Lewat Djam Malam* restoration was presented, among others, at the 2012 Busan International Film Festival and the 2013 Hong Kong International Film Festival. Perhaps the asymmetry of power that Cheah observed was slowly changing with more archives and festivals in Asia being interested in showing archival films (Iordanova 2020).

Expanding the Track

The *Lewat Djam Malam* project enabled wider access to an old film as well as the circulation of knowledge and network. It initiated public support for restoration in Indonesia, which can be seen until today, where the Indonesian government responded by allocating budgets to restore four film titles since 2013 (Maharani 2019). However, the process of *Lewat Djam Malam*'s restoration served to solidify the existing canon of Indonesian film.

Figure 45.2 Still from *Aladin*. Source: Sinematek Indonesia.

In 2021, Usmar Ismail was acknowledged as a national hero by the Indonesian Republic (Nugraheny 2021).

The technical restoration standard of *Lewat Djam Malam* became a benchmark that is perceived as a standard of a good restoration. At the same time, however, it generated negative responses, such as the statement by film critic Totot Indrarto: "This restoration project is a work that has shamed us, [because it's] foreign people who performed this" (Detik.com 2012; Indrarto 2012). This statement, rather than a sign of antipathy, is an expression of criticism for lack of active engagement and investment of resources, as well as a paralyzing concern that restoration perhaps can only be done abroad with foreign resources.

The restoration of *Aladin* was a proposition to react to this frustration, utilizing acquired knowledge from previous restoration and exploring possibilities with a simpler budget structure and a combination of locally available technology. *Aladin* was restored by Indonesian film archivists working for a community organization specializing in film digitization, called Indonesian Film Centre (IDFC), founded in 2010 by Jakarta-based Dutch filmmaker, Orlow Seunke.

Emphasis on Encountering the Lesser Known

The aim of the IDFC restoration project in 2017 was to reintroduce lesser-known archival films to the public. The process of restoration started in January 2017 by looking at different categories of films and its condition (Rahman 2017). In 1991, American visual anthropologist Karl G. Heider (1991, 14) wrote that Indonesian films made before 1950 are all lost. This statement is obviously inaccurate as at least 13 titles listed in the catalog of Sinematek Indonesia's (SI) collection are identified to have been made between 1935 and

1949 (Rahman 2017). Heider's was one of the earliest books published in English about the subject and probably the widest known and referenced by international observers of Indonesian film history. Many film scholars had already found out that his statement was not accurate, but very few have ever witnessed the remaining artifacts.

Among the films in the SI collection, it is obvious that the films produced between 1935 and 1949 have very different features compared to their successors. These films are produced by companies owned by Chinese migrants, such as Star Film Company or Tan's Film, featuring fantastic stories like *Aladdin, Tales from the 1001 Nights*, or locally invented action heroes, such as *Matjan Berbisik* (released in 1940) and *Gagak Item* (De Zwarte Raaf; released in 1939). This is significantly different to the post-independence films of Usmar Ismail's cohort, which are realist in style and often adapted from theater or proses by European writers (see, for example, information on Ismail's 1949 film *Harta Karun*), which was an adaptation of Moliere's play *L'Avare*). The visibility of Indonesian archival films other than those produced by Usmar Ismail is very limited, especially due to the existing discourse of Indonesian national film history, which is aimed at celebrating pioneers such as Ismail, due to his *pribumi* or native origin. There has been criticism toward this racially motivated discourse, and propositions to acknowledge the contribution of filmmakers from migrant backgrounds, especially from the Chinese community (Sen 2006; Setijadi-Dunn and Barker 2010), as they have been consistently investing and producing films in Indonesia since the 1930s.

The surviving copies of films registered as being made before 1949 are incomplete. However, they could be reintroduced in a good way to the public, with the right presentation treatment. The fact that the film is incomplete is crucial to emphasize, as it will stress the importance of preserving and restoring them so that what was left will not disappear. Although all of the surviving pre-independence films are equally important and interesting, they pose very different technical challenges due to the variety of decays and damages. After a series of discussions between the preservation staff of SI and the IDFC team, a decision was made to begin hands-on training with a film which has a single surviving copy, and was in relatively stable chemical condition (Rahman 2017).

In the *Lewat Djam Malam* project, the whole technical workflow was conducted in one laboratory in Italy. The IDFC restoration process had to be designed differently, bringing together knowledge and technical equipment that was available in Jakarta. Since the film material did not contain title cards nor credit titles, the real title of this film was subject to further research. The team worked with the provisory title *"Aladin Dengan Lampoe Wasiat,"* taken from articles announcing the start of production for a film with a character called Aladin in *Pertjatoeran Doenia* magazine, published respectively in January and February 1942 (30). Physical damage, such as tears, as well as chemical decay, such as fungus and dirt, were removed using digital restoration software. The IDFC staff members received special training in basic digital cleaning techniques using the Diamant restoration software. The Diamant software training was conducted by Walter Plaschzug (founder of HS-Art Digital, the creator of Diamant software) in a series of on-site and remote consultations. From January until October 2017, IDFC allocated more than 350 hours of learning/working hours for the digital restoration of this title, documenting the workflow for future references (Rahman 2017).

Through the training series, the restoration team learned to adopt technical knowledge and adapt it to the condition of the materials, as well as to the technical possibilities in Jakarta at the time. Following the digital cleaning phase done by the IDFC team, the final steps were done in collaboration with film post production facilities for sound restoration (Satrio Budiono/Fourmix) and also color correction/mastering (Rivai Chen).

During the technical workflow, parallel research was conducted by Lisabona Rahman at the library of Sinematek Indonesia, additionally utilizing the Internet-based Indonesian Film Catalog and search engine. Once the scanning process was completed, the result could be used for further research into the content. The provisory title *Aladin Dengan Lampoe Wasiat*, a film estimated to be from 1941 or 1942, was found to be inaccurate since the actors and storyline of the film are different from what was written in the articles of *Pertjatoeran Doenia*. Another entry in the Indonesian Film Catalog (Film Indonesia n.d.) showed another film version of a similar story, made in 1953, with very little information of cast, crew, and plot. A further search in November 2017 involving the name of the main actor, A. Hamid Arief, yielded more accurate results, pointing to the title of *Aladin* in 1952 and 1953 (Sud 1953). Afterward it was possible for the restoration team to find the right title of the film and production date, as well as the names of cast and crew, to reconstruct the title sequences.

In September 2019, running up to the premiere screening of the restoration at the Busan International Film Festival, an article about Tan Sing Hwat was published by *Historia*, a popular web magazine on history, by Andri Setiawan (2019). His article chronicled the life of Tan Sing Hwat, a Chinese migrant who was a journalist and filmmaker and who was also very active in the labor union and anti-colonial movement. Tan was one of the most productive writer-directors among Indonesian Chinese filmmakers. In 1950, Tan Sing Hwat was working as a full-time director at the Golden Arrow production company in Jakarta and was also a union leader of Sarikat Buruh Film dan Seni Drama (Sarbufis), associated with Indonesia's political left. The process of *Aladin*'s restoration created an opportunity to understand the diversity of cinema culture in the 1950s from the work of a Chinese migrant whose career was thwarted after the military regime took over power in Indonesia in 1966.

Aladin is one among few surviving examples of entertainment films from Indonesia's post–World War II period, more specifically from the fantasy genre. Next to the more well-known auteur cinema of the time, which was produced by nationalist directors like Usmar Ismail, a different kind of cinema exists where a scene of prewar entertainment cinema resurfaces, being a combination of well-known popular theater plays and music. These films featured fantastic tales using magical visual effects with stories that come from the repertoire of *The 1001 Nights* or ghost stories. *Aladin* tells the story of a petty thief who saves his country from corrupt ministers and evil sorcerers, acting on his love for the princess. The film was made using various camera and optical tricks to produce special effects showing a giant genie, disappearing technique or magic mirror, which was a rare skill among the existing film technician working in Indonesia in the 1950s and 1960s (Masak 2016, 206). Fantasy films like *Aladin* provide a continuity between the film scene before and after the establishment of the republic, since they are made by filmmakers who were already active since the end of 1930s.

Conclusion

The restoration of *Lewat Djam Malam* and *Aladin* started out from the intention to support increasing the visibility of the Sinematek Indonesia collection. Each project utilizes a different method of engagement with film heritage, with *Lewat Djam Malam* adopting a classical approach of highlighting a monumental work for restoration for the purpose of gaining international financial support and visibility. This choice of method generated enough interest in support of film restoration, as well as enabling the adoption of technological skills and network. Coming back to Armijn Pane's remark about film as a seed of knowledge implemented in a hybrid socio-cultural context that enables democratization, although he was writing in 1953 to describe the growth of Indonesian filmmaking, the process of circulation and the growth of knowledge about film restoration is reflecting a similar pattern. The path that opened up with the *Lewat Djam Malam* restoration made further experimentation possible, which allowed the restoration of *Aladin* to take place.

The *Lewat Djam Malam* project was not simply lauded by the media but also triggered sentiments of inferiority. The *Aladin* project, on the other hand, had less media exposure because of the film's obscurity. The position of Indonesian activists in *Lewat Djam Malam* was as recipient of financial support, film laboratory client and students learning about the knowledge of film restoration. In the *Aladin* project, this knowledge was applied with a lot of adaptations, using locally available means. The acquisition of knowledge and its implementation enabled further production of knowledge that challenged the mainstream historical canon, as well as the silencing and marginalization of leftist filmmakers. Despite the contrasting nature of the two cases, since it was clear that one thing enabled another, both approaches should continue to coexist to enable polyphonic listening to history's multiple voices.

References

Ardan, S. M. 1979. *Apa Siapa Orang Film Indonesia 1926–1978*. Jakarta: Yayasan Artis Film dan Sinematek Indonesia.

Biran, Misbach Yusa. 1973. "Sebuah Gagasan Tentang Cinematek Indonesia." Project Proposal.

———. 2009. *Sejarah Film 1900–1950: Bikin Film di Jawa*. Jakarta: Komunitas Bambu.

Biran, Misbach Yusa, and Ediyami Bondan Andoko. 1999. "A Moving Experience: Relocating the Sinematek Indonesia Collections." Speech/Report for Southeast Asia Pacific Audiovisual Archive Association.

Cheah, Philip. 2012. "Watching the Wheels (Life is what Happens when You are Busy Making Other Plans)." *NMS Cinémathèque Quarterly* (April–June): 72–75. https://www.nhb.gov.sg/nationalmuseum/~/media/nms/documents/nms_cq-apr-jun2012.pdf

Cipriani, Martino. 2021. "Mapping Digital Cinema in the Kingdom: The Transition from Analog to Digital Technologies in the Thai Film Industry." *Communication and Media in Asia Pacific (CMAP)* 4 (1): 23–32.

Detik.com. 2012. "Wow, Film Klasik 'Lewat Djam Malam' Diputar di Cannes Film Festival." *Detik.com*, June 4. https://hot.detik.com/movie/d-1932637/wow-film-klasik-lewat-djam-malam-diputar-di-cannes-film-festival-.

FIAF (International Federation of Film Archives). n.d. "Past FIAF Summer Schools". Accessed February 22. https://www.fiafnet.org/pages/Training/Past-Summer-Schools.html

Film Indonesia. n.d. filmindonesia.or.id. Aladin (1953). http://filmindonesia.or.id/movie/title/lf-a006-53-549378_aladin#.Ym6kmrixUWo

Fossati, Giovanna. 2018. *From Grain to Pixel: The Archival Life of Film in Transition*. 3rd rev. ed. Amsterdam: Amsterdam University Press.

———. 2021. "For a Global Approach to Audiovisual Heritage: A Plea for North/South Exchange in Research and Practice." *NECSUS European Journal of Media Studies* 10 (2): 127–33.

Gilliland, A., and S. McKemmish. 2014. "The Role of Participatory Archives in Furthering Human Rights, Reconciliation and Recovery." *Atlanti: Review for Modern Archival Theory and Practice* 24: 78–88.

Ginanjar, Ging. 2012. "A Crystal Clear Curfew." *Tempo* 41, no. 12 (June): 10.

Heider, Karl G. 1991. *Indonesian Cinema: National Culture on Screen*. Hawaii: University of Hawaii Press.

Indrarto, Totot. 2012. "Sahabat Sinematek: Inisiatif Warga Menyelamatkan Sejarah." In *Lewat Djam Malam Restored*, edited by Adrian Jonathan Pasaribu and J. B. Kristanto, 103–8. Jakarta: Sahabat Sinematek.

Iordanova, Dina. 2020. "Archiving and Film Restoration: The View from Asia." *Frames Cinema Journal* 17. https://framescinemajournal.com/.

Ismail, Usmar. 1963. "Film Saja Jang Pertama." *Intisari* 1: 121–27.

Ismayanto, Darma. 2012. "Film Nasional Rasa Asing." *Historia*, October 22. https://historia.id/kultur/articles/film-nasional-rasa-quot-asing-quot-D8LpD

Kamil, Ati. 2012. " 'Lewat Djam Malam' Segera Masuk Gedung Bioskop Tanah Air." *Kompas*, June 5.

Lee, Sang Joon. 2020. *Cinema and the Cultural Cold War: US Diplomacy and the Origins of the Asian Cinema Network*. Ithaca: Cornell University Press.

Maharani, Esthi. 2019. "Kemendikbud Restorasi Film 1981 Kereta Api Terakhir." *Republika*, December 18. https://www.republika.co.id/berita/q2pfhg335/kemendikbud-restorasi-film-1981-kereta-api-terakhir.

Masak, Tanete Pong. 2016. *Sinema pada Masa Soekarno*. Jakarta: Fakultas Film dan Televisi IKJ.

Mydin, Iskander. 2012. "The Singapore Connection: An Archipelago View." In *Merdeka! The Films of Usmar Ismail and Garin Nugroho. Program Catalogue*. Singapore: National Museum of Singapore.

Nugraheny, Dian Erika. 2021. "Usmar Ismail, Bapak Film Nasional yang Kini Jadi Pahlawan Nasional." *Kompas*, November 10. https://nasional.kompas.com/read/2021/11/10/12101361/usmar-ismail-bapak-film-nasional-yang-kini-jadi-pahlawan-nasional.

Pane, Armijn. 1953. *Produksi Film Tjerita di Indonesia; Perkembangannja Sebagai Alat Masjarakat*. Jakarta: Badan Musjawarat Kebudajaan Nasional.

Pasaribu, Adrian Jonathan, and J. B. Kristanto. 2012. *Lewat Djam Malam Restored*. Jakarta: Sahabat Sinematek.

Rahman, Lisabona. 2013. "Archiving Outside of The Frame, The Story Continues." MA Thesis, University of Amsterdam.

_____. 2017. "Film Restoration Report for *Aladin*." Project Report for Indonesian Film Centre, October 23.

Read, Paul, and Mark-Paul Meyer. 2000. *Restoration of Motion Picture Film*. Oxford: Elsevier.

Sen, Krishna. 1994. *Indonesian Cinema: Framing the New Order*. London: Zed Books.

_____. 2006. " 'Chinese' Indonesians in National Cinema." *Inter-Asia Cultural Studies* 7 (1): 171–84.

Setiawan, Andri. 2019. "Riwayat Tan Sing Hwat." *Historia* 11 (September). https://historia.id/kultur/articles/riwayat-tan-sing-hwat-vo1mN/page/1.

Setijadi-Dunn, Charlotte, and Thomas Barker. 2010. "Imagining 'Indonesia': Ethnic Chinese Film Producers in Pre-Independence Cinema." *Asian Cinema* 21 (2): 25–47.

Shibata, Kenta. 2020. "Japanese Film History and the Challenges of Imagica West Corp." In *Routledge Handbook of Japanese Cinema*, edited by Joanne Bernardi and Shota T. Ogawa, 301–13. New York: Routledge.

Suara Pembaruan. "Martin Scorsese Hidupkan Kembali Film Lewat Djam Malam." *Suara Pembaruan*, June 21, 2012. www.suarapembaruan.com.

Sud, M. "Abdul Hamid Arief." *Minggu Pagi*, August 9, 1953. https://seputarteater.wordpress.com/2017/03/16/minggu-pagi-1953-abdul-hamid-arief/.

Wardany, Irawaty. 2013. "Dibutuhkan Energi yang Luar Biasa untuk Mengurus Sinematek Indonesia." *Fovea* 1 (Winter Edition).

46

THAI FILM ARCHIVE AND EARLY THAI QUEER CINEMA

Sanchai Chotirosseranee and Atit Pongpanit

Introduction

In 1993, the Thai Film Archive (TFA) discovered a short film, *Kathoey Pen Het* (Because of a Transgender) directed by Ledger, a group of amateur filmmakers. Presumably, the film was shown within a limited circuit in 1954. The 16 mm film print had been donated to TFA by Manop Silpi, the nephew of Charlee Silpi, who was one of the Ledger members, together with a number of his other home movies. This discovery upended the history of Thai queer cinema because *Kathoey Pen Het* is arguably the oldest cinematic representation of Thai queer issues in the Thai mediascape, as opposed to *Pleng Sut Thai* (The Last Song) directed by Pisal Akaraseranee in 1985. When the first Thai feature film, *Choke Song Chan* (Double Luck), directed by Pleng Suriya, was released in 1927, the discovery of *Kathoey Pen Het* inspired us that it was possible that there might be other Thai films prior to 1985 that represent queer issues whether with or without a homosexual focus. This chapter, therefore, aims to better complete the history of Thai queer cinema by exploring early Thai queer films collected at TFA.

To emphasize the significance of TFA to Thai cinematic studies, the first section provides a brief history and overview of the tasks and challenges of TFA. The second part reviews the history of Thai queer subcultures to provide an anthropological background and framework to better understand and discuss queer representations in the Thai Film Archive's collection in the final section.

A Brief History of the Thai Film Archive

In 1981, film historian Dome Sukvong discovered a warehouse full of abandoned, half-decayed film reels from the reign of King Rama VII (1925–35). Realizing the importance of film archivism and the need to consolidate Thai film history, Dome began a public campaign and proposed that a state-funded department exclusively tasked with film preservation must be established in Thailand. He foresaw the unresolvable difficulties of Thai cinema studies if there were no official film archive to professionally collect, store, and

DOI: 10.4324/9781003266952-59

preserve Thai films and their related materials. With his continuous effort, the Thai Film Archive was founded in 1984.

At the beginning, TFA was allocated limited financial support and other resources from the government. There has never been a legal deposit law in Thailand, one that would mandate film producers or owners to submit copies of their works for preservation, and thus, the effort to set up a film preservation agency had always been challenging. At the present time, even though TFA has been sufficiently funded compared to when it started out nearly four decades ago, the effort to track down, acquire, and collect as many films produced in Thailand as possible remains difficult. One of the main obstacles is that the majority of original film materials cannot be found, and many of the prints that arrive at TFA are damaged.

As of 2021, TFA has 2,416 features or approximately 47% of the total Thai features in its collection with a variety of audiovisual formats. Apart from the audiovisual collection, TFA has also preserved other film-related materials such as film posters, film scripts, film booklets, showcards, and handbills. Those audiovisual and printed materials include content which explicitly and implicitly presents the issues of Thai same-sex subcultures. The next section provides a brief anthropological background to build a framework for the later discussion of queer representations in the TFA's collection.

A Brief History of Thai Non-heterosexualities

Thailand has long assigned a space in society for non-heterosexual individuals. Historical evidence reveals the tripartite, or three categories, of gendered identities in Thai public discourses, namely, normatively masculine "men," normatively feminine "women," and an in-between category, or *kathoey*s (Morris 1994, 19; Jackson 2000, 409). A *kathoey* refers to both male and female individuals exhibiting hermaphroditic features, or having inappropriate behaviors from their gender, and has long been called a "third gender/sex," or เพศที่สาม (*phet thi sarm*), in Thai society (Jackson 2000, 409).

The given space for same-sex subcultures, nonetheless, should not be equated with social acceptance toward sexual minorities. The allowed social terrain may reveal the familiarity of Thai mainstream heteronormative society toward non-heterosexuality; this does not mean that Thai queer identities and practices have been unconditionally accepted or equally treated. Historical records reflect negative attitudes of Thai society toward homosexualities as a source of shame or moral wrongdoing (Terdsak 2002; Jackson 1993, 1999).

Jackson (2003) interestingly notes that since the 1940s, Field Marshal Phibun Songkhram's vision of "civilized" masculinity and femininity had become firmly established in Thai law, bureaucratic structures, and medical practices. In the 1950s, the Thai press began reporting extensively on cross-dressing *kathoey*s. Because of these new normalized forms of gender difference between masculine and feminine, there has been a notable rise in the creation of gender and sexual identity categories in the mid-1960s. These new categories, including *gay king* (inserter gay men), *gay queen* (insertee gay men), *tom* (masculine lesbians), *dee* (feminine lesbians), *seua bai* (bisexuals), and *kathoey*, have emerged in public discourse and become the basis of new homosexual and transgender identities and cultures' formations in various Thai cities, particularly Bangkok. Jackson (2003) further points out that in the 1960s, Thai physicians and psychologists began to draw upon Western biomedical discourses to negatively address the issues of cross-dressing and homosexuality as "abnormal" and "deviant." The epidemic of HIV/AIDS in Thailand in 1987 became another significant factor, similarly to the rest of the world, fueling negative attitudes toward same-sex subcultures in society (Terdsak 2002, 171). In terms of Thai popular entertainment, especially cinematic representations, Fuhrmann (2016, 124) observes that within the Thai mediascape, *kathoeys* have become increasingly common from the early 1980s. Ünaldi even further notes that after the 1997 Thai New Wave Cinema, films portraying *kathoeys* became part of the country's cinematic culture (2011, 59).

On the contrary, the portrayals of *gay* (or masculine homosexual) men, and even more so lesbians, had been underrepresented, and gained significant representation in screen cultures only after the 1990s (Fuhrmann 2016, 124). This is well-supported by the growing dominance of the genre of male homoerotic intimacy called boy love, or *Y* series in Thai, on both mainstream and online platforms, reversely putting *kathoeys* and effeminacy to a peripheral position in the Thai mediascape (Natthanai 2019; Atit and Murtagh 2022).

While it is still debatable whether or not the specific genre of boy love, or *Y* series, has contributed to positive social perceptions of masculine male (or non-*kathoey*) homosexuality, studies of other Thai queer films, particularly those after the 1980s, reveal the repetitive representation/narration especially from mainstream cinema on the issues of same-sex subcultures with stereotypes, stigmas, abnormality, mental pathology, inferiority, shame, degeneracy, and ridicule (Oradol 2008; Atit 2011; Käng 2012). A great number of off-mainstream cinema, on the other hand, projects a more natural, complicated, and even positive turn on Thai same-sex behaviors and identities (Oradol 2008; Farmer 2018; Fuhrmann 2018).

Since most of the current literature begins its exploration of Thai queer films after *Pleng Sut Thai*, the next section will explore Thai films, both with and without a queer focus, prior to Pleng Sut Thai preserved at TFA to further complete and build on a more comprehensive archival database for the studies of early Thai queer cinema.

The Thai Film Archive and Early Thai Queer Cinema

Due to the limitation faced by Thai film archivists mentioned earlier, the list of the films mentioned here may not be represented as a complete list of all queer films in Thai film history. Also, this chapter does not intend to analyze each film in great detail but offer a synthesized database for the convenience of those who wish to do further studies on the subject. The discussion will be divided into two parts. The first section explores the oldest Thai film with a focus on a *kathoey*, or transgender, story. The second part focuses on Thai films with a non-queer focus, but which contain queer elements in their narratives.

The Early Thai Queer Film with a Homosexual Focus

From our research, we found one short film at TFA that can be counted as the very first Thai queer film so far. TFA received *Kathoey Pen Het* in 1993. It is a silent, black-and-white, 11-minute film made by the collective of amateur filmmakers, Ledger, working full-time at Monthon Bank in the 1950s. Unfortunately, there has been no record so far regarding whether or not the film was shown to the public at that time. This makes it impossible to determine how Thai society responded to the very first film with a clearly non-heteronormative character. Yet a conversation with Dome, the founder and former director of TFA, reveals that during the 1950s, there was a trend for amateur filmmakers to make and screen their films among themselves in private screenings. If our assumption is correct that the

Figure 46.1 In *Kathoey Pen Het*, or *Because of a Transgender*, a male character fools around with the kathoey character without knowing that she is not a woman. (Source: Thai Film Archive Public Organization)).

filmmaker had no intention to show the film to the public, this might explain why they had the conviction to make *Kathoey Pen Het* in the first place. The same way that alternative or art-house films today are screened only in selected circuits, this very first *kathoey* film may have not been conceived to gauge the public's responses and expectations toward the representation of non-normative gender and sexuality.

Kathoey Pen Het is a comedy, though the very first intertitle informs the audience that it is "a great tragedy." The story concerns a group of men fighting over a beautiful woman, before they find out later in the film that she is, in fact, a *kathoey*, not a real woman. This leads to the tragic ending of the male characters but brings much laughter to its audience.

Atit Pongpanit and Ben Murtagh (2022) discussed the film in detail. They notice that while the *kathoey* character represents a source of laughter and disappointment, her femininity is highly sexually desirable by all the male characters. This reflects the ambivalent "tolerant but unaccepting" position of *kathoey* in the early Thai mediascape. *Kathoey Pen Het* is therefore the oldest Thai film with a focus on transgender issues collected at TFA that reveals the social perceptions and position of *kathoeys* in Thai society. Though portrayed as a source of laughter and humiliation, the *kathoey* character is being tolerated by the male characters. No blame or punishment is meted out on her for deceiving the men by presenting herself as a woman.

While we have found only one short film with a queer focus at TFA, the next part reveals a great number of early Thai films prior to 1980s that even not focusing on homosexualities, they obviously include and re-present the elements of queer issues.

The Early Thai Queer Films with a Non-homosexual Focus

Our survey of the films with a non-homosexual focus in the Thai Film Archive has revealed about 40 films which contain queer elements in various aspects. We categorize the representations of queer characters in these films into three following different characteristics.

i. Early Thai Films with Kathoey *Characters as Comic or Supportive Roles*

The first category is films that feature male or female homosexual characters in their narrative. In *Setthi Anatha* (Poor Millionaire 1955), the first film to win best picture from the first national film award (Phra Surutsawadee Award), a *kathoey*/transgender bar was shown for the very first time in Thai film history. The film shows a few transgenders, together with female showgirls, in the bar singing and dancing to entertain their clients. A woman arrives at the bar looking for her husband, who is dancing intimately with a *kathoey* dancer, though the wife does not know she is a *kathoey*. They got into an argument, and the wife pulls out the *kathoey*'s wig in a comic sketch. The wife uses the term "*kathoey* bar" (บาร์กะเทย) to describe the setting of the scene.

In a *Wiwah Pa Fun* (Dreamy Marriage 1971), a housekeeper character is a *kathoey*. But the character is played by Suwin Swangrat, a famous actor who was usually cast in the role of macho antagonists. The character dresses and acts like a woman, albeit with a fully formed mustache. The contradiction derived from such confusing gender appearance serves as a comic turn to the story. The film also casts a famous real-life *kathoey* at that time, Ratchanok Na Chiang Mai, to play an unnamed *kathoey*. The male protagonist, in his attempt to make his wife jealous, pretends to get intimate with the *kathoey* character, who is presented as a sex object that the husband can touch everywhere. The wife, in order to take revenge, responds with the same strategy. She has a tomboy character, played by a female actor, Juri Osiri, dressed up in a man's suit and a mustache, and asks the tomboy to flirt with her. The jealousy strengthens the love and relationship between the two main heterosexual couple, who later reconcile. The use of the effeminate transgender and masculine lesbian characters therefore works as a key plot point in restoring the heterosexual relationship of the lead couple in the film.

The films with *kathoey* characters in the 1960s to 1970s also reveal that at that time the term "*kathoey*" did not refer only to male or female homosexuals. It also encompassed those who displayed behaviors deemed inappropriate for their biological gender, and this reflects the historical understanding of *kathoeys* as "the third sex" in Thai society before 1960s as discussed. In *Wiwah Pa Fun*, the effeminate Prince Chiang Miang is labeled by another character as "having a touch of *kathoey*" due to his flamboyant attire and camp aesthetics. Nevertheless, the prince expresses his heterosexual desire by engaging in flirtatious interactions with women.

Apart from *Wiwah Pa Fun*, we have also found the synopses of some action movies in film magazines describing their male characters as *kathoeys*, as in *Koa Mungorn* (Nine Dragons, 1963), *Yoey Fah Tah Din* (Challenging Fate, 1964), *Bua Luang* (Royal Lotus, 1968), and *E-Soaw Baan Rai* (Farming Girl, 1970). From the synopses and photos, these *kathoey* characters are hetero- or non-homosexual but display effeminate characteristics.

In the late 1970s up to 1984, *kathoey* characters are assigned a new role as the protagonist's best friend and portrayed with modernized/Westernized characteristics. In *Ta Yat Pong*

Pang (Pong Pang's Heir, 1978), a *kathoey* character is a fashion designer who gives the male protagonist a makeover, transforming his traditional Thai-Chinese appearance into a more Westernized one. In *Kaew* (1980), a *kathoey* character is a matchmaker who introduces the leading couple to each other, then grooms their relationship toward a happy ending. In *Madam Yee Hub* (1982), a younger brother of the male protagonist is a *kathoey* who helps the female protagonist achieve her urbanification goal and transform her from a gawky country girl into a well-educated "madam." In *Nang Soa Yen Ru Dee* (Miss Yen Ru Dee, 1983), a *kathoey* character is a personal trainer for a beauty pageant. The *kathoey* does not only express their *kathoeyness* by being effeminate but is also presented as being foul-mouthed. In *Kongpan Ta-harn Kane* (The Conscript Army, 1984), a *kathoey* is conscripted and trained with other male privates. The contrast between their effeminate mannerisms and the hyper-masculine environment of the barracks is played out mainly for the audience's laughter.

According to this archival survey on Thai films with *kathoey* characters, before 1970, we see a number of films that reveal male and female homosexuals were still understood within the traditional discourse on "the third sex." Being a *kathoey* is not necessarily related to homosexual desire; rather, the term signifies behavioral patterns considered incompatible with the norms of the gender binary, namely, "normatively masculine men" and "normatively feminine women." We can also see a hint of sexual fluidity in the *kathoey* characters who display effeminate mannerisms while also having heterosexual desire. Between 1970 and 1984, however, the representation of the *kathoey* characters became more fixed on men who perform an effeminate gendered identity while their sexualities are not mentioned. The *kathoey* characters were assigned supportive roles to main heterosexual characters, but their sexual practices were rarely discussed.

Altogether, from the films with *kathoey* characters before 1985, we are able to discern certain stereotypical representations of *kathoeys,* both in Thai society and almost in all Thai films later on. For instance, being a *kathoey* must be "useful" to the (heterosexual) society in some ways, as in *The Iron Ladies* (2000), *Beautiful Boxer* (2003), and *It Gets Better* (2012). In terms of personality, they have to be loud, foul-mouthed, funny, and ridiculous, as in Poj Arnon's eight-film franchise *Hor Taew Take* (*Haunted Tranny's Dorm*) (Atit 2011, 2013). The next category discusses the practice of gender-crossing in Thai cinema with a non queer focus before 1980s.

ii. The Politics of Gender-Crossing in Early Thai Cinema

The practice of crossing the gender binary had been a repetitive motif presented in Thai films prior to the 1980s. We found a film by a Thai amateur filmmaker, Prince of Kamphaengphet. He experimented with the early movie camera to present film tricks and named his work, *Trick Cinematograph* (1927–30). As part of his experiment in optical illusion, he swaps a female dancing body with a male head. This is thus arguably the first Thai film depicting "gender-crossing," a spectacle in the early cinema period. To further explore the gender-crossing practice in Thai films before 1980s we found in TFA, we divided the cinematic representations of gender-crossing into two main practices.

a. The Practice of Cross-Dressing

The act of cross-dressing or having a character in disguise as the opposite sex has long appeared in Thai cinema. A romantic drama, *Chua Fah Din Sa Lai* (Forever Yours, 1955), has a brief comic shot in which Suang Supsomruai (also known as Lotok), a famous come-dian, dresses up as a woman with his mustache intact to seduce a male character. It is worth noting that even though the male character seems appalled at first, he later tries to kiss the cross-dressing character, who in turn tries to get away from the man. In *Sao Dao Tiam* (Miss Dao Tiam, 1960), two policemen disguise themselves as women to get close to the leading female character and to investigate a crime. In a comic sequence in *Wiwah Pa Fun*, Sombat Matanee, a famous, heavily muscled male actor, dresses up in several female national costumes, such as a Japanese kimono, a Korean hanbok, and an Indian sari, to entertain a gang of pirates.

While male-to-female cross-dressing is mostly used for comic relief, the practice of female-to-male cross-dressing often leads to a dramatic turn in early Thai cinema. In *Muan Fun* (Dreamlike, 1976), the heroine passes herself off as a man in order to gain access into a nightclub and to kill her enemy. Although that scene is featured only briefly in the film, the poster highlights the image of the heroine in a man's suit holding a gun. Likewise, in *Sua Pu Khao* (Mountain Tiger, 1979), the leading female character disguises herself as a man to take revenge for her father.

Apart from these, although the film copies have not been discovered, we have come across film-related materials such as promotional synopses, posters, and booklets that reveal the practice of cross-dressing in their narratives. In *Muang Mae Mai* (A Widow City, 1935), the male protagonist and his friend need to disguise themselves as women to enter a widow city, whose population is exclusively female. In *Phra Ruang Khom Dum Din* (Phra Ruang, 1943), a female protagonist poses as a male solider in order to join the army along with her husband. The four leading actors in *Phol Nikorn Kim-gnuan Talui Harem* (Phol Nikorn Kim-gnuan Hit a Harem, 1959) sneak into an Arab prince's harem. One of them ends up impregnating the prince's concubine, and they need to remain in disguise as female belly dancers in order to stay safe. In *Mangkorn Dum* (Black Dragon, 1965), a group of policemen are shown in the promotion stills in female costumes.

The film-related materials also reveal the practice of male-to-*kathoey* cross dressing in Thai films. In 1964, two action movies, *Kao Mahakarn* (The Great Nine) and *Ratchasee Krung* (The City Lion) have their main male characters, played by Mitr Chaibancha and Sombat, respectively, the most virile and most famous actors at that time, dressed up in disguise as *kathoey* to solve criminal cases. *Ratchasee Krung's* synopsis describes the main male protagonist as follows: "He's somewhat a *kathoey*. When he confronts his enemy, he curls up like a timid pangolin, shier than a hot-blooded teenage girl [จะเป็นกะเทยสักหน่อย" และถ้าเขาอยู่ต่อหน้าศัตรูของเขา "เขาจะกลายเป็นตัวนิ่มที่อายเสียยิ่งกว่าผู้หญิงวัยกำดัด]. In *Nua Khoo* (Soulmate, 1968), a male villain disguises himself as a *kathoey* to get close to women. He and his philandering friend are human traffickers, and their targets are rich women.

While these films and filmic materials re-present the cross-dressing plots that focus on the character's outward appearance, the practice of crossing or blurring the gender norma-tive line is also often concerned with characters' gender confusion in early Thai cinema.

b. *Crossing/Blurring the Gender Normative Line*

A good example of a filmmaker's attempt to address opposition toward the gender binary appears in *Kung Nang* (1976). The female protagonist has been raised as a boy, and the film plays around with her gender and sexuality. The heroine perceives herself as a boy until she meets the male protagonist who puts an end to her gendered confusion and restores her normative-heterosexual femininity. In *Sawasdee Khun Khroo* (Good Morning, Teacher, 1978) the gender binary is also blurred. The female character is a "tomboy," and the male character is a *kathoey*. Yet in the end, the film restores heteronormative law and order by having these two characters fall in love with each other. While this may seem like a progressive move in terms of sexual expressions and fluidity, the film also sends a message that being queer is just a phase and not a natural/genuine sexual desire. The same production company went on to make another film with a similar storyline, *Wai Rean Pean Rak* (Crazy Love Student, 1985). The film sends out a strong message that it is the parents' direct responsibility to give "correct" advice to children to prevent them from becoming homosexuals. The film shows that with the right upbringing and care children who lose their ways and become a homosexual can return to "the correct path." A lesbian character who does not receive such correct guidance becomes mentally ill. The ending of the film presents a didactic moment to the audience that parents must take good care of children to prevent them from being homosexual.

Also, having main female characters appear masculine like a "tomboy" is one of the classic plots in Thai cinema: she may dress, act, or fight like a man, but deep down the heroine is still a woman, waiting for the right man to put a stop to her performance and turn her into the normative feminine. A good example is *Matador Jom Pean* (Crazy Matador, 1985). The female protagonist is an attractive matador who believes that she is a man. She flirts, hugs, and kisses many women. Until one day, the male protagonist comes along and physically touches her. The matador is shocked and confused, then another character explains to her that "she has become a full woman by feeling sexually aroused by the male protagonist."

From this list of films, we can see that the Thai cinemascape has long been familiar with the practice of crossing the gender binary. Cross-dressing as a plot device has been used to serve specific purposes, such as male characters appearing as *kathoeys* to fight crimes, to get close to women to commit some evil deed, or to bring comic relief to the story. The act of crossing the gender binary is therefore temporary and does not represent the characters' gender identities. On the other hand, particularly in films after the second half of the 20th century, when the characters express their non-heteronormative gendered identities, the films strongly present such behaviors as wrong, abnormal, and non-inherent and must be "cured" to maintain social heteronormativity.

The last characteristic of non-heterosexual elements we found in early Thai cinema with a non-queer focus at TFA straightforwardly portrays queer issues with a negative light. In these films, the *kathoey*/queer characters are characterized as evil, deviant, and dangerous.

iii. Queer as Evil

It is worth noting that the portrayals of non-heterosexual characters as evil, deviant, and harmful happened mainly in films made after the 1970s. This reflects a shift in social attitudes that began in the 1960s wherein homosexualities were perceived as social inappropriateness and mental illness (Jackson 2003; Terdsak 2002).

In *Khon Kin Mia* (The Wife Eater, 1974), a queer character falls in love with his own nephew. Whenever the nephew gets married, he poisons and kills his wives. There is a scene showing him trying to sexually abuse another male character and flying into a rage after the man rejects him. Being a homosexual here is thus associated with incest and violence. The character, nonetheless, expresses heterosexual desire in a scene showing him having sex with a woman. The film interestingly suggests that the woman takes the active sexual role (we see her wearing a mustache). The disturbing nature of the scene is compounded by the display of drug abuse and "unusual" pornographic pictures in the room of the *kathoey*. His sexual fluidity is not thus progressively represented, but on the other hand, it still becomes an element emphasizing his deviant characteristics.

In *Thevada Derndin* (Earth Angles, 1976), the film tells the story of three rebellious teenagers who become outlaws and are dubbed "the three earth angels" by the media. One of them is a *kathoey* character who is portrayed as courageous, loyal, and addicted to drugs. The film addresses nearly every significant social issue in Thailand, including modernity and capitalism, poverty, law and justice, the power of the media, drugs, borders and minority groups, and religious minorities in the Deep South of Thailand. In one scene, the film shows the male and female characters having sexual intercourse while the homosexual is taking drugs in the same room. The *kathoey* character with his/her drug use thus adds another layer to the film's subversion of social (hetero-)norms. While they are criminals, the film presents the three characters as social victims forced to behave immorally because of the pressure and injustice of a capitalist society, for instance, the film explains that the *kathoey* character becomes an outlaw because his middle-class parents neglect him.

Another film, *Chong Wang Rawang Huajai* (The Gap Between Hearts, 1976), features a bisexual character who attempts to seduce a young man and has an affair with his friend's wife. The story is challenging to understand, as TFA only possesses the mute original camera negative of the film. The character is portrayed as having an obsessive interest in sex and engaging in sexual misconduct, such as consuming both male and female pornography and committing adultery. This film is also noteworthy for being the very first Thai film to vividly depict male-male intimacy and sexual exposure. The bisexual character tries to force oral sex on the young male character twice. In the second incident, the two men are alone in a room, half-naked and wearing tight white shorts. Although the young man rejects him both times, a queer reading or even Y (boy love) reading of the story suggests a wonder how the young man allows himself to be half-naked with the bisexual character for the second time when he was being already molested once.

Chong Wang Rawang Huajai is also groundbreaking in its explicit portrayal of full graphic nudity. The movie features scenes in which the bisexual character is shown reading both female and male pornographic magazines. The film intentionally visualizes both full frontal nudity of the female body and, notably, the male genitalia. It is worth noting that since TFA possesses the original camera negative, there is a significant chance that this version may not have the Thai censorship board yet. The specific scene in question might have been removed in the released version.

In *Games* (1976), the female protagonist finds out that her boyfriend has cheated on her with her male friend. This causes her unbearable pain. Its synopsis explicitly mentions that homosexuality is harmful to women. Similarly, in *Sapai Lukthung* (Rustic Daughter-in-Law, 1982), a male homosexual character deceives a woman into marrying him as part of a financial scheme to obtain money from his parents, which he intends to share with his boyfriend. The film serves as a reflection of the evolving landscape of gender and sexual identities that emerged since the mid-1960s in Thai society, incorporating terms such as gay, gay king, and gay queen.

In the low-budget comedy film *Hor Sao* (Female Dormitory, 1984), a male character passes himself off as a woman to get into a female dormitory. He ends up in a room with a bisexual man who sexually harasses him. Female homosexual characters were also portrayed as deviant and violent in several films from the period. In *Hua Jai Tee Mai Yak Ten* (Weary Heart, 1977), a female English tutor has a secret relationship with her lonely female student. She finds out later that the student is having an affair with her brother's boyfriend. The teacher shoots both of them dead and later turns the gun on herself. Similarly, in the last scene of *Wai Rean Pean Rak,* a lesbian comes to her former girlfriend's wedding with a gun to kill the couple before losing her mind. In *Hor Sao,* one scene shows a lesbian character pointing a gun at her girlfriend when the girlfriend is about to leave her for a man.

A plot device in which female and male homosexual characters commit sexual harassment within a prison setting is a repetitive trope in Thai films. *Khung Pad* (The 8th Prison, 1974), the film portrays a women's penitentiary in which the female protagonist faces a sexual threat from a lesbian inmate. *Haek Khai Narok Dien Bien Phu* (Escaping from Dien Bien Phu Hell, 1977) also shows a brief scene in which a brutal male warden sexually touches a male leading character's body and behind. After the success of *Khung Pad,* the same production company produced *Khung Daeng* (The Red Prison, 1981), which, according to its synopsis, features an encounter between the leading male character and a sexually perverted inmate. The film synopsis teases the audience to see for themselves whether the male character will lose his virginity.

Accordingly, these films evidently preach the negative effects of the interventions from the public and academic discourses on homosexuals in Thai society. The decade of 1970s marks the beginning of the negative portrayals of homosexuals in Thai mediascape.

Conclusion

Our exploration of the queer films and film related materials preserved in TFA reveals that while a thorough work still needs to be done to complete the history of Thai queer cinema, we have come across some significant findings. Before *Pleng Sut Thai*, homosexual elements had frequently been portrayed in the Thai cinematic queerscape. While being perceived as inferior, unauthentic, comical, or inappropriate, the films prior to the 1960s hardly represented non-heterosexuality as pathological abnormality, deviance, or a threat. *Kathoey* seems to have a place and space in society or at least the mediascape. More importantly, being labeled as *kathoey* in the films in that period only identifies the characters' gendered identity, signifying their effeminate mannerism, but the *kathoey* identity does not affect sexual identities or preferences. Their effeminacy does not equate to homosexuality. It was after the 1960s, particularly with the interventions of Western medical discourse and the influence of the Thai press, that Thai films apparently and significantly began to project homosexual elements as mental illness, moral wrongdoing, and harmful behaviors.

In terms of gender and sexual diversity, while it is true according to this film collection that the *kathoey* characters represented prior to 1970 express more sexual fluidity, there was less than 10% of the total films that represent other alternative gendered and sexual identities, especially female homosexual and gay (or masculine homosexuals). While the famous *Pleng Sut Thai* and its sequel, *Rak Toramarn* (Torture Love) released in 1987, had a solid storyline about lesbianism, after these two movies in the 1980s, it is still the case that female homosexuals have been significantly underrepresented in the Thai mediascape. This is opposite to *kathoeys* and male (masculine) homosexuals who have received continuous and increasing attention from Thai, as well as Asian, media markets in various platforms, be it in cinemas or online.

While these films offer a significant opportunity to explore queer issues in Thai society, from the earlier discussion, there is a number of films that do not have the original negative or access prints. Most of them, including *Pleng Sut Thai*, only have poor-quality digital copies transferred from magnetic tapes or VHS copies. The visual and audio contents have been degraded, and thus, it is difficult to scrutinize the films in great detail. Losing good-quality, viewable filmic materials mean we are losing significant historical records and evidence. This problem is therefore a serious threat to Thai film studies in general and Thai queer cinema studies in particular.

References

Atit Pongpanit. 2011. "The Bitter-Sweet Portrayals of Expressing and Maintaining Non-Normative Genders and Sexualities in Thai Mainstream Cinema From 1980 to 2010." PhD diss., SOAS University of London.

———. 2013. "It Gets Better: Transgenderism/Transsexualism and 'Thai Theravada Buddhist Beliefs' in Thai Cinema." *Manutsayasat Wichakan* 20 (2): 111–42.

Atit Pongpanit, and Ben Murtagh. 2022. "Emergent Queer Identities in 20th Century Films from Southeast Asia." In *Queer Southeast Asia*, edited by Shawna Tang and Hendri Yulius Wijaya. London: Routledge.

Farmer, Brett. 2018. "Queer Cinema: *Love of Siam/Rak Haeng Siam*." In *Thai Cinema: The Complete Guide*, edited by Mary J. Ainslie and Katarzyna Ancuta, 193–208. London: Tauris Academic Texts.

Fuhrmann, Arnika. 2016. *Ghostly Desires: Queer Sexuality and Vernacular Buddhism in Contemporary Thai Cinema*. Durham: Duke University Press.

———. 2018. "Queer Cinema: *This Area is Under Quarantine*." In *Thai Cinema: The Complete Guide*, edited by Mary J. Ainslie and Katarzyna Ancuta, 193–208. London: Tauris Academic Texts.

Jackson, Peter A. 1993. "Male Homosexuality and Transgenderism in the Thai Buddhist Tradition." In *Queer Dharma: Voices of Gay Buddhists*, edited by Winston Leyland. San Francisco: Gay Sunshine Press.

———. 1999. "Tolerant But Unaccepting: The Myth of a Thai 'Gay Paradise'." In *Genders and Sexualities in Modern Thailand*, edited by Peter A. Jackson and Nerida M. Cook, 226–42. Chiang Mai: Silkworm Books.

———. 2000. "An Explosion of Thai Identities: Global Queering and Re-Imagining Queer Theory." *Culture, Health & Sexuality* 2 (4): 405–24. https://www.jstor.org/stable/3986699.

———. 2003. "Performative Genders, Perverse Desires: A Bio-History of Thailand's Same-Sex and Transgender Cultures." *Intersections: Gender, History and Culture in the Asian Context* 9. http://intersections.anu.edu.au/issue9/jackson.html.

Käng, Dredge Byung'chu. 2012. "*Kathoey* 'In Trend': Emergent Genderscapes, National Anxieties and the Re-Signification of Male-Bodied Effeminacy in Thailand." *Asian Studies Review* 36: 475–94.

Morris, Rosalind C. 1994. "Three Sexes and Four Sexualities: Redressing the Discourses on Gender and Sexuality in Contemporary Thailand." *Positions* 2 (1): 15–43.

Natthanai Prasannam. 2019. "The Yaoi Phenomenon in Thailand and Fan/Industry Interaction." *Plaridel* 16 (2): 63–89.

Oradol Kaewprasert. 2008. "Gender Representations in Thai Queer Cinema." PhD diss., University of Essex.

Terdsak Romjumpa. 2002. "Discourses on 'Gay' in Thai Society, 1965–1999." MA thesis, Chulalongkorn University.

Ünaldi, Serhat. 2011. "Back in the Spotlight: The Cinematic Regime of Representation of *Kathoeys* and Gay Men in Thailand." In *Queer Bangkok: Twenty-First-Century Markets, Media, and Rights*, edited by Peter A. Jackson, 59–80. Hong Kong: Hong Kong University Press.

INDEX

Please note that *italicized* page numbers in this index indicate illustrations.

9 781032 199405